THE HALF-L

MW01104374

Since her untimely death in 1975, the life and work of the Vancouver poet Pat Lowther have often been referred to as 'the Lowther legacy.' In *The Half-Lives of Pat Lowther*, Christine Wiesenthal seeks to convey what that legacy actually entails.

Combining biography with an analysis of literary and cultural history, Wiesenthal examines the critical legacy of a writer whose remarkable life and poetry have remained overshadowed by her notorious death. Working within a new form of biography, which employs multiple narrative arcs – or 'half-lives' – that interpret Lowther's life and poetry within and across several interpretive frameworks, Wiesenthal retraces the influences on the public memory of the poet. She charts Lowther's complex creative evolution from her modest beginnings as a high school drop-out and single mother to her emergence as one of the most distinctive poetic voices of the 1970s.

A wealth of previously uncollected and unpublished letters, notebook entries, court documents, interviews, and archival materials illuminate Pat Lowther's manifold achievements in her domestic, political, and intellectual lives. *The Half-Lives of Pat Lowther* is the premier work on this remarkable figure.

CHRISTINE WIESENTHAL is a professor in the Department of English and Film Studies at the University of Alberta.

The Half-Lives of
Pat Lowther

Christine Wiesenthal

UNIVERSITY OF TORONTO PRESS
Toronto Buffalo London

© University of Toronto Press Incorporated 2005
Toronto Buffalo London
Printed in Canada

Reprinted in paperback 2006

ISBN 0-8020-3635-X (cloth)
ISBN 0-8020-9480-5 (paper)

Printed on acid-free paper

Library and Archives Canada Cataloguing in Publication

Wiesenthal, Christine S. (Christine Susan), 1963–
Half-lives of Pat Lowther / Christine Wiesenthal.

Includes bibliographical references and index.
ISBN 0-8020-3635-X (bound)   ISBN 0-8020-9480-5 (pbk.)

1. Lowther, Pat, 1935–1975.   2. Poets, Canadian (English) –
20th century – Biography.   I. Title.

PS8573.O9Z95 2005   C811'.54   C2005-901012-6

University of Toronto Press acknowledges the financial assistance to its
publishing program of the Canada Council for the Arts and the
Ontario Arts Council.

This book has been published with the help of a grant from the Canadian
Federation for the Humanities and Social Sciences, through the Aid to Scholarly
Publications Programme, using funds provided by the Social Sciences and
Humanities Research Council of Canada.

University of Toronto Press acknowledges the financial support for its
publishing activities of the Government of Canada through the
Book Publishing Industry Development Program (BPIDP).

for Zo-Zo, just beginning
&
Elizabet, unbowed to the end

Contents

IV Philosophy's First Molecule

Illustrations follow page 236

Abbreviations

Works By and Including Pat Lowther

AB	*The Age of the Bird.* Vancouver: Blackfish P, 1972.
DF	*This Difficult Flowring.* Vancouver: Very Stone House, 1968.
FI	*Final Instructions.* Vancouver: West Coast Review / Orca Sound, 1980.
MS	*Milk Stone.* Ottawa: Borealis P, 1974.
SD	*A Stone Diary.* Toronto: Oxford UP, 1977.
TC	*Time Capsule: New and Selected Poems.* Vancouver: Polestar Books, 1997.
Fifteen	*Fifteen Canadian Poets Plus Five.* Ed. Gary Geddes and Phyllis Bruce. Toronto: Oxford UP, 1978.
FNFC	*For Neruda, for Chile.* Ed. Walter Lowenfels. Boston: Beacon P, 1975.
Forty	*Forty Women Poets of Canada.* Ed. Dorothy Livesay and Seymour Mayne. Montreal: Ingluvin, 1971.
MMD	*Mountain Moving Day.* Ed. Elaine Gill. New York: Crossing Press, 1973.

Other

CATT	Court of Appeal Trial Transcripts. *Her Majesty the Queen against Roy Armstrong Lowther.* 4 volumes plus supplemental volume of closing addresses. Vancouver, B.C. Provincial Law Courts.
Crim. Rep.	R. v. Lowther, *Criminal Reports* (Summary of Appeal Case). 1978 7 C.R. (3d). Vancouver, B.C. Provincial Law Courts.

FCR Family Court Registry. Divorce and Matrimonial Causes file 1001/62. Patricia Domphousse v. William Harvey Joseph Domphousse. Vancouver, B.C. Provincial Law Courts.

PHTT Preliminary Hearing Trial Transcripts. *Regina v. Lowther.* 10 vols. Criminal Registry file # CC 760402. Vancouver, B.C. Provincial Law Courts.

RLJ Roy Lowther. Unpublished casebook transcripts. 2 vols. In the possession of Ruth Lowther Lalonde.

Chronology

1888	Jan. 24: death of William Wilks, PL's maternal great-grandfather.
1923	May 28: death of Arthur Tinmouth Sr, PL's paternal grandfather.
1935	July 29: PL born, to Virginia Louise (Wilks) (1907–98) and Arthur Tinmouth Jr (1908–70).
1935–41	Tinmouths reside at Lynn Creek water intake station.
1951	June: PL drops out of North Vancouver High School.
1953	Oct. 2: marriage to William Harvey Joseph Domphousse (1925–99).
1954	April 1: First child, Alan, born.
1956	Sept. 30: Second child, Katharine Dawn, born. Family moves to Deep Cove.
1959	Oct.: separation from William Domphousse.
1960	April: regains custody of Kathy through 'Equal Guardianship of Infants Act.'
1963	March 15: Divorce from William Domphousse finalized. July 20: marriage to Roy Armstrong Lowther; move to Vancouver City.
1966	Aug. 9: Third child, Heidi Elizabeth (Beth), born.
1967	Nov. 19: Fourth child, Christine Louise (Christie), born.
1968	June: *This Difficult Flowring*.
1969	April: first Canada Council Grant. May: Roy loses teaching job. Nov.: first solo trip to 'Poet and Critic' conference, Edmonton.
1970	April 25: PL's father, Arthur Tinmouth, dies.

1971   Fall: submission of *Milk Stone* to Ingluvin Press.

1972   *The Age of the Bird.*
        Spring: first multimedia show, 'Canadian Mosaic.'
        June: assumes position as League of Canadian Poets represen-
        tative for British Columbia.
        Fall: second Canada Council grant; meets Eugene
        McNamara.
        Oct.: League biennial meeting, Edmonton; League 'Western'
        reading tour.

1973   part-time job as Little Mountain NDP constituency secretary.
        June: submission of *A Stone Diary* to Anansi; NDP provincial
        convention.
        Sept.: Chilean coup and death of Neruda; Ingluvin collapses;
        part-time job as creative-writing instructor.

1974   Jan.: submission of *Milk Stone* to Anansi; return of *A Stone
        Diary* and *Milk Stone* manuscripts.
        Feb.: re-submits *Milk Stone* to Borealis Press; friendship with
        Milton Acorn ends.
        Aug. 12–26: performances of *Infinite Mirror Trip: A Multimedia
        Experience of the Universe* (begun in 1972).
        Oct.: *Milk Stone*; Ontario League reading tour; elected League
        Chair in Fredericton.

1975   March: appointed to NDP Interim Arts Board; UBC sessional
        appointment for fall.
        May: re-submission of *A Stone Diary* to Oxford UP.
        July: P.E.I. reading; Toronto reading; Mayne Island summer
        holiday.
        Aug.: assumes teaching duties at UBC; finalizing organization
        and publicity for League meeting, Victoria, 10–13 Oct. 1975.
        Sept. 9: *A Stone Diary* accepted for publication.
        Sept. 23–4: death.

What is the structure of a peculiarly historical consciousness?
– Hayden White, 'The Historical Text
as Literary Artifact,' 1978

Introduction

Toward a Half-Life of Pat Lowther

No other figure in the history of recent Canadian writing has been remembered *and* forgotten with quite such urgent simultaneity as the poet Pat Lowther, killed at the age of forty by her husband, just as she seemed poised on the cusp of 'whatever fame and fortune Canadian poetry has to offer,' as Robert Fulford put it at the time.[1] To Pat Lowther goes the dubious, if not fatal, distinction of having accrued the most sensationally tragic of contemporary literary reputations. In a mainstream culture generally untroubled by the existence of poets, good, great, indifferent, or bad, the memory of Pat Lowther troubles, and allures.

Lowther's murder in the fall of 1975 coincided closely with the most significant successes of a brief, but remarkable, even unlikely, literary career. Her beginnings had not been particularly auspicious. Born during the Depression to a working-class family in North Vancouver, she quit high school, became pregnant and first wed at eighteen, and was divorced by her mid-twenties. Her status as a single mother by 1960 was a hard-won privilege, for she had to fight to regain even partial custody of one of her two children from that first marriage. Thereafter, she droned away at a series of mind-numbing, ill-paying clerical jobs – this phase, a Cold War, proletarian version of the stultifying stenographic life captured by the poetry of P.K. Page in the preceding decade. Yet though poverty would prove an intransigent shadow of her existence to the end, by the time of her death Lowther had achieved a degree of quiet literary prominence that was nothing short of amazing. In the very same month she died, for instance, her third collection of poetry, *A Stone Diary*, was officially accepted for publication by Oxford University Press; she was in the final stages of organizing the Annual Meeting of the League of Canadian Poets, the national association to which she had been elected Chair the previous fall; and she had just taken up her first important – if also temporary – teaching job, as a sabbatical replacement in the Creative Writing Department at the University of British Columbia. In addition to consolidating a highly credible reputation as a poet and arts administrator, Lowther, a recognized political activist on the left, had that summer also begun work as a newly appointed member of the B.C. Interim Arts Board, an influential cultural policy committee formed under David Barrett's NDP government.

Though Pat Lowther had been reported 'missing' by late September 1975, her murder could not be confirmed for an agonizing stretch of time, until her body was recovered. Some three weeks after her disappearance, on a Thanksgiving weekend, members of the League of Canadian Poets assembled at the Empress Hotel in Victoria for the Annual Meeting which Lowther and her executive secretary, Arlene Lampert, had been working ferociously, months in advance, to organize. 'To say that the ... conference in Victoria ... was darkened by the disappearance of its chief organizer, Pat Lowther, would be a grave understatement,' Dorothy Livesay later wrote. 'Reading poetry seemed to be an exercise in futility with Pat not there': her absence 'numbed all other sensibilities.'[2] Amid swirling news reports that police were investigating the disappearance of a 'Victoria' poet 'in her early thirties,' the League members did, however, persevere with their readings and meetings.[3] And on Thanksgiving Monday, October 13, as they prepared to disperse again, Lowther's remains were accidentally discovered at Furry Creek, near Squamish.

She had been bludgeoned to death, her body later moved to Furry Creek and dumped about a mile and a half upstream from where it was eventually recovered. On October 21, just over a week after the grisly discovery was made, Roy Armstrong Lowther was arrested, and subsequently tried and convicted of his wife's murder. While Pat Lowther's family and friends had almost immediately augured the worst when she went 'missing,' news of her murder left the literary community from coast to coast shocked and stunned, saddened and angry. In the terse words of Dorothy Livesay, Lowther's death represented nothing less than 'a body blow to the cause of poetry in Canada.'[4]

The painful, dramatic circumstances of Lowther's abrupt demise continued to unfold in the immediate aftermath through media coverage of the case, and over the course of Roy Lowther's highly publicized – and strikingly theatrical – 1977 trial. At the same time, a spate of com-

memorative essays, poems, eulogies, and brief retrospectives of Pat
Lowther's life and work also began to appear during the late seventies.
In late fall of the year she was killed, CBC Radio impresario Peter
Gzowski aired a special tribute to Lowther produced by Allan Safarik,
one of her former small-press publishers. In 1976, Paul Grescoe's biographical essay, 'Eulogy for a Poet,' received national exposure under
the front-page headline of 'The Poet as Victim' in *The Canadian*, a weekend magazine supplement to newspapers such as the *Toronto Star* and
the *Vancouver Province*. Small literary magazines of the sort that Lowther
had frequently published with – notably, Livesay's *CVII* and Fred Candelaria's *West Coast Review* – began to print tributes, mainly in the form
of poems; similar commemorative pieces, by Margaret Atwood and
Patrick Lane, among others, appeared in anthologies, NDP newsletters,
and League publications. The posthumously published *A Stone Diary* was
widely reviewed when it appeared in 1977. In 1978 former West Coast
Tish kid Frank Davey coached into print a book of poems by a young
former student of Lowther's: Gail McKay's *The Pat Lowther Poem*, which
deploys newspaper coverage of the Lowther case as an extensive intertext, became the first full-length creative work based on the poet's
death.

Though the initial shock of Lowther's abruptly brutal end inevitably
faded, she has never been entirely forgotten, especially in her home
town of Vancouver, and by the literary organization she so briefly, but
efficiently, steered – the League of Canadian Poets having named an
annual poetry prize after Lowther in 1981. The decade that ensued witnessed the posthumous appearance of some early and unpublished
poems, *Final Instructions*, edited by Fred Candelaria and Dona Sturmanis (1980); in Quebec, a small selection of Lowther's poems were translated for a French audience; another small selection were translated
into Spanish by Lake Sagaris for a Chilean audience; and two new critical essays appeared, one in English, one in French.[5] In her 1983 entry
for Lowther in *The Oxford Companion to Canadian Literature*, Rosemary
Sullivan saluted Lowther's 'permanent place in Canadian poetry' (474);
likewise, in her 1986 entry for Lowther in *The Dictionary of Literary Biography*, Hilda Thomas concluded that although 'the body of her work is
small, it has been truly described as "a major legacy to Canadian
poetry." Her place in Canadian literature is assured' (278). These assessments would seem to be ratified by Lowther's continued appearance in
major anthologies of the late seventies and eighties, including the influential second edition of Gary Geddes and Phyllis Bruce's *Fifteen Cana-*

dian Poets Plus Five (1978), J.R. Colombo's *The Poets of Canada* (1978), Margaret Atwood's *The New Oxford Book of Canadian Verse in English* (1982), and Rosemary Sullivan's *Poetry by Canadian Women* (1989).

And, rather than receding from cultural consciousness during the nineties, Lowther has enjoyed a resurgence with the last century's turn. In 1997 novelist and literary critic Keith Harrison published an essay in *Canadian Literature* which later became part of an experimental 'non-fiction novel,' *Furry Creek*, closely based on Lowther's murder and its criminal investigation. In 2000, Toby Brooks brought out a biography, *Pat Lowther's Continent: Her Life and Work*, a study that simultaneously positions Lowther as a poet of particular interest to second-wave feminists and as a writer of timeless relevance. Most recently, there has been a newly released documentary film, *Water Marks*, by Anne Henderson (2002), and one more new critical essay on Lowther.[6]

The recent interest in Pat Lowther's life, and to a lesser extent her work, may be attributed, at least in part, to the 1997 release of *Time Capsule*, a selection from her published works, along with some previously unpublished and uncollected poems. *Time Capsule* has accorded Lowther's work renewed visibility, ensuring its accessibility for younger generations of readers. What reviewers tend to call 'the Lowther legacy' has also extended into a new generation through the 1999 publication of a book of poems, *New Power*, by one of Lowther's daughters, Christine. The collective trauma of that blunt-force 'body blow' that Lowther's death dealt Dorothy Livesay and her contemporaries, not to mention Lowther's own family, has now had a generation to assimilate, to find the breath to articulate itself in coherent narratives. Whatever the specific historical factors underpinning her present 'recovery' as a subject for biography, criticism, and creative work may be, however, at least one thing is clear: Lowther is a poet who has indeed inspired a rather 'unusually prolific afterlife' (Higgins 1997: 191).

Given the attention she has continued to attract over the past three decades, in fact, there are those who would argue that Pat Lowther has already been remembered, if not too well – which would be too crass a thing to say – then at least out of all reasonable proportion to her actual literary accomplishment, as a writer of such limited output, however promising. There is some truth to this. Relative to the amount of attention inspired by other, far more established West Coast women poets – say, P.K. Page or Phyllis Webb – or even relative to the amount of attention accorded that sizeable host of other Canadian poets who have met regrettably early deaths – say, Raymond Knister, Bronwen Wallace, Marie

Uguay, John Thompson, or even Anne Wilkinson or bp Nichol – the case for a historical neglect of Pat Lowther is not a straightforward one to make.

At the time she died, Lowther had published only two full–length collections with small presses, *This Difficult Flowring* and *Milk Stone*, her strongest, *A Stone Diary*, was yet to come. Her serious writing career spanned only a single decade, from 1965 to 1975. This is a long time if one is talking about the Viet Nam War, but extremely brief for an artistic career. Few poets can commission a posthumous collected and selected on such a small slice of life's work, even those who are able to keep their books in print while they are alive. When she died, Lowther had fulfilled her duties as Chair of the League of Canadian Poets for less than a year. Is it ungenerous to note that Raymond Souster, who had served faithfully in that capacity from the League's inception in 1966 through to 1972, has no League award named after him? Similarly, though some of our major poets have become subjects of National Film Board documentaries, it is a rare few who, like Lowther, have rated an independently produced, prime-time television documentary. And so on. The cynical conclusion, only too easily arrived at for those of such disposition, is that Pat Lowther's 'legacy' hinges crucially on our abiding fascination with – and potent susceptibility to – the terrible pathos of her end, or the romantic idea of 'the poet as victim,' to echo the plangent headline of *The Canadian* magazine. It is, such sceptics would suggest (when they dare), Lowther's powerful appeal as an icon of tragic femininity, and her consequent availability as a handy poster girl for feminist and socialist political causes, that essentially props up her entire reputation to this day.

We may not like it, but in the absence of any substantive work on Lowther's actual poetic achievement, such scepticism needs to be acknowledged and addressed in order to be properly refuted. It needs to be said that *despite* consistently strong and numerous reviews of her work throughout her career; and *despite* Lowther's inclusion in important anthologies over three decades; *despite* the editions of her early and unpublished work; and *despite* the posthumous energy of her 'afterlife,' the critical literature to substantiate any claims made for the 'major legacy' of her small body of work, and for her 'assured' place in Canadian literary history, is extremely thin, almost non-existent (Thomas 1986; Sullivan 1983, 1997). And this fact begins to point up how the same 'unusually prolific afterlife,' which 'has helped preserve the memory' of Lowther's 'fine poetic gift' (Higgins 1997: 191), has simultaneously

relied upon an obscure sense of that 'fine poetic gift' and of the diffi-
dent, intensely private woman who struggled against considerable odds
to develop her uneasy possession of that 'gift.'

What exactly *is* 'the Lowther legacy'? What is the nature and scope of
Patricia Louise Lowther's bequest from the past – her specific contributions to literary culture, politics, and poetics of the seventies? Somewhere in the rhetoric of sanctified 'legacies,' what seems to get lost is the
simple fact that, at the time of her death, despite her apparently high-
profile position as head of a national literary organization, Lowther's
work was well known by only a dozen or two people in a position to recognize and encourage literary talent.[7] These included, chiefly, Milton
Acorn, Dorothy Livesay, Patrick Lane, Seymour Mayne, bill bissett, Joy
Kogawa, Margaret Atwood, Gary Geddes, George Woodcock, Eugene
McNamara, and Fred Cogswell, the indefatigable editor of *The Fiddlehead* magazine, where Lowther got an important start. And even
Lowther's associations with many of these writers – such as Lane, bissett,
and Kogawa – were lifeblood connections to young writers almost as
unestablished as she herself was at the time, writers not nearly as influential then as they are now. Other literary figures, such as Milton Acorn,
were to some degree political and poetic kindred spirits, but played no
significant, pragmatic role in promoting Lowther's writing career. Peter
Gzowski was perhaps overstating the case when he said, in the immediate wake of Lowther's murder, that she was, except 'in the eyes and the
ears of the poets ... in crassest terms, a nobody.'[8] But there was a kernel
of truth in that, too.

In fact, Lowther's claim on the critical memory has never been anything but extremely tenuous. It is telling, in this regard, that the very
first essay of literary criticism produced on Lowther, published in *Canadian Literature* the year that Roy Lowther went to trial, was almost withdrawn by its author before it hit print and eventually published only
under a pseudonym. When he wrote and submitted an essay on the
poetry of 'Florence McNeil and Pat Lowther,' Eugene McNamara had
no way of knowing he would become publicly involved in Roy Lowther's
murder trial. Between 1972 and 1975, McNamara and Pat had enjoyed
an intermittent, long-distance affair. But after he was subpoenaed to
appear at Roy's 1977 trial, McNamara sought to distance himself from
the painful memory of Lowther; in part, his concern over the article was
that his real identity could only compromise her work since his commentary on it would not be viewed as critically objective.[9]

From these fraught beginnings, the critical uptake has been slow, sporadic, and spotty in terms of calibre. Probably the finest scholarly work on Lowther to date has been by Jean Mallinson, who included Lowther in an excellent, unpublished PhD dissertation on contemporary women poets, and who went on to publish an important 1986 article on the sources of Lowther's 'Woman on/against Snow.' Mallinson's work and Keith Harrison's essay, the following decade, both offer highly insightful readings of individual (and important) Lowther poems; they do not aim at any comprehensive assessment of her poetic contribution. Judith Cowan's 'La poésie de Pat Lowther' in *Ellipse* is a brief and unremarkable general introduction to a selection of Lowther's poems. Toby Brooks's research has provided a valuable foundation for the study of Lowther's life, but her recent biography is marked by significant omissions and inaccuracies. The poetry that is taken up in *Pat Lowther's Continent* tends to be approached as transparently biographical. Whatever the oft-trumpeted 'Lowther legacy' is, it is a 'legacy' that remains largely unexamined and therefore open to casual dismissal.

Indeed, what emerges from a review of the extant published and archival literature on Pat Lowther is a poet far more often recognized by name than read; a poet whose place on the literary map of her time remains a nebulous question mark. What emerges is a poet whose memory is readily mobilized in some quarters for a variety of (more or less) legitimate political ends, and avoided in others for a variety of (more or less) legitimate personal ones. She is a poet whose own main archive has been fairly well trodden, but who has been virtually obliterated from the records of others, who have had to forget. In Lowther's instance, then, it's not so much the case – as it is with many authors – that her literary reputation deserves rehabilitation for a new historical moment (though this is also true). It is instead that the sensational details of her death, and its 'afterlife' fallout, have to a significant degree inhibited the development of any substantive critical inquiry in the first place. Our collective memory of both her life *and* her work has not yet fully recovered from the violent fact of her murder.

So the question of critical objectivity, phantasmal and banal at the best of times, nevertheless remains *the* major challenge in reading Lowther's life and poetry since her murder. As Sharon Thesen remarks, 'it is nearly impossible to read [a collection like] *Time Capsule* without the template of that tragedy casting its form over every poem' (Thesen 1997: 19). Indeed, the looming fact of *that tragedy* has skewed perspective on Lowther's writing life in the past by prompting an awed overemphasis on the extent to which her poetry is 'death haunted' and seems uncannily to predict the poet's end. The titles of Dona Sturmanis's 1985 article – 'A Poet's Haunting Legacy' – and of Susan Musgrave's recent review of *Time Capsule* – 'Slain Poet's New Work Eerily Prescient' (1997) – are fairly typical of this strain. The element of the uncanny that is so frequently invoked in discussions of Lowther's 'afterlife' reinforces her legendary mystique, as though she were somehow supernaturally premonitory for simply recognizing – as her correspondence indicates she could not fail to do – the increasing volatility of her domestic situation with Roy over the twelve years they spent together.

Cassandra, tragic prophetess of doom, is one of the fetchingly mythic subtexts of the reviewers here. About which Lowther, who herself tended to approach myth from more sharply analytic Marxist and feminist perspectives, might have had a few things to say. It was, after all, she who by 1964 was writing essays on the social utility and 'institutionalization' of myth in contemporary culture; and she who by 1973 was explicitly rejecting stereotypes of the poet-as-preternatural-prophet when she wrote of the poet's role: 'We can't believe ourselves to be some sort of mystical vanguard. We're not creating the flow, we're part of it.'[10] And it was, after all, she who went on to lampoon exactly this notion of the 'mystical vanguard' in *A Stone Diary*, namely, at the wind-slapped 'Intersection' of Fraser and Marine:

> it was just here
> at this bus stop
> I lost my glove
> my forty-cent transfer
> my book
> of unwritten profundities
>
> I tell you they fell upward! (*SD*, 78)

For reasons which may already be apparent from the preceding overview, this book does not offer a conventional 'life.' Shaped around the literal fact of a life half-lived – a half-life, summarily truncated by the hand of another – the following pages merge literary and cultural history and analysis with biography in the hope of finding a form adequately responsive to the range and complexity of their subject's demands. These demands, it seems to me, include grappling with the difficult significance of Lowther's murder *and* assimilating her literary and political contributions in life. They include reinforcing the value of Lowther's poetic 'legacy' apart from the circumstance of her death, while acknowledging also the effects of that death as a pre-text for inter-pretation and as a factor in the (somewhat superficial) visibility of that 'legacy' today.

To this end, Part I, 'The Craft of Memory,' opens with an account tracing the formation of the collective memory around 'Pat Lowther' during the three decades since her murder. The overwhelming problem of Lowther's notorious *death* is the first issue that needs to be addressed, and carefully, as a prerequisite to any other reconstructive efforts. Indeed, the 'life' that comes after the fact of Lowther's death, her so-called 'afterlife,' is an essential part of 'the Lowther legacy.' It is inescap-ably so, in the way that the present always filters and infiltrates our knowledge of the past. But in the case of this posthumous 'life,' it is also essential for how the past continues to infiltrate the present, extending and perpetuating the sorry 'legacy' of Lowther's killer. Roy Armstrong Lowther died in prison in 1985, far more readily recognizable as his wife's murderer than as her first biographer. In effect, however, the author of Pat Lowther's death also set the type for the script of her enthusiastic 'afterlife.' Rigidly unoriginal and otherwise almost entirely unremarkable a man, Roy was not only the catalyst for the demise of his wife's finer and stronger soul, but remains deeply insinuated in the ways we have most ardently wanted to remember (and forget about) Pat Lowther to this day.

In addition to ensuring the on-going indent of Roy Lowther's heavy hand, the absolute lack of any critical attention to Lowther's murder, to her husband's trial, and to the subsequent body of commemorative lit-erature and cultural debate around her since 1975 has enabled other misconceptions and false claims to proliferate, as well. Scattered across literary journals, newspaper reports, radio broadcasts, legal documents, and various forms of tribute literature, these materials need to be brought together and read in relation to one another. Only then does their real complexity as cultural events and as representational acts emerge, and only then do their lingering implications for the 'legacy' of 'Pat Lowther' come into clear focus.

The circumstances of Lowther's death pose problems related to time, memory, and meaning's reliance on both. As a woman at the prime of her life; as a poet perched ever so tantalizingly on the 'edge of fame'; and as the League official who vanished just prior to her first formal debut before a jury of her peers in Victoria, it is as much the brutal timing of Lowther's silencing as the brutality of that silencing itself which has contributed to the 'uncanny' poignancy of her memory, often to the detriment of that memory's historical integrity. Her death, and our attempts to remember or forget both it and her, thus raise the basic questions with which the opening chapters of this book begin. Namely: whose timing? whose pathos? whose memories, and whose meanings? These chapters confront questions about the functions of personal and cultural recollection, about memory and time as legal entities, about memory as a category of medicine, art, ethics, and politics too. They confront questions about literary politics, the cultural uses of literature, and a strange entanglement of 'Verses and Verdicts,' or poetry and the law. They attempt to chart the significant continuities between Roy's crime and his murder trial, on the one hand, and the literature and debates around *Pat* Lowther in the wake of her death, on the other. Ultimately, too, they attempt to document how the history of Lowther since her murder amounts to a story of ambivalence that is distinctly our own – to confusions that have expressed themselves as sharply in the ways that we have tried to conserve her memory as in the ways that we have begun to debate its meaning and 'legacy.' Especially in relation to the history of Roy's crime and its punishment, this is the story of a posthumous 'life' that asks as many difficult questions about class as it does anything else.

In beginning with Lowther's last half-life, her posthumous one, my aim is to work through the primary, usurping problem of her sensational end in order to discharge its obvious climactic appeal, and clear some new ground for the biographical narratives which follow in Parts II, III, and IV. While this strategy does not 'solve' the problem of *that tragedy*, it does productively complicate one's sense of Lowther's identity as a 'victim,' and it should (I hope) render a little more opaque the glass through which we are necessarily looking when we try to see the life that came before, the one that follows in subsequent sections of the book. That said, I have also come to the conclusion that no organizational design is going to neutralize the risk of sensationalism. Unless I were radically to censor my research or sidestep entirely the events around Pat Lowther's death, this history is inherently scandalous. Not attempting to deal with it closely because of that unpalatable fact still seems to me by far the more serious of the two risks I could choose to run.

Similarly, an awareness of Roy Lowther's hand in subsequent projections of Pat Lowther after her death did not 'solve' the very real dilemmas he posed for me in writing this book, deceased though he is. For one thing, like Toby Brooks before me, I am to some degree indebted to the man who killed Pat Lowther for copious records that include details about her work and home environment. Much of this information appears in Roy's court testimonies. Some of it appears in the even more voluminous legal casebooks he prepared for his lawyers, two single-spaced volumes of transcribed oral journals, which Roy's daughter from his first marriage, Ruth Lowther Lalonde, graciously permitted me to consult.

Roy's casebook journals, like his court testimonies, contain the world according to Roy. Nevertheless, they are valuable: not only are his distortions of truth and lengthy litanies of woe telling in themselves, but Roy also recorded minute details of the sort that only a spouse would know – his wife's work habits, for example, or dates of composition for certain poems and notebooks. Though not always accurate anyway, these are details of the kind that Roy had little incentive to falsify intentionally. (Often, in such instances, the opposite was true: he was self-consciously attempting to record his wife's 'biography.') In many cases, Roy's journals provided important leads for which I was able to find corroborating – or conflicting – evidence elsewhere.

Certainly the most problematic, but also an indispensable, source of information outside of Pat's own records, Roy was also not just his wife's murderer. Or, at least, though he may have been the simple cause of her death, he was not a simple factor in her life. Nothing will change the appalling crime he committed in 1975. But merely to excoriate or dismiss Roy for his pathetic destructiveness (as Brooks's biography tends to do), without recognizing precisely the ways in which he contributed – for ill *and otherwise* – to Lowther's life and her career, is only to diminish, unhelpfully and inaccurately, the complicated realities of their relationship, and its subtly changing social contexts, over more than a dozen years. Such an oversight would be to diminish the very complexities of experience that continued to bind Pat to a man who was falling apart, and dangerously so.

One truth is that the husband who ultimately took Pat Lowther's life was also pivotal in helping, initially, to stimulate her career ambitions. It was through Roy, for example, that Lowther first began, in the early sixties, to submit poems to small magazines such as *The Fiddlehead*, thus initiating an important decade-long correspondence and, eventually, good friendship with its editor, Fred Cogswell. Of course, Roy encouraged such contacts early in the marriage without knowing that, before long, his wife's literary career would eclipse his own artistic aspirations. By the time that eclipse came about, his mode had also changed considerably, to one of more or less constant surveillance and acts of sabotage, both petty and dramatic.

So, in retrospect anyway, I suppose it should not surprise me that when I first sat down to begin writing this book, I discovered that I had 'accidentally' lost an entire file of material which I had accumulated over years, and which included a key document that I needed to begin chapter 1 – namely, a copy of a poem by Roy called 'September 23rd.' While Beth Lowther came to my rescue in helping me track down a replacement copy of the poem, I never did recover my lost file. (Nor, to this day, can I recall where or from whom I obtained my original copy of Roy's text in the first place.) On page zero of my draft, the sudden absence of my file came as nothing if not damning evidence of my own memory's craft. At the time, I was too distressed to think of Pat's poem 'Losing My Head.' But I think of that now. A terrible reality something vaguely like hers must have been sinking into me. Try as I might, there was no way I could successfully 'lose' Roy Lowther in the task that lay ahead, any more than Pat could escape him in life. And just as she had no choice but to rely on him at times, so I would also have no choice but to resort to him as one of my sources. To him, and the troubled, troubling powers of his prior surveillance.

Uncatalogued and held in several old cardboard boxes by her daughter, Beth, Pat Lowther's own main archive presents a confusing disarray. Many of the notebooks are falling apart, one or two are torn in half or replaced by photocopies, and several, written in pencil, are already barely legible. Her papers bear the traces of past visitors: of Roy, and the Lowther household's artistically exuberant children, Kathy, Beth, and Christie; of anonymous, posthumous donors to the archive; and of one of the detectives assigned to the criminal investigation, Roy Chapman. His ubiquitous initials, 'R.E.C.,' mark the upper-right-hand corner of much of the material in careful, black felt. The collection held by Beth Lowther contains comparatively little material pertaining to the period prior to Lowther's marriage to Roy in 1963, and very little juvenilia. Absent also are at least a few items which appear to have disappeared without a trace, including one manuscript, 'A Treehouse for Everyone,' to which Lowther made several references during the seventies. Perhaps she tossed it (or, in her case, maybe, lost it).

To cast it in geologic terms, this is the archive as earth's outer crust. In comparison with the cubic feet of material left behind by writers like Dorothy Livesay, Lowther's papers are not only modest in proportion to her shorter life. Her literary remains raise unique concerns. In his case-book journals, Roy reports collecting 'two or three bags of waste paper ... for recycling' during the investigation into his wife's disappearance: unimportant 'old documents' related to his wife's 'meetings, briefs, that sort of thing' (RLJ, 1:39). Perhaps so. Like the torn notebook and Detective Chapman's initials, however, Roy's remark comes as a re-minder that not every archive has been vulnerable to quite the same degree of invasive interference as Pat's.

Of the 'old documents' that *do* exist among Lowther's surviving papers, though, is a draft from the sixties entitled 'Split Rock.' An early precursor to the stone poems of *A Stone Diary*, this poem begins with the announcement, 'I am divided / like a cleft mountain':

> and the I of me
> that's a monolith
> that would speak a word
> luminous and whole as
> a rock
> is apart from the I
> that stands dazzled
> before luminous rocks.[11]

The 'cleft' 'I' of 'Split Rock' voices an awareness of self-division and the plurality of experience to which Lowther would return frequently in the years to come. 'The I of me' was a metaphor, and more, for the 'mono-lith' of a self divided in and by language, by her own 'luminous' con-sciousness, and by the off-spring she bore. But it also signals a process of self-multiplication enacted in daily practice by the separate lives that Lowther eventually began to lead, as her literary career flowered, and she attempted, increasingly, to dissociate herself from Roy by forging her own professional and personal identities.

Lowther's own, eventually acute, sense of her life as a formation fis-sured like a 'split rock' or 'cleft mountain' is the idea that structures my approach to it in the sections which follow Part I. Rather than one con-tinuous 'luminous and whole' biography – *the* life, or even *a* life of Pat Lowther – these narratives are offered instead as a series of overlapping, partially recursive biographical histories, coextensive and enfolded time-lines, each of which examines different (but interrelated) aspects of her life and work. Several half-lives, they seek to read Lowther within and across multiple interpretive frames that accord close attention to her still under-read poetry and its historical contexts. Readers wishing a direct through line on a given subject or work may consult the chronology and the index.

By way of establishing an initial foundation, Part II, 'Complicated Airflows in the House,' begins with a fairly comprehensive account of Lowther's domestic life: her immediate family background, marital experiences and relations, early literary education and associations, and the poetry to which these gave rise. Part III, 'Ready to Learn Politics,' reverts to more remote chapters of relevant family history before pursuing Lowther's rapid development in her more public roles as an activist, professional artist, arts consultant, and administrator. Concomitant with her engagements in these political spheres were Lowther's attempts to cultivate also a more 'public' voice in her political poetry (chapters 12 and 13).

The fault line separating the domestic and political lives of Parts II and III reinscribes Lowther's own sometimes desperate attempts to hold her private and public worlds apart. This, as she fully appreciated, was a 'schizophrenic' practice that contradicted even her routine feminist assertions of the inseparability of personal and political spheres. The division of Parts within this book is similarly permeable, as the 'continuities' that thread through these half-lives should demonstrate.

Indeed, far from 'schizophrenic,' the coherence across different aspects of Lowther's existence comprises the keynote of the final section, 'Philosophy's First Molecule.' This last part of the book recounts the natural history, as it were, of Lowther's connections to the physical world of her West Coast home, and her interests in the organic, physical universe more generally. These chapters retrace the 'root' of that 'I' who stood 'dazzled / before luminous rocks' as a context for reading the most significant strand of her mature poetic achievement (chapters 15 and 16). In doing so, they reveal an intellectual life at once integrally personal and political in its expressions, intimate and vast in its curiosity and focus.

Cumulatively, then, the last three sections of this book explore some of the paradoxes at the heart of Lowther's life, in their place and time. They trace the life of a woman always greatly challenged as a housekeeper, for example, but organized *tout de suite* as an extremely able 'housekeeper' of the League of Canadian Poets. They explore the complex literary milieu of Lowther's Vancouver, where the much-vaunted postmodern poetics of *Tish* coexisted with a tenacious, residual, pre-modernist literary traditionalism that placed the emphasis on the British of British Columbia. They consider the life of a woman generously active as an advocate of almost every good welfare cause, but nevertheless unable to safeguard herself; the life of a writer whose emergence as a professional artist was a triumph that pointed at once to future solutions for present problems, *and* troubled her bred-in-the-bone convictions as a democratic socialist. And they follow the life of a writer whose 'evolution' resulted in a strange species of poetics at once remarkably visionary and materialist.

An eclectic reader, Lowther embraced a wide field of interests that included, crucially, a surprising assortment of contemporary sciences, ranging from astrophysics and archeology to evolutionary biology. Ultimately, it was the physical and sub-physical nature of the universe – enigmas of matter, energy, space, and time – that prompted some of her most ambitious projects and finest accomplishments in late works such as the multimedia *Infinite Mirror Trip* (1974) and *A Stone Diary*. Fascinated by the limits of empirical inquiry, *and* the possibilities of science fiction (for feminist *poetry*!), Lowther drew increasingly on the vocabulary and images of science in order to capture 'the excitement and complexity of a natural world' that she very pointedly contrasted against 'current concerns with mysticism and the supernatural' (quoted in Mertens 1974: 29).

The title of this book is drawn from the same physical sciences which so strongly attracted Lowther. In chemistry and physics, the concept of the half-life denotes a measurement of 'values' over time. Concerned with rates of decay (or longevity), it denotes a negative calculation of diminishing returns, a means of charting the eventual transformation of elemental energy into something other, something smaller and less than whatever 'luminous' molecular 'whole' it once was. Essentially, it represents the naturalistic equivalent of an afterlife – an un-mystical, non-supernatural one.

Imported as metaphor into the cultural field, physical half-lives present a suggestive correlative to processes of historical memory and their variable rates of erosion. In this sense, they serve to emphasize especially the transformative work of memory: its craft as a form of energy that is both finite and *inclusive* of the (negative) energy that it takes to forget, to diminish, or to lose from sight. In this sense, too, the half-life offers more than just an appropriate way of thinking about the literal fact of Lowther's half-lived life, which, despite its apparent posthumous energy, has in effect been half-forgotten. By extension, it is a metaphor that applies as well to broader qualitative 'measurements' that include biographical efforts such as this, which is also (fundamentally) the product of many memories and their failures, foremost among those being the diminishing returns of my own.

It is, in the end, through the form of the half-life that this book attempts to reconceive the limits of biography and the problem of 'measuring' the endurance of a life's 'value' over time. If the several 'half' accounts that follow make obvious the artificiality of my presentation of Lowther's life, then they do so to acknowledge the subjectively 'constructed' nature of biography in a way that specifically links this issue to the broader (epistemological) problem of the limits to a secure knowledge of physical reality in general – a problem that cuts across biography, history, and the sciences too. In Lowther's own time, historiographers like Hayden White recognized 'the threat of "infinite regress" that lurks at the interior of the very complex of historical "facts"' (1978: 44). Such '"infinite regress"' applies as well to the assembled '"facts"' (and they are facts) of this book. Rather like a black hole, everything knowable points to an 'interior' converging tunnel that eventually disappears into something invisible, indivisible, and unknowable from where we search in space and time. In physical theory, this is essentially the gist of Werner Heisenberg's famous Uncertainty Principle, which not only proved that any human attempt to *observe* tiny, subatomic properties *disturbed* the behaviour of those properties, but also that any attempt to 'measure' the location *and* momentum of an atomic particle would be necessarily delimited – by half. The physicist, he concluded, could calculate the answer to one question *or* the other, but never know both – the *where* and the *how* of the particle – at the same time.

That subjectivity *physically* conditions and contains knowledge in ways that we cannot yet pretend to understand is one basic premise behind this book's attempt to articulate its basis in knowledge that is necessarily partial. And in redescribing the half-means that most of us must rely upon in taking our 'measures,' it is both inevitable and unsurprising that, like a 'split rock' – or an atomic particle – 'Pat Lowther' will keep shifting about, as she does 'In the Continent behind My Eyes,' where (*or,* should that be *how?*) –

How like a pool in the afternoon
I create every
possible existence
while behind me night
erases beginnings (*MS*, 28)

PART I

The Craft of Memory

Icons
have no need
for language
– *The Age
of the Bird*

Chapter 1

Three September Twenty-Threes

The long night train.
So often,
south to north,
with wet ponchos,
grain,
boots clogged with mud,
in third class,
you ran on, unwinding geography.
Perhaps it was then I began
my diary of the earth.
I learned the kilometers
of smoke,
the spread of silence.
> – Pablo Neruda,
> 'The Night Train,' 1964

Smoke from the aerial bombardment of La Moneda Palace had scarcely dissipated over central Santiago when Ricardo Neftalí Reyes Basalto, better known to the world as Pablo Neruda, slipped from consciousness and then into death on 23 September 1973. He was sixty-nine years old. Only twelve days earlier, on September 11, Chile's most famous poet and communist had listened in alarm to radio and television broadcasts announcing the military overthrow of President Salvador Allende's Popular Unity government, the first democratically elected Marxist administration in Latin America. Neruda had helped to propel Allende, a friend and leftist ally, to power in 1970. At the time of the coup, battling prostate cancer and apparently feverishly dictating the final pages of his

Memoirs to an amanuensis, Neruda was ensconced at his beloved beach home near Valparaíso, an hour outside Santiago. 'Isla Negra' is a stone house, an old sea captain's residence, with a turret tower that faces the Pacific Ocean. Here, looking out over sea swells and spindrift, the Nobel Prize–winning poet had always retreated to write and to indulge the luxury of (sometimes) not answering the phone.

With the U.S.-sponsored fall of the Allende government that September, however, the military junta promptly closed roads and placed the port city of Valparaíso under twenty-four-hour curfew. Overnight, it became virtually impossible to obtain medical attention and medication. Neruda was granted permission to move to a Santiago clinic only when it was already desperately clear he was dying. He breathed his last just as Chile, the country he had helped make over into cantos, sweepingly epic, descended chaotically into an era of dictatorial repression from which it has yet to fully recover. Because the 'two events' coincided so closely in time, Allende's downfall on September 11 and Neruda's death on September 23 'will forever be linked in the memory of Latin Americans' (González Echevarría 1991: 5). Moreover, it was, perhaps, also 'inevitable' that the deaths of Allende and Neruda, together, would come to be widely perceived as 'a symbol for the death of Chile' (Bizzarro 1979: 164).[1]

Geography unwinds. Some 10,576 kilometres of jagged coastline separate Valparaíso from Vancouver on the Pacific Northwest. But in Canada, and particularly in British Columbia, many followed the disturbing, erratic newscasts from Chile with consternation. In her rented home at 566 East 46th Avenue, Pat Lowther was no exception. In the fall of 1973, Lowther was working as a constituency secretary for Phyllis Young, the NDP member for the provincial riding of Little Mountain. This stop-gap job placed Lowther at the bottom clerical rungs of a new, leftist provincial government that was, for various obvious and also less apparent reasons, interestingly linked to the political upheavals in the far-flung southern hemisphere. In the context of Nixon-era North American politics, anyway, David Barrett's election in 1972 as British Columbia's first NDP premier struck some as a 'very radical' event, with the province being portrayed in the American media as 'the Chile of the North.'[2] Conversely, within British Columbia, as Tom Wayman recalls, 'Allende was widely seen as a social democrat in the mold of NDP leaders, and his overthrow suggested to NDP supporters that any actions of a popularly-elected B.C. NDP government whose initiatives threatened U.S. interests in our province might well see the same sort of destabilizing (economic, if not military) intervention as Chile suffered.'[3]

Of course, it was not just as a British Columbian and a socialist, but also as a poet who had recently started her own, stone, 'diary of the earth' that Pat Lowther tracked the news from South America closely that September. Like many writers of the early seventies, she had long since discovered in the translated works of Pablo Neruda a compelling poetic influence, just as, in Neruda's dual career as a diplomat and Communist Party leader, she had found a prominent exemplar of the social responsibilities she associated with the artist's role. By coincidence, on September 22, the eve of Neruda's death, Lowther had written to her long-distance lover, Eugene McNamara: 'I'm very worried about Neruda. I believe he was ambassador to the UN, so [I] am hoping he was out of the country. [H]ave you heard anything?'[4]

Not only was Neruda *not* safely 'out of the country,' but, as Lowther's concluding question indicates, the precise circumstances around both his and Allende's respective fates were largely obscured in the immediate wake of the coup, a result of disinformation compounded by telecommunications breakdowns – American interests in international telephone and telegraph services having played no small part in the Chilean government's overthrow in the first place. Though Allende's death had been swiftly reported, rumours swirled as to whether it was really the result of suicide, as the junta alleged. Neruda's death, on the other hand, seems not to have been immediately reported, at least not by the *Vancouver Province*, whose coverage for Monday, September 24, includes a headline about the closure of Chilean borders, but no mention of the poet's death. It was, indeed, almost the end of September before 'the news came through' to Pat Lowther in East Vancouver. At that time, she mentioned Neruda's demise in a letter to Doug Barbour, then co-Chair of the League of Canadian Poets:

> I've been troubled by the death of Neruda, since I had heard only hours before the news came through that he was among the political prisoners – two reports, one that he was being held on a ship that was being used as a floating prison, and another, that he was under house arrest. Possibly, both were true at different times, but it's impossible to get any reliable information out of Chile.[5]

So it would go from September of 1973. Obfuscation and censorship clouded public accounts of a military juggernaut that, like 'The Night Train' Neruda recalled tearing through the rainforests of his childhood, left 'kilometers / of smoke' and 'the spread of silence' in its wake, from South to North.

Back in Vancouver, Lowther had also a different sort of silence to contend with at home. That September her youngest child, Christie, had started school, leaving the house strangely empty and quiet during the daytime. Her youngest daughter's departure for school was a ritual that Lowther marked with ambivalence, acknowledging grudgingly, 'It's a liberation of sorts, I suppose.'[6] That 'liberation of sorts' amounted to more freedom for her to work, namely at various part-time jobs, since by the fall of 1973 her husband, Roy, was pretty much chronically unemployed. She taught a night class, a poetry workshop, in New Westminster. She did unpaid work for the League of Canadian Poets as the regional representative for British Columbia. And, for a few days each week, she worked as Phyllis Young's secretary at the NDP's Little Mountain constituency headquarters, Hillcrest Hall. On Main Street near 28th Avenue, Hillcrest was an old building where Lowther was promised her own 'office' – 'of sorts.' As she explained to Fred Cogswell,

> I have been doing my NDP work at home, but today have moved into an office of sorts – an old meeting hall where they plan to partition off a corner – wall me in like a cask of Amontillado. Where I am now sitting waiting for the telephone co. to come and install a phone so I'll have some work to do. Or at least be in communication with the outside world.[7]

While she waited for the phone to ring, Lowther took the opportunity to communicate 'with the outside world' in her own way, by writing poetry, as well as letters to friends. 'A hi-fi has been installed in my office,' she reported to Eugene McNamara: 'I'm playing the Messiah and ... Bach's Easter cantata. Slowly writing a poem about Chileans imprisoned in disused nitrate mines.'[8] 'Chacabuco, the Pit,' which Lowther worked on during slack hours at Hillcrest Hall, was one of her most immediate poetic responses to the events of September 1973. Taking up the grim subject of the mass round-up of Chile's political prisoners – and North America's complicity in those atrocities – the poem would eventually become a part of the book she herself would not live to see published, *A Stone Diary*.

By 1973, a decade into her second marriage, the author of 'Chacabuco, the Pit' had also had some important first-hand experience with personal sorts of pits, emotional abysses of extreme duress. Evidence suggests that while Lowther initially experienced her union with Roy Lowther – a dozen years her senior – as passionate and intellectually stimulating, the bloom was off the rose, as they say, even before the couple's first anniversary rolled around. It was very soon clear to the newly remarried Pat Lowther that Roy was unable to make a functional break with his past life at the outset of his new one. He struggled, in particular, with despair and anger over his loss of custody of the children from his former marriage.

Through a complicated custody decision that awarded one child to each parent, Lowther herself had lost custody of the son from her previous marriage, Alan, who joined his new step-family mainly on weekend visits. To the five children of their previous unions, the Lowthers had added two children of their own in rapid succession. A year after Lowther published her first book, *This Difficult Flowring*, in 1968, Roy was let go from his job as a music teacher, turning instead to substitute teaching. Those sporadic posts eventually also dried up. Money became an increasingly pressing problem. Tensions between Roy and his soon teenaged step-daughter, Kathy, escalated with the passing years and, as might be expected, sometimes caught Pat awkwardly in the middle. The departure of Kathy from the Lowther household, at the age of fifteen, worried her mother deeply. At the same time, there were compelling reasons for Pat not to contest her daughter's youthful judgment in leaving the family home.

Amid the panoply of stresses on the complexly blended Lowther family, Pat, like most working mothers, found herself fretting at the intractable problem of finding a balance among her family life, her writing life, her political commitments, and the miscellaneous jobs she was obliged to seek to support the family's income. Yet while her husband's professional aspirations had by 1973 largely derailed, her own career ambitions had come quietly, steadily, into ever clearer focus. And, despite a few setbacks of the sort faced by most writers – the usual rejections, and a manuscript too long in limbo with a press that would fold before her book appeared – Pat Lowther's professional goals were also generally being realized, just as quietly and steadily.

Exacerbated by the growing disparity between their public lives, relations between the Lowthers, already estranged and rocky by the late sixties, deteriorated rapidly in the final years of the marriage. According to

Roy, the couple had struck a 'commitment policy' – namely, 'to stay together because of [the children] and look after them.' By early 1975, this 'policy' included the tacit understanding, initiated by Pat, that monogamy was no longer necessarily part of 'the arrangement.'[9] Roy was contemptuously opposed to 1960s-style polysexualism, disputing 'the new morality' as merely 'old immorality in a new form' (CATT, 3:392). Lowther herself was a more complicated case: as an intelligent feminist, she too was sceptical of what she once jokingly referred to as the '"*eros über alles*" approach.'[10] But that didn't mean she wasn't also, for various reasons, susceptible to the lure of 'free love,' with its promises of pleasure without responsibility. In any event, Roy's 'period of discovery,' as he called it, of his wife's infidelities could not have been entirely unexpected. Nor was such a 'discovery' entirely accidental, given that Lowther specifically directed intimate mail to her home address and seems to have made little attempt to conceal it.[11]

In the midst of increasing arguments about how 'open' an 'open' marriage could be without threatening 'the commitment' pact, Roy also began, from the fall of 1974 onward, to take advantage of his wife's absences from home by rummaging through her bookshelves, her stacks of notebooks and work papers, and, especially, her black briefcase, 'in order to smoke out information' (RLJ, 1:55). What upset Roy – who, by his own account, at any rate, eventually threw himself into a few consolatory extramarital affairs of his own – was less the fact of his wife's affairs *per se* than her apparent casualness about keeping evidence of her assignations from him. Even *more* damaging, to his mind, was the appallingly 'bourgeois' 'sex poetry' she was publishing as a result, he felt, of her liaisons: 'literary pornography' which he was convinced transparently identified him 'to everybody who reads Canadian literature' as a risible 'cuckold' (RLJ, 1:53, 73, 59–60). Roy thus began a year of reading through all of his wife's recent work, published and unpublished, documenting textual evidence of his public humiliation. He began to suspect affairs with virtually any man his sexually profligate (as he thought) wife had known occasion to be alone with. He began to see her – semidisguised, perhaps, but not successfully so – in nude art photos of a recent issue of *West Coast Review*. (The photos are not of Pat.)[12] And, especially after Lowther's temporary teaching appointment at the University of British Columbia came through in 1975, Roy became increasingly fearful that his treacherous, sadly debased wife would, in fact, desert him.

Lowther's own correspondence from the period bears the strained signs of Roy's growing paranoia and desperation. Crisis letters to close friends and reports of migraines or 'sick headaches' increase in frequency and pitch. 'Today, my husband left the house in an ambulance to be X-rayed for possible skull fracture – self-inflicted,' begins one such weary letter. 'This is the kind of thing that's been happening off and on for many years and it's been especially heavy this fall [1974] – self-mutilation, suicide threats, and an absolute refusal to try to get help from anyone but me.'[13] To her friend, the poet bill bissett, Lowther reported, simply: 'I've fallen into a hole.' Innocently, bissett thought she was referring to trouble with writing.[14] 'The fact is,' however, as she confessed to Fred Cogswell in an anguished letter the spring before her death,

> I'm living in a hell that was completely beyond my imagination before I got into it. And I'm so deep in that there's no way out. I thought for awhile it was getting better, but it's worse again now, worse than it's been for almost a year. It must be cyclic. It's building up again to more and more episodes of irrational violence. There are no moderate laws to deal with this kind of thing – it's either committal or nothing. No one can be compelled to have medical treatment. If he would just go on tranquilizers I feel sure it would make a tremendous difference.[15]

The unnameable, indeterminate 'it' behind her husband's behaviour had transformed Lowther's second marriage into her own private Chacabuco, a pit of dread, mental anguish, and apprehension 'so deep' that she saw 'no way out.' She spoke of her sense of entrapment especially frequently in the final years of her life. Indeed, in the same letter she had written on the eve of Pablo Neruda's death, expressing her concern for his welfare, she had also compared her own domestic situation to that of a prisoner 'doing time': 'I'm getting too tired to withstand the nasty surprises that always seem to be lying in wait. I used to think I could do my time and come out with some resources still left but that begins to seem unlikely.'[16] Years of 'nasty surprises' like Roy's self-inflicted head wounds and suicide threats were taking an emotional and physical toll that not even her 'tranks,' as she referred to her medication, could adequately mitigate.

What would appear to be Roy's final suicide threat came over the phone on 11 September 1975, exactly the second anniversary of the Chilean coup. The call came just as Lowther, at her Brock Hall office on the UBC campus, was attempting to get her first classes of the new term under way (RLJ, 1:89). Between dealing with her unstable husband, making a good first impression with students and faculty at UBC, organizing the impending Victoria meeting of the League of Canadian Poets, and absorbing the mid-September news of Oxford University Press's acceptance of her *Stone Diary* manuscript, the pressures on Lowther during the final month of her life were not all bad, but certainly numerous and very intense.

To the extent that the teaching job, the League meeting, and the new book were all ringing indications of his wife's success and growing independence, they were clearly pressures on Roy Lowther, too. He, however, claimed to feel particularly hurt by having been excluded from a roster of poets slated to read at an NDP 'Poetry Evening' at the Ironworkers' Hall on September 27th. The evening was to feature the poetry of Patrick Lane, David Day, Peter Trower, and – as the only woman writer – Roy's own wife. In the early seventies, Roy's ties to the NDP were as close as Pat's were, but he had also long styled himself as both a 'revolutionary' political dissident and a populist 'working-man's' poet and musician. (His pal, Milton Acorn, was a strong influence on this rôle.) Especially since he had become convinced that his wife's poetry was taking a pernicious turn toward apolitical 'bourgeois immorality,' anyway, Roy felt his exclusion from the NDP Ironworkers' reading as a keen injustice (RLJ, 1:51A).

As founding member of the Vancouver Writers' Guild and Labour Poets' Workshop, as past secretary of the Vancouver Poetry Society, and as a prolific poet of 'labor and CCF-NDP poetry for thirty years,' Roy's position, which he lobbied for over the phone to Patrick Lane and by letter to Rita Lalik, an NDP administrator, was adamant: 'In this crowd, I deserve twenty minutes [as a reader] too.' In his letter to Lalik, Roy reminds party members that he had once been called 'the Poet Laureate of the NDP' by 'one MLA,' whom he doesn't name. Roy's last-ditch petition for inclusion at the Ironworkers' Hall reading also repeatedly refers to his wife in the formal third person, as 'Pat Lowther,' an odd attempt to override their obvious relation. 'Pat Lowther' is referred to as though a nodding acquaintance on the literary circuit, rather than as the letter-writer's wife and mother of his youngest children. For example, in assessing the respective credentials of the poets on the program, Roy wrote: '[David] Day himself is pretty new. He's ... so new as a poet that I overheard Pat Lowther the other day tell someone she didn't know him, and she knows all of them.'[17]

Partly, no doubt, a poor attempt to downplay his own opportunism, Roy's defamiliarization of 'Pat Lowther' in the Lalik letter is telling in other ways, too. Within weeks of composing this letter, Roy Lowther would maintain that 'somebody,' a 'stranger' or an 'intruder,' broke into his bedroom and murdered his wife (CATT, 3:352; RLJ, 1:38). If Roy, however, already regarded his wife as, in effect, a 'stranger' to himself and could represent her as such to others, then one might discern an element of strangely distorted truth in this testimony. By September 1975, 'Pat Lowther' had become a virtual stranger to Roy; ergo, was he not also a 'stranger' in relation to her? The Lalik letter is only one example of the warped logic that Roy's behaviour would reinforce in the weeks preceding and following his wife's death.

With Roy deeply aggrieved and insecure, and Pat stretched for time, energy, and patience, September in the Lowther household proved a month of uncomfortable silences punctuated by arguments that escalated in duration and intensity. Pat suspected Roy of having placed a threatening call to her long-distance lover and confronted him with this suspicion. Roy 'denounced' his wife for her refusal to exert herself on his behalf in the Ironworkers' matter, and for 'openly hazarding' 'the commitment' 'for the first time.' He wondered how best to handle 'so sick a woman.' There were arguments over the teenaged Kathy (RLJ, 1:90–1, 92, xvii). It is evident from Roy's journal that Pat feared for her safety during these arguments, which culminated in two, prolonged confrontations the weekend prior to her murder (RLJ, 1:91).

Roy offers no recollection of when *it* happened, of when the violence he had so often (though not always) in past directed suicidally toward his own head turned outward instead, into a homicidal rage directed at his wife's. By his account, Pat retired to bed on the evening of Tuesday, September 23, with a migraine. Though ill himself, he rose the next morning to see the children off to school, kindly checking in on his wife and inquiring as to her well-being before leaving the house at 9:00 a.m. to go for a drive and contemplate how he might yet finagle 'a chance to read' at the Ironworkers' Hall on Saturday (RLJ, 1:4). That was the last time he saw her alive, he claimed. When he returned a few hours later, shortly after 11:30, he discovered his wife's body, badly damaged at the head. He sat down on an old, gray trunk at the foot of the bed – 'I don't know for how long' – and surveyed the scene in sickeningly meticulous detail. When he finally registered 'a feeling,' 'it was a sweeping thing': 'it was a feeling of pity for her, for what had happened to her,' but also, and more ambiguously, 'this pity for what she had become, what she was becoming.'[18] In the immediate context of the passage, Roy is apparently referring to the pathos of his wife's demise just as she was 'becoming' better known as an accomplished poet in literary circles or, as he put it, 'really getting in there' (RLJ, 1:6). But in the broader context of his voluble journal as a whole, the phrase 'what she had become, what she was becoming' also resonates more ominously with Roy's obsessions and growing delusions about 'the sexual promiscuity of Pat Lowther,' the 'barracuda' who was publicly shaming him by publishing 'literary pornography.'[19]

Then something else dawned on Roy. 'It came gradually, as I sat there and looked at her, it came to me that I had walked right into the worst trap I could ever imagine': 'I had walked into the trap of all time' (RLJ, 1:6; CATT, 3:351). The husband is always the first suspect in cases like this. With his background as a 'revolutionary' ex–student-radical and communist sympathizer, as a man who had a record of run-ins with the law before, Roy would never get a fair shake from the police or courts: 'Everybody would believe that it was I who killed her.' Therefore, as he soon decided, he would have to go to the extraordinary measures that he did, in attempting to dispose of the body and other evidence. Before he left the bedroom, however, Roy made a point of pausing to inspect the dresser mirror. What kind of self-image reflected back to him, he doesn't say (RLJ, 1:5–6).

That Pat Lowther was murdered sometime over the night of September 23, two years to the day of Pablo Neruda's death, might be easily dismissed as an intriguing but irrelevant coincidence. Roy's crime, after all, appeared to be a so-called crime of passion, the sort that ostensibly doesn't lend itself to advance calculation. But a third 'September 23rd' comes into play in this case. It is a text, a poem by that title, written by Roy Lowther and published in *Pegasus*, the mimeographed magazine he produced and edited for his current poetry club, the Vancouver Writers' Guild, in December 1974. 'September 23rd' is a melodramatic allegory about the death of a season – the high season, summer.[20] Roy might have claimed that he wrote this poem about his Uncle Maurice, who had died earlier that fall, at the age of eighty, and who was buried, 'give or take a day,' on his birthday, September 23. In his journal, Roy connected the memory of Uncle Maurice's funeral to the recollection of an 'incredible' expression of disdain which he perceived on Pat's face that day. He noted that his wife's expression matched a 'similar expression on another relative who was there' – that of a youthful male relative he also suspected her of having an affair with (RLJ, 1:61D). He zeroed in on 'a long-felt suspicion that something was going on involving Pat.' 'A day or two later,' the magazine *Quarry* showed up at his house with a poem in it by his wife, entitled 'Wrestling.' Roy read this poem as a 'sex poem.' (Lowther herself talked about it as a poem about writing.) The same issue contained a (completely unrelated) poem by Eugene McNamara. These events were associated in Roy's mind as interlinked signs, all and somehow equally proof of his wife's seemingly insatiable capacity for sexual deceit (RLJ, 1:48A). September 23 therefore stuck in his mind, as his later court testimony also indicated: 'I first learned of Eugene McNamara sometime between the 23rd of September, 1974' – the day of Uncle Maurice's burial – 'and October '74' (CATT, 4:549).

Roy *might* have claimed that he wrote 'September 23rd' as a way of unpacking the significance, for him, of Uncle Maurice's death. But he didn't. When the issue came up during his trial eighteen months later – for the prosecution was very interested in this poem, when they discovered it – Roy explained it had been written 'I don't know how many years ago' – 'it would be in the sixties.' 'The unfortunate date on the top of it is September 23rd,' the court noted. 'Would you look at the thing entitled "September 23rd" which is a very significant date,' the judge continued: 'The poem deals with death ... Why the date September 23rd?' To which Roy replied: 'It happened that I wrote the poem on that date and the night before there was a storm or something of some kind, and the summer went out on that date and the fall was coming in, that is all it was, the impression is there that summer died the night before' (CATT, 3:469–70).

At issue during the trial was whether or not the prosecution, headed by John Hall, would be allowed to introduce the text of Roy's poem as 'rebuttal evidence.' 'That's evidence by the prosecutor that comes after the defence evidence,' Roy's former defence attorney explains. 'Very unusual – you're not usually allowed to do this':

> But the rebuttal evidence he [John Hall] wanted to call had to do with this poem I'm talking about. He wanted to put the poem in and invite the jury to infer that Roy had planned this all along, or at least ever since he wrote that poem. And I successfully opposed that. Thank God. Not that it did Roy any good [in the end].[21]

Though there was 'something in that poem' which 'at the time' plainly suggested to Roy's own defence counsel 'that [Roy] could have written it in the knowledge that he might end up killing [Pat], or, alternatively, that he killed her on that day, because of the date in the poem,' the defence prevailed in blocking the rebuttal evidence, and 'the thing entitled "September 23rd"' was withdrawn from the jury's potential purview.[22]

Leaving aside, for the moment, the legal ramifications of 'September 23rd,' Roy's poem provides a fair indication of his penchant for melodramatic symbolism. And the symbolic investiture of that particular date for him seems an inescapable conclusion. September 23 was a date he associated with death. It was a date he associated with suspicions of adultery. And finally, it was also a date that, as he was very well aware, held special significance for his wife, as the anniversary of Neruda's death. Pat Lowther had, in fact, only recently commemorated that anniversary in her 'Anniversary Letter to Pablo,' a poem published in the American anthology *For Neruda, for Chile* (1975). Maybe it upset Roy that here was his wife writing an 'anniversary' letter to another man – a dead one, yet – more proof of his public humiliation. His attitude toward his wife's interest in Neruda had certainly soured to rancid cynicism by this point.

Ineluctably, Roy's sense of timing superimposed the fact of his wife's death onto the still fresh public memory of Pablo Neruda's – international literary icon and heroic synecdoche for the violent 'death' of socialist democracy. Roy Lowther's sense of timing, in other words, like his poem, needs to be read as a dramatic statement in itself, and it is a statement crucial in first inscribing the political martyr that 'Pat Lowther' symbolizes to this day: the 'murdered socialist poet, still thought of with blood,' to cite the lugubrious headline of one tribute article.[23] Political martyrs, however, usually die (and, usually, willingly so) in relation to some cause that is meaningful *to them* – love of freedom, justice, nation, religion. Not because their jealous husbands happen to believe they wore a highly suspicious expression on their face at a family funeral. Pat Lowther's own primary 'cause' was poetry. But this was a 'cause' she pursued and practised in order to save, not sacrifice, herself.

Obviously, as with any instance of spousal homicide, Roy's crime would have conveyed broader political overtones on any day. Five years after Lowther's death, the internationally prominent Marxist theorist Louis Althusser murdered his wife, Hélène Rytmann; in a cutting riposte to the generally sympathetic public response surrounding Althusser's case, Geraldine Finn points up the wider relevance signalled by the 'personal tragedy' of domestic violence: '... the violence, the contradictions and the struggle which characteriz[e] ... particular relationship[s] are intrinsic to and constitutive of all patriarchal relationships and sexual relationships in particular' (29). At the most basic level, Pat Lowther's death was, quite simply, *the* most infamous Canadian example of its time to underscore a host of socialist-feminist concerns, from class

inequities and lack of social resources for women in abusive relationships; to backlash against the second-wave 'women's lib' movement; to
the effects of a dominant culture that continues to reinforce patterns of
aggression and violence in response to change and difference. It is
indeed impossible to overlook the historical coincidence of Lowther's
murder with the emergence in Canada, during the late seventies, of the
first public campaigns against domestic violence; the first establishment
of 'transition' houses for women and children at risk; and the first landmark studies documenting the societal prevalence of the problem
(Duffy and Momirov 1997: 29). These are clearly shaping factors when it
comes to the question of her place in cultural memory.

Nevertheless, as Roy's 'September 23rd' indicates, there is nothing
basic or quite simple or neatly representative about the 'example' of Pat
Lowther's victimization, which was quite strangely timed and bound up
with specific political events and associations that were reinforced and
amplified from the start. Almost as certainly as they included Neruda's
death, these self-conscious associations on Roy's part likely included a
feminist frame of reference. Because, like the September date, 1975 was
not just any old year, either. That year, almost a full calendar year from
the time his poem appeared in *Pegasus*, happened to be the same one
declared International Women's Year by the United Nations, a year celebrated, as he also knew, by feminists like his wife. Roy himself was of the
opinion that most of what passed for feminist 'rebellion' against the traditional roles of 'women/wives/mothers' was really just 'self-pity' (RLJ,
1:125). As it happened, his timing of his wife's death would also forever
surcharge the memory of that death with an irresistibly poignant relevance, a terribly tragic irony. 'Pat Lowther' would become a woman
remembered not only (somehow, vaguely) as a political hero, but also as
a woman put to death in the very year most recently proclaimed as the
advent for her emancipation. Now wouldn't *that* give the feminists something to pity and lament.

Roy's scripting of his wife's death on 'September 23rd,' 1975, was
more or less deliberate – who knows? But at least two things seem clear.
The first is that Pat Lowther's uniquely distinctive posthumous power as
a tragic heroine, a rallying point for socialist-feminist causes, is inescapably cast along the lines of her husband's hyperbolic imagination. The
scripts embedded in Roy's initial, murderous action have influenced Pat
Lowther's 'afterlife' in ways that have yet to be examined by those who
would continue to identify and represent her specifically *as* a blood-
soaked political martyr and *as* a tragic victim of affective femininity –

'the darling of the Canadian poetry scene of the 60's and 70's ... brutally murdered by her husband,' as the *National Post* put it in 1999 (Howard 1999: B4).

A second and related point is that the evidently motivated timing of Lowther's death reveals an associative subtext fundamentally self-serving for her murderer, however precarious his mental state at the time. Whatever it was that Roy Lowther, poet manqué and spurned husband, might have been trying to communicate by cementing his wife's death to the memory of Neruda's, the associative implications of the linkage only help to reinforce his fiction of personal detachment from the crime of actually killing 'Pat Lowther' – that woman Roy once overheard talking with some poets about other poets. For politically rationalized murders are by definition impersonal events, and in Neruda's case, it may be recalled, the death hastened along by the military junta was also *inevitable* anyway. The cancer-stricken Neruda was already gravely ill, just as Pat Lowther was, in her husband's estimation, 'so sick a woman': '... she was a cancer for us to be rid of ' (RLJ, 1:91, 90).

The gesture of association with Neruda's canonical 'greatness' also implies a paradoxical commitment to honorifically entrenching the memory of the very life Roy Lowther committed himself to extinguish. In this regard, the symbolically charged timing of Lowther's murder needs to be recognized as a grotesque culmination of Roy's deeply dichotomized perceptions of his wife, whom he had come to revile as a woman and sexual being, but whom he valorized as a poet. Despite his rants about her 'bourgeois' 'sex poetry,' that is, Roy perceived 'Pat the poet' in awestruck terms as 'one of the finest minds that ever got into Canadian literature' (RLJ, 1:6). He was profoundly impressed by the extent and quality of her literary contacts, and by 'how important' her work was 'becoming.' When she took the witness stand during Roy's preliminary hearing, Virginia Tinmouth, Pat's mother, recalled her son-in-law having lectured her on this point: 'I don't think you realize how important Pat's work is becoming,' he had admonished. 'She's really getting up there now ... She's travelling all over Canada to the best places. Her work is being read in the best places. She's meeting fine writers' (PHTT, 10:757). Roy was every bit as intensely proud as he was intensely jealous of his wife's literary achievements. This might help account for his otherwise inexplicable thoughtfulness in taking the pains he did to imbue her death with a special aura of momentous historicity. Because by timing Pat's death to coincide with the anniversary of Neruda's, Roy did help ensure that it would be remembered as an essentially portentous political event, an event in which the death of the individual inevitably gets cast in iconic terms of a larger, national narrative – 'this *Canadian* tragedy,' as Dorothy Livesay phrased it.[24]

Roy had once written music for a multimedia production Lowther created. It was a planetarium show titled *Infinite Mirror Trip*, and its song lyrics included the refrain 'we are children of a minor star.'[25] By hitching his wife's ascending star – it was 'really getting up there' – to the glorious zenith of Neruda's, Roy, in effect, positioned Pat Lowther as Ursa Minor to Neruda's Ursa Major. His coupling of Pat and Pablo in death represents a radically ambivalent gesture that reflects his own hopelessly split vision of his wife as *both* a traitorous woman and a 'great' poet. His homicidal act over the night of the twenty-third bespeaks, on the one hand, a viciously vengeful send-off of the unfaithful wife, so that she might meet her 'anniversary' date with the 'other' man – while that man is still, in good misogynist form, bigger and brighter than she is. Conversely, for 'Pat the poet,' the symbolic coupling with such stellar company as Pablo Neruda was also perhaps intended as a token of beneficent admiration, a compliment. One that to every mind but Roy's easily reveals itself as among the crudest of backhanded compliments ever played out as a criminal travesty.[26]

Roy's bifurcated thinking about his wife is worth remarking because it, too, underscores the enduring significance of his definitive hand in setting 'the template of that tragedy,' to recall Sharon Thesen's phrase (1997: 19). To the degree that many subsequent claims about Pat Lowther have tended, as we will see, to replicate polarized extremes of critical over- and under-valuation, one could say that Roy Lowther's own perceptions of his wife initiate a dehiscence that continues to run throughout discussions of 'the Lowther legacy.' So, too, the dissonant ambiguities of 'tributes' offered in her name, which only begin with Roy's initial – and self-gratifying – symbolic linkage of his wife with a 'major' literary 'star.' 'We can't all blueprint the future,' as Roy once pointed out (CATT, 3:437). He himself strove to prove the exception to the rule. And for this reason, as much as any, history owes it to 'the darling' Pat Lowther that we be as precise as possible about Roy's role and influence in his wife's posthumous 'legacy.'

 ⁀

To return, briefly, to 'the thing entitled "September 23rd."' When it was ruled inadmissible as 'rebuttal evidence' during the trial, the text that might have been construed as foreshadowing Roy's crime on that date caused his defence counsellor, Alex Henderson, to release a sigh of relief – 'Thank God.' Because as evidence of some element of premeditation, 'either version [of its reading] is very damning, from a legal point of view.'[27] Importantly, however, it was not that such 'very damning' evidence would have made a difference in the nature of the charge against Roy. That charge was 'murder' – a charge that presupposed the notion of 'intent to kill or the apprehension of causing death' – as opposed to the lesser homicide charge of 'manslaughter,' under which so-called 'crimes of passion' fell. Legally, what 'September 23rd' signified was another powerful piece of circumstantial evidence against Roy in a case where it was already fairly easy to establish 'beyond a reasonable doubt' that Roy Lowther – not the 'stranger' or 'intruder' he theorized about – killed his wife. In the end, what is perhaps most instructive about the aborted legal history of 'September 23rd' relates to the principle of law which precluded its courtroom admission in the first place. Apparently, the primary criterion governing 'rebuttal evidence' is not how relevant (or even 'very damning') the new evidence may be. It is, rather, the fundamental importance of the *timing* of its introduction to trial proceedings, given that any new evidence introduced after the fact of defence evidence clearly poses a serious disadvantage for the defendant.[28] In other words, the judicial privileging of chronology over content leads in this case to a rather striking paradox: the one piece of evidence that most suggestively pointed to the significance of time in Roy Lowther's crime was suppressed on legal grounds upholding the importance of that very same principle.

Beyond its brief courtroom appearance, though, the text of 'September 23rd' introduces to the history of Pat Lowther's murder lingering questions about memory and truth that are less easily resolved – and that, since Roy's death in prison, in 1985, must go unanswered in any event. It's disconcerting enough that anyone so inclined can easily read Roy's allegorical poem as an oblique commentary on his wife, who, at barely forty, was in the full 'summer' bloom of her life when she died – exactly the half-way point of Uncle Maurice's natural lifespan, to be precise. Even stranger is a melodramatic poem about a 'storm or something' that in the context of the ensuing murder points to something like the oxymoron of an apparently foretold 'crime of passion,' a raging 'storm or something' over the night of 23 September 1975. In this sense, Roy's poem announces a crime scenario at some level pre-envisioned and allegorically rehearsed, if not coherently premeditated as such. The poem, with its ominous intimations of an anticipatory knowledge – on the part of Roy, let it be stressed – presents a remarkable counter to the apparent absence of any retroactive knowledge about the murder in Roy's casebooks and trial testimony. His accounts elide any memory of an explosive 'storm' but represent this elision, not as a failure of memory, but as a 'truth.' For Roy's defence was a narrative fully committed to the fiction of his physical (not mental) 'absence' during the murder – an absence supplanted by an 'intruder's' presence, that is.

Gail McKay, who had just undertaken a poetry tutorial at UBC with Pat Lowther when the murder occurred, and who would go on to follow Roy's trial closely in preparation of her book, *The Pat Lowther Poem*, is soft-spoken and thoughtfully articulate when she thinks back to this time. 'In a way,' she says, 'I believed that [Roy] believed that he didn't do it.'[29] If McKay is right – and she is certainly not alone in venturing this opinion – then the circumstances of Pat Lowther's death must be seen to involve the effects of delusion and compulsive 'forgetting' side by side with the effects of highly elaborate, self-conscious acts of memory and commemoration. The first strategist and dupe in the chequer-board of absence and presence, memory and repression, truth and fiction, that comprises the 'Lowther legacy' is Roy Armstrong Lowther himself, who, much like the 'bad poet' T.S. Eliot exposed long ago, 'is usually unconscious where he ought to be conscious, and conscious where he ought to be unconscious' (1919: 32). As a man predisposed to both melodrama and paranoia, to fits of tears as well as rage, it is Roy Lowther who proves a 'subject of pathos' in Shoshana Felman's sense of that term, as 'a subject whose position with respect to fiction (even when he is the author) is not one of mastery, of control, of sovereign affirmation of meaning, but of ... *loss of meaning* ... [and] *the non-mastery of [his] own fiction*' (1985: 49; emphasis in the original). Which doesn't mean that such 'non-mastery' can't be influential as it spins out in its historical effects. Roy Lowther's very successful positioning and projection of Pat Lowther as a distinctively heightened *object* of pathos and often under-critical reverence attests to this.

But historical effects, though they may be overdetermined, are rarely single in nature. Gail McKay's life, for one, changed tracks largely because of what she absorbed as a peripheral witness to the events that unfolded after 23 September 1975. Once she finished writing *The Pat Lowther Poem*, the young poet crossed professions and went on instead to establish a feminist law practice.

Chapter 2

Not about Poetry

This trial isn't about poetry ... This is a murder trial, but the poetry comes into it in an indirect way. You can't ignore it.
   – Crown Prosecutor John Hall, closing address to the jury, 1977

On the morning of the Ironworkers' Hall poetry reading, a warm and clear Saturday, September 27th, Kathy Domphousse, Pat Lowther's second child by her first marriage, pulled up to the front of her mother's two-storey house on East 46th Avenue. Beyond Roy and the two youngsters, Christie and Beth, then respectively seven and nine years old, Kathy had been the last family member to see her mother alive on September 23, having dropped by the Lowther household that evening for a visit. She hadn't stayed long that night – her mother, she discovered, was ill with a migraine – but the two women had made some plans for the weekend. It was Kathy's nineteenth birthday in a few days, and Pat had wished to indulge her eldest daughter with some shopping that Saturday. When she arrived at the house, Kathy discovered Roy out front, packing the family car, an old blue and white Ford jalopy. Pat had deserted the family and 'gone back East,' he informed his bewildered stepdaughter. Just where 'back East,' he didn't know; he mentioned Toronto. Roy told Kathy that her mother had left on the morning of the 24th, just after Kathy's visit. As for himself, instead of preparing to picket the poetry reading at the Ironworkers' Hall, as he had only recently obsessed about doing, Roy was now in the process of packing up his two young daughters and moving to the Gulf Islands.

Four days after the murder, Roy's encounter with his stepdaughter marked the first time he had to deliver, in person, an early version of an increasingly elaborate cover-up story he would tell, retell, amend, and improvise over the coming month. Though Kathy was the first to actually arrive at the house looking for Pat there had already been troublesome phone calls. Arlene Lampert had called from Toronto more than once, urgently requesting to speak with Pat about plans for the League's Victoria meeting. Her first call had been placed at 8:15 a.m., Vancouver time, on the morning of September 24. A few days later, after Lowther had failed to show up, without warning, for her Thursday poetry seminar at UBC, a disgruntled Robert Harlow, head of the Creative Writing Department, had called to demand an explanation from his new hire. Someone else had called for Pat regarding the Ironworkers' poetry evening.[1] Roy had been putting all callers off with the story that Pat had been called to Victoria early on the 24th for an 'emergency' meeting related to the League conference; he promptly added the bit about his wife 'going back East' when it occurred to him that 'no one goes missing from Victoria' (CATT, 3:419). So he began to tell people that his wife had phoned him after leaving for Victoria – 'she sounded very far away'[2] – to tell him she was leaving for good.

Of course, Roy's fabrications were also the account perpetuated in the earliest newspaper reports of Lowther's disappearance – red herrings that, in turn, led to at least one false public report of a posthumous sighting.[3] 'The purpose of the deceit was to buy more time,' Roy later admitted in court. He realized that the immediate inquiries of colleagues such as Lampert and Harlow were just the beginning (CATT, 4:555). Soon, the rest of his wife's family and friends would be asking questions, phoning, demanding answers. Then, inevitably, the police would arrive. No wonder the Gulf Islands never looked so good.

In the meantime, though, he had been preoccupied with other pressing concerns; namely, disposing of the evidence of the murder he claimed he did not commit. He had started in the bedroom, cleaning up. That took several hours. Before he wrapped the remains of Pat Lowther in a sheet, he fastidiously clothed the partly clad body because he 'didn't like the idea of her being naked' (CATT, 3:355). Then he temporarily moved her corpse, stowing it in the closet of an upstairs workroom which had once been Kathy's bedroom but now served as an office where his youngest daughters rarely ventured. Into this room, he dragged also two mattresses from the master bedroom, cutting away evidence and taping new material over bloodstains. When Beth and Christie returned from school, Roy told them their mother had gone to Victoria on business.

On the evening of the 24th, Roy moved his car from where it was usually parked, in the front street, and backed it into a narrow, unpaved parking stall next to the garage, behind the house. That night, he waited until both the children and the downstairs boarder, Don Cummins, were sound asleep. In the early hours of the 25th, sometime between three and five in the morning, Roy moved his wife's body into the trunk of his waiting car. The mattress – one of two he had doctored – was even more problematic to move, 'but it made less noise.' He left it leaning against the car, 'the taped end down on the ground,' trusting blithely 'to the custom of people to mind their own business' and not disturb it before he fixed it to the roof of the car later that morning. He went back into the house one more time – to fetch a cardboard box into which he had placed other evidence and to round up 'other things ... that would be considered necessary if anyone was going to make a trip.' 'Anyone' would need her purse, a toothbrush, some toothpaste, and a white poncho she had bought earlier that year for a reading tour and business trip 'back East.' And, her new, black briefcase. Then he went to bed. 'Anyone's' contact lenses he forgot about (RLJ, 1:14–15).

The morning promised, again, to be a fine and unseasonably warm day, as most of September had been that fall on the lower mainland. Roy ushered the children off to school 'as usual,' giving them lunch bags and telling them he'd be gone for a long drive that day, but home by the time they returned from school. On the highway on his way up to Squamish, he noticed in the rear-view mirror that the sheet he had affixed to the mattress on top of his car 'was working loose, hanging down' – in effect, flapping in the draft like a large white flag of surrender. 'Chances were the bloodstains were showing,' he later testified, adding, with more than a hint of self-satisfaction, that other motorists 'seemed to be amused by it' (CATT, 3:358). In his mind, every 'bungle,' every mistake he made – and he made many – could be viewed as an index of innocence, proof of his lack of guile and calculation, of his panicked desperation. In court, he therefore not only freely owned up to evidence of his own ineptitude, he actually emphasized and embellished such gaffes in his narratives of self-defence. But the troublesome mattress he did quickly ditch at the nearest picnic spot off the highway (RLJ, 1:17).

From the highway, to a gravel road and bridge that crossed Furry Creek, uphill to a rough and rocky logging road, Roy took his wife's body back to where they had once spent part of their honeymoon in 1963, near the South Valley Dam, a macabre pilgrimage prompted, perhaps, by some remnant of love sickened beyond recognition as such.

Once out of the car, however, he was unable to move the body very far, certainly not up to the dam as he had intended. So, 'leaving all kinds of signs,' he dropped the body into the creek bed in a 'semi-concealed' alcove of rock, visible from neither the trail alongside the creek nor the bridge below (RLJ, 1:19). It was 'a spot where,' as he would later coyly describe it to the police, 'the creek bends like a question mark' (CATT, 4:544). At the time, he was quite confident in his belief that the body would remain in this crook, on its flatbed of rock, at least over the winter. He threw his wife's purse down after her, exactly one dollar intact.[4]

As for the box with the 'spoiled articles and the poncho,' Roy drove back down the road to 'an old disused dump,' where he discarded these. That left the briefcase. As the container of letters and documents testifying to both his wife's literary success and her infidelity, Pat's new, black briefcase had come to embody for Roy 'a symbol' of all the impotent and too potent rage and hurt he could not own. It was 'a symbol' for which he reserved a special animosity:

> This black briefcase went wherever she went, and in the house was ... staring me in the face evening after evening while we read together or watched television ... And most often in the kitchen when it confronted me whenever I worked there, cleaned up, ... washed dishes, whatever, for twelve months, knowing its contents ... It was a symbol. I took that black briefcase and I threw it into the bushes as far as I could.[5]

Precisely because 'that black briefcase' 'went wherever she went' in life, Roy made sure to separate his wife from this 'basic tool of her trade' in death (CATT, 4:544).

This had been the trail of events leading to Roy's preparations for departure from the mainland via the Horseshoe Bay ferry on September 27th. No doubt partially as a way of distracting his young daughters, whom he now informed of their mother's putative desertion, Roy had hit upon the grand idea that he could – with some help from Pat's relatives – 'build a new life' with his girls on Mayne Island (RLJ, 1:21). For many years, the Lowther family had spent their summer vacations with Bill and Elsie Wilks, Pat's uncle and his wife, who owned a seaside property on the island. Roy called the Wilkses from Vancouver with his tale of desertion and asked if he and the girls could stay at Sleepy Hollow, a guest cabin, which – despite the bucolic name and location – was unheated and leaky, an accommodation intended strictly for summer use. The Wilkses agreed, with the proviso that Roy find more permanent lodgings soon, if he intended to stay on the island. Only once he had retreated to the romantic fiction of 'Sleepy Hollow' did he decide it was time to contact Pat's immediate family.

But in fact Pat's family had already swung into action, even as Roy attempted his escape. After her 'fishy' encounter with Roy on the Saturday morning she had arrived for her mother, Kathy, sensing immediately that something was seriously awry, had paid a visit to her grandmother. In her modest North Vancouver home, Virginia Tinmouth was 'putting the finishing touches' on some slipcovers when her granddaughter arrived to inquire whether she'd heard from or seen Pat lately. The very next day, most of Pat's family, including Virginia, Kathy, and Pat's siblings, Brenda and John, made the first of several, desperate return trips to the house at 566 East 46th Avenue: 'I don't know why we [first] went there,' Virginia recalled many years later, 'except that I knew Kathy wanted something done.'[6]

Though initially they may not have known precisely what they were looking for, the family's searches of the Lowther household at least helped focus their concerns by pointing to an absence due to suspicious malfeasance, and not, as Brenda had also briefly and plausibly fretted, to a possible medical problem potentially linked to her sister's terrible migraine headaches (CATT, 1:124). Inside the house, they found the master bedroom stripped bare of even the drapes. Only one mattress and most of Pat's clothes and belongings remained. Pat's mother immediately noticed a favourite outfit that Pat had been wearing lately 'on a regular basis,' a recent birthday gift from Kathy (CATT, 2:232). Virginia was also quick to observe that her daughter – who did not possess any luggage of her own – had not borrowed her suitcase, as she normally would have done, if going on a trip. On a repeat visit, looking for a photograph to provide the police, John, at the time a young man in his twenties, discovered the alterations Roy had made to the one remaining mattress (PHTT, 6:488–9).

Her nineteenth birthday come and gone with no word from her mother, Kathy reported Pat missing to the police on October 1. In the almost two weeks that elapsed between that day and the discovery of Lowther's body on Thanksgiving Monday, the 13th, the family's repeat visits – aided also by Pat's brother Arden and by Kathy's brother Alan, among others – took on the inexorable, surreal quality of a nightmare. That the weather turned for the worse heightened this sense of unreality, as perhaps only fog-enshrouded coastal inclemency can. The rains came so heavily that early October that the Lowthers' landlord, Mr

Gutknecht, feared the basement of his property at 566 East 46th Avenue would flood. It was on one such drenching night that Pat Lowther's family found themselves digging up the back garden at the house, where they had noticed freshly turned earth. 'You just do things you never, ever imagined yourself doing,' Kathy recalls of this incident, quietly, after the interval of a quarter century. 'Trying to find things, and terrified that you're going to find them, and then devastated when you don't find them.'[7]

∽

It was crucial that the investigation into Pat Lowther's disappearance began as a 'missing person's' case. To some degree, it was incumbent upon her distraught family to persuade the police that this was likely not a straightforward 'missing person's' case at all. According to Pat's mother, Virginia, 'We had an awful time to get them to investigate':

> They said, 'We're used to this sort of thing. A woman leaves home because she's got a sweetheart somewhere ... It will turn out fine where she is eventually' ... When they finally started to investigate, they said, 'We were slow to investigate because it was just too, too trite.'[8]

Indeed, the police observed their own protocols. When Kathy first filed the missing person's report with the Vancouver police, a Constable Menzies followed up immediately by contacting sources, including Roy, who agreed to return from Mayne Island on October 2nd for an interview. Because Roy, unsurprisingly enough, had his own very precise ideas about the ideal time-line and order which the investigation should follow – *his* plan had been to 'start the police looking' somewhat later that week (RLJ, 1:29) – Kathy's pre-emptive move in filing the missing person report flummoxed him somewhat. This pattern would recur over the course of the investigation whenever reality deviated from the temporal sequence he plotted in his head. Armed with evidence of his wife's love affair, he showed up for his meeting with Constable Menzies, but later he also dropped by the house in East Vancouver, removing the incriminating mattress which John had inspected and taking it with him back to Mayne Island on October 3rd.

Roy's attempts to settle with his daughters into more permanent rental quarters on Mayne Island were soon thwarted by another police summons to Vancouver. This time, Detectives Roy Chapman and Ken Hale of the homicide division took him back to the house on 46th Avenue. But the officers' forty-minute 'search' of the house was 'routine' and extremely cursory. Though they indeed thought it 'strange' that a woman should depart without taking much of her clothing, and that Roy had removed the mattresses from the bed ('What did you think she would sleep on, if she returned?'), they were 'treating it as a missing person' case and 'talking to [Roy] as an aggrieved husband at the beginning.'[9] Thus, although they told the media from the outset that Lowther's 'complete' disappearance was suspicious,[10] in the house itself that day, they merely checked the bathroom and surveyed the master bedroom briefly from the hallway door, trying to determine only what items an absconded Lowther may have taken with her.

The detectives' main impression of the Lowther household was of its impoverishment, with the single exception being an excessive profusion of books – books everywhere, 'a great number of books ... I would say hundreds.'[11] The books, they couldn't miss – and, in fact, remarked upon frequently in court, as though at a loss to explain this domestic peculiarity. Like the earlier family members, though, what Chapman and Hale did not see on their initial visit was the less manifest profusion of small blood spots on the walls of the master bedroom, evidence camouflaged by both a red-patterned wallpaper and bad light. Later that same month, when the detectives returned, this time specifically looking for evidence of violent crime, they first discerned 117 and later, according to Hale, 248 such traces on the walls, valance, ceiling, and bed frame before they gave up counting (PHTT, 9:704).

As for the Lowthers' private library, no one in the family can remember exactly where all those hundreds of books went when the household on 46th Avenue was eventually liquidated. As Brenda points out, with her brother John nodding in concurrence, 'You know, we were all in a terrible state; I find there are huge blanks in my memory.'[12]

Ken Hale, the detective who can today recount precisely how scientific advances in blood typing and DNA evidence have revolutionized police work, was in October of 1975 a rookie on the homicide squad, only recently promoted. The Lowther 'missing person' case was one of the first he'd been assigned to in this capacity, which is perhaps why it has 'always stuck' quite vividly in his memory. Books and poetry came up during his earliest conversations with Roy. Roy took advantage of the detectives' attention to show them some of his wife's work and air his (auto-)biographical explications of its references to her affairs and his ignominious status as a 'cuckold.' Handed some recent samples of Pat's publications, Hale confessed that 'this type of poetry' was not his 'cup of tea'; he himself was more of a Rudyard Kipling man.[13] While Hale implies, in retrospect, that this expression of literary taste was tossed off by way of prompting Roy to reveal something of the poetic rivalry that would come under scrutiny during the trial, the former detective is also candid about the 'sympathy' he came to feel for a man whose obituary he carried around in his wallet for years: 'I felt sympathy for the man because he was his own worst enemy. He was [always] making a run for his own bank.'[14]

Setting back into place the fact that Roy proved a worse 'enemy' to Pat Lowther than he ever did to himself, it is true that he soon made another characteristic 'run for his own bank.' After the detectives departed from their first survey of the Lowther home, Roy scribbled a note which he left conspicuously taped to the dining-room table that had once served as his wife's primary work space; it read, in part:

> Pat,
> I hope you return soon and are well. Some sort of solution will have to be worked out, for this problem, [sic] with legal aid. We are living on Mayne Island. The children are happy and well ... Everyone has been extremely worried about your disappearance. Please contact us. (PHTT, 9:683–4)

It was Kathy who, on a subsequent tour of the premises, found this latest addition to Roy's charade and turned it over to the authorities (RLJ, 1:36). 'The English in the note was strange,' Detective Hale testified at the preliminary hearing. He recounted confronting Roy about it: 'You write the words as if she would read it someplace else. You wrote, "I hope you return soon and are well." Surely you would have wrote [sic], "I'm glad you're back" or something in the present, not in the future tense.' 'I guess I am a suspect,' was Roy's response (PHTT, 9:685). As far as he was concerned, his own *idée fixe* about 'the trap' he'd stepped into in the bedroom – the husband is always the first to be fingered – was merely being confirmed.

The pivotal event in the investigation into Pat Lowther's disappearance was occasioned, not by the police, but instead by an unsuspecting head waiter employed by the University Club of Vancouver. The man had taken his family for a holiday weekend picnic to Furry Creek and had ambled a quarter mile downstream on his own (PHTT, 2:99). His discovery of a woman's body on that October Thanksgiving had, in turn, been literally precipitated by precipitation – by the same rains which had threatened to swamp landlord Gutknecht's basement and which had beleaguered Lowther's family in their futile searches for any trace of Pat. The past few weeks of downpour, drizzle, and downpour had swollen the creek's water levels to such a degree that the body dislodged from the crook where Roy had dropped it and was carried downstream, closer to more frequented recreation areas. In effect, the creek that hooked 'like a question mark' ended up throwing Roy at least one good curve which he could not anticipate.

Though it would take some time for an autopsy and a positive identification of the remains through dental records, the early consensus was fairly certain that the newly discovered body was that of the 'noted' and 'missing poet, Pat Lowther.'[15] On the same October 13th that the RCMP gathered at Furry Creek, taking pictures and interviewing the shaken head waiter, many of Pat Lowther's literary friends and acquaintances – poets such as P.K. Page, F.R. Scott, Al Purdy, Joy Kogawa, and Dorothy Livesay – were, of course, departing from the annual League meeting, which had proceeded in Victoria despite the uneasy absence of its Chair. 'See you soon, *God willing* as Alden Nowlan put on his "if" slip,' Lowther had written just a few months earlier, in reference to an imminent cross-country trip. She was citing Nowlan's words for his tentative plans to attend the Victoria meeting that fall.[16] Though the last months of her correspondence reflect every expectation that she, too, would be present for the October meeting, like Nowlan, the cancer-haunted Maritime poet, Lowther was also clearly living with a heightened awareness of the conditionality of all 'plans' by 1975. As it turned out, 'God willed' to Alden Nowlan a longer '"if" slip' than that extended to Pat Lowther, though before too very long, Nowlan would also be dead, and also too early, at just fifty. In retrospect, one of the poets who did attend the 1975 meeting, P.K. Page, is wistful but realistic about the fact that the program of taped readings then sponsored by the League of Canadian Poets caught up to neither Lowther nor Nowlan before their deaths: 'We made up a hit list ... according to age,' she says, resplendent at eighty-four, in the verdant backyard of her Victoria home. 'And the hit list doesn't work because you don't know who's going to die; you can only surmise' (Bowling 2002: 26).

A similar breach between the realms of speculation and fact had to be crossed in the investigation into Pat Lowther's disappearance. Only once her body was recovered and positively identified could the police finally let go of 'the missing person's scenario' and actually pursue the concerns that had gripped Lowther's family from the beginning, the 'suspicion [that] this could be more than meets the eye here.'[17] Almost immediately, the detectives, Chapman and Hale, flew by helicopter to Mayne, in order to 'notify' and quiz Roy about the body's discovery. At this point, on October 15th, they seized from Roy's cabin a hammer and the second mattress, which he had hauled to the island, and sent both off for tests. Eventually, Chapman asked the 'aggrieved husband' point-blank: 'Did you kill your wife?' Roy answered as might be expected, and then asked to call a lawyer. The detectives seized his car and returned to Vancouver to reinspect the house on 46th Avenue more thoroughly, this time with the aid of fingerprint and serology experts. Though they were unable to type and date the trace amounts precisely, the police discovered blood on all of the seized evidence, as well as in the house, facts for which Roy, when pressed, had no explanations (PHTT, 7:557–77). All the time that the detectives intensified their focus upon him, and pursued the conclusions that the evidence plainly pointed to, Roy protested his innocence; at the same time, however, he could also not resist occasionally teasing the police with the self-gratifying promise of his own drama: 'You will find more if you go deeper' (PHTT, 7:557).

Four weeks to the Tuesday, September 23rd, of his crime, Roy Lowther was arrested on Mayne Island. Having already named himself as a prime suspect from the outset, he had, of course, anticipated this event, watching and waiting for Chapman and Hale to make their 'final move' (RLJ, 1:41). Under pressure, he had by this point finally divulged the fact of their mother's death to his daughters. But on that Tuesday, October 21, he had not anticipated the alacrity with which Social Services personnel would arrive to take custody of his children, during their school hours. By the time he learned that welfare officers had arrived to seize Beth and Christie, and by the time he raced to the ferry dock at Miner's Bay, he barely had time to say goodbye to his traumatized daughters before they were sprinted away in a police boat across the choppy gray waters of Active Pass. From the girls' perspective, their father appeared as a rapidly receding figure on the dock. It was the last they ever saw of their one remaining parent.[18]

Beth and Christine Lowther were headed onward that day into futures which they themselves have best begun to reconstruct, in their public interviews and writing as adults. At the time, however, and unfortunately for them, the girls were not present when, a few days after Roy's arrest, Pat Lowther's family and local friends were finally able to pay their last respects at a memorial service, held at the Unitarian Church of Vancouver on West 49th Street. The service that preceded the poetry readings was conducted by the same Unitarian minister who had married Patricia Domphousse to Roy Lowther in 1963. Among those who benefited from the small but essential balm of a formal good-bye were old friends, such as Patrick Lane, newer friends, such as Marya Fiamengo, and some of Lowther's students, such as the quietly observant Gail McKay.

Apprehended and held briefly in the 'Van City Bucket,' the municipal jail on Main Street, Roy was soon arraigned and out on bail, the cash put up by an unidentified friend. The price of temporary freedom for the charge of non-capital murder? In this case, three thousand dollars. 'I do not condone people killing their wives,' Justice J.C. Bouck, who set bail, was cited as saying. 'But when they do, it is more likely to be an act of passion unlikely to be repeated on someone else.'[19] Luckily only for Roy, this judge had no way to fathom the calculated symbolism of his presumably spontaneous 'act of passion.' Nor, for that matter, was the judge who granted bail apparently aware of Roy Lowther's previous track record when it came to the prospect of 'people killing their wives.' Prior to his 1963 marriage to Pat, Roy's stormy first marriage had ended badly, a break-up precipitated by Roy's violent assault – some sources say attempted murder – of his first wife. This had earned him a brief incarceration at a psychiatric institution.

As a result, the man perceived by Detective Hale as 'his own worst enemy' was free to use the interval between the granting of his bail and his court hearings to live some of the time on the Gulf Island of Saturna with a friend, a living he somehow continued to manage without actually doing (in Hale's phrase) 'a lick of work.' Within a few months of being released on bail, Roy was also back in the local news for an unrelated reason, a bizarre traffic incident in which his runaway car, left in gear with no one in the driver's seat, rammed a police cruiser (repeatedly) in a Kitsilano Beach parking lot. Apparently, Roy was afraid the law would forget him – forget him just as completely as he himself seemed to have forgotten a few things. As the now retired Ken Hale muses from the far end of his constabulary experience, in one way or another 'the mind tunes itself into what most troubles it.'[20]

Yet for a man who could repudiate any memory of the actual murder of his wife, Roy's memory was quite copious when it came to the all-important rationale for the measures he undertook to cover up the crime that, as he alleged, a 'stranger' had committed. His master narrative of entrapment ensured that after September 23 his fate would unfold with the magical logic of a self-fulfilling prophecy – each inch on the road toward his legal conviction as a murderer only reinforcing an already entrenched emotional conviction of his persecution as a 'revolutionary' and as a man. By indicting himself, even despite himself, at almost every turn, Roy could know himself as omniscient all along. It was a drama of victimization fundamentally based on strategies of reversal and projection, and it was a drama of self-martyrdom that hung upon the twin nails of sex and politics.

As for Roy's claims of sexual discrimination, even Ken Hale, the somewhat 'sympathetic' detective (Chapman is since deceased), recognized that this 'was very clichéd' as grounds for a cover-up, especially for a husband in a marriage known to be – at the very least – unhappy: 'I mean, ninety-nine – no, I won't say ninety-nine – [in] ninety-seven per cent of [such homicide] cases, it's the husband [who is responsible], you know. I mean, you can't ignore that.'[21] 'I remember him always feeling that the husband gets the raw deal when people split up,' Roy's former defence lawyer also recalls, apparently rather well:

> I remember him going on and on and on about that, and probably writing me a long memo on it ... When a wife is murdered, the husband is always the first person suspected. Which is probably true, but that's because about three-quarters of those murders are committed by the husband ... So what [Roy is] saying is true, but there's a good reason for it.[22]

Roy's stated motive of political persecution, on the other hand, was based largely upon what he liked to characterize as his past involvements with student radical movements during the 'McCarthy-hysteria era.' After graduating from UBC with a second-class honours degree in philosophy and psychology in 1945, Roy had moved for a time to the University of California at Berkeley to undertake an MA in philosophy (on aesthetics) – this degree, by his own account, 'written for and failed.' Around the time that his student visa expired anyway, in 1949, he claimed to have been 'deported for political (communist) activity.'[23] Alex Henderson, Roy's defence counsel, would later stress his client's unhappy career as a student communist during the 'infamous era of Senator Joe McCarthy' during his closing address in Roy's 1977 trial (CATT, Supplemental: 8). Today, Henderson has 'a vague recollection' of this aspect of his 'difficult' former client's history: 'I can also say that Roy would probably be prone to exaggerate something like that ... he'd make himself out to be leader of the rally, when he was really [a] fourth spear-carrier in the back row.'[24]

Whatever the precise circumstances of Roy's first American deportation, he made another 'run for his own bank,' to reprise Detective Hale, the following year, when in 1950 he illegally re-entered the United

States, this time to pursue an avowedly romantic (not political) inter-est.[25] 'We all knew Roy was constantly angry and believed the world was persecuting him,' says Bethoe Shirkoff, a former NDP associate of the Lowthers in Vancouver. 'He *had* been persecuted by the U.S. govern-ment, but he courted that persecution by deliberately crossing the bor-der after [his] expulsion in the McCarthy days.'[26] The consequence of this 'courting' – the more successful of the two kinds he pursued – was a year-and-a-half jail term at the McNeil Island Penitentiary in Washing-ton State, plus a substantial fine of one thousand dollars.[27]

When he returned to Canada, Roy joined the Labour Progressive Party (formerly the Communist Party of Canada) and married his first wife, also a communist activist at the time, in Toronto. 'He was some-thing of a student of Marxism' before he shifted over to become 'quite active in the NDP,' recalls Hilda Thomas, an English professor who knew Roy through her left-wing connections in Vancouver. '[But] he wasn't an imposing person intellectually.'[28] As was also the case with Roy's involvements with arts organizations such as the Vancouver Poetry Society, his choleric and dogmatic personality led to uneasy relation-ships within Labour and, later, NDP circles; indeed, according to Tho-mas, Roy's move to the NDP occurred because he had been 'kicked out of the Communist Party' – 'one of the few people,' she adds, 'to have enjoyed that particular privilege.'[29] It is worth noting that Roy's political history in this respect resembles that of Milton Acorn, the Lowthers' friend and sometime-boarder during the sixties, whose 'cranky individu-alism' likewise defined his 'belligerent' and 'persistent' 'quarrels with partisan authority' (Doyle 1997: 74–5).

Roy's personal story of persecution as a 'pioneer political prisoner' was another cliché, this one of the Cold War climate that nurtured him. A derivative thinker, he appropriated the dominant keynotes of his time, just as he also tended to appropriate and pervert his wife's literary metaphors. He used the pretext of political persecution toward the essentially self-serving end of masking or disguising – from himself as much or more as from anyone else – the actual motives for his behav-iour on and after September 23.

გუ

When the time came, two key aspects of Roy Lowther's 1977 murder trial – the weakness of the accused's own narrative of self-defence and the strength of what the prosecutor called the 'tight web of circumstantial evidence' against him – served to expedite the judicial process (CATT, Supplemental: 18). The preliminary hearing, held in early April to determine whether there was sufficient evidence to proceed to the more expensive, federal assize court, quickly determined that there was. Roy's trial by jury – nine men and three women – lasted nine days between April 10th and the 22rd. At the time of the trial, the new Arthur Erickson–designed provincial court buildings downtown on Howe and Smithe Streets had not yet been completed, so the case was heard in the old courthouse on Georgia, a few blocks away, in the brick, glass-domed building that is now home to the Vancouver Art Gallery.

These days, Roy's former lawyer, Alex Henderson – like his counterpart, John Hall – is a high-profile judge on the B.C. Supreme Court. Their offices, hidden within the labyrinthine and tightly secured corridors of the law courts complex, are filled with oak-panelled walls, red leather chairs, and long rows of legal books and binders bearing the identical spines of serial runs. In April of 1977, though, Henderson was a young and relatively inexperienced lawyer brought in to serve as Roy's counsel 'at the last minute' request of the Legal Aid Society. As Henderson recollects, the accused had already 'gone through at least two other lawyers who "fired the client," as we say.' Roy's would be only the second murder trial of Henderson's professional career to that point, and certainly, he says, his 'first well publicized case.' With only a few weeks to prepare a case file that other, evidently exasperated lawyers had begun, the defence chose to rely on only a single witness, the accused himself – as against the prosecution's list of twenty-five witnesses and its lengthy list of exhibits. Given that Roy was prone to rambling diatribe, not to mention such habits as cutting off his own lawyer in mid-question, and insulting both the prosecutor and the judge, he was, of course, not his own best defence. 'He was the most difficult client I've ever had,' Henderson sighs, 'and I've had thousands.'[30]

At the end of the nine-day trial, the Crown prosecutor, John Hall, summarized the case quite bluntly for the jury: 'Mr. Lowther professes himself to be very alarmed at authorities, etcetera, etcetera ... The key issue gets down to [be]: can you believe the bilge that the accused has told you?' Indeed, by the time of his closing address, the prosecutor had seen and heard enough of 'Mr. Lowther' to include in his final remarks a collegial pat of sympathetic commiseration for the defence team. The jury took less than three hours to deliberate a guilty verdict. Roy was sentenced to life in prison with no chance of parole for ten years. His appeal the following year, under a new defence lawyer (after Henderson also 'fired the client'), and under new grounds of 'provocation,' was summarily dispatched as 'frivolous.'[31]

On the face of it, the case against Roy Lowther was fairly straightforward. As John Hall asserted in his closing address, this was *not* a trial about poetry, but first and foremost a trial about a particularly 'violent, insensate type of crime' (CATT, Supplemental: 25). The vicious nature of Pat Lowther's death was all too awfully apparent from three of the central exhibits entered by the Crown: an 'ordinary 16 ounce standard hammer' with traces of blood in its claws (CATT, 4:508); the tampered but still bloodied mattress the detectives had retrieved from Mayne Island; and, by far the most painful piece of evidence, almost unspeakably so, a portion of the poet's shattered skull. In his testimony, the pathologist who removed the occipital bone for courtroom exhibition acknowledged that this was an 'unusual course' of procedure to follow; his primary aim in doing so was to enable the prosecution to more precisely link the murder weapon to the injuries sustained by the victim – to show that the skull, that is, 'Exhibit P' in the preliminary hearing, bore depressions caused by blows from a weapon very much like the hammer, 'Exhibit Q' (CATT, 4:501; PHTT, 3:162–200).

Some of the twenty-five witnesses taking the stand for the prosecution were members of Pat's grieving and angry family, who testified to Roy Lowther's violent predilections. Under cross-examination by Henderson, Pat's mother, Virginia, said that though she had never directly witnessed Roy strike her daughter, 'I have seen evidence [of abuse] on her body.' Henderson persisted for the unconditional, monosyllabic answer he sought: had she, he repeated, ever *seen* her son-in-law hit Pat? 'No,' Virginia responded. This was her final reply as a witness before the defence dismissed Pat Lowther's mother from its cross-examination, and for Virginia, it must have been a bitter final word (CATT, 2:237). Kathy, however, described under cross-examination witnessing at least two physical altercations during the years she lived with her mother and Roy. She, along with other family members, could also attest to examples of Roy's fits of blinding, explosive rage, during which he could 'bend pot lids' and 'crack doors with his fists.' Most of the doors in the house on East 46th Avenue bore the traces of this rage (PHTT, 4:257–8; 5:313).

Coupled with Roy's own imprudent lack of self-governance on the stand, the prosecution's 'tight web' of evidence and the testimony of its witnesses revealed with sufficient detail a 'violent, insensate type of crime,' a fact proven well 'beyond a reasonable doubt' in Courtroom 406 that April, eighteen months after Pat Lowther's death. At the same time, however, as with Roy's crime itself, the trial proceedings were not so simple. Although 'this trial' was 'not about poetry' – it was a murder trial – 'poetry' nevertheless entered into it in an essential way. As the prosecutor reminded the jury, poetry was 'very much a side issue,' but 'you can't ignore it.' More broadly, it was a whole ensemble of issues related to literary aesthetics, culture, and politics that consistently usurped the attention of the assembled jurors, judge, and spectators for the duration of the trial. With respect to the murder of a poet, the 'side issue' of literature was more than just marginalia; it was a peripheral 'issue' simultaneously central to the case in ways that seem both obvious – and, in hindsight, at least – surprising.

On the most obvious level, the trial *was* about poetry in the sense that poetry was, inescapably, its main referential frame. Over the course of the preliminary hearing and the trial, jurors and audiences were initiated to the world of small literary magazines, such as *West Coast Review* and *Event*; to esoteric literary organizations, such as the League of Canadian Poets ('The *what*, please?' as the uncomprehending judge asked [PHTT, 5:354]); and to an international array of poets, from the American Charles Bukowski, to the Chilean Nobel laureate Neruda ('N-E-R-U-D-A'), and the Canadian Dorothy Livesay ('L-I-V-E-S-A-Y, of Victoria') (PHTT, 6:421). Not all literary references proved equally obscure, though. Lowther's 1972 reading tour with Margaret Atwood was mentioned at one point, for example, and the judge, for one, was evidently impressed. When he delivered his Charge to the Jury, 'the court,' as he is referred to in trial transcripts, felt it only fair, 'in case you all don't know,' to note 'that Margaret Atwood was [*sic*] a big name in contemporary Canadian Literature, so big that I should take judicial notice of it. It is a commonly known fact, so that is big name stuff' (CATT, 4:558). N-E-R-U-D-A, though, still needed to be spelled out.

In addition, aside from letters, photographs, and physical evidence retrieved from the crime scenes, many of the twenty-seven exhibits introduced during the trial were actually literary texts, mainly poetic, of one sort or another. There was, of course, 'the thing entitled "September 23rd,"' which the prosecution tried unsuccessfully to enter as rebuttal evidence, given its 'very significant date' (CATT, 3:469). But the poetic texts introduced as evidence in court were mainly works by Eugene McNamara, Pat's long-distance lover, and poems by Lowther herself. The broader implications of such legal uses of literature for artistic freedom and censorship were not, in and of themselves, raised as issues during the trial.

Summoned from his home in Ontario to appear at the trial, Mc-
Namara testified that when Lowther died, it had been a full year since
he'd last seen her. Nevertheless, books he had sent her over the course
of their relationship – his 1974 collection, *Diving for the Body*, and a previous 1972 volume, *Passages and Other Poems* – were placed before the
court for scrutiny. These were books that Roy had found at home and
were part of the cache of literary 'evidence' which he had been assem-
bling in the 'case' against his wife; the detectives had seized this bundle
of documents from him upon his arrest. In court, the defence tried to
suggest that the books, along with other, individual McNamara poems,
contained work written specifically for Pat Lowther and about his relationship with her. When the defence asked McNamara to confirm or dis-
pute that theory, though, the judge ruled this line of questioning
'inadmissible' on, basically, the New Critical grounds of the intentional
fallacy: '... it is irrelevant what the author thought or what he intended;
it is what the poem says as interpreted by the Jury [that counts]' (CATT,
2:169). It is interesting to think to what extent such moments of courtroom 'judgment' have as much to do with the literary training of legal
professionals as with principles of jurisprudence. At the very least, it
seems no random accident that principles of New Criticism clearly
inform the trial's interpretive proceedings, given that it was the method
historically prevalent at the time that the judge and lawyers involved
would have received their respective undergraduate educations – from
professional counterparts, incidentally, of Eugene McNamara, the English professor in the witness stand.[32]

A range of Pat Lowther's works also factored in the trial. These
included a feminist anthology in which some of her work appeared,
Mountain Moving Day, and, interestingly, 'seven poems' from a new,
unfinished project provisionally entitled 'Time Capsule.' This latter was
the same project she had described at a 1975 reading as 'a complex kind
of witness' to 'things like history, and context, and continuity.' Along
with McNamara's poems, these were among the texts carefully copied
and compiled by the unhappy husband as 'proof' of his wife's betrayals.
Although his lawyers tried as far as they could to restrain Roy's testimony, he nonetheless used the forum of the court to expound upon
what he had described to a friend as an 'intellectual type of poetry' 'personally directed at him' (CATT, 4:524).

To readers familiar with Lowther's sometimes confessional poetry, it
will not come as any surprise that some of the poems Roy singled out for
courtroom attention *are* (auto-)biographically inflected. For example, in

the early seventies, Lowther had written a long dramatic poem entitled 'Sandy Humbleton,' which recounts, by way of a male persona, a paranoid protagonist's Orphic descent into madness. It is not a strong poem, and there is no record that she ever published it. Roy, however, claimed in court that not only had it been published *and* broadcast on a local radio station, but that he had also 'learned' from his wife 'that I was the model [for it].' This was one of many texts, according to him, 'in which I appeared in a rather negative fashion' (CATT, 3:388).

Whether dramatic or lyric, however, the poetic 'I' is, to reprise Pat Lowther's own phrase, 'a complex kind of witness': an unpredictable amalgam of biographical and other experience (including the absorption of other texts), imaginatively transmuted into a literary construct. This distinction between life and art was one that Roy had trouble grasping. For him, life spilled into art and vice versa with an astounding lack of probity. This fact is reinforced by a startling confession he made to the lawyer who handled his appeal case: in the immediate aftermath of the murder, he had actually made a few phone-call 'inquiries of officials' as to the penalties for interfering with the scene of a crime, 'under the pretext of needing the information for the work of a plot line in a story I was doing' (RLJ, 1:48). At the same time, Roy railed against 'the everlasting' 'symbolic or abstract "you"' that contemporary poets like his wife 'claim ... are not really describing a particular [person]' (RLJ, 1:56, 49). Unsurprisingly, then, most of the time Roy was quite radically off the mark in his (mis)readings of his wife's poetry, not to mention also of her personal correspondence. His interpretations, fuelled by narcissistic paranoia, reflect a 'hermeneutics of suspicion' strangely akin to that which operates in the realm of detective or sensation fiction, those omni-significant crime genres in which every sign is a symbol, and every symbol, another paranoia-inducing possible clue (Miller 1988). But there is nothing fictional about the consequences of Roy's interpretive habits. People have often rightly observed that Pat Lowther died because of her husband's jealousy at being the lesser writer. That he was also, quite drastically, the less capable reader of the two was a related problem, just as fatal.

To the extent that Roy believed there was a direct connection between the 'bourgeois immorality' of his wife's infidelity and that of her writing, poetry was as integral an element as adultery in both his crime and its public trial. In this regard, the notion of poetic rivalry was another important literary issue that came up for the jurors' attention during the proceedings. Roy firmly rejected the idea of poetic competitiveness when it was put to him, maintaining that 'we were not rivals in the same field': 'She was a contemporary, a modernist [poet]. I'm a labour poet whose forms tend ... to the traditional rhyme and rhythm, bread and butter subjects. She wrote in free verse poetry based on imagery rather than in rhythm or anything' (CATT, 3:384–5). Roy's rigid alignment of 'labour' poets with verse traditionalism, and 'intellectual' or 'establishment' poets (he used the adjectives interchangeably) with 'modernist' free verse, prompted John Hall to inquire what kind of poets had organized the Ironworkers' Hall reading in which Roy had wished to participate, alongside his wife. Well, they were poets of the 'establishment' sort, who 'have books published, [are] funded by the Canada Council, have the small [elite, literary] audiences, [and] write in those [free verse] forms' (CATT, 3:386). The prosecutor saw his opening and pointed out the contradiction to the witness: if this was an 'arty meeting' of an 'intellectual' crowd that Roy, as a 'bread and butter' poet, saw himself as defined against, then why had he been so adamant about getting on the program for September 27th?

The defendant's answer to that question had to do with his political precedence in the NDP party, which had co-sponsored the reading, but the reply itself is less important than the exchange it prompted about aesthetic standards and the relationship between politics and poetry, which bears citing at some length. Pressing Roy about the unusual references to 'Pat Lowther' in his letter to Rita Lalik, the prosecutor remarked,

Q   Now, I suggest to you that one of the things that you as a literary man
     would consider relevant in deciding whether poetry was good or bad
     would be style, content, that sort of thing, right?
A   These are two very different things, style or content, Mr. Hall.
Q   There are some standards that do apply in literature, generally?
A   Yes.
Q   I mean, there's good poetry and bad poetry. Do you agree or disagree?
A   Of course ...
Q   ... The major criterion, Mr. Lowther, I suggest, in deciding whether or
     not a person should be giving a reading would be whether or not that
     person writes good poetry that's worth listening to, right?
A   Yes. Taking into account the fact that there are different standards for
     different groups, different audiences.
Q   And you would agree with me that political considerations should be
     left aside from artistic considerations?
A   This is a false divorce. (CATT, 3:400–1)

One of the more discomfiting questions raised by this dialogue is with whom we actually agree by the end. For now the prosecutor has stepped into the judge's shoes as the New Critic, advocate of universal aesthetic 'standards,' and of a neat apartheid between 'artistic' and 'political considerations,' while Roy Lowther – though not immune to 'false divorces' of his own – here attempts, at least in part, to take into account 'different groups, different audiences.' It is Roy who articulates a populist position of diversity and difference which contemporary readers are more likely to recognize for its critical currency today.

In this case, however, courtroom debates about aesthetics and ideology also warrant close attention because they clearly reveal the extent to which the presumably 'private,' domestic disputes which led to Pat Lowther's premature and violent death were in fact shaped, if not prescribed, by broader 'culture wars' and class tensions related to clashing perceptions about the nature and function of art and the people who produce it. Roy's adversarial opposition between 'traditionalist' and 'modernist, free verse' poetry, for instance, only repeats tensions identical to those that, until very recently, anyway, have long been upheld as structuring the rise of modernism in Canadian literary history (e.g., see Arnason 1986; Norris 1982; Precosky 1983).

That Roy was hopelessly rearguard – the proverbial 'fourth spear-carrier in the back row,' to recall his lawyer's words – in failing to take into account the obsolescence of modernism itself by 1977 is beside the point. For the split Roy was really getting at in his division between 'traditionalist' and 'modernist' poets was in fact that widening breach between 'the different groups' and 'different standards' of amateur (i.e., 'popular') and professional (i.e., 'artsy') writers, a distinction he is lucid enough to make elsewhere in those terms.[33] This was a breach that widened considerably during the post–Massey Commission decades of the sixties and seventies, an era during which newly formed, state-sponsored organizations such as the Canada Council and the League   of Canadian Poets, organizations that sought to spur the growth of 'a national literature,' actively and self-consciously promoted the professionalization of literature in direct (and often openly antagonistic) opposition to such presumably less (or non-)professional groups as the Canadian Authors Association and the Vancouver Poetry Society. The rapid consolidation of the professional artist as a formal social category during this period not only advanced a distinctive version of 'the literary' as an official 'standard'; it also ensured a growing rift between the 'serious' *literati* – the 'big name stuff,' such as Margaret Atwood, in the judge's view – and all the leftovers, that tribe of the common *littera*.

In other words, the arguments inside 566 East 46th Avenue that eventually ended in Pat Lowther's horrible death were not simply 'about' messy personal affairs better left shut up. They were arguments quite integrally bound up with historical formations of class conflict that directly and dramatically bisected the Lowther marriage, pitting the defensive amateur husband resentfully against his apparently 'establishment' wife and her literary friends, with their published books, their social prestige, and their Canada Council grants. If this goes some way toward explaining Roy's special hostility for his wife's new briefcase, the emblematic *accoutrement* of the professional, it perhaps also points toward the utterly complicated position that Pat Lowther found herself in by the mid-seventies, as an impoverished socialist thinker and poet, who had yet also in some ways rapidly 'professionalized' to become a representative and gatekeeper of an official literary 'standard,' as that standard was exemplified by the League of Canadian Poets – and the University of British Columbia. To this extent, then, the tragedy of Pat Lowther's half-life portends a narrative of social division and conflict that is inseparable from larger questions raised by the literary culture and politics of her period.

Given the class-inflected literary politics at work, it is also perhaps not so surprising that what Alex Henderson remembers decades later as the 'nice literary touch' of Roy Lowther's trial[34] is a 'touch' that tends to cluster at the extremes of a steep hierarchy of genres, alternately manifesting itself as low-brow melodrama and high-brow canonical tragedy. The inherently theatrical forum of the courtroom connects the two ends of the spectrum. (It was not for nothing that the old courthouse on Georgia was later transformed into a gallery for art.)

The criminal trial with which Pat Lowther's memory is today still bound up displayed all the definitive elements of melodrama. This is no less significant to her subsequent 'legacy' than the apparently 'too, too trite' aspect of her disappearance was to the initial reluctance to investigate her murder. By the time of her death, Lowther had grown into a poet capable of wonderful subtlety. And she had always, even as a child, been a private person. Yet, despite character testimonies to that effect by the family members and friends who knew her well, her husband's trial, insofar as it became an early public representation of her life and death, listed heavily in an antithetical direction.

The headlines of newspapers tell much of this story: 'Poetic Rivalry Blamed in Murder Case'; 'Slain Vancouver Poet Wrote of Bloody Death'; 'Witness Recounts Melodramatic Vow'; 'Slain Poet Led Double Life'; 'Affair with Slain Poet Related at Murder Trial'; 'Lowther Says Maniac May Have Killed Wife.' With headlines like these, it was only to be expected that Roy's 'bizarre trial ... kept the courtroom at overflow point.'[35] In fact, attendance was so robust by the time the trial neared the verdict stage that officials actually had to move it, holus-bolus, to a larger courtroom on the third floor. The new courtroom, with its heavy, plum-coloured curtain, pulled to mask the jury from the spectators and vice versa, only heightened the dramatic sense of spectacle and suspense.

When Bethoe Shirkoff, who had been a friend and NDP associate of the Lowthers, arrived on the last day of the trial, she found a 'giggling, chattering crowd' waiting for the proceedings to begin. The courtroom was 'hot ... and steamy' that day, the stickiness intensified by the packed crowd of gossiping auditors. Shirkoff took notes throughout the hearings, and her diary provides an interesting glimpse into the otherwise unrecorded dimension of the trial as a public event: the small knot of people who 'snigger[ed]' over Roy's last session of testimony; the 'curly haired reporter' who scribbled; the yawns of the 'white-haired' male court clerk. 'Seated two rows ahead' of Shirkoff, Detective Chapman leaned forward in his seat, 'elbows on his knees,' absorbed by something.[36] Or perhaps just waiting for the judge to appear on his elevated platform. Waiting for order to arrive in the court.

Shortly after the jury had re-emerged from behind its plum-coloured curtain and rendered the verdict that would send Roy to jail, the *Vancouver Sun* ran a full-page spread entitled 'Verses and Verdicts.'[37] It was accompanied by a photograph of Roy, walking with bowed head, toting a tattered, document-stuffed paper bag (not briefcase), and looking a lot older than his fifty-two years. The article is remarkable for its dramatic reconstruction of the Lowther murder trial, which it frames not just as artifice – a theatrical production complete with 'courtroom voyeurs' and 'a cast of characters most hear about, but never see in the flesh' – but, even more explicitly, in terms of a specific genre of crime melodrama: a 'whodunit' with a few 'literary touches' (in Henderson's phrase) of gothic romance thrown in for good measure. Readers of the

Vancouver Sun were thus notified of all the key plot elements: 'There is a lover, a madman, and a poet. There is a missing woman, a bloodstained hammer, and a threatening phone call. But when all is said and done, the question is – whodunit?' In addition to suspense and, of course, a villain, the 'whodunit' usually features a vulnerable dame: 'one of the woman jurors,' who 'sits on the edge of her seat' as the accused 'describes the [murder] scene' with its ghastly detail, adequately fits this bill, nicely filling in for the 'missing woman' where the central female 'character' should be. But 'perhaps the best way to appreciate [this] non-capital murder trial,' as one might 'appreciate' any good entertainment, 'is to imagine yourself' as a 'neutral and uninvolved' spectator in the public gallery, say an audience member like 'Margaret,' a source/ 'character' introduced at the article's outset: 'Margaret (the girls at bingo call her Meg),' is 'a tiny English woman who climbs the four flights of stairs each day, a bag lunch in one hand, a copy of the *National Enquirer* folded neatly in the other.'

If the distinctions between life and art proved problematic for Roy Lowther, he was evidently not alone, joined as he was by at least one journalist with tabloid inclinations, who also proved a less 'complex kind of witness' than Pat Lowther herself would have wished to imagine. 'When all is said and done,' 'Verses and Verdicts' is just as problematic as Roy's own drama of self-defence in how crudely it turns fact to face fiction, solders story to history, and stages life as a 'real show' (as the article ambiguously phrases it). Through the framework of a crime melodrama, actual people become formulaic caricatures: Eugene Mc-Namara is described as an academic 'Ernie Hemingway,' and the prosecutor, John Hall (in one genuinely 'nice' gothic 'touch'), is likened to an 'Anglican priest sermonizing die-hard Catholics' in his 'ritualistic knee-length black robes.' As for 'Margaret' – if such a woman really existed – we are most assuredly not likely to mistake her with any 'big name' Margarets. Indeed, with her '*National Enquirer* folded neatly' in one hand and 'bag lunch' in the other, 'Meg' is a 'tiny English woman' far more reminiscent of a 'courtroom voyeur' straight out of Dickens – a contemporary update of the impoverished but genteel Miss Flite, who minces her way to Chancery Court day after day, dragging her little reticulated bag with her, in Dickens's brilliant indictment of the law in *Bleak House.*

However, while Roy's own attempt to script an alibi 'under the pretext of ... a plot line in a story I was doing' soon disclosed itself as a discursive vehicle with no one in the driver's seat, Don McLellan's 'Verses and Verdicts' deploys its narrative codes quite adeptly. The ethics subtending such journalism are questionable, but the entertainment factor of 'Verses and Verdicts' is such that the central irony of choosing to represent the Lowther trial as a 'whodunit' is easy to miss, even though it's right in front of us. For as far as the question of 'whodunit' went, the suspense factor in this case was actually pretty poor, as Pat Lowther's family could readily attest. The entertainment of the 'news' article comes at the price of misrepresenting the strength of the circumstantial evidence against the accused, not to mention reducing real people and real pain to the level of amusing stereotypes. It may also bear mention that, before she became 'the missing woman' of Don McLellan's shrewd 'whodunit,' the real and living Pat Lowther had met and been interviewed by this same journalist.[38]

As might be expected, the *Vancouver Sun* article – like most press coverage of the trial – touches only briefly on the literary politics at stake; here, they are boiled down to a mere matter of some 'semantic debate on poetry' and the Crown's contention that Roy 'coveted the prestige [his wife] was receiving from Canada's literary elite.' Yet even as it deflects the reader's attention to the more salacious and popularly recognizable aspects of 'this cast of characters,' 'Verses and Verdicts' also confidently reassures its reader that, 'unlike so many murder trials ... – drunken husbands, jealous wives – this one is more complex.'

There is a more or less direct link to be drawn between the sensationalism of such media coverage as 'Verses and Verdicts,' on the one hand, and the melodramatic sensibility of Roy Lowther, on the other. For one thing, Roy's histrionic propensities had come up for discussion in testimony by family members and had thus been a subject for report in the press. Similarly, other articles also reveal the extent to which, in its coverage of Roy's own testimony, the media took its stylistic cue from the man on the stand, sometimes actually buffing his poor melodrama to a higher lustre than the defendant himself was capable of providing. For example, in his journals and court testimony, Roy placed a smug emphasis on the fact that he had managed to move his wife's body from the house to the car under 'a full moon' without being detected: the night was so bright, 'anybody looking could have seen' (RLJ, 1:13–14). The 'full moon' detail was too good to be true for setting up *A Mid-Summer Night's Dream* that already promised to include 'a lover, a madman, and a poet' (*and* the further tantalizing prospect that these roles were exchangeable among the principal 'characters' involved).[39] It provided the perfect 'touch' for lurid headline banners: 'Lowther Tells of Moving

Body by Moonlight' blares one such piece, sliding in the 'Bloodstained Mattress' as a bolded sub-heading. First, this article succinctly restates Roy's panoptic fantasy: 'Residents of an East Vancouver street would have witnessed a macabre scene had they looked out of their windows in the early hours of September 25, 1975.' It then proceeds to describe 'the spectacle' of 'murder suspect Roy Lowther, bathed in moonlight, carrying his wife's body ... and placing it in the trunk of his car.' Thus 'bathed in moonlight,' the struggle which by Roy's own journal account was grotesquely clumsy and strenuous is effectively airbrushed into something approximating a soft porn / pulp romance 'spectacle' with dimly Frankensteinian overtones.[40]

'It is a sorry fact in this case,' as John Hall concluded in his closing address, that Roy Lowther 'rather enjoyed giving evidence ... There are so many touches here of a mind of a very strange cast' (CATT, Supplemental: 19, 21). The judge summed up the Crown's case this way:

> The Crown puts to you this rhetorical question: what do you think of the histrionics in the box? [Roy's] story is fantastic and improbable. Then it added touches, for instance the full moon as he carried the body out. He enjoyed ... fencing with Counsel when he is on trial for murder. At last he is on the center stage ... The Crown would suggest his entire performance in the box was bad acting. (CATT, 4:566)

In its conclusions about the 'poor theatre' provided by the defendant, the assize court confirmed what Detective Hale had already suspected while Roy was still out on bail during the preliminary hearing. Left alone in the empty courtroom with Roy one day, Hale recalls Roy quizzing him about witness box protocol: must one sit down, or could one stand up while testifying? Hale replied that both were options:

> I said, 'Go in the witness box, there's nobody here now. See if you'd rather stand up or sit down.' So he stood there ... And he stood there, and he looked around the court. And [as] he was standing in this empty court with his hands on the [witness stand railing], looking around, ... I thought, *gotcha*.[41]

Gotcha. The trap metaphor introduced by the defendant himself had run throughout the trial proceedings, extended and strongly reinforced, for one, by Roy's defence lawyer, whose closing address deploys the word 'trap' nine times in fairly rapid-fire succession over the space of one, four-paragraph segment alone. The conceit of the 'trap,' which had come with Roy Lowther's first 'wave' of 'feeling' on September 23, was also literally his last word at the trial. As is the convention, he was given the opportunity to make a final remark after the jury's verdict had been delivered. After first taking the time to offend the judge by implying that the trial had not been fairly conducted, he reasserted his innocence, his 'strange English' hinting at his guilt once again – 'God help all of you if the real killer will ever have the guts to confess.' Then he grandiloquently pronounced: 'The trap is closed. That is all I want to say' (CATT, 4:580). He sat down as he shut his 'trap,' for he had, of course, chosen to stand up during his time on the 'center stage.'[42]

Perhaps it was an association triggered by the trope of 'the trap' that led to the introduction of yet another literary intertext in this trial that was 'not about poetry.' For it was another kind of 'court' drama, a regal one, that John Hall explicitly enlisted in his prosecution of the man responsible for what he would not let the jury forget was Pat Lowther's 'violent, insensate' death. Famously, *Hamlet* features a play-within-a-play that is all about detecting 'occulted guilt': 'The Mousetrap,' to be precise ('The play's the thing / Wherein I'll catch the conscience of the King') (3.2.80, 66; 2.2.535–6). Given the prominence of the 'entrapment' motif in the accused's defence, it is probably not entirely accidental that the prosecutor was led, in his closing remarks, to counter Roy's fiction of having 'discovered' his wife's body by citing from, of all things, this same Renaissance revenge tragedy: 'It was, in the words of Shakespeare, "a consummation devoutly [*sic*] to be wished for" [for Roy] to be rid of his wife' (CATT, Supplemental: 21).

Today, Justice John Hall can't recall exactly why that famous drama should have occurred to him as a source text then, except to observe, 'I probably, in my study of English, became reasonably familiar with Shakespeare, and there's an awful lot of Shakespeare that one can quote dealing with almost any aspect of life.'[43] True enough. It is also true that the borrowed line was strategic as a subtle reminder to the jury of the literary hierarchies that factored into the crime, a reassertion of a sublime literary 'standard' which the 'poor theatre' and 'bad poetry' of the accused could be measured against as 'almost spectacularly unsuccessful' (CATT, 4:565). For this was not just any 'nice literary touch,' to recall Alex Henderson's phrase, but a line from the most famous ('To be or not to be') soliloquy of the most famous William Shakespeare's most famous play. As would not be the case with a line from, say, 'L-I-V-E-S-A-Y, of Victoria,' Hall could count on Shakespeare as an arbiter of high culture who wouldn't have to be spelled out for anyone – whether or not they had ever read *Hamlet*.

The counter-note of canonical tragedy which surfaces as a slightly mis-quoted but direct allusion in Hall's closing address, however, had also already tacitly insinuated itself over the course of the trial proceedings in even more remarkable ways, as a result of the prosecutor's own appar-ently dramatic courtroom stage presence. Presumably, as with poetry, there's bad acting, and then there's good acting, and the lawyer likened by the popular press to an 'Anglican priest' in his flowing, black robes appears to have belonged to the more effective of those thespian catego-ries – by all accounts except his own, that is. The cameo portrait of Hall exuding a Hamlet-like air of 'Sunday afternoon melancholy' in the *Van-couver Sun*'s 'Verses and Verdicts' must be considered in the context of the source. So too, then, the recollections of other sources, such as those of the defence counsellor who faced the prosecutor in court.

Alex Henderson, who appears to have retained quite a vivid memory of Roy's case, except where it comes to areas of solicitor-client privilege that include Roy's previous history of domestic violence and incarceration, has some jarring memories related to 'John Hall and the skull.' 'You didn't ask me about the skull,' he notes, unprompted, toward the end of an interview. 'There's only one other thing I'll tell you, because every-body wants to know about that':

> This was the case, which is kind of famous locally amongst lawyers, because of John Hall and the skull ... I don't know, maybe you don't want to hear this ... This is more of a lawyer's thing ... [Hall] put Pat Lowther's skull in evidence. Which is the one and only time I've ever seen that done ... Hope I never see it again. He also had the hammer in evidence – which is fair enough. And every time I'd be up cross-examining a witness, making some headway, making some good points, I'd look over at the jury and I'd find that they didn't look like they were paying attention. Then I'd look at Hall, and he'd have this piece of skull in his hand, and the hammer, and he'd be sort of fitting the head of the hammer into the hole in the skull. And [the jury would] be mesmerized by this ... [It] may be exaggerated by now, but it's become a sort of famous trial-lawyers' story – how to divert a jury, just get the skull into evidence.[44]

The use of human remains as a diversionary courtroom tactic, a trick spectacular enough to enter trial-lawyer lore, smacks on the surface as even more shocking than a journalist's insensitive fictionalized caricature. Yet, even if 'exaggerated' in retrospect, the 'famous trial-lawyers' story' of 'John Hall and the skull' tellingly reinforces the role played by literature as an imaginative subtext of the law in the 1977 murder trial that followed Pat Lowther's death. Far from being 'more of a lawyer's thing,' that is, the dramatic courtroom use of Exhibits 'P' and 'Q' subtly re-enacts a scene from the tragic drama that houses 'The Mousetrap' that the prosecutor would eventually spring on Roy (and the jury) outright.

It's in the opening scene of the final act of *Hamlet*, 'The Gravedigger's Scene,' that Shakespeare's contemplative Prince encounters the *memento mori* of the human skull, holding a specimen up for close, self-absorbed inspection. Whether it was intentional or not, the scene called up by Hall's similarly rapt preoccupation with a portion of Pat Lowther's skull is worth remembering. For in direct contrast to what might otherwise be dismissed as gratuitous or expedient courtroom antics, the Shakespearian scene informing Hall's jury-mesmerizing tactic occurs at a moment when the play focuses spectators' attention precisely upon Hamlet's tender sense of moral affront at the gravedigger's casual insouciance in handling human remains. Watching the clown carelessly chuck up a couple skulls, Hamlet is led mournfully to opine: 'That skull had a tongue in it, and could sing once. How the knave jowls it to the ground ... Did these bones cost no more the breeding but to play at loggets with them? Mine ache to think on't' (5.1.58–9; 69–70).

Maybe before the plum-coloured curtain got drawn, the jury, watching Hall 'sort of fitting the head of the hammer into the hole in the skull,' was intuitively prompted along those lines in a less Elizabethan idiom. Or even no language at all. In another of the many paradoxes generated by this case, the callous spectacle of the Crown prosecutor in effect 'playing at loggets with' the skull of Pat Lowther was probably the most efficient means of directing the collective elbows of the jury, provoking their sense of outrage and pathos. In this regard, Hall's *tableau vivant* of a classic Renaissance scene is also a classic example of stooping to conquer in the service of a compelling end. At the very least, John Hall accomplished restitution for Lowther's murder far more efficiently than Hamlet ever managed to deal with Claudius's crime.

John Hall does not see himself – has, in fact, never thought of himself – as particularly 'given to dramatics or histrionics.' And, frankly, sitting in his office at his huge oak desk, thoughtful and even a touch stiffly earnest, he does not exactly convey that predilection at first impression, either. While the apparent gaps in the memory of Roy's former lawyer, Alex Henderson, are perhaps predictable, the former prosecutor inter-

estingly claims no 'independent recollection' of the dramatic manoeu-
vre at the basis of the 'the famous trial-lawyers' story,' which his defence
colleague remembers as the most effective of Hall's prosecutorial strategies in Roy Lowther's trial.[45] It may be that Hall also retains no conscious recollection from his days as an English undergraduate that, in
the Shakespearean tragedy he was – for no apparent reason – led to
quote in his closing address to the jury, the second skull chucked up by
the gravedigger, is, Hamlet thinks, that 'of a lawyer,' whose bones, it
seems, are no more immune than anyone else's from being 'played at
loggets with': 'Where be his quiddities now, his quillets, his cases, his
tenures, and his tricks?' (5.1.75–6). A big question, perhaps, for a
young, aspiring prosecutor, an undergraduate – like Hamlet himself –
attracted to the role of framing all the crucial questions, rather than
being obliged to answer them.

When, how, and why the associations that make up memory work – or
what works to stump memory, yet sometimes allow its embedded half-
lives to persist, elsewhere or otherwise – are questions easier to speculate about in relation to certain individuals involved with this immediate
posthumous phase of Pat Lowther's history than they are with others.
And conjecture remains an incomplete answer, at best. One thing more
certain, however, is that mnemonic associations, especially when forged
under traumatic and dramatic circumstances, once established, tend to
stick. Roy Lowther's *idée fixe* is the extreme example of this, but the
enjambment of Pat Lowther's history with the memory of her husband
is a related problem.

　Of the 'nice literary touch' that characterized *Roy's* court case, Alex
Henderson says, 'In a sense, it was kind of – a little bit of *her* legacy'
(emphasis added). He goes on to mention one of Lowther's poems,
'Kitchen Murder,' which 'seemed, in some ways, to foreshadow [her
fate],' and then recalls the allegorical melodrama that Roy wrote, 'September 23rd.'[46] The slippage between the history of the husband and
the poetic 'legacy' of the wife, and the smooth slide from the work of
the one to the work of the other as equally premonitory, is representative of the problem that confronts readers of Lowther today. It is indicative of the inevitable – yet, in this case, also crucial – phenomenon of
unconscious association and overlap with Roy in the historical memory
around Pat Lowther. Not in the least, such slides reinforce the easy

interchangeability of a generic 'poet' role and status that was anything but the actual case in the Lowthers' marriage, where that role and status was a primary sore point of contestation.

Whatever the 'Lowther legacy' may consist of, it has fairly little to do with the literary 'legacy' which accrued over the course of the investigation into and prosecution of Pat Lowther's murder. Contrary to Roy's assertion at the close of his trial that it was his wife 'who was really the central person in this drama' (CATT, 4:579), the public records of this period are texts informative chiefly for what they reveal about others' perceptions of poetry – including, but not only, Pat Lowther's work – in the context of others' poetic tastes, philosophies, and literary 'standards,' especially Roy's. From Roy's embattled, populist defence of a 'traditional' poetics; to Detective Hale's shared affinity for Rudyard Kipling; to the pop culture and gothic romance referents of Don Mc-Lellan and other journalists; to the more canonical and 'serious' literary orientations revealed by legal professionals, the trial that was, manifestly, 'not about poetry,' on the one hand, was emphatically 'about poetry,' on the other – just not primarily or even essentially 'about' Pat Lowther's poetry, or her ideas about it.

Yet, as with Roy Lowther's initial conjoining of his wife and Pablo Neruda in a politically and emotionally freighted 'anniversary' of death, the *Hamlet-as-whodunit* collaboratively scripted after Lowther's murder has had lingering implications for posthumous representations of her life's 'legacy.' As far as Pat Lowther's prospective critical 'legacy' was concerned, in fact, it is not much of a stretch at all to say that the 'nice literary touch' of her husband's trial was as good a 'touch' as that of the mythical Midas. A fabulous brew of potboiler melodrama and Shakespearean high tragedy, this peculiar mix of popular-canonical extremes persists as an abiding feature of much writing about Pat Lowther. To this day, the works of Eugene McNamara, Jean Mallinson, and a handful of others are exceptions in a cultural 'legacy' that still too readily seizes upon tropes of classical tragedy (Lowther's life as 'star-crossed' or as a 'Greek tragedy')[47] while simultaneously, and often unintentionally, reinforcing most of the elemental adjuncts of melodrama in its focus on her victimization.

Pat Lowther herself worried about what she recognized as the 'melodrama' of her domestic life 'affect[ing]' her 'imagination.' And where it came to canonical writers, she was not shy about proclaiming her preference for 'N-E-R-U-D-A' over Shakespeare any day.[48]

؏

The judge who decades ago presided over *Regina v. Lowther* still recalls Roy's voluble final statement at the trial's close. It was a performance, he says, unparalleled in his forty-seven-year law career. Just shy of noon in the Georgia Hotel, not far from the courthouses, old and new, the elegantly attired octogenarian presents himself as a man of brisk temperament and intellect, neither of which is softened by the Bloody Mary he nurses over lunch. A tape recorder placed on the table is impatiently nixed, and question after question waved away as uninformed and probably irrelevant anyway. With the young waiter, he is also gruff, irascible.

The retired judge is also singularly helpful, having taken the trouble to retrieve his old bench book in order to refresh his memory – and later, taking the time to ensure access to various court records. Reading through the notes he took during the 1977 trial has, it seems, jogged for the judge an unwritten memory related to an earlier bench book belonging to another judge: this one being the judge who had in 1964 overseen the custody hearings related to the dissolution of Roy Lowther's first marriage. At some point during those proceedings thirteen years earlier, in the left-hand margin of *his* bench book, the divorce court judge had apparently scribbled in reference to Roy: 'this man can be dangerous.' More than likely sitting in that family courtroom on that day in May 1964 would have been, not only Roy, but Roy's second wife, the newly remarried Pat Lowther. But it was a prediction which the family court judge felt impelled to share with 'the court' of *Regina v. Lowther* only after the fact of the 1977 murder trial.[49] Felt impelled to share, no doubt, because, as Roy Lowther well knew, there is nothing quite so gratifying as a personal prophecy fulfilled. As John Hall had remarked to the jury in 1977: 'It's a situation where you have a picture of man with a very queer view of life and a set of rails that are sort of leading to this very tragic set of circumstances' (CATT, Supplemental: 19).

In the Georgia Hotel, the retired judge takes an angry little stab at his Cobb salad, as though at the exfoliate of these multiple pasts. Then he puts down his fork and leans across the table, keenly. 'How good a poet was she, anyway, *really?*'[50]

Chapter 3

Canonicity and the 'Cult of the Victim'

[W]hen a writer is young and has died violently, how should we respond? ...
A review of a living poet cannot help being written with one eye on the
poet; she will read it, whether it's a good review or not, and she will judge
us. But reviewing a dead poet pressures the reviewer into declaiming like
Brutus over Cæsar's corpse ... The pull towards elegy is strong.

                                                      – Margaret Atwood,
                    'Last Testaments: Pat Lowther and John Thompson,' 1978

Lowther wasn't the only Canadian writer whose poor judgement and
appalling taste in men blunted her creativity, and her life. The otherwise
brilliant Gwendolyn MacEwen married malodorous Marxist Milton Acorn
and died of untreated alcoholism. One-book wonder Elizabeth Smart bore
a litter of children by her callous married lover.

    Lowther, MacEwen and Smart are now saints in CanLit heaven ...
                    – Kathy Shaidle, 'Women, Poetry and the Cult of the Victim,' 2000

Only twenty-two years, less than a blip in evolutionary time, separates
the self-reflexive musings of Margaret Atwood in the proximate aftermath of Pat Lowther's death from the accusatory contempt of Kathy
Shaidle, writing from the (apparently) confident vantage point of a
succeeding generation. Two poets of two different generations, each
bearing a markedly different relationship to the name 'Pat Lowther.'
Atwood, who had been an acquaintance of the person, Pat Lowther,
writes as an impersonal, informed advocate of Lowther's and John
Thompson's poetry in the American literary review *Parnassus*.[1] Shaidle,
who once attended a commemorative fund-raiser in honour of the

League's Pat Lowther Memorial Award, writes, decades later, in a major Canadian newspaper, as an impassioned critic of the 'self-sabotaging' lives of certain falsely installed 'saints in CanLit heaven' (2000: B2). Among other things, these two extracts from either side of a generational divide throw into relief a curious paradox: namely, while a friend and ally of the dead poet can evidently summon the capacity for critical caution at precisely that historical moment when a fresh gust of grief makes 'the pull towards elegy ... strong,' a poet with no such immediate personal connection to Lowther yet reacts much more viscerally to her subject almost a quarter century later – not 'declaiming like Brutus,' as in Atwood's scenario, but rather decrying in no uncertain terms the 'poor judgement and appalling taste' of a predecessor whom Shaidle regards as little more than a 'victim' 'elevate[d] ... to heroine status' by misguided 'feminists' (2000: B2).

When it comes to the question of Pat Lowther's posthumous 'legacy,' the disparate perspectives of Atwood and Shaidle appear to present a version of canonical history as a form of half-life – as, that is, a negative measurement of value over time, and so, quite literally, a calculation of steadily diminishing returns. But it is Lowther's undiminished visibility in 'CanLit' which is precisely what Shaidle's article is concerned to emphasize. Moreover, the complexity of the initial question which Atwood poses – 'when a writer is young and has died violently, how should we respond?' – reveals itself quite vividly within the excerpts quoted above. Apparently, the answer may depend on whether we are speaking of how to respond to the *work* of that young and violently dead writer (as with Atwood's focus), or how to respond to the perceived *life* of that writer (Shaidle's focus). The fact that two inextricably interlinked yet different objects of 'judgment' come into play in debates about the 'Lowther legacy' is worth noting at the outset, since it marks a distinction that as frequently as not gets overlooked even as it tacitly underpins commentary about Lowther since her death. As Shaidle's exclusive preoccupation with the 'appalling' lives of *women* poets also begins to intimate, gender-specific (as well as class-specific) terms of judgment come to factor in this sometimes blurry equation as well.

It is equally instructive to pause, in Atwood's words about 'Last Testaments,' over the supersession of one Shakespearean tragedy by yet another. The invocation of *Julius Caesar* provides a deeply resonant literary frame for Pat Lowther's own 'rich legacy'; indeed, to the extent that Shakespeare's eponymous hero dies because of his apparent ambition, his demise, like Lowther's murder, betrays 'mistrust of good success'

(5.3.66). Moreover, in 'declaiming' over the corpse of the slain leader of the Romans, both Brutus and Marc Antony indulge the kind of eulogistic apotheosis that Atwood sets out, in her review, to resist, and that Shaidle, in her article on the 'cult of the victim,' vociferously posits as the thin substance holding Saint Lowther's star in the firmament of 'CanLit heaven.' 'Let but the commons hear this testament,' Marc Antony says, waving the freshly dead Caesar's last will and testament before the crowd in the market place, where his body has been borne:

> And they would go and kiss dead Caesar's wounds,
> And dip their napkins in his sacred blood,
> Yea, beg a hair of him for memory.
> And, dying, mention it within their wills,
> Bequeathing it, as a rich legacy,
> Unto their issue. (3.2.132, 134–9)

In Shakespeare's text, the assassination of the Roman emperor thus leads directly to his 'canonization' as a martyred saint: Julius Caesar figures as a sort of pre-Christian Jesus Christ, one whose remains become 'sacred' relics even as politically motivated factions begin to develop (along with the declaiming) over his corpse in the market place. As a review of the literature produced in the wake of Pat Lowther's death indicates, both of these elements of Shakespeare's tragic plot – the metaphorical 'canonization' of the victim, and the not-so-metaphorical partisan schisms among the survivors – also apply to the history of the murdered leader of the League of Canadian Poets. Incidentally, as a plot about the plotting of internecine political revolt, *Julius Caesar* signals a drama that could easily work to re-entrench the heavily symbolic script plotted by Roy Lowther, who timed his wife's death to coincide with the politically charged anniversary of the death of Chilean statesman/poet Pablo Neruda. Atwood, it should be reiterated, evokes the 'pressure' of this drama precisely as a plot to be resisted.

The fact that Lowther's murder prompted a response dominated by the conventional touchstones of tragedy, elegy, eulogy, and romance (including faint echoes of the crime melodrama) is not surprising, but it is important. Posthumous representations of Lowther entail fundamental implications for readers today, necessarily conditioning our understanding of her life and her art. Stephen Scobie has in the past noted the power of 'public images' with regard to such poets as Phyllis Webb (the nun-like 'recluse') and Leonard Cohen (in his youth, the 'brooding' and 'tortured' Byronic hero). These images, he writes, 'may be reductive and clichéd ... but there is a sense in which [they] are now, whether the writers like it or not, *part of their work*': 'The writer's public image, whether deliberately created or not, *is* a text, and must be read as such' (1991: 61; emphasis in the original). This is also profoundly true of the 'public images' produced in the void of Lowther's shockingly sudden absence, from 1975 onward. As with the emplotted narratives generated by Roy Lowther's crime, his trial, and its media coverage, the avalanche of tributes, poems, newspaper eulogies, reviews, and other art touched off by Lowther's death has settled with time to become a 'part of [her] work' that needs to be reckoned with. Maybe in Lowther's case even more urgently so than with the poets discussed by Scobie. Phyllis Webb and Leonard Cohen may or may not worry about bromide projections of their public personae, but at least neither of them has to entertain seriously the more radical prospect that those 'public images' might be mistaken as sufficient substitutes for reading their books. To the extent that a vague awareness of Lowther's tragic/melodramatic status as a murder victim generally far outstrips familiarity with her life's work, this is a real concern in her case.

There are headstones so wreathed about by foliage planted by mourners that it's impossible to tell who is buried in the plot beneath. Some of the literary tributes written in honour of the author of *A Stone Diary* are memorable accomplishments in themselves. But to extend Stephen Scobie's argument, it is also true that, once offered, none of the tributes produced in memory of Lowther, however skilfully or crudely executed, can ever be entirely prised from the text of the poet's 'original' tablet – no more so than lichen already insinuated into rock. But rather than pointing to the prospect of an authentic bedrock 'buried' beneath it, the predominantly elegiac cultural text scripted around the memory of Lowther's loss needs to be read as an extension of her corpus: 'marginalia' as essential to our understanding of Pat Lowther and her writing today as the subject of poetry was to the 1977 murder trial that was 'not about poetry.' To proceed as such helps to clarify the cultural politics around Lowther's 'afterlife,' since it is essentially the posthumous activity around her absence that functions as the cumulative thesis to which recent critics such as Kathy Shaidle react – react, that is, less to any specific defect of Lowther's poetic craft, than specifically to perceptions of her as a 'victim' and to the aura of sentiment and pathos which has, however understandably, lingered to suffuse the memory of a poet who was young, and who died violently.

⟡

In the period most immediately following the confirmation of Lowther's death, what Atwood terms 'the pull towards elegy' was not only for obvious reason 'strong,' but virtually irresistible. Articulated in states of horror and sorrow, the earliest tributes and eulogies for Lowther are trauma narratives in the classic sense of the term. Dorothy Livesay was not the only friend to represent Lowther's loss in terms of the literal, physical trauma of 'a body blow' of the sort that actually killed her younger friend; in describing the impact of the news of the death, Hilda Thomas and Arlene Lampert also resorted to similar images of a blunt-force 'blow on the back of the neck' or 'knock' on the head. In so voicing their pain, Livesay, Thomas, Lampert, and others rearticulate trauma as 'the moving and sorrowful *voice* that cries out, a voice that is paradoxically released *through the wound*' (Caruth 1996: 2; emphasis in the original).[2] An elegy by Lowther's early publisher, Patrick Lane, entitled simply 'For Pat Lowther,' works extensively with this metaphor. Published just a year after *A Stone Diary* had posthumously appeared, Lane's poem unites the trauma of 'one just dead' with the trauma of birth, the trauma of the 'I / before the I':

> The poem of one just dead
> is the opening a mouth made in our flesh
> before the flesh could speak, the I
> before the I, the unhealed wound of all we ever knew.
> (In Dempster 1978: 62)

By comparison, Dorothy Livesay and Hilda Thomas spoke of the 'body blow' of Lowther's death in the context of what was – aside from the family memorial service that had been held in lieu of a funeral – the first widely public tribute to Lowther. That context was a CBC Radio show, hosted by Peter Gzowski on 2 November 1975, and also featuring commentary by Patrick Lane, George Woodcock, Seymour Mayne, Marya Fiamengo, Milton Acorn, and Lowther's mother, Virginia. Despite the spontaneity and apparent ephemerality of its broadcast medium, the influence of this radio program as a source for subsequent discussions of Lowther can be discerned in echoes that resonate right up to 1997's *Time Capsule*.[3] It therefore warrants attention.

Gzowski's 'special report' opened with a recorded reading by Pat Lowther of a short poem entitled 'Nightmare.' Somewhat like earlier poems such as 'Baby You Tell Me' or other, discernibly swaggering

Lowther pieces, 'Nightmare' is a trifle of black humour that ultimately turns upon a dark pun – something like the equivalent of a playful Halloween *boo!*

> Edgar Allan Poe &
> Disney combined
> couldn't have done it
> better: the tall black house
> the dungeon
> the secret book
>
> Later, the pale determined
> men with dogs.
> I try to cry out:
> *I'm harmless!*
> but the words can't
> get through my fangs. (*SD*, 15)

When she finished reading this poem at an outdoor poetry festival in July 1975, Lowther herself couldn't suppress a small, self-amused snicker, provoked perhaps by the chortles from the audience, which eclipsed the birds twittering in the background. A bit of the laughter, in fact, remains audible on the re-recorded opening clip of Gzowski's show. But when the spliced recording of Lowther's reading ends, Gzowski's nice nicotine baritone comes on to solemnly intone, '*This*, also, is a true nightmare': '*That* woman, the poet, Pat Lowther, whose voice you just heard, is dead now.'

Summoned as an eerily lingering 'presence' by virtue of the July recording of her voice, Lowther 'speaks' in this broadcast through the very, very raw wounds of survivors left to pick up her slack. That the poet's mordantly clever little 'Nightmare' is re-recorded as 'a true nightmare' for the living requires no explanation or apology. At the same time, it would be a mistake to read this poem now as the ominous self-dirge that the 1975 radio tribute implies, through a eulogistic framework that pretty much entirely subverts its facetious tone.[4]

In his prefatory remarks, Gzowski introduced the conventional metaphor of 'canonization' that would stick around long enough for critics in a new millennium to object to as a matter of fact:

Her name was Pat Lowther ... and according not only to the people who
knew her best, but to the most influential figures in Canadian literature,
she'd been on the verge of joining that small but treasured group of artists
who rank as major stars in the constellation of Canadian letters ... Although
the rest of us may not have heard of her until her murder, Pat Lowther was,
in the eyes and ears of the poets, a very important person.

Thus launched into heaven, Lowther is sent off with the dubious distinction of an anonymous VIP, a writer simultaneously recognized by an
'influential' elite, but basically (in 'crassest terms') 'nobody' to 'the rest
of us.' It should matter that this oxymoronic formula is strikingly reminiscent of Roy Lowther's own riven perceptions of his Very Important
'anyone.' For the related fact that Lowther happens to figure in
Gzowski's program as a lesser star – a nebula just 'on the verge of joining that small but treasured group ... who rank as *major* stars' (emphasis
added) – also unwittingly reinscribes a vision that accords quite nicely
with her murderer's apparent desire to 'commemorate' his wife precisely as such. Roy might have taken some satisfaction in this pre-autho-
rized, as it were, 'introduction' of his wife to the general public as a
relatively little dipper.

'I tell ya, I was lucky I was drunk when I heard the news, because I could
cry ... without being embarrassed – and I did not – uh, I *did* cry.' Of all the
remarks actually made by Lowther's friends on Gzowski's show, perhaps
the most revealing come from the celebrated 'people's poet,' Milton
Acorn, who caught himself in a bit of a verbal slip during this opening
statement. But this admission proved a mere preface to a much longer
disquisition on the significance of Lowther's death, a question that
appears to have been posed to most of the writer-participants on the program. Even when one takes into account the crisis atmosphere of the
immediate circumstance; Acorn's own characteristic bent for outrageous
and self-aggrandizing polemics; and the further fact that the author of
I've Tasted My Blood had his own manly wound to lick where it came to Pat
Lowther, none of these variables can adequately salvage a diatribe that
virtually exonerates Roy Lowther of the actual crime of murder.

At moments literally incomprehensible with a stuttering, apoplectic
rage that print insufficiently captures, the tenor and substance of
Acorn's jeremiad are best approximated by quoting it, much as it was
heard on Gzowski's program, in one long torrent:

The murder of Pat Lowther was an artistic finale for the artistic murder which she had been suffering for a decade. And she was not alone. Generally, the poets of the West Coast were being systematically excluded from national recognition by the poetic Eastern Mafia. These poets kept on developing while I was in Vancouver, and by the time I left, Pat Lowther, and bill bissett, and Patrick Lane ... were developed poets – that was ten years ago! Why didn't anybody help her? Because of the unmistakable note of *truth* in her voice! That's why the Eastern Mafia never recognized her! Of course, they had no way of knowing that she was a nationalist, or ... a socialist, or ... that she had appeared at benefits for the fighting people of Viet Nam. But they saw that proud note of truth in her voice, and for that, they damned her! And now, you have this Robert Fulford coming out in the [*Toronto*] *Star* and saying, '*O*, we were just about to grant our *holy* recognition to her!' He and his gang had suppressed her for ten years! ... Now look. When I was coming up, you only had to write *one good poem* to be known from coast to coast among those who knew poetry. But since then, poetry has become a propaganda game to lay ... the mighty burden of the Stars and Stripes and all its inhabitants upon us, and the statement has come out that we must be Americans! And we must write like Americans!

[Calmer.] Now okay, she died by violence; she died by murder – but this is not uncommon amongst writers, it seems to me. Writers arouse strong emotions ... and after all, murder is not as cruel as cancer or half a dozen other diseases. No, the murder I'm talking about is the murder of Pat Lowther as an artist.

In choosing to speak about the 'artistic murder' of Pat Lowther, Acorn largely deflects attention from the fact of her actual murder, which is eventually – and bizarrely – downplayed, as though such a fate is, firstly, a fairly routine ('not uncommon') occupational hazard for writers, and secondly, an affliction 'not as cruel as cancer or half a dozen other diseases.' (One can't help but wonder what someone like the cancer-stricken Alden Nowlan might have had to say about this questionable comparative pathology.)

Oddly enough, if one recalls Roy Lowther's melodramatic allegory about 'September 23rd,' Acorn was almost right about Lowther's murder as a weirdly 'artistic finale.' But in his view, this 'finale' would appear to have virtually nothing to do with Roy Lowther at all. Instead, very much as in the political drama of *Julius Caesar*, Lowther's 'artistic murder' is represented as the result of a nefarious conspiracy plot, this one driven by competing regional and national, as well as imperial, forces.

In Acorn's restaged tragedy, cultural critic Robert Fulford stars as Brutus, and it is Fulford and 'his gang' of 'Eastern Mafia' co-conspirators who are primarily responsible for 'the murder of Pat Lowther as an artist.' By Acorn's account, this 'murder' marks a historical process that began 'ten years ago' – which is to say that at virtually the moment Lowther's publishing career begins, around 1965, Acorn sees the dominant 'Eastern' literary establishment 'systematically' setting out to actively 'suppress' and exclude her, and her West Coast compatriots, bissett and Lane. Listeners of Gzowski's show were thus presented with the genuinely prescient phenomenon of an 'artistic murder' that commenced at birth, as it were.

At any rate, Acorn, residing at that time in Toronto and still emotionally scarred from his split with his (Toronto-based) ex, Gwendolyn MacEwen, eventually gets around to the subject that had been a favourite hobby horse of his since his quarrels with *Tish* in the early sixties: 'the mighty burden of the Stars and Stripes' and the business of writing 'like Americans.' Regional alienation directed against a Toronto-centric literary 'Mafia,' cultural nationalism, and American imperialism are the real axes to grind here, a personal political agenda which entirely swamps the focus from the fact at hand: a poet murdered by her husband.

Acorn was, of course, correct in his general assertion that literary politics and culture played a significant role in Lowther's death, but his characterization of those conflicts differs dramatically from the tensions revealed in Roy Lowther's writings and the trial records. Whereas Roy, it may be recalled, focused resentfully on his wife's presumably achieved 'establishment' status as a recognized 'professional' poet – an artist validated by peer-adjudicated literary magazines and federal granting agencies, as well as one invested with enviable literary capital as a member, and then an official, of the League – Acorn focuses resentfully on exactly the opposite: namely, Lowther's presumably un-achieved *lack* of literary 'establishment' status, as a beleaguered outcast always and to the bitter end struggling against a dominant 'Eastern' elite who spurned and excluded her.[5]

Though it was Milton Acorn who ranted most bitterly, he was not alone in forwarding this view of Lowther as a poetic exile 'damned,' like the mythical Cassandra, for the 'proud note of truth in her voice.' In separate reviews of the posthumously published *A Stone Diary*, Lowther's former Blackfish Press editors, Brian Brett and Allan Safarik, reinforced the idea of Lowther's lack of literary community and clout *vis à vis* the 'Eastern' establishment. Both reviewers, like Acorn, specifically took exception to Robert Fulford's belatedly fulsome words of praise for Lowther – which by this point, in 1977, had been irritatingly reprinted by the 'moguls' at Oxford University Press on the back cover of *A Stone Diary* (and widely quoted ever thereafter). As Brett wrote,

> She published three books in her lifetime, all of them excellent and all of them absolutely unnoticed by the literary gods that be, for she was an outsider and took no part in the political idiocies necessary for success ... [A]nd since she belonged to no back-slapping coterie that could help her, she was ignored ... It was typical that it took her violent death for the Gods of Toronto to notice her. And it is even more typical that there was no Robert Fulford to sing her praises in the past. (1977: 22)

Similarly, Allan Safarik recapitulated views he had already publicly expressed in press interviews after Lowther's murder:

> [S]he had great difficulty in convincing the mandarins of the Eastern Canadian publishing industry that she had anything worthwhile to offer them. She did not fit into any of the cliques that inhabit the Vancouver sandbox literary scene. In effect, she was isolated from the mainstream. She had no facility for self-promotion and the necessary social climb, so often synonymous with the rise to literary reputation ... However, it seems that death by suspect circumstance is a great cure for obscurity. [Quotes Fulford.] It is depressing that Pat Lowther did not receive more than a glimmer of official reception from the establishment of publishing, criticizing, and broadcasting moguls.[6]

Other West Coast writers – for example, Patrick Lane, on the Gzowski radio tribute – were somewhat more circumspect in their assessments of Lowther's career, but also echoed the idea of Lowther's social isolation and lack of connection in the literary world. As a young Lane put it: 'There was no establishment there, couching her world, you know?'[7]

Commentators such as Brett, Safarik, and Lane had their own reasons for the note of cynical grievance that informs their perspectives on Lowther's apparently lonely struggle against the Eastern 'mandarins.' Small-press West Coast writers, editors, and publishers were, after all, the ones who had taken those first crucial leaps of faith in Lowther's work. Brett, Safarik, and Lane (in his comments elsewhere) are right in their assertions that Lowther did not 'fit into' any cohesively defined poetic group, either inside or outside Vancouver. To have Toronto-based cultural 'mandarins' and publishing 'moguls' come in at the eleventh hour to grant a now-dead B.C. poet their '*holy* recognition,' as Acorn put it (drawing out the vowel), could only be galling.

Nevertheless, such assessments of Lowther as, in effect, a heroically independent babe-in-the-woods also need to be questioned. Like Acorn's more prolix diatribe, such representations idealistically overplay the distance between Lowther and the literary formations and 'power politics' of her time. They overlook certain basic facts, such as her extensive involvements with such groups as the B.C. Interim Arts Board and the League of Canadian Poets. While Lowther may not have been covered with 'sandbox' grime, to reprise Safarik's metaphor, her work with such organizations compelled her to watch the activity in the local playground pretty closely – and she was typically conscientious about any jobs she accepted. That was already a good part of her job as a regional representative for the League, for instance, and by the time she was elected League Chair, she was writing letters to Ernest Hall, the provincial secretary of David Barrett's new NDP government, mentioning her newly 'influential position' and her desire 'to be doing something to further the cause of socialism in the literary community.'[8] Similarly, as a League executive, some of the issues she inherited were, if not 'political idiocies,' in Brett's phrase, then at least intensely 'political,' including the on-going contentious debate over League membership criteria and qualifications. Nor did Lowther lack either the desire or the ability for 'self-promotion' and 'the necessary social climb,' in Safarik's words. In this, her younger male friends underestimated her. In fact, the distance she had already 'climbed' was a factor that worked to imperil her life in the end.

Acorn's extravagant plot of an intentional 'artistic murder,' with its uncomfortable resonances, in this case, to Roy's own fictions of persecution, was one thing. In comparison, those West Coast writers who portrayed Lowther in less extreme, though also romanticized, terms, as a marginalized 'outsider' (Brett 1977) or a 'poet from the underground' (Safarik 1977), were no more right – or wrong – than the poet's murderer himself had been in casting 'Pat Lowther' and her literary peers ('and she knows all of them,' he'd assured Rita Lalik) as the very embodiment of a dominant artistic 'establishment.' In either case there is an element of half-truth, depending, of course, on one's frame of reference. To Roy, as an 'amateur' versifier in a debased poetic subculture that was more or less aware of its own 'traditional' obsolescence long before the seventies, it stands to reason that 'Pat Lowther' would have appeared as a Very Important Person in the 'modern' world of 'free verse' and 'intellectual' Canadian poetry. She had a new briefcase, new clothes, new jobs, new professional titles, and a new, official League letterhead address stamp to prove it.

In turn, Lowther's fellow small-press literary crowd, who took as *their* frame of reference the wider national scene of 'serious' contemporary poetry, knew that in terms of publishing and literary careers, the really imposing 'big name stuff,' to recall the judge's phrase for Margaret Atwood, usually happened east of the Rockies – and not in Alberta, Saskatchewan, or Manitoba either. Indeed, while Vancouver may have been a particularly vital poetry scene during the sixties, for all practical purposes, the West Coast remained an exotic 'margin' in the seventies (Bowering 1994: 121), and only the big Toronto publishing houses controlled the proverbial means of production for a national literary reputation. It was, in fact, precisely because of their frustration with a lack of publishing venues for emerging poets of Canada's so-called 'third solitude' – including, especially, themselves – that aspiring writers such as Patrick Lane, Seymour Mayne, Jim Brown, bill bissett, Brian Brett, and Allan Safarik began their West Coast presses in the sixties and seventies. So, Very Stone House, TalonBooks, and Blackfish all got their start (see, for example, Norris 1984 and Woodcock 1974).

In other words, accounts of Lowther's neglect by the 'Gods of Toronto' or 'the mandarins of the Eastern Canadian publishing industry' need to be read as reflecting the regionalist politics subtending the contemporary West Coast writing scene more than anything else. They may have applied '*generally*,' in Milton Acorn's phrase, to 'the poets of the West Coast,' who were perhaps perceived by *some* as 'being systematically excluded from national recognition.' But they are accounts that do not tally persuasively with the specific facts of Lowther's own individual career. Even before *A Stone Diary*'s success with Oxford, Lowther had met with considerable good fortune in the land of the 'mandarins' for a writer only yet establishing her name: *Milk Stone* had been published by an 'Eastern' press, though a small one; her first books were very well reviewed in prominent 'Eastern' magazines such as the *Canadian Forum*; she had recently completed a thorough-going reading tour in Ontario, where her auditors had included an enthusiastic Carol Shields, among others; and, in her appointment as Chair of the League, she headed an organization that was making a conscious effort to move its executive base beyond the borders of Ontario in order to foster a broader cross-section of national membership. In short, by the time of her death, not only did Lowther have extensive literary contacts across Canada, but some of her most important critical reception and personal alliances came from Ontario.

Nevertheless, it is the account of her terribly sorry neglect by an indifferent, if not downright hostile, 'Eastern' literary 'establishment' that is still taken for granted in recent discussions (Brooks 2000: 147; Howard 1999: B4), thereby in effect collapsing the history of Lowther's actual victimization with a specious history of her 'artistic victimization.' With her 'victim' status in this way doubly inscribed, it becomes even harder to see past or around it. In this regard it is not surprising that subsequent elegiac tributes would include Lowther's portrayal as the proverbial sacrificial lamb.[9]

This heightened emphasis would certainly seem to be the case with West Coast journalist Paul Grescoe's 1976 'Eulogy for a Poet,' which appeared as the front cover feature of *The Canadian Magazine*, with a full-page profile photograph of Lowther and, at bottom right, the textual epitaph: 'The Poet as Victim: Pat Lowther.' Largely a biographical piece, Grescoe's article cites as one of its sources the Gzowski radio program on which Milton Acorn had disburdened himself of the theory of Pat Lowther's 'artistic' persecution. Unsurprisingly, then, it too recycles the idea of her 'relative neglect by the publishing establishment in Eastern Canada'(19).

Among other things, Grescoe's article records a slanted version of a public skirmish occasioned by the original *Gzowski on FM* radio program. On November 4th, two days after the tribute aired, Gzowski had permitted the Maritime poet Andy Wainwright to read a poem critical of the show, which Wainwright felt had been 'sensational' and 'maudlin in the extreme, dwelling as it did on [Lowther's] personal life in ways that left the poetry in the shadows.'[10] Wainwright's 'For Pat Lowther' was a direct apostrophe to the absent Lowther: 'On CBC last night, they made you human, / stripping away your poet's mask, / making you wear their own: / Pat the welfare girl whose teeth were bad / patriot Pat, who never was American / poor Pat we never told how much we loved.' Wainwright's criticism of the program's profile of the 'first FM martyr, Pat,' in turn, provoked Gzowski's 'response department' to air on the *next* day's program a 'response to a response' by an angry Allan Safarik, who had prepared the original audio 'portrait' and who characterized the Maritime interloper as 'a stranger at a funeral.'[11]

The acrimony that erupted after the initial radio tribute expressed sincere concern and anger, from – literally – diametrically opposed positions on a map: a West Coast friend of the deceased and a detached, East Coast 'stranger.' Theoretically, journalists (and biographers) are supposed to take these things into consideration, but Paul Grescoe's 'Eulogy for a Poet' is not interested in journalistic objectivity. Citing the first few lines of Wainwright's poem (inaccurately), Grescoe's piece basically reiterates Safarik's point that the Maritime poet 'didn't know Pat Lowther' and was therefore speaking out of turn as 'a stranger at a funeral' (16). Lowther, we read, 'was not a public poet': she 'wrote out of the soul-scarring experience of [her] life, about the exquisite anguish of being something that makes an Andy Wainwright wince: that is, being human' (16).

But the 'soul-scarring,' 'exquisite anguish' of the romantic rhetoric here is the journalist's own, not (unless you want to count her juvenilia) Lowther's. And Grescoe's recourse to the idea of the primacy of lived experience – as against the ignorance of a 'stranger' 'who didn't *know* Pat Lowther' (emphasis added) – also has serious implications for the way Lowther's *work* gets represented in 'Eulogy for a Poet,' an article whose bolded epitaph, 'The Poet as Victim,' is a headline act that 'Pat Lowther' has yet to fully recover from. For while the dual subjects of a poet's life and her work may elicit vastly different judgments, they are also interrelated in ways that make it easy for assumptions about the one to get transposed, *ipso facto*, onto the other. Since Grescoe's article posits experiential knowledge of the woman, Pat Lowther, as privileged ground, it follows also that it is the autobiographical poems, apparently written 'out of the soul-scarring experience' of the poet's 'life' as 'a wife and a mother, and a lover, as a feminist and a socialist,' that get priority here (16).

This autobiographical emphasis overlooks the important fact that as many of Lowther's most powerful poems come from carefully re-searched reading as they do from 'her life as a wife and a mother, and a lover, as a feminist and a socialist.' Lowther's Chilean and Arctic poems, for example, were manifestly about places and peoples she didn't 'know' first-hand – places and peoples that, as some might now be inclined to argue, she herself was a 'stranger' to, as another White, North American interloper. In fact, the question of experience, its authenticity and authority, was a problem that Lowther herself 'wrestled' with during her brief but thoughtful poetic career. In a workshop essay entitled 'A Kind of Wrestling,' she wrote:

> The limit of my own experience is a barrier I cannot cross, and don't want
> to cross. I have not climbed mountains, gone to sea, or visited foreign
> countries. I have not been a doctor, a dock worker, or a detective. I have

lived as a person, with and among other people. That is my material, and I
want to do it justice, to the best of my ability.[12]

Lowther never did enjoy the range of vocational possibilities she
alludes to, nor the opportunity to visit the 'foreign countries' that especially fascinated her. Yet, to her simply stated 'material' of living 'as a
person, with and among people,' she brought a poetic intelligence sufficiently complex to contradict her modest sense of the 'barrier' posed by
her 'own experience.' For example, the fact that Lowther never actually
crossed borders into 'foreign countries' didn't preclude her writing
about a Chilean prison camp 'authentically' enough to convey the
impression of her having died *in situ*, as one American reviewer of *A
Stone Diary* duly misinformed her readers (Morehouse, 1977). In short,
Lowther's poetry, like any good art, is as often as not based on mediated
rather than directly experiential forms of knowledge; her poetry has as
much to do with her ability to project herself with focused emotional
precision into *un*-lived experience as anything else. This fact must qualify any understanding of the neighbouring fact that Lowther herself was
more keenly self-conscious about: namely, the truth of the materially circumscribed 'limit of [her] own experience' as a high-school drop-out
and working-class woman and mother.

To his credit, Paul Grescoe tried to separate out these issues, sort of.
Having first placed 'soul-scarring experience' as the basis of Lowther's
life and work alike, 'Eulogy for a Poet' goes on to attempt a distinction
between the two. At the 'eulogy's' close, Lowther's friend Lorraine Vernon is quoted, 'talk[ing] about Pat Lowther as victim'– not as *a* victim,
mind, but condensed, like the definitive epitaph, '*as* victim.' '"She was
so incredibly passive,"' Vernon is quoted as saying: '"warm and beautiful, but passive."' 'As *a person*, perhaps,' the next paragraph begins: 'But
as *a poet*, Pat Lowther was *the kind of woman* who, as Pat Lane says, scared
most men, "scared the hell out of them"' (19, emphasis added). Person
/ poet / (scary) 'kind of woman' (poet): the attempt to separate the
'person' and the 'poet' is already undone by the end of the thought,
which offers a definition of Pat Lowther 'as a poet' in terms of the sexually intimidating 'kind of woman' (writer) she appeared to be. Just as
instructive as the alacrity with which the distinction falters, though, is
the stark disparity between the perceptions of the two friends cited, a
contradiction that carries some fairly fundamental implications for any
narrative that is willing to lean heavily and uncritically on the idea of
experiential knowledge. Unlike Andy Wainwright (or Robert Fulford

and 'his gang' of 'Eastern Mafia'), both Lorraine Vernon and Patrick Lane undeniably '*knew* Pat Lowther' quite well by the time of her death. Yet all that this fact really proves in 'Eulogy for a Poet' is that Lowther appeared a different person to different people: to an older female friend, she appeared a 'passive' woman; to a younger male friend, she appeared, quite conversely, as a rather 'scary' woman-poet.

Such contradictions serve as a reminder that first-hand knowledge is not automatically equivalent, in and of itself, to sufficient understanding – of any person, place, or problem. However important embodied experience is – and it *is* important – its most serious 'limits,' in Lowther's word, are made manifest when appeals to it turn custodial of the truth. In this respect, the 'sandbox' controversies and questions that spring up in the public forum over 'Pat Lowther' in the immediate wake of her death point to some of our most rudimentary and potent territorial instincts as human animals yet. The need to mark hierarchies of grief and stake possession of the corpse accordingly fuels the most passionate claims over who did or did not 'know' Pat Lowther; who did or did not 'suppress' her career; who was or was not 'invited' to her funeral.[13]

Shakespeare, who of course isn't famous for nothing, knew at least this much about our creature compulsions when he wrote *Julius Caesar,* a play in which conspirators and mourners alike are inclined to bathe their hands in the blood of the victim. In this regard, too, Lowther's is a posthumous 'legacy' which underscores the more immediate, *legal* question of ownership posed in 1975 by the presence of her literary corpus in the market place, in the absence of its author. Contrary to journalist Sean Rossiter's assertion in Anne Henderson's film *Water Marks,* Lowther did not have time before her death to respond to Oxford University Press's letter of acceptance for the manuscript of *A Stone Diary.* No contract was signed. In more ways than one, she left an unsettled estate.[14]

To commemorate Lowther's death, many turned, aptly, to the medium of poetry, producing yet another set of cultural documents essential to her 'legacy.' 'As a memorial to Pat, whom I knew intimately for ten years,' Dorothy Livesay wrote from Winnipeg, 'I have asked poets who knew and loved her to write something for *CV/II,* either in prose or verse.' By the time the January 1976 issue of *CV/II* went to press, under a double-bill cover of 'AL PURDY in conversation' and 'PAT LOWTHER a

tribute,' Livesay had 'gleaned' several '"flowers for her [friend's] garden."'[15] As Livesay's nod to the conventions of pastoral elegy indicate,
most of the Lowther 'tributes' she received were verse elegies, though
P.K. Page, Anne Marriott, and Marya Fiamengo also each contributed
short, astute prose pieces. Elegiac tributes to Lowther also appeared, a
few years later, in *West Coast Review* (January 1978) and in a collection of
poems edited by Barry Dempster, entitled *Tributaries: An Anthology,
Writer to Writer* (1978). Dempster's anthology includes poems written
'For Pat Lowther' by Patrick Lane, as well as by Margaret Atwood and
Dorothy Livesay herself. Many friends 'who knew and loved' Lowther
also published elegies separately, in their own collections.

It is generally agreed that, whatever else they may manage to accom-
plish, elegies – like any ritualization of grief – are always in part strategies for recovery, exercises in assimilating the shock and non-sense of
death, even in those instances where the formal convention of consolation is resisted or rejected by the poet. Along these lines, some of the
poetic tributes to Lowther remind one more overtly than others that elegies are inevitably as much or more about the mourner as they are the
mourned. Some make their 'lyric self-concern' (Bruffee 1983: 47) inadvertently transparent, openly revealing the anxious concerns with
self-mortality that often lurk, unspoken, between the lines of poems
lamenting the death of another. Others, like Robert Gibbs' 'The Premonition' and Dorothy Livesay's 'Book Review,' both published in Dempster's *Tributaries* and both inscribed 'for Pat Lowther,' are more complex
poems, though also not so much 'about' the woman to whom they are
dedicated as they are 'about' the phenomenon of survivor guilt.[16]
Gibbs's poem laments what is presented as an incommensurable gulf
between the 'plain fact' of the dead poet's 'un / sufferable pain' and
the speaker's own 'numb dumb pushing' grief, which searches for
expression in words of 'love' (Dempster 1978: 59). 'The Premonition' is
a poem of sorrow that points primarily to a speaker disconsolate with his
own sense of the paradoxical inadequacy of his healthy, beating 'physical heart,' 'its tough / indifferent muscle' (Dempster 1978: 59).

Similarly, Livesay's 'Book Review,' motivated by the 1977 appearance
of *A Stone Diary*, is a poem of self-reproach above all else. 'It was / that we
did not know you enough / treasure your look / your casual word,' the
speaker begins: 'we saw only the outer dress / the thin sharp bones, the
skinniness' (Dempster 1978: 63). Coming from Livesay, who had, as she
stressed, known Lowther 'intimately for ten years,' the speaker's public
representation of having glimpsed 'only the outer dress' of her deceased

friend is worth noting. Berating herself and her surviving peers alike with the plural 'we,' the speaker of 'Book Review' suggests that Lowther's 'presence' was taken 'carelessly for granted,' before she concludes: 'It was as if / the fire burning in your eyes / failed to ignite ours / until now, facing your stones / we are blinded.' Confronted with the astonishing 'stones' of their friend's last 'diary,' colleagues such as Gibbs and Livesay were moved to self-recrimination for what their grief cast as their own insensitivity: in the first instance, a stone-hearted inability to appreciate Lowther's 'pain'; and in the second, a blindness to Lowther's inner 'fire' and talent during her lifetime. In Livesay's case, for one, there is plenty of evidence to contradict the self-chastising charge.

But it is intriguing to compare 'Book Review' with a later Livesay poem, 'Two Lives,' dually dedicated to Lowther and to Sharon Stevenson, a fellow socialist Vancouver poet (and an acquaintance of Lowther's) who committed suicide in 1978. While 'Book Review' takes the form of an apostrophe to the recently dead author of *A Stone Diary*, 'Two Lives,' first published in 1984, signals a major shift in both its structure of address and its theme.[17] As its title suggests, the poem juxtaposes the 'two lives' of 'Pat,' who 'believed in the new world' but 'was murdered by her husband,' and 'Sharon,' who 'believed in the new world' 'but murdered / herself.' 'Were they dream-besot / or star-guided?' the speaker asks. In the last half of this brief poem, the interrogatives continue to pile up: 'Who will now speak for them as poets?'

> Who will stand up
> and be counted
> for their sake
> will stay alive
> womanning the last barricade
> till the end of falsehood? (Livesay 1999: 220)

No longer a direct run after a gapingly absent 'you,' a tongue that can't stop readdressing that 'unhealed wound of all we ever knew' (Lane, in Dempster 1978: 62), 'Two Lives' uses the more remote third person to speak about the dead poets. In doing so, it shifts grounds from an elegiac quest to speak *to* the deceased, to the more polemical and ethical question of 'who will *now* speak *for* them' (Livesay 1999: 220; emphasis added). Whereas the fresh absence that is the premise of 'Book Review' primarily takes a measure of the speaker herself, and finds that speaker wanting, the spare biographical facts and rhetorical questions of 'Two

Lives' call for feminist solidarity against the broader social and political fact of the violent 'falsehood' of patriarchy.

Though a poem of two dozen lines struggles to do it justice, the implied drama of 'Two Lives' is that of 'fallen' sisters in a wider and not always well camouflaged historical war against women. The individual *deaths* of Lowther and Stevenson, which essentially define their respective *lives* in 'Two Lives,' thus become emblematic of a feminist cause for which one should 'stand up / and be counted.' But even more to the point is how the keenly felt tragedy of Livesay's earlier 'Book Review' – 'It was / that we did not know you enough' – gets recast in the later poem. In 'Two Lives,' it is a more confidently knowable tragedy that is taken up by Livesay, who *will* say what 'they' – the two dead poets – 'believed in,' and stood for, and fell on account of. The perhaps more unsettling consideration that we might, in fact, have known 'only the outer dress' of the departed appears to have dissipated with time.

As Patrick Lane's image of the inarticulate, open-'mouthed' wound in 'For Pat Lowther' accurately indicates, the recurrent concern of elegy is with giving voice, alternately or both to the pain of the mourner and to the remembered 'voice' of the deceased. In some instances, a measure of solace in face of the fact of Lowther's murder is attained when the poet is able to reconnect with the 'voice' of the departed. Written, like 'Book Review,' in the immediate aftermath of Lowther's murder, another Livesay elegy, 'The Continuum,' seeks the consolation indicated by its title despite its austere setting during 'the first snow' of an on-coming Winnipeg winter.[18] Standing beside 'Riel's river' and watching the 'soft shroud' of snow fall 'upon olive-green water,' Livesay's speaker is led to think of her friend's 'life' – implicitly compared within the poem to that of the Métis leader, 'Riel's' – 'chopped off at prime / victim of violent hate' (Livesay 1998: 213). Lowther's West Coast imagery and her Neruda poems 'return' to wash over the speaker as she contemplates the Red River flowing past: 'I feel your poems falling clean / upon our living / alive with your pleading, / incisive tongue' (214). The dead poet's voice is still 'alive,' yet her absence remains an open wound, as the speaker's last wish suggests: 'O may your words / return   return / to heal our griefs / seal cicatrice' (214).

The first of the four poems dedicated to Lowther in Dempster's *Tributaries*, Margaret Atwood's elegy 'for Pat,' 'Another Night Visit,' represents an interesting variation on this theme, opening with an invocation of those very emblems of 'Edgar Allan Poe' romance that Lowther herself had played with in her 'Nightmare.' Thus, Atwood's title announces that it is 'night,' and in the opening stanza, under 'the height of moon,' in a house 'floating on wind,' the speaker holds a 'cat' against her beating 'heart, heart' (Dempster 1978: 60). As might be expected from a writer who was already on guard about 'declaiming like Brutus over Caesar's corpse,' though, these clichés of Halloween gothic are invoked only to be rejected. Interior to the ironic romance frame of 'Another Night Visit,' a more poignant, private search for the lost friend unfolds: 'Which stone / are you in?' A *Stone Diary*, the 'book' that Livesay also 'reviews' and that Atwood sent on to *Ms* magazine in hopes of actually having it reviewed,[19] comes 'in the mail' here as a kind of visitation:

> This is your voice I hold,
> it came in the mail
> ...
> Is that you, in the wind or
> as you said, in stone
> But this is not a stone,
> it is your voice,
>
> alive still, moving
> around each word like
> wind, these words un-
> earth you. (Dempster 1978: 60–1)

Failing a last glimpse of the departed friend 'in the wind or' 'in stone,' the poet settles instead, like Livesay in 'The Continuum,' for the comforts of prosopopoeia, the 'voice' of the absent, 'alive still.'

The poetic tributes to Lowther include several other accomplished examples which feature as their central concern the poet's renegotiation with the voice of the dead. Like Atwood's and Livesay's, most of these are cast as direct addresses to the absent presence of Lowther. But unlike the foregoing, some of these elegies ultimately discover degrees of hope or consolation as much in their visions of Lowther's canonicity as in their reconnections with her 'voice.' In Livesay's 1976 tribute issue of *CV/II*, Lowther's friend Elizabeth Brewster contributed a poem bearing the same simple title as Patrick Lane's 'For Pat Lowther.' Brewster's elegy begins with the speaker's own reaction to 'hearing of your death / in violence' (Brewster 1976: 16). Interweaving allusions to and from some of Lowther's own 'tidal poems,' such as 'To Capture Proteus' (*MS*, 78), Brewster's elegy figures Lowther as both prophet and revenant:

I realize you must have dreamed
just this death
and in my own dreams lately
you have walked white-faced,
blood on your forehead,
wearing a seaweed-black
trailing skirt

but speaking
in a voice
gentle as water
your tidal poems

In the Saskatoon poet's 'dreams,' Lowther emerges as a kind of phantasmagoric Ophelia, trailing her 'weedy trophies' and 'clothes spread
wide' (*Hamlet*, 4.7.174–5). But this is only her preliminary incarnation
as a 'gentle ghost' in Brewster's poem. Confessing that she 'envied'
Lowther for some of her poems, the speaker – like other guilt-ridden
survivors – goes on to beseech pardon from a predecessor who gradually takes on a stature somewhat more divine than Shakespeare's tragic
heroine:

Forgive me, gentle ghost.
Haunt my mind's
passageways
with your grace.
Haunt me with your words.
Let your spilled blood
renew my veins.

Rise, and walk
on all the waters
of your tears,
like sunshine stepping
on the waves
of the life-and-death creating
end-of-all-journeys sea.

Brewster's echoes here are to Lowther's long poem 'In The Continent
behind My Eyes,' where the sea – 'even now ... inventing/ sex and

death' (*MS*, 25) – is indeed envisioned as the naturalistic 'end-of-all-journeys,' and where Lowther, does, in fact, recall having accomplished the impressively Christ-like feat of walking on water. In Lowther's poem, however, this miracle is recalled in the context of a childhood memory of visiting Rice Lake with her father, who once worked there as a water supply maintenance man. The passage occurs in the opening stanza of the poem's third section, which revisits a child's exquisite satisfaction at a special mark of paternal favour – a young girl's pleasure in sharing the mysteries of her father's strange and exciting 'wor[k] with water' ('adjusting flow and level, / going out from his bed / into 3 in the morning storms'). As a municipal watershed, Rice Lake was strictly off-limits to the public when a young 'Patsy Lou' had been escorted there by her father:

> And once he took me to Rice Lake
> where no one is allowed –
> the water was flat as pavement
> papered with fallen leaves
> and flat wooden walkways
> and there I walked on water (*MS*, 24)

In Lowther's original text, the memory of having 'walked on water' at Rice Lake thus unfolds as a form of double-consciousness: a child's excited perception of the placid reservoir ('And ... and ... and'), looking just like 'pavement' and 'papered' over with 'leaves,' is filtered through and blended with the adult poet's tempered awareness of the 'flat wooden walkways' skimming that reservoir's 'flat' surface, and thus ironically flattening (or literally supporting, depending on your inclination) such a 'miracle.' The result is an interlude which conveys both the speaker's nostalgia for *and* her subtle bemusement at a younger self's divine inspirations.

In Brewster's elegiac tribute 'For Pat Lowther,' on the other hand, the Christ-like allusion is called up as an unqualified injunction to 'rise, and walk on all the waters' – not just Rice Lake, and with no supporting props in sight. In Brewster's elegy, too, it is the reservoir of her own spent tears upon which the dead poet walks. No fond memories here. Not even Brewster's final rays of 'sunshine,' as prefigured by the hoped-for renewal of the living poet, and the visionary resurrection of her dead predecessor, can quite dissipate that copious 'sea' of tears a transfigured and beatified Lowther treads.

West Coast poet Marya Fiamengo's 'Requiem (For Pat Lowther – October 24, 1975)' offers a similar iconography and is also similarly complex in terms of its elegiac engagement with, and adaptation of, 'the music' of Lowther's own 'words' (Fiamengo 1978: 15). Published in Fred Candelaria's *West Coast Review*, 'Requiem' takes the form of a prayer: 'Earth and salt water / bless and absolve / the burning of this flesh / which walked the hard road / of genesis.' Like tributes by Brewster, Livesay, and others who 'knew and loved' the poetry of Pat Lowther, Fiamengo recalls the words of the deceased poet, enjoining that poet 'to sing to us now / through caves of space':

> All her mortal bones
> undressed
> sing to us now
> through caves of space
> requiescat lady, rest
> your white heart
> burns clean and live
> as hottest star
> or farthest nebulae.

'Requiem' is a moving lyric, sensitive to the citations and metaphors it mobilizes. The lines 'All her mortal bones / undressed,' for instance, allude unobtrusively to 'The Dig' from *A Stone Diary*, where 'the diggers,' 'with very gentle fingers,' 'lift up the bones of a woman' and 'tenderly ... take off her stockings of earth' (*SD*, 90). In calling up the archaeologists of Lowther's poem in the process of her own poem's attempt to address the 'bones' of Pat Lowther, Fiamengo points to the fact that Lowther herself could at times speak as a deeply ironic elegist. For while 'the diggers' of 'The Dig' are 'gentle' men – the very antithesis of *Hamlet's* grave-digging, skull-lobbing clowns – they are also undercut as hypocrites in a poem that swiftly punctures its elegiac mood to focus on the archaeologists' less respectful treatment of their own: 'They have not such love / for the living / who are not finished / or predicted' (*SD*, 90).

With its 'hard road / of genesis' and burning 'white heart,' 'Requiem' – like Brewster's 'For Pat Lowther' or Daniel David Moses' 'Our Lady of the Glacier'[20] – could be read as reinforcing in its imagery the posthumous projection of Lowther as a 'saint,' a projection to which later critics such as Kathy Shaidle react. Yet Fiamengo's poem introduces small and welcome modifications to the recurrent metaphor of the celestial sphere that is sometimes taken for the sweet home of 'CanLit heaven.' To represent Lowther 'as hottest star / or farthest nebulae' as Fiamengo does is not quite the same as pitching her as Ursa Minor in relation to the Really Big Stars, a trope surcharged with the unfortunate significance of reinforcing the competitive logic of the man driven to end Pat Lowther's life. In its emphasis on intense heat and immense distance, Fiamengo's envisionment of Lowther's posthumous 'star' instead preserves the idea that disappears between 'the outer dress' of Livesay's 'Book Review' and the inner assuredness of 'Two Lives': namely, the idea of a body so remote it is no longer fully knowable, and certainly not directly touchable.

While some of Lowther's literary friends found a degree of relief in the enduring 'presence' of her 'voice,' or resorted to traditional theological visions of ascension and resurrection by way of elegiac consolation, Lowther's former UBC student Gail McKay had been busying herself with a more extensive project dedicated to the memory of her poetic mentor. Before she went off to law school, McKay found herself in Montreal in 1976, where she encountered Frank Davey in a poetry seminar. Davey, in turn, shepherded into print what evolved as McKay's creative MA thesis, *The Pat Lowther Poem* (1977). As Davey suggests, McKay's long poem, much like Atwood's *The Journals of Susanna Moodie* (1970) or Florence McNeil's *Emily* (1975), reflects the concern of a distinct phase of Anglo-American feminist literary history with the recovery of foremothers.[21] But you'd never guess this from glancing at the book's cover. Like many things related to the history of Pat Lowther, the cover appearance of *The Pat Lowther Poem* doesn't quite do justice to the text it encloses. Against a grainy, film noir-ish background of black and white, the Coach House Press cover features a lone female figure in high heels. She appears to be either poised to run or already running down a dark street lit by a single, garishly bright street lamp. If we were to read only so far, we might be forgiven for mistaking McKay's book as a slim crime melodrama.

And indeed, constructed as a *bricolage* of voices, *The Pat Lowther Poem* does deploy excerpts from newspaper sources, setting the poet's private quest for the absent '*sister*, artist' (xxvi; emphasis in the original) off against the jarringly impersonal and sensational 'facts' of Lowther's murder and Roy's trial, as those 'facts' were reported by the media: the 'one hundred seventeen / blood spots / on the wall' (xliii); the 'spectacle of murder suspect, Roy Lowther, bathed in moonlight carrying his wife's body' (xxvi); the spectacle of Roy on the witness stand blended with quotations from the *Vancouver Sun*'s journalistic 'whodunit,' 'Verses and Verdicts' (xxxiv), and so forth. Against these deliberately intrusive, block-capital passages of newspaper headlines, however, excerpts from Lowther's own poems are set off, and both of these source texts are interwoven with lyrics exploring McKay's relationship to Lowther and to her own family past in the B.C. interior.

Actually, the younger poet's own personal history, though only occasionally introduced, provides material for some of the strongest poems in *The Pat Lowther Poem*: tersely witnessed, these segments capture a painful past of 'logging accident[s]' and thwarted artistic aspirations (xvi); of trapped wild animals (xxxiv) and summarily executed domesticated ones – as with the shooting of a loyal 'old black nag' 'crippled up bad' and 'almost finished' anyway ('You have to understand / the way we do things in the country' [xxv]). But McKay's long poem opens with the image of 'Professor Lowther['s]' 'empty office' (xi, i), and it is the mentor's absence that acts as a 'black pearl / under the tongue' of the younger poet, a 'grain of sand the muscle / worries over' (vii). As the 'muscle' of McKay's 'tongue' runs after its lost object, it questions myths of origin and end (lix, lx) and constructs 'Pat Lowther' in various, artful shapes and incarnations: as silhouetted saint 'against the stained- / glass window' (xi); as Nerudian sacred relic (xlv); as Dante's Beatrice, from whose 'breast the white / dove startles' (xix); as blood-bespattered 'Lady, MacBeth' (xlii); and as Lady Godiva, 'the shoulders o the breasts / the thighs ... / bare,' 'on a white horse,' with a flowing 'mane' 'lace[d]' into its rider's own long 'hair'(xxiii, xiii, x).

As the sensual details of Lowther-as-Lady-Godiva intimate, what complicates the romance tropes of *The Pat Lowther Poem*, making them in the end less conventional than they first appear, are the homoerotic undertones that shape the younger poet's quest for her sister/foremother. Heterosexual fantasy is introduced only to be quietly subverted. In the concluding poems, for example, the poet interpellates herself (and the reader) as the direct addressee of these lines from Lowther's 'Hotline to the Gulf' (*SD*, 81): 'write to me, darling / from the other world' (liv). Elegist and reader are similarly positioned to intercept Eugene McNamara's inscription in a book sent to Lowther, as reported by the press in its coverage of the trial: 'Always I am with you. Even if I were blind I would find you' (lxii).

Despite the elegist's attestation that 'here in the dark / under the skin / of my small left breast' there is 'no wound' (lxi), *The Pat Lowther Poem* ultimately comes to rest in loss, 'always, from breath to breath ... / saying goodbye' (lxiii). With this citation from Lowther's '100,' a poem that casts an unflinching but compassionate gaze on a dying centenarian (*SD*, 64), McKay gives final word to the voice of the woman to whom her book pays tribute. Formal closure and consolation elude the (soon-to-be-lawyer) poet, who at the end of her long poem is still 'always, from breath to breath ... / saying goodbye' to the half-life behind '100.'

Of the extensive and variegated bouquet of poetic 'flowers' gathered in homage to Lowther, nowhere is the loss so incisively represented against the traditional terms of pastoral elegy as in Leona Gom's 'Patricia's Garden.'[22] In this case, what begins in the initial stanza as 'a perfectly-kept garden,' orderly and 'well' 'grown,' quickly transmutes into the nightmare of 'a life split open somewhere / a small, wasted garden':

> tomatoes break open, bleed into earth.
> ...
> cabbages crack like torn brains.
> carrots push up swollen orange knuckles
> from the soil. everything is balanced
> on the rim of rot. (Gom 1991: 236)

And the poem does not let us forget that 'what is wrong' with this picture 'depends on us':

> the woman who planted this
> is simply
> not here.
> one of us knows
> where she has gone,
> one of us knows

In its veiled allusion to Lowther's murderer – the 'one' who 'knows / where' the disappeared poet 'has gone' – Gom's poem insists on Roy's inclusion as 'one of us.' In doing so, it implies a broader social indictment for Pat Lowther's murder without offering any reassuring diagnosis for 'what is wrong' with 'us.' As there is 'simply' no solace for Lowther's absence here, so too there are 'simply' no quick ways to account for the 'rot' and 'waste' her death represents. Aside from its terrifying malformations of broken fruit and 'swollen orange knuckles,' part of the nightmarish quality of 'Patricia's Garden' is organic to the poem's very silence on this point – its refusal to make any sense of the gravest question it poses: 'what is wrong' with 'us'? In effect, 'Patricia's Garden' leads its readers to 'the rim of rot' and leaves us there, to 'balance' on our own.

∞

It was, then, within an overwhelmingly eulogistic and elegiac framework that reviewers of *A Stone Diary* took up their unenviable task when Lowther's last book, after some contractual delays, finally appeared in 1977. Among the more than dozen reviews initially produced, very, very few reviewers, like Suniti Namjoshi (1977) and Robert Quickenden (1977), managed to pull off the rather remarkable feat of writing reviews focused entirely, and perceptively, on Lowther's poetry, without a single, direct reference to the biographical fact of her recent death. Far more often, reviewers were self-conscious about the precarious potential pitfalls of wading critically into 'Patricia's Garden.' Such reviewers, like Atwood in her *Parnassus* piece and Gwendolyn MacEwen writing in *Quill and Quire* (1977: 44), felt impelled to address the issue up front.

Deflecting attention immediately from the questions of what Lowther 'might have become' or 'how she died,' Christopher Levenson warned: 'If we are to avoid a Canadian Plath cult, we must now look carefully at the poems themselves and isolate their peculiar qualities' (1978: 352). While Levenson felt confident enough to predict, by the end of his review, Lowther's 'assure[d] ... major place in future Canadian anthologies' (1978: 354), others assumed a more cautious, wait-and-see approach. At the conclusion of a review entitled 'Tone, Tune of True Poet,' Ottawa poet Catherine Firestone signed off as follows: 'One can only hope that this diary of bloodstone and seed, of fragmentation and foreboding, will receive the equitable literary judgement it deserves before the events surrounding Lowther's murder distort her poetry through the fallacies that are so often animated by myth.'[23] But by the time these words were written, 'before' was already too late: 'the events surrounding Lowther's murder' had *already* begun to complicate her poetry, if not – in Firestone's more pejorative term – 'distort' it.

Gary Geddes, typically one of Lowther's more astute readers, began a fairly extensive review in the *Globe and Mail* by noting that 'for those who love literary gossip more than literature, *A Stone Diary* will provide abundant material for speculation upon the relation between Pat Lowther's life and her tragic death.' It was fellow poet and editor Geddes to whom Lowther had turned for advice while preparing *A Stone Diary* for submission, and while privately Geddes confided after her death that 'the Lowther manuscript is like a ghost,'[24] in his review he was careful to distance himself from his own sense of the uncanny. He thus emphasized immediately the 'superficial[ity]' of any resemblance between Lowther's work, with its 'fascination with death by violence,' and 'that of Sylvia Plath, who courted suicide in her work long before she took her own life.' Sensibly qualified in its praise of the poetry, Geddes' review arrives at the conclusion that Lowther's is 'a body of work that must already be reckoned with' and that 'in due course, as her best work is brought together in a selected poems, we will be better able to appreciate the range and uniqueness of her legacy' (1977: E27).

Much as with the rule of law responsible for blocking the admission of 'the thing entitled "September 23rd"' from Roy's trial, most of the critically valuable review literature written in the immediate wake of Lowther's death is marked, then, by an awareness of the importance of timing in relation to judgment, even if that literature differs markedly in its sense of the timing at stake. (Hence, Levenson's emphasis on judgment '*now*,' Firestone's emphasis on judgment '*before*,' and Geddes' emphasis on deferring judgment '*in due course.*')

In all too many other instances, however, this question was ignored by other reviewers, who were too caught up instead with the apparently uncanny temporality at work *in* Lowther's life and poetry. This holds as true for reviews of the recent *Time Capsule* as it does for reviews of *A Stone Diary*. 'The death of the Vancouver poet Pat Lowther casts an eerie shadow over her first and last major collection of poetry,' as Robert Fulford wrote in *Saturday Night*: '... the poems in *A Stone Diary* are such that it's impossible to forget her death, even for a moment' (1977: 71). Which anticipates very closely later reviewers such as Sharon Thesen: 'No matter how much one would like to forget the fact that Pat Lowther was murdered by her husband ... the template of that tragedy cast[s] its form over every poem' (1997: 19). Or Susan Musgrave, who introduces 'Pat Lowther' as 'a rising star on the Canadian literary scene in the late '60s and '70s':

Knowing the painful details of her death ... Lowther's poetry [*sic*] becomes all the more ironic and haunting. Death, and violent death in particular, obsessed this poet right from the start ... The reader gets the chilling feeling from these poems that Pat Lowther had premonitory knowledge of the future ... For her short life, and in death, let us praise her. (1997: G1, G8).

As Musgrave's prose suggests, almost invariably accompanying reviewers' focus on Lowther's 'obsession' with death is the familiar representation of her as an otherworldly prophetess of 'chilling' premonitory powers, and the eulogistic/elegiac element of reverential 'praise' for the deceased. (Obviously, the latter is not in itself objectionable – if one is writing a eulogy or an elegy.) But Lowther's 'haunting legacy' (Sturmanis 1985a) has not been done any favours by reviewers, journalists, and critics (among them, many fellow poets writing in those capacities) who have positioned her, however sincerely, along these lines, as a prescient Cassandra who 'crystallize[d] ... her destiny into an almost mythic concision' (Ormsby 1998: 33) – or who even forecast the actual year of her own death in a fabulous book inscription.[25]

The proliferation of 'literary gossip' and gothic fascination with the aura of uncanniness surrounding Lowther and her poetry has led to the recording of some unusual triumphs over basic physics of time and space. Given Lowther's own interest in that subject, she might have been amused (or not) by more than just that one, hopelessly lost American reviewer who pinpointed her death 'in Chile.' Rather like those mis-sightings of the poet right after her disappearance, for instance, an editorial mis-sight in Ralph Gustafson's 1975 anthology, *The Penguin Book of Canadian Verse*, results in a biographical note informing us that Lowther is dead, but nevertheless still 'presently' serving as 'co-chairman of the League of Canadian Poets' (329). Other slips reflect the same sort of confusion between the overlapping identities of Roy and Pat that is evident in early newspaper coverage of the two apparently interchangeable 'poets.' Thus, in Dona Sturmanis's 'A Poet's Haunting Legacy,' Furry Creek, where Lowther's body was discovered, becomes a childhood haunt of the poet herself, which is a more poignant and appealing version of the truth that the site was in fact Roy Lowther's childhood haunt (1985a: 6).[26] Similarly, among the errors in Sharon Thesen's 'Earth's Dark Anvil,' the Professor Lowther who 'taught at UBC' becomes Roy, not Pat. This error is introduced in the service of making a feminist point: Roy's apparent professional entitlement is juxtaposed with his wife's life, 'circumscribed by the domestic' as 'a woman poet working at home and outside the support and contacts of the academic community' (1997: 19). A reversal of basic fact once again clearly in sync with the persistent temptation to amplify Pat Lowther's oppression, this inaccuracy unwittingly illustrates its own point about the 'circumscrib[ing]' power of traditional gender roles and expectations. In other words, it is an error that matters because it is exactly the *subversion* of those roles and expectations which are actually key to the feminist significance of Pat's history.

Among the earlier review literature, work by Dona Sturmanis is particularly important in that it points to the ambiguous publication history of what would become, after *A Stone Diary*, 'Pat Lowther's' next major posthumous appearance in print, in 1980's *Final Instructions*. In two separate accounts provided by Sturmanis, as co-editor of that collection of Lowther's early and unpublished work, this history is quickly and vaguely glossed over. In 'A Poet's Haunting Legacy,' readers are simply told that 'in 1980, Vancouver inventor Ward Carson proffered a ream of [Lowther's] poems that she had produced at 25 and never shown anyone. They eventually found their way into a volume entitled *Final Instructions*' (1985a: 6).[27] In fact, this 'ream of ... poems' was apparently 'proffered' by Ward Carson to the article's author, Dona Sturmanis, herself. Moreover, it was not on their own that these poems somehow 'popped up' (1985b: 4) and 'eventually found their way' into print (1985a: 6). While working as a journalist for the *Vancouver Province*, Sturmanis had inadvertently discovered Carson's link to Lowther while profiling the 'Vancouver inventor['s]' work; she brought the material that Carson entrusted to her to Lowther's surviving League co-Chair and then-editor of the *West Coast Review*, Fred Candelaria. Together, Sturmanis and Candelaria decided to publish the poems 'as a posthumous tribute' to Lowther, under the joint imprints of *West Coast Review* and Orca Sound.

Who was Ward Carson, and what was his connection to Lowther? In the late fifties, when Pat was still married to her first husband, Bill Domphousse, she met Carson through a creative writing course in North Vancouver. The two eventually began a relationship, which ended, according to both her and Carson, on unhappy terms. During the subsequent dissolution of her marriage with Bill, Pat made it clear that Carson became an obstacle for her in her struggle to retain custody of the children from her first marriage. Carson, it seems, was unwilling to cover up their affair in order to protect Pat against her husband's threat to take 'full advantage' of the situation and sue for full custody on grounds of adultery. Pat went ahead and denied the affair anyway, without Carson's backing – the fault-based divorce laws of the time gave her no real options but to do so. In 1960 this struggle resulted in a temporary decision awarding the son of that first marriage, Alan, to his father. It was a decision that cost Lowther no small amount of anger, grief, and guilt. Alan was barely six years old at the time.[28]

While Dona Sturmanis probably had no way of knowing the painful complications around Carson's past personal connection to Lowther, she did apparently know a few things about the 'Vancouver inventor' himself – at a later stage in his life, anyway. In a lengthy magazine profile of Carson's independent work as an 'inventor' – he had been an electrician by trade, as well as an early member of the Mensa organization – Sturmanis probed her subject as 'a brilliant "man of ideas" – but his ideas keep meeting strange fates' (1980: 3). Entitled 'Investigation of an Inventor,' the article remarks that 'Carson's stories are sometimes so incredible, it is hard to take him seriously' (1980: 4). She describes his 'cluttered little' East End house: 'Everywhere – even in the bathtub – are piles of papers, magazines, and books. The two dozen rabbits he keeps in his basement might lead some people to call him an eccentric' (1980: 5). The article about the 'inventor' who 'everyone keeps telling me ... is actually a genius' (1980: 5) is ultimately an ambiguous testimony to an 'eccentric' history of only partially verifiable accomplishments and near-accomplishments. As one source is quoted as saying, by way of conclusion: '"Everything about Carson just became mysterious at some point"' (1980: 5).

'Mysterious' or not, Ward Carson is the original source for the early, previously unpublished poems that appear in *Final Instructions*. In their preface to the 1980 collection, however, co-editors Sturmanis and Candelaria seem inclined to sustain the mystery, thanking Carson, among many others, for 'help and encouragement' with the volume, but not actually identifying him as the source of the early poems in their introduction:

> Early this year, a small collection of some of Pat Lowther's earliest, unpublished poems was given to Dona Sturmanis by an old and dear friend of Pat's. Some were typed on Pat's typewriter; others were handwritten. Wildly romantic, they were composed while Pat was attending some of her first creative writing classes in her mid-twenties ...
> Other uncollected verses by Pat were found scattered in various periodicals and are presented here along with the early poems. (*FI*, n.pag.)

The paratactic construction describing the early, unpublished material – 'Some were typed on Pat's typewriter; others were handwritten' –

102 The Craft of Memory

implies that the handwriting, like the typewriter, belonged to Pat, which it may well have. At least this is the conclusion Toby Brooks makes explicit in *Pat Lowther's Continent*: 'Some were carbon copies from Pat's typewriter; some were in Pat's own handwriting' (235). In a 1997 interview with Brooks, however, Carson states: 'She [Lowther] was a great person in most ways. Some of her writings, I can still remember a lot of them. But the ones *that I had written out and that*, and I loaned them to whatchamacall [Dona Sturmanis] ... of course, I never saw them again.'[29] When queried on this point, Carson is quite adamant that he himself did not transcribe any of the poems, either from memory or from other manuscript sources, as his apparently elliptical statement to Brooks might easily be taken to indicate. However, at the same time, now quite elderly and infirm, Carson also has no clear recollection, today, of even giving the poems to Sturmanis in the first place, or of how and when he first encountered her.[30]

Carson's claim that the materials he 'loaned' (not 'proffered') to Sturmanis were never returned to him also points to the evidently open question of the whereabouts of the original typescript/manuscript(s?) that formed the basis of *Final Instructions*. While some of the previously unpublished early poems that are printed in *Final Instructions* exist in the papers now in possession of Beth Lowther, the original 'ream' of poems Carson gave to Sturmanis does not. Sturmanis thinks it possible that she may have lost track of the papers after an offer to donate them to UBC's Special Collections was declined.[31]

For his part, Lowther's former League associate, Fred Candelaria, has no recollection of where Sturmanis even got the original 'ream' of unpublished poems, but he does recall that when she approached him with the material and the idea for *Final Instructions*, 'I said, well wonderful, let's see the manuscript. And then when I saw it, I realized that the leading poem, the leading idea ['Final Instructions'] – was in fact not Lowther's.'[32] Evidently, among the poems that Carson retrieved from his cluttered little house and 'loaned' to Sturmanis was one that was not Lowther's at all, but rather a poem by C. Day Lewis. The stray Day Lewis poem is also a detail taken up, briefly, by the editors in their introduction to *Final Instructions*:

Part of Pat's personality is reflected in the title of this book. Her social awareness and commitment showed in her early interest in the British poets of the 30s. She had gone to the trouble of copying out C. Day Lewis' poem, 'Final Instructions.' It was found with her early work and we thought it appropriate to use the title for this final book. (*FI*, n.pag.)

So it comes about that the title of 'this final book,' intended as 'a posthumous tribute to a very fine poet,' is not that 'very fine' poet's at all, but donated, as it were, by C. Day Lewis and well-meaning friends.

Lowther, it should be noted, was indeed in the habit of collecting poems she liked, or that others sent to her; there are quite a few such examples of works by other poets, some identified as such and some not, in the boxes kept by her daughter. There is also good reason why she may have transcribed the poem that her first posthumous editors 'thought it appropriate to use' as a title. Day Lewis's 'Final Instructions' is not a poem reflecting 'social awareness and commitment,' but rather, an intimate lyric that gives voice to a parent's tender, parting advice to a son ('So luck is all I can wish you, or need wish you' [Day Lewis 1992: 512]). The poem that Lowther had 'gone to the trouble of copying out' – wherever it is, today – records the private story of her misery over the prospect of losing custody of her own son, Alan. But it is this story of maternal grief that gets obscured from view along with the role and identity of the 'eccentric' and 'mysterious' Ward Carson – that 'old and dear friend' who, in the words of Pat's sister, Brenda, 'couldn't stand up for her when she needed him' during her divorce from Bill Domphousse.[33]

The real issue posed by *Final Instructions* is its implications for our understanding of 'Pat Lowther' today. If its sketchy (to say the least) textual history should raise concerns, then its organization, which is based on loosely grouped thematic sections rather than chronology, also limits its usefulness in terms of enhancing any sense of Lowther's development as a poet. In short, the very opening claim made by the editors in their introductory note to *Final Instructions* – 'Pat Lowther's place in our literary history is secure' (*FI*, n.pag.) – is a claim seriously contradicted by too many factors that suggest exactly the opposite. From the wild card of Ward Carson, the estranged ex–lover and 'Vancouver inventor'; to the absence of an original manuscript that can be collated against the papers now in the possession of Beth Lowther; to the collection's admittedly borrowed title and governing conceit, yet ignorance or suppression of their real biographical relevance; to its neglect of Lowther's own chronology as a poet – this is just not the posthumous collection of a writer in any way 'secure' in 'literary history.'

Perhaps more than anything else, what also deserves to be noted is the larger historical shift occurring at the cusp of a new decade. As though anticipating the very moment that *A Stone Diary* would slip away, quietly remaindered by Oxford in April of 1981, a mere four years after its appearance, two 1980 posthumous 'tributes' to 'Pat Lowther' displace the author in the cultural memory. The first comes bearing another poet's title, and the open question of another man's matter-of-factly inventive hand, among other concerns. The second comes up with the idea of inaugurating a literary competition to honour the memory of a writer who died, as much as anything else, as a result of ill will born of 'poetic rivalry.' And, as Kathy Shaidle's denigrating remarks about 'the "Lowther"' in 'Women, Poetry and the Cult of the Victim' indicate, within the space of the next generation, this annual, women-only poetry competition will itself become the most visible lightening rod for subsequently questioning the talent of 'Pat Lowther.'[34] As Dona Sturmanis so aptly put it in her piece on Lowther's 'haunting legacy': 'People want to remember Pat Lowther, and they don't' (1985a: 6).

∽

By comparison with *Final Instructions*, the preparation of the posthumous *Time Capsule* seems reassuring. For this selected and new collection, Polestar Press and a truly 'old and dear friend' of Lowther's, Lorraine Vernon, drew up an initial list of poems, which they then finalized in consultation with Lowther's three daughters, Kathy, Beth and Christine. 'Our priority in almost all cases was the integrity of the entire collection,' according to Polestar's Michelle Benjamin, who also referred to Gary Geddes' measured words about *A Stone Diary* while she worked with Vernon.[35] In particular, the volume's modest inclusions from *Final Instructions* are sound, all the poems chosen for reprint from this source existing either as previously published poems or in manuscript form among the papers in Lowther's archive.

Nevertheless, despite its value as an accessible representative selection of Lowther's work, *Time Capsule* is also not fully reliable in terms of editorial accuracy.[36] Moreover, a distinctly selective sort of historical memory also surrounds the marketing of this volume, which in some ways works to reinforce Lowther's mythos as a ghostly prophetess. This is in part an effect of the title, which *is* Lowther's this time (or, at least, it was by way of a working title for a very incomplete, new project). Like a 'space capsule,' the idea of a 'time capsule' sounds somewhat futuristic. Yet only superficially so, the fantasy behind 'time capsules' being not

magical access to the future but, on the contrary, an inherently anticipatory nostalgia – the past announcing its own pastness to itself and to the
unknown future. Perhaps the ambiguity of the title concept helps
explain why pre-publication notices for *Time Capsule* announced the
book as one 'to be unveiled,' like a ghost, on 31 May 1997, rather than
'launched' like most books (and space/time capsules), hoping to find a
future.

The 'Time Capsule' project Lowther envisioned as a 'complex witness' to 'history and continuity' was probably 'complex' as a result of
her awareness of the intriguing temporal illusions set into play by the
title idea. As someone who liked clocks, especially the way they seemed
to go 'backwards' in mirrors, she was interested in perceptions of time.
Moreover, as a writer who believed that she lived 'in a culture that functions basically by mind-manipulation' (*MMD*, 80), Lowther would have
likely recognized in the social diversion of 'time capsules' a 'mind-
manipulating' attempt to manufacture the *frisson* of the uncanny by
means of distinctly kitschy, elaborate artifice. We also speak of 'time-
release capsules,' which connote other strands of associations, especially
in relation to a poet who suffered from chronic migraine headaches.
And so on. The point is, the title itself is only superficially 'uncanny' and
indicates very little about the particular inflections Lowther may or may
not have been planning to bring to bear on the idea as a generative metaphor for a new body of work.

Michelle Benjamin's prefatory framing of *Time Capsule* as 'a gift' of
'magic' to novitiates 'who have not yet been introduced to Pat Lowther's
pure and original voice,' however, does subtly reinforce the sacral note
of prophetic writing (16). Another 'uncanny' component of the Polestar text relates to the autobiographical narrative which is key to its history; namely, the description of a now-adult Beth Lowther's 'chance
excursion' into her brother's 'attic,' which yielded the previously
'unseen' *Time Capsule* poems (*TC*, 17). Invariably played up in publicity
for and reviews of the book, Beth Lowther's account of her unexpected
discovery of her mother's poems is a discovery that should *not* be mistaken for our own. This material was indeed a 'new' 'discovery' for
Lowther's youngest daughters, who scarcely had a chance to know their
mother before she was taken from them, and for whom the papers kept
by their half-brother Alan must have come as a powerful shock.

Other, older family members such as Kathy, Brenda, and Virginia,
however, were aware of the boxes that eventually passed to Alan through
various family members' possession over the years. More importantly,

they, and anyone else who was old and alert enough to care in the seventies, might have recalled that a certain group of 'Time Capsule' poems were among the literary evidence submitted and discussed at Roy Lowther's well-publicized trial. The discovery of a file called 'Time Capsule' that Pat had referred to as a 'forthcoming book' came up during the preliminary hearing (PHTT, 6:419) and again during the ensuing trial, the judge in his Charge to the Jury even reminding auditors of these particular 'seven poems' Roy had collected as 'evidence' against his wife (CATT, 4:549). Before that, Lowther herself had talked about this new project during one of her last readings, a discussion recorded on tape. But in the historical memory around Pat Lowther, the looming fact of her murder, which 'is impossible to forget ... even for a moment' (Fulford 1977: 71), 'no matter how much one would like to forget [that] fact' (Thesen 1997: 19), is a memory that comes at the expense of obliterating a myriad of other, less dramatic memories, memories that are essential in terms of demystifying Pat Lowther's too largely legendary 'legacy.'

That it was once public knowledge but until recently had been 'forgotten' that Lowther prior to her death had begun working on a project tentatively entitled 'Time Capsule,' is a truth that underscores Cary Nelson's observation that 'we recover what we are culturally and psychologically prepared to recover.' '[A]nd what we recover,' he adds, 'we necessarily re-write' (1989: 11). The recovered memory of Lowther's 'Time Capsule' poems in 1997 is at once more and equally suggestive today in comparison with 1977. The title is *more* suggestive now than it was before the future happened – the twenty-year interval that would make the release of a 'time capsule' meaningful, and that would, in effect, make Lowther's 1975 remarks about her project as a 'complex kind of witness ... buried and dug up in the future' *come true,* in a way. But the response to *Time Capsule* is also *equally* suggestive of the same sort of retrospective reading that inescapably conditioned the reception of *A Stone Diary.* Thus, Susan Musgrave's pronouncement about *Time Capsule* – 'knowing the painful details of her death' makes 'Lowther's poetry becom[e] all the more ironic and haunting' (1997: G1) – is a sentiment that might as well have been published in 1977, because that's pretty much exactly what most reviewers were saying then, too. Or, to put it differently: as a collection already writ large with 'eerie' foreknowledge in 1977, *A Stone Diary* from the start foretold the appearance of its equally uncanny *Time Capsule* successor somewhere down the road. What is really poignant, depressing, or amusing – take your pick – about this 'legacy' is the unshakeable tenacity of the suspicion that what Lowther's poetry must mean is that she was somehow super-psychic or endowed with a 'chilling ... premonitory knowledge of the future' (Musgrave 1997).[37]

Lowther's history might point, instead, in the direction of Walter Benjamin, another complicated visionary materialist with whom she shared at least that basic hybridity. As far as our relationship to her posthumous 'legacy' goes, we could think, especially, of Benjamin's famous backwards-facing 'angel of history,' the parable by which he demonstrates his thesis that the hideous spectacle and irresistible lure of the past makes for a constantly blind encounter with the future.[38]

The contingence of meaning upon time persists as the most fundamental problem for readers of Lowther. Paradoxically, the sheer horror and fascination of what she called the 'dung and debris of generations' (SD, 57), and what Walter Benjamin called the 'wreckage' of the past, keeps on resulting in a strange disregard of chronology and history when it comes to discussions of Lowther and her work. In a recent review of Pat Lowther's Continent, for instance, Bina Freiwald is prompted to 'explore new ways of thinking about' Lowther's poetry as a result of Toby Brooks's book. 'One might begin,' she suggests, 'by reading Lowther not only with [Elizabeth] Smart, but also with Daphne Marlatt, whose "Musing With Mothertongue," Brooks reveals, was found among Lowther's papers' (Freiwald 2001: 69). This statement implies the revelation of a 'new,' biographically motivated cue for 'ways of thinking about' Lowther's poetry, an approach based on what has been 'found among Lowther's papers.' However, unless we are to construe from this newly uncovered fact that Pat Lowther read Daphne Marlatt's essay almost a decade before Marlatt wrote and published it in 1984's Touch to My Tongue – which would really do wonders for Lowther's transcendental status – the significance of Brooks's revelation of what is clearly a posthumous addition to the poet's archive is not apparent.[39]

Similarly, if the editors of Final Instructions neglected chronology in their collection, then the publishers of Time Capsule also make an interesting error with time in their capsule, eagerly anticipating the book's arrival into the material world with a misprinted '1996' copyright date; the book actually appeared in May 1997, or, exactly twenty years down the road or a half-life away from the appearance of A Stone Diary. This tiny but telling anachronism literally places Time Capsule in the company of certain other key texts in the modern history of the cultural unconscious, like Freud's similarly misdated *The Interpretation of Dreams.*

Speaking of 'spectacularizing speculation[s] on time,' Jacques Derrida asks: 'What is a specter? What is its history and what is its time?' (1994: 100). In posing these questions, Derrida makes apparent why the roles of prophet and revenant so often go hand in hand, as they do in posthumous constructions of Pat Lowther. Just as 'time capsules' appear future-oriented but are manifestly about mourning the passing present, so 'specters,' though conventionally regarded as visitations from the past, are premised upon our latent perception of their advance of us: '... the specter first of all sees *us* ... It looks at us even before we see *it*, or even before we see period' (Derrida 1994: 100–1; emphasis in the original). In other words, it is in the ghost's prophetic futurity, its spectral foreknowledge of our being here (wherever 'here' is) to 'visit' and 'haunt' in the first place, that its *unheimlichkeit* resides. So it is with the 'strange familiarity' of *Time Capsule*, which 'unveils' a ghostly voice from the past, a voice already endowed with the power of having anticipated itself (and us) as a future imperative. Interesting though it is in many ways, Lowther's posthumous typecasting as a spectral prophetess does not really help 'unveil' anything much about that one young 'Patsy Lou' who would go on to write intricately filtered poems about blissful illusions, like walking on water.

One thing that becomes evident in the course of rereading the history of Pat Lowther's posthumous 'legacy' is the necessity for reasserting a firm distinction between 'canonization' as a (theological) metaphor, and literary canonization as an actual effect of on-going social and institutional processes. As John Guillory has pointed out, though the concept of a 'canon' derives, etymologically and historically, from practices based on the formation of the early Christian 'biblical canon,' 'the analogy' between them 'has proven misleading at best' (1995: 239). While both types of 'canons' entail doctrinally driven 'standards' of selection, neither aesthetic nor ideological 'value' can adequately account for the complex web of factors that combine to determine the ways in which a specific society 'organize[s] and regulate[s]' 'the social practices of reading and writing,' according to a host of criteria, including (not only) gender and class, and by means of various state functions, especially educational institutions (Guillory 1995: 239).

But it is precisely this distinction between metaphors of 'beatification and canonization' and social processes of literary institutionalization that escapes critics such as Kathy Shaidle. She opens her article 'Women, Poetry and the Cult of the Victim' by recalling a recent papal 'blessing' of an eighteenth-century victim of domestic abuse, before sliding right over into a lateral critique of the 'women-only' Pat Lowther Memorial Award, and the perceived life of the woman that award is intended to honour (2000: B2). There is no disputing the fact that Shaidle finds so objectionable: Lowther has indeed been 'canonized,' cast in larger-than-life mythic and heroic terms, not only in literary tributes but, more problematically, in 'critical' periodical and review literature that is also sometimes tempted to portray her as an 'immaculate poet' (Safarik 1977: 31) or an 'angel' (Brett 1977: 22). Yet the fact that a figurative form of 'sainthood' has been projected upon her by others after her death cannot and should not be mistaken as the equivalent of literary canonization, only the actual fact of which ensures an afterlife postal address in 'CanLit heaven.' Indeed, Lowther's metaphorical 'sainthood' points to the crux of the problem afflicting her life's 'legacy' today: her reputation as a poet still remains largely an outgrowth of the elegiac 'canonization' and romanticization of an earlier and more immediately traumatic historical phase of homage. On-going claims for the security and prominence of her place in Canadian literary history (Levenson 1978; Sturmanis and Candelaria in *FI*; Thomas 1986; Sullivan 1997) are essentially statements of *faith* based on metaphorical projections of her transcendental 'canonicity.'

Ironically, then, Shaidle is partially correct in her assertion that Lowther's 'canonicity' is to some degree a matter of smoke and mirrors. However, while Shaidle attributes this to Lowther's lack of more than 'passable' poetic talent – in an article that, oddly, given that claim, does not address Lowther's poetry at all – the illusoriness of the 'canonical' status Shaidle raises has to do instead with the very (false) analogy which inspires her article. In terms of its actual institutionalization in Canadian literary history, the memory of Lowther has always been a far more dicey affair. As John Barton rightly reminds readers, 'Until the publication of *Time Capsule*, none of [Lowther's] collections of poetry has been available, except in libraries and the odd second-hand bookstore' (1997: 64).

As for Lowther's current inclusion in 'social practices of reading and writing' – whether 'systematically regulated' or not – she is, in fact, almost solely represented by whatever of her work continues to be chosen for popular anthologies, especially those which make it onto classroom curricula designed to reach new readers. The first such influential posthumous anthologization, which helped open space for Lowther in subsequent anthologies by Margaret Atwood (1982) and Rosemary Sullivan (1989), was Gary Geddes and Phyllis Bruce's *Fifteen Canadian Poets Plus Five*. In that expanded, 1978 second edition, Lowther was one of the 'plus five,' and even at that, her inclusion was by no means a *fait accompli*. Geddes, as a matter of fact, recalls some rather prominent resistance to this editorial decision:

> [W]hen I was editing that anthology and talked to Michael Ondaatje and Eli Mandel, a few people like that ... all of them to a one said, 'No, Lowther's not good enough to put in that book. You shouldn't include Lowther.' They all discouraged me. Now, why do you think that was? I respected them ... I respected their opinion, but I thought they were wrong in that case. It just makes me wonder what it was.[40]

It's the rare anthology indeed that doesn't bring up disagreements over individual inclusions (and exclusions), but in this instance Geddes' perplexity also points directly to sharp differences in appraisals of Lowther and her work – as well as to the role of her death in complicating those responses.

As will become more fully apparent in the following sections of this book, *before* Lowther's murder, her poetry was not only promoted by editors like Geddes, who had already anthologized her in his *Skookum Wawa: Writings of the Canadian Northwest* (1975). Lowther had also more than once been singled out even before the appearance of *A Stone Diary* by critics such as Diane Bessai and George Woodcock as the most promising emergent writer among cohorts that included a then little-known Carol Shields, as well as more acclaimed names such as Miriam Mandel, the 1973 recipient of the Governor General's Award for poetry. In 1975, Woodcock, then editor of *Canadian Literature*, described Lowther as a poet of 'impeccable verbal appropriateness' and concluded that 'Pat Lowther is writing verse on a level with poets who are much better known in Canada, and better verse than some winners of awards' (1975: 94).[41]

But then 23 September 1975 arrived, and with it the poet's discursive deification by an ensuing chorus of voices projecting 'Pat Lowther as victim' (Grescoe), as 'artistic victim' (Acorn), as seraph (Brett) or saint (Brewster), and so on. With the passing of that sickening murder, too, comes Lowther's posthumous conscription as a luminous 'icon' or representative for more than just one righteous social cause or another. At a wider historical remove, the grounds for Atwood's 1978 concerns about the declamatory perils of reviewing the recently dead are pretty clearly played out: over the past quarter century, Lowther's metaphorical canonization has in effect pre-empted her availability for critique, conferring upon her life's work a kind of immunity she herself would not have sought. As a recent reviewer of *Time Capsule* puts it, 'How can anyone begin to critique an icon?' (Barton 1997: 64). But being treated as more than human is only negligibly better than being regarded as less than so; sooner or later, incense burning at the altar is bound to attract sceptics. Lowther's phrase 'the stench / of divinity' comes to mind (*MS*, 28).

Dissenting voices, when they have dared to speak, have sometimes been gentle: '... there is an occasional tendency (understandable if misguided) to crown her with a martyr's aureole,' as Eric Ormsby politely phrases it (1998: 33). Seymour Mayne is similarly diplomatic: '... it's unfortunate she's been a *bit* pumped up.'[42] But the tragic sentimentalism and 'eerie' sensationalism that are lingering elements of Lowther's posthumous 'legacy' also account for excessively impatient, hyper-critical dismissals of her. In 'Women, Poetry and the Cult of the Victim,' Kathy Shaidle asserts Lowther's artistic mediocrity without in the least offering to substantiate that judgment, because the chain she really wants to rattle pertains, of course, not to the poet's work at all but to her *life* – as she evidently apprehends that 'self-sabotaging, often amoral' life on the strength of having 'dutifully attended' one fund-raising event (2000: B2). Calling herself a feminist 'of the old-fashioned variety' harkening back to 'Eleanor Roosevelt' (who apparently, like Nancy Reagan, basically said *just say no*), Shaidle alludes to an 'elder-statesman poet' at the fund-raiser, who provided an emotional testimonial to 'all the times he'd rented a truck' in an attempt to 'spirit [Pat] and the kids to safety.' At this point, Shaidle writes, the speaker's 'thoughts were painfully obvious to the stone-silent, mostly female audience: Why didn't the dumb broad just up and leave?' It is thus the culture of confession and commemoration surrounding Lowther 'as victim' which directly provokes Shaidle's nastiest dismissal of that victim. That this latter-day feminist must resort to the misogynist and class-inflected rhetoric of hard-boiled detective fiction in order to do so is only one of the ironies that might be registered. For Shaidle's rebuke of 'the dumb broad' also begs the question of why an acolyte of 'old-fashioned' feminist self-reliance apparently felt 'dutifully' obliged to attend (or remain at) an event so to her distaste in the first place. On a purely rational level, since simplistic rationalism is the underlying premise here, the question posed of Lowther reflects more aptly on its questioner.

J.R. Colombo, by contrast, actually met Pat Lowther once, long enough to form first 'impressions about her' – and even about 'her poetry,' this time. Colombo met Lowther during the last year of her life, when she stopped in Toronto en route back home from her reading of 'Nightmare' and other poems at a poetry festival in Prince Edward Island. During her stopover, Lowther gave a reading at the reconstituted 'BoEm' in the newly opened Harbourfront Cultural Centre, the less famous (and less 'bohemian') successor to the original St Nicholas Street establishment. Colombo was the 'regular master of ceremonies' there and had introduced Lowther to 'an appreciative response' on the evening of 16 July 1975:

> At the time, unmodified by details of her background or information about her subsequent life, I had two distinct impressions about her, one about her poetry, the other about her person. I felt very strongly that she was talented but was lacking the necessary distance and discipline to develop that talent to any great extent. She felt compelled to write but could not see her own work with any objectivity. The overwhelming sensation I had was that she was a member of the lower class and was unaware of this fact, and that she would retain its standards and expectations until such time as she became aware of their strengths and limitations, if ever ... I realize this is not a politic point to make because we pay lip service to the classless society, but this was how I felt then and now. Truth to tell, she had victim written all over her and seemed already battered.[43]

'Truth to tell,' for a poet already buried under the epitaph of 'victim' and problematically, if also lovingly, 'rewritten' by a veritable *trauerspiel* choir of voices as Christ, Neruda, saint, sacrificial lamb, Louis Riel, Lady Godiva, and Ophelia among many others, the real question is instead: how can 'Pat Lowther,' today, *not* have 'victim written all over her'? Indeed, can she be remembered any other way? Colombo's attempt to recall his 'impressions' of Lowther 'at the time, unmodified by details of her background or information about her subsequent life,' points to a foundational problem. 'How exactly is it that we come to know the past?' asks Linda Hutcheon. She is not alone in answering that question via 'the present': '... the past exists *for us* – *now* – only as traces on and in the present' (1989: 92, 73; emphasis in the original). That it is impossible to remember 'Pat Lowther' outside of the present moment *and* 'prior textualization[s]' of history and literature (Hutcheon 1989: 78) only makes it more imperative that we pay close attention to the tensions inherent in that temporal doubleness for our understanding of her '*for us – now.*'[44]

What is arresting about Colombo's 'impression' of Lowther's poetic 'talent' is how precisely it contradicts claims made by proponents of her work such as George Woodcock, who emphasize exactly the elements of technique and craft that Colombo perceives as radically 'lacking' in Lowther's raw 'talent.' Cast by Colombo as a diamond in the rough, unendowed with the necessary 'objective' 'distance and discipline' of the craft, Lowther is at best a compulsively 'confessional' poet; at worst, a contemporary recrudescence of those spontaneously effusive Victorian 'pain girls' that modernists like Louise Bogan had fun skewering. In either case, Colombo's appraisal is exactly antithetical to laudatory estimations of Lowther as a superbly self-conscious perfectionist, 'a craftsman' no less precise than a jeweller: 'every poem [being] smoothly polished like a stone until it was finally ready to be set on the page. She had all the talents' (Brett 1977: 22). In itself, this dichotomy recalls Roy Lowther's black-and-white perceptions of his wife's poetry as at once very, very bad (in terms of its 'immorality') *and* virtually 'great' ('second only ... to Milton Acorn' or Neruda, of course).

Also important is Colombo's admittedly less 'politic point' regarding his 'impression,' not of Lowther's poetry, but of 'her person.' Colombo is careful not to conflate these intertwined issues in his comments, but in this instance, the perception of Lowther's 'person' nevertheless correlates closely with the aesthetic valuation that precedes it. Apparently untutored and purely intuitive in her poetics, Lowther, it also follows, must have been 'unaware of [the] fact' 'that she was a member of the lower class.' This would have come as a bitter surprise to Lowther, an anti-poverty activist and occasional welfare recipient who was reminded of her 'lower class' status on an almost continual basis. As her notebooks also reveal, it was exactly the 'standards and expectations' of working-class womanhood that Lowther had already been attempting to shuck in advance of her debut with *This Difficult Flowring* (1968) – and this was a process that unfolded even more self-consciously and rapidly thereafter. In this respect, Colombo's memory of Lowther as a gauche and under-cultured 'member of the lower class' perhaps points back to the grounds for complaint voiced by her West Coast compatriots about patronizing 'Eastern' attitudes.

At the same time, though, Colombo is calling a spade a spade: he is absolutely right that ours is a culture that 'pay[s] lip service to the [ideal of a] classless society.' It is precisely the uncomfortably complex issue of class which has been paid 'lip service' in accounts of Pat Lowther's life and death, which never fail to mention her 'working-class' beginnings and chronic indigence, but leave it at that, as though the mere mention is somehow sufficient as an explanation for anything. It is precisely the history of class tensions between various fields of literary production that has been repressed, if not entirely elided, in posthumous invocations of her memory (despite the fact that these invocations have usually been at least nominally 'leftist' in aim and leaning). The literary competition established in Lowther's name is only the most prominent example of this seemingly wilful historical blindness. In short, to the extent that it throws the difficult problem of class difference and conflict into stark relief, Colombo's 'impression' of the 'person' of 'Pat Lowther,' impolitic though it may be, is important.

If Lowther cuts an uncanny figure in the cultural memory, then it is not because she in any way inexplicably foresaw her own death or her own 'afterlife' resurrections in *A Stone Diary* and *Time Capsule*. If she is uncanny, then it is for the same reason that the uncanny unconscious is always uncanny: because it is the trace of a function that can be nowhere firmly located, a trace knowable only through its effects. And the sense in which Lowther is most difficult to 'locate' is in terms of the multiple social strata she inhabited during the final years of her life, social class being, of course, a function not only of material wherewithal but also of the various forms of so-called 'symbolic' capital that help determine relations of power and influence – including one's education, 'taste,' and inclusion or exclusion by various collectives or status groups (Bourdieu 1984, 1993).

As John Hall had noted during his closing address at Roy's trial, the Lowthers were 'not really in the chips,' ever, financially, 'but she [Pat] was starting to work out of that fairly well' by 1975 (CATT, Supplemental: 19). Indeed, the more Roy Lowther's talented wife was able to 'get into Canadian literature' (in his phrase) by virtue of her poetry, the more that talented wife also became eligible for administrative and professional offices offered to her on that basis, which in turn were also making it increasingly possible for her to get *out* of the ranks of the working-class poor – by, quite literally, writing, administering, and teaching her way out. 'She was devoted to her "career,"' Roy sneered in his journal, 'through which she saw prospects of university teaching' (RLJ, 2: n.pag.). It was the consolidation of those '"career"' 'prospects' as a fact that the husband could not handle when his high-school drop-out wife actually did land a teaching position at *his* alma mater, the univer-sity which was once supposed to have been *his* launching pad to a life of middle-class professional success.

For Lowther herself, 'getting that job at UBC was probably a turning point,' as colleague Hilda Thomas speculates: 'That meant she could support herself and her kids. And to think of supporting yourself and your kids on a sessional lecturer's stipend at that time isn't quite as laughable in itself [as it is today] ... it was probably more than she was used to, anyway.'[45] Still poor, yes, and a child of the working class by birth, Lowther was nevertheless no longer impoverished in terms of the artistic 'capital' she had begun to accumulate by 1975. She died at a decisive moment of social transfer that was every bit as threatening to her emotionally and financially dependent husband as any signals of his wife's sexual autonomy. The two forms of departure were inextricably related.

Toward the end of her life, Lowther was, in one sense, un-classed: no longer in any simple or conventional terms 'a member of the lower class' (as Colombo would have it), nor yet by any means a full member of an entitled professional 'establishment' (as her husband would have it). What is 'written all over' 'Pat Lowther' by now is as much an anxious narrative of class as it is a more exploited story of victimization. Hers is a history that points to the *spectre* of class as an essential *and* inherently unstable category in our cultural imagination, one that depends pro-foundly on internalized functions of perception and representation – those reflexes by which we reinforce and renegotiate the shifting sand-banks of privilege, tolerance, and exclusion that shape the social order of the day. It is both the insistence *and* the instability of class identity that are thus 'written all over' the radical range of Lowther's posthu-mous figurations as a woman who – to take only her poetic incarnations – gets refracted in one poet's line as 'Pat, the welfare girl' (Wainwright); in another poet's line as the middle-class intellectual, 'Professor Lowther' (McKay 1978: xi); and in still other poets' elegiac lines as 'Lady' Lowther, titular emblem of a truly high-brow aristocratic nobility en route to sainthood – that one last, transcendental class barrier.

In life, Lowther was an inveterate bus-rider because she did not drive. And in a sense, she also died in public transit – somewhere between the neighbourhood of working-class poor and the prospect of something else, a different socio-economic niche enabled by her artistic and intel-lectual 'capital.' But, rather like a ghost, she died neither here nor there. Our wildly disparate representations of her since her death reflect our own confusions.

❧

'I am not sure,' John Barton says, 'that much real knowledge of [Lowther's] work has been carried forward to interest today's readers and writers' (1997: 64). He is right. Despite the flurry of publicity around *Time Capsule* and Lowther's recent treatment in film, the continuing dearth of critical work on Lowther is the best index of the precariously liminal 'canonical' status she inhabits today. Less than a handful of articles, two unpublished PhD dissertations, and one MA thesis provide a pointed indication of how infrequently her work has been read and studied over the decades since her death. Thanks entirely to her husband's actions, Lowther has had a far more powerful posthumous appeal as a muse and inspirational icon for activists and artists than she has had any power to sustain the focused critical attention which she had begun to attract from poets and critics such as Dorothy Livesay, Gary Geddes, and George Woodcock during her lifetime.

Recent works about Lowther by activists (Brooks) and by artists (novelists and film-makers these days, less so poets) reflect distinctly semicritical approaches. This is perhaps most deliberately so the case with Keith Harrison's *Furry Creek*, a boldly experimental 'non-fiction novel.' Like Gail McKay's *The Pat Lowther Poem*, Harrison's novel is also constructed as pastiche from a variety of source texts. The sources here, however, are far more heterogeneous, including not only excerpts from newspaper coverage, trial records, and Pat Lowther's poetry, but also miscellaneous correspondence with Lowther's daughters; the texts of their respective autobiographical essays in *Time Capsule*; the pre-publication announcement of *Time Capsule*'s 'unveiling'; and the essay text of Harrison's previously published 'Notes on "Notes from Furry Creek."' Around this dizzying array of material, Harrison's book fictionalizes the story of Lowther's murder from the perspective of various characters involved with Roy Lowther's criminal trial.

For reasons apparent when one recalls Don McLellan's 'Verses and Verdicts,' and also outlined by one of Beth Lowther's letters to the author in the 'novel,' Harrison's is an inherently uneasy, though calculated, undertaking. Intended as a postmodern composite of fiction and fact, *Furry Creek* is like many of the elegies offered in Lowther's name in that it 'uses her death to illuminate something else': '*Furry Creek* isn't about Pat Lowther ... Not her life. Not her killer's life' (Bridgeman

2000). Yet, perhaps because Harrison's novel *does* reproduce key testimony from Roy about walking into 'the trap of all time' (198) and because it also alludes, at various points, to both *Hamlet* (117) and *Romeo and Juliet* (169), it is a non-fiction/fiction that coincidentally extends the (real) non-fiction/fiction of Pat Lowther's death and Roy's trial in terms of dramatized Shakespearian tragedy. At least that is the leitmotif probably not fortuitously accentuated in reviews of the 1999 'non-fiction novel':

> *Furry Creek* is, Polonius like, a book that is very indirect, a book that circles gory death and spies on its *dramatis personae* from a safe distance, as a means of tactfully and honourably approaching the murder of poet, teacher and activist Pat Lowther ... Lowther's troubled shadow looms behind the text, a body in water, a ghost, a grainy photo on a Web site, a powerful presence even though she is not seen directly, is faceless.
>
> This [novel] is ... a labour of love, a monument to a writer's memory, to a writer who had a blunt, domestic instrument laid to that delicate pink brain. Remember me, asks the uneasy ghost, and Harrison remembers. (Jarman 2000: D10).

The gist of what is actually 'remembered' here as constituting 'a monument to a writer's memory,' a 'writer' well 'remembered,' is telling: 'Pat Lowther' 'looms' once again as Ophelia ('a body in water'); as the 'uneasy ghost' (of Hamlet, Senior: 'Remember me'); as a prophet able to find us in the digital future ('a grainy photo on a Web site'); as a transcendental deity ('a powerful presence,' but 'faceless'); and, last but not least, as a feminine crime victim ('that delicate pink brain').

Readers like Mark Jarman find that 'the fictional elements' of Keith Harrison's *Furry Creek* 'are less interesting than the real and horrific events' of history (2000: D10). Yet the fact that those 'real and horrific' events were themselves played out in strangely aestheticized terms of a 'real show' (as Don McLellan put it back in 1977), in dramatically distorted terms that also ask to be recognized and 'remembered,' because they too have a bearing on the 'memory' of the 'writer' in question – *this* goes without so much as a hiccup of notice. The strategy of 'tactfully and honourably' 'spying' on one's *'dramatis personae* from a safe distance' would thus seem to be laden with significant risks of its own.[46]

The absent presence of 'Pat Lowther' is also the case with Anne Henderson's recently released *Water Marks* (2002), a film that takes as its focal point less Lowther herself than Lowther's 'legacy' in the form of her surviving family members, especially her daughters. Interspersed with filmic 'dramatizations' of Lowther's poems, and interviews with Allan Safarik and journalist Sean Rossiter, who comprise the main sources of information about Lowther's career, the film records the autobiographical narratives of Beth and Christine Lowther, and to some degree also of Kathy, and of Ruth Lowther Lalonde, in their respective struggles with the memories of their traumatic family past. As the film's title hints, 'water' imagery and sounds provide a lyrical background for this account of Lowther's life, death, and its impact on her children's lives. Anne Henderson, the director, is a relative of Roy's former defence lawyer. By her account, she was drawn to the subject of Pat Lowther without being aware of her brother's previous connection to Roy Lowther – the 'most difficult' client, among 'thousands,' that Alex Henderson ever had.

In comparison with other tragedies of premature death – the John Thompsons, Marie Uguays, and Sharon Stevensons of our literary history – 'a lot of printers' ink has been spilled' on the 'interesting, dramatic, newsworthy' 'case' of Pat (and Roy) Lowther (CATT, 4:490, 510). In some ways, Pat Lowther seems to matter more to us than these lesser known writers who died from suicide or cancer, also before their lives were finished and their careers could be completed. But in other respects, Pat Lowther herself hasn't really mattered all that much, or at least she has mattered less than the artistic and political causes her death has inspired and been used to symbolize. Patricia Louise Lowther has been artfully rewritten and artlessly forgotten as often or more as she has been well remembered and recalled. Hers, in the end, is a posthumous 'legacy' of troubled 'tribute,' troubled most of all for what it reflects, not about Pat Lowther, but about the craft of our own collective memory.

'How can I begin?' Lowther mused at the outset of her second collection of poems, *Milk Stone*. 'So many skins / of silence upon me' (*MS*, 13). She wasn't thinking then of her own posthumous figurations, but today the question resonates in this context too, through a dense overlay of voices that include those of Roy, of legal experts, of journalists and critics, and of many other poets and artists. But while 'icons' may 'have no need / for language' (*AB*, 2), Pat Lowther was a writer, and writers do.

PART II

Complicated Airflows in the House

The complicated airflow in the house
stirred by my passing sets
the doors to opening and closing
one and then another
    – *This Difficult Flowring*

Chapter 4

'At, Rat, Cat, Sat, Pat'

The North Vancouver district that Pat Lowther was first born into as Patricia Louise Tinmouth, in 1935, was a cedar-scented hinterland of shingle-bolt production, ship manufacture, and small, isolated communities nestled along the eastern base of the North Shore mountains. The population of North Vancouver City, incorporated in 1906, was still only 8,510 by 1931. Down the long slope of Lonsdale Avenue – once a skid road traversed by oxen hauling lumber – one could take the ferry to mainland Vancouver, a bustling metropolis of 350,000. The steel-span links between the two municipalities across Burrard Inlet were as yet tenuous. The Second Narrows bridge had just reopened in 1934 after falling down four years earlier – its successor collapsed in 1958. And the famous Lions Gate or First Narrows bridge had not yet been built by the Guinness family empire. At North Shore establishments like Fawcett's Store, however, North Vancouverites who could afford to grocery shop might have found most anything they sought. Pot roast sold for five cents a pound; tins of Heinz soup, three for a quarter; and Miss Lydia Pinkham's Vegetable Compound, touted as the best 'tonic and regulator' for 'feminine complaints,' was also discreetly available.

Virginia Tinmouth preferred Campbell's soup over Heinz. And, long before Andy Warhol thought to immortalize the Campbell's logo as a pop art artifact, Virginia also discovered a brilliant new practical application for this Depression-era staple. Faced, circa 1937, with one inquisitive toddler, limited means, and the reality of living on the rainy outskirts of the North Shore district, Virginia enlisted Campbell's soup as a tutorial aid for rearing her first-born child, 'Patsy Lou.' 'We taught her to read with a Campbell's soup can. That's the way we started,' Virginia recalled of the 'lonely' years she and her husband, Arthur, spent at the Lynn Creek water intake station, beyond the outer limits of town. Teaching Patsy Lou her alphabet was a snap; she soon graduated from the soup cans:

> [Then] we got a little chalkboard and taught her how to build her words like *at, rat, cat, sat, pat*; and then we changed the end letter: *car,* or *can, pan.* You know? And my goodness, in no time at all ... she was reading all sorts of things. Before we left the Intake – I guess she was six years old when we left – ... she had read all the *Oz* books, as many as we could get for her – we used to go to the library and bring home an armful of books for her.[1]

As Virginia's words hint, regularly replenishing a fresh 'armful' of books for a pre-school child was not such a snap, at least not in North Vancouver during the thirties and forties. Both the complicated topography of the region, with its terraced slopes and glacial valleys, and its history as a centre for raw resources and, later, for heavy marine industry during the 'prosperous' years of the Second World War, make for a rather fascinating local past where it comes to book culture. Like the settlement patterns that dotted its slopes, sources for books on the North Shore were small and isolated. During the Depression and war years, the population was served by one, chronically itinerant, fee-for-service public library in the City of North Vancouver itself, and by a haphazard sprinkling of tiny, volunteer-run book associations in the outlying regions, for the surrounding *District* of North Vancouver was (and remains) a separate municipal entity, a region of huge rolling swaths of Douglas fir, western hemlock, spruce, yew, yellow and red cedar – areas not yet connected by a convenient upper levels highway.

The library in the City of North Vancouver was established during the twenties and run by volunteers of the Ladies' Auxiliary Club. The ladies raised funds for their books through afternoon teas and card parties, especially during the thirties, when whatever modest municipal and provincial grants had been available dried up. Around 1930, they charged a dollar per annum for a membership fee (there was a two-book limit per patron) and two cents a day for the newest books, which thus paid for themselves over time. Their little 'literary emporium' bounced about from place to place in the main shopping area of Lower Lonsdale – at times in 'a room above a butcher shop, and for a while ... above a milkman's unheated garage' (Black 1992: 2). Undeterred by an un-leisured, working-class community that was not especially conscious of the local 'emporium' for literary 'leisure' in its midst, the library ladies 'refused to run up the white flag of surrender': '[s]heer determination kept the library going,' and by the end of the Second World War, a monthly circulation of about six hundred books had been achieved. The city library's first semi-permanent home was in the old Wartime Administration Building, quarters into which it moved in 1949 (Black 1992: 1–2).

As for the small, enforested subdivisions of the District, only the postwar years brought official public libraries to these regions – by which time, the Tinmouths had left their lonely post at the Lynn Creek water intake and relocated in the city of 'North Van.' But the 'humble beginnings' of the Capilano Public Library Association, similarly formed by a group of determined housewives in 1952, provides further indication of the conditions under which literacy managed to flourish 'in those early days' (Dickinson 1964: 25). The Capilano group's initial collection of 150 books immediately posed another familiar logistical 'problem':

> The problem of a place to put [the] books was a pressing one ... First shelves in a dry goods store and then an abandoned newspaper hut were tried. More satisfactory was the shack built for their use by the local Home Owners' Association. This shack had the added attraction of being built on skids for ease of movement from one empty lot to another, as the lots were sold and built on. (Dickinson 1964: 26–7)

Until it found a permanent home, Capilano's first modern library, literally a 'travelling' 'shack' of a library, depended on essentially the same device of wooden 'skids' that, a century earlier, had facilitated the movement of lumber from the forest to the dock at the port of old 'Moodyville.' In the mid-twentieth century, over in Russia, meanwhile, scientists were working on Sputnik technology.

And in comparison with the Lynn Valley region to the north, Capilano's establishment of the District's first public library 'shack' actually represented the progressive cutting edge. The Lynn Valley area where Patricia Louise Tinmouth spent the first six years of her life – learning her letters from Campbell's soup cans and a mini-chalkboard – was not served by its own separate library system until 1964. By then, the former Pat Tinmouth was a year removed from the North Shore region in which she had grown up – gone for good, as Pat Lowther, for the bigger city that sparkled at night across the black neck of Burrard Inlet. Even by that time, in 1964, North Vancouver District Library records estimate the ratio of books per capita at 0.51 books per person.[2]

❦

Importantly, though, by 1935, when Patricia Tinmouth was born on July 29 at the North Vancouver General Hospital, her mother, Virginia, had already acquired a taste of the wider world, as a former music-hall dancer. Virginia herself had made her first debut in 1907 as Virginia Wilks in Butte, Montana. She was one of seven children – six of whom survived – born to Annie McCain and James Wilks, a mine union organizer. Virginia, the second youngest of the clan, was named after the one who didn't make it, an infant who had been baptized and buried as 'Virginia' before her. In later years, Virginia's siblings called her 'Ginnie' or 'Jean' instead.

When James Wilks's work brought the family back to Canada, the Wilkses settled in North Vancouver. Growing up there as a 'very puny' child, Virginia was sent by her parents to the Grace Goddard dance school 'in the Cotillion on the corner of Davie and Granville,' presumably as a means of shoring up her 'puny' physical frame. Virginia took seriously to dance, however, and in doing so, soon followed in the footsteps of her glamorous older sister, Isabelle. 'Belle,' as she was known, was thirteen years Virginia's senior, and a celebrated vaudeville performer who toured the States, Mexico, and Canada with a very successful musical comedy revue, 'The Speeders,' during the twenties. Hailed by the American press as 'destined to make a place all her own in musical comedy and to some day have her name in the bright lights,' Isabelle was bragged about by the local *Vancouver Daily World* as 'a native daughter of British Columbia' who was 'on her way to the top rungs of the vaudeville ladder of fame.'[3] Isabelle had a dashing American lover named Harry Stover, a pianist and composer. She even introduced him to her parents once, probably when 'The Speeders' swept into her hometown for a triumphant 1923 performance at Pantages Theatre. By this time, Virginia was already taking a cue from her big sister, soon joining a local dance troupe that also ventured to the States. Virginia's group, The Attree Dancers, travelled 'in a big Hudson sedan' to perform at 'barnstorming' engagements, stopping in places like Chicago before hitting New York, where Isabelle was based. In New York, Virginia stayed with her independent and successful vaudevillian sister.[4]

While she was there, a twenty-two-year-old Virginia decided, on a whim, to sneak a peek at the recently opened Roxy Theatre, the ornate movie 'cathedral' and music hall that once stood in mid-town Manhattan at 7th Avenue and 50th Street, off Broadway. When it opened in 1927, not long before Virginia showed up at its doors, the Roxy was simply *the* latest word in theatre architecture, engineering, and technology. With a seating capacity of almost six thousand – or roughly two-thirds the population of North Vancouver City – it was the largest such motion picture and dance-hall theatre in the world. The auditorium was air-conditioned, with foot lighting and seat indicator lights. Beneath a sixty-foot proscenium arch, the stage was divided into four parts, two of them set on hydraulic lifts; also installed beneath the stage was a state-of-the-art Kimball organ player with three separate consoles. At just the right moments, the invisible organ player could intone just the right notes for such place of worship as a motion picture 'cathedral.' When the stage shows ended, three different types of film projectors, 'superior to anything else in existence' at the time, took over. The Roxy employed its own 110-piece orchestra, chorus line *and* ballet corps, seamstresses, stage-hands, set designers, carpenters, mechanics, and ushers – the latter group, one of the first such to be uniformed in 'clothes that rivaled an admiral's.' 'Here,' as one awe-struck contemporary observer put it, 'modern science works wonders for your amazement and entertainment': 'when you enter [the Roxy's] portals you step magically from the drab world into a fairy palace whose presiding genius entertains you royally.'[5]

According to Virginia, one of the 'presiding' geniuses of the Roxy, an up-and-coming ex-Texan choreographer named Russell Markert, caught sight of her as she lingered in a doorway, watching a dance rehearsal. He asked if she had come for the rehearsal. She said, 'No.' He asked if she was looking for a job. She said, 'Yes, I guess so.' He asked what she could do. Pointing to the stage, she said, 'I can do what *those* girls are doing.' The choreographer once quoted as saying, 'If you can walk, I can make you dance,' hired her on the spot.[6] And so, Virginia embarked, for a short time anyway, upon a career as one of 'Markert's Roxyettes, a swell group of steppers' compared to 'the West Point cadets of show business' for their precision dance routines.[7] Virginia's connection with the 'Russell Markert Dancers,' with whom she eventually 'tour[ed] the Eastern States for quite a few weeks' after her stint at the Roxy, ended before Russell Markert went on to make his name as the man behind the famous 'Radio City Rockettes' during the early thirties. Nor was Virginia's career ever destined to attain the promise of her older sister, Isabelle's.

Sometime around the 1929 'stock-exchange tragedy' of Black Monday, Virginia Wilks and her sister Isabelle both returned to their family base in North Vancouver. Perhaps the advent of the Depression prompted James and Annie Wilks to summon their footloose 'girls' home to settle down – a summons perhaps enabled by the fact that James had that year just landed a new job. Or perhaps the sisters' eye-witnessing of the panic precipitated by the collapse of the New York stock market – 'people were jumping out of windows and committing suicide; I was there at that time,' as Virginia recalled – prompted a mood of sober retrenchment that led the Wilks daughters back home of their own accord. Or perhaps 'Belle,' then thirty-five years old, had her own reasons for quitting New York and her stage career at that time. Virginia herself recalls simply that she 'got homesick' at this point.[8]

The homesickness must have been powerful, because Virginia traded in her New York salary as a dancer – then, an extremely lucrative fifty-five dollars a week – for a 'job at Woodwards ... demonstrating Chanel wax products.' For these services, she remembered being paid eighteen dollars and fifty cents per week.[9] Sometime while demonstrating those wax products, she met – or re-encountered – a local boy named Arthur Tinmouth. The handsome man Virginia Wilks would marry in 1932 had never been to Chicago or New York. He had grown up in North Vancouver and stayed put, the youngest son of a mother widowed early, when he was only fourteen. Also from a prolific family, Arthur had been born in Sunderland, England, the last of eight children born to Arthur and Harriet Tinmouth. As immigrants, the Tinmouths had settled briefly in Alberta, and then in Atlantic Canada, before eventually migrating across the country again to North Vancouver, in search of work. In comparison with Virginia's side of the family, the Tinmouths are less prominent in both personal family accounts and public records. A 1919 North Vancouver school photo shows Arthur, aged eleven, looking thin, pinched, and very serious, at a desk squeezed against the wall, midway down a row furthest from the camera. Within a few years, Arthur's father, Arthur Sr, would die in a hideous workplace accident at the Burrard Dry Docks. That same employer would later become the son's own economic life-line for the bulk of his working life, during which he laboured as a sheet-metal operative.

During the early years of his marriage to Virginia Wilks, however, Arthur worked as a water intake caretaker. Perhaps, in first taking the job at the remote Lynn Creek intake, Arthur Jr had been attempting to avoid the shipyards, the all-too-obvious employment 'opportunity' that the region offered to him. Or maybe there was simply nothing else available during the Depression. Whatever the case, Arthur earned substantially less for the job of ensuring a safe supply of drinking water to an entire community, than his wife had formerly earned as a New York City chorus-line dancer.[10] And Virginia was not especially happy at her 'lonely' new post out at the Lynn Creek intake. Though she never had her married name legally changed to 'Tinmuth,' it was Virginia's initiative to drop the *o* from her husband's surname – a practice that accounts for its variant spellings to this day. Complicating the young wife's adjustment to her new life was the fact that, around the time Virginia recalls teaching Pat her alphabet, Arthur fell ill with meningitis – perhaps contracted from cleaning out a chicken coop.[11]

By 1939 war had been declared, and Arthur and Virginia had not just one, but two, daughters to think about: Pat – not yet quite school-aged, but almost, and Brenda, a brand new addition. The couple's move back to 'North Van' around 1941 must have come as a relief for Virginia, but Arthur's turn at this time to a new job at the Burrard Dry Docks also appears as part of a larger wartime workforce migration, one that saw an unprecedented increase in manufacture – a staggering employment spike of 1,500 per cent over the years 1940 and 1942 alone – as the shipyards struggled to meet the demand for corvettes, mine-sweepers, and cargo vessels.[12] 'It was at once exhilarating and painful to see our quiet, sleepy town of North Vancouver become riddled with the roar of shipbuilding, the traffic of industry,' as Dorothy Livesay remarked by way of preface to her 1943 'West Coast' sequence of *The Documentaries*: 'From across Canada thousands of men came ... to work in the shipyards' (24).

As one of those shipyard-bound 'thousands of men,' Patricia Tinmouth's father did not have much time for reading – he was not a 'bookish' type, though he did keep up to date with current events in the newspapers. He was a man who sometimes went out with hunting parties, but more to 'keep the chipmunks company' than actually to hunt.[13] Above all, what did characterize Arthur, according to his family, was a lively sense of humour as an entertainer, and an inclination for extended 'family parties' featuring music and dance. 'He could pick up anything and play it,' Virginia recalled fondly, many years after her husband's death, but 'his favorite instrument was the swinet.''S-W-I-N-E-T,' Brenda interjects helpfully: 'a washtub with a broom handle and a string.' Arthur and Virginia's enthusiasm for music and dance naturally enough rubbed off on the four children they would eventually raise – Pat, Brenda, Arden, born in 1946, and John, who followed in 1949. All four danced, sang, picked tunes at the piano or guitar, and, according to their mother, Virginia, demonstrated 'good rhythm.'[14]

∽

But it was really the pleasures of linguistic 'rhythms' and rhymes that resonated most profoundly with Patsy Lou from the time her parents first taught her 'how to build her words,' thereby opening up fabulous worlds of possibility that belied the child's actual Depression-era circumstances. These fabulous possibilities included a virtually infinite selection and combination of letters that could make her very own name, *Pat*, rhyme with whiskered animal nouns, like *cat* or *rat*; with bland function-words, like *at;* or even with action verbs like *sat* or *pat*. And so the possibilities of English grammar and vocabulary invited the Tinmouth's eldest child to entertain the singular notion that the sound of her very own name could be used to mean, not a person at all, but rather, an affectionate action. And furthermore, that the simple flip of one letter could transform a girl named *Pat* into a homely kitchen utensil – a frying *pan*! In fact, just one more flip, and that girl, *Pat*, could also *become* a Campbell's soup *can*! These were lessons in a strange magic, a craft of continual metamorphosis that an adult Pat Lowther never left behind.

No doubt as a result of the early encouragement she received, Patsy Lou's abilities as a reader and writer flourished – there are many family tales of her precociousness as such.[15] Surviving records support these accounts of her early indications of talent. Her first publicity came at the tender age of four, when 'Patsy Lou's' picture appeared in the *Vancouver Sun*, for having 'amazed' the children's columnist, 'Uncle Ben' (of the 'Uncle Ben's Sun Ray Club'), with her ability to read 'the Sun-Ray page and the comics as easily as you or I.' The 1939 newspaper clipping identifies the young whiz kid as 'Patricia Louise Wilkes Tinmouth,' and records both her mother's and her aunt Isabelle's 'noted' careers 'on the stage' 'before marriage.' 'Her father,' the blurb also adds, 'is the keeper of the water intake.'[16]

One notebook of juvenilia, dating from her early elementary school period, is inscribed with a child's scrawl inside the front cover 'Pat Tinmuth, 233 E 12th' – the way her mother taught her to spell her name – and then, proudly, 'Poems and Stories made up by me.' The scribbler includes at least one poem in which the young poet attempts scansion, and several 'fairy'-themed verses. Among these is 'Winter in Fairy Land' – an early effort that, despite its shaky line breaks, already demonstrates a nose for effective reversals of mood:

All the little fairies
dancing on the snow
Big wings, little wings, now you
know.
Each little
fairy has on
her wings
A shawl of gold
for winter stings.[17]

More remarkable is an apparently collaborative dramatic script enti-tled 'Song of the Forestland,' a juvenile play that testifies to more than just Virginia's theatrical background and Arthur's similar penchant as the family 'showman.'[18] Written with a girlfriend when Pat was around ten or twelve years old, 'Song of the Forestland' features a hilariously complicated plot, including detailed dramaturgical instructions, narra-tive time lapses, and wildly clashing romance and realist registers. The names and roles of the various 'DRAMATIS PERSONAE' are the first cue: there is 'Poldi (the village playboy), Ilka (his beautiful sister), Theresa (Girl who loves Poldi), Mark (a pilgrim), and Poldi Jr. (son of Poldi and Theresa).' Missing from the list of players at the head of the script is the fearsome 'Grabku' – the word is ornately written throughout and barely decipherable – 'a horrible beast' who lurks in the forest, endangering 'the villagers' until the hero-pilgrim, Mark, slays him during a climactic encounter. With the death of the forest monster, Ilka finally recognizes the pilgrim as 'the dark hero' of legend and as her true love, 'which is no news to anybody but her,' the young playwrights add. (Notably, Pat and her girlfriend were in too inspired a rush to actually ascribe any dia-logue to the characters in their play – it is written out entirely in narra-tive form.) The play thus couples the ascetic 'pilgrim,' Mark, with Ilka, 'the beautiful, shy sister' of the village 'playboy.' Both Mark and Ilka eventually become angelic creatures: 'surrounded by light,' 'they exit up center,' 'hand in hand' at the play's conclusion.

As for the saucy village 'playboy,' Poldi, and Theresa, the 'Girl who loves Poldi,' their story is somewhat different. 'Song of the Forestland' opens with Poldi acting out true to character, 'pinch[ing] one girl' in public and 'hiccup[ping] in the face of another.' 'To heck with mar-riage,' he cries, before he begins singing songs 'on the glories of drink-ing and flirting, assisted by a chorus.' When Theresa enters and sings

out a query as to why Poldi won't marry her, 'the playboy' responds with
a song 'portray[ing] the disadvantages of marriage,' and then 'starts
grumbling about women in general.' In fact, though, Poldi does marry
Theresa. And as the play reveals when it jumps ahead in time to a
twenty-year 'anniversary' party in honour of the now long-married couple, it is 'the disadvantages of marriage' *for women* that the pre-pubes-
cent playwrights are concerned to 'portray.' The lovelorn Theresa gets
her man, but at a cost. During the anniversary party scene, a 'song by
Theresa on how to catch a man' is 'pantomimed by dancers.' Poldi Jr,
the product of her union with Poldi Sr, is revealed to be a drunkard and
a lout. Both he and his identically miscreant father, Poldi Sr, ruin the
party by insulting the angelic Ilka, leaving Theresa to fix her misbehav-
ing men with a 'big black look.'

Hugely entertaining in its exuberance, 'Song of the Forestland' also
comes as an early indication of 'Patsy Lou's' ironic intelligence. In particular, the drama's disillusioned end to Theresa's narrative of fulfilled-
but-unfulfilled desire anticipates later concerns in Lowther's writing
with both gender stereotypes and romance expectations. Before too
long, it was less amusing domestic tensions, or 'complicated airflow[s]
in the house' (*DF,* 17), that would mark the first dominant, exploratory
theme in her adult writing about sexuality and marriage.

For an accomplished young reader and writer like Pat, however, the
attention that such skill inevitably drew from adults was an additional
bonus. As the eldest daughter in an increasingly crowded, small household – especially once brothers Arden and John appeared – 'Patsy
Lou's' feats of composition and advanced reading emerged as perhaps
the most distinctive characteristic to set her apart from the typically utilitarian role of oldest girl and mother's helpmeet. In Pat's case, that role
was pronounced not only by her age difference from her siblings, but
also by the fact that Arden, born with cerebral palsy, absorbed Virginia's
special care and attention.

Toby Brooks is no doubt correct in her assertion that Pat 'saw herself
nudged from the centre of the family nest' with some apprehension as
these beloved new arrivals and rivals joined the scene (2000: 26). As evidence, however, Brooks points to the same passage from the same poem
that Roy Lowther alludes to in his own 'biographical' account of his
wife, an account that also isolates competition for parental attention as a
key factor in her childhood development.[19] The poem in question is
'Watershed,' in which the speaker reflects on 'the nest' her parents first

made out at the Lynn Creek 'watershed,' where 'the road ends' and 'the mountains ring / with woodpeckers':

> my father took my
> mother's nipple,
> squirted milk at me:
> 'See, it doesn't
> like you anymore.
> It belongs to the new baby.'[20]

'Watershed,' however, is a more ambiguous poem than this single stanza adequately indicates. The same speaker who recalls this memory of her dramatic childhood displacement by 'the new baby' opens by recounting the memory of a treasure hunt staged by her parents solely for her own pleasure: 'my parents made a nest / in the long grass / filled it with easter eggs / for me to find.' 'Watershed' is, as much as anything, an interrogation of artifice and nature: of fake 'nests,' filled with 'easter eggs,' and of real nests, human and ornithological. Ultimately, too, it is a poem which ends on a decidedly indeterminate note, dissolving into the aural memory of a persistent 'hammer' tap sound that is both unlocatable – out there 'somewhere' – and indistinct – either 'man'-made or 'woodpecker'-produced. The speaker is unsure which, and the ambiguity is left to stand as an oblique comment on the paradox of memory itself, as a crafty process of natural manufacture. What is finally most interesting about this overtly 'autobiographical' poem, then, is its subtle questioning of 'watershed' moments remembered: those very, key memories the poet calls upon to make up the story of the life she tells.

In her notebooks, Lowther later remembered her childhood world as 'seething like a hive with honey and stings.'[21] The 'stings,' which appear to have included Arthur and Virginia's sometimes distant marital relations, were of the normal sort. There is no evidence of unusual childhood trauma or distress which might be conscripted to help 'explain' anything much about Pat's later history. Unmarked by any obvious signs of serious dysfunction, Pat's childhood does reflect a growing reticence born of an awareness of her own difference. For if it is true that Patsy Lou's precocious talents sometimes brought her attention from the adults in her life, then it is also true that, from very early on, she often eschewed the attention of everyone in the 'hive.' Her younger sister,

Brenda, can still vividly recall one day happening upon a box that Pat kept in the basement of the tiny wartime house that her father built on East 10th Avenue. It was a box that shrewdly anticipated its discovery by some family member or another living in close quarters, for written upon its lid was a very unambiguous message: 'Curiosity killed the cat. You wouldn't want that to happen to you.' (Brenda gingerly restored the box, contents unseen.)[22]

In some ways, the box in the basement seems emblematic. By her mother's account, Pat was generally a compliant and mild child: 'she wasn't a showoff at all; she was very quiet' – so quiet, in fact, that whereas Virginia could hear her other children from 'half a block away' as they returned from school, Pat's 'shoes at the front door' would be the first indication that her eldest had apparently come home at some point, too.[23] But her family also recognized a part of Pat's being that was not just 'quiet,' but somehow more firmly removed. For one thing, Brenda says, 'you never had Pat's total attention, because she [always] had a book while she was talking to you.'[24] Preoccupied with print, and her own imagination, Pat could be intensely 'private' – a closed book or box – even with her closest circle. At the core of this reserve lay an uncommunicative surfeit of expression with nowhere obvious to go.

Children have sounder instincts for safety than adults are often willing to give them credit for. This probably holds true for the contained silence of a hungry young bookworm who, as she grew up during the forties, must have realized that 'all sorts of things' she was reading, in her mother's phrase, were beginning to prompt questions – vague ideas and stirrings of possibility – that were, however, nowhere clearly reflected in the daily round of her conventional North Shore world. That was a limited world in which, as 'Patsy Lou' clearly knew, men might grumble about the 'disadvantages of marriage,' but most women's futures still rested 'on how to catch a man.' In Pat's case, moreover, the self-protective fear of nonconformity that is part of most adolescences, especially that of an embryonic artist's, was further compounded. At twelve, she developed a severe skin condition which resulted in 'sausage'-size blisters not only grossly visible but sinister enough to hospitalize her during the affliction's first onslaught.[25] From this point on, her skin was permanently sensitive to all kinds of variables, including heat – and, later, that enthusiastically mass-marketed though understudied harbinger of sixties' reproductive freedom, the pill. An unpublished poem draft entitled 'Summer Sickness' recalls, in part, a memory of 'sitting pale and clothed / among tanned bodies' 'at Horseshoe Bay': 'I was more alien even / than they could guess.' 'My hands burned like cities.'[26]

The inclination to remain guardedly incommunicado about what was going on inside strengthened with age. Around fourteen, Pat Tinmouth started smoking – like her dad. Matinées, eventually more than a pack a day. What survives of her high-school record suggests an indifferently average student: C+ in science, C+ in French, C- in math. She was an 'assistant editor' of the journalism class 'Press Club' during 1950–1 – even had her photo taken with that group. That year, she contributed a few poems to her school yearbook, just before she dropped out, at sixteen. One of the yearbook poems, a hyper-romantic lyric entitled 'Legend of the Hills,' bid her farewell to the halls of academe. The poem envisions the mythic 'figure' of 'the wind God,' 'leaping from crest to crest' among the mountaintops and singing his 'wierd [sic] passionless songs' with sublime abandon to everything, spelling evidently included.[27]

She marched home and abruptly announced to Arthur and Virginia that she had decided to quit school, get a job. According to her mother, 'Patsy Lou' never offered to elaborate, and though they weren't happy about her decision – 'we thought it was terrible because she was a real natural scholar' – they didn't protest either. 'It wasn't that unusual, you know,' her sister Brenda offers, by way of reminder: at that time, 'people quit school – lots.'[28] More concretely, in 1951, a whopping 'lots' of 36.4 per cent of Canadian women aged fifteen to nineteen would not complete high school (UNESCO 1977: 56), a number that may well have been higher in working-class neighbourhoods like Pat's. Perhaps, as Virginia speculated, 'if she'd been born into a different family, she'd have [had] a much better chance' for staying in school.[29] On the other hand, the lack of a high-school diploma did not in the end thwart Pat Lowther's development; like Gwendolyn MacEwen and other prominent autodidacts from earlier generations, she would go on instead to become another exemplar of the truth that there is no simple correlation between literacy levels and years of formal schooling.

'Anyhow,' as Virginia recalled, 'in a couple of days, she came home with a job.' Miss Tinmouth's first taste of the so-called 'real' world was as a keypunch operator for the local firm of Evans, Coleman, and Evans. It was the first in a string of such clerical jobs she would take. If high school had bored her, then what must have soon become clear to the working girl now was that she had just traded in one form of drudgery for another. An undated pencil draft entitled 'In the Tabulating Room' captures the monotony of feeding 'columns of cards' into 'the precise click- /ing teeth' of 'squat / machines,' an endlessly mechanical digestion of 'info.: debit /and credit, pounds / shipped and dollars owed.' The poem ends with the poet making a mental note to herself about the number-crunching 'squat / machines': 'they'll eat your life / if you're not careful.'[30] The same notebook includes an untitled short story in which an aspiring (male) writer is accused of not having a 'real job': 'You sit up there day after day with that typewriter that hasn't produced anything yet.' To which the author's first-person male alter ego replies: 'I figured ... I'd bought myself some time. Doing work I hate. Grinding the edge off my brain with columns of figures in ledgers. Vomiting debits and credits into my dreams all night.'

Perhaps hoping, like her male character, to find a job that would merely 'give me enough to subsist on, and leave me free to goof off and fiddle around with words,' a young Pat Tinmouth discovered instead that it is precisely one's time and vital energy for 'goof[ing] off and fiddl[ing] around with words' that jobs tend to 'eat,' rather than enable. And, of course, in addition to the serious problem of 'grinding the edge' off one's brain, the clerical opportunities that confronted Miss Tinmouth in the early fifties didn't pay particularly well, either. A stray pay roll record stub from 1961, when she was already a decade into this pink-collar workforce, shows that she had drawn a considerable advance on her month's wages, which suggests she may have had difficulty living on her income, especially with children to help support, as was the case by then.[31]

But, to alter P.K. Page's emphasis in 'The Stenographers' just a bit, there was always the 'brief bivouac of Sunday' beyond the 'forced march' of the work week (1997: 1:102). Outside of work, Pat hung out with her single girlfriends and female cousins, perhaps, in their spare time, making a quick 'bivouac' to Ambleside Beach or up the Grouse Mountain trail for the occasional picnic, as the 'tourists' from Vancouver City liked to do. It was through her friends, Lorraine, Eleanor, and Thelma, that Pat Tinmouth met her first husband, a local man of Scottish-French ancestry named William Harvey Joseph Domphousse. By this time, between 1952 and 1953, the Evans, Coleman, and Evans office girl had moved to a job at the Burrard Shipyards, where the steel plater also worked, eventually as a longshoreman out on the docks. 'Bill,' as he was known, had also left school early, working at a shingle mill in Vancouver before moving to the Burrard Dry Docks, like Arthur Tinmouth, during

the war years. Six feet tall, blonde and blue-eyed, Bill was a full ten years
Pat's senior – 'a great big, burly guy,' as Virginia recalled. He was, she
added, 'very fast about everything, and very efficient.'[32] Clearly he was,
because he was very soon and without much fanfare married to Patricia
Tinmouth, who gave birth to their first child, Alan, on 1 April 1954.
'Mom was, I think, eighteen when she got married,' her daughter Kathy
recalls, and 'she was pregnant when she got married ... Back then, I guess
there wasn't much choice *but* to get married.'[33]

The quiet wedding took place on 2 October 1953, at the quaint St
Andrews Church in North Vancouver, after which Arthur and Virginia
hosted a small party for the couple and their retinue of family guests.
The newlyweds first lived for a while in a row house at 210 West 15th
Street, right next door to Pat's friend Lorraine Plowman, who remembers giving the new mother tips on infant care after she brought her son
home from the hospital. Lorraine was somewhat anxiously solicitous
with her maternal advice because, to her mind, the baby's mother
'always seemed up in the clouds somewhere.'[34] Indeed, according to
Virginia – in retrospect, anyway –

> It would be hard for any man of [Bill's] nature to put up with a girl like Pat
> because she was a daydreamer. She was always into books, and she had
> never done any housework and never done any cooking or anything like
> that, and I told him all this when they got married. I said, 'She's not ready
> to take care of a home or anything like that.' 'Oh, that's alright. I'll help
> her, ' [he said].[35]

After the birth of their second child, Katharine Dawn, on 30 September
1956, the family moved within North Vancouver City again, in 1957, to a
residence on West 17th. Early the next year, they moved again, this time
to Deep Cove, in the outlying District beyond the city.

Though the Domphousses' newly rented home was apparently as
bucolic as their address at 315 Sunnyside Lane sounded, the tucked-
away, weekend–regatta club community of Deep Cove offered few
respites for a twenty-two-year-old mother at home with two toddlers and
no means of transportation. If there was a local library in Deep Cove at
this time, it would have been one of the tiny, irregular-hours, volunteer-
run kind – hardly more than a few dozen books on somebody's shelf
somewhere. Unsurprisingly, Pat appears to have become restless. She
had been restless in high school when she submitted the 'Legend of the
Hills' to her last high-school yearbook, and now she sought an outlet

from the cloistered responsibilities of full-time domesticity by going back to school. She enrolled in an adult-education creative-writing course offered in North Vancouver. It was in one such course that she met Ward Carson, later, 'the Vancouver inventor.' He was also living in Deep Cove at the time and began to give his classmate rides to and from their evening courses.

One class that she enrolled in produced a mimeographed pamphlet showcasing its work at the end of the year. 'This winter of 1957–8 has been a memorable one,' the sage course instructor wrote by way of preface: 'We have been shown "how" to write. Now, knowing the technique and construction necessary for a good article or story, it behooves us to apply this knowledge with imagination.' The first entry in this homemade anthology is an ode by Patricia Domphousse, entitled 'To a Tall Tree' – no shortage of those wherever she looked around her North Shore environs. Though the poem opens with a hackneyed formal salutation 'to' the 'tall tree' in the title, the next line, which describes it as being 'wrought by slow explosion through the fertile years,' warrants pause.[36] The promising image of an arboreal 'slow explosion' would stick, but it 'behooved' a more mature poet to ditch the tutored 'wrought' archaisms and contrived form of the apostrophe for a more naturalistic form and colloquial register by the time of 1974's *Milk Stone*: 'I think of a tree / as a slow paradigm / for an explosion' (*MS*, 43).

Patricia Domphousse's enrolment in creative-writing courses brought the young wife into contact with others who, like Ward Carson, but unlike her more practical and rough-edged husband, Bill, liked 'to fiddle around with words.' It was likely also through these courses that she first heard about the *Alberta Poetry Yearbook* annual contests, which provided the aspiring poet with a venue for some of her earliest publications. By far the longest-running of other such contest anthologies across Canada, the *Alberta Yearbook* was sponsored by a local branch of the Canadian Authors Association (Harrington 1981: 249). The contests tended to invite work in traditional genres and were entered by a preponderance of female writers. Even at the time, the reputation of annual anthologies like the *Alberta Yearbook* was hardly auspicious; dismissed as vanity publishing, such anthologies have generally been regarded – when they have been regarded at all – at the 'lightweight, popular end' of a *belles lettres* tradition (Kelly 2000: 4).[37] Basically, just more stuff from the 'scribbling sisterhood,' to evoke Henry James's famous insult from the preceding century.

Despite their perceived lack of literary merit, however, it was 'vanity' publications such as the *Alberta Yearbook* anthology series which provided a young mother in Deep Cove, B.C., with her first visible inclusion and recognition in *any* sort of wider literary community. It was a foundation essential in helping to encourage Patricia Domphousse's still very tenuous self-identification as a writer (who *me?* a *woman?*), and it was a foundation that thus made possible other, subsequent connections to (presumably) more serious and non-vain literary circles. It was, simultaneously, 'vanity' publications such as the *Alberta Yearbook* series which provided Roy Lowther with an award in the 'sonnet' class for an almost incoherent 1959 poem advocating pacifist means of social change.[38]

Many of the works that the apprentice poet submitted and saw printed in the *Alberta Yearbook* series were, like 'To a Tall Tree,' traditional verse forms such as sonnets. But some were also more experimental, even as they clung to traditional subject matters. 'Requiem of a Phoenix,' which won an 'honorable mention' in the 'Short Poem' class for 1959, for example, recurs again to a 'figure' from 'legend,' but unlike 1951's 'Legend of the Hills,' this poem is written in free verse and rejects its own mythological premise as a 'bitter lie': 'Poor bird, you believed your own legend / that was your folly.' The poem is extravagantly overwritten, but its critical edge charts the distance travelled in the eight years that elapsed between the last high-school yearbook and the first *Alberta Yearbook*. A teenager's rhapsodic visions of unfettered freedom give way to the scepticism, even anger, of the young wife and mother. Perhaps the vehemence with which the 'bitter lie' of a fable of rebirth is renounced here had to do with Mrs Domphousse remembering that she had once known such scepticism all along – or at least she had, as a sassy pre-adolescent.

However unimposing they were, these first, rudimentary beginnings of Pat Lowther's literary career also spelled the beginning of the end for the Domphousse marriage. Pat's friendship and eventual liaison with Carson, her fellow poetry enthusiast and Deep Cove neighbour, were symptomatic of a more profound cleavage in orientation between husband and wife. As Kathy ruefully observes, her parents were a couple who, with the exception of a surprise pregnancy, and eventually two children, 'had absolutely nothing in common.'[39] Certainly, by October 1959, when her relationship with Carson came to light, Pat's life with her husband was, she wrote, 'completely miserable' in ways that included physical intimidation and violence. Bill in effect threw her out of the house on Sunnyside Lane, 'seized the children by force, and refused me access to them.' She had to initiate proceedings under the Equal Guardianship of Infants Act before custody of Kathy was legally restored to her the following spring.[40]

According to Virginia, the decision of 'the stupid judge' to split up the youngsters, Alan and Kathy, was intended as a paternalistic 'little nudge to get [the parents] together again.'[41] Inescapably, though, the removal of Alan from Pat's care at such a young age also appears a puni-tive measure intended as a stern warning to a wife once gone astray: infi-delity in women, even a whiff of it, would not be tolerated. Such women were not fit mothers, and they could – and would – stand to lose their children (especially the boys). This may have been a lesson that lingered when the time came for Pat Lowther to think about leaving another marriage.

And so, as the decade popularly celebrated for its 'swinging' sexual groove was about to loosen some belts, Patricia Domphousse found her-self back in her parent's 'nest,' one fledgling of her own along with her this time, and smarting from the absence of the other. She and her little daughter moved into the basement of the small Tinmouth family house at 309 East 10th Avenue, the same North Vancouver basement where 'Patsy Lou' had once kept her secret box full of secret, special things. Public directories of the time listed occupations as well as names, and hers appears in 1960, under 'Domphousse, Mrs Patricia': 'key punch operator, Vancouver Machine Accounting Services.' She was twenty-five years old, a single mother, and looking hard into a future filled with 'the precise click- / ing teeth' of tabulating machines.

Chapter 5

5823 St George Street

Though strained by ongoing child custody disputes with Bill, the basement years, from 1959 to 1962, were not all bad; Kathy, understandably enough, recalls the period spent at her grandmother's home with particular fondness, as a time of calm contentment in comparison with the years that would follow with Roy. While Kathy went off to the same elementary school, Ridgeway, that her mother had attended before her, and that Arthur Tinmouth had attended before *her*, Pat headed by ferry to work in downtown Vancouver. Little Alan came for Saturday visits. Virginia remembers her daughter also frequently having friends over for visits during the evenings: 'She had company, and she seemed to be quite happy. And he also came to the house at that time.'[1] *He* was Roy, of course, who entered the picture toward the end of this period in the spring of 1962. Exactly where and how Patricia Domphousse initially met Roy Lowther isn't certain, but it seems most likely that they first made an acquaintance at a meeting of the Vancouver Poetry Society, of which Pat may have learned while browsing through bookstores in Vancouver, or through her creative-writing classmates in North Vancouver.[2] As he would rarely fail to notify people, Roy presided over that group as its secretary during this period.

Like Bill Domphousse (and Ward Carson), Roy Lowther was substantially older than Pat. In 1951, while a teenaged Pat Tinmouth had been making her decision to join the ranks of the labour force, Roy was already a university graduate, grad school drop-out, and ex-convict, released late that year from a Washington State penitentiary and his first scrape with the law. By 1960 he was a father of three, whose own first marriage was about to grind to a volatile, official end. His occupations during the fifties appear to have been peripatetic; he worked at 'odd jobs' and collected unemployment insurance 'through [to] 1962.'[3] In the early sixties, he returned to UBC to obtain his teacher's certificate.

The bespectacled Roy was not a physically prepossessing man, although according to Virginia, 'he was very presentable at the time ... slim and not bad looking.' All accounts indicate how this would change: over the years, Roy's personal appearance would gradually run to the dishevelled, after the direction of his notoriously unkempt friend Milton Acorn. By the end, 'he was always ragged,' as his brother-in-law John puts it.[4]

If the Domphousse coupling had seemed unlikely from the outset, then so too did Pat's second union. Her choice of Roy seemed so unobvious that it still tends to bewilder friends who knew them both. 'Why did she ever marry him?' Hilda Thomas wonders aloud. 'It's absolutely astonishing to me that someone like Pat could ever have been attracted to someone like Roy.'[5] When Bethoe Shirkoff first saw the couple together at an NDP meeting, 'passing the children back and forth from her knee to his,' 'I thought ... that she might be his daughter. That he might be grandfather to those children.'[6] In the mid-sixties, Lionel Kearns once showed up at a downtown reading where Pat was 'introduced and championed by bill bissett'; Roy Lowther also read at that event, and Kearns was struck by the incongruity between the husband and wife as 'an improbable reading duo.' 'His [poetry] was old-style rhymed and metered, left-wing rhetorical ... Hers was modern, focused, personal, and surprisingly well written ... She quickly gained a reputation as an interesting young poet with an embarrassing husband.'[7]

And yet, despite the disparity in age and the 'embarrassing' contrast, by the mid-sixties, in their aesthetic styles, Patricia Domphousse was clearly drawn to something about the man who came a-courting while she was living in her mother's basement. No doubt it was a compelling combination of what Roy did and did not have in common with her that provided a basis for the attraction. Most immediately, what they shared was the experience of an unhappy first marriage. These were both still in the process of unravelling, since, notably, although she initiated litigation to regain partial custody of her children right away, Pat did not begin divorce proceedings against Bill until after her relationship with Roy became serious, around Christmas of 1962. The trials and tribulations of divorce and custody struggles were definitive factors in the new courtship and eventual second marriage.

Similarly, Pat and Roy would have discovered their shared family backgrounds in relatively isolated North Shore communities. Also an eldest child, Roy, born in 1924, had grown up in Britannia Beach during the thirties, at which time that small town was remote even by North Vancouver standards. His father, Armstrong John, much like Pat's father, Arthur, at the intake station, had worked for the Howe Sound Mining Company as 'a watchman-repairman' at Furry Creek Dam and its pipelines. Roy's mother, Winifred, like Pat's mother, Virginia, was a musical woman, a piano teacher (RLJ, 2: 'Biographical'). Politically, both families leaned toward active trade unionism and labour reform. All of which pointed to a shared interest in music, literature, labour politics – as well as a shared love for the thickly forested, rock and snow-capped spurs of the Coast Range region. In both cases, too, that love for the mountainous rainforest of their youth mingled with the memory of a somewhat lonely, bookish childhood within the predominantly working-class culture the region supported. Indeed, Roy probably dwelt at length on the ostracism he apparently suffered in Britannia Beach.[8] And this is where the differences between her and Roy may have begun to intrigue Patricia Domphousse.

Not only had Roy, unlike Pat, graduated from his local high school, Britannia Mines High, but he had parlayed his academic proficiency into a post-secondary degree and then some. By virtue of his age and education, Roy in his mid-thirties could project a much wider, worldly experience and authoritative source of knowledge than anyone else Pat had ever closely encountered. He could regale her with tales of undergraduate life at UBC – of his involvement with debating clubs and jazz societies and social events like campus 'smokers.' As a result of his studies, he knew a few things about philosophy and aesthetics, and could probably recommend some strange books by people like Plato and Theodor Adorno. And though he may have left out the details about the expired student visa and the sought-after girl who prompted his 1950 arrest for illegal entry to the States, Roy could also tell his new girl some truly shocking tales about sunny California in the post-war years. He might, for example, have spoken credibly and convincingly about the relentless pursuit of political dissent in America, especially at such places as the University of California at Berkeley, a unique epicentre of communist paranoia during Roy's graduate tenure there. Indeed, the insidious militarization of intellectual life at Berkeley alone could have yielded an endless amount of perfectly plausible fodder for Roy's overblown stories about his personal political 'persecution.'[9]

In partially answering her own question about what Pat may have seen in Roy, Hilda Thomas speculates that it was likely the intensity of Roy's self-professed commitments as 'a student of Marxism' that was 'attractive to her.'[10] Indeed, what sources such as bill bissett and Tom Wayman accurately characterize as Roy's tendentious 'old school socialist' or 'Stalinist' views on politics and literature,[11] probably first appeared – and appealed – to a young Pat Domphousse as a mark of superior intellectual confidence and focus. To a young woman still just beginning to come to terms with her own artistic inclinations, and just beginning to rethink, critically, her own social circumstances as a single mother, Roy's clear-cut convictions about culture and politics may have seemed to offer a model of certainty worth investigating, if not emulating. Certainly, the Marxist or 'small *c*' communist theories he brought with him (CATT, 3:379) offered one way to explain and understand the frustrations and difficulties of the narrow prospects she herself now confronted.

In addition to his tale of political imprisonment, Roy could tell Patricia Domphousse about his subsequent travels to Toronto and across Canada, a sojourn he was planning to commemorate in a book of verse called *Cross-Country Rhymes*. A jazz, classical, and folk song afficionado, Roy knew about music and could play the piano, as Pat thought, better than she. As an executive member of a long-established Vancouver poetry club, Roy could also introduce Pat to new workshop and publishing opportunities, including the small literary magazine, *The Fiddlehead*, to which he had been (with much tenacity but little success) submitting work since the mid-fifties. Roy self-identified as a 'labour man,' yet despite the checkered employment history that he had accrued since his return to Vancouver, his new teaching credentials at least held prospects for the sort of professional, middle-class job he would eventually land in 1964 as a music teacher with the Maple Ridge School District.

In all these ways, Roy was the antithesis of Pat's first husband, Bill. And yet, though no longshoreman by a long shot, Roy was not exactly physically anaemic, either. Somewhat of an outdoors man, he did know the area around Britannia Beach (and its history) intimately, as a hiker and a camper; he was also a skilled canoeist.[12] Finally, although his road skills apparently weren't so skilful, Roy also had a car and a driver's licence. Part of his courtship with Pat Domphousse in 1962 consisted in driving her out to explore places she had never been, but which would impress her deeply, like Furry Creek.

So, for a young woman living in her parents' basement, there were all kinds of inducements for pursuing the relationship, which she did, by filing for a divorce from Bill early in 1963. On March 15 of that year, she appeared in court – ill, with her skin allergies – asserting her right to seek full custody of Alan in future, in the hope that she might yet 'personally raise the children together as brother and sister.'[13] But tensions with Bill over this issue were mounting, rather than subsiding, and the matter of access was left unsettled at the finalization of the divorce. Above all, what emerges from court documents filed at this time is the extent to which the aggravated circumstances of Pat's divorce contributed directly to her marriage with Roy a mere four months later. For by July of 1963, when he discovered that Pat and Roy had begun to live together (in 'open adultery,' as he charged), Bill Domphousse announced his intention to make 'an immediate application' for custody of Kathy *and* to revoke Pat's access to Alan, who was scheduled for a summer holiday with his mother and sister that August.[14]

Pat's second marriage took place soon after that, nine days before her twenty-eighth birthday, on 20 July 1963. Roy, whose own divorce had just been finalized in May, was almost thirty-nine at the time. Once again, as with her decision to leave school, there was no advance discussion about it with family members; brother Arden was the only adult family relative present at the wedding, which caught even Virginia and Arthur off guard. The wedding ceremony, officiated by a Unitarian minister, took place at 5823 St George Street, the couple's first East Vancouver residence. Pat was characteristically unenthusiastic about being photographed, so it is a little surprising that in addition to the usual special occasion photos, a later portion of the celebration, showing the smiling bride, was actually also filmed. With her dark hair bobbed short and ornamented with a lace fillet, she wore a tailored, turquoise blue, Jackie Kennedy–style dress suit. The new Pat Lowther made for a stylish catch. Roy certainly thought so. A month after the wedding, he bragged to one of his Vancouver Poetry Society friends: 'Pat, by the way, is Pat Lowther now, as of July 20, and Pat Domphousse no longer ... I pledge not to make this sort of thing a rule with female recruits to V.P.S.'[15]

But over the summer of 1963, Bill Domphousse had also begun to discover other grounds on which he planned to contest his ex-wife's care of their children. Having done some research into Roy's history, he learned of the violent behaviour which had ended Roy's first marriage, and furnished the court with evidence relating to Roy's mental condition. It was a letter from the psychiatrist who had discharged Roy from the clinic where he had been incarcerated until February 1962, just before he'd first met Patricia Domphousse. The doctor had diagnosed Roy as 'paranoid schizophrenic,' 'although,' he added, 'he conceals a good deal of this with his verbal and intellectual ability.'[16] But this evidence came in an affidavit filed on 7 August 1963, several weeks after Pat was 'Pat Domphousse no longer,' and Roy had already bagged his new prize.

⌒⌒

After a brief honeymoon on Mayne Island, and canoeing along the North Shore, with one night up at the South Valley Dam by Furry Creek, Roy and his 'female recruit' settled down in East Vancouver. Like many of the less affluent areas east of the Main Street corridor, the neighbourhood into which they moved was one of lower- to middle-income families and immigrants from still largely European backgrounds – Greek, German, Polish, Ukrainian, Jewish – an ethno-cultural mix that reflected 'preferential' federal immigration policies until well into the sixties (Hiebert 1999: 37–8). The Lowther home on St George was east of Main Street and west of Fraser, with its small meat shops, fruit stands, and community centres. Access to downtown Vancouver by public transit was convenient. On clear days, if Lowther walked north up Fraser Street to East Broadway, she could see the mountains of her North Shore home across Burrard Inlet. Walking south, she got to the bus stops at the windy corner of Fraser and Marine.

With a symbolic economy that calls to mind Emily Dickinson, the Lowthers' rental home on St George Street, which still stands, directly faced an elementary school in the front and abutted a cemetery in the back. For a woman who would soon be writing about the 'complicated airflow' in her house, the physical situation of the residence between school and grave aptly glosses the earliest period of the Lowther marriage, which was likewise marked, on the one hand, by an immediate and urgent desire for children and, on the other, by ghosts of relationships past.

Even as the honeymoon initially continued – with an eye toward increasing the student population of the school across the street – and even as Lowther's notebooks and letters to editors begin to indicate a frank new concern with sexual pleasure and 'married love,' subtle currents of counter-tension enter to complicate the early picture of marital satisfaction. A rough but relatively promising poem draft from this period, entitled simply 'House,' sounds a parodic note in its celebration of domestic inadequacies: the poet thumbs her nose at her household's lack of cleanliness and the 'perpetual arrears / on the gas bill.' More interestingly, she chooses to celebrate a couple's wedded bliss – 'our noisy loving / in the freezing bedroom' – through negative definition, by imagining that couple's absence: 'we could be kicked out tomorrow,' and yet the 'little furry creatures' and 'doves' who also nest among the 'rafters' would 'never miss us,' '[nor] the smell of my cooking, / nor Mozart arranging tensions / in the living room.' Reinforced by 'the wind blowing through the closed windows' of the 'freezing bedroom,' the conditionality of the couple's presence points to their status as temporary residents or renters. As such, they are, in the end, ciphers: if not they, then '[s]omebody else would pay / the eighty-five a month.'[17] 'House' is a celebration of a peculiarly precarious conjugal intimacy that is about as far from John Donne's splendid sun-and-centre-of-the-universe-usurping lovers in 'The Sun Rising' as it is possible to get.

'Sometime, I think it must be well over a year now,' Lowther wrote to one magazine editor around the time she married Roy, 'I sent some poems to you under the name of Pat Domphousse.' She was writing because she wanted confirmation that she could resubmit the poems elsewhere, but her problem also, quite typically, was that she couldn't remember exactly which 'half a dozen' poems she'd sent the editor in the first place. The draft letter to an editor she did not appear to know personally is uncharacteristically chatty: 'I was at that time [of initial submission] preoccupied with some messy personal problems and I let our correspondence lapse. Since my problems have been happily resolved (or at least exchanged for a more interesting set) I'm beginning again to submit my work to magazines.'[18] The parenthesis speaks volumes. Her second marriage was not like leaving high school, to go off bravely and blindly in hopes of 'leaping from crest to crest' among the mountaintops to sing her 'wierd ... songs.' It was, rather, as she this time recognized, to 'exchange' – not 'resolve' – one 'set' of 'problems' for another, as she hoped, 'more interesting set.' The next three words after the parenthesis also speak volumes: 'I'm beginning again.' Without believing in the legend of any mythical phoenix, another rebirth, a difficult flowering, was now under way.

∽

Lowther's new 'problems' began as new opportunities, some more promising than others. Roy may have been the first person she fully opened up to, and he was probably the first man who seriously listened to and encouraged her ideas and artistic aspirations – at least, in this initial phase, while she was still his unthreatening protégé. With their marriage, Roy also helped to widen and reconfigure Lowther's social milieu in a way that made for an 'interesting set' of literary cross-connections indeed.

When she first arrived in greater Vancouver with Roy in the summer of 1963, Lowther was likely not aware of her proximity – geographically, anyway – to what was at that very moment in the process of becoming the most distinctive, if not also most influential, poetic movement of the period, the intellectually avant-garde 'Black Mountain North school' of *Tish*. Famously kick-started by a group of young poet-students and their faculty mentors at the University of British Columbia, the excitement and the arguments sparked by the postmodern 'poetic revisionism' of *Tish* helped to energize Vancouver as the hippest literary scene in anglo-Canada (Neuman 1990: 60). But what makes Vancouver during the sixties especially intriguing, as Lowther's own literary education reveals, is the wide spectrum of heterogeneous and protean literary subcultures and classes that it continued to support as it birthed postmodernism. These included historically entrenched 'schools' of pre-modern traditionalism which, contrary to the memories of post-modernists like George Bowering, fought off extinction well beyond the Second World War.[19] Roy's Vancouver Poetry Society was probably the most prominent example of such a less-than-cutting-edge 'school,' which 'recruited' and graduated the likes of Pat Lowther (whom VPS records show was a member during 1962–7). She was in good company: Dorothy Livesay was an alumnus too.

Thus, while *Tish* poets like George Bowering and Frank Davey were busy projecting themselves into the finer points of Charles Olson's 'projective verse,' the new Mrs Lowther was inducted into the living, breathing midst of a literary community similar to that represented within the pages of the *Alberta Poetry Yearbook*. Predating even the establishment of the Canadian Authors Association in 1921, the Vancouver Poetry Society was the oldest literary society on the West Coast, first founded in 1916 by Dr Ernest P. Fewster and 'seven fellow enthusiasts.' Serving as president until his death in 1947, Dr Fewster is fondly recalled in VPS historical records as 'gently and earnestly discoursing on the spiritual essence of poetry' 'with his halo of silver hair' radiating about him. Bliss Carman and Sir Charles G.D. Roberts are listed among the 'galaxy of distinguished people' involved as honorary presidents at one time or another.[20] In the thirties, Mr Duncan Macnair and his wife, a certain Mrs Dorothy Macnair, also signed on, just in time for the launch of the VPS's members-only magazine, *Full Tide*, in 1936.[21] *Full Tide* was still publishing in 1962 when it began to print early work by, first, 'Patricia

Domphousse' and, later, 'Patricia Lowther.' The poems are much like those which appeared in the *Alberta Yearbook*.

The goals of the Vancouver Poetry Society were also much like those of the editors of the *Alberta Yearbook*: they were 'the encouragement of native poetic talent and the development of a distinctive Canadian culture.'[22] In these aims, the mandates of literary groups like the VPS clearly anticipate and dovetail with the broader post-war attempt to 'popularize' high culture as a nationalist bulwark against American mass media – the very rationale of the influential Massey-Levesque commission of 1949–51, and its major new initiatives for funding and promoting arts and letters in Canada.[23] Something of the same sort of 'peculiar mixture' of liberal democratic idealism and cultural elitism that marks the Massey agenda (Litt 1992: 252) thus also leaves its 'peculiar' print on satellite cultural groups such as the VPS, which – especially with people like Roy at the helm in the early sixties – strongly endorsed populist principles of art for and by 'the people,' all the while stalwartly adhering to a legacy of high art forms from an earlier European tradition that also first inspired Dr Fewster and his 'fellow enthusiasts.' If anything, this tension was perhaps especially pronounced in the case of the VPS, which by the sixties also appears to have become something of a refuge for socialists of the Old Left.

In a sense 'born old,' like the much-maligned Canadian Authors Association (Harrington 1981: 235), the VPS was uniquely a 'society rooted in the past.' By the late sixties, even the local Vancouver chapter of the CAA, seeking to strike a coalition of sorts, was pressuring the VPS to open itself to external influences and introduce some change. Having 'withstood' the onslaughts of 'Georgian philistines, old-line leftists, new line leftists, [and] beat poets,' the VPS was at this time portrayed by the press as every bit as antiquated as a Dickensian Pickwickian club: a 'society' of 'inflexibility and courtly manners – a style of life that went out with the gas light era but still flickers within the ageing heart of the [Vancouver] Poetry Society.' Pressed to address this issue publicly, the Society's president, Ken Symes, conceded that

> come to think of it ... we don't have a [beatnik] beard in the outfit, but that doesn't mean to say we're afraid of the way-out group. We're interested in all forms of poetry and it wouldn't be fair to say our interest stops around the age of Tennyson. But I suppose our interest does lean more towards the conservative type of poetry and perhaps, by and large, we like to go our own way as much as the modern poets see fit to do.[24]

'By and large' the subject of open ridicule by the sixties, the public profile of the VPS seems to have passed the point of damage control sometime after mid-century. Though in good part a result of their own complacency, the waning fortunes of groups such as the VPS and the CAA were also officially helped along by the new forms of cultural authority established in the wake of the Massey Commission. While the mandate of the newly minted Canada Council ostensibly included fostering 'relations with national voluntary [arts] associations, [and] aid for local arts activities,' it was also largely 'designed to extend the federal government's support to *refined levels* of cultural activity that it had never before reached' (Litt 1992: 214, emphasis added). And in practice, as Lyn Harrington's history of the CAA shows, the implementation of the Canada Council's policies during the fifties and sixties tended to exclude groups that it deemed inadequately 'refined' because 'non-professional writers comprised too large a percentage of the membership' (1981: 245). In a sense, then, the new arts bureaucracies formalized the distinction between professional poets and amateur poetasters that F.R. Scott so memorably threw into relief in his parody of the CAA, 'The Canadian Authors Meet' (1945: 37).[25]

Like Livesay before her, Lowther soon knew enough to move on, decamping from 'the teacup-tinkling' scene, as she called it, by 1967. Tired of assigned workshop themes on 'inane' topics, she took a cue from F.R. Scott and privately parodied the VPS in her notebooks ('Have I spent all my hard-lived time / to diddle with an inane rhyme?').[26] All the same, a part of her would not forget the VPS, some members of which, like Lorraine Vernon, would remain good friends. Like the *Alberta Yearbook* anthologies, associations such as the VPS served their own enabling function – one from which aspiring writers from non-literary backgrounds, like Lowther herself, stood to benefit. At the very least, such groups opened a space for literary community and for imagining an artistic life, if only by upholding a poetics that a contemporary writer would have to develop against, in negative definition, as she eventually did.

While, on the one hand, her union with Roy connected Lowther to an enclave of 'populist' literary traditionalism headed for inevitable superannuation, it also led to more productive contacts. For almost a decade prior to his second marriage, Roy had been quite steadily bombarding Fred Cogswell, the editor of the eclectic and respected *The Fiddlehead* magazine, with submissions that were by and large graciously declined.[27] The fact of these submissions to *The Fiddlehead* contravenes Roy's later claims that he and his wife 'were not rivals in the same field' of artistic production (CATT, 3:385); at least initially, he clearly aimed for the same select, 'literary' audience that Pat, apparently on his advice, also began to aim at. For soon after she was married to Roy, Lowther herself began sending poems to Cogswell, and scoring hits, beginning with her very first submission, when Cogswell accepted her 'Poem for Schizo-phrenics' in 1964.

The correspondence between 'Dear Dr. Cogswell' and Pat Lowther begins deferentially and self-consciously on her part. 'If your backlog is too big for you to be reading submissions right now, just shoot them back and I'll try another time,' one such letter reads. Or, half a year later: 'I hope I'm not bugging you by submitting too frequently ... If this is too much, please kick me in the return mail.' But, far from 'kicking' her, Cogswell sent encouragement. He wouldn't meet Lowther in per-son until 1972, a few years before she was appointed League Chair over the University of New Brunswick professor, who had also been consid-ered for the post. But Lowther's election did not affect what had by then already developed into an easy-going, close friendship by mail; Cogswell continued to send Lowther new batches of Fiddlehead books and to steer younger poets migrating to the West Coast, like Leona Gom, in her direction. The affable Maritime editor seemed to inspire the trust of younger women writers such as Lowther and Joy Kogawa, both of whom he corresponded with extensively. The very last Lowther letter on record, affectionately signed 'love, Pat,' is to 'Dear Fred.'[28]

Similarly, the second marriage and move to Vancouver were direct catalysts for Lowther's first contact with Milton Acorn, who had arrived on the Coast in the same year she married Roy. The reputation of Acorn, then perhaps still best known as the author of *In Love and Anger* (1956, self-published), preceded him. Or, at least, it did in the drafty new Lowther household on St George. In the spring of 1963, just prior to Acorn's appearance in Vancouver, *The Fiddlehead* magazine had pub-lished a special issue devoted to his work. As a long-time subscriber to the magazine, and also as a member of a group called the Labour Poets Workshop, Roy already knew about the up-and-coming 'working-class' Maritime poet, who, like Roy himself, was not really working-class and, like Roy too, had been a member of the Labour Progressive Party until he became disaffected with it. In her very first letter to Fred Cogswell, Lowther specifically mentioned *The Fiddlehead*'s spring, 1963 issue on Acorn – gratefully, since, as she noted, his books were 'impossible to obtain' in Vancouver.[29]

So, it was unsurprising that Roy and Pat appeared at the readings Acorn soon organized at the League for Socialist Action on Granville Street. It is also not terribly surprising that Acorn and Roy apparently hit it off quite well. According to Patrick Lane, '[they] could have long arguments about Communism and Leninism and Trotskyism and all that sort of stuff. Milton could wax for twenty hours on that ... No one else would listen to him probably but Roy.'[30] Before long, Acorn became a sometime room-and-boarder with the Lowthers, staying with them off and on during his West Coast sojourn. In return, Acorn agreed to act, at least once, as a go-between to help Roy secure Fred Cogswell as a referee for a 'workingman's' anthology which Roy wanted to (though never did) edit.[31]

While her husband and the boisterous, cigar-chomping Maritime poet no doubt bonded over shared political grievances, ·Lowther was free to make the acquaintance of others who congregated at the LSA readings. Others, for example, such as a young poet named bill bissett, who would very soon become a co-founder of Very Stone House Press, which would eventually publish her first book. Bissett recalls that Acorn's LSA events were held in a Longshoreman's Association hall (quoted in Lemm 1999: 142), a detail that points again to the overlapping and shifting currents that made up Vancouver literary culture circa 1965. Not only did Lowther first meet younger – and very contemporary – poets like bissett in a hall that her first husband, another Bill, and a genuine longshoreman, might have occupied at other times, for reasons very other than poetry. Here, her poetry – and Roy's too – was also first heard by members of the city's academic avant-garde, like Lionel Kearns – whose presence at LSA readings comes as a reminder that even *Tish* aficionados were not so insular unto themselves as to neglect the doings of their less famous, non-academic 'associates downtown' (Bowering 1994: 128). The Vancouver Lowther inhabited was a place 'where all sorts of movements and groups and little collisions of talent' could and did happen, like particle physics, on a fairly regular basis.[32]

Maybe the sea air invigorated him; Acorn was soon a busy man about town. In addition to the LSA reading series, he also began to organize readings and 'Thursday night "Blab" sessions' at the Advance Mattress, a 'non-profit coffee house' on the outskirts of Kitsilano. The Advance Mattress, initially on '10th Avenue near Alma Street,' became an 'important part' of the local 'scene': 'Named after the former tenant in this warehouse, the coffee house became Acorn's west coast version of the Bohemian Embassy. He read, hosted readings, and, of course, hung out, tirelessly talking about politics and poetry' (Lemm 1999: 143). In fact,

Acorn's first column for the inaugural, ten-cent issue of a radically new 'underground' free press, the *Georgia Straight*, was about the Advance Mattress – or, rather, about the 'deliberate, cynical persecution of the Advance Mattress' (in Pauls and Campbell 1997: 33). If that sounds a suspiciously familiar Acorn theme, the context in this case nevertheless bears him out. Local authorities apparently looked askance at Acorn's Advance, judging it to be little more than an acid-head shop and centre for subversive long-hairs; it was thus evicted from its original premises in short order. These were, after all, years during which the downtown Hudson's Bay store still employed its own uniformed guards to enforce a 'No Hippies' policy in its Malt Bar, and also an outdoor window washer, equipped 'with a hose,' to prevent hippie 'filth' from 'congregating around the corner of Georgia and Granville' (Cummings, in Pauls and Campbell 1997: 16). The volatile mix of politics, drugs, youth, and reactionary authoritarianism is a factor that complicates literary formations of the time: as with the case of the Advance Mattress, it was a combination that frequently made for spontaneous combustion in the form of ephemeral, fly-by-night groupings and organizations.

Promptly plugged into multiple circuits of 'way out' 'long-hairs,' less psychedelic Old Left hardliners, and straight-laced tea-drinking Tennyson fans, Lowther must have experienced her earliest years of marriage in Vancouver as incredibly stimulating, if initially somewhat disorienting, too. If she could not fail to mark a certain 'schizophrenic' contrast between the atmosphere and the ideas she encountered at the Advance Mattress or the League for Socialist Action, on the one hand, and those of the Vancouver Poetry Society, on the other, then one of the first benefits she gained from this wider exposure was simply a new appreciation for the relativity of her own 'viewpoint.'As she at this time wrote to Jacob Zilber, editor of *Prism* magazine, she was submitting some poems that tried to capture the realism of 'married love' from 'the viewpoint of the woman, or housewife – which,' she now added, 'is somewhat enclosed and even a little frightening thing to be.'[33]

⌒∽⌒

It is clear from her notebooks that Lowther, like many women in the sixties, was beginning to give serious thought to the implications of domesticity as a career – even as she and Roy were actively seeking to reconfirm her 'somewhat enclosed' role as 'housewife' and mother, by trying for a child of their own. Though she rarely used her notebooks for standard journal entries, in one remarkable exception – a long, melancholy, prose entry from the St George Street period of her marriage – she addressed the reality of her new domestic life. The entry begins in contemplation of 'the orange-gold light in a house window across the graveyard' – the evening view across her backyard.[34] What emerges subsequently is that, aside from 'the one saved child,' Kathy, the Lowthers were feeling acutely bereft of the children from their previous marriages. Pat, in particular, was concerned about the emotional toll of divorce on the children – on her step-children, as much as her own. But she was also struck by its dramatic toll on the new husband who had so lately, as Patrick Lane says, 'swept her off her feet.'[35] Despite the good fortune of having found relatively stable work as a substitute teacher, Roy began to reveal a singularly black despair about a year into the marriage, a despair that coincided with the end of the 1964 custody hearings that awarded the children of his previous marriage to his former wife. At this time, Roy could already share with his new wife a terribly bitter conclusion: 'There is nothing to live for.' This remark rang in Lowther's head; it recurs throughout her long, meditative notebook entry as a bleak refrain, reiterated in disappointment and disbelief.

At some point that evening, while she contemplated the distant glow of a home across the cemetery, Lowther realized she'd smoked all her cigarettes and finished her coffee and Curacao. '[C]annot exist without cigarettes,' she confessed. And then, a fretful worry: 'Why is there no baby?' Whatever tensions had already begun to mark their relation, it seems that the answer to them would, surely, be a new baby. In particular, a new family might be the potential cure for the unhealthy outrage and abjection her husband was displaying over the final outcome of his divorce, a hopeful means of mitigating 'the crying and hate [that] cripples our born children, and reaches into us where we make our bed.'

Yet, even as Lowther tuned anxiously into her own still-empty womb, 'wanting to be fed,' she was admonishing that 'blind, deaf little animal' and asking herself an essential question: 'Is there no wanting beyond this?' Was it strictly as a woman capable of bearing children that she 'wanted' in this world? Or were there other creative powers that also 'wanted' employment? Around 1964, this was a question still without any clear answer. But the fact of its being asked at all was a 'watershed' moment for the former Pat Tinmouth, who would go on to explore this business of 'Wanting' in the books ahead of her (MS, 46).

In the meantime, though, she had her hands full with Roy. Having been named as a co-defendant in the divorce suit brought by Roy's first wife, Lowther attended at least some of the custody hearings related to her husband's first marriage. In a draft letter to Ken Symes, the president of the Vancouver Poetry Society, she condemned another female VPS member's 'fantastic character assassination' of Roy during her testimony against him at one of those hearings. That club member's representation of Roy as 'arrogant' and prone to purple-faced anger is vehemently rejected by Pat as a 'shock[ing]' 'falsehood' told by a 'vicious fanatic' – an 'ardent Communist' who is motivated by a Party agenda in seeking to harm Roy, the ex-Communist Party member. In this draft (was it ever sent?), Roy's new wife, then, sounds more like Roy himself than anyone else. But it also reveals the sincerity of a young wife's sympathetic belief in her husband's grievances: 'I ... feel greatly concerned for my husband,' the letter states toward its end: 'He has been through a terrible ordeal.'[36]

Roy regularly vilified his former spouse, and, according to Kathy, 'in later years, as Roy became more and more violent, [Pat] did begin to doubt his stories about his first wife.'[37] But the evidence suggests that 'later' may have been sooner, in this case. The same notebook which contains the defensive draft letter to Ken Symes also contains another interesting draft: a thinly veiled, autobiographical short story concerning a couple dealing with the phantom presence of the husband's past relationship. In this 'fiction,' titled 'Thrift,' the artist figure is, significantly, the woman, a visual artist who one day undertakes a painting that begins as a completely black canvas. Not until the next day do 'forms begin to emerge out of that blackness.' The 'forms' that eventually 'emerge' are those of the husband's past wife, 'her shape grown out of many-colored darkness, only her pale arms and face lighted.' She is holding out a loaf of bread, 'like an offering.' In other words, it is an entreating portrait, and one to which the husband in the story strongly objects. His negative reaction inwardly distresses the artistic wife, since she herself considers the work promising. After the husband's rejection of the portrait, the disillusioned artist / wife sees 'what she rarely noticed, or thought of – the difference in years between them': 'He looked tired.'[38]

Similarly, the same 'Standard Life' notebook which contains the letter defending Roy's reputation is also filled with poem drafts that indicate how soon Lowther knew she had a badly wounded man on her hands. 'Division' hints at the intricacy of later Lowther poems. It begins with a couple's physical parting: 'When our mouths have slid apart / from the last blurred kiss / and landed, quenched in pillows / he closes on a private agony / and sends his last thick thought from me.' That physical separation is followed by the speaker's focus on the internal 'division' signalled by her mate's ' private agony.' She knows that 'flesh has not healed his scissored heart': 'the spinning female thing that lives in me / and all night weaves a blunt, blind skin/ over the day's ruptures and incisions / ... lives not in him.' The poem ends: 'Then shall I mourn the whole / and silken sphere of me, a mate to this / bloodied rag and lace / of a heart that took my hand.' With its faint allusions to 'spinning female' prototypes like Arachne and Ariadne, 'Divisions'' construction of a 'spinning female thing' introduces an important leitmotif. In her later domestic poetry, Lowther would go on to spool and un-spool this metaphor, with interesting variations, again and again.

Rolling bandages for the Red Cross had been part of the patriotic war effort undertaken during the forties by many Canadian women and children – including a school-aged Patricia Tinmouth, who had also grown up watching her mother nurse Arden. By extension, part of what is 'mourn[ed]' in a poem like 'Division' is the speaker's own fading belief in traditional ideals of femininity as a source of altruistic healing power. Here, there is no room for any Florence Nightingale fantasy: the speaker's mate, with his 'bloodied rag and lace / of a heart,' is already beyond her capacity for repair. Long before the full extent of her husband's festering emotional wounds were even apparent, a newly remarried Lowther acknowledged as much to herself during her long notebook meditation at the St George Street house: 'What will cure my love, crucified on his pillow, and all those back-handed by hate, is past the power of this *I*.'

Nevertheless, despite the red flags that appeared early on, life in Vancouver was already proving 'more interesting' and expansive than life in Deep Cove or 'North Van' ever had. Besides which, there were very soon new grounds for Lowther to hope that her husband's disturbing anguish might fade. Roy was temporarily placated by the appearance of his *Cross-Country Rhymes* in 1965, a collection of sentimental nationalist verse, self-published through his Labour Poets Workshop. Lowther herself continued to write poems and send them off to a steadily expanding repertoire of little magazines, including *Prism*, *Fiddlehead*, *Cyclic*, *blewointment*, and bp Nichol's *Ganglia*. The couple's literary contacts also continued to grow and solidify, at least in part through Roy's invitations to writers such as Patrick Lane and bill bissett to join poetry gatherings which he hosted at home.[39] It was by similar invitation to one of these poetry nights that Dorothy Livesay, who had returned to the West Coast from Zambia in 1963, also first met Pat. While November found Lowther working – 'in a #@! *insurance office*' – to address family 'financial problems,' 1965 was by and large a more upbeat year than the previous.[40]

That December, Dorothy Livesay threw a Christmas party at her place on 3347 West 8th Avenue. Among others, she invited the Lowthers, the Lanes, Seymour Mayne, Milton Acorn, Jamie Reid, and bill bissett. A widow since Duncan MacNair's sudden death in 1959, Livesay had returned from her work with UNESCO in Africa to find herself feeling a little out of place in Vancouver's now profoundly changed literary scene. Much like P.K. Page, who also returned to the West Coast from abroad in 1964 with similar feelings, Livesay was not overtly receptive to the new 'Black Mountain offspring' and once confessed to Seymour Mayne that she 'never felt accepted' upon her return to British Columbia – 'except by the chosen few, you – all young ones.' Livesay's 'chosen few' were a fairly diverse congeries; a '*salon des autres*,' in Mayne's phrase. He adds also: 'Dorothy was a great catalyst.'[41]

For Lowther, landing in Livesay's living room must have felt a little like finding home. Here was an established poet who was both a mother and a professional – in fact, a kind of professional mother through her training as a social worker. Here, too, was a woman poet who had travelled widely, but yet also shared Lowther's own specific ties to North Vancouver, right down to good old Deep Cove. And finally, here was a woman who could surround Lowther with other talented, politically like-minded young writers interested in contemporary writing. The literary circle that Livesay formed around herself at this time, as a kind of den mother and mentor to this set, would have a definite impact on the decade of Lowther's writing life ahead.

And there was shortly another important reason for optimism. By the summer of 1966, Lowther found herself so very pregnant that she fully expected 'two or more whopping boys' to come of the bulk she lugged around. Who appeared instead, early that August, 'in a great rush, but in good health' was 'one rather smallish girl,' Heidi Elizabeth, whom her delighted parents immediately nicknamed 'Beth.'[42] The new baby kept her mother busy, but she also energized and inspired her. Three and a half months after Beth's birth, Lowther wrote to 'Dee' Livesay, who had recently moved to become writer-in-residence at the University of New Brunswick: 'I haven't stopped [writing] altogether, and have sent three poems for your consideration.' Of Dorothy's new job, she added: 'I understand a post like this is supposed to leave you lots of time for writing, which is terrific, if true.' Part of her may have coveted the mobility, the 'time for writing,' and the 'lofty eminence' signalled by Livesay's new 'post.'[43]

But by the mid-sixties, no doubt stimulated by well-read friends like Livesay, Lowther also began reading some contemporary feminism, and realizing that she wasn't alone in the prescriptive domesticity she sometimes chafed against. One poem draft of the period takes its title from Betty Friedan's 1963 *The Feminine Mystique*, one of the hallmarks of modern North American feminism. Lowther's 'The Feminine Mystique' is primarily an exercise in fun, but also interesting for the glimpse it affords into the unfolding process of a poet's self-understanding. Written in sestets with a regular rhyme scheme (*aabccb*), it is a poem that witnesses her formalist upbringing in Vancouver Poetry Society quarters, except for its overtly facetious tone and intent, which recall a much younger Pat Tinmouth's keen awareness of the social imperative to 'get a man, get a man / catch him any way you can':

> There's a story that they tell
> And the magazines all sell,
> That domestic life is every female's true affinity.
> You may cook and clean and sew,
> But beyond that don't dare go
> ...
> If a business girl you'd be
> (Can't you try embroidery?)
> You must keep your mind on business – get yourself a groom.[44]

One of the personal contradictions Lowther registers with this only partially tongue-in-cheek burlesque is that, while as a girl, her reading and composition skills had led to laudatory applause – indeed, to being singled out in grade school for special IQ testing – as an adult, she was socially expected to camouflage any sign of sentience from the neck up. Or as she put it, with better cadence: 'Keep your voice and neckline low / learn to murmur, "I don't know."' In the unpublished draft of 'The Feminine Mystique,' Lowther made 'biological' rhyme with 'never think at all.'

It both is and isn't surprising that she apparently read, and was provoked to riff on, *The Feminine Mystique*. Friedan's book sold millions of copies in the decade after it was first published and galvanized the discontent of a generation of suburban housewives. Though not particularly original in its thesis (quietly borrowed from Friedrich Engels), Friedan's book effectively critiqued the illusory 'mystique' of the traditional female domestic consumer, and strongly endorsed entry to the paid workforce, and especially professionalization, as the answer to middle-class women's 'self-realization' (Horowitz 1998: 201–3, 4). All the same, Lowther did not exactly fit the conservative middle-class demographic that *The Feminine Mystique* was squarely aimed at, and it is likely that she would have found the book's 'watered down' Marxism (Horowitz 1998: 216), and recourse to a 'post-material agenda' of personal growth, a little questionable (Herman 1995: 277).

Likely, she would have been more interested in how and why Friedan's own remarkable early history of radical working-class feminism and Popular Front labour activism was gradually erased and unwritten as that author 'reinvented' herself as a more lukewarm sixties' liberal feminist.[45] Lowther would also, no doubt, have been interested to know that as the Ivy-League American was writing her pivotal bestseller (with the help of a nanny) in an upper New York State mansion during the early sixties, Friedan's husband, Carl, was busy cursing 'that bitch' who was scribbling at the dining-room table instead of getting dinner ready; that Carl and Betty Friedan's 'sadomasochistic free-for-all' marriage included hurling sugar bowls and mirrors at each other; and that the run-away success of Betty's 1963 book exacerbated tensions in the stormy marriage to the point that 'Mr. Betty Friedan' and Mrs. Betty divorced, in a lingeringly bitter and acrimonious split (Horowitz 1998: 200, 154, 225). Writing away in the drafty, rented 'House' on St George Street, Lowther had more in common with the privileged and educationally pedigreed American than she could have ever guessed from the 1963 book that inspired her poem.

Chapter 6

A Difficult Flowering

While Lowther was busy by the mid-sixties mothering, gradually writing her way out of the Vancouver Poetry Society, and reading her way into a sharper feminist consciousness, some of her new young male friends, bill bissett, Patrick Lane, Seymour Mayne, and Jim Brown, were also busy with a bold new venture of their own. Frustrated with a lack of venues for their work, they came up with the idea for a press of their own, and so, exuberantly, on 6 June 1966, Very Stone House was born at bissett's house. Unofficially, the enthusiastic novice publishers occasionally used a past participle verb for the 'stone' part of their new 'house.' The Montreal-born Mayne was only twenty-two, ambitious and smart, and already committed to completing a doctoral degree at UBC. Jim Brown already had the poetry magazine *Talon* to look after, and would soon go his own way with the very successful Talon Books. Lane and bissett, at twenty-seven apiece, were in chronological years not much younger than Lowther, but considerably less settled in their lives at that point. While bissett encountered medical and legal troubles that would soon see him head for 100 Mile House, the sixties in general were also 'a traumatic time' for Patrick Lane. A series of personal crises, including the sudden death of his brother, the murder of his father, and the disintegration of his first marriage, all resulted in a 'quite deranged' Lane 'back then': 'I lived excessively in every possible way: alcohol, drugs, women, etc. etc. I was, to put it mildly, quite wild and extremely irresponsible' (in Bowling 2002: 63). Nevertheless, it was onto the shoulders of the unlikely duo of Patrick Lane, the talented but wild 'Okanagan outlaw,' and (especially) Seymour Mayne, the more cosmopolitan young Jewish intellectual from Montreal, that the bulk of the new Press's work fell. The first four books that Very Stone House published in rapid succession were four books by the four 'publishers' themselves: Lane's *Letters from a Savage Mind*, Mayne's *From the Portals of Mouseholes*; bissett's *The Jinx Ship and Other Tales*, and Brown's *The Circus in the Boy's Eye*.

It was clear from the start that the young poets had no real idea of what they were getting themselves into – which lends to the history of this shaky little Very Stone House an appealing touch of comedy. When Seymour Mayne cheerfully informed Earle Birney that Very Stone was planning to publish Lane's *Letters from a Savage Mind* even though Lane had not yet officially heard back from 'McStew,' where he had already submitted the manuscript, the senior man of letters growled back about protocols for first rights of refusal: 'You gotta do it business-like and legal if you're to launch a press, man,' he admonished.[1] But protocol was nothing compared to 'fucking' government forms, tax regulations, cash to cover printer's costs, fund-raiser readings to come up with that cash, distribution logistics, cohesion on editorial policy, and other pleasant, business-type distractions of running a small press. By January 1967, little more than six months into the project, bissett and Brown had departed, and Mayne, left to struggle with mounting debts, was already lamenting the future of the press. Even when Mayne temporarily left Vancouver during holidays, he didn't exactly leave his publishing house duties behind; instead, he was writing detailed housekeeping instructions – and the occasional reprimand – to his less business-oriented partner, Lane, apparently prone to filling out those 'fucking' government forms incorrectly without him. In short, 'the confusion reigning' at Very Stone lasted until the 'final spasms' of the Press in July 1969, when Lane and Mayne, having 'lost interest' and 'chosen rootless paths for the next year,' finally threw in the towel.[2]

Pretty much lurching from crisis to crisis and never safely out of debt during the three short years of its life, Very Stone House nevertheless lasted long enough to see through a year of publishing books by people other than its publishers. Since the editors made a conscious and firm decision 'to publish West Coasters first before Easterners in this press,'[3] the immediate prospect they thought about, after their own books were out, was Pat Lowther, whose poems they had all seen in small magazines, and whom they had all heard read, by then, at places like the League for Socialist Action and the Advance Mattress. 'We approached her and said, "Do you want a book?" ' Lane recalls, 'and that's how *This Difficult Flowring* happened.'

Over the course of 1967, and into the next spring, Lowther's new editors 'offered a certain amount of critical advice,' but largely they sifted through the 'fairly finished' poems Lowther had accumulated by that point, with her, to decide which to include in the collection.[4] Preliminary Table of Content lists and loose-leaf typescripts among Lowther's papers show the manuscript's gradual evolution: with a few surprising exceptions of strong and thematically relevant poems which she for some reason yanked (and, in one case, later published in *Milk Stone* under a new title, 'Touch Home'), Lowther gradually weeded out weaker efforts and lightly revised those slated for inclusion, frequently changing their titles. As her editors discovered, though, one title she was adamantly wedded to was that of the collection as a whole: '[we] argued with her about the "flow'ring" versus "flowering,"' as Lane remembers, with a laugh. 'We tried to talk her out of that, and she just would not have it.'[5]

'Thrilled' with the prospect of her first book's appearance, Lowther was probably also aware, as Mayne speculates, 'that there would be jealousy and negativity coming from her husband' when it did appear.[6] But the mere fact of her being invited to prepare a collection by young, male writers whose acquaintance Roy himself had courted was already enough to put a new strain on the marriage. In May 1967, when Lowther was into the first trimester of a new pregnancy with what would be her fourth and last child, Christie, Lane wrote to Mayne in Montreal, alluding darkly to both social turbulence in the city and domestic turbulence at the Lowther home:

> The fuzz are becoming more brutal in their attacks on the hippies and many are being arrested and evicted – the Lowthers were evicted (not by the fuzz or anything like that) and Pat's pregnant again ... and they're fighting the endless emptiness of their lives like lonely goldfish in private bowls of despair.[7]

The Lowthers were not exactly 'evicted' from their St George Street residence. According to a neighbour and friend of the family at the time, Pauline Bennett, the landlady needed the space for herself, and Pat actually 'felt sorry' for the landlady because the landlady 'was upset at having to give them notice.'[8] All the same, the Lowthers did not choose to move. They were renters, however, and renters sometimes have such decisions made for them, new babies on the way or not.

But they didn't have to move far. Just a few blocks away, in the same neighbourhood, the family moved that July into landlord Gutknecht's old two-storey house on East 46th Avenue. Situated midway on a block between the busy shopping street of Fraser and their old street of St George, the new Lowther abode stood diagonally across from the Martin Luther Church at the corner, with its black-shingled, steeple roof. Four months after the move, Christine Louise made her appearance, on November 19.

On 20 June 1968, Seymour Mayne and Patrick Lane personally dropped off Lowther's author copies of *This Difficult Flowring*. '[H]ers was the first really well-designed book we did,' Lane recounts. 'We actually put some time and effort into it ... [and] did a nice-looking book.'[9] Weighing in at a modest forty-two pages, *This Difficult Flowring* was clearly a source of pride for its publishers, who had not only elected to use 'green-colored paper' for the pages of the book, 'because of the title,' but who had also commissioned artist Steve Slutsky to design the butterfly-ringed cover.[10] That cover image is, thankfully, a subtle antidote to the alarmingly Freudian illustrations which accompany the text inside, all of which feature voluptuously naked women and overtly sexualized, phantasmagoric landscapes, after the style of the time. In one final detail that Roy Lowther would not have missed as distinguishing this book from his own *Cross-Country Rhymes*, the colophon page of *This Difficult Flowring* attests to its being underwritten by Canada's official, 'cross-country' culture industry: 'published with the assistance of the Canada Council, June 1968.' This was no amateur production or vanity publication, though, interestingly, that's precisely how Very Stone House also, in effect, began – as a vanity press for a group of young writers who were not exactly professional publishers themselves.

As its awkwardly self-conscious title indicates, *This Difficult Flowring* signals more than just a simple announcement of poetic arrival with the appearance of some of Lowther's first fully mature blooms in poems such as 'Two Babies in Two Years,' 'The Complicated Airflow,' and 'Leaning from City Window.' In this instance, the strained pun on 'flowring' reinforces more than anything else the qualifier that precedes it: the 'difficulty' of this book's own long gestation. That the collection came into being in the first place at the instigation of Lowther's friends – and not as a result of her own initiative – is in itself telling. If Lowther's expeditious pursuit of little magazine publication from 1963 on is any gauge, a book publication would have presented itself to her sooner or later as the next logical step in another 'wanting beyond this.' Nevertheless, the external nudge it took for her first 'flowring' to appear does suggest that by 1967, at the age of thirty-two, she had not yet made a connection between what she saw was possible for her younger (male) friends, and what she saw as possible for herself. Still caught in the 'who, me?' mode when it came to signs of writerly self-identity, Lowther discovered herself as a poet through a series of surprises – or 'shocks of recognition,' to use her own favoured phrase (from Adorno).

That *This Difficult Flowring* charts the uncertain, sometimes regressive, sometimes circuitous trajectory of its author's struggle toward the confidence of a natural contemporary voice is suggested by 'Angel,' the poem which lends its final line to the collection's title. The 'Angel' in question here is the poet's *anti*–muse – a self-subverting 'incubus' that is figured as both male and very malevolent – a Satanic 'angel' of damnation, in fact. 'He' is a 'monstrous' 'creature' that the speaker has 'worked' 'rites of exorcism against,' to no avail: 'he rises out of someone else's poem / fits his face on the moon's dead face, / mocks me in mirrors' (*DF*, 26). In its attempt to dramatize a 'difficult flowring,' the title poem registers a troubled disjunction between the woman speaker and the masculine images reflected back to her – by moon, mirror, or 'someone else's poem.' These images are not only male, but mockingly so: they 'jeer' at her. At the same time, 'Angel' attempts to define the terms of a personal poetics. In this effort, it clings to a romantic equation between art and suffering even as it recounts the speaker's 'most potent exorcism' against that attraction (*DF*, 25).

Jean Mallinson was the to first observe, back in 1981, that the conflict in poems like 'Angel' 'is between the woman as woman and the woman as poet' (21). In *This Difficult Flowring*, the result of this conflict is – to reprise an earlier Lowther title – 'a kind of wrestling' with tone, which oscillates between the open vulnerability of 'Angel,' on the one hand, and an affected, macho posturing elsewhere – an over-compensation attributable to the very real pressure that many women at the time felt, to 'act like a man' if they wanted to be taken seriously. In 'Baby You Tell Me,' for instance, the woman poet, the 'babe,' is told to toughen up intellectually, 'to grow teeth in [her] cranium.' This gauntlet is quickly picked up and thrown back with cavalier cockiness: 'Anybody's going to eat me / he's going to know/ he's had a meal' (*DF*, 19). The final stanza's faint echo of Gwendolyn MacEwen's 'A Breakfast for Barbarians' ('by God that was a meal') also points to contemporary female voices that Lowther turned to, with especial attention, around this time. Both MacEwen's *A Breakfast for Barbarians* and Atwood's award-winning

Circle Game had been published in 1966. If Lowther's poems, like everyone's, were going to 'rise out of somebody else's poem,' then what better than the poem of another woman of her own generation, a writer confronted by similar struggles for social parity and intellectual respect?

Fundamentally, Lowther's first book represents an expansion on the theme of tenuous domesticity that she had been testing out in unpublished drafts such as 'House' and 'The Feminine Mystique.' The book's opening poem is darkly titled 'Damn Doom':

> Damn doom to
>   day after day
>   break our bright wishes
>   on this work:
> to carve a simple beauty
>   out of chaos.
> To make
>   in this multi-motioned grid
>   a lattice loop
>   of space/time tamed
> as air is tamed in a vase
>   or a woven basket.
>
> Best break the world
>   like a wild horse
>   or house
>   the wind (*DF*, 7)

'This work,' on which 'bright wishes' are broken is both the work of domestication, 'of space/time tamed / as air is tamed in a vase,' and *this* work, the green pages of *This Difficult Flowring*. '*This* work,' with its wishes cast in the infinitive – 'to carve' and 'to make' – is answered with a sceptic note that already anticipates the mocking 'Angel': one might as well try to tame 'the world' at large, 'or house/ the wind.' In an earlier incarnation, 'Damn Doom' had been entitled 'Love Is to Go on Living with Each Other.' It was written when Lowther was only about three years into marriage with a man who apparently felt that it was burdensome enough to just go on living, period. As he had said by 1964: 'there is nothing to live for.'

This Difficult Flowring's focus on domestic themes – maternity, mar-

riage, sexuality – suggests Lowther's participation in the larger project
of Canadian women's writing (and visual art) in the sixties. As Jean Mallinson, Nadine McInnis, and many others have remarked, this entailed
both a concerted reclamation of female experience as a legitimate 'literary' subject, and a self-conscious re-vision of the predominantly male
tradition of erotic love poetry in which women figured as muse (or
'babe'). In this respect, alongside works from the period by writers like
Atwood and MacEwen, Lowther's first collection recalls Dorothy Livesay's *The Unquiet Bed* (1967), with its artful demand for equal elbow
room: 'the woman I am / is not what you see / move over love / make
room for me' (Livesay 1972: 292).

As successors to Livesay's robust 'mid-life love poems,' Lowther's
poems similarly insist on the specificity of a female perspective on sexuality, and also simultaneously articulate a younger woman's 'struggles
against being silenced' in 'this uncharted poetic territory' (McInnis
1994: 63, 65). The book's closing sequence, an interestingly experimental, if uneven, long poem sequence entitled 'The Insider: A Poem for
Voices,' soliloquizes an anonymous 'woman's voice' in sonnet form:

> I am a woman; all that I might be
> is like a cloud or mist in which I live.
> Dragging my sex like a great dark sack with me,
> I learned that this was all I had to give.
> I brought to him my gift of female thighs,
> my sex in a silken bowl of belly and hair;
> he entered me with groans and hungry cries,
> then washed himself as though I were a whore.
> He'd read the pamphlets from the Board of Health
> and knew that girls who give must be unclean,
> yet knew of nothing else to choose from wealth
> of all a giving woman might have been.
> Now, though I curse my sex, this heavy heat,
> I will not give unless the giving's sweet. (*DF*, 40).

'Christ! I've never read poetry like this by a woman!' an overwrought
male reviewer of *This Difficult Flowring* gasped: 'In the intricate genre of
modern love poetry, the Canadian poetess ... has her male counterpart
dragging his uncouth tail. Pat Lowther's bio-logic-poetic mystique roils
the male ego, and rolls in the humming womb' (Gasparini 1969: 232).
The 'poetess' was not amused by this hyperventilating review of her 'bio-

logic-poetic' feminine 'mystique,' which she dismissed as 'embarrassing.' To her sincere dismay, it was, however, reprinted on the back cover of her next book.[11]

But the example from 'The Insider' – and the response such poems prompted in readers – indicate more than just Lowther's growing facility with adapting traditional forms in the service of new declarations of sexual self-determination: 'I will not give unless the giving's sweet.' The poignant undercurrent of the unresolved 'curse [of] sex, this heavy heat,' was the abiding dilemma she shared with emancipated predecessors from Edna St Vincent Millay to her more immediate mentor, Dorothy Livesay. Lowther's own 'wide-wombed' ability to 'pour forth litters of children / mouthfuls of kisses and shrieks' in the 'smeary congress of kitchens,' was clearly a deeply satisfying cause for celebration (*DF*, 18). But the happy creative chaos loosed by her own fecundity also marked a site of tension, a deeper ambivalence about sexuality and maternity that Lowther would return to and revisit throughout her career.

'Wanting,' for instance, a poem first published in *Intrepid* in 1969, before its appearance in *Milk Stone*, captures the paradox of female sexuality as a source of both empowerment and potential vulnerability. As its title suggests, the poem signals both the imperative of the woman poet's desire and her simultaneous 'fear' that she will be *mis*-taken by a lover conditioned to see her only in his own terms, as a sexual other whose 'wanting' amounts, basically, to an absence or 'lack':

> I am arrogant
> knowing
> what I can do
> for a man
>
> I am arrogant
> for fear
> I may be broken
> utterly open
> and he not see
> the flower shape of me. (*MS*, 46)

The trope of sexuality as an ambiguous form of 'breaking' – 'a terrible pleasure' or 'a soft explosion / miraculous as rain' – persists throughout *A Stone Diary*, as well. Addressing 'the bones' of long-buried 'sisters,' Lowther would remember again 'how love broke us / in that helplessly desired / breaking, and men / and children ransacked our flesh' (*SD*, 92).

To the young writers who gathered at places like the Advance Mattress when the author of *This Difficult Flowring* read her intimate poems of domestic triumph and trial, Lowther struck some, like Patrick Lane, as a strange curiosity. For one thing, 'she didn't take drugs,' as he recalls:

> She'd stand up [at readings], and there would be this nicely dressed woman – she didn't go [to readings] in a pair of jeans and make sure her hair was dirty before she read. She was a mother, she was raising kids. There she was, standing in front of these hairy people who were all smoking grass and talking about their latest acid trip, and she was reading a poem like the Mediterranean one ['Two Babies in Two Years'], about this woman going through the whole process of moving into middle age. (Quoted in Grescoe 1976: 17–18)

Older (and, apparently, cleaner) than the 'hairy,' spaced-out hippies and students who crashed at the Advance, Lowther was in some ways slightly out of sync with the very crowd responsible for encouraging her book into being in the first place.

But though she may not have 'fit' quite seamlessly into the literary scene that people like Lane remember, Lowther had already begun to use her own sense of the relativity of her position as material for her work. Even as the poems in *This Difficult Flowring* contributed to a broader contemporary effort to *make space* in the literary public domain for women's private, domestic experience, the domestic spaces realized in Lowther's poetry are also marked by a distinctive awareness of the complexity and fragility of that experience itself. Domesticity, she had clearly come to recognize, denoted not just a 'somewhat enclosed' space, a location providing a 'viewpoint' for 'the woman, or housewife,' as she had written to Jacob Zilber at *Prism* a few years since. As books like Betty Friedan's would have suggested to her, the housewife's 'house' was also a socially determined structure for women's experience – a set of conventions naturalized, not a 'natural' container or place holder.

In Vancouver during the late sixties, this was precisely the idea also taken up by visual artists such as Gathie Falk, whose first ceramic installation work, *Home Environment* (1968), featured a living room plastered in cloying pink, with the odd chicken carcass and dead fish strategically placed out of place. Lowther's poetic destabilizations of domestic space were rendered in somewhat darker hues, reconfirming her sense of the housewife as 'even a little frightening thing to be.' In 'The Complicated Airflow,' the bottom drops out – the foundations of the 'house' are the first to go:

> The complicated airflow in the house
> stirred by my passing sets
> the doors to opening and closing
> one and then another
> in an unknown order
> like a pack of cards playing
> its own solitaire.
> The echoes fade like wooden etudes.
> I think sometimes my passage
> through this hall is like a falling
> down a clef into the sea
> and where I hit, a hissing
> fault springs on the surface
> (warp in a spider web,
> spidering of a mirror)
>
> What is whiter than hurt water?
> What is more flawed than a broken
> stave of sound? (*DF*, 17)

By the time of 1974's *Milk Stone* there is an even more radical de-naturalization of hearth and home, in 'Toward a Pragmatic Psychology':

> Every night at midnight the house falls.
> Stairs fold like pleated paper.
> The walls slide down
> a straight incline
> like wooden rain.
> Pigeons desert the eaves and fly east.
> The roof is swept away
> a pointed arc
> beaching at last on some intersection
> under trolley wires and pruned trees.
>
> Every morning we have to
> compose the house anew

> paper the walls
> reinvent principles of engineering
> make sure we have elbows,
> mouths, places to sit.
> Every night we lie down
> without prayer. (*MS*, 71).

First, the pitfall into a 'sea' of white, 'hurt water.' Then a whole household flimsy as origami and obliged to 'reinvent' itself on a daily basis. Lowther's domestic poetry exceeds a critique of houses and housewives as necessarily manufactured 'things.' As utterances inspired by her own family life, such poems also record her plunge into the despairing 'sea' of her husband's 'hurt water,' the discordant note of his 'broken / stave of sound.' At the same time, they are poems that trace the architecture of a domestic experience 'complicated' by low income: the record of a consciousness never entirely free from the prospect of another arbitrarily imposed decampment. And, finally, they are poems which also locate Lowther in the specific geography of her West Coast home, where fog and moisture do insinuate human dwelling space; the weather does transfigure reality in profound ways; and the land mass is, indeed, unstable. There was not one, but many reasons why '[e]very night' the walls supporting domestic convention and invention might begin to shake, begin to fuel the next landslide: 'down / a straight incline / like wooden rain.'

About seven hundred copies of *This Difficult Flowring* were printed and sold for two dollars a copy, at a time when two Canadian dollars still commanded its own pink paper bill. Patrick Lane and Seymour Mayne remember the print run selling out. Following on the heels of the two healthy babies she had birthed in 1966 and 1967, the appearance of her first book should have been a happy time in Lowther's life. But in the months following the book's publication, one 'male ego' truly 'roil[ed]' by *This Difficult Flowring* (Gasparini 1969: 232) began to flare, and Roy became very unhappy. He found great fault with Kathy, just then approaching her thirteenth birthday and vigorously testing parental limits, as thirteen-year-olds sometimes do. At this time, Roy was still hanging onto a full-time teaching job, but the family's budget, with debts, rent ($160 a month), maintenance payments, and living expenses, was extremely tight (CATT, 3:438). It seemed to rankle at Roy that he paid more in monthly maintenance to his former wife, for three children, than Pat received from her former husband, for one child. He observed that his wife earned one hundred dollars during this period from poetry readings – 'she was pleased and proud of it; deservedly so' – but he complained that she was careless and irresponsible with her money.

In the weeks leading up to Christie's first birthday, Roy stormed off, temporarily deserting his family for a hotel room in New Westminster, and citing his wife's failure to rein in Kathy as the main reason (RLJ, 1:ix–x). Patrick Lane registered his concern in a letter to Seymour Mayne on 8 November 1968: 'Roy Lowther left Pat and things [are] pretty much mixed up there – he might be back by now – I told her if she got uptight I'd give her $50 from Very Stoned.' Mayne wrote back a few days later: 'As for Pat Lowther – you mean Roy left her with two kids, why didn't he leave her alone from the beginning – I suppose we could give her fifty now, and maybe more later.'[12] Roy came back of his own volition, of course, in a week – apparently without any prompting or communication at all from Pat in the interim (RLJ, 1:ix).

A few weeks after Roy's return, Lowther wrote another missive to Dee Livesay, this time apologetically explaining her 'inexcusably churlish silence':

> What happened was that shortly after our last conversation, problems began erupting in my family – some of them foreseeable, but others completely unanticipated. They kept coming one after another, and just seemed to heap up and overwhelm me. I've really been so distraught these last several weeks that at one point I felt in danger of losing my ability to function at all. Certainly I've been functioning on a minimal level.[13]

However, 'things' were 'a little calmer at the moment,' she added. And the reason she was writing, anyway, was to thank Livesay for having written an important letter of recommendation. It was a letter that would soon help secure Lowther's first Canada Council grant.

Chapter 7

That 'Spinning Female Thing'

Over the winter of 1967, as Lowther had been preparing the final manuscript for *This Difficult Flowring*, Milton Acorn was staying downstairs again, for several months.[1] He didn't confine himself to the nether regions of the house, though. Patrick Lane remembers him coming banging upstairs at 566 East 46th Avenue, 'black cigar stub clenched in his teeth' and 'fists clenched,' 'raging about Gwen MacEwen, how she [had] once more betrayed him,' and about 'the betrayals of the Trotskyists, the Marxist-Leninists' (1995: 30). 'What a crazy man, yeah,' Kathy recollects, affectionately. From her own adolescent perspective, the 'loud' and 'almost scary-looking' Acorn was, nevertheless, a welcome presence for the inadvertent oddities and spectacles he afforded. For one thing, he enlivened the dinner table, once shaking the salt cellar so vigorously in mid-peroration that the lid flew off, covering his plate with an unexpectedly generous dump of salt – and bringing his declamations to an abrupt end. Moreover, Acorn was a distraction for Kathy's stepfather, who otherwise had the family walking 'on eggshells most of the time,' for fear of triggering one of Roy's ranting temper tantrums.[2]

Between Roy Lowther and Milton Acorn there would have been no shortage of ranting in the household. Among other things that Roy (like Betty Friedan's husband) ranted about in the years that followed his wife's debut book was the 'untidiness' of the 'damn bitch' he had married, his 'harried, nondomesticable, intellectual wife' (RLJ, 1:61G, iii). According to him, 'poverty can reflect on the man, but untidiness tends to reflect on the woman' (RLJ, 2:118).

The first installment of that 'intellectual' wife's first Canada Council grant arrived in April 1969, and it was income every bit as valuable to Lowther for the new level of literary validation it symbolized, as for the welcome cash infusion it brought. Though 'plagued by a succession of minor illnesses' that spring, the happy grant recipient joked to Livesay about 'hoarding and mumbling' over 'the first cheque' when it arrived. But she also added, in a more serious vein: 'I have several projects planned . . . and feel quite confident of being able to work well soon ... Simply the freedom that this grant makes possible is bound to make a great difference.' In the same letter, she notified Livesay of a poem she'd written after reading *The Unquiet Bed* and an unspecified 'book on gardening, some of which is plagiarized in the poem.'[3] 'Growing the Seasons,' a poem of tribute to Livesay, was published that fall in *Quarry* magazine, and – for whatever reason – the perpetually money-strapped Lowther never did cash the cheque she received in payment for that poem. That five-dollar cheque, signed by Tom Marshall and dated 29 October 1969, still exists among her papers.

Lowther's first official writer's grant was modest – two thousand dollars was the first installment of the three-and-a-half grand total – but it came at a crucial time. Because before she could even finish 'hoarding and mumbling' over her new fortune, Roy came home one day the following month to announce that he'd lost his full-time job with the Coquitlam School Board. According to him, the 'smashing of [his] teaching career' was 'a grave wrong' that amounted to the school administration's 'suppression of [his] innovative tactics in choral music' (RLJ, 1:57; 2:106). Roy appealed his dismissal and was additionally put out, since he felt that he 'should have had [his] wife with [him] in the struggle' against the school board, as was only befitting for 'wives of socialists.' But by 1969, Lowther was no longer the trusting 'recruit' she had been in 1963, and no longer prepared to 'go to bat' for her husband any more (RLJ, 1:92). Ineligible for unemployment insurance, at least for the summer months ahead, Roy was also unlikely to find yet another new position and so would have to turn to social assistance. Which meant that Lowther's new-found 'freedom' grant would have to be reported as family income. Roy portrays his wife as both 'incensed' and tearfully upset by seeing 'the money go up in smoke for us to keep the family,' instead of being used as she saw fit, for writing purposes (RLJ, 1:57).

Roy remembered his firing, 'most unfortunately,' as having come 'on the same day' as his wife's Canada Council cheque 'arrived in the house,' which is not exactly accurate, if his memory of the date of his own dismissal 'on a particular day in May 1969' is to be trusted (RLJ, 1:57). Lowther's own correspondence with Livesay indicates that the cheque's arrival predated Roy's firing by some weeks. It is possible that she didn't tell her husband about it right away; she had been thinking of using at least part of her grant money for travel. It is also possible that Roy conflated time in retrospect; certainly, his version of history is more striking for its intensification of the black-and-white contrast between his latest professional disgrace and the most recent sign, after *This Difficult Flowring*, of his wife's professional elevation. At least for him, he remembered the spring of 1969 as signalling a 'full turn' in their marriage (RLJ, 1:56).

Lowther's own records on the subject of her marriage are typically more oblique and fragmentary; her correspondence with Livesay from this period alludes to 'certain paralyses of will' setting in 'when things go badly (as they usually do),' and to her awareness of 'sex often being a sublimation for other drives.'[4] But by now there were patterns beginning to establish themselves in the six-year-old union which she could not fail to miss: in a sort of perverse, inverse correlation to one another, any sign of growing literary achievement on her part was answered by an increasingly dramatic sign of Roy's inability to cope.

And yet, despite this disturbing disequilibrium, and the new strain of Roy's unemployment, Lowther persevered with her work. In fact, regardless of her inability to use her Canada Council grant as she would have wished, the recognition and the legitimacy it conferred upon her seems to have been enough to usher in an intensely productive period of writing by the decade's turn. During 1969–70, Lowther made real leaps, writing some of the strongest poems that would eventually appear in *Milk Stone, A Stone Diary*, and the posthumously published *Time Capsule*. These included 'Woman on/against Snow,' 'Coast Range,' and 'The Chinese Greengrocers,' all of which were first published in little magazines and anthologies by 1971. Not only that, but she also struck a healthy new determination to 'considerably cut down on my smoking,' as she advised Livesay during the summer of 1969. Which she virtuously did, for awhile. 'Nobody has even noticed,' she added, though, in a bit of a sulk.[5]

Banishing the demon weed was a resolution that would come and go; within a couple years, she was again writing about her struggle with the habit, this time informing Fred Cogswell that she had been ill: '... a lung sprung a leak, causing quite a lot of pain and fatigue, but it seems to be healing itself without any treatment except that I cut down drastically on my smoking.'[6] By that time, Lowther had good reason to be monitoring her Matinées. On 25 April 1970, her father, Arthur, the man who had given his eldest daughter magical childhood memories of Rice Lake, died suddenly of a heart attack, at sixty-four.

Lowther had registered a shift in the formerly happy-go-lucky Arthur in his later years. Not only had he never warmed to his surprise son-in-law, Roy, but as he aged, the spirits of the family 'showman' seemed to flag – perhaps, at least in part, a toll exacted from decades of toil at the shipyards which had also claimed his father. In *This Difficult Flowring*, Lowther had written about her father, that once 'confirmed / lamp-shade-on-the-head man' and 'ukulele' soloist, in a poem called 'In Praise of Youth':

> Gone are the grass skirts
> the turned out hats
> the bundles of leeks behind the ears.
>
> Man it makes me old
> to see him fat and sixty
> doing his drinking sitting down
> while the lampshades
> stay on the lamps. (*DF*, 33)

Arthur's death may have led Lowther to confront some of her own assumptions – about herself, as much as the men in her life. It may or may not have been a coincidence that after he died, she never again looked to men markedly senior than she herself for companionship; her next two lovers were in her own age bracket. Certainly, for a woman who had already come to observe that sex – like money – was 'often . . . a sublimation for other drives,' a prompting bound up with other needs and insecurities, Arthur's passing may have provoked Lowther to recognize the paternalistic ideals lurking in her past attractions to older men like Bill Domphousse, Ward Carson – and Roy.

If so, then it was an insight that by 1970 pointed up a cruel irony: namely, that Roy, who in the early years of their courtship had appeared a self-assured source of knowledge, guidance, and even potential economic stability, was not only none of the above, but proving ever more regressively erratic in behaviour and judgment, and reliant upon her as a consequence. Far from functioning as any sort of competent figure of paternal authority, Roy, as Patrick Lane suggests, was gradually becoming 'just . . . another child to her . . . someone she had to look after.'[7]

Except for stints as a substitute teacher, which also dwindled away over time, Roy's years of reliable employment ended with his 1969 dismissal. And, despite her best diligence, the repercussions for Pat were obvious and immediate. Expected to 'produce' artistically by the terms of her Canada Council grant, Lowther was now faced with the extra pressure of finding ways to generate income for the family whenever and wherever possible. At the same time, while Roy took on some child-care duties from this point forward, his presence at home did not exactly divest Lowther of the responsibilities and the expectations placed upon her as a mother and housewife, by Roy himself, among others – responsibilities to which the ubiquitous scraps of grocery lists and school PTA notes among her papers attest. By 1970, more than ever, she needed to summon that creative and regenerative energy that she had earlier dubbed 'the spinning female thing that lives in me.'

As a means of focusing that constructive energy, Lowther withdrew – emotionally, sexually, and intellectually – from Roy in the years immediately following *This Difficult Flowring*. Her part in their 'commitment' pact necessitated her physical presence in the household, but that presence was now more and more discernibly directed toward the children alone. The umbilicus, that 'partway-unwound / spiral of bloody cord,' was the most fundamental thread of her feminine creativity, the 'omphalos' of her world, and it bound her to the daughters in the household – daughters whose birthright as girls was, as she saw it, to replicate her own 'spinning': 'each is the weaver of her province: / spinning a tight fuzzy world out / of her own body / and distracted mind' (*DF*, 8, 40, 18). To the children of her two marriages, Lowther tried to remain as fully available as possible. So, when she wasn't on her red pleatherette chair, tapping away at her Remington in the dining room, or off to readings (on her own, now), she would likely have been in the 'smeary congress' of her kitchen, supervising the crayon productions that also constitute part of her archive, and making meatloaf, ling cod, or tuna casserole. These were meals which the family would then eat, as Kathy recalls, around her dining-table workspace. Elsewhere, too, Lowther would be throwing herself into some 'foolish' domestic project or other: painting her daughters' bedroom; making 'puppets or fruitcake'; or, as she undertook one Christmas, building them a magnificent 'castle out of huge cardboard boxes.'[8] Not exactly a castle in the air, but one made, pragmatically, out of materials she had to hand.

The few quiet hours of leisure that Lowther had to herself, she occasionally spent over chips and wine with her old VPS friend, Lorraine Vernon. More often, maybe while listening to music by a favoured com-

poser like Jean Sibelius, she put those early Rice Lake lessons in structural linguistics to work at her favourite hobby: playing solitaire
scrabble, which she did with a passion. (In his journals, Roy offered esti-
mates of the time and frequency with which she indulged this pastime;
he was jealous of her scrabble too.) Quiet hours of 'fiddling around with
words' in solitary board games, though, as with other peacefully creative
pastimes, were offset by what her correspondence, notebooks, and
friends all reveal as the barely contained chaos of her routine home life,
a life that more often than not threatened to spin out of control by
sheer virtue of the distractions and claims it placed upon her. Trying to
get a new grant application together in a 'fine, last-minute frenzy,' she
abruptly signed off one missive to Livesay: 'I'll end now, as one of the
children just vomited.' Or, to Fred Cogswell:

> Dear Fred,
> Happy new year. My Christmas went like this: Beth, my middle girl, had flu,
> I had sick headache for five days running, flooded the livingroom ceiling
> (don't ask), Christie, the youngest, dropped a brick on her foot, and was
> just getting over that when she came down with chickenpox. So you see, in
> some respects I do live a typical domestic life.[9]

There were 'typical' domestic crises and accidents, though, and then
there was the chronic state of disorder at 566 East 46th Avenue – no
longer a joking matter, as the 'perpetual arrears / on the gas bill' had
once been for the newly married St George Street poet, with fewer
stresses and burdens. 'Dear Arlene,' Lowther would handwrite to her
executive secretary at the League of Canadian Poets in a future, 'fine,
last-minute frenzy,' distractedly misdating her letter by a year: '#! typewriter's on the blink again. And it was just repaired! *Four* typewriters in
this house and not one working!'[10] Along with the broken doors and
Roy's poorly maintained old cars, the unreliable typewriters added to
the clutter of dysfunctional household stuff that to some degree mirrored the deteriorating relationship of the cohabitants on East 46th. In
a painfully vivid magazine vignette entitled 'Pat Lowther, c. 1973,'
Patrick Lane reconstructs his impression of the household:

> The house is filthy, dishes stacked in crusty piles on the counters, in the
> sink, on the table; broken garbage bags by the back door, food spilling out,
> rotting vegetables and bones. The children's clothes, hers, Roy's, are
> strewn across the floor, piled in corners, nests for the cats and children. Pat

is oblivious. She steps over, around, through the wreckage of the kitchen to the dining room where books and papers, half-finished poems, shreds of manuscript lie in piles on the table and the floor. (1995: 30)

It is a portrayal of the Lowther household that accords with too many other sources to be very far off-base.

The fact that Lowther lacked a private office space to work in (Roy took over Kathy's bedroom for this purpose when the eldest daughter left) and that her poetry arose out of the very eye, as it were, of this household maelstrom is worth noting, if for no other reason than that it accounts for her perpetual problems with keeping track of her poems, her briefcase, and even (in one instance) an entire manuscript. 'You'll think me terribly disorganized, which I am,' one such confession to Livesay begins, 'but at this point I'm not at all sure which poems of mine you have. After I sent you the first batch, I sent some more very hastily and without keeping a proper record.' And a few weeks later: 'If you ever do find that original group of poems I sent you, could you shoot them back? I seem to have lost my only copy of one of them.'[11]

Patrick Lane observes that Lowther's work environment also testifies to the self-absenting nature of creativity: 'It's like a strange kind of schizophrenia where one world does not touch the other. You can go off and ... do the writing while everything around you is in a state of collapse.' He offers the anecdote of the poet John Newlove as a counterpart for Lowther:

John [would] sit in the middle of a room, in a chair, with a typewriter and a steel table, with a circle drawn around it with red crayon about three feet on either side of the thing, and outside of that, the kids would scream and yell, [but] they weren't allowed to come across or step inside the circle ... The outside of the room was surrounded with empty beer bottles and empty cartons and kids' toys and the kids pooping their pants, and inside the circle the floor was swept and clean, [and there was] John with his nice pair of slacks on, and a clean white shirt, and a circle with a red crayon ... So there's the lives of poets, you see. Pat was the same way. Pat could live in the squalor of that home and go [to] work at a typewriter, and that [squalor] would just disappear.[12]

Similar, yes. But not exactly 'the same.' As a mother, Lowther drew no red circles around herself: there simply was no inviolate zone. The children's doodles and scrawled messages that sometimes illustrate her notebooks and typescripts reinforce this fact. Likewise, if a child vomits or poops, *someone* has to stop working.

While she may have seemed to others 'oblivious' of the physical 'wreckage' of her home, Lowther was actually keenly conscious of it. If the 'squalor'of her surroundings 'disappeared' while she composed, then it also reappeared in sharp and taxing relief whenever something or someone made her surface from her work. Her housekeeping skills – or lack of such skills – had already been a subject of concern for her mother and for friends like Lorraine Plowman at the time of her first marriage to Bill Domphousse. Now that she had more children than ever to mind, Roy railed about her not putting 'traveling' household things back in their place; about her lack of acquaintance with the broom (especially 'after 1968'); about her 'poetry submissions, poetry ms., personal things on and in the dressers, etc' (RLJ, 2:97). Over the years, she had already enjoyed frequent opportunities to measure herself against standards of domesticity that were supposed to be 'every female's true affinity.'

'I am a spider / spinning a bandage / out of my guts. / Some day the roll will run / empty': 'WHAT WILL I DO?'(*DF,* 22). In *This Difficult Flowring,* Lowther posed this upper-case question, half-facetiously, as an Arachne affecting hysterical discomposure in the fifth of 'Seven Purgative Poems' about the purgatory of domestic life. But in reality, the unruly state of the household was no laughing matter. It testified to the increasingly hectic schedule that an often overwhelmed Lowther juggled after 1968, and to the minimal cooperation she received on this front from Roy – who might have chosen to exercise the broom more frequently himself, rather than taking off in his ancient Ford or Viva to head for some nearby park and contemplate his sorrows, as he liked to do (CATT, 3:380).

Clearly, somewhere among the 'wreckage' Lowther lived in was a fierce repudiation of the traditionally prim bourgeois housewife. For her, no less than for Gathie Falk, a world in which there was a 'correct' place for everything, and everything was in its 'proper' place, was basically a fascistic nightmare. On the other hand, at some point, creative over-'flowring' spilled into disabling chaos. Even if she'd borrowed John Newlove's red crayon, the mess was making it harder for Lowther to find a place to draw this line.

As a gamesome twenty-seven-year-old with still untapped reserves of idealism, Pat Domphousse had in good faith taken on her second husband's suffering causes: his painful childhood, his painful political 'persecution,' his painful first marriage and its painful aftermath. But by the turn of the decade, 'the spinning female thing' which had once sought to sooth that suffering was weary of it, and otherwise preoccupied with a busy household round of toddlers and teenagers – not to mention with a burst of creative energy that marked, among other things, the beginnings of *Milk Stone* and *A Stone Diary*. While her domestic life unravelled, the poems spun out. And one of the themes Lowther now redoubled her focus upon was precisely the relationship between making art and the art of home-making, between making and unmaking, between doing and being undone.

In its winter 1970 issue, *The Fiddlehead* magazine published her four-part poem 'Penelopes.' The turn here is to Homer's famous legend of Odysseus and his faithful wife, Penelope. During an epic absence by her husband, off at sea, Penelope stalls the many suitors clamouring for her hand by saying she will choose a new husband when she has finished a shroud, which she weaves by day and unweaves every night. As Lowther's plural title accurately indicates, multiple post-Homeric versions of the myth abound, including versions that render the faithful wife as a whore who succumbs to all of her one-hundred-plus suitors in succession and conceives the lecherous god Pan in the process. Some versions have Odysseus returning to discover Penelope's infidelity and either banishing or killing her in retaliation (Smith 1967: 183; Grimal 1990: 337–8).

Lowther's own 'Penelopes' are variations on a theme: four different scenes, each connected by a thread of 'un-learning.' The first section focuses on dance, the art of movement that Lowther's mother and Aunt Isabelle knew well. The dancer's grace makes the dance seem effortless: 'we do not think of years unlearning / earth's hard facts. / or of the sweat it takes / to break the pattern the mind makes' (*MS*, 54). The second section focuses on the stasis of a tapestry panel, a fourteenth-century arras of a lady and a unicorn, 'woven perhaps by some less faithful dame' – whether 'less faithful' than the virtuous Penelope or the speaker herself, the poem leaves ambiguous at this point. The eroticized encounter between 'maid and unicorn' is a lesson in 'twin duplicity': the maid is left to hope 'that innocence may be as it appears,' while the 'timid unicorn' 'must now renounce all learning of his life / and willfully walk forward to be caught' (*MS*, 55). In the poem's third part, two levels of art merge as the speaker's identity merges with that of the mythical Penelope in the past tense: 'when I was Penelope,' she tells us,

'[I] unravelled every night / what I had learnt of pain.' Hers is the work of 'slyly tearing, thread by thread' whatever she has learned of 'enemies,' of love ('the heart's maze'), and of ratiocination ('the demon-perilled journey between / first   and second thought') (*MS*, 55–6).

The fourth and strongest section of the poem is a contemporized retelling of the Homeric myth from Penelope's point of view: 'So the old boy came home, / burst brawling into the anteroom, / interrupting forever covert yawns / scurrilous anecdotes / sweet songs – .' After Odysseus's violent re-entry – he dispatches his 'scurrilous' rivals by 'hack[ing]' their limbs, and then 'howl[ing]' to his 'woman' for a 'towel' to clean up – his presence at home is one of morose and restless boredom. He examines Penelope's 'tapestry' and decides to 'accep[t] her as loyal.' But there is 'distance' and 'veiled inattention' 'in his eyes' now. Preoccupied, 'the old boy' dozes 'over wine,' makes love 'indifferently,' his eyes always 'suck[ed]' back out to sea: 'in a matter of weeks / he was off again.' Penelope is 'left with her flawed work,' and has a 'choice' to 'face':

> whether to let her age-long labor fall,
> grow old and bitter, turn her face to the wall,
> or somehow to gather will,
> begin unpicking the pattern of her life,
> and weave again
> > designs
> > > of innocence and disbelief ... (*MS*, 56–7,
> > > ellipses in the original)

Heightened at times by deliberately sing-song end rhymes, Lowther's ironic deflation of classical Greek mythology in 'Penelopes' – especially her re-telling of 'the old boy's' heroic story from the perspective of his disillusioned wife – reinforces her rapid attunement to the pulse of the poetic present. Jay MacPherson, P.K.Page, Margaret Atwood, and Elizabeth Brewster were among the Canadian writers experimenting with such adaptations, subversions, and transformations of canonical myth as a strategy for feminist poetics around this period (Mallinson 1981: 47–91). In Lowther's case, though, the abiding significance of myth for contemporary culture was something of a hobbyhorse, anyhow. She   had certainly been thinking about the subject since her St George Street period, when she wrote an essay entitled 'Rumpelstiltskin, Dr. Freud, Adam and Eve, and Others.' The essay traces the appropriation and 'manipulation' of myths – Greek and Christian – within the pop-

Freudian consumer culture of the sixties. Echoing Plato's *Republic*, the essay concludes that the real 'fable-makers of today, at least in North America,' are 'ad-writers and the producers of commercial television.'[13]

Lowther's essay casts a critical eye on the uses of myth in therapeutic and economic arenas, where canny 'fable-makers' like 'Dr. Freud,' or the 'Rumpelstiltskin' spin-men of the advertising industry, 'revive' and 'distort' old fictions for newer ends. In this regard, feminist poets like Lowther were now giving back as good as they got. But in addition to the political question of the uses of myth, 'Penelopes' also raises subtler questions about knowledge and ignorance. The quartet's recurrent exploration of the gaps between appearance and reality, 'innocence and disbelief,' creation and destruction, 'first and second thought,' also spans the deep fault between 'un-doing' and 'un-learning.' Though it might take some 'sweat,' 'the pattern of [a] life' can be picked apart and un-done. But 'un-learned'? Like many Lowther poems, 'Penelopes' ultimately charts an irrevocable, Blakean 'fall' into experience, acknowledging the impossibility of fully un-learning what is once known or experienced. These ambiguities of knowledge mark the poem's unanswered questions, in the end. We never do 'learn' for sure whether 'the old boy' Odysseus was deceived or right in 'accepting' Penelope as 'as loyal,' for example.[14] Nor do we ever find out what 'choice' it is that Penelope actually makes in the final section. Trailing off into open-ended ellipses, the poem leaves the reader suspended indeterminately somewhere between the 'twin duplicity' of knowledge and ignorance.

A sequel to the 'spinning female' poems of *This Difficult Flowring*, 'Penelopes' reworks the theme of domestic, feminine creativity that Lowther also began to explore around this time through Inuit mythology in poems such as 'Woman on/against Snow' and 'String Figure Man outside the Door' ('Didn't I too catch the sun / in a cradle spun / from my own gut-string?' [*MS*, 17]). The poems based on Native mythology demanded a good deal of research and reading, which Lowther snuck in where and when possible. Most weekends, Roy and she took the children to North Vancouver to visit their grandmother, and Lowther would bring her books and scribblers along. There, she would jot notes while having a cup of tea with her mother, or answer her sister Brenda over the rim of whatever she was reading.

New opportunities were also opening up fast. By the summer of 1972, the same year that her unbound portfolio, *The Age of the Bird,* appeared, Raymond Souster approached her to serve as a League representative for British Columbia, and she was also invited to join in as Atwood's opening act for a multi-city reading tour. 'I feel confident I have a direction in my work now,' an exuberant Lowther wrote to Livesay that summer: 'I have not one, but two, clearly defined projects ahead. Wow! Love, Pat.'[15] The 'not one, but two clearly defined projects' were *Milk Stone* and *A Stone Diary,* which she now began to shape and separate out from one another as the poems appeared contemporaneously.

But Lowther's increasing activities with the League, which had begun to involve brief periods of travel away from home for readings and annual meetings, were also beginning to reshape her world. In Vancouver during October 1972, she met for the first time in person an editor with whom she had corresponded in the recent past, Eugene McNamara. Later that fall, the two met up again at the League's annual meeting in Edmonton. American born and educated, McNamara was at the time a writer and a professor at the University of Windsor, where he taught creative writing alongside novelist Alistair MacLeod. Urbane and accomplished, McNamara was only five years Lowther's senior; like her, he was also married with a family. In Edmonton, the initial attraction between the two developed into a relationship (CATT, 1:167). Predictably enough under the circumstances, Lowther's liaison with McNamara was for the most part destined to play out through Canada Post as a discursive long-distance romance. Over the three years of their relationship, they only met in person five times, and fewer than that as a couple, each time in a different city (CATT, 1:163–5).

According to Brenda, Pat knew that such a far-flung relationship was not likely to presage 'a real future.' But Brenda is also astonished, in retrospect, that her sister even confided in her about the matter – that, in itself, 'was so out of character.'[16] Lowther was discrete about her new love. Like her first, precious Canada Council cheque, she was inclined to 'hoard' it to herself. She probably told her sister about it because, although she recognized the affair for what it was – just that, and not 'a real future' – McNamara's appearance in her life filled her with a renewed sense of hope that was hard for her to contain. At thirty-seven-years old, she wrote to Livesay: 'I know it's silly, but I'm as excited as a young girl.' 'After seeing nothing like this in my future,' she added, with nary a hint of Cassandra-like clairvoyance.[17] What McNamara offered was a temporary release, an occasional respite from the whirlpool of Lowther's daily, domestic round. The infrequency of their meetings made such escapes from her 'bandage spinning' role as nursemaid / spider woman more imaginary than actual, of course, but even the long-distance relationship was enough to sustain a crucial sense of anticipation, possibility, literary stimulation. 'Your letters mean so much,' she wrote to 'Gene': 'proof that there is another life with some sanity and joy.'[18] Perhaps most importantly, McNamara's correspondence provided a source of support for the work of emotional self-resuscitation that Lowther now found herself regularly undertaking as a result of Roy's 'rampages' and 'nasty surprises.'

Unsurprisingly, Lowther's extra-domestic activities and growing profile as a writer continued to provoke fresh outbursts of stormy and aggrieved reaction from her spouse. April of 1973 was 'brilliant' – weatherwise – with 'everything flowering, [and] birds shitting all over the clean laundry.' A stretch of uninterrupted sunshine could almost let Lowther forget 'what a gray day [was] like.'[19] But it was only April 'objectively,' as she put it. Subjectively, the 'it' behind Roy's destructive behaviour was again plunging her into misery that month – this time, an 'absolute despair' of alarming depths. As she wrote to McNamara:

> I seem to be having my semi-annual mini-breakdown – which only means I stand around and shake a lot, I don't do anything. That's the whole trouble I never do anything [sic]. I feel driven to absolute despair requiring some desperate action and there's no action I can take. I can't even die because it would be abandoning my children.
>
> It's only temporary. I'll find some way of living with it again. I always do.[20]

But shaking the fatalistic mood, as she 'always' did, to 'find some way of living with it again,' wasn't easy. A few days later, it was Good Friday, and Lowther was still feeling so far from 'good' that she wrote an even more despondent letter to Joy Kogawa, the young Vancouver poet whom Lowther had come to know in the late sixties, through her Very Stone House associations:

> Weather here is brilliant, all the trees are flowering, and I feel buried alive forever. Amen. It will pass – the feeling, not the fact.
>
> My whole life seems so evil sick disastrous I can't believe in possibilities anymore. When you've been this wrong there aren't any more chances.[21]

With Kogawa, born the same year as Lowther, and also a divorced mother of young children, the self-prognosis was, if anything, less hopeful: only 'the feeling, not the fact' of being 'buried alive forever' would 'pass.' She had already been 'wrong' in her choice of a first husband. That 'choice' had been made as an eighteen-year-old with few options, and even that 'choice' had not yet been remotely 'this wrong.' Now, with the guilt of an 'evil' extramarital affair weighing on her conscience, she faced the 'sick disastrous' consequences of her second marital choice. On that dismal Good Friday, she could not believe in any more 'possibilities' for beginning again, any more 'chances' for resurrection.

The chronic and worsening cracks in her marriage with Roy meant that Lowther, like her Penelope, inevitably came to a point where she realized she had another 'choice' to make. Could she 'somehow ... gather [the] will / [and] begin unpicking the pattern of her life' by leaving the marriage? This would mean taking action – like Odysseus, not the stay-at-home spinner, Penelope. Lowther's friend Lorraine Vernon recalls an aborted attempt Lowther made around this time:

> Pat phoned and asked if . . . I could help her find a suite of her own. She was leaving Roy, she said. We drove her all over town, but found nothing. The following day, I went to her home . . . where she had packed her belongings into cardboard boxes, and I swept and tidied the house to help her in her intention to leave. Roy was away on a canoeing trip in Howe Sound and it was her intention to leave before he returned. She did not leave.[22]

Somewhere in the 'demon-perilled journey between / first and second thought' (*MS*, 56), the Odysseus in Lowther faltered, and her 'choice' derailed, went un-done. It's possible that the 'cardboard boxes' Lorraine Vernon remembers as being 'packed' full of Lowther's 'intention to leave' were the same 'huge cardboard boxes' she later, in a more hopeful mood, converted into a 'castle' for her daughters in December 1973.

To Patrick Lane, who had seen enough of Roy's churlish behaviour since his days as an editor and publisher of Very Stone House, and who also attempted to help Lowther see through her 'intention' of leaving Roy, the situation at 566 East 46th Avenue was getting intolerable to witness. During that same dark spring of 1973 that Lowther wrote in despair to McNamara and Kogawa, Lane gave a reading at the Advance

Mattress and publicly dedicated a poem to Lowther. It was a disturbing poem about exhibitionistic *faux*–masochism – a man who hammers pins into a nerve-dead limb, 'saying: / *It doesn't hurt at all.*'[23] It caused a small scandal among those present that night, and the audience included Lowther.

Chapter 8

It Happens Every Day

'You are quite right – I do know you well enough not to have been insulted.' So Lowther wrote to Lane, who soon apologized for the episode at the Advance Mattress. In accepting Lane's amends, Lowther did, sincerely, what she had in earlier years done for Roy – that is, take on the role of damage control:

> I guess what happened was that being just slightly sloshed, you didn't say exactly what you meant. I understood but others didn't. There has been talk about it, and whenever I've heard it, I've tried to set it straight. I think some people just like to have an excuse for feeling indignant.

Graciously, she went on to elaborate her circumstances in a way that she did only with people she trusted:

> My kids are fine – fascinating & exasperating like all kids I guess. As for Roy, I see now [*sic*] way out of continuing to live with him. I've finally escaped the emotional bondage, much, much too late. Leaving would mean having to be a full-time mother with not [*sic*] time or energy for writing or simply being the person I have to be. Some people could do it but I know my limits. I'd end up so neurotic and bitchy I'd be no good to my kids either. But living as a family is dishonest and harmful too. It's the kind of situation psychologists devise to drive white rats crazy.[1]

Clearly, by Easter of 1973, Lowther felt she had reached an impasse, that she was caught in the kind of maze laboratory scientists might 'devise to drive white rats crazy.' The conflict between her *desire* to leave, on the one hand, and her *reasons* for staying, on the other, is graphically inscribed in the first accidental typo of her letter to Lane – that slash through the '*w*,' which transforms 'now' into 'no.' In a literal sense, that one letter which made the difference between '*now*' and '*no* way out' spelled the real abyss between 'first   and second thought.'

Above all, however, Lowther's response to Lane reveals hers as a dilemma having little to do with the reckless embrace of a 'self-sabotaging' life (Shaidle 2000: B2). Hers was a 'situation' far more complicated than could be solved by strength of will or intention alone. As she expounds it, her conclusion that there was 'no way out of continuing to live with [Roy]' was, rather, based on a grim logic: the factual calculus of time and money squared against the demands of her evolving literary career. What only she herself could determine as a realistic and self-knowing assessment of her own 'limits' as a person, she calculated against her needs as a writer, and against the press of material circumstances that pitted those 'limits' and needs into direct conflict with each other. A family crisis centre of the sort Lorraine Vernon urged her friend to contact may have provided a temporary refuge, but it would not have solved the problem of reconciling full-time parenting with preserving 'time or energy for writing' – the very vocation that, by 1973, Lowther already had reason to hope might some day provide a viable means of escape, if she could only firmly establish her name first.

Indeed, here was one important aspect of the maddening catch: with *Milk Stone* hung up in publishing limbo by this time, Lowther felt a particular pressure to continue producing at this precise moment in her writing life. In order to secure more Canada Council grants (she had applied for her second in 1972), and to gain teaching experience (as she would begin to do in the fall of 1973), she needed, above all, to keep working and publishing in the meantime – *now*. To leave Roy at this point would have necessarily meant putting the brakes to her career, if not taking an enforced temporary hiatus, at the very same time that she felt she could least 'afford any more delays.'[2] The alternative was to stay in the marriage, at least for now, keep the writing going, and, as she would begin to tell friends in the last year of her life, get out once Christie and Beth, by then just seven and nine years of age, were a bit older, and she herself was on a more firmly employable, if not employed, footing.

Lowther's concern to respect her own needs and 'limits' as a woman and a writer (in itself, not the trait of a 'self-sabotaging' masochist) was inextricably bound up with her worries about being an effective parent; as she remarked to Lane, what she wanted most to avoid was placing herself in a position where she would end up 'so neurotic and bitchy [that] I'd be no good to my kids either.' Being an effective parent meant not merely providing financially for her offspring, as she now scrambled to do, but providing for them well over the long haul, by ensuring for herself the livelihood she most wanted and needed, financially modest though that literary livelihood promised to be. She had only to look to Roy to see that a thwarted and resentful being could not be a healthy example for younger beings.

Back on St George Street, Lowther had already contemplated in her notebooks the effects of a bitter divorce and adult 'hatred' on the 'fear-eyed' children and step-children of her new household. It could not have helped assuage her anxieties about the potential trauma of family breakdown for children that she embarked upon motherhood at a time it had become a virtual 'public ritual' for the 'experts' – social theorists and psychologists of the fifties and sixties from Dr Spock to Erik Erikson – to blame the inadequacy of mothers 'for everything from children's misbehavior to the alarming state of Western civilization' (Herman 1995: 279ff). The readiness of Lowther's society to lay blame on women, especially mothers, for all manner of social ills also, of course, held doubly true in cases where women strayed from the norms of that society. Lowther's memories of her own first divorce could attest to this. Under the fault-based statute that still prevailed in the divorce act of the early seventies, it was not impossible that Lowther could have lost custody of her two daughters with Roy, had she left the marriage and details of her extramarital affairs been divulged in court.[3] In this regard, the same relationships that she looked to for temporary relief from her life with Roy were also potentially serious legal snares.

Indeed, Lowther's decision to abide, at least for the time being, by what Roy called their 'commitment pact' – to stay together for sake of the children – reflects exactly the course of action popularly prescribed at the time by family 'experts,' among them, the judge who had overseen the initial custody arrangements of Mr and Mrs Domphousse in 1960. In even contemplating another marital split, Lowther would have been led to think not only about Kathy's painfully under-aged departure from her second home in 1972, but also the even more pronounced absence of Alan – the son she had once hoped 'to be in a better position' to regain custody of, but never did.[4]

And, more than any other factor Lowther had to weigh, there was Roy himself – the biggest obstacle. As she knew, and once confided to Lor-

raine Vernon, any attempted departure from her dysfunctional marriage would almost certainly provoke Roy to 'follow her.' 'He would
come after her,' Vernon recalled Lowther explaining to her: 'especially
if she had the children ... [T]he only way she could escape would be to
leave the city entirely.'[5] Leaving the city 'entirely' would mean leaving
her older children, Kathy and Alan, behind altogether. It would also
mean leaving the only remaining supports which were available to her
as a parent; namely, close female friends like Vernon and Lowther's
extended family, Virginia and Brenda, in particular.

And so, she remained. Her decision to stay the course in the marital
'hell' she found herself in was an overdetermined 'decision' made in
full recognition that, as she admitted to Lane, 'living as a family is dis-
honest and harmful too.' At the same time, not leaving was not tanta-
mount to simple passivity or non-response, either. Crucially, it was
exactly the same self-absenting capacity for creative withdrawal which
allowed Lowther to compose poetry in the chaos of her home, that she
also attempted to use as a survival strategy for 'living with *it*,' as she'd
written to McNamara. If she could just extricate herself from 'emotional
bondage' to Roy, zone him out and disown him in all but name, then
she might be able to continue functioning as a semi-disengaged agent.
In this regard, Lowther's response to '*it*' – the one thing which, despite
her knack for poetic precision, she never could bring herself to name –
was, fundamentally, an imaginative response too.

So, though she stayed, in her own way, she also departed. Locally, she
reinforced a strict cleavage between her public and private lives. Joy
Kogawa called it Lowther's 'double life.'[6] As Lowther became involved
in League activities after 1972, for instance, the meetings were always
held anywhere but at her own residence, usually at the homes of Fred
Candelaria or Leona Gom. Gom recalls having invited Lowther to read
for a class she was teaching at Columbia College around 1974, and driving her guest home afterwards:

> The closer we got to her house, the more nervous she became, and sud-
> denly at a light [several blocks from her house], she just jumped out. Per-
> haps it was because she didn't want to inconvenience me, but it also
> seemed to be more than that; she didn't want me to see her home, possibly
> to have to invite me in.[7]

Gom's impression of the virtual apartheid Lowther eventually attempted to maintain between the half-lives of her private and public being is one echoed with complete unanimity by the poet's Vancouver friends and acquaintances, most of whom never did visit her house, and many of whom never did clap eyes on Roy.

Patrick Lane is probably right to point out that to some degree, this state of affairs simply reflects the nature of literary community as 'very much a public event,' a form of social 'camaraderie' that always concludes, at the end of the day, with writers 'retreat[ing] back to their own private worlds.' At that time in Vancouver, as he recollects, 'there weren't that many people making a cross-over in the private worlds.'[8] But in Lowther's case, Leona Gom's intuition that 'it also seemed to be more than that' is accurate too. In the final years of her life, Lowther worked *actively* to contain her domestic and literary lives in 'separate spheres,' as the Victorians once called it. As her purchase of a new briefcase around 1974 suggests, she was becoming more self-conscious about cultivating a 'professional' public appearance in the outer world. It was a profile she did not, for obvious reasons, want compromised by the disordered reality of her home life with her 'embarrassing' husband, Roy.

Even when she did allow someone to make a rare 'cross-over' into her domestic world, Lowther now took strict precautions to preserve the compartmentalization of her lives, by keeping her husband out of the picture. When Fred Cogswell visited Vancouver on a sabbatical in 1974, she made an exception and invited her Maritime friend to her home. As Cogswell remembers, it was an invitation extended for the express purpose of proudly introducing him to her two youngest daughters – those children who, as Lowther marvelled, somehow continued to 'grow like flowers on / a geologic fault' (*TC*, 230). But she made sure Roy was out while the editor of *The Fiddlehead* magazine visited: '... she didn't want me to meet him. She said that ... he wouldn't understand, whatever that meant.'[9] What it 'meant,' of course, was that Lowther knew that Cogswell's presence, now as her personal friend and colleague, would only inflame Roy's sense of himself and his 'labour poet' cohorts as 'writers of a now despised generation' (RLJ, 2:115). As the figurehead of a little magazine which had spurned Roy's work, but advanced Pat's, Cogswell was far too fraught a figure in the literary class war that was playing itself out on a micro-level at East 46th. Better to wait till Roy went out, before presenting Fred to Christie and Beth.

As Lorraine Vernon said of her friend in 1975, 'It was as though she put Roy out of her life.'[10] Physically, Lowther did 'put Roy out of her life,' by taking other lovers and taking flight, whenever she could, for trips, readings, and meetings. McNamara was the most important new emotional and sexual tie for her, but in early December 1973, when Salvador Allende's widow, Hortensia Bussi, had come to Vancouver to speak about the situation in Chile, Lowther had also befriended a man named David Morgan. A local who shared her interest in left-wing politics, Morgan taught, at the time, at an alternative school for high-risk kids and drop-outs. Soft-spoken and thoughtful in nature, Morgan was also part of a volunteer group working to establish a co-op radio station at Hastings and Powell, right in the heart of Vancouver's skid row. Lowther took an interest in these activities, and, according to Morgan, the friendship turned into a brief affair during the spring of 1974. To Morgan, Lowther made no secret of her marriage; she informed him also of her relationship with McNamara; and she broke it off with him by the summer. But the two remained friends until the end of her life.[11] It was Morgan who took the picture of the typically camera-shy Lowther which appears on the back cover of A Stone Diary and the front cover of The Canadian Magazine's 'Eulogy for a Poet' issue.

According to Roy, the photographs Morgan took of Lowther in Stanley Park were the same pictures he 'discovered' while one day digging 'deep in the central portion' of his wife's new 'black brief case' in December of 1974. Since the photos, enclosed in a lavender envelope and signed simply, 'with love, David,' indicated no surname, Roy's 'discovery' led him to entertain thoughts that his wife might be having affairs with every 'David' she knew – including David Evanier, the editor of Event magazine, and David Lowther, her nephew by marriage, among other Davids (RLJ, 1:61E). Lowther eventually came to suspect Roy's snooping through her personal papers at home, and his behaviour revealed the limits – and contradictions – of her survival strategy. The sort of demarcation she attempted to draw between her domestic and non-domestic lives was never more than partial, and so, terribly fragile, at best. To McNamara, she confessed at this point: '... my schizophrenic life is getting more difficult.'[12]

Lowther had once stated to Lorraine Vernon that 'when one ceases to accept responsibility for another, everything falls into place.'[13] But this detached, theoretical declaration of independence was necessarily belied by the fact of her on-going existence within a domestic ecology that included, if not subsumed, her. A late poem like 'Kitchen Mur-

der,' which elicited nervous laughter when Lowther read it during her
Prince Edward Island tour in 1975, is disturbing for the very reason
that the speaker figures herself as literally plugged into the loop of a
domestic 'circuit' that is *at once* purely functional *and* potentially
deadly:

> i'll wire myself
> into a circuit:
> the automatic perc,
> the dishwasher, the
> socket above the sink
>
> i'll smile an electric
> eel smile:
> whoever touches
> me is dead. (*SD*, 75)

Citing this poem as an example of the 'kitchen gothic' initiated by
Sylvia Plath, Jean Mallinson notes the speaker's significance as the
charged extension of a dangerous household voltage: '... the violence is
turned outwards, but it includes her' (1981: 160, 161–2). In reality, too,
the more strenuously Lowther attempted to disown her 'emotional bondage' to Roy, the more aggressively he sought to meddle in the affairs of
her 'outside' life. In the tug-of-war-of-wills that ensued, 'everything' that
should ideally have fallen 'into place' began to fall apart anew. The fact
was that Lowther remained legally and emotionally bound to Roy, and if
not 'responsible' for his behaviour, then anything but immune from its
effects. The tranquilizers she had her physician, Dr Forbes, prescribe for
her around this time were just one reminder of that.

Lowther's sister recalls a curious story from their childhood. The Tinmouths kept a box of old skates in the basement, and in the winter,
Brenda would sometimes ask her sister to take her skating. Once, when
she was about ten or twelve, Pat agreed; but only on the condition that
the little sister not only lace up her elder's skates, but physically pick her
up and carry her onto the ice rink.[14] Brenda laughs in bemusement at
the memory of Pat's imperious childhood whim, but the incident anticipates the composite personality traits that go unremarked in such biographical profiles as Paul Grescoe's 'Eulogy for a Poet.' Long before

Lorraine Vernon and Patrick Lane, Brenda glimpsed facets of her sister that were at once 'incredibly passive' *and* quite imposing or 'scary' (Grescoe 1976: 19). Like the smiling housewife of 'Kitchen Murder,' a medium who is passively powerful ('whoever' presumes *to touch her* 'is dead'), Lowther could be neutrally inert and defiantly so at the same time. Like many women of her era, she had been schooled well enough in that feminine art of passive aggression, whereby deliberately projecting an intellect no higher than one's décolletage, for example, was all part of the bigger game plan to 'get a man, get a man.' The limp ice princess role Lowther affected for her little sister around 1945 is a good dramatization of this gender imperative, in unselfconscious caricature. And it is a mode of active inaction that also appears, decades later, as an element in Lowther's struggle to separate herself from the husband whom she could not, for fairly compelling reasons, simply get up and leave – at least just yet.

So while she did not abandon her husband, Lowther was becoming increasingly vocal about her dissatisfaction in the union. Nor did she go to excessively great lengths to keep her relationships with other men a secret from Roy after about 1973. Without a doubt, Roy was a shameless spy, but there seems to be some truth to his assertions that Lowther was not as scrupulous about concealing the tokens of her affairs as she would have been, had she truly wanted to keep them clandestine. As with Morgan's photographs, for instance, she also for the most part received and kept McNamara's letters and packages at her home address (CATT, 1:165). At least one letter from McNamara, from January 1975, has crayon artwork signed by an eight-year-old Beth on the reverse side of it, suggesting that it was left within open reach of the youngster's hands. In doing so, a daring part of Lowther seems to have been trying to serve notice of her intent to vacate, inviting her husband to recognize the prelude to a wholesale departure. At other times, especially after the UBC teaching position came through in the summer of 1975, this was exactly the message Lowther found herself explicitly and fearfully back-pedalling on, in an attempt to assuage Roy's agitated suspicions that she would 'pull up stakes if she wanted,' as John Hall put it (CATT, 3:436, 427).

Incidentally, Beth's picture on the back of the letter shows two figures – one going 'up up up' a flight of stairs, and the other going 'down down down.' The drawing is remarkable for what it hints of a child's intuitive grasp of the tensions splintering her family household. 'There's that . . . downward mobility of Roy and upward mobility of Pat,' as Patrick Lane observes in retrospect, 'and they sort of meet in the mid-dle . . . like an earthquake zone.'[15]

The situation in the Lowther home had deteriorated into a veritable 'earthquake zone' by the New Year of 1975. Unsurprisingly, Roy appears to have found the letter with Beth's drawing on it; it was one of the pieces of textual evidence later entered into court proceedings. Accord-ing to Roy, it was around this time, in February 1975, that he and Pat also came to an agreement on an 'open' marriage, after his wife also 'admitted' to her brief fling with David Morgan the previous year. 'What it meant was that the commitment from then on to the kids did not bind either of us to the other' (RLJ, 1:61F; CATT, 3:425; 4:564). But the apparent rapprochement on extramarital activity was never a good deal, as far as Roy was concerned.

With *Milk Stone* having finally appeared in the fall of 1974, another manuscript in the wings, and her appointments with the League and with David Barrett's NDP Arts Board, Lowther's responsibilities and travel schedules multiplied along with Roy's obsessions in 1975. When he wasn't rifling through his wife's possessions during her absences from home, Roy would 'mind the children' by taking them to Virginia in North Vancouver, or to Brenda at her lakeside trailer retreat on Cul-tus Lake. This was a good thing for the girls, but for Pat's mother and sister, it also meant having to deal more often with Roy's litanies of mis-ery and woe, crying spells, and unstable behaviour. Lowther herself took this into account whenever she made travel plans. 'Problems at home make it unlikely that I'll be able to stay more than a few days,' as she wrote to Arlene Lampert regarding a stop-over in Toronto on League business during the summer of 1975.[16] Business or pleasure, her trips were always quick.

Frequently, though, when Pat was gone, Virginia and Brenda would encourage Roy just to leave the girls with them, and come back later to collect them. At Brenda's weekend trailer home, where space was lim-ited anyway, Roy would leave reluctantly, only to be discovered sleeping someways off in his car at the side of the highway, in the same dirty clothes he now wore to pieces day in and day out.[17] Virginia recounted in court one visit Roy paid her at home in her daughter's absence. When Roy expressed envy at his wife's opportunity for travel, she responded by casually hoping that her daughter was 'having a little bit of fun while she's about it.' That was more than enough to set Roy off into another bellicose demonstration of the same possessiveness he had shown when gloating over his new wifely 'recruit' in 1963. Knocking over a chair in the process, 'he brought his hand down on the table very firmly, and he said, "well, I'll tell you this, your daughter is the only exciting woman I have ever known, and no other man will get her!"' (PHTT, 10:759; CATT, 2:235–6).

The incident Virginia recalled indicates the extent to which the 'open marriage' concept never was more than a charade for Roy, even though he apparently went through the motions of proving it 'open' for himself, as well. Moreover, his turn to Virginia in Pat's absence reconfirms Patrick Lane's sense of Roy's dependency status. If he encountered a problem while his spouse was out of town – such as once, when his car wouldn't start after he'd taken his daughters canoeing – he would phone his mother-in-law, in tears, asking her for advice on what he should do.[18]

The widening breach in Roy's marriage was leaving him an abysmally helpless and dangerous wreck. Around the house, he started to speak, vaguely, to young Beth and Christie about the 'risks' associated with their mother's lifestyle, and the probability of 'accidents.'[19]

Both Lorraine Vernon and Patrick Lane, two friends who knew Pat Lowther better than most, point to denial as an element in her 'silence and . . . reluctance to discuss [Roy's] obviously worsening state' by this time.[20] As Lane sees it, denial is insidious because it works to normalize the abnormal: '... from someone else looking at it, you'd just think, 'My God, these people are really living in insanity' ... [but] somehow you have this illusion when you're in that kind of a trap that everything's normal – that this is normal life. And it's not. It's utterly abnormal.'[21]

But what is remarkable in Lowther's case is just how *consciously* she struggled with her own 'denial.' Not only did 'denial' always coexist for her with a recognition of the problem, but the records she left suggest that she never did acclimatize to the apparent 'insanity' of her life along the lines suggested by Lane. On the contrary, she wrote with acute self-awareness to Livesay about the 'paralyses of will' that stymied her. To Fred Cogswell, she pointedly qualified hers as 'a typical domestic life' only 'in some respects.' She contrasted her own 'schizophrenic life' to that represented for her by McNamara ('another life with some sanity and joy'). To Joy Kogawa, she spoke of a kind of living death that was 'sick' and 'disastrous.' It is an understatement to say that Lowther *knew* things with Roy were not right, and that, increasingly, she *knew* some 'desperate action' was called for.

In other words, it might be more precise to say that her 'reluctance' to speak of '*it*,' and her tendency to become, in Vernon's words, 'more and more closed as to Roy's behavior'[22] presented a form of *failed* denial. To all external appearance, Lowther may have seemed successfully 'oblivious,' but her own writing recounts a more peculiarly complex series of self-conscious attempts to acknowledge the state of denial, a 'state' that Lowther seemed to straddle, with one foot in and one foot out.

Among her papers is an undated typescript of a poem entitled 'A Death and Resurrection,' which begins with an observation and a question: 'The house has fallen where we lived, made love / ... How shall bruised hands and broken tongues / Build whole again?' What follows testifies to a dual recognition of both serious household 'rot,' and the speaker's own predilection to 'look away' from that 'rot':

> When did the rot come? How can we know?
> Infection is everywhere. The streets are not clean.
>> When the floors began cursing my footsteps,
>> I dared not know.
>
> ...
>
> So when I saw the fungus spreading on the wall,
> the dust crawling with blind feelers through the cracks,
> I looked away.[23]

As with the Good Friday letter to Joy Kogawa, the 'resurrection' called for by this poem goes unachieved in the end. It is one of many drafts that now begin to thematize what Lowther elsewhere constructs as 'green living rooms / Built / on the edge of denial' (*TC*, 214).

Some of the strongest of these new poems 'Built / on the edge of denial' would eventually appear as the so-called 'death-haunted' and 'premonitory' poems of *A Stone Diary* and *Time Capsule*. 'City Slide / 6,' one of a suite of poems that reflects Lowther's interest in experimentation with visual and mixed-media forms, is one such example. Its first stanza, in particular, has been frequently cited as eerily prescient: 'Love is an intersection / where I have chosen / unwittingly to die' (*SD*, 72). Compact and deceptively simple in its matter-of-fact tone and language,

'City Slide / 6' is a poem that presents readers with a rich array of suggestive paradoxes, beginning with the paradox of a slippery speaker who is, in effect, conscious of being unconscious, and therefore not really unconscious. Her statement in the opening stanza, that she has 'chosen / unwittingly to die,' articulates a contradiction in terms, since her awareness of the 'choice' she has made makes that 'choice' anything but un-knowing or 'unwitting.' If, on the other hand, the pivotal adverb, *unwittingly*, is read as modifying the infinitive verb which follows, a similar conundrum presents itself. There are no two ways about it: one cannot die witfully; 'to die' *is* to part with one's wits, to yield to the 'unwitting.' In this case, then, there is no real 'choice' to have been made in the first place. In either case, the 'choice' the poet is pointing to is pointedly specious, and the poem's first stanza amounts to a trap of logic, a snare ('the kind of situation psychologists devise to drive white rats crazy,' perhaps).[24]

In 'City Slide / 6,' love's 'intersection' is thus an 'X' marking the spot of a 'choice' that is at once made and un-made by the poem. The connections to earlier works such as 'Penelopes' are manifest: the focal interest of this 'Stone Diary' poem is not so much death *per se* as it is, once again, entrapment and the 'twin duplicity' of knowledge and ignorance, of doing and undoing. Lowther's earlier work, that is, helps to contextualize her much-remarked-upon 'obsession' with death in the late poetry as part of an already unfolding – and much more encompassing – fascination with the limits and nature of knowledge and consciousness in general: 'the large holes / and the fine holes / . . . silted with data' 'inside us' (*SD*, 67).

Whereas concerned friends like Vernon and Lane were fretting over Lowther's seemingly obdurate avoidance of reality while she was writing such poems as 'City Slide / 6,' 'Kitchen Murder,' 'To a Woman Who Died of 34 Stab Wounds,' and 'It Happens Every Day,' readers of the late Pat Lowther's poetry have often quoted such texts as approximations of exactly the opposite: her uncanny attunement to reality and prophetic anticipations of it. After all, such poems take up the subject of death or murder, and the poet who wrote them soon after died by murder. The first three lines of 'City Slide/ 6' appear to predict the poet's death at love's 'intersection'; and for some, this is enough. It doesn't matter that this apparent prediction is presented as an enigmatic riddle designed to catch readers up in a recognition of what it means not to have real 'choices.' Or, for that matter, that the poem's first stanza is followed by these lines:

Next year the blue lights
will still be here
lighting up the columns of rain

I'll be in a room
in this same city
with my sick headache
reflecting on accidents
of all kinds (*SD*, 72)

Forecasting that the speaker 'will still be here,' '[n]ext year,' 'in this same city,' with another 'sick headache,' the poem is foreboding in tone, but not actually premonitory of the poet's fate in any particular way. Nor does it qualify as a 'tragic irony' either, a term that presupposes the 'unwittingness' of the poet who here innocently and wrongly assumes her continued existence. By the last year of her life, Lowther cohabited with a man who had taken to making veiled verbal threats around the house, a man who was doing exactly what the poem figures the speaker as doing: 'reflecting on accidents / of all kinds.' To the degree that poems like 'City Slide / 6' 'reflect' an autobiographical situation, they 'reflect' little more or less than Lowther's generalized awareness of the essentially amorphous threat posed by Roy – the potential for what he may have mentioned as being 'accidents / of all kinds.'

Nevertheless, the later poems of domestic violence are inescapably unsettling. There is, for example, the unpublished typescript 'Contexts,' which reads, in part:

Behind the closet door
which is kept firmly closed
after dark
corpses are propped up
waiting to be discovered
...
yes and a parallelogram
of light from another room
lies on the small beds
the children asleep
while the closet door is closed.[25]

There are other 'corpses . . . propped up / waiting to be discovered' in Lowther's oeuvre, but none which captures the immediate aftermath of her own murder in quite such horrifying detail. If there are any lines that might be taken as evidence for a 'haunting legacy,' these would have to be candidates.

But Lowther seems to have written 'Contexts' in the same spirit as her darkly playful 'Nightmare' (*SD*, 15). The same distinctive toy-gothic atmosphere of 'Nightmare's' 'Edgar Allan Poe & / Disney combined' (*SD*, 15) also comes through clearly in the lines which intercede the segments of 'Contexts' quoted above. Thus, after the 'corpses are propped up' 'behind the closet door,' '[g]houls munch their flesh / Dracula sharpens his fangs,' and 'Frankenstein's monster / does finger exercises.' Though it is impossible to know what sorts of 'accidental' scenarios Roy may have been pitching around the house, his anticipatory threats factor as a context for 'Contexts.' Alternatively, it is just as likely – maybe even likelier – that Roy gleaned his own ideas from reading such typescripts as 'Contexts.' By the end, he was inspecting his wife's papers and lifting her metaphors on a regular basis, anyway. Above all, he was most certainly digesting the contents of her work according to a plot replete with fantasies of self-fulfilling prophecy.

As Gary Geddes, Margaret Atwood, and a few others pointed out in the immediate wake of Lowther's death, there is nothing incomprehensibly otherworldly about her work, including the disturbing poems of domestic violence she was producing toward the end of her life. Lowther herself is her own best witness in this regard. In the final summer of her life, she told the back story of 'To a Woman Who Died of 34 Stab Wounds.' The poem speculatively envisions the circumstances of the gruesome murder indicated by its title, concluding of the murderer, 'at the end, coiling, striking, / his rage was for himself' (*SD*, 65). She was speaking to an audience on Prince Edward Island when she elaborated:

> It's funny, that was actually ... a friend of mine who *was* murdered, while on vacation in Hawaii – don't ever go to Hawaii for a vacation. I had not seen her for about ten years, and yet I imagined – you know, having known her – I imagined she *must* have been involved with this man [who killed her], simply because she was a tremendously open and very proud person. Despite the fact that she would have been about sixty at this time, I could just see this kind of thing happening. In fact, the story was even more sordid. She just woke up while her room was being robbed, and was . . . [voice trails off]. But I thought, anyone who stabbed somebody that many times, there must have been some real anger there.[26]

Lowther's confession that she had jumped to a conclusion in the case of her vacationing friend's murder points to how she was both right *and* wrong in terms of the 'kind of thing' she 'could just see happening.' The profligate violence of a crime committed in 'real anger' by a spouse (whose 'rage' 'in the end,' 'was for himself') would prove true of her own murder. The 'context'of her own experience with a progressively destructive mate could not fail to tune her antennae to precisely this 'kind of thing.' As is often the case in her crisis letters to friends, however, Lowther explicitly draws attention here as much to what was *un*foreseen by her as anything else – to the 'even more sordid' 'fact' of a random, *ad hoc* killing that she had not, in this case, envisioned. As she had written to Fred Cogswell by May 1975, in a similar vein, about her own marriage to Roy: 'I am living in a hell that was completely beyond my imagination before I got into it.'

Highly conscious and conscientious though she was, especially about her own defences, the limits of Lowther's knowledge are crucial to recognize – and not just as a means of demystifying her phantasmagorical cachet. Without recognizing what she could *not* foresee, it is impossible to appreciate the magnitude of horror and mortification Lowther had begun to express to friends like Joy Kogawa by April 1973, when she realized the extent of the trouble she – and Roy – were in. 'I can't believe in possibilities anymore,' she had written then: 'When you've been this wrong there aren't any more chances.' Even if she had come across allegations related to Roy's mental history after the fact of her marriage, it would have been extremely difficult for Lowther to envision the disintegration of personality that she would witness in him a decade later. As she asked in her draft poem 'A Death and Resurrection': 'When did the rot come? How can we know?' What had begun with an unnerving depression and outbursts of purple-faced ranting had progressed to episodes of head-banging self-mutilation, pot-lid crunching 'irrational violence,' paranoia and threats. But Lowther did not experience her twelve-year marriage with the compressed coherence of its retelling. Of a mutual acquaintance, she had once written to Fred Cogswell that she was *relieved* to hear that their friend had suffered 'a severe physical illness' rather than the nervous 'breakdown' they originally feared he had: 'I found this reassuring [news] – it's not like an intangible thing that keeps cropping up for years.'[27]

It would take years for the 'intangible thing,' the 'it' Lowther lived with, to evolve into patterns she could recognize. More years before her realization that, whenever 'it' had arrived, and by whatever impercepti- ble gradations 'it' had spread, like a 'fungus,' the household 'rot' and 'infection' were now serious. When that realization did hit home, Lowther was especially devastated by what she took on as a personal fail- ing: an unforgivable error in judgment or lack of perspicacity on her part. How could she *ever* have been so blind, so very and profoundly '*wrong*' about Roy? How could she *not* have 'just see[n] this kind of thing happening'? *Not* have guessed anything predictive of this 'hell' in advance? In confronting, head-on, the enormous and terrible implica- tions of 'it,' Lowther's confidence in her own judgment was radically undermined at precisely the moment when she needed more than ever to exercise and trust that faculty. The self-doubt and self-blame now only compounded the 'paralyses of will' she had early on written to Livesay about. Which she knew. Which brought on more migraine headaches.

Nineteen seventy-five was 'a hell of a busy year.' Between the full-tilt pace, the 'sick headaches,' and Roy 'making it difficult for [her] to work,' it is astounding that Lowther even managed to keep writing.[28] But write she did, and some of the new poems she produced during this period continue her attempts to make sense of the frightening predica- ment she found herself in, rather than foreclose it outright, or simply 'loo[k] away.' While the writing reflects her on-going struggle with an only half-denied 'denial,' the new poems also reinforce the pragmatic will that allowed Lowther to ease her family off social assistance in July 1975, thanks to a combination of income she derived from poetry read- ings and the salary stipend from her new Interim Arts Board job (CATT, 3:426). By August, she was preparing for her new teaching stint at UBC. She had to keep on writing. The poems – the basis of her literary career – could one day lead to a way out.

By now, the public profile of Lowther's work ethic and lengthening track record suggested nothing but an impressive quick-study of compe- tence and generosity. But the strain of her private life had also begun to show. When Patrick Lane returned to Vancouver after travels eastward in the early seventies, he saw Lowther again after an interval of four or five years, and the alteration he noticed in her appearance shocked him. 'When I first met her in the early sixties,' he reminisces, 'she was really an attractive, beautiful woman.' But in the decade between 1963 and 1973, he says, it seemed that 'she aged thirty years' – 'those ten years had taken an immense physical toll on her.'[29] There were the inevitable signs of aging, of course, like graying hair and deeper stress lines at the mouth and brow. But Lowther's temperamental skin condition also sometimes left her complexion sallow, and Lane recalls that in later years her face seemed puffy – perhaps a result of the 'tranks' she was on, or of sleep deprivation, or both. She wore a dental plate, but – as her friends would note on Gzowski's radio tribute – her teeth were still in need of further repair. One observer from the seventies described her as looking 'frail': 'one is . . . struck by something in her self, something that has suffered heavily.' Margaret Atwood counters: 'She was thin, of course – that sometimes makes people think one is frail.'[30] A black and white picture taken on Prince Edward Island during the summer of 1975 shows Lowther looking un-puffy and smiling mildly, her lips closed. She may have been self-conscious about her teeth, but her shapely mouth is wide and generous, like her eyebrows. Her gaze is averted from the camera. The photo is a close-up, but in her eyes, she looks far away.

A weariness that sapped Lowther's reserves was setting in, even as she fought on with her work. 'I'm getting too tired to withstand the nasty surprises that always seem to be lying in wait,' as she'd admitted to McNamara. The note of fatalism that creeps into her correspondence after 1973 also begins to manifest itself more insistently in her final notebooks from around 1974–5. A 'Canadian Music Dictation' scribbler from this time includes drafts of some of the previously unpublished poems that appear in the posthumous *Time Capsule*. 'Random Interview' is one of these. Only the middle section of the three-part poem reprinted in *Time Capsule* appears in this notebook. It begins as follows:

> i am tired of pain
> i am tired of my own pain
> i am tired of
> the pain of others
>
> i am tired of lives
> unwinding like a roll
> of bloody bandage
> i shall roll up
> the sky, pinch the sun (*TC*, 243)

With this, Lowther's Arachne, that industriously 'spinning female thing,' comes to the end of the roll, a prospect Lowther once joked about in the period of her difficult flowering. For her to write of 'pinch[ing]' out the sun, as though snuffing a matchstick taper, is remarkable. West Coast born and bred though she was, she was no fan of its 'depressing' 'drowning weather,' which she frequently complained about in letters. Usually, she celebrated the sun, even if her jumpy skin wouldn't allow her to be out in it for long.

'The Sun in November' is another late poem from this period, bound, in its holograph form, as the only entry in its own separate, stapled and unlined notebook. The notebook's pages are pale green, rather like the pages of *This Difficult Flowring*. Confessional in more than tone alone, the poem equates the fleeting transience of 'two days' sunshine in November to the ephemeral, but lingering, gratification of a love tryst (*TC*, 226). But the eleven-part poem takes a sharp left turn in the ninth section, where the focus swerves from the speaker's love relationship to a clinical setting, a mis-encounter between doctor and patient which is cleverly portrayed as a secular version of the Catholic's 'confessional.' It is all unhearing instruction on the side of authority, and fruitless appeals for understanding on the side of the patient. Lowther italicizes and capitalizes the misfired monologues to make the point:

> *Have your medical card ready.*
> *Sit here. You will be called.*
>
> dr. you must understand i am
> not a woman with strong
> reasons for living:
> my children maimed
> as much as cherished
> grow like flowers on
> a geologic fault
> my every step shudders
> disaster . . .
>
> ...
>
> *Raise your arms*
> *over your head. Breathe.*
>
> My lover is a catholic
> with children in
> parochial schools no one

i've loved has been
ultimately any better
for it you must understand
...
Good news: your x-ray shows
spontaneous healing. The hole
in your lung is closing.
There should be no pain.

you understand i have lost
my reflection in windows
even my eyes have turned
pale the hole is
a constant trap i have
never stopped falling
like a ruined house
open to weather it is
snowing or raining

Here is a prescription
for 292s. Avoid anxiety.
Take the sun.

Take the sun.
the sun
take
                the (*TC*, 231–2)

While its final stanzas seem to echo Ibsen's *Ghosts*, 'The Sun in November' more explicitly reinvokes all those 'ruined house[s]' 'open to weather' in *This Difficult Flowring* and *Milk Stone*.[31] Exposed to the elements, 'a constant trap,' home is no shelter here either.

Unlike the case in some of the earlier domestic poems, though, this 'house' – and the self who inhabits it – are not necessarily recomposed on a daily basis. 'Listen,' Lowther had written in her experimental 1974 prose piece 'The Face': 'every morning I take a razor to the fabric of my life, I cut out a woman shape, I step into it, I go out, I perform, it works. But every morning it has to be done again' (40). The boredom of repetitive performativity, the labour of daily self reinvention, now gives way instead to a more profound sense of the self's insubstantiality, that of a

woman who has 'lost' more than just her tolerance for artifice and pre-
tense. 'Lost' is the speaker's own 'reflection in windows.' Missing too are
the pupils of her 'eyes,' those 'windows' onto the 'I': 'even my eyes have
turned / pale the hole is / a constant trap.' 'Holes' of emptiness and
absence replace visible reflections of presence, wholeness. The woman
articulates a deep fatigue that the 'dr.,' despite all entreaties, will not
'understand': 'dr. you must understand i am / not a woman with strong
/ reasons for living.'

As with most 'confessional' poetry, 'The Sun in November' draws
closely from autobiographical experience, and behind her persona's
admission of weak 'reasons for living' are the corrosive, cumulative
effects of Roy's abject credo from 1964: 'there is nothing to live for.' A
dozen years of living with the demands of Roy's despair inevitably
sapped Lowther's considerable resources of spirit. Her husband's
embittered hopelessness was a toxin expelled with every exhalation
into the household atmosphere, and no one living at 566 East 46th was
immune to it. Not Lowther with her blinding 'sick headaches,' nor her
too often vomiting children. Long before 1975, a part of her realized
what she was up against: she was living with the Man of Sorrows himself. And she wrote poem drafts accordingly: 'Think of the Wives of
Martyrs,' 'There Goes My Love All Curst and Blest,' and so on. On the
other hand, despite the intellectual flowering ushered in with the late
sixties, Patsy Lou, mother's little helper, the responsible older child,
never did disappear entirely, no more so than the 'Mrs Patricia' of the
fifties, tutored in a 'domestic life' that was supposed to be 'every
female's true affinity.'

And what had come of all that? The houses she had grown up to keep
as a woman had never measured up to *Good Housekeeping* standards, and
she knew it. One marriage had failed soundly, and the next had led to a
train wreck she'd never seen coming. By legal fiat or personal choice, her
two eldest children had left her care prematurely. Because she found 'no
way out' of the walls she touched at every turn, her two youngest children were under the partial care of a husband she knew was not emotionally well. Her mother and her siblings shared the unhappy
consequences and burdens of this, her supposedly sober 'second
thought' about marriage. Her lovers and even her friends were liable to
be drawn into the vortex of Roy's angry jealousy at any moment. The ide-
alistic side of Lowther – the side that wanted to believe in betterment
always just ahead, on the horizon – had brought her and those in her
personal sphere nothing but disillusion, even catastrophe. And now she

blamed herself for this, coming to an especially rough self-judgment: '... no one / i've loved has been / ultimately any better / for it ...'

∽

More than once, Lowther wrote to friends about not being able to die. 'I think of lying down, sleeping it off forever,' she said in her Good Friday letter to Joy Kogawa. '[B]ut I know I can't because all the wrong would just go on happening, even compounded by my absence.' Or, to McNamara: 'I can't even die because it would be abandoning my children.' Though the desire to 'sleep it off forever' is immediately checked or negated outright – 'I can't even die' – the fact that Lowther came occasionally to think of death as a potential means of relief indicates the extremity of her weariness.

Kogawa, for one, was alarmed enough by Lowther's April 1973 letter to immediately place a call from Ottawa. And this was a detail that Lowther herself mentioned with 'embarrassment' in the next letter that she wrote to Fred Cogswell, dated 3 May 1973:

> I've been very down and, much to my embarrassment, wrote a terribly despondent letter to Joy, to which she responded by phoning all the way from Ottawa. I hate to think what my thoughtlessness and her good heart cost her in cash, which she has to earn herself now.

Less than two weeks after she confessed her temptation for 'sleeping it off forever,' Lowther had revised her outlook substantially; her letter to Cogswell goes on to chat about some new poems she is busy 'researching,' and to political gossip about the Watergate scandal.[32]

Similarly, it is also worth noting that Lowther had long fantasized about 'not dying,' even at much lighter and more liberating moments of her life. When she left high school in optimistic high hopes of finding freedom in a wage, for example, one of the farewell poems she submitted to her school yearbook was entitled 'Let Me Not Die.' Contrary to the title's cue, the poem stipulates the kind of death that an operatic adolescent Pat Tinmouth did not think she would want (a boring and 'quiet' one) only in order to better define the kind she *did* think would be okay (a 'raging storm' and a 'moaning surf' were the preferable accompaniments).[33]

While Roy Lowther would remain comfortable with such clichés of the dark and stormy night in his own death allegory, 'September 23rd,' Pat had long since moved on to thinking about death as an epistemological problem. How to grasp the reality of a state available to the living only as an abstraction? This is the question posed by 'The Egg of Death,' which goes on to observe that '[t]he thought of one's / own death lies in a crypt of mind' (*DF,* 31). In a lengthy essay entitled 'Thoughts on War and Death' (1915), Freud had promoted the notion that 'the thought of one's / own death *lies*' in the sense that such 'thoughts' inevitably belie the actual fact – and acceptance – of 'one's / own death.' Lowther, never particularly persuaded by the arguments of 'Dr. Freud,' nevertheless sums this argument up in one neat line which projects the mortality of the self as the occluded kernel, the sealed 'crypt' buried and inaccessible within the living 'mind.'

As much as anything else, then, death, as the ultimate riddle, was an object of abiding intellectual fascination for Lowther, a solitary scrabble-playing poet who liked to find sense in nonsense. While her husband's genuinely suicidal behaviour by 1973 prompted a note of fatalistic resignation to surface in her own writing toward the end, Lowther's attraction to the idea of death as a respite from the *sturm und drang* of her private life was never more than a transitory sign of emotional exhaustion against which she continued to rally. Even where she frankly acknowledged that debilitating fatigue, fear, and confusion, she resisted it. 'Random Interview,' the same poem in which she testified to being 'tired of lives / unwinding like a roll / of bloody bandage,' is representative of her continued resilience. Triptych in structure, the poem's first two sections, subtitled, '1, the fear' and '2, i am tired,' are in the end countered by an affirmative final section unequivocally headed '3, what i want': 'what i want is to be blessed / what i want is a cloak of air / the light entering my lungs' (*TC,* 244). There was always a 'wanting' beyond this. She'd find a way to live with 'it,' and the pitfalls into panic and exhaustion that 'it' caused. She always did. Shortly before Fred Cogswell headed back to New Brunswick after his sabbatical year on the Coast, he met up with Lowther in 1975 for a hasty farewell coffee. 'What she said was, as near as I can remember, this: "In ten years the children will be old enough to look after themselves, and I'll only be fifty." '[34]

In the final section of Phyllis Webb's *Naked Poems* (1965), entitled 'Some Final Questions,' one half of the split lyric 'I' asks the other: '*But why don't you do something?*' And the rejoinder from the other half is, simply, 'I am trying to write a poem' (Webb 1982: 106). Similarly, as Lowther's worried friends ardently wished she would *do* something, she was. She was clearing some space at the cluttered dining-room table and sitting back in her red pleatherette. She was picking up her pencil, maybe giving it a little twirl. She was beginning to 'weave again,' her own 'designs / of innocence and disbelief ...'

PART III

Ready to Learn Politics

Often now I forget
how to make love
but I think I am ready
to learn politics.
— *Milk Stone*

Chapter 9

The First 'Red Flag'

James Wilks, Pat Lowther's colliery-bred, British-born maternal grandfather, arrived on Vancouver Island in 1870, a year before British Columbia's entry into Confederation officially drew a new 'Dominion' over its traditional Aboriginal territories. James was three years old at the time, and although he didn't realize it then, he came as part of a much wider wave of later-nineteenth-century West Coast settlement, as English, Scottish, Irish, and American immigrants flooded into the region looking for work, gold, coal. Not coincidentally, also docking at the edge of this overextended British Empire, along with the settlers, were creeds which took up the cause of the working classes, signalling the advent of an unprecedented new era in British and international trade unionism. From London and Paris, Chicago and Moscow, labour reform movements began to march, inspired by Marxist-socialist theories that even made the unlikely voyage via steerage to tiny, White settler outposts like Nanaimo, British Columbia – where the family of James Wilks settled. Sometimes, such notions came as part and parcel of the immigrants' worldly goods – as bundles of political pamphlets or labour newspapers, their pages curled and salt-water stiffened. Or sometimes, as with Jim Connell's famous workingman's anthem, 'The Red Flag,' they were simply carried along by heart, as songs.

Born at Scotland Gate, Bedlington, in Northumberland, James was the eldest child and only son of William and Isabella Wilks, who also had three girls. 'They were coal miners in England, and they came out to Canada because his father didn't want his sons to work in the coal mines,' Virginia recalls. 'And then they finally wound up on Vancouver Island, working in the coal mines.'[1] Though William Wilks actually set up shop as a hotel-keeper after he transplanted his family, this was a business venture that, as Virginia's remark indicates, had to be supplemented by continued work in the mines. Already by the 1870s, Nanaimo had developed into the largest coal-mining community on the Island, and depending on vagaries of the local economy, it was common for men to patch together a living in this way.

Hopeful to secure a better future for James, William and Isabella sent their boy off for a rudimentary education at a Catholic parish school, the only school likely available at the time. Though it was, of course, primarily aimed at converting as many of the Island's original Kwakiutl and Sne ney mux inhabitants as possible, the Catholics lived up to their name when it came to potential recruits. Or so it would appear from the records of James Wilks, still listed as a Methodist in 1881, but claimed as Catholic in the census taken a decade later. Recounting her father's early school years among 'a few White boys, but mostly Indians,' Virginia says that James's formal education 'didn't go very far.' But, she adds, 'he was a self-educated man,' 'a great man with words.' 'Everything he ever read or heard, he remembered it.' She was very proud of her father. 'He would quote Shakespeare at the drop of a hat.'[2]

But the Bardic fluency was a development of later life. James was probably not quoting Shakespeare while he was down in the mine shafts of Nanaimo as a young man, which is where he appears to have ended up working for a time, after his schooling. The coal beds around Nanaimo were among the earliest developed in the province, and among the most perilous in the world. Explosions occurred with appalling regularity, in part, a result of the lethal combination of the miners' open-flame Kilmarnock lamps and poor ventilation systems, unable to flush methane gas from the mine shafts.[3] In 1887, nearly 150 men died in one such explosion at Nanaimo. Less than a year later, on 24 January 1888, there was another huge disaster. This blast happened on the eastern slope of the Wellington Number Five mine and killed over 60. 'A repetition of last year's fearful accident at Nanaimo was something to be dreaded and, alas, feared,' the *Daily Colonist* opined. What made this 'repetition' of history worse, according to the *Colonist*, was that the Wellington Number Five site 'was considered the safest mine on the island,' even by the miners themselves.

Among the men who happened to be working the eastern slope of Wellington Number Five on that unsafe morning in 1888 was James Wilks's father, William, the aspiring hotelier. He is listed among the fatalities as 'Wm. Wilks, aged 49, [of] Northumberland.' He was one of the few casualties who had lived long enough to leave behind a substantial family. Most of the dead were young, unmarried men in their teens and twenties. Even more, the majority, in fact, were Chinese labourers, employed as runners and loaders. Their names were not listed among the dead in the newspapers 'as they were known only by numbers.'[4]

Along with his mother, Isabella, and his three younger sisters, Margaret Alice, Mary Elizabeth, and Hannah, James Wilks, then aged twenty-one, would have been among the crowd of men, women, and children who gathered at the wrecked Number Five pithead as news of the accident spread. 'Crying in a heart-breaking way, and bewailing their loss,' the mourners created what a journalist at the time rather expediently termed 'an indescribable scene, such as always occurs at such an event.' The force of the explosion had destroyed the hoisting gear and blocked the bottom of the mine shaft with rubble and debris. It took hours to rig a block and tackle and lower the first brave 'exploring party.' It took days to retrieve the bodies of the victims, and what eventually came up was a hideous sight. The great majority of the dead 'were fearfully mutilated and blackened, their skins being burned off, and their heads especially battered. The terrible force that knocked them about played sad havoc.' The 'poor battered and charred corpses were in every position,' in cases where limbs remained intact. The remains were taken by railway to the local blacksmith's shop in preparation for burial. Some, like those who died with their hands held up 'in a rigid attitude of defence,' needed to be prised into shapes that would fit a coffin.

On Friday afternoon, 27 January 1888, William Wilks, who had come to Canada to escape the mines, was interred back into the earth from which his body had been hoisted. He appears to have belonged to some working men's associations, for 'the burial ritual of the Workmen' was read by surviving fellows at his funeral. Around the same time he was buried, a sycophantic editorial in the *Daily Colonist* reported a 'general' 'sympathy' for the mine owner, Robert Dunsmuir, 'since it was felt that his sensitive heart would feel keenly the untimely cutting off of so many of his employees.' Plus, it would be at least four or five profitless weeks before Wellington Number Five would be 'ready for a renewal of work.'[5]

Especially on Vancouver Island, it was not just the constant threat posed by coal dust, fish oil, methane 'firedamp,' and cave-ins that miners confronted. In a province whose mining industry was at the forefront of organized labour movements from the start, Nanaimo was, by 1888, an established centre of violent labour strife and unrest. And the single most effective countervailing force to miners who sought to better their lot through collective action was the legacy of Robert

Dunsmuir, the largest mine owner on the Island, and himself a former indentured miner. Virulently anti-union and ruthless when it came to undercutting pioneering efforts at organized labour, Dunsmuir was known for evicting striking miners' families from company-owned property; importing strike breakers from San Francisco; and hiring a good third of his labour force from the 'cheap' pool of Chinese immigrant workers, who were, in turn, frequently set upon by the White community and invariably blamed for most of the accidents at the mines.[6] When the miners of Vancouver Island had formed their first union, the Miners' Mutual Protective Association, and gone on strike in 1877, Dunsmuir called in the militia, though this was five years after trade unions had been legalized in Canada. 'King Grab,' the coal baron, died not too long after the 1888 Wellington explosion, but his legacy extended through his equally purse-proud widow and sons, the heirs of his empire and his considerable political clout.

Census records suggest that the widowed Isabella Wilks and her three girls left the Nanaimo area shortly after William's devastating death, leaving James, by 1891, as the only remaining Wilks in the vicinity. James seems to have found employment as a blacksmith, perhaps at the same smith shop that prepared his father's body for burial. Chronic industrial accidents of the sort that killed William Wilks and hundreds of other men appear to have prompted the young man to leave the mine pits. More than that, his father's death evidently got James thinking about the need to redress working conditions in the mines. He would soon leave the blacksmith job for a career in labour activism and education, a career that his family history had by this point already decisively turned him toward.

But there was one other reason why James Wilks apparently chose to hang around Nanaimo after his father's death, as a single man, living in lodgings. There was a new Irish lass in town who had caught his fancy. She was Annie McCain, the second-eldest child of Samuel and Eliza McCain. Annie's father, and also her eldest brother, William, age sixteen, toiled in the same Dunsmuir collieries that James had recently walked away from. Her mother, Eliza, had been born in England, and was Anglican, but had given birth to all of her children in Ireland before the family resettled in Nanaimo around 1890. In 1891, Annie was fifteen; in 1892, she was married. James was in his mid-twenties when he wed her, in the newly incorporated City of Vancouver, on November 8. In what is said to be their wedding picture, she looks vastly older than her years, all in black, and with a large, plumed hat. Annie was emotionally 'tough' and inclined toward stockiness; James was tall, slim, and stylish. Like her mother before her, Annie would bear her own husband seven children, including, of course, James's admiring daughter, Virginia.

After their marriage, James and Annie Wilks returned to Nanaimo, where their future vaudeville star, 'Belle,' named after James's mother, Isabella Wilks, was born in 1894. But soon after Isabelle's birth, the family returned to the mainland, where James now began in earnest to pursue work as a mine union organizer. The family travelled about in the interior, through Rossland, Fernie, and Nelson, south to Butte, Montana, where the two Virginias were born. These were hard-scrabble mining towns, and the Wilks family's movement reflects the development of mineral resources in the Kootenay region of British Columbia at that time. Some of the union locals that appeared in such towns as the Wilkses traversed between 1895 and 1903 were militant American unions whose incursion into Canada reiterates the strong north-south links of both the coal and base metal industries. According to labour historian Paul Phillips, 'with much of their ideology borrowed from European socialism,' radical American unions like the Western Federation of Miners were 'prone to direct action and meeting force with force' – so much so that by 1897, local chapters were urged to form their own rifle corps (1967: 28). North of the border, 'the new radicalism' was less vigilante in character: Canadian districts tended to reflect a stronger 'interest in setting up libraries and lectures to educate the membership, and in collecting statistics on unemployment, employment and wages' (Phillips 1967: 29). Devoted to self-education and improvement, such working mens' resources in the Kootenay were likely based on British models of Mechanics' and Literary Institutes that had already begun to appear throughout the province during its pre-Confederation years (Perry 2001: 84–9). It is conceivable that James Wilks, as a 'great man with words,' was involved with the work of such libraries and lectures in his capacity as a union organizer. Newspaper articles published at James's death state only that he eventually became 'President of the Kootenay branch of the Miner's Union for some years and was a well known figure for many years among organized miners in the West.'[7]

'The new radicalism' of organized labour and class consciousness in the early twentieth century was manifested not only by the increase in numbers of unionized workers, but by labour's extension into the political arena, with the proliferation of new – and often short-lived – parties. With this expansion of the left came division and factional schisms that deepened over the decades leading to the Depression. At least on the

West Coast, one of the most contentious causes of the 'widening rift' between 'old line . . . trade unionists and the rapidly rising radical socialists,' between good old-fashioned 'business' unionism and the newfangled political socialism, was the issue of Asian immigration, labour, and enfranchisement (Phillips 1967: 38, 88, 112). Orthodox unionists tended to oppose them all, rather strongly. But radicals differed on this point, and some began to regard the trade unions sceptically, 'as not being consistent with principles of scientific socialism,' even resorting, on occasion, to disrupting meetings by breaking out into a rousing round of 'The Red Flag' (Phillips 1967: 47, 87). By the thirties, this split in labour politics was thrown into relief by the 1933 election platforms of two major provincial parties: the newly formed Co-Operative Commonwealth Federation, which advocated enfranchisement for the Asian population; and the Liberal party, which capitalized on anti-Asian sentiment of the sort reflected by the establishment of the 'Asiatic Exclusion League' of 1921. The two parties split the labour vote (Phillips 1967: 109; Barman 1996: 254–5, 374).

This context is important for understanding the later phase of James Wilks's career. Sometime after he left Butte, Montana, James also turned from union organization to direct involvement with party politics. But not on behalf of any of the new labour parties or the CCF. Instead, he became a 'front man' for the splashy Liberal politician Gerry McGeer, at one point even serving as the Liberal party's provincial organizer. 'They were pretty close,' Virginia remarks of her father and McGeer.[8] By all accounts a colourful and loquacious politician, McGeer held multiple posts, sometimes more than one at the same time: he won the Vancouver-Burrard seat for the Liberals in the abovementioned 1933 provincial election, and soon after added the title of Mayor of Vancouver to his MLA status. As mayor, he literally read the Riot Act after a strike by the city's unemployed left him fearing an incipient communist revolution. He was something of a Christian social reformer, 'declaring war on gambling' and thus ridding Vancouver of one thousand pernicious slot machines, while also indulging his inclinations as 'a lay preacher, discussing "Christian Economics" ' (Davis 1976: 193–4). Gerry McGeer, paraded in effigy by the unemployed men of Vancouver's relief camps in 1935, was the candidate that an older James Wilks backed.

While there were probably many factors behind the ex-coal miner's political reorientation as a 'lib-lab' or moderate labour socialist in later life, the fiercely divisive issue of Asian labour and enfranchisement seems to have played a role in it. From his own experience, and even more so from the memory of his father's fate in the dank and dangerous mines of Vancouver Island, James Wilks may have harboured hard feelings against the Chinese immigrants whom 'captains of industry' like Robert Dunsmuir used to undercut and thwart the protests of White workers. He may have even blamed 'them' for the personal tragedy of his father's death. Although Virginia's fond reminiscences of her father contradict this view, James's support of the anti-Asian Liberal party at least points to this conclusion. More unequivocal were the views of his wife, Annie McCain Wilks, whom older family sources can recall openly voicing antagonistic opinions on the Chinese.[9] It was a bias typical of the White working class she and James stemmed from, a generation that attained middle and old age with 'the heyday of British Columbia's whiteness' and the 'zenith of its anti-Asian legislation' in the first half of the twentieth century (Perry 2001: 201). It is also one of the factors that, two generations down the line, would prompt Pat Lowther's own conflicted attitude toward the 'Inheritance' of her family history (*SD*, 14).

Eventually, James's connections to Gerry McGeer and the Liberal party helped secure him 'a government position' as the first licensed liquor vendor in North Vancouver. 'He was appointed by – I guess it would be [called] a patronage deal,' Virginia says of her father's sinecure.[10] First appointed to the job in 1929, James Wilks was still in the employ of 'the Vancouver branch' of that government liquor-vending 'service' when he suddenly died on 28 February, 1937, of a heart attack. He was sixty-four. The pall bearers at his funeral were 'presidents of the local Liberal association or their representatives.'[11]

'Patsy Lou,' who had appeared along with Pablo Neruda's *Residence on Earth* in 1935, was a baby, about eighteen months old, when her maternal grandfather died. At the time, her mother, Virginia, would nurse her to sleep by singing 'The Red Flag.' It was a 'great tune' for 'walk[ing] back and forth with a baby in your arms,' she said.[12] The song, originally written by a blacklisted dockhand and Irish expatriate on the occasion of the Great London Dock Strike of 1889, voiced a rallying cry for class solidarity that eventually became a well-known communist standard. 'The Red Flag' usually borrowed its melody from the German Christmas carol 'Tannenbaum,' making it a 'great tune' in emphatic iambic tetrameter, despite its dire lyrics:

The people's flag is deepest red,
It shrouded oft our martyred dead,
And ere their limbs grew stiff and cold,
Their hearts' blood dyed its every fold.

Then raise the scarlet standard high.
Within its shade we'll live and die,
Though cowards flinch and traitors sneer,
We'll keep the red flag flying here.

While Virginia later laughed at the memory of having reinvented Jim Connell's old 'Red Flag' as a nursery song, in 1937 the former Roxyette chorus-line girl was married into a family of dock- and ship-workers whose own history underlined both the original labour context of the song, and the importance of her own father's early work as a union organizer. Though the mortality and injury rates for longshoremen and waterfront workers were not as astronomical as those in the mining industry, this, too, was difficult and sometimes perilous work, as the fate of Virginia's father-in-law reinforced.

Arthur Tinmouth had still been a wan-faced, gaunt adolescent when his father, Arthur Sr, left for work at the Burrard shipyards one Monday in 1923, and never came home again. He was a steel caulker by trade, an experienced and 'highly respected' employee who had been with the company for a number of years. On the morning of May 28, Arthur Sr had been among a small crew of men assigned to make minor repairs to a liner called the SS *Niagara*. His mates reported that he had gone, alone, into the ship's 'deep tank to do some caulking'; when he failed to appear for lunch, they began to search for him. Later that afternoon, they finally found him:

> [T]he body was found jammed head and shoulders through the narrow opening to the bilges below the deep tank. His hips and legs were in sight, but his head and the upper part of his body were covered in about two feet of crude oil ... A great bruise on his forehead led to the belief that he had fallen from the tank and struck his head, being rendered unconscious as his body crashed into the bilges, and he was then smothered in the oil.[13]

Arthur's lunch was still in his trouser pocket.

His widow, Harriet, was left to raise her youngest six children on her own, with a small pension provided by the company. Newspaper reports of the accident couldn't seem to manage the task of naming the dead 'shipyard worker' accurately. The *Daily Province*'s headlines informed readers that an 'Arthur Kinmouth' had met a 'Horrible Death in Accident.' The *Vancouver Sun* went instead with 'A. Timmoth Meets Death on SS. Niagara in Mysterious Manner.' Over in North Vancouver, in the meantime, the weekly *North Shore Press* didn't even bother running a report of the latest fatality at the docks. It simply assumed the community's familiarity by word of mouth with Harriet Tinmouth's 'recent sad bereavement,' printing the widow's 'card of thanks' for flowers received, and trumpeting elsewhere in the same issue the 'Vancouver Port's Splendid Record.'[14]

In fact, though, Vancouver's 'splendid' ports were also producing an increasingly contumacious workforce in the years following Arthur Sr's death, and accident rates in the industry were among the workers' concerns. This discontent culminated in 1934 with a particularly violent longshoremen's strike that the *Vancouver Province* called 'the bloodiest hours' in waterfront history.[15] The violence occurred on the Vancouver side of the port when deckhands, freight handlers, and dock workers from various unions joined the longshoremen in a massive sympathy march on Ballantyne Pier. The police used tear gas and clubs to break up the demonstration; some of the protesting strikers hurled rocks and bricks. A handful were arrested, and scores were injured in 'the general melee.' Mayor Gerry McGeer was quoted as saying that the strike amounted to a brazen 'open declaration of war,' and placed the blame for such 'belligerent terrorism' squarely on the shoulders of 'Communist agitators' inciting the longshoremen to riot. He vowed to keep the port open for trade and commerce.[16]

It is interesting to speculate how the Ballantyne Pier riot, and the ongoing, serious waterfront disputes that coincided closely with the birth of Patricia Tinmouth in the summer of 1935, may have divided the family into which she was born. Given the political connections of Virginia's father to Mayor McGeer, on the one hand, and Arthur Tinmouth Jr's likely support for the longshoremen's cause, on the other, the subject of 'communist agitators' in the waterfront trade unions may have been the source of some debate between Arthur and his father-in-law, or between the Wilks and Tinmouth sides of the family more generally. With his wartime shift to the dry docks, Arthur himself later joined one of those large unions in which, as Mayor McGeer knew, communist organizers had indeed played an early, influential, and efficient role.[17]

Virginia's own incidental comments about the family's political affiliations suggest that the Tinmouths were never more than nominal sorts of 'communists': not converts to the Party so much as to a generalized social gospel that 'everybody was talking about,' at least before the war, when 'everybody was out of work, and everybody was a socialist.'[18] Indeed, by the mid-thirties, the Depression had plunged the entire City and District of North Vancouver into receivership. Municipal government was reduced to one-man rule by an appointed Commissioner, who promptly confessed 'that he was appalled when he first looked into the city's financial situation' and announced a debt approaching three and a half million dollars, not including money still owed for the Second Narrows Bridge.[19] As a result, services were slashed and taxes sky-rocketed to the point that many property owners lost title to their land. At least for as long as they lived at the caretaker's house by Lynn Creek, Arthur and Virginia Tinmouth could follow the dock disputes and the distress of the town below at somewhat of a distance. There were few municipal services up at the end of Lynn Valley Road anyway.

Virginia once quipped of her nursery room methods that if 'you walk back and forth with a baby in your arms singing "The Red Flag," it's got to have some effect on somebody.' She wondered whether that was why all of her children later tended to socialism. Virginia also recalled at least once taking a pre-school Pat with her when she went to go cast a vote; it was as a result of this early exposure to the electoral process that the scintillating tract *Instructions for Poll Clerks in Provincial Elections* could thereafter be added to her daughter's precocious reading repertoire. ('She hadn't a clue what it meant, but she read it.' And, of course, everyone was 'astonished.')[20]

Certainly, a young Pat grew up in a home where she learned quickly that politics mattered. Just how perceptively attuned she was to the adult world of politics is best revealed by some of the 'poems and stories made up by me' in her elementary school scribbler. 'Sea Bird,' for example, is a fairy tale about an underwater kingdom that suggests the parable of Jonah and the whale. But it also shows how the social reality of war shaped Pat's emergent consciousness. 'Sea Bird,' a beautiful and brave princess, lives with her father, the King, in a castle of 'white coral.' But she is also the heroine in a battle between nations. Instead of 'once upon a time,' the young writer begins: 'Once there was a great nation under the sea ... Now, you may think that being such a great fearless nation they would occupy the sea and have nothing to fight. But no indeed!' No indeed: the 'great nation' comes under attack from a 'great monster fish,' a leviathan who starts a war by swallowing a hapless 'mer-baby.' This prompts the fearless Princess Sea Bird to fly to the defence, followed by her 'whole nation': 'Sir Swordfish' and 'Sir Saw Fish' first, then the whole 'tuna' regiment, and finally the King himself, 'the Old Man of the Sea,' bringing up the rear. The encounter begins with the Princess's stern reprimand of the big 'fish' and ends with the whale not only contritely disgorging the 'mer-baby,' but also wanting to defect to Sea Bird's 'great nation.' He promises to be a loyal 'subject' and 'never be bad anymore.' In one more nice flourish, the whale's name is 'Romeo.'[21]

A fable of girl heroism, 'Sea Bird' also inescapably suggests the young author's awareness of the conflict of nations, which by 1941 was every-where apparent in her North Vancouver world, but nowhere directly so. There were great battles happening *somewhere*, but they weren't to be seen. They had something to do with the jerry-built houses slapped up on every square foot of unused land near the docks, foundries, and ironworks around Lower Lonsdale. And with the people streaming to and from the Vancouver ferries like schools of fish, into the shipyards and dry docks, day after day. Most of all, they had something to do with the sea itself, and with the leviathan-sized ships and aircraft carriers being built and refurbished at the very doorstep, as it were, of her dominion. As they began to emerge as distinct shapes within their incredibly intricate scaffolding, the curved girders and hulls of ships being built at the dry dock did indeed resemble the rib cage of a 'great monster fish.'

Unbeknownst to Patsy Lou, then busy writing her 'stories by me' in her school scribbler, one of her neighbours, Mrs Dorothy Livesay Mac-nair, was riveted by the same buzz of wartime activity. 'One day, fired with the excitement around me, I got permission to visit the North Van-couver shipyards myself, to observe first-hand how a ship was built,' Live-say recounts in *The Documentaries* (1968: 24). The resulting 'documentary' poem was called 'West Coast' (1943): 'And all about men flatten out the steel / with hammer beat, beat hammer, hammer beat, / shape it with sweat and muscle, shaped to fit / the muzzle of a ship, a new sea-bird' (26).

∽

For Livesay, the 'excitement' and energy of the war effort were tem-pered by the doubts raised by 'years of pacifism,' though she was also one of those leftists led to rethink communism before the last of those 'new sea-bird[s]' was sent off in defence of 'great' nations (1968: 24). The attentive child-writer, on the other hand, recognized the war as an important, but unfathomable, mystery. An adult Pat Lowther would later reflect upon the 'Rumours of War' she gleaned during her 'very early years.' It was the 'ominous news broadcasts / on the radio' that prompted a childhood dream about 'the Black Forest' 'moving across a map':

> Austria Poland Hungary
> would have meant nothing
> to me
> but the Black Forest
> came right up our ravine
> down over the mountains (*SD*, 10)

As though spilling right down over the tops of Mount Crown, Grouse Mountain, and Mount Seymour, the marching wood of the Black Forest 'moving across a map' brought enemy territory far too close for comfort. But by the time this poem was written, the war was a hazy childhood memory, and the path back to 'Patsy Lou's' rumoured Black Forest seems to have led through the Great Birnam Wood of *Macbeth*.

By that time, though, at least one thing was more clear. From the ancestors blown up in mines and smothered in bunker fuel, to 'Patsy Lou's' first 'red' lullabies and electoral tracts, to her early submarine fairy tales of war and peace, Pat Lowther was 'ready / to learn politics.' She had never been anything but.

Chapter 10

The Local Left

Even while still married to Bill Domphousse, Pat had begun to submit some of her short stories for publication. None of these attempts seems to have gotten past editors, though the 'curiously uneven' quality of some did arouse enough 'interest' to elicit fairly expansive rejection letters.[1] One such 'curiously uneven' work from around 1959 is economically entitled 'Red.' It is, *à la* Ernest Hemingway, a *very* short story – two pages, single-spaced. The title takes its cue from the main character, Harry Reddy, who, in turn, acknowledges that his name 'matches' both the colour of his 'hair' and his 'politics.' 'Red' is an old hand, a welder by day, a drinker by night. The plot, such as it is, focuses almost entirely on the ebb and flow of tension in a drunken political discussion that Red and his younger bar-room buddies find themselves drawn into. Set off by the plight of a laid-off co-worker saddled with 'three kids' and a wife 'up the stump again,' Red is angered by the indifference of the 'young bastards' who are more interested in the heads on their beers, though he himself is a long way into 'beer-bought belligerence.' As he slides into a mood of sloppy sentimentalism, a detached narrative voice takes over to articulate Red's disillusioned 'vision of universal brotherhood': 'The dream of Russia, that had held so much hope for so many, had died, had become only one more enemy.' Lurching back unsteadily to that hopeful vision for a moment, Red blurts out a message of fraternal love for his companions, throwing his arm around one of them 'in an excess of joy and comradeship,' and knocking over several beers in the process. This gesture is misconstrued as the overture of a 'lousy pervert' by the young man he embraces, and things head downhill from there. Red is soon escorted from the establishment by a bouncer. 'Hearing and tasting the word "pervert," and beginning to understand,' he staggers home, 'his shoulders hunched and his raw, red face completely blank.'[2]

With its protagonist caught between dismay at the legacy of Stalinist totalitarianism, on the one hand, and bewilderment at the defensive masculinity of a post-war generation, on the other, 'Red' is a perceptively observed scenario of alienation and confusion. Though the prose strains at times ('His heart felt as full as an aching bladder'), the neat narrative counterpoint between perversions of socialism and a perverse homophobia reflects the story's real potential. In addition to its focus on generational difference, it suggests an awareness of the banality of what passes for political debate in beer parlours – pubs of the sort that, say, Bill Domphousse usually spent his Friday nights at, around North Vancouver. The story's concern with unemployment is also drawn from life. As records from the Burrard Dry Docks indicate, recurrent lay-offs of the sort 'Red' laments were a significant problem for workers like Bill in the immediate post-war years.[3]

More importantly, 'Red' stands out as one of the relatively few works on explicitly political themes which survive from this phase of Mrs Domphousse's writing life. And if she had already been thinking about 'the dream of Russia' before Roy Lowther's first appearance, then the tutorial in Marxist-Leninist ideology no doubt began in earnest with his arrival in 1962. For in addition to Roy's prior involvement with the Labour Progressive Party, former associates also recall his affiliations with the 'Stanley Park Club,' 'a group of former Trotskyists.'[4] Roy's influence can definitely be discerned in the political poetry which Pat began to produce in the very early sixties, as her involvement with him first developed. Along with Roy, she began to write scads of pacificist verse, published during the early sixties in Labour Poets' pamphlet collections with names like *Poets for Peace* and *Poems for Life*. None of this work is particularly promising. Nevertheless, it reiterates the fact that Roy to some degree acted as a spur in the politicization of his younger wife, providing a form of socialist tutelage to a consciousness that was already flagged 'red' by the labour and trade unionist family background of which she was a product. Similarly, records suggest that Pat Lowther's life as a public activist and her involvement with party politics began only after her first marriage ended, and she became Roy's prized 'recruit.'

At the same time, Lowther's evident readiness for politics during the sixties clearly signals the effect of a cultural influence vastly broader and more plural in nature than the influence of any one individual, however overbearing or proselytizing that one man may have been. For many people, the decade itself unfolded as one long political catalyst. In America, the amassing of a large military presence in Viet Nam by 1962 prompted early stirrings of the anti-war protest that would crest with the rise of the New Left, and the introduction of a wider – and Whiter – conscription net, after mid-decade. In Canada, the New Democratic Party arose like a phoenix from the ashes of the old CCF in 1961, fanning widespread hopes for a revitalized and viable national socialist movement. And in Vancouver, the Old, the New, the counter-, and the anti- came together and 'over-lapped' in an 'active and differentiated' local landscape.[5]

Among the 'Old' well-entrenched communists, factional groups like the Maoists and Trots bickered amongst each other, splitting ideological hairs. Younger student radicals differed sharply from their elder 'comrades' in terms of their embrace of a more individualistic ethos, among other things. For this reason, younger leftists often found more common ground with other 'subversive' counter-cultural formations that were not necessarily, or only incidentally, political in nature (Blum 1991: 273–4). The old guard, on the other hand, Roy Lowther among it, viewed the openly hedonistic, hippy, drop-out and drug crowds with a suspicion and moral disdain that united it with the far right. As feminists would have to work diligently to convey, none of these leftist groups lived up to their 'radical' self-billing where it came to the concerns of the many women among them. Former Vancouver activist and friend of the Lowthers, Brian Campbell, sums it up: '... the political debate was much richer certainly than it is today.'[6]

It would have been this type of variegated local left that Lowther confronted during the anti–Viet Nam demonstrations she attended early in her marriage. In 1965, with Kathy and Alan in tow, she stood on the steps of the same Law Courts building that would later house Roy's trial, and read her anti-war poems. Not coincidentally, Lowther's participation in such rallies occurred during Milton Acorn's residency in the city. Acorn was an organizing force behind a committee called 'Artists against Viet Nam.' The group was established 'in the belief that artists perhaps more so than others can use their special awareness and their creative powers to combat the disease of apathy, which threatens everyone in our society,' and to 'bring an end to one of the most unjust, immoral, inhumane and destructive wars in the history of mankind.' Preparing flyers to advertise this artists' coalition was one of the projects Acorn was busy with at the time that Patrick Lane heard him banging about the Lowther abode in 1967.[7]

But Acorn's 'Artists Against Viet Nam,' like his Advance Mattress, was not long-lived. As Lane recalls, sometime in the spring or summer of 1968, Joe Rosenblatt and he 'finally put him on a railroad train and sent him packing back east.' It seems that the ever-itinerant Acorn had become too much for his friends to handle. 'Joe and I packed his stuff and put it in boxes and put him on the train, and said, "Don't come back,"' Lane laughs. 'What? Where am I going?' Acorn had asked. 'We said, "You're going to Toronto. And don't kill Gwen MacEwen when you get there."'[8]

Formed and dissolved in the space of a few years or even months, protest groups like 'Artists against Viet Nam' were fleeting in comparison to Lowther's far more continuous and significant political commitment to the NDP at both the municipal and provincial levels. In less than a decade, between 1963, the first year the NDP ran provincially, and 1972, when David Barrett finally won his unprecedented victory for the party, there were four elections in British Columbia. Lowther was active on behalf of the NDP almost from the start (as was Roy). By the fall of 1965, she was election canvassing for the unsuccessful 1966 race; thereafter, she became extensively involved with her constituency riding, an investment that tapered off only partially with her later assumption of new duties with other government and literary organizations.

One of the first roles Lowther assumed was as a constituency delegate to a newly formed group called the Vancouver Area Council, an NDP venture into municipal politics. Topping the list of this group's priorities was the call for a fundamental overhaul of the city's power structure. Vancouver's municipal system was unusual for a city its size – over the one million mark by the mid-seventies – in that its original ward system, thought to foster parochialism, had been long abolished. In effect, the absence of wards guaranteed a preponderance of 'professional-managerial' types on city council. It was this business-oriented segment of the population that tended to run for civic office, in no small part because, until the sixties, property qualifications for holding public office effectively shut out lower income, working-class residents like Pat Lowther. The 'professional-managerial' classes also, of course, tended to live in the wealthier neighbourhoods west of Main Street, leaving the city's east side pretty much voiceless (Tennant 1976: 179). The Vancouver Area Council, headed at different times by Pat's NDP friends, Hilda Thomas and Brian Campbell, thus lobbied for the re-establishment of a full ward system for the city, one that would ensure equitable representation for all neighbourhoods, and one that would ensure firm local control over such issues as zoning, development, and traffic controls.

Naturally enough, Lowther soon put her writing aptitude to work for her political causes, as well. On a purely practical level, she frequently acted as recording secretary during her riding association's monthly meetings, every third Thursday. For a woman who was rarely without a scribbler and a pencil anyway, and who would give up writing on a bus only when the bumps truly ruled out legibility, she probably figured she might as well employ herself constructively during these sometimes dry and dilatory meetings. Occasionally, she started notes for poems while taking the minutes, but generally she was a good listener – as could not be said for all of her fellow civic activists. More often, though, it was as a regular contributor to the *Mountaineer*, the newsletter of her local NDP riding, Little Mountain, that she applied her skills. In these pages, she interviewed people like Hartley Dent, the Party's provincial secretary, asking bluntly about the exact nature of his job ('That's a good question') and Dent's self-identification as a 'Christian Socialist.' She submitted calls for consumer boycotts of questionable corporate citizens, like Kraft Foods Inc., and she reported on symposia she attended and on standing committees that she chaired. She wrote capsule film reviews of National Film Board documentaries, and at least one short biographical profile, of NDP 'pioneer' Tom Anderson, a trade unionist whose history resembled the early career of her own grandfather, James Wilks.[9] And, she wrote on events related to the far left of the NDP, to which – with a few reservations – she inclined.

Demands for a 'more radical NDP' emerged on a national scale during the late sixties when some adherents became 'eager to challenge a party leadership' which had so far consistently failed to deliver electoral victory at the federal level (Morton 1977: 92). This alliance called itself 'the Waffle,' a name 'wryly adopted' in response to 'the intentionally broad generalities' of the group's 'original manifesto' (Waffle 1969: 1). The idea was, when in doubt, waffle to the left. By the early seventies there was a British Columbian wing of the Waffle; many of its members overlapped with those of the Vancouver Area Council. Heading into the 1972 provincial election, the B.C. Wafflers wanted to field a leadership candidate of their own, against David Barrett. In one of her most extensive articles for the *Mountaineer*, entitled 'Slicing Up the Waffle,' Lowther declared herself 'A Sometime Waffler.' She was against the idea of running a Waffle candidate because it seemed an empty 'gesture' to her. More importantly, she was dismayed by the in-fighting among fringe groups at the pre-convention meeting she attended, and provided a deft analysis warning of premature action and the potential consequences of dissension among the ranks:

> It seems obvious that the B.C. Waffle is not sufficiently cohesive, not even sure enough of where and who its political allies are, to engage in power struggles. Its single unifying issue is extra-parliamentary action, and this is, I think, where the B.C. Waffle must place its emphasis for the next space of time – on urging and jostling the NDP into actions which will help build a mass base.

In her reference to 'extra-parliamentary action,' Lowther was taking a page out of *The Waffle Manifesto*, which exhorted the Party to redirect its energies from 'winning an electoral victory' to the prerequisite goal of 'building a socialist base both within and outside of the ranks of the NDP' (46, 47). But she continued 'slicing up' her subject:

> If division within the Waffle should render it ineffective or sectarian, the effect for the Party as a whole would be disastrous. It's no secret that the NDP had been recruiting fewer and fewer young people until the advent of Waffle. It's also no secret that young people are joining the Party specifically to take part in Waffle. Without a really meaningful Waffle group now, we won't have a viable Party ten or twenty years from now.[10]

Aside from her critique of the provincial Waffle group's lack of tactical judgment and unity, Lowther sympathized with its agenda in principle, and her qualified support for her Party's left wing points to a very specific socialist platform. The Waffle went beyond the traditional labour-socialist call for 'public ownership of Canadian resource industries,' advocating state control also of Canadian 'financial institutions, including banks and trust companies' (Waffle 1969: 16, 29). Moreover, the group's *Manifesto* proposed that 'compensation' to owners and investors 'be made through low-interest long-term bonds,' adding the stern warning that 'corporations which obstruct nationalization by means of economic sabotage or other undemocratic means will be appropriated' (29–30). Chilean president Salvador Allende was in the process of nationalizing just such 'enterprises' when the frankly 'undemocratic means' of transnational capital effectively 'sabotaged' his plans. The political scandals that led to the debacle of the Chilean coup only entrenched the Waffle's already adamant stance against 'American corporate capitalism,' which it likewise identified as 'the major threat to Canadian survival today' (8).

Issues of sovereignty also stamped the Waffle's domestic policy: at a time when the FLQ was sufficiently terrorizing Ottawa for it invoke the War Measures Act, Wafflers unequivocally supported 'the recognition of Quebec nationhood as essential to the building of an independent socialist Canada' (20). And Lowther's own notebook jottings reiterate in one form or another most of *The Waffle Manifesto*'s program on 'Women's Liberation': the 'establishment of user-controlled day-care centers in all locations'; the 'removal of abortion from the criminal code'; the establishment of 'publicly financed birth-control and abortion centers for both information and medical care'; and income tax relief for working parents to defray child care costs (33).

Indeed, with Hilda Thomas, Bethoe Shirkoff, and others, Lowther specifically worked on behalf of the Party's local feminist caucus, which organized conferences and formulated policy papers on 'women's' issues such as 'safe and inexpensive birth control' and leave with pay for working mothers during children's illness. '[The] NDP,' one of her notebook entries states, 'regards the family as the basic social unit and believes that one of a government's most important functions is to assist the family in providing a harmonious, satisfying life for all of its members, particularly for the children.' By the seventies, she would have found herself affirming party proclamations like this with the discordant truth of her own inharmonious domestic life ringing in her ears.[11]

Poverty was a related 'women's' issue. Among others, journalist Ian Adams had pointed this out in *The Poverty Wall*, a popular 1970 book that Lowther appears to have read:

> Imagine a city, a walled city of 350,000 adults and more than 1.1 million children. A city larger than Winnipeg, as big as Vancouver, but different. The weird thing about this city is that there are no men; there are only women. If you can see such a city in your mind's eye, then you are looking at the real and enormous number of abandoned and forgotten people who live silently among us. Because ... there are that many women in this country, bringing up their children on marginal incomes and the subsistence that is welfare. (Adams 1970: 61)

As one of the '350,000' women inhabiting Adams' citadel, Lowther was one of the vocal contingent who chose not to 'live silently' among surrounding affluence, and she had begun to speak for herself. Around the time Adams's book appeared, she was writing poems with titles like 'Address to Welfare Mothers' and speaking on behalf of SHARE, 'a self-help organization for lower-income mothers.' 'We are the margarine eaters, the Army & Navy sale day shoppers,' she wrote of the group she represented, which was opposing proposed rate hikes at B.C. Tel.:

> Not all of us in SHARE are welfare recipients, but many are. These families do not have an allowance for utilities. The telephone bill, like the heat and the light, has to be squeezed out of the food allowance. It's hanging by a wire now. Put [rates] up even another 75¢, which is a pound and a half of hamburger, if you know where to get it at that price, and a lot of people are going to have to do what they have become expert at doing – do without.[12]

The 'freezing' old house on St George Street may have been behind her, but 'perpetual arrears' on basic utilities were still a perpetual worry.

As an extension of her work with community coalitions like SHARE, Lowther became involved, late in 1971, with helping a group of NDP women to organize a conference on poverty. The invited keynote speaker was the author of *The Poverty Wall*, Ian Adams. Bethoe Shirkoff remembers at least two things about the 'all-woman planning meeting' she and Lowther attended in advance of the event. One is that Pat was 'chain smoking' while 'she mentioned . . . that she was trying to cut down on the cigarettes.' She was trying not to inhale, she said. And two is that the progressive wing ran into some trouble that night, 'with the arrival of two vigorous young men, heavy thinkers in the NDP at that time, who scrapped half of our carefully laid plans, which they said exceeded the terms of reference with which we had been entrusted.'[13] Even among the ranks of the egalitarian NDP, it seems, there were a few good men who preferred to keep Ian Adams's 'Hidden City' of voiceless women just that.

Over the next few years, Lowther found herself declining nominations for higher profile but time-consuming executive positions within her riding association. If she was going to take on more work, at least some of it had to be paid. She was sanguine about the part-time position she landed during the summer of 1973 as a secretary for the constituency office at Hillcrest Hall. To Eugene McNamara, she described her job as 'a sort of PR secretary for Phyllis Young, who is minister without portfolio in the B.C. Government and will head a new Consumer Affairs dept. in the fall.' 'I'm hoping,' she added, 'my new job will sustain me through the summer – keep me from wallowing in self-pity and frustration.'[14] The 'new job' did, eventually, give her a windowless 'Cask of Amontillado' office of her own for a few months, and even a few hours to write poetry. But the work wasn't as impressive as she described it, or as sustaining as she may have hoped. Rita Lalik was the minister's actual executive 'PR secretary'; Lowther, as an office temp, actually worked as an intermediary between her fellow constituents and the higher-ups, mainly stuck with mundane tasks like fielding phone calls, tallying the results of questionnaires, and directing mail. Nor did the job last out a year. She moved on, probably because she was increasingly busy with other work, or bored silly, or – as Lalik speculates – because Roy made the job more difficult than it was worth – because 'Roy objected to everything Pat did.'[15]

At the same as time she turned down a 1973 nomination for vice-president of the Little Mountain NDP association, Lowther nevertheless accepted another volunteer position as Chair of the riding's Education Committee, a post that reflected her commitment to fostering 'the development of socialist consciousness' (Waffle 1969: 8). This was 'kind of a fun job,' as she put it, which mainly involved arranging a series of panel discussions and visiting speakers. During the year that she assumed the post, Lowther brought in speakers for talks on topics ranging from consumer problems to the situation in Chile, before and after the coup – the latter, a prelude to the appearance of Allende's widow elsewhere in Vancouver late that year. As part of their 'educative purpose,' local affiliates of the NDP ran such lecture series on a continuing basis. Members also heard about the 'Evolution of Parliamentary Democracy' and 'The Evolution of the Welfare Society,' as well as 'Economic Theories and Systems' and 'Canada's Future vis à vis Foreign Economic Control.'[16] Late in the fall of 1974, the Little Mountain association brought in Claire Culhane, a former medical administrator in Viet Nam, whose first-hand account (and film) of conditions in Quang Ngai moved Lowther to write about the obligation of the political witness – and the refusal of that role.[17] The film nights at Hillcrest Hall, made barely possible by a temperamental borrowed projector, were an extension of the NDP's educational program, and the Friday night 'pub nites,' which Pat and Roy by this time usually attended separately, on alternate weekends, were a sociable extension of the informal film gatherings.

While she seems to have made a conscious decision to try to contain her work with the constituency, Lowther was a bit too effective for her

own good when it came to her local activism. Passionately committed to
the printed word herself, she could nevertheless stand up at meetings of
the Vancouver Area Council to point out that the whole assembly was
'too print-oriented.' As Bethoe Shirkoff recounts it, she said

> that many of us find it easy to turn out a leaflet, easier than walking a picket
> line ... or speaking up on unpopular issues before a hostile crowd. We find
> reading easy, she said, and we fire off bulletins and articles and manifestos
> and think these will cure social ills. But a lot of people don't enjoy reading,
> she said, and how are we to reach those people [?][18]

It was, no doubt, moments like this which transformed the greenhorn
from North Vancouver into a recognized and well-respected member of
the civic left wing during the years 1965–75. Many of her fellow activists,
like Shirkoff, 'had no idea she was a poet.' Shirley Miller, a neighbour
and NDP feminist whom Lowther worked with fairly closely over the
entire decade, discovered Lowther's identity as a writer only in the
spring of 1975.[19]

As a result of the community profile she established over the decade,
Lowther was also, much to her husband's chagrin, repeatedly elected
as a riding delegate and representative to NDP provincial conventions, in Vancouver in 1973 and in Penticton in 1975. It was a direct
step from her inclusion in such provincial forums to the real plum:
her final appointment to the advisory council of the B.C. Arts Board.
Late in the fall of 1974, the provincial secretary, Ernie Hall, had established an 'interim' Arts Board 'to advise on cultural matters until such
time as regional arts panels' could be established in the province. The
role of the interim council was tantalizingly capacious: it was, simply,
to 'suggest new policy in the arts' and then lobby vigorously for it.[20]
This time, when Lowther mentioned her new job to friends, she
wasn't overestimating its importance or its ability to 'sustain' her. In
fact, literary friends who had first helped her into print quietly took
note of the appointment among themselves: '... she is in a position to
make things work [for] B.C. writers,' as Seymour Mayne now
remarked to Patrick Lane.[21] Especially since she had already learned
her way around the office of the provincial secretary, this was a role

Lowther could really sink her teeth into. She got down to work right away.

During the spring of 1974, the government had circulated 'a draft cultural policy . . . to interested groups for feedback.' As a first step, Lowther took the pulse of that feedback. She noted that 'comments of local artists range all the way from "light years ahead of anything we've ever had before," to "a pile of shit." '[22] Undeterred, she then set about formulating her own priorities, namely, access and funding (priorities not so very different, after all, from the child custody matters that had preoccupied a newly separated Mrs Domphousse). On the first issue, she wrote: '... the most important thing [that] an NDP cultural policy should provide is indeed access to the arts.' She was particularly concerned that 'a socialist cultural policy' accommodate isolated rural communities 'not serviced by a large university or college,' or by other advantages of 'urban centres' where artists tended to converge. To that end, she proposed provincially funded reading tours, with a particular mandate to reach smaller communities, and to help artists from those communities, especially in the remote 'northern parts' of the province, gain exposure themselves. She wanted to ensure the existence of community resource facilities, which would provide free means for 'all citizens to participate in art activities.' That meant everything from access to adequate 'rehearsal space' to a 'minimum' complement of publicly available office equipment, like typewriters and a 'duplicating machine.' She argued that 'art instruction – such as music lessons, etc.,' be subsidized for low-income adults and children. She advocated more extensive use of artists in classrooms. And, her wish-list included the proposal for a bookmobile project, which would see B.C. books and Canadian authors brought to every region in the province.[23] Big-city urbanite though she had become, Lowther had not forgotten the lessons of Rice Lake, Deep Cove, and North Vancouver – right down to the idea of the old 'portable' library, only this time on wheels, rather than skid runners.

In itself, the ideal of unfettered access seemed simple enough. In tandem with the issue of funding, however, a coherent 'socialist cultural policy' suddenly became a much more delicate balancing act, one that asked Lowther to make some very deliberate decisions about the distribution of public wealth. The tension between the principle of 'grassroots' inclusiveness, on the one hand, and the inherently meritorious cause of 'art,' on the other, is manifest from the outset of her draft posi-

tion paper, which proposes parallel but separate 'goals' for two different
levels of arts funding:

<u>Goals</u>:
1   To encourage the creative power of everyone in B.C., especially in the
    areas of creativity which a profit-minded society neglects.
2   To provide special encouragement and support for individuals and
    groups who have demonstrated exceptional talent in their field, espe-
    cially where this support leads to a dissemination of their skills in B.C.

Lowther insisted that by separating out these double 'goals,' both could
be pursued in a fully compatible way. 'Funds administered by regional
art panels,' she argued, 'should be clearly separated for assistance to two
categories of applicants: amateur and professional. Amateur and professional artists should never be in a position of competing for the same
funds.' It is hard to miss the force of conviction behind that *never.*

   She could try to pre-empt 'competition' and potential conflict
between 'amateurs' and 'professionals' by creating separate resource
pools. She could try to democratize the 'professional' by adding the
funding caveat about the obligation to 'disseminate' such 'skills.' And
she could state, categorically, if also with an oddly convoluted syntax:
'The idea that an artist who is not conspicuously at the top of his field is
a failed artist must be rejected by socialists.' But the bottom line was that
a two-tiered funding system – one for 'everyone in B.C.' and another for
a select set deemed to 'have exceptional talent' – reinforced a stub-
bornly preferential social distinction that nagged uncomfortably at
Lowther's 'red' sensibilities. From her own most exacting socialist point
of view, her plan was inescapably problematic. When in doubt, she was
supposed to be waffling to the *left.* Instead, here she was, using a position of real political influence to promote a scheme that would necessarily direct a disproportionate (as some might argue) amount of public
resources to a small minority – or 'elite' – judged to have 'exceptional
talent.' Even more troublesome, the system she advocated was based
upon potentially self-replicating recognition, since the adjudicators of
such 'exceptional talent' were to be 'authorities in various art disciplines,' that is, 'professionals' and 'professional' artists, in the first
place. This internal dissonance made for some vigilant self-editing in
the handwritten preliminary draft fragments of Lowther's document: 'If
art is ~~not to become the monopoly of a small elite~~ to truly inform and
enrich society, it must be nurtured by society at the grass-roots level.'

But as a government adviser *and* an artist, it's hard to say what else she might have proposed. In 'Notes toward a Socialist Cultural Policy for British Columbia,' the socialist in her went to conscientiously detailed lengths to ensure the healthy proliferation and inclusiveness of what she called 'a people's culture,' one enhanced by at least the possibility of creative expression and practice at all levels. Conversely, the poet in her – and by this point, the League Chair, too – recognized the 'professional' card as the most effective leverage that artists had to distinguish themselves from the multifarious claimants to government funding – agencies that tended to understand the concept of 'culture' better when it came as an adjective clinging like a wet sponge to words like 'industry' or 'business.' By 1975 the mark of the 'professional' artist could not be abandoned, despite the real risks of importing the language and regulatory ethos of 'professionalization' and rationalized production into the domain of creative endeavour. These included the risk of rather grossly misrepresenting an underclass of 'professional' artists, many of whom could at best hope to eke out a subsistence-level living from whatever government largesse fell their way.

In a sense, Lowther's two-tier proposal for provincial arts funding was simply trying to take into account that, as Roy would later put it, 'there are different standards for different groups, different audiences' (CATT, 3: 401). While Pat was agonizing over her blueprint for a 'socialist cultural policy,' Roy had, in fact, been trying, without success, to secure a municipal grant for his Vancouver Writer's Guild, an 'amateur' group he ran after his involvement with the Vancouver Poetry Society ended. In a 1974 editorial he wrote for the organ of the VWG, *Pegasus*, Roy prophesied that David Barrett's new NDP government would spell 'a new day for the amateur' – 'if' its cultural policy was 'not subverted by hungry and vociferous professionals.' 'The amateur writer, musician, painter, filmmaker, hobbyist, ethnic folk artist: the *people* [will] become – tentatively, but with need – artists.'[24] But Roy's prediction of a new artistic legitimacy for amateur producers was seriously rattled when he discovered, a few months later, that his wife would be among the handful of those invested with the power of shaping and implementing any new government arts policy. This was a discovery he made while Pat was away on a Canada Council–sponsored trip to a Canada Council-sponsored League meeting in Fredericton. As he later elaborated in his journals:

In principle, Pat supported the cause of amateur writing more earnestly than most. But the Vancouver Writer's Guild, its members and their works were anathema to her ... So ... when I learned that applications were being accepted by the Provincial Secretary for the 14 positions on the new Arts Board, it was from someone else . . . ten days after the deadline passed! I got confirmation that Pat Lowther, who was then in Fredericton, rocking her peers with her poetry readings ... had sent in her application in September. She had told me nothing. (RLJ, 1:79)

Here was all the living proof of a disaffected 'amateur' artist anyone could need. Roy later admitted that he and his wife 'differed ... on some of those things' related to Arts Board policy and appointments (CATT, 3:392).

Roy accounts at least in part for the great lengths to which Pat went, in her draft 'socialist cultural policy,' to ensure some level of official validation and financial support for amateur groups. Though Roy was too blinded by anger and humiliation over his exclusion from the ranks of the 'hungry and vociferous professionals' to see it, she *was* attempting to address the real problems of social and literary distinction that were contributing to the estrangement between them. And while Roy was probably right that his Vancouver Writer's Guild had become 'anathema' to Pat by the time she assumed her Arts Board position, at some level, her entitlements as a 'professional' poet, leaving her husband behind with the aspiring masses, appear as another factor in what Patrick Lane calls her 'strange confused concern for Roy' (1995: 30). Along with everything else that clamoured for her attention there was a 'strange confused' sense of guilt about defecting from the ranks of a 'comrade' whom she once believed had preceded her in the struggle for a truly transformative, 'red' socialist democracy. That probably felt like a long time ago.

James Wilks and four of his children in Butte, Montana, ca. 1909.
Two-year-old Virginia is second from left, holding her father's hand.

Isabelle 'Belle' Wilks at the height of her stage career during the 1920s.

The caretaker, Arthur Tinmouth Jr, and his first child,
at the Lynn Creek intake, ca. 1937.

Rice Lake reservoir, ca. 1929: 'And there I walked on water.'

'Annie McCain bequeathed to me her lace': Patsy Lou and the grandmother
of her 'Inheritance,' ca. 1938.

Big sister with her younger charges, Brenda (right) and cousin Karl (middle),
Bowen Island, ca. 1945.

Mrs Domphousse and her first two babies, Alan and Kathy, ca. 1958.

The newlyweds at 5823 St George Street: Roy looking up to his
'recruit' from the start.

Christine (left) and Beth Lowther, ca. 1975.

Relativity — Small Arctic sun, curving space
around her.

Song arranges itself at The door of (my, one's) mouth

mother   O.V. — Figure without landscape
midwife,   (woman on/against snow)
responsibility,

        trapping — rabbit, fox, weasel (ermine)
                lemmings, squirrel,

Song arranges itself   She is a small Arctic sun,
at The door   curving space around her.
of one's mouth   This world swirls,
abraded One is beaten by grief   changes with every wind.
1   like snow with many teeth   she must shape The world
        The walls drip water   by being alive
        and glaze
        Words name The dead   Figure without landscape
        for a time   white with The many names of snow
        breathing song   she makes her house
        one is not alone   of skin and snow.

        Give me a bone for my hunger Alone,
kuliguk   for The others are dead,
        I will turn it in my hand
        till it speaks
        I will call from it
        shapes, faces,
        with my ulu
        I will call from it

Notebook draft page showing Lowther's method of composition for
'Woman on/against Snow.'

'Milk stone' on Mayne Island.

The League 'Chair Creature,' 1975.

Chapter 11

The Age of the Bird

As it turned out, Lowther would not see the 'socialist cultural policy' she sweated over during the summer of 1975 put to the test anyway. That year, Premier David Barrett called an election with two years remaining in his government's mandate, and it wasn't a good move. Apparently to its own surprise, the NDP lost the race, to a coalition led by the son of the previous premier, W.A.C. Bennett. The NDP's day in the fleeting British Columbian sun was over: the tenure of the so-called 'Chile of the North' had lasted barely three years, bracketed on either side by a sturdily conservative Social Credit dynasty.

The vicissitudes of provincial politics over such a short period of time parallel the rapid and significant changes in Pat Lowther's life during the seventies. Between 1970 and 1975, she not only came of age politically, but also made her major literary contributions. In those same years, she was coming of age in a more literal sense, too. When Lowther first took up her official duties with the Arts Board in early June of 1975, she was approaching the mid-life milestone of her fortieth birthday. While a teenaged Pat had lusted after 'legends of the hills,' the adult Pat, a more experienced 'mountaineer,' recognized summits for the ambivalent places they were – apexes both glorious and worrisome. And while middle age matters to most everyone, it mattered quite a lot to Lowther, whose literary prospects had to do not simply with productivity, but more specifically with productivity in relation to her age. This is a recurrent theme in her correspondence from the seventies.

Patrick Lane, for instance, had once sent Lowther a batch of poems by Peter Trower, a poet recently celebrated as British Columbia's very own 'people's poet,' but in 1973 struggling to obtain recognition as a writer. Lowther wrote back to Lane with assurances of her support for

Trower's work. Of Trower's so far unsuccessful application for a Canada Council Arts Bursary, she also added:

> I wonder how much of a factor his age is. I heard somebody, I can't remember who, who had been on the [Canada] Council, say that they don't really consider applications from people over forty. Anne Marriott got one [grant] this year, but she's probably the exception.[1]

The truth or falsehood of the rumour is in some sense less important than Lowther's attention to its very existence. Her remark reveals that when she wrote these words in 1973, she was more or less consciously trying to prove or disprove it for herself, by keeping mental tabs on who was and was not getting funded, and how old they were.

In the context of the emphatic 'youth culture' of the time, Lowther's concern with perceptions of age as a handicap for 'late' artistic bloomers, especially women, cannot be dismissed. Age factored overtly into the politics of the literary culture of her era when it came to celebrating the youthfulness of the 'new.' When Al Purdy published his anthology *Storm Warning: The New Canadian Poets*, in 1971, at least one mathematically minded reviewer took the time to carefully calculate 'the average age' of the 'new Canadian poets' represented between the book's covers. 'Twenty-five' was the sum triumphantly announced: 'they are the generation of first post-war babies who came of age in Canada's centennial year'; 'their poetry reflects a young, back-to-the-land movement.'[2] The anthology was deliberately manufactured to solicit this sort of attention. Purdy had agreed to the condition of an 'arbitrary' 'upper-age limit ... cut-off point' imposed by Jack McClelland and 'the McStew editors,' and the book played up this specific demographic both in its back-jacket blurb and in the biographical profiles (and photos) of its young 'new Canadian poets.'[3]

At the same historical moment that being 'young' had begun to matter more than ever, few people – like Lowther's anonymous Council source – were willing to admit that *not* being particularly young might make a difference, too. As a liability, the issue of age either went unspoken or was privately acknowledged between friends, like Lowther's small-press publishers, Allan Safarik and Patrick Lane. 'One problem in this land is that there are such catagories [*sic*] as young poet or established poet,' Safarik wrote to Lane, about a year after Lowther's death. Safarik was alluding to another anthology then being planned along the lines of Purdy's *Storm Warning*. 'We are attempting to put Pat Lowther into this anthology,' he informed Lane. 'Of course,' he added, matter-of-factly, 'she was left out of the first *Storm Warning* for being too old.'[4]

In Purdy's first, 1971 *Storm Warning*, virtually all of the 'new Canadian poets' were men, and his anthology tilted decisively toward a masculine mythology of the writer-as-scrappy-frontiersman and/or alienated-labourer. In this respect there was evidently more to the omission of a poet like Lowther than the factor of her age alone.[5] Nevertheless, Safarik's candid reminder that Lowther could be 'left out . . . for being too old' reinforces Patrick Lane's perception of her as a more mature and conspicuously un-drugged reader during the fitful days of the Advance Mattress. Both recall the fact that her career was promoted at the outset by small-press publishers who, if they did not actually belong to a 'younger' and distinctly self-defined generation that 'came of age during Canada's centennial year,' then at least they identified with that generation. Though her early publishers recognized the promise of her work, Lowther was not anymore a part of their 'scene' than she was a part of the generation of senior mentors and 'established' poets such as Dorothy Livesay, who also worked to advance her poetry.

It does not go quite far enough to say that, demographically, Lowther fell between the crests of two highly influential literary generations of forties modernists and sixties *New Wave* centennial 'babies.' True, she herself had 'come of age' during the fifties, 'this largely reactionary period' in our 'literary situation,' as Raymond Souster put it, in his preface to *New Wave Canada* (1966). Nevertheless, she was closer in age – in some cases, very close, indeed – to many of the writers who appeared in anthologies like Souster's *New Wave Canada* and Purdy's *Storm Warning*'s. But she was neither a pedigreed postmodernist, as was the case with the mostly *Tish*-affiliated 'young Canadians' profiled in Souster's *New Wave Canada*, nor a sturdy, bushwhacking backwoodsman, part of the 'young back-to-the-land movement' reflected by the *Storm Warning* group – Ken Belford, Patrick Lane, Sid Marty, Andrew Suknaski, and Tom Wayman, among them. Lowther's Cold War coming-of-age, *in combination with* her relatively late self-discovery as a writer, better accounts for her slightly eccentric, slightly out-of-sync relation to many contemporary literary currents of her period. That her later start as a 'serious' writer had profoundly to do with the double-barrelled circumstances of her working-class womanhood was of little interest in a literary market place that had recently begun to place a heavy commodity premium on newness, youth, and early-onset genius. It was a literary culture vastly changed from the one that had published F.R. Scott's first *Overture* in 1945, when that poet debuted at the age of forty-six. Consequently, during the seventies, Lowther had at least partial grounds to worry about being regarded as 'too old' or somehow belated. Until she died, that is. After that, she would be universally regarded as tragically young.

It was at the very outset of the decade, in 1970, that Lowther first met Allan Safarik and his publishing partner, Brian Brett, through Seymour Mayne. Safarik and Brett were young undergraduates, in their early twenties, who attended the new university up on the mountain, Simon Fraser. At the time, they defined themselves as 'anarchists.'[6] The 'anarchists' were dedicated craftsmen when it came to their literary productions. They started a little magazine, *Blackfish*, which began publishing an interesting mix of poetry, not just by the usual local talents – Earle Birney, P.K. Page, Dorothy Livesay – or even the familiar, not-so-local talents – Al Purdy, Milton Acorn, Margaret Atwood. One issue also included translations of Japanese and Chinese poetry by writers truly 'unknown' in Vancouver, and most issues also published poetry by home-grown up-and-comers like Patrick Lane and, by 1971, the editors' new friend, Pat Lowther. For its ambitious range, as well as for the quality of work by newcomers like Lowther, *Blackfish* was a magazine that 'immediately' struck George Woodcock 'as several cuts above the ordinary little magazine brought out for two or three issues by frustrated poets trying to get their own work into print' (1975: 93).

The fall 1971 issue of *Blackfish* included a number of poems from Lowther's newly compiled *Milk Stone* manuscript – including 'Woman,' 'Psyche,' 'Arctic Carving,' 'Moonwalk Summer,' and 'Now.' 'Coast Range,' from the still in-process *A Stone Diary*, also first appeared in this issue.[7] When Safarik and Brett decided to branch out into a series of limited-edition broadsheets, they approached some of their Vancouver-based contributors, including Lowther, for projects to design. The result was the appearance of Dorothy Livesay's *Disasters of the Sun*, Seymour Mayne's *Face*, and, in 1972, Lowther's *The Age of the Bird*. Lowther's was fourth in the Blackfish broadside series. *The Age of the Bird* was described in a press circular as 'a long poem in eight sections, each on a separate sheet of parchment paper. Inserted loosely in a green Spanish-leather-weave heavy card folder, hand-sewn and painted.' One hundred and fifty of the elegant, oversized broadsheets were printed, signed and numbered by the author.

'Brian and I went to a great deal of trouble,' Safarik remembers of producing *The Age of the Bird*. With scarcely a scrap of money to their name, the Blackfish duo relied on a borrowed printing press (Simon Fraser University's) and their own time and ingenuity. For Lowther's broadsheet, at her suggestion, they first headed on one gray and rainy day to her place on East 46th. Since Lowther's long poem was based loosely on the death of the Marxist guerilla leader Che Guevara, she thought that they might find some suitable illustrations among Roy's old books – he had 'thousands,' many of them library rejects with their 'pages falling out.'[8] They found some vaguely Aztec-looking designs, cut them out with an Exacto knife, and later proceeded to hand set the illustrations among the text. They determined that *The Age of the Bird* was not *that* long a long poem. So, since Lowther 'was writing a pile about Chile' at the time, Brett and Safarik decided to append 'Regard to Neruda' to the unbound chapbook as well. They were simply fitting in as much as they could produce, Brett explains.[9]

In his review of Brett and Safarik's publications, Woodcock concluded that *The Age of the Bird* 'was easily the best of the Blackfish Press cycle of broadsheets.' In the same breath, he speculated that Lowther's treatment of Guevara's 'guerilla campaign' was 'garnished, one suspects, by memories of *Green Mansions*' (1975: 94) – W.H. Hudson's popular novel from 1904, subtitled 'A Romance of the Tropical Forest.' There are general correspondences between the texts: both deal with political turmoil in remote jungle regions, and both invoke mythological figures, half-human, half-bird. Perhaps Lowther had read Hudson's tale at some point; it had become a best-seller after Alfred Knopf issued an American edition around the time of the First World War, and it's quite feasible that a dusty copy or two lingered among the modest and mostly dated library offerings of Lowther's North Vancouver. What is more certain is that Lowther wasn't relying only on 'memories' of a distant romance in writing her poem: her handwritten preliminary drafts of *The Age of the Bird* make self-conscious reference to what 'my sources don't say' and 'my research doesn't tell,' lines she wisely pruned at a later stage.[10]

In daring to write a poem about a Cuban revolutionary in South America, Lowther was mightily engaged in 'A Kind of Wrestling,' as she'd called it in her earlier essay. The poem's foreign subject matter meant that she found herself apprehensively 'pushing and pulling against limitations I am constantly discovering,' struggling with the 'truism that a person can write only about what he knows.' For a non–Spanish-speaking poet who had scarcely left the borders of her native land, the leap into Latin American revolutionary politics was a long one.

Still, as Eugene McNamara soon pointed out, *The Age of the Bird* was also, importantly, 'about' larger historical and temporal processes: 'The image of the bird is emblematic of [that] stage in the evolutionary process, immediately after the reptilian age, just on the brink of the time of mammals and the coming of man' (McNamara 1977: 23). The attention of Lowther's new long poem to prehistory and evolutionary time is consistent with an emerging preoccupation in her other work too, in both *Milk Stone* and *A Stone Diary*. In this respect, *The Age of the Bird* reflects a poet newly intrigued by the confluence of mythology and science – each, in its way, a quest for origins. It is an interest that points as much to the example of Pablo Neruda's *Canto General* – in itself, a sweeping poetic re-vision of Darwin's *On The Origin of Species* – as it may to the precedent of W.H. Hudson's exotic romance, *Green Mansions*.

Not long after the appearance of the Blackfish chapbook, Lowther was invited 'to do the Western tour' with Margaret Atwood, as she'd excitedly written to 'Dee' Livesay. At the time, the League of Canadian Poets was sponsoring reading tours which routinely paired established writers with less well known colleagues. Gerald Lampert, the organizer, was a little vague on specifics about the tour at first, creating a series of confusions about scheduling and leading Lowther to the 'impression' that the tour would consist of three provinces, or at least three dates.[11] It was on this assumption that she initially contacted Atwood by mail. When she discovered, 'piecemeal and unofficially,' that the touring 'arrangement' would consist of only two provinces – British Columbia and Saskatchewan – she dashed off an anxious note to Atwood, correcting herself. She didn't want her error to be misconstrued as naked presumption: 'It's left me feeling rather foolish, as I feel it may have made me appear to be seeking advantages that others aren't getting.'[12]

By current standards of travel, it may not appear of much consequence whether Lowther's first reading tour as a professional poet would span two or three provinces. But the year of *The Age of the Bird* marked the most extensive flight that Lowther had taken, to that date, from 'the land of rain and riots' she called home.[13] Aside from a few day trips across the Washington State border as a teenager, she had travelled out-of-province only once before, to attend a poetry conference Livesay organized in Edmonton in 1969. Apart from that, she had never, to age thirty-seven, left British Columbia. But the fall of 1972 changed this, thanks first of all to the League's Third General Meeting, held October

6–8 in Edmonton, to which Lowther travelled again, over the Rockies by train, and where, this time, she would re-encounter McNamara and ignite that relationship. She was barely home from that pivotal trip when it was time to get on a plane for the Saskatchewan leg of her readings with Atwood in Saskatoon on October 23rd, and in Regina the following day.

Already a Governor General's Award winner for her first book of poetry, *The Circle Game* (1966), the ever-prolific Atwood published two books in 1972 alone: *Survival*, her critical survey of Canadian literary culture, and her second novel, *Surfacing*. Four years Lowther's junior in age, Atwood had also already published five books of poetry, including the recent *Power Politics* (1971) and *The Journals of Susanna Moodie* (1970). She was impeccably educated, with a degree from Toronto and graduate experience at Radcliffe. Saskatchewan was not the furthest afield she'd ever been.

On her 'western tour,' it was impossible for Lowther not to be overshadowed by her already eminent contemporary. Andrew Robertson, the poets' host at their October 24th University of Regina reading, introduced Atwood as 'the woman who has been referred to as Canada's foremost literary talent.' His introduction of Lowther, on the other hand, had already been the subject of some rather anxious correspondence in advance of her appearance:

> Dear Pat,
> ... I have offered to introduce you when you come to read at Regina on October 24th. I must confess that I have been unable to find any book of yours other than *This Difficult Flowring* here in Regina; and anthologies are hardly a fair picture. First of all, then, can you tell me where I can write for them – and speedily!? Can you tell me when *Milk Stone* is going to be available?
>
> The biography that Lloyd [Person] had to pass on is almost non-existent. I don't want to pry, but nor do I want to be totally oblivious. Perhaps you could drop me a line soon ...[14]

There's no record of how Lowther responded to this plea to pad out her 'almost non-existent' biography. On the actual evening of the reading, her host settled on introducing her as a poet who 'continually tries to broaden the horizon of her experience.' Before handing over the stage to Lowther, Robertson then reminded the audience – like they needed reminding – that Atwood would follow the break.[15]

Second fiddle was the assignment, but if any publicity is good publicity, then being paired with a hot ticket like Atwood had its obvious advantage, too. Atwood's name guaranteed good crowds and a new level of exposure for Lowther. The October 30th Vancouver reading following those at Regina and Saskatoon, for example, proved a fire marshal's nightmare, packed and filled to overcapacity. That reading, the tour's culmination in Lowther's home town, took place at Simon Fraser University on a Monday evening. Among 'the attentive overflow crowd' in the lecture theatre was at least one student journalist, smitten gaze trained firmly on 'the smooth Botticelli face' and 'Dali eyes' of the star attraction: 'The lights and cameras were on Margaret Atwood, whose novels and poems have earned her a definite position among Canada's best contemporary writers.' As for Lowther, the reporter for the *Peak* concluded: 'Her softness [of voice] and smaller reputation kept her in an odd sort of supporting role.'[16]

The *Vancouver Province* was in the packed house that night, too, in the person of Andreas Schroeder, a journalistic regular on the local poetry beat back then. He accorded Atwood a highly respectful review, on account of both her excellent work and the apparent fierceness of the persona she projected: '... here was a woman who could not only go for the jugular, but knew how to keep an unyielding grip on it as well.' The review's final paragraph, given over to Lowther, does not bode well at the outset: 'Reading on the same occasion was Vancouver poetess Pat Lowther, author of the volume of poems *A Difficult Flowring* [*sic*].' But Schroeder went on to praise the poetry Lowther had read – that night, largely work from the new broadsheet, *The Age of the Bird*. He cited her as 'one of the very few poets writing about political matters who doesn't become hopelessly strident or sloppily sincere in the process; the poetry doesn't get buried under the message.'[17] And 'the lights and cameras' of the press also caught both poets that evening, in pictures that accompanied the *Peak*'s review. Atwood looks more dreamily abstracted than fiercely jugular. Lowther, in a puffy-sleeved peasant blouse, just looks like she's having a good time, a thin *S* of smoke tapering upwards from the Matinée in her hand, and a bemused smile on her face.

⁂

Unless she hitched a ride home that night, Lowther would have taken the long bus ride through Burnaby and back down Hastings Street into eastside Vancouver after this final reading of her first real 'tour.' She would have had good reason to feel buoyant and self-satisfied, taking in the usual city scenes through her bus window. After that one October –

a good four years since the appearance of her first book – she was beginning to feel directly plugged into a writers' loop beyond the circuits of
Vancouver. She'd met a range of new writers in Edmonton, reached new
audiences in Saskatchewan, and caught the ear of Margaret Atwood,
who would take an interest in her career from this point on. 'I had beautiful times reading with Margaret, and I think all went well,' she
reported to Gerald Lampert after the tour. 'I keep wondering what
she'll be like at say 65.' Then she signed off with a contented, one-word
'Peace.'[18]

Soon after, Lowther received a 'note of thanks' from her SFU host,
David Stouck, 'for the very fine reading.' He enclosed a copy of the student newspaper's 'article about you and Margaret,' along with their
'very fetching' photos.[19] What she did not receive so soon after was payment from the League for the readings. 'Still have not heard from
Gerry Lampert,' she informed McNamara around mid-November:
'Where's my money? Supercapitalists on the Canada Council are lighting cigars with it.'[20] Her half-mock impatience with the 'supercapitalists'
of the government's arts bureaucracy, though, was nothing in comparison to her smoldering dissatisfaction with the indeterminate fate of *Milk
Stone*, the book whose availability her Regina host, Andrew Robertson,
had pressed her about. She'd given the manuscript to Seymour Mayne
for Ingluvin Press a full year ago.

One of Lowther's first expressions of frustration about *Milk Stone* was
to her new acquaintance, Margaret Atwood. Not long after their joint
readings, Lowther had, at Atwood's request, sent her some poems for
possible inclusion in a 'new anthology.' Trouble was, as usual, she
couldn't find the 'record' of which poems she'd actually sent Atwood.
So she soon wrote, requesting 'a list of what I gave you.' But their time
together on the tour had obviously involved some shop talk about
projects on the go, and before winding up her letter, Lowther also confided: 'Ingluvin eventually got their Canada Council money. God knows
what's holding them up now. I wish I had the patience to withdraw my
ms. and start over with another publisher.'[21]

Ingluvin, named after 'a patent medicine of the nineteenth century,'
was the brainchild of Seymour Mayne and a Montreal compatriot, Kenneth Hertz. They started the press after Very Stone House 'sputtered
out.' But this time, the publishers involved actually *bought* a press: 'We
set up a printing shop in Montreal, doing small commercial jobs, and
in the other time ... printing books.'[22] In this way, Ingluvin published
Livesay's feminist anthology, *Forty Women Poets of Canada* (1971). That
anthology included Lowther, whose contributor's note alludes to the

'second book of poetry' she was expecting to appear in '1972.' Hertz
was in charge of the Ingluvin enterprise while Mayne went back to British Columbia to finish his PhD. Hertz apparently did not cope well in
Mayne's absence. Over Christmas of 1972, Mayne headed east for the
holiday break. Four days after Lowther had written to Atwood about
wishing for the patience to pull her manuscript from Ingluvin, Mayne
wrote to Lowther, from several provinces away:

> Dear Pat,
>   Sorry I did not get the chance to call and say good-bye before I left two
> weeks ago, but with so many things to do at the last minute I managed to
> leave with many things undone ...
>   Last week Kenneth Hertz and I met to review Ingluvin Publications and
> our on-going projects. We are, as you know, hamstruck with lack of help
> and our schedule is off again. We have to re-schedule the eight new books
> that we have ready. Meantime our new catalogue for 1973 is ready ... We
> have eight new books on hand ... including your own. But I must tell you
> that it will still take time. Kenneth figures that *Milk Stone* should be out by
> the spring. I know that is disappointing, but we cannot do any better. The
> pressure is great, we are operating under duress and limitations ... If you
> are concerned about the upcoming Canada Council Senior Grant competi-
> tion this April, I suggest that you apply. [Your] book will be advertised by
> then and will be known to the literary community ... I know that [you] and
> our other writers are anxious to see their books, but please remember that
> we are no supermen, and that no other publisher will provide any [other]
> set-up, no matter what they may say or promise.[23]

Ingluvin's update struck Lowther as very 'disturbing' in its vagueness.
On 5 January 1973, immediately after she received Mayne's letter, she
wrote back. 'I do feel at this point I must have something more definite,'
she declared. 'Frankly, Seymour, this unpublished book has begun to
feel like an albatross hung around my neck.' She prodded him for specifics:

> You say Kenneth figures *Milk Stone* should be out by spring. What does
> 'should' mean, and what does 'spring' mean? ...
>   My understanding is that Ingluvin's Canada Council grant finally came
> through. Since you did say you'll answer any questions I might have, could
> you tell me what portion of the grant you've allocated to my book and how
> many copies you plan to print?

You(re [*sic*] quite right that royalties are not my major concern. I *am very* concerned that this book get out and distributed – soon.

Her letter also went on to make crystal clear her anxieties over age as a critical factor in her emerging literary career:

There are some things you should understand about my own position: In the first place, I'm 37 years old. I've had only one book published, besides the Blackfish thing [*The Age of the Bird*]. I'm chronically broke and have no other resources such as teaching. I haven't a hope in hell of getting even a junior grant from the Canada Council without at least one more book out. They have told me so in politer words. I feel reasonably sure that once this book is published, and if it's decently distributed, I can get more readings on the strength of it.

What I can't do is wait till June, then be told more problems have come up, and it should be out in the fall, and so on.

She closed on a slightly more conciliatory note:

I don't want to be heavy, Seymour, but I'm convinced that my career is hanging on this thing and at my age I can't afford any more delays or uncertainty ...

I realize you've had a lot of problems [at Ingluvin], and I hate to be adding to them. If I'd had another book since 1968, I'd be content to let things ride now, but I really feel very strongly that I can't now. I hope to hear from you soon.[24]

Lowther heard back from Atwood sooner than she did from Ingluvin. 'Do keep me informed about the Ingluvin project,' Atwood wrote: 'I hope the book comes out. If there are difficulties, you know I would be interested in seeing the work, but I don't want to cut in on Ingluvin.'[25] Sure enough, by the spring of 1973, Ingluvin, as Lowther lamented to Fred Cogswell, was 'still not producing anything that I can see': 'My last word from them is that if books are not out by June, authors are free to take back their manuscripts. So I'm waiting til June 1 to withdraw my poor stepchild book, and then hope Anansi will do it.'[26] That was 3 May 1973, right around the time she was writing her letters of despair to friends like Joy Kogawa, trying to explain her inability to leave Roy.

Seymour Mayne had returned again to Montreal that spring and checked into the company's books, to find that it was in serious debt.[27] On her self-imposed deadline of June 1st, Lowther wrote to her 'Dear Gene' in Windsor:

> So much has happened it seems like another age. Katharine, my oldest daughter, was in a car accident, got her face cut; it appears that some of the scars will be permanent. But is lucky to be alive.
>
> Ingluvin came through with the type-setting proofs just two weeks before the deadline I had decided on. Of course, that's no guarnatee [*sic*] of promptness. And the next day got a letter from Atwood saying, sure, if Ingluvin doesn't come through, send it to us. I've decided the only thing to do is to write it off, forget it, let them limp on, and start thinking about the next one. So [I] have put together a new *ms* which I am sending (today) to Anansi.[28]

The 'new *ms*,' 'the next one,' was *A Stone Diary*, which she shipped out while the dismal saga of *Milk Stone* continued to unfold.

Now she had two irons in the fire, which was a good thing. Because by the fall of 1973, Lowther's fading hope that 'the mythical Ingluvin puts out my mythical book' was finally extinguished for good.[29] On September 21, while she was keeping close tabs on the upsetting news out of Chile, she got a special delivery letter from Mayne, which she promptly summarized in a letter to McNamara: 'Ingluvin has finally gone splosh.' And to Livesay: 'Ingluvin is finished ... [the] Canada Council has withdrawn its grant. None of this is very surprising to me, but I wish I'd known a few months ago, before Atwood left Anansi.'[30]

Lowther's last remark about Atwood's newly severed ties from the House of Anansi pointed to more disappointment ahead, for both of her books. She had submitted *A Stone Diary* to Anansi expressly because she was hopeful that Atwood's support, as a poetry editor, would improve her manuscript's chance of success there. But the same summer that Lowther sent Anansi her 'new *ms*,'Atwood resigned from the editorial board, evidently not on the most comfortable of terms. She later wrote Lowther, explaining the situation, and assuring her of Anansi's 'continuing interest' in her manuscript, despite her own departure. By then, Atwood had also heard the 'rumour' 'that Ingluvin is closing up shop.' 'If the Ingluvin book is off,' she suggested, why not consider an 'amalgamation of the two *mss*'?[31]

Lowther's response indicates a certain weariness. What with Roy's worsening outbursts, bad news out of Montreal and Santiago, and sick kids over Christmas, it had been a draining fall and early winter. 'Dear Margaret,' she wrote,

> Thanks for your letter. I had heard about your resignation from Anansi ... [Yes,] Ingluvin has finally given up. I've been trying to think about whether or not to combine the two *mss.* but without being able to come to a decision. So I guess I'll take your advice and send the Ingluvin *ms.* to Anansi, and get an opinion from there. I hear from Pat Lane that you are enjoying rural life. Best wishes for the coming year.
> Sincerely,
> Pat[32]

Within a week, she followed through with her intentions, sending her 'poor stepchild' and 'albatross' of a manuscript on to Anansi also, by 4 January 1974. Why not? It was the best prospect she had, and besides, these were the first hopeful days of another new year. In her cover letter to Shirley Gibson at Anansi, she mentioned that she was submitting *Milk Stone* 'on Peggy's advice.' She clearly explained the history of this 'earlier manuscript of mine' and raised the possibility 'about combining the two.'[33]

After this second submission, Anansi's double rejection was impressively swift. It came by return mail within three weeks. Despite Lowther's clarity in her letter to Shirley Gibson, Anansi's response indicates that the editorial board was either confused or careless about the chronology of the two manuscripts. It is possible that they had already reached a negative decision on *A Stone Diary* by the time that the earlier completed *Milk Stone* manuscript arrived. In any case, Anansi's assessment offered a constructive, if also oddly diffuse and evasive, reading of Lowther's two manuscripts. It was written by James Polk, the Anansi editor from whom 'Peggy Atwood' had recently parted personal ways. *A Stone Diary* was deemed insufficiently cohesive or 'nutritional' as a book, despite the acknowledged incandescence of certain poems. *Milk Stone* was judged as a progressive step toward longer poems, but less original and craft worthy than the strongest sections of the *Diary*. In sum, the editors just did not feel that Lowther had yet written the book she could, probably, some day write. They hoped that didn't sound too vague and assured her that the work had been given due consideration. Maybe, Polk added, Margaret Atwood would have some better suggestions.[34]

By this point, Lowther wasn't the only one getting concerned about her seemingly stalled writing career. Her B.C. small-press publishers were watching, too. Allan Safarik maintained that Lowther was a much better poet than most, 'but,' he concluded in a letter to Patrick Lane, dated 10 August 1974, 'she'll never make it': 'It's been four years since I meet [sic] her and every month since then, she's told me her book is just about to happen, and it will never come out.' He added the news about her latest disappointment with Anansi.[35]

∽

Within a month of Anansi's rejection, a grimly determined Lowther informed her friend Fred Cogswell that she had two newly revised manuscripts back out in circulation. And, she said, her old friend Milton Acorn was back in town. Lowther hadn't seen Acorn since his friendly deportation back east in 1968. As a writer whom she'd made time for from the very beginning of her Vancouver period, 'the people's poet' had continued as a source of inspiration for her even after he'd left. According to Lorraine Vernon, Acorn was the basis for 'Mr. Happyman Is Coming,' the celebratory poem that eventually rounded out her *Milk Stone* collection (*Forty*, 78; *MS*, 93).[36] This seems plausible, given the existence of other undated poem manuscripts inscribed 'To Milton Acorn' among Lowther's papers. 'I see you as a hand curled / around a growing thing, / sheltering,' one such tribute begins.[37]

But Lowther's letter to Cogswell about Milton's return to the Coast was distressed, not joyous:

> Milton Acorn is in Vancouver. I saw one of his readings, which was nothing short of disastrous. He's reading at SFU today – it's got to be better, there's no way to go but up. Meeting Milt again has been very disappointing and upsetting. We had had a very close warm friendship, but it's been six years since we've seen each other, and I guess many of those years have been lonely for him. Anyway, he has somehow fantasized that relationship into something it never was and never could be, with the result that I really don't want to see him again, and there's a good friendship down the drain.[38]

And that is the last mention of Milton Acorn in Lowther's surviving correspondence. 'Milton,' Cogswell ventures, 'was very complex and a very strange kind of person, half in love with Pat. In a certain way he attempted to be more to Pat than he was.'[39]

On Peter Gzowski's radio tribute shortly after Lowther's death, Acorn recalled how 'very, very pretty' Lowther was when he had first met her around 1963. In his eyes, she had become only prettier by the time he saw her again in 1974. By then, he said, 'she was a stunning beauty.' He also recalled sexual jokes they had shared in the past, a running banter about the 'average' number of lovers one could expect in a lifetime.[40] Clearly, what Lowther perceived as nothing more or less than 'a very close warm friendship' led Acorn in 1974 to some sort of sexual trespass serious enough for Lowther to write off a valued friendship. Thirty-nine years old when she experienced her unpleasant re-encounter with 'Milt,' Lowther was in a doubly unenviable position. If the new youth culture of her time implicitly cast her as too 'old' to decently qualify as a 'new' or 'emergent' writer, then she was nevertheless apparently not yet too old a bird to be hit upon either.

Milton's betrayal hurt. First, know where your allies are: this had been the gist of Lowther's political counsel to the Waffle in 1971. By 1974, she had long since come to believe that she had found a trusted friend – a 'sheltering' 'hand' – in Milton Acorn. Just as she once believed she'd found a guiding light in Roy Lowther.

Chapter 12

Longitudes, North

As *The Age of the Bird* suggests, Lowther's own conviction of the inseparability of art and politics finds its most pronounced articulation in the
poetry that she produced from the early seventies on. The poems in
This Difficult Flowring were already political, of course, to the extent that
they rattled cultural ideals of domesticity, while also revaluing as productive women's 'private' experiences within the housewife's curiously
unpaid, middle-class space. But the development of an explicitly politicized poetics comes to the foreground in the work of her mid-to-late
career, synchronous with Lowther's rise from foot soldier in the cause
for an 'independent socialist Canada' to provincial government arts policy consultant. That sphere of her political life was local and provincial
in scope, and so was the focus of some of the new 'political' poetry.

In works such as 'Burning Iris I' (*MS*, 50) and the 'City Slide' series
(*SD*, 67–73), for example, Lowther began to cast her eye on the question of class as it was refracted through the minutiae of the modern city
around her. She was observant where it came to the grittier corners of
the city she travelled through – or sometimes arrived at, to meet friends
like David Morgan downtown for beers at the Cecil Hotel. Such city
poems make a point of sketching in her scenic hometown 'from a gum
wrapper's viewpoint' – literally, the meanest street level of detritus and
litter, junk shops and drunks (*SD*, 69). They chart the contrasts of comfort and poverty that could be glimpsed beneath the city's 'revolving
neon' lights, where 'elegant' men with 'tidy clothes' and 'wellkept' bodies approached 'ragbag broad[s]' 'smoking in doorways' (*MS*, 50). In
this documentary impulse, Lowther's new urban poems were similar to
Daphne Marlatt's *Vancouver Poems*, a book whose appearance she duly
noted in 1972.[1] But while Marlatt took in the city through a breathless

tidal wash of unstopped lines and impressionistic image fragments, Lowther's technique was beginning to integrate her fascination with contemporary visual technologies in equally interesting and distinctive ways.

Slide projectors and film projectors (or bus windows, for that matter) intrigued her for their capacity to frame and manipulate experience – crop it, arrest it, slow it, or speed it up. An opening sequence of the long poem 'In the Continent behind My Eyes' illustrates how she began to adapt such filmic techniques on the page:

> The city like an open brain
> zaps messages
> lights   avenues
> A hillside suburb
> lights up like a bloc
> of dogma memorized
>
> *The first lamp post is*
> *a block away*
> *the next is half a block*
> *and then a quarter*
> *then closer faster*
> *mene mene pencil strokes*
> *how fast can you*
> *run runrun rn* (*TC,* 58)[2]

The imagistic acceleration of the sequence, from the static 'bloc / of dogma memorized' to the 'lamp post' moving 'closer faster' is striking, but the movement is also brilliant by way of the playful 'pencil strokes' through '*mene mene*' compressed idioms and registers of language. Utilitarian shorthand notation, scriptural mysticism, phonetic puns, the serial blur of graffiti: all these possibilities combine to displace and voice-over one another during this opening '*run runrun rn.*'

Lowther thought about television and film at least in part because she was among those critics of the Viet Nam War who had come to recognize such visual media as enormously powerful tools in advancing commitments to particular versions of truth and reality. Mass media coverage of current events like Viet Nam – and the alternative wide angle provided by people like Claire Culhane, the Quang Ngai medical official brought in by Lowther's constituency – were highlighting in dra-

254   Ready to Learn Politics

matic new ways the ideological stakes behind the images 'passively' con-
sumed by North American viewers. So it is relatively unsurprising that
Lowther also extended her exploration of filmic techniques and analo-
gies to her most overtly political poems, works like 'Chacabuco, the Pit.'
By the same token, given that she 'continually trie[d] to broaden the
horizon of her experience,' as Andrew Robertson noted, it is not surprising that most of the poems which take up explicitly political events
and subjects are, in fact, not local or provincial, but international – or at
least far-reaching – in compass.

Far-reaching, but not random. In 1972, Lorraine Vernon gave Lowther a book called *The Singing Cells: Modern Greek Poetry.* There had been
a military coup in Greece in 1967, and *The Singing Cells* was a selection of
poems stemming from that political overthrow. The book included work
by George Seferis, the 1963 Nobel Prize winner for literature. But neither
the Greek situation nor Seferis's work – nor even Viet Nam, for that matter – ever caught Lowther's poetic attention the way that Chilean politics
and Pablo Neruda's writing did. Indeed, the geography of her political
imagination appeared to run in a distinctly longitudinal direction, from
Latin America in the far south, to the polar extreme of the Canadian
Arctic in the far north. The Nerudian title of *A Stone Diary* and the original title of *Milk Stone, Ice Crucible,* point up this antipodal orientation.[3] (It
was not just because Lowther was thin that Dorothy Livesay once
described her as an '*elongated* sort of person, very intensely interested in
political commitment to the issues of the times.')[4]

To a certain extent, the Northern and Aboriginal focus of many of the
Milk Stone poems – 'Woman on/against Snow,' 'Arctic Carving,' 'Vision,'
'String Figure Man outside the Door,' and 'There Were Giants in the
Earth,' for example – indicate Lowther's 'political commitment' to the
self-conscious nationalism that preoccupied many artists of the period.
Yet the Arctic was, notably, the only Canadian region outside of her
home province that Lowther chose to write about. Unlike, say, Al Purdy,
who liked to think of 'Canada' as his 'home town' (Purdy 1993: 290), or
even Roy Lowther, with his *Cross-Country Rhymes,* she did not make a
point of aspiring to write across the Maple Leaf from sea to shining sea.

In conjunction with Lowther's projection south to Chile, her interest
in the North might recall George Woodcock's detection of a latently
romantic sensibility at work in *The Age of the Bird* – an 'elongated'
embrace of the classic extremes of fire and ice. In 1976, however, Frank
Davey argued that such a range could be construed as yet one more posture of 'an international stereotype':

The most 'colonial' [writers] are, ironically, the independentists often accepted by Ontario-based CanLit for their recognizable and familiar styles – Robin Skelton, Susan Musgrave, Pat Lane, Tom Wayman, the late Pat Lowther and Stanley Cooperman; these are colonial in the sense that their work could be written in any number of places by any number of internationally exchangeable writers. The independentist stance is, paradoxically, an international stereotype, expressed in either proud or perverse rejection of human community. Humanists anywhere can adopt the roles either on [*sic*, of] non-accountable eccentric (Cooperman, Layton, Musgrave, Lane, Wayman) or of existential sufferer (Atwood, Lowther, Newlove). (1976: 18–19)

From the perspective of a *Tish* proponent in 1976, it was the *Tish* postmodernists – like Fred Wah, George Bowering, Daphne Marlatt, and Davey himself – who were less likely to be 'accepted by Ontario-based CanLit' because their poetics were based on a specific 'sense of *belonging*' that writers of other regions (and theoretical inclinations) just didn't get: 'the sense of belonging to a specific geography, of belonging to the political and social life of that geography' (19, emphasis in the original).

But, in fact, when she was writing about a nitrate mine in the Atacama Desert, no less than when she was writing about Vancouver or the Gulf Islands, the scope of Lowther's poetry indicates a historical imagination that firmly and fundamentally bespeaks 'the sense of belonging to a specific geography' and 'belonging to the political and social life of that geography.' At least since the advent of nineteenth-century industry, British Columbia, despite its name, looked specifically to the north and to the south, economically and culturally, as well as geographically. This was especially true of the mining resource industry, which, on the one hand, ran north to the Alaskan panhandle and, on the other, ran south, even beyond the sources of American capital, in centres like San Francisco, to the first Spanish 'mining ventures' in Mexico and Peru (Angus et al. 1970: 264). The province's strong historical ties and trade links to the south and north had to a large degree dictated the footsteps of Lowther's own 'pioneering' ancestors, like James Wilks and his vaudevillian daughters, Virginia and Isabelle – the latter had toured along the coast from as far south as Mexico, in her performing days. Similarly, at least one 'great uncle Johnny' followed the lure of the Klondike, as Lowther recalled in a poem titled 'History Lessons' (*TC*, 191). During Lowther's own day, moreover, a sizeable Chilean diaspora settled in British Columbia, a Canadian province that, like Chile, was more 'elongated' than it was wide, was sealed off from the land mass to the east by a mountain range, and was economically reliant on natural resources.

In this sense, the trajectory of Lowther's poetry does not simply encompass 'any number of places' that 'any number' of writers might also have written about. It signals, rather, a field of vision coherently focused by the migratory coastal culture that preceded her, and that also influenced her directly during her own lifetime. To the degree that this history reflects a peculiar mix of transnational exchange *and* regional specificity, it reflects a combination not so different from that circulation of ideas which formed the basis of a 'Black Mountain North' poetics of place and '*belonging*.' Except that Lowther's more elastic sense of place was markedly material in derivation, based on a history that involved the circulation of working bodies and cash, and on a reality of suffering that was not only 'existential' in nature. The 'longitudinal' internationalism of her poetry thus uniquely says as much about '*community ... geographic historicity ... particularism* and *localism*' as does the poetry generated by the Olsonite revisionism of the early sixties (Davey 1976: 23; emphasis in the original).

c/o

'Does the museum or the university at Victoria have a good collection of native Indian music, do you know? I never get time to go out to UBC, but maybe I could listen to some tapes while I'm in Victoria.'[5] So Lowther concluded a letter to Livesay that had started out as a giddy anticipation of a weekend tryst with her lover at Livesay's cabin on the Island, at Cadboro Bay. Evidently, she was not quite so head-over-heels-far-gone as to overlook the possibility that she might also squeeze some valuable research time into her Victoria interlude. More readily, in fact, than she might 'get time to go out to UBC' while she was at home in the city.

Lowther's query about Native music in 1973 was not her first expression of interest in Aboriginal culture, history, and art. A few years earlier, she had written film reviews for the *Mountaineer* in response to a series of short documentary films about First Nations peoples. The National Film Board offerings she saw at Hillcrest Hall in November 1971 included *Age of the Buffalo* (1964), which she praised as 'visually magnificent'; *Cariboo Hunters* (1951), about a trap-line hunter leading a 'quiet, almost solitary life' in 'the high latitudes'; and *Circle of the Sun* (1961), a film that predicted the impending cultural extinction

(Lowther called it the 'gradual disintegration') of the Blood tribe of Alberta. The last – and shortest – film was called *The Ballad of the Crowfoot*; it was billed as 'made by a member of an NFB film crew composed of Canadian Indians.'[6] In a draft of her review, Lowther concluded:

> [I]t was left to the only film actually made by Indians to provide the evening's most dramatic confrontation with history. Made by Willy Dunn, a Micmac Indian, with assistance of the NFB, *The Ballad of the Crowfoot* packs its ten minutes with maximum impact. The only audio commentary is in the form of a long Dylanesque ballad written by Dunn, and against this background, timing is used in a crescendo effect. At first, only stills are used – ... from various archives. About half way through ... motion is introduced and the tempo picks up ... building to a swift montage of treaties, edicts, newspaper headlines (back page headlines, that is, because since when do stories about conditions of life for Indians make the front page?). And again and again throughout the film, faces, dispirited faces, angry faces, proud, bitter faces.[7]

Around the same time that she was commenting on the 'magnificently visual' 'timing ... effect' and 'tempo' of films like *The Ballad of the Crowfoot* and *The Age of the Buffalo*, Lowther would have been at work on *The Age of the Bird*. But in August 1971, Dorothy Livesay had also written asking her for permission to publish 'Woman on/against Snow.' A heatwave in Edmonton had left Livesay feeling 'a bit blotto,' she confessed, but it wasn't just the title of 'Woman on/against Snow' that struck a wilting 'Dee' as refreshing. '*I like it finely*,' she stressed, of Lowther's ambitious new poem.[8] And so, in the fall of 1971, Lowther also saw the first appearance of 'Woman on/against Snow' in Sheila Watson's little magazine, *White Pelican*.

Rather like the film *Cariboo Hunters*, Lowther's newest work focused on a 'quiet, almost solitary life' in 'the high latitudes.' The 'woman' figured by the title is the lone survivor of her family in an arctic world that 'swirls, / changes with every wind' (*MS*, 14). 'Woman on/against Snow' is both lyric and dramatic in form. Like 'The Insider,' a less successful predecessor from *This Difficult Flowring*, it is, in effect, another experimental 'poem for voices.' Only this one throws into contrapuntal relief the voices of 'insiders' and 'outsiders,' juxtaposing a citation from the diary of a White Northern explorer with the embedded monologues of an Inuit woman, who is 'named' for readers only as she hears herself named 'by the whole night' that engulfs her: 'Small Small / Here-by-

chance / Belonging-nowhere-meaning-nothing' (*MS*, 15). The voices of
the Northern explorer and of 'Small Small' are in turn framed by that
of the speaker, who functions as the lens through which readers appre-
hend a world indefinitely 'white with the many names of snow' (*MS*, 14).

'Woman on/against Snow' was one of the poems Lowther read while
she was in Regina on her 'Western tour' with Atwood, a year after its initial publication in *White Pelican*. The prefatory comments she addressed
to the audience about the poem that evening are especially intriguing.
She had started the reading off with 'some poems about the Coast,' but
now, she announced, she would move from the Northwest to the *True*
North:

> To go from the West to [the] North, which I thought was real, but which
> turned out to be partly a mythical North: I think it was [in] a book on
> architecture [that] I came upon this story of an Eskimo woman who had
> been alone for some months and had managed to survive, and not only to
> survive, but to create art – to create beautiful objects and decorate her
> clothing, and so on. It took me a long time to trace down this reference; it
> went through several different books, until finally, it was in Samuel
> Hearne's *Journeys* [*sic*] – and it was *not at all* [about] an Eskimo woman – it
> was [about] an Indian woman below the treeline. But by that time I had
> written a poem, and was committed to the figure of the Eskimo woman.[9]

The 'book on architecture' to which Lowther alludes as an initial source
for her poem is almost certainly Gyorgy Kepes's 1966 essay collection
Sign, Image, Symbol, an interdisciplinary study of representational systems
which includes several essays on architecture. It was to Kepes's book that
Jean Mallinson first traced the main intertexts of 'Woman on/against
Snow' in her 1981 doctoral dissertation, and then, more definitively, in
her 1986 article, subtitled 'A Poem and Its Sources.' Specifically, Mallinson pointed to two essays within Kepes's collection, both by American
anthropologists: Edmund Carpenter's 'Image Making in Arctic Art' and
Paul Riesman's 'The Eskimo Discovery of Man's Place in the Universe.'
Though she lacked any other evidence that these were sources Lowther
actually did use, when Mallinson compared Carpenter's and Riesman's
works against the text of Lowther's poem, unmistakable correspondences emerged (1981: 35–9; 1986).[10]

What Lowther's public comments and notebooks add to our understanding is that Carpenter and Riesman were among multiple other
sources she used in writing her poem, including Samuel Hearne's origi-

nal report of his astonished encounter with the lone woman. Lowther's poem quotes from the same passage of Hearne's journal that she initially came across as a second-hand citation in Carpenter's essay. Rather unhelpfully, though – for a professional anthropologist anyway – Carpenter provided no specific reference for his own quotations of Hearne, thus obliging Lowther to chase them down 'through several different books' until she finally found her eighteenth-century *ur*-text in *A Journey from Prince of Wales's Fort in Hudson's Bay to the Northern Ocean, 1769–1772.*

Without doubt, she was diligent. But her anecdote of the hunt is also the story of a disappointment, a consternation, and her comments to her Regina auditors in 1972 begin to reveal the extent of her poem's complex relations to its subject matter and source materials. Tracing the story back to Hearne's original text was a disconcerting eye-opener, confronting Lowther with striking evidence of the potential unreliability of her ethnographic sources, contemporary 'experts' though they were. Only when she read Hearne for herself could she see that 'this story of an Eskimo woman,' 'was *not at all* [about] an Eskimo woman' or an 'arctic' encounter, as Carpenter's essay misleadingly represented it. According to Hearne, the lone survivor he met in the winter of 1772 was a member of the Dogrib Nation, and he chanced upon her not in the middle of the 'desolate Canadian tundra' (Carpenter 1966: 206), but in the boreal forests along the shores of Athapuscow Lake, now known as Great Slave Lake (Hearne 1958: 168–9). That locale was apparently circumpolar enough for the purposes of 'Image Making in Arctic Art,' but Lowther was quite rightly miffed by Carpenter's inaccuracy and sleight of hand in what was purportedly a factual, scholarly essay.[11] The discovery suddenly altered the imaginary landscape she had constructed around the story, though it did not make her rewrite her 'Eskimo' poem, which at this point, had already come to life in a world whitened, so it now seemed, by more than just snow.

Occasional factual imprecision was not the extent of Lowther's problems with source materials, including Hearne's book itself. It did not escape her notice that these documentary accounts were unsupplemented by Aboriginal perspectives of contact, counter-narratives that might well prove 'the most dramatic confrontation with history,' as she had said of Willy Dunn's *The Ballad of the Crowfoot.* Ethnographic social science of Lowther's era had yet to confront the Western manufacture of its own blind authority, never mind the need to think through the nagging influence of various literary models on its 'scientific' representations of 'reality' (Hunan 1996). In 1966, Arctic anthropologists like

Edmund Carpenter could still marvel that classic psychoanalytic theory made 'no sense' in relation to 'the Eskimo artist,' before promptly forging ahead to 'apply' Freudian notions of Natives' 'parallels with primitives' such as 'children,' 'the senile,' and 'the mentally ill,' among other sub-literates (216, 219, 212).

For a writer who grappled continuously with the 'limitations' of her modest experience – and who was sometimes reminded of her 'almost non-existent' biographical small smallness by others, too – Lowther's research for 'Woman on/against Snow' was a distinctive process. It highlighted in a concrete, new way the limitations inherent not so much in herself as in the extraneous sources of knowledge she relied upon, especially the books that served as her essential pipeline to the world. Most of those books about her Arctic subject were themselves based on the direct experience and 'fieldwork' of scientists and artists, armed with the freedom to strike out for the 'high latitudes' on their own. If the 'first-hand' impressions they gathered were direct, then they were not unclouded for that fact. Experiential or not, knowledge was problematic, and for Lowther, the result was a clear-sighted appreciation that 'the North' of her imagined Inuit woman was 'partly a mythical North.'

Indeed, Lowther's determined 'commit[ment]' 'to the *figure* of the Eskimo woman' reinforces her recognition of the necessarily metaphorical relationship of the southern White artist to what pianist Glenn Gould aptly titled the 'The Idea of the North' in celebration of Canada's centennial in 1967. Simultaneously projected as 'the testing ground for and the graveyard of independence,' the North, as recent critics have shown, traditionally 'represents' for non-Native southerners a powerfully paradoxical '*tabula rasa*,' a site constructed as 'empty, desolate, and silent,' on the one hand, and 'full of promise,' on the other: 'promise for spiritual rebirth, for technological innovation, for the realization of national, corporate, and personal desire' (MacLaren 1996: 9).[12] As such, it had already proven irresistible in the popular imagination, as 'virgin' territory for metaphorically minded artists and intellectuals of generations preceding Lowther's – from Robert Service on through F.R. Scott and Lawren Harris, to name a few.

But as the timing of Gould's 'The Idea of the North' intimates, interest in the 'high latitudes' crested to a centennial high amid the 'promise' and anxiety of cultural sovereignty during Lowther's lifetime.

Gwendolyn MacEwen and Lowther were relative anomalies among the cadre of artists, largely male, who turned to the North during the sixties and seventies, in effect staking out the claims and boundaries of a national imagination. In addition to musicians like Gould, these artistic Northern explorers included contemporary visual artists such as Jean-Paul Riopelle – whose interest in Inuit string figures coincided with Lowther's during the early seventies – and, of course, writers from Farley Mowat to Robert Kroetsch and Rudy Wiebe. 'Playing with the myth of the North as a blank page, but starting to question it at the same time,' as Lorraine York notes, was also the 'idea' behind the work of contemporary poets like Al Purdy and Lowther's friend Patrick Lane (1993: 48).

As one among those footloose souls who actually made an Arctic trek (with some help from the Canada Council), Al Purdy casually shared his doubts about the venture from Pangnirtung, Baffin Island, with the American poet Charles Bukowski:

> Ya, 6 weeks in the Arctic. 24 poems, about 10,000 words of prose ... Trouble with this whole biz tho, is here I am writin poems I'm not really involved in – I mean, this isn't like writin about a union or a woman I know etc. etc. I come up here like a goddamn phoney reporter. So I look at what I see then write poems ... It's the wrong way around. The material should come to me naturally, not me to the material. No more will I do this sort of thing. (In Cooney 1983: 93, 95).

By the end of his trip, Purdy was dying for a beer and 'sick to death of the Arctic' (in Cooney 1983: 95). His careful measurement of output ('24 poems ... 10,000 words') is almost poignant – as though he needed the numbers to convince himself of his expedition's productive value. But he had felt impelled to make the journey because, as he said to Margaret Laurence, 'no book I'd read had given me the feeling of what it was like to be there, the colour, the smells etc., just the reality' (in Lennox 1993: 43).

The search for 'just the reality' of the North was clearly as elusive for Purdy, left feeling like 'a goddamn phoney reporter' up in Pangnirtung, as it was for Lowther, back in the mild climes of Vancouver, and facing difficulties of her own with books unable to adequately capture 'just' that same Arctic 'reality.' Unlike Purdy and his male counterparts at the time, though, Lowther never would enjoy the privilege of seeing what a place like 'Pang' might make of her, and she of it. For her, an expensive

'6 weeks' Arctic odyssey was out of the question anyway – even if she'd had a grant to do so. With no grounds to mull over the ethics or the aesthetic value of journeys up North, she did, instead, what she always did: like Homer's Penelope, she stayed home and wove poems.

Specifically, she wrote poems with titles like 'Notes Toward a Journey,' an unpublished, undated draft that unequivocally constructs the Northern adventure as a male prerogative. Written in the second person, this poem's speaker addresses a 'you' who feels the 'need' to 'leave friends, wife, [and] all who have been / heart-holds, [to] journey toward the north,' in an epic search for his essential self – and the north pole, 'the world's centre.' The speaker's opening declaration is intriguing: 'it is not enough to have reached / the white space on the map.' Ultimately, though, the poem falls back on the cliché of the Arctic as a sublime crucible, the return from which endows the male adventurer with 'certain' spiritual truths and 'powers.'[13] As Penelope un-wove her tapestry, so Lowther quietly set this draft aside in the reject pile. It was apparently written before she discovered that, as it turned out, this North too – as a footsore and dry Al Purdy might attest – was also 'partly a mythical North.'

Indeed, the crucial difference between an attempt like 'Notes Toward a Journey' and 'Woman on/against Snow' is that while the former addresses 'the white space on the map' by way of a familiar romantic metaphor of self-discovery, the latter imparts the originality and freshness of vision of a poet in the actual process of self-discovery. This is true even of an early, handwritten draft of 'Woman on/against Snow,' which appears, appropriately enough, in a 'Canadian Exercise' scribbler. In the notebook version, most of the poem's stanzas appear in apparently random sequence, with a numerical order and some arrows indicating 'move up' or 'down' pencilled in along the margins. The compositional process suggested comes as a reminder of Lowther's avid passion for solitaire scrabble, that happy diversion for an imagination that may have been spatially 'elongated,' but was also non-linear. The scrambled-stanza holograph also indicates a plastic sense of structure and meaning, of gradually discovered and contemplated form, that is integral to the Arctic landscape and the theme of Inuit art-making that 'Woman on/against Snow' takes up.

The opening stanza of the poem establishes the idea of fluid form even as it introduces 'the figure of the Eskimo woman':

> Alone
> for the others are dead,
> she is a small Arctic sun

curving space around her.
This world swirls,
changes with every wind.
She must shape the world
by being alive. (*MS*, 14)

Sometime during the year between the poem's original appearance   in *White Pelican* and her reading of it in Regina the following fall, Lowther went back to work on the text and specifically amplified the notion of releasing an artwork's 'hidden' or immanent form from within the artist's raw materials, rather than imposing an intentional design on them from the outset.[14] The emphasis on artistic production as the birthing or release of latent form and idea is reflected in new lines Lowther added to the first speaking part of the Inuit woman artist within the poem, when 'Small Small' invokes the mythical figure of Nuliajuk to sustain her, physically and spiritually, by providing her with a 'bone' to appease her 'hunger' for both food and art: 'Give me a bone for my hunger, / Nuliajuk / I will turn it in my hand / till it speaks / I will call from it / shapes, faces, / with my ulo' (*MS*, 15).

Once Lowther had, similarly, culled a final 'shape' from her 'scatter poem' stanzas, 'Woman on/against Snow' emerged as an intricately choreographed arrangement of voices and structures of address.[15] The speaker who initially introduces 'Small Small' as 'figure without landscape' proceeds in the next stanza to cite Samuel Hearne, verbatim:

> 'It is scarcely possible to conceive
> that a person in her forlorn situation
> could be so composed
> as to be capable of
> contriving or executing
> anything that was not absolutely necessary
> to her existence' (*MS*, 14)

Unintroduced, uncontextualized, and unattributed, Hearne's disbelief is literally suspended within Lowther's text – left to hang like a patch of ice fog between quotation marks that throw the bland abstraction of the male explorer's language into stark relief against the 'crackle and hiss' of the surrounding poem (*MS*, 15).

The ensuing text alternates between the voice of the speaker, addressing the Inuit woman artist in the third person, and that of 'Small Small' herself, who speaks in the first person to address only Nuliajuk, the powerful embodiment of female creativity and of life source in Inuit mythology.[16] These two voices, of Native artist and non-Native poet, physically cross over each other on the page, interchanging left- and right-hand justified stanzas, marking a crossing place of identity. At one point, the artists' voices merge ambiguously to utter the meditation of 'one' who could be either 'Small Small' or the poet 'composing' her 'song':

> Song arranges itself
> at the door
> of one's mouth
> One is abraded by grief
> like snow with many teeth
> The walls drip water
> and glaze
> Words name the dead
> For a time breathing song
> one is not alone (*MS*, 16)

Through this interplay of voices 'on/against' each other, Lowther's poem signals an incomplete and composite relationship between its non-Aboriginal speaker and the Inuit woman who is positioned as both object and subject within the poem. The title's double prepositions specify this relationship as one of partial contact ('on') and of partial difference ('against'). The stanza above offers a good example of how Lowther managed to arrange the polyphonic effect of the poem's two main speakers – who never do address one another directly – as overlapping, but not identical, discursive orbits. To the English ear, the impersonal 'one' who 'is not alone' when 'breathing song' may well imply a formal convergence of the speakers' identities. At the same time, the pronoun also carefully registers a subtle, but fundamental, difference of the Inuit speaker as 'against' her English counterpart. In her preliminary workbook scribblings, Lowther had busily taken notes on Inuktitut: on the language's sound patterns; its names for English words like 'yes'; its names for words without English equivalents; its conventions of speech and connective phrases. The resulting poem attempted to acknowledge and inflect what she had been able to learn about the existence of that Native tongue. As with the poem's many hyphenated compound phrases, and its other apparent peculiarities of prosody and syntax, Lowther's deliberate use of the formal pronoun was designed as a grammatical reminder that the 'first-person pronoun, which in

English is so important we make "I" upper case,' is not so important in
Inuktituk, which tends to de-emphasize the 'participation of self in
experience.'[17]

With its dramatic 'montage of treaties, edicts, [and] newspaper headlines,' Willy Dunn's documentary film, *The Ballad of the Crowfoot*, had
provided a graphic reminder of the instrumental role played by language in officially disenabling Canada's First Nations. Similarly, Lowther's attempts to Inuktitut-ize English in 'Woman on/against Snow'
reveal that she did not simply take her own medium for granted, anymore than she did the 'print-oriented' culture of Vancouver's local left.
As a 'welfare mother' who avoided costly bricks of butter and shopped
at thrift stores (long before it was chic to do so), Lowther was fully aware
that her poem was as much about the power and prerogative of naming
– as 'against' being named – or being nameless – as it was a poem about
'making art':

> Lost as the sun
> among all stars,
> she hears the whole night
> name her,
> Small Small
> Here-by-chance
> Belonging-nowhere-meaning-nothing.
> She says stubbornly nothing
> but poems come from her hands:
> she finds food.
> ...
> Being-alone has been
> a name for death.
> Being alone when light fails
> and the traps are empty,
> she will sit crouched
> in her body
> and her hands stiffen
> still working. (*MS*, 15, 16)[18]

'One can only tactfully surmise,' Jean Mallinson wrote in 1986, that the
story of a 'woman alone, in desperate plight, still using her energy creatively,' 'correspond[ed]' forcefully with Lowther's 'sense of her own

case' (1986: 18). Certainly, like her 'figure of the Eskimo woman,' Lowther knew a little something about working in a difficult, constantly demanding, and unpredictable environment, one that could turn treacherous 'with every wind.' Likewise, the poem's potently conjured song of Small Small's metaphysical inconsequence in a vast 'white world' points to the imprint of Lowther's own history. That history could quite accurately christen her existence or 'being-alone' as a 'here-by-chance' happenstance that occurred in 1935 despite the string of occupational 'accidents' and family illnesses that might easily have precluded it. As for being named, and named 'Small Small': so she had been, by the social convention that sought to erase her identity by renaming her as the 'Mrs' of William Domphousse and then Roy Lowther; by the paternalistic disapproval of the custody judge who removed Alan from her care; by the stigma of being branded a 'welfare case' – a likely indolent and increasing 'burden' on 'property taxpayers,' as the local press informed her.[19] Even sympathetic poverty activists were apt to figure her kind as invisible and mute within a 'Hidden City' (Adams 1970: 61). She would not have needed any reminders about the function of 'representation' as a verbal noun, always signalling 'something done to something, with something, by someone, for someone' (Mitchell 1994: 180).

As a socialist, too, the more Lowther discovered about the remote North, the more she discovered that the Inuit's pragmatic philosophy of art already made perfect sense to her. The idea of art as interwoven with other practices of daily living, as reflected by Small Small's need to produce art from/with food and clothing, for instance, dovetailed precisely with the politics of her own cultural materialism, which called for the recognition of the 'artist as a worker who is creating a socially useful product.'[20] It also dovetailed quite nicely with her practice as a mother who recycled Christmas castles from cast-off cardboard boxes. In short, almost everything she learned about the Arctic and its indigenous artistic culture effectively discovered *her*, even as she discovered *it* through her travels along the bookshelves at home or at the library. These multiple bases for identification with her subject were more than enough to obviate concerns about 'writin poems I'm not really involved in,' as Purdy had found himself fretting about the Arctic 'material' he more actively pursued as poetic fodder.

Yet the personal correspondences linking Lowther to the Inuit artist, who, in turn, looks to the mythical Nuliajuk as an inspirational embodiment of creative female survival, remain unobtrusive, quietly implicit in the speaker's descriptive passages. Just as the significance of the poem's unidentified citation from Samuel Hearne's journals depends on extra-textual knowledge, so too, the autobiographical valence of 'Woman on/against Snow.'

If anything, what Lowther did attempt to register were obstacles that complicated full contact or identification across race and culture. From the start, her work was remarkably self-aware about its own observer status as 'white-skinned' and 'round-eyed.'[21] Perhaps a little too self-consciously so. In *This Difficult Flowring*, the poem 'Midterm Exam' probed the experience of a White woman, both a new mother and a new graduate of a history course. 'It seems that history's / given for my final mark / a conditional pass,' the speaker states, noting dryly that she also needs to do 'a little more work on / the minor virtues.' But the ironic humour of the newly minted 'conditional' historian evaporates as she contemplates patterns of historical probability, and her own gleaming white face in a 'mirror new washed':

> ... I am assured of
> regular meals
> a domestic furnace
> time for the occasional composition of
> a poem   a child
> protection from certain kinds of rain
>   and therefore probably a natural death
>
> The life expectancy of the average Canadian woman
> is
>   (white-skinned   round-eyed)
>
> My white-skinned round-eyed baby
> cries and is answered
> at the first cry (*DF*, 20)

By the time of 'Woman on/against Snow,' on the other hand, Lowther could let the trope of 'whiteness' speak for itself to much more subtle effect. Here, the idea that the poet is part of a 'white world' that 'circles' and observes a 'living' Native centre is succinctly captured by a zoom lens close-up of 'Small Small' in her Arctic landscape: 'The white world circles / blank as a zero / In the centre of white, / a dark speck, living. / She is the pupil of that eye' (*MS*, 16). The image reinforces the 'on/against' alterity that structures the relationship between the 'eye' of the outside observer and the 'I' of the Native subject, with Small Small serving as the 'pupil' of the poet's ocular image, but the poet, even in the process, also revealing herself as the 'pupil' who looks to learn from the example of the poem's first-person Aboriginal 'I.'

The self-reflexive procedures, linguistic experimentalism, and polyvocal structure of 'Woman on/against Snow' indicate the significance of Lowther's work, alongside that of contemporaries like Al Purdy and Patrick Lane, as part of what Lorraine York terms a 'transitional' phase of English-Canadian artists' consciousness about identity politics and place: a period marked by a nascent awareness 'that the North and the page are not the *tabulae rasae* of the aesthete's dreams, but rather, a postmodernist palimpsest' (1993: 48). Like the Northern poems of her male counterparts, Lowther's work also realized a landscape layered over with multiple realities of difference and flux, cultural and physical realities resistant to the comprehension of the non-resident, non-Native artist. However, since the highest latitude she ever actually attained was 53° (Edmonton), her artistic passage through this 'postmodern' North marked a journey distinctive from that of the male trailblazers of her time. Ironically, her stationary route showed her more quickly than Purdy's trek did that it was 'not enough to have reached / the white space on the map.' Some 'places,' both internal and external, can defy 'conversion': 'They say it's a country of dream:/ so few go there / a cold place inside us / the body can't convert' ('Arctic Carving,' *MS*, 34).

Less than two weeks after Anansi's quick rejection of her two manuscripts in the new year of 1974, Lowther hove *Milk Stone* out into the hands of Canada Post again. She had added two new sequels to the original 'Burning Iris I,' but otherwise left the manuscript intact. As a result, most of the poems represented work produced in the period 1969–71, during that spurt of intense creativity that coincided with her first Canada Council grant and her father's death. She arranged 'Woman on/against Snow,' her first major metapoetic statement, as the centrepiece of several Inuit-themed poems that opened *Milk Stone*. Thematically, these poems connect to other significant efforts such as 'In the Continent behind My Eyes,' a work whose glacial reach spans time, rather than space. Lowther thought of this long poem, 'largely concerned with the Ice Age,' as the 'core poem sequence' of her collection.

'[A]t this point,' as she wrote in her covering letter to the new publisher, she was submitting a 'xerox' copy, rather than an original typescript, because 'I can not, can not, re-type this manuscript one more time.'[22] The new publisher she was trying was a small press with the aptly Northern-sounding name of Borealis. It was run out of the University of Ottawa by Glenn Clever, an acquaintance of Seymour Mayne's. Mayne, feeling somewhat 'responsible' for the plight of Lowther's manuscript after Ingluvin's sinking, helped put Lowther in touch with Clever.[23]

She resubmitted the *Milk Stone* manuscript on 13 February 1974; by mid-March, she had a contract in hand and was discussing matters of production. Borealis commissioned Steve Slutsky to do the cover design again, and Lowther wanted his illustration in black and white, with 'the frame and back cover in deep blue, on matte, not glossy paper.' 'Since the core poem sequence is largely concerned with the Ice Age,' she explained, 'I'd like to carry over to the outside a sort of cold, remote feeling.' (Besides, she disliked 'pastel shades.') She was relieved to 'have the book in such business-like hands.'[24] Some seven months later, in October, on the very 'eve' of an important reading tour to Ontario, her author's copy of *Milk Stone* arrived from Ontario. Though she wasn't entirely satisfied with the book's appearance in the end, its black and white colour scheme was at least stark enough to convey a 'sort of cold, remote feeling.'[25] The 'albatross' had finally landed.

Chapter 13

Longitudes, South

Milk Stone is a book that thaws out and heats up as it goes on, which may be why Lowther eventually rejected its first title, *Ice Crucible*. From the high Arctic and remote Ice Age, the poems chart their way back into the present of a 'green country' below the tree line, into worlds of water, fire, burning irises, 'trumpet daffodils,' 'summers of nasturtiums,' and 'scattering' suns (93, 63). In part, this gradual climate change is also the result of the warmly appreciative tone of several tribute poems. Closest to home, these were the poems inspired by 'Dee' Livesay and (implicitly) by Milton Acorn – or, at least, by the 'Mr. Happyman' Lowther thought she knew before he returned to Vancouver in 1974 and their friendship abruptly ended. These were rounded out by tributes to a pair of poets, one North American, one South American, with whom Lowther was not personally acquainted: 'For Robert Bly Saying Poems' and 'Regard to Neruda.' Not coincidentally, Bly was one of Neruda's more influential English translators during the sixties and seventies.

Milk Stone's 'Regard to Neruda' dates from the 1969 presidential race that Neruda briefly joined as a candidate for the Chilean Communist Party, before he stepped aside to make way for Salvador Allende's Popular Unity Front. 'When I heard that / the world's greatest poet / was running for president,' Lowther's poem begins, 'being north american / I would have laughed' (*MS*, 66). 'Would have' is the operative term, for the poem is written from the perspective of a 'north american' genuinely intrigued by a culture that could support a poet's campaign for presidency. Neruda's nomination for his country's highest public office implied a striking 'regard for' the occupation of the artist as a role of real social relevance. To this extent, Neruda confirmed for Lowther the possibility of a socially engaged artistic life in much the same way that

Inuit aesthetic culture also did. Both the Arctic and sub-equatorial zones offered examples of artists not only involved with the work of everyday life, but involved with transforming that life through word and deed. It was enough to make a poet from the middling northern meridians want to forget about love, and get ready to learn about politics all over again.

And indeed, 'Regard to Neruda' was just the start, the first Chilean spark, as it were. Both before and after Neruda's death in 1973, Lowther worked on a whole series of sequel 'letters' addressed to him: 'Anniversary Letter to Pablo,' 'Letter to Pablo 2,' 'Letter to Pablo 3,' 'Letter to Pablo 4,' and 'Last Letter to Pablo.' The 'Last Letter' addresses news of Neruda's death, and Lowther's own reliance on 'newscast' hearsay about it:

> Cancer the newscast said,
> and coma   but
> what of the sea
> also full of bones
> and miracles
> they said was your
> last prison? (*SD*, 57)

Soon after she finished this final 'letter' in 1974, she sent it on to Livesay, who accepted it for publication in *Woman's Eye*, an anthology she was currently putting together. But 'Dee' had some editorial issues. Could Pat do something about the poem's 'weak similes'? 'You do not need those "likes"!' she exhorted. Livesay didn't like the title either and rather boldly proposed 'The Alchemist' instead.[1] Lowther met her halfway in response, and her reply gives the clearest indication of the chronology of her Pablo 'letters.' 'Dear Dee,' she began,

You are perfectly right about those 'likes.' I'll have to scrutinize current poems for that, too. I feel I must keep the title, though – this poem being very definitely a post-script to an earlier group of 'Letters to Pablo' written about a year and a half ago [1972]. I hope eventually they will all be published together in some collection.[2]

Historically, Lowther's growing fascination with things Nerudian was part of a discernible North American shift toward contemporary Hispanic literature during the sixties and seventies. Tired of a 'post-war poetry' still predominantly influenced by the aesthetics of New Criti-

cism, dissident North American poets and critics like Robert Bly and
W.S. Merwin turned during this period to Spanish and South America
poets – Juan Ramón Jiménez, Federico García Lorca, César Vallejo, as
well as Neruda. Their hope was to reinvigorate modern poetry by opening it to non-traditional influences outside the English language; Spanish modern poetry, in particular, appealed to readers like Robert Bly
because of its distinctive 'surrealist impulse' and its 'moral commitment
on social and political issues' (Marras 1984: 33, 35).[3]

It was down in the States, at places like the University of California,
that some Canadian poets like Tom Wayman, in turn, discovered the
Spanish moderns as part of their experience of the student movements
of the sixties. There, Bly, a left-wing activist before his *Iron John* years,
appeared as a reader to share his translations of Vallejo and Neruda,
blowing away young auditors like Wayman, who 'had no idea there *was*
poetry like this' (Wayman 1993: 86). Others – Al Purdy, Earle Birney,
Patrick Lane – trekked down to South America to assess the heights of
Macchu Picchu for themselves. For her part, Lowther, as usual, tuned
into the new South American current in poetics closer to home,
through books. At the very least, the household on East 46th Avenue
appears to have contained a copy of *The Heights of Macchu Picchu*, one of
the first parts of Neruda's *Canto General* widely translated into English.[4]

Neruda was the biggest Latin American import commodity of all. By
the end of the sixties, about to embark upon the fifth decade of his
career, he was one of the most widely translated poets of his time, and certainly the one figure who had 'the greatest impact on English-language
poets' (Agosin 1986: 132). At least in the United States, Neruda's critical
reception was not hurt by the fact that he proclaimed his own poetic pat-
rimony as stemming from none other than Walt Whitman, that great
American singer of himself and seer of democratic Yankee vistas. (This
artery of influence also extended to Lowther, who attended carefully to
her copy of *Leaves of Grass* and more or less knew the opening lines of
'Song of Myself' by heart.) Neruda's international popularity was thus
already firmly established even before he was officially crowned 'the
world's greatest poet,' in Lowther's phrase, by the Nobel Prize, an
honour bestowed upon him in 1971. The Nobel Prize prompted a whole
new flurry of translated editions and criticism. In conjunction with the
international scandal of the *golpe de estado* that ended in Allende's murder
and Neruda's demise shortly thereafter, the Nobel fanned Neruda's fame
over the ensuing decade as 'The Poet' of all poets (Bizzarro 1979).

So when Lowther wrote to Doug Barbour at the League, in September

1973, that she couldn't 'help feeling that writers here and elsewhere ought to take some kind of stand on the whole situation' in Chile, 'if only to honor [Neruda's] memory,' she was anything but alone in her feeling.[5] The editor of one tribute anthology recalled in his preface how, 'in the United States, from coast to coast, and throughout the world, there were memorial services and read-ins' at the news of Neruda's passing. Walter Lowenfels believed that the international range of his anthology, *For Neruda, for Chile*, reflected the 'millions of people' who had 'been moved by the Chilean tragedy' (*FNFC*, vii). *For Neruda, for Chile* included work by American, African-American, Bulgarian, Canadian, Chilean, French, Greek, Hungarian, Italian, Japanese, Lebanese, Portuguese, Russian, Slovenian, Spanish, Swedish, and Turkish poets. Tom Wayman and Lowther were among the Canadian contributors, whose international ranks also included Allen Ginsberg, Victor Jara, Ishmael Reed, Robert Hass, and Evgenii (Yevgeny) Yevtushenko, among many others.[6]

It is possible, as Tom Wayman speculates, that Lowther encountered Neruda's work even prior to the sixties – in a distinctly political context, that is, through Communist Party organs such as *Masses and Mainstream*, which published English translations of Neruda's political poetry as early as 1950.[7] But if so, she was evidently unprepared to admit it as an influence in her own poetry right away. For it is really only in *A Stone Diary* that the Chilean poet becomes a pervasive and manifold presence, conjured as a touchstone not only in the 'letters' to Pablo but also in occasional poems touched off by the turmoil in Chile, such as 'Chacabuco, the Pit,' and, more diffusely, in the elemental, materialist vision of *A Stone Diary*'s nature poems, which indirectly evoke Neruda's *Elementary Odes* in their earthiness and simplicity.

Necessary for all new beginnings, literary predecessors are also necessarily troublesome ghosts. Neruda proved no exception. In the end, the effect of his example on Lowther's writing was uneven, and she herself at least sensed it: the guiding spirit of her *Stone Diary* was not always her better 'angel.' He could obtrude as 'someone else's poem' to make this latest 'flowring' difficult, too (*DF*, 26). Not only that, he wasn't the only strong predecessor she had to contend with. Never exactly a shy or retiring presence, Livesay exerted an effect that extended in significant ways to Lowther's political poetry, too.

∽

Between 1972 and 1975, when she wrote her 'letters' to Pablo, the volume of Lowther's correspondence by mail swelled enormously. Much of the bulk was a result of her increasing involvements with the League over this period. But not all of it. She had come home from the League's meeting in Edmonton in the fall of 1972 dizzy with fresh infatuation, and a fair amount of the letters that ensued were going to, and coming from, Eugene McNamara in Windsor. 'Your letters,' she wrote in one, rushed note to him, 'are nourishment, sustaining me': 'Every day I think they'll stop, the postal system won't let us go on like this, but they keep coming. Bless you.'[8] Actually, their 'letters' to each other were usually more like their brief encounters in reality, except less intermittent – quick affairs of a few paragraphs, or even just a few lines. This was typical for Lowther, who for the most part wrote longer letters – that is, a full page or more – only when she was in crisis mode. (Her business correspondence was another matter.) Her exchange with McNamara was also typical in terms of its running literary content, including, in particular, observations about Neruda and Walt Whitman's influence on him.

In effect, she was working away at two sets of long-distance 'letters,' one personal, one poetic, which were connected by more than merely the simultaneity of their composition. The 'letters' to Pablo in *A Stone Diary* highlight an epistolary form that held a special significance in the context of the Chilean poet's political history. Especially given that Neruda may have appeared on Lowther's political radar first, she was probably aware of his famous 'Carta íntima para millones de hombres,' a document literally transcribed as the 'Intimate Letter to Millions of Men.' Neruda wrote this open letter in 1947, in his capacity as a communist senator who had worked to get a left-wing party headed by a man named González Videla into power. Once elected, Videla, it seems, reneged on promises for reform, targeted labour unions and communists, and became a friend to 'the old Chilean landed oligarchy' (González Echevarría 1991: 9–10). Feeling bitterly betrayed, Neruda soon published his scathingly accusatory 'Intimate Letter' in a prominent national newspaper. Along with a subsequent fiery speech in the Senate, his efforts earned him an arrest warrant – and he fled into exile, writing the last part of his massive *Canto General* while in hiding.

Neruda had used the letter form memorably, then, as a weapon to make public a personal statement of political defiance. In her stone 'diary,' Lowther similarly deployed 'intimate' forms such as 'letters' to make public her personal affirmation of Neruda's poetry and politics alike. But the concept of Neruda's 'open letter' itself also quietly suggests a possible inspiration for the dangerous experiment that she began to test out in practice around the house, at this time, by making no special effort to conceal the correspondence from her relationship with McNamara. Her seemingly casual use of McNamara's letters as flags to Roy – that she was serious about the 'openness' of their 'open marriage,' and ready to step out the nearest functionally open exit – was a statement made in the same defiant spirit, if not scope, as Neruda's 'intimate letter.' 'Everything here's a weapon,' as she wrote in 'Kitchen Murder.' In that poem, the 'weapons' include meat forks, Drano, and the automatic percolator (*SD*, 75); in reality, that arsenal of 'everything' seemed to include the love letters that her children occasionally doodled upon, and that her husband claimed to have discovered 'accidentally' among loose papers on the kitchen counter: 'Yes, he always mailed his love notes to our house ... The love notes were everywhere, esp. on the counter beside the stove; it was usually 2 or 3 days and sometimes weeks before they went into the briefcase side pocket' (RLJ, 2:102).

Set against each other, these two sets of 'letters' also point up the persistence of the idealized, older male authority figure in Lowther's consciousness. In actuality, this was exactly the relational anchor she was breaking away from through her liaisons with younger men like McNamara and (more briefly) David Morgan. No more lopsided paternal seniority. She would have men of her own age, men she could meet on more equal footing. All the same, as an aesthetic mentor, Neruda took his place in Lowther's repertoire of idealized older men, which – in another lifetime – had once included Roy. And before him, had also included her father, the man who worked magic with water, as well as her mother's beloved father, James Wilks, the prominent family patriarch and 'great man with words.'[9]

Lowther's literary 'correspondence' with Neruda thus deferentially addresses a venerable 'old man' – one Rabelaisian in appetite, but 'more lustrous / than flowers.' Neruda is the divine made incarnate: a 'Buddha contemplating / the heart / of the plural self,' but a deity who 'move[s] past the image / to honour the belly' (*SD*, 54, 55). 'Neruda,' as one reviewer summed up the series, 'appears in the poems as the modest magician, capable of finding or making life in unexpected places, and of delicately transforming the inanimate world. "Letter to Pablo 3" speaks in an idiom which neatly links Neruda to Odysseus. The "Last Letter to Pablo" ... seems to suggest Auden on the death of Yeats' (Hosek 1978: 164–5). Here is part of that 'Last Letter':

> We are weary of atrocities;
> the manure of blood

you said grows
something so frightful
only you could look:
you smoothing wounds
we shudder from –
...
now you too lie with skeletons
heaped about you;
our small crooked hands
touch you for comfort (*SD*, 57)

By turns Buddha and Odysseus, Pablo emerges by this 'Last Letter' as a giant among men, endowed with legendary courage and uncommon powers of vision: 'only you could look.' The passage comes perilously close to reinforcing the sort of iconic hero worship so deftly deflated in other works like 'Penelopes' or *The Age of the Bird*. The only thing that saves 'Pablo' from the status of fetish object or sacred relic here is the image that firmly embeds him in a 'heap' of other, anonymous 'skeletons,' an image that humanizes the great man as but one of many, equally vulnerable victims of political terror. That, and the fact that in contrast to *Milk Stone*'s 'Regard to Neruda,' Lowther was now putting herself on a familiar, first-name basis with 'The Poet' of all poets.

Compared to some of the elegies which apotheosized 'Pablo' in anthologies like *For Neruda, for Chile*, the quasi-sacramental treatment of Neruda in Lowther's 'letters' is relatively restrained. Nor did she live long enough to measure the political martyr of 1973 against the auto-biographical self projected in Neruda's posthumous *Memoirs*. When the first English translation of the *Memoirs* appeared in 1977, it disillusioned other North American Neruda enthusiasts, such as Tom Wayman, for among other things, this book revealed a man who could come off by his own hand as decidedly self-aggrandizing (not to mention criminally crude in his treatment of women).[10] It is virtually certain that Lowther, too, would have come away from the often immodest and un-magical *Memoirs* with a seriously qualified 'regard for' Neruda.

It says something about the sharp crosswinds of Lowther's historical moment, though, that more than one of her poems in high praise of 'the world's greatest poet' were nevertheless first published in specifically feminist, or at least, alternative 'women's' anthologies like Livesay's *Woman's Eye* and Elaine Gill's *Mountain Moving Day*.[11] If not firmly based on the premise of a poetics distinctive to gendered subjectivity – a

Woman's Eye – such anthologies as Gill's *Mountain Moving Day* at least raised the issue as the feminist question *du jour*: was there, after all, an appreciable 'difference between the poetry written by men and the poetry written by women'? Gill, for one, waffled nervously in her editorial introduction, first suggesting no, then yes. And then explaining: 'In the past women have tried to imitate the sound of men's voices ... [But] Mountain Moving Day is truly upon us – women are beginning to speak out with their own voices' (*MMD*, 7). As her own contribution toward this appointed 'moving day,' Lowther included 'Regard to Neruda' and prefaced her work with an author's statement that focused on the idea of transitions. Old habits die hard, she acceded, but 'new assumptions' were definitely displacing the old patriarchal world order: 'I see the women's revolution as part of a new outreach of consciousness. The liberation of women from imposed self-images *is* happening' (*MMD*, 80; emphasis in the original).

'*Is* happening.' The continuous tense speaks directly to the apparent contradiction of her poetic idealization of Neruda at precisely the same time that feminism, that insurgent 'outreach of consciousness,' was also prompting her to question and discard outmoded ideals of male authority as never before. Assimilating her feminism from the vantage point of maturity, Lowther, like her 'Penelope,' had a lot of retroactive 'un-learning' to do. In her case, growth into a 'new' feminist 'consciousness' also involved 'un-learning' the ingrained ideals of an old-school socialism that was nothing if not hierarchical and thoroughly paternalistic in nature. So while it was scarcely possible for any writer interested in contemporary political poetry to ignore Neruda's work, for women writers like Lowther, it was exactly the sort of problems aired in feminist publications like *Mountain Moving Day* – problems of 'voice' and 'imposed self-images' – that the example of Neruda would pose. He renewed with a vengeance questions of legitimacy and authority that she had struggled with from her earliest male alter-egos in fictional drafts to the mocking male 'Angel' of *This Difficult Flowring*.

In their respective centuries and hemispheres, both Neruda and Walt. Whitman before him heralded poetic legacies radically antithetical in almost every conceivable way to anything 'Small Small.' Both men cast a good long booming voice on the page, and each in his time perfected the illusion of a larger-than-life poetic persona, figuring himself as the endlessly virile progenitor of the nation and people whose mythologies he celebrated. Indeed, like Whitman before him (and Homer before *him*), the singer of the *Canto General* epitomized a bardic tradition of the poet as a visionary-patriot-sage: a vocation emphatically, exclusively, and immemorially male. When Lowther tried to tap this august tradition, as she did in the inaugural 'Regard to Neruda,' she inevitably found herself writing from a default position, expressed in this case by way of the timidly wishful subjunctive mood:

> Could I see with his high vision
> (Man with thick hands and belly
> full of good things)
> ...
> could I wash my country
> with songs that settle
> like haloes on the constituents
> I'd campaign
> to be prime minister
> without kisses (*MMD*, 84; *MS*, 66)

'Regard to Neruda' attributes the consecrating powers of the bard's 'songs' to his 'high vision,' without pausing to consider how positions of social prominence – like a senator 'running for President,' say – might also support such transcendent 'vision.' The poem posits Neruda's 'high vision' as an unattainable ideal for the woman speaker, without probing the silent prohibitions that lurk behind the poem's 'could's' as shadowy 'not's.' It did not seem to occur to Lowther that the apparently more myopic limits of the woman singer 'could' have something to do with the fact that she was not likely to be elected to any senate or to campaign for any job as 'prime minister' – with or 'without kisses.' The closest the poem comes to articulating connections between cultural agency and literary achievement is in the final stanza's pointed acknowledgment that, unlike 'love,' 'politics' was one of those realms of public experience that women 'could' *not* be presumed to know anything about – and thus had to get 'ready / to learn.'

When she attempted to situate herself in relation to the model of epic authority that Neruda typified, Lowther was thus apt to encounter something that harked back vaguely to Samuel Johnson's spectacle of the literary woman as a dancing dog. It was, in the words of Irish poet Eavan Boland, to find oneself having 'blundered into an ancient world of customs and permissions' that recognized women only as metaphor, emblem, or muse of the beloved/cruel/victimized homeland or nation-state (1995: 27). Women could be poets, maybe, sometimes. But as

Boland was also discovering in Dublin during the sixties, the very attempt to venture beyond the sanctioned themes of children, family, love, sex, or nature, and to address 'serious' 'public' subjects like history, nationalism, or politics was a sure-fire guarantee for women poets to find their 'poetry and ... sexuality on a collision course' (28). Lowther wasn't aware of Boland's existence, but she would have known exactly what her Irish contemporary was talking about. In her notebooks, she recorded the incidents of such 'collisions,' pithily, as the discordant sound of her 'fake / Adam's apple.'[12]

That 'fake / Adam's apple' sticks out on occasion, in some of the political poetry that coincides with Lowther's Neruda phase. 'Chacabuco, the Pit,' her Hillcrest Hall meditation on the plight of political prisoners rounded up in the wake of the Chilean coup, is perhaps the most salient case in point. Hailed by reviewers as 'powerful' and 'masterful' in its own time and ours (Barbour 1975–6; Barton 1997), 'Chacabuco' has also been dismissed in its own time, and ours, as a 'long and tedious,' 'hopelessly dated' poem that 'discovers nothing, but hovers rather on the edge of rhetoric' (Ormsby 1998; Levenson 1978). As others such as Phyllis Gotlieb have suggested, it reflects, that is, an achievement somewhere in between (1977: 88).

For some of those Allende supporters who made it out of Augusto Pinochet's initial, clearing-house detention centres, Chacabuco, an abandoned nitrate mining town in the midst of Chile's northern Atacama Desert, became home.[13] As Lowther's poem registers, it was the thirty-seven-hectare town site of Chacabuco, a dusty 'grid of streets,' and not the actual mine 'pit,' that was converted into a prison camp of brickstone barracks, barbed wire, chained gates, and wooden watchtowers (*SD*, 18). In composing her poem, however, she was supplementing the partial information available to her at the time with her imagination of 'pit' conditions: 'There are men in that pit / imagine that they are chained / (they may be)' (*SD*, 19). Among other things, this was an imagination likely fired to some degree by family tales about her grandfather's and great-grandfather's lives in the coalbeds of Vancouver Island.

'Chacabuco' is a longer poem, composed of six sections of varying length. An opening headnote situates the poem historically, followed by epigraphs which juxtapose two forms of 'private' communications, secular and sacred. Appearing first are two damning excerpts from the International Telegraph and Telephone Company's infamous '18-point plan,' calling for the overthrow of Allende's government and 'immediate retaliatory measures' against its plans to nationalize Chilean resource and service industries (Sobel 1974: 118). Hammered out behind closed doors with other large American corporate players, ITT's 'plan' had been clandestinely submitted to the Nixon administration in the fall of 1971 and leaked to the media in March of the following spring. Set off against these fragments of political subterfuge is a line from an unidentified 'ancient Mayan prayer': 'I shall speak to the Lord of Heaven / where he sits asleep' (SD, 16). With this express hope for communion with a slumbering 'Lord of Heaven,' the epigraphs leave off.

The poem itself opens by evoking the landscape of the 'Atacama desert.' By day, it is a place of blinding sun and dust: 'blurred glitter between / creased squinting eyelids.' By night, it turns arctic, a place 'cold to the utter bone' (SD, 17). The opening sequence then moves to dramatize its own 'suspenseful / approach' to the edge of 'the pit.' The speaker not only challenges the reader to look, but repeatedly exhorts her to 'notice first,' 'note that,' and 'watch until' Chacabuco's 'pit' appears:

> A huge, gouged cavity
> flickering like a bad film,
> the whole scene twitching
> on and off
> in and out of existence:
> is God blinking? are you
> shuttering your eyes, tourista? (SD, 17–18)

If the confrontational taunt of the 'tourista' falters as a momentary attempt to mimic an 'authentic' Latin American voice, then it also arises as one of those tough-talking, pistol-packing verbal swaggers caught up in Lowther's 'fake / Adam's apple.' She could try them on for size, but such overtly imposing rhetorical postures were basically foreign to 'Patsy Lou,' and she never could pull them off in a fully convincing way. (By comparison, Livesay, in her more 'ornery' moments, could.) Unlike her restlessly roving 'Okanagan outlaw' friend, Patrick Lane, Lowther could no more comfortably inhabit the role of the gaucho than she could assume the role of the prophet Neruda – who, of course, with his 'real,' God-given Adam's apple, *could* do tough-talking confrontation with all the conviction of the Old Testament itself.[14]

Eric Ormsby cites the 'tourista' passage of 'Chacabuco' as awkwardly 'forced' evidence of Neruda's 'especially destructive' influence on Lowther's work, an influence to which he attributes the injection of 'false notes of condescension and political self-righteousness into her otherwise rather pure, if restricted, lyric voice' (1998: 33). Like Neruda, however, Lowther was in her own way specifically intent on working 'Towards an *Impure* Poetry,' and that she still found her 'voice' subtly 'restricted' to the culturally permissible zone of the more ladylike 'lyric' was exactly the problem she was up against in such efforts as 'Chacabuco.' If anything, her deliberate attempt to muddy the waters of poetry (and prayer) with the dirty politics of the day in 'Chacabuco' suggests that she was not so much responding to Neruda, anyway, as she was listening closer to home, to the example of her more tangible modernist fore*mother*, Dorothy Livesay.

Livesay once confessed to harbouring a soft spot 'for the Pat Lowthers and Pat Lanes' of the world, who had to 'fight [their] way up,' as she felt she did.[15] In addition to dispensing editorial advice and occasionally loaning out her cabin at Cadboro Bay, Livesay acted as an informal tutor to her younger 'set,' sharing her knowledge of the literary landscape and helping, at least in Lowther's case, to direct her reading. Just as importantly for Lowther, 'Dee' also provided a relatively rare, home-grown precedent for an openly politicized female voice, especially in her long social poems. Both *The Documentaries* (1968) and the theoretical narrative Livesay constructed around that book, 'The Documentary Poem: A Canadian Genre,' were particularly relevant texts that Lowther knew.[16]

In her foreword to *The Documentaries*, Livesay noted her turn toward political poetry during the thirties, and concerning her decision to leave poems written earlier 'untouched, as a record of the times,' she stated: 'I believe that the veracity of the material and mood is more important than the occasional sentimentality of expression or the lack of polish in style. I am "ornery," and I like authenticity in reportage' (v). In the critical essay that followed, she defined the 'documentary' genre against 'great American epics' like *Leaves of Grass* or William Carlos Williams's *Paterson*: 'My premise is ... that the Canadian longer poem is not truly a narrative at all – and certainly not a historical epic. It is, rather, a *documentary* poem, based on topical data but held together by descriptive, lyrical and didactic elements' (1971: 269).

'Chacabuco, the Pit' is a 'documentary' poem in this sense, mixing its 'topical data' with 'descriptive, lyrical and didactic elements.' But while

Livesay sketched out an 'experimental' hybrid form that was – like her own long poems – primarily designed 'to be heard aloud, often specifically [written] for radio' (1971: 269), Lowther was interested in renovating the concept for the more visual, multimedia culture of her own generation. The ideas of new media theorists like Marshall McLuhan were an influence here. Among other places, Lowther would have come across McLuhan's famous essay 'The Medium Is the Message' in Eli Mandel's *Contexts of Canadian Criticism* – the same book in which Livesay's essay on the Canadian 'documentary poem' appeared in 1971. In synthesizing these home-grown influences, 'Chacabuco' raises concerns about the connections among technology, politics, commerce, art, and religion, indicating the contemporary direction that Lowther was trying to take Livesay's 'documentary tradition.' Indeed, if it is true that, 'increasingly, the political poetry of the twentieth century has become a poetry of witnessed atrocity' (York 1993–4: 325), then Lowther's focus on acts of documentary 'witnessing' highlights the crucial question of their dependency on 'increasingly' simulated forms of reality.

It is no coincidence that 'Chacabuco' 'flicker[s] like a bad film' of the sort that Lowther and her Little Mountain NDPers regularly attempted to view on the sputtering projector at their Hillcrest headquarters (*SD*, 18). That was, after all, the place where she first drafted the text at the tail-end of 1973, while listening to music on a new office 'hi-fi' installed in her 'Cask of Amontillado' office. This context obliquely informs the opening dramatization of the initial 'ceremonial / suspenseful / approach' to Chacabuco's 'pit': 'Carefully now (place / records on a turntable) / remember those 1940s movies / where virgins were sacrifices / to volcanoes' (*SD*, 17). Old 'movies' and 'records on a turntable' are among those seemingly dust-encrusted details that have, no doubt, led some readers to reject 'Chacabuco' as 'hopelessly dated' (Ormsby 1998: 33). Like the long-faded scandal of Chacabuco itself, the poem's 'topical data' appears, to echo Livesay, as quaint an 'untouched ... record of the times' as Lowther's gratified mention of her by-now antique office 'hi-fi.'

Less passé, however, is the idea of assimilating suffering through technologically processed means, from an apparently detached, even safely entertaining, distance. With its invocations of background mood music and melodramatic Hollywood movies, 'Chacabuco' immediately raises this question of mediatized experience. Literally set to a soundtrack and filtered through the spectacle of mass entertainment, this form of eye-'witnessing' is structured by the poem as both voyeuristic and radically unreliable. Neither the 'blurred glitter' of the desert landscape nor the 'flicker[ing]' 'pit' itself is brought into stable focus for the reader. Much of the poem is presented as flashes of discontinuous vision between 'moments of darkness' and 'negative light,' or as a parallel form of memory circuit failure: 'on and off' blackouts of 'forgetting' spliced between moments of conscious remembrance (*SD*, 17, 19, 20). Obviously, one effect of this technique is to call into question Livesay's 'ornery' premise of 'authenticity in reportage' and 'veracity of . . . material.' A further implication is that the blinking tourist-witness, or 'tourista' of terrorism, like the inmate of Chacabuco, is also in some sense a captive: if not physically imprisoned, then nonetheless crucially contained and constrained by the media which structure her apprehension of reality, and her memory.

Already by the end of the poem's opening section, Lowther reveals herself very much in step with Marshall McLuhan and the media theorists of her time, who were also setting out to parse the 'subliminal grammar of technology' and disturb its 'hypnotic spell' (Kroker 1984: 63, 74). In 'The Medium Is the Message' (1964), McLuhan had cogitated on 'the effects of technology':

> The effects of technology do not occur at the level of opinions or concepts, but alter sense ratios or patterns of perception steadily and without any resistance. The serious artist is the only person able to encounter technology with impunity, just because he is an expert aware of the changes in sense perception. (150)

McLuhan argued brilliantly that 'any medium has the power to impose its own assumption on the unwary,' even as his own 'message' interestingly reified the 'assumption' of the class divide between the 'professional' and the non-expert (or amateur) artist at this time. Only the carefully qualified 'serious' 'expert' could demonstrate for the masses a sufficiently wary defence against technology's 'subliminal charge,' and 'he' was, predictably, a 'serious artist' defined not only in opposition to popular culture but also to femininity (147, 151).

It is precisely the implications of technology as a 'subliminal' extension of human experience that Lowther, both female and the product of vulgar artistic origins, was beginning to probe. This is true not just of her 'documentary' poems like 'Chacabuco' but of a whole range of works, including *Infinite Mirror Trip*, 'The Electric Boy' (*MS*, 87), 'Intersection' (*SD*, 76), and 'Hotline to the Gulf' (*SD*, 80), to name a few. Phones, televisions, radios, electric circuits, electric amplifiers, electric instruments, wires, cables, 'extension cords' and 'electrodes,' neon signs, traffic lights, street lights, suburban lights, and machinery of various kinds increasingly pervade the poetry in general, as McLuhanesque reminders of so many 'bloc[s] / of dogma' already 'memorized,' without conscious memorization (*TC*, 58). A more or less direct result of Lowther's constant awareness of her own enforced reliance on print and electronic technologies for knowing the world, this 'wired' vision is one of the more suggestively 'postmodern' aspects of her work. Notably, it is also a version of nascent 'postmodernism' (of the strain that would beget McLuhan's more fatalistic, Gallic heir, Jean Baudrillard) that differs significantly, in this regard, from what was recognized in the early seventies as the prevailing model of West Coast poetic 'postmodernism,' as exemplified by *Tish*.[17]

'Chacabuco,' however, accentuates the role of technology specifically as a means of organizing its 'didactic' agenda. In particular, the metaphor of film, introduced as the source of both voyeuristic pleasure and of imprisonment within altered 'patterns of perception,' implicitly develops the poem's social critique. Of all the new 'technostructures,' film best embodied for Lowther the complex *imaginary* working conditions of the postmodern political 'witness.' It was a fascinatingly ambiguous medium: unprecedentedly immediate in its multiple sensory effects, yet at the same time premised upon a built-in assumption of distance and disconnection between viewer and viewed. In the magical machinery of cinematic representation, Lowther recognized two equally seductive illusions: on the one hand, the illusion of the watcher's 'real' relation to the thing watched; and, on the other hand, the simultaneous illusion of the watcher's fortified detachment from the thing watched. If no other medium at the time could generate such an absorbing facsimile of 'authentic' experience, then none other also reinforced quite so powerfully the comforting fiction of the witness's immunity from any 'atrocities' witnessed. 'We are probably the most passive people in the whole of history,' she lamented in one notebook entry. 'Everything points to some tremendous violence. Even the way we are deliberately and systematically being deadened, as though we were being anaesthetized for major surgery.' Lowther saw the numbing of society as a cause and effect of vapid consumerism, in general – 'they lull us with *things*' – but also, of mindless image consumption, in particular. In another of her political poems, an unpublished draft entitled 'newsreel,' she underlined this focus: 'a machine gun fires / directly at the camera / the film splinters white / but we do not wake up.'[18]

By extension, what 'Chacabuco' aims to document as a causal factor in the political 'atrocity' it witnesses is the essential relationship between technology and 'businessmen's cheque hands' (*SD*, 23) – exactly that blind spot which tended to elude Marshall McLuhan's liberal imagination.[19] For Lowther, ITT's involvement in the Chilean coup came as both ample and crude indication that the challenge posed by technology was not just the inherent 'power' of new communications media to alter 'perception steadily and without any resistance.' The problem was also, inextricably, the appropriation and privatized control of technology – of all kinds – by corporations which were proving ever more decisive determinants of 'power' in a wire-tapped, electronic world. In 'Chacabuco,' technology itself thus emerges as less culpable than the self-proliferating, acquisitive logic of capitalism. The poem makes this point in very plain language, when it portrays the social conditions of Chilean nationals under Allende's reforms as an interlude of peaceful sleep and forgetfulness. But the sleep of these 'collective dreamers' is abruptly ruptured by the 'stealth' and 'strength' of foreign corporations, like the ominously named Anaconda Mining Co.:

> They forgot lifetimes of exile
> years of held breath and stealth
> seeing so many strong
> they forgot the strength of I.T. & T.
> United Fruit Co.,
>   Anaconda
>
> who do not easily give up
> what they have taken. (*SD*, 20)

In her draft notebook version of 'The Pit,' as it was first titled, Lowther played around with the tempting possibilities of 'Anaconda,' spiralling the letters down the page in a serpentine form, so as to more visibly shake loose the 'o' and the 'canada' in it. But it was only a near-anagram, presumably not good enough to meet her scrabble-honed criteria for a letter-perfect match. So she changed it back.

The national anthem was an ironic subtext she wouldn't have missed for good reason: Allende had disclosed in 1972 that Canadian banks were among the lenders who had suspended credit to Chile pending disputes over its seizure of American-owned copper enterprises (Sobel 1974: 92). Canada's less publicized involvements with the 'Chilean tragedy' were, of course, reinforced in NDP literature of the time. In one example, a political cartoon depicted Uncle Sam with a long straw, drinking an outline of Chile dry, with a tubby little Canadian beaver in a bowler hat, tugging at Sam's trouser pocket for a sip.[20] At the time she wrote 'Chacabuco,' however, Lowther was in no mood to find any humour in North Americans' collective exploitation of the South. As one reviewer immediately noted, the poem's social critique is aimed directly at underscoring 'the complicity between public acts and private lives' (Quickenden 1977: 3); and as such, its indictment extends beyond 'statesmen' and 'businessmen' to include complacent suburban consumers. No one can claim immunity from 'the horrors of / what we allow to be done' elsewhere in the world, beyond our own 'pleasant lawns':

> Even now in our cities
> churches   universities
> pleasant lawns   we are
> scrabbling with broken nails
> against rock, we are
> dying of flies and disease.
> Until that pus is drained
> we are not healed. (*SD*, 26, 25)

Against this corruption of the body politic, 'Chacabuco' keeps coming back to questions of faith and spiritual renewal – a 'counterpoint, maybe,' she said. It was the last day of the year, 31 December 1973, and 'the first sunny day in weeks' when Lowther wrote to Eugene McNamara about her Chilean poem. His last correspondence had taken almost two weeks to reach her. Rejuvenation was on her mind. 'Darling,' she wrote,

The mail slowdown has finally arrived. Your correspondence posted the 19th reached me today. A beautiful day. The first sunny day in weeks, crisp and frosty. I fear for all the poor trees and bushes that have been thinking it's just a cold spring. Just before Christmas I went into the garden to cut some branches and found leaf buds everywhere. On the lilac tree, wisteria vine, currant bushes.

A hi-fi has been installed in my office and I'm playing the Messiah and a scratchy old record of Columbus Boys Choir singing Bach's Easter Cantata. Slowly writing a poem about Chileans imprisoned in disused nitrate mines, and it seems to be mixed up with this kind of music. Counterpoint, maybe.[21]

In her poem, the 'scratchy old record'of the 'Columbus Boys' and the surprising 'leaf buds' of Lowther's winter garden enter 'Chacabuco' in the third section, which contrasts the miserable plight of captive Chileans against 'Choirs of young boys' singing 'hymns in cathedrals,' and 'fruit trees unfold[ing] their blossoms / petal by petal': 'we are continually born / but these, captive, stumble / in gross heat' (*SD*, 22). Side by side with 'our absurdities' and worse, 'Chacabuco' also documents the 'casually accept[ed] splendour' of existence, in an effort to mitigate 'horrors of ... mind' and deed, with evidence of 'the grace of the soul' (*SD*, 25, 26).

That the poem was 'mixed up' in Lowther's mind with devotional music like Handel's extended choral piece, *The Messiah*, and Bach's *Easter Cantata*, is also of wider significance. With their many voices in unison, these choral 'towers of sound' reinforce the poem's allusions to a fairly heterogeneous range of Jewish, Christian, and Native Meso-American mythologies. Yet Lowther also transposed into 'Chacabuco' the emphasis of her Baroque musical sources on Christian resurrection and salvation. The poem's final section is prefaced by a scriptural extract from Paul's First Epistle to the Corinthians: 'And the dead shall be raised incorruptible' (15:52). In its closing sequence, 'Chacabuco' appears to narrow to a conventional Christian moral. In sum, the substance of the final stanzas suggests that, as we are all accountable for what happens elsewhere on earth, so we shall all be held accountable elsewhere, in the higher court of an after-life Judgment Day: 'When their names are called / will you answer / will I?' (*SD*, 26). At the same time, the poem shifts into a heightened, vatic key reminiscent of Neruda: 'For I tell you the earth / itself is a mystery / . . . and our people a holy mystery' (*SD*, 26). By the end of the poem, then, the focus seems to have shifted away from the 'topical' problem of witnessing violence by way of new technologies, to the eternal promise of a faith witnessed by way of the New Testament. Not quite the expected course from someone of her materialist, postmodernist sensibilities.

Yet Lowther suspended the final act of Judgment in the form of open questions: 'will you answer to their names?' 'Will I?' She also chose to punctuate her meditation with a last 'Amen,' explicitly resurrecting, as it were, a mode of prayer first evoked in the epigraphs, and reiterated in the poem's opening section. The closing stanzas call attention to a distinctive discursive *form*, that is. And in doing so, 'the medium is the message' here, as much as anything else. At this point, moreover, that 'message' inevitably resonates with the ambiguity of the first pagan 'Mayan' prayer presented to the reader: 'I shall speak to the Lord of Heaven / where he sits asleep' (*SD*, 16, 18). So, with God as her 'witness,' the poet speaks to 'to the Lord of Heaven' at the end of 'Chacabuco.' Whether the Lord – or at least one of them, anyway – is actually awake to hear what she says, and not sleeping – like the 'collective dreamers' of Chile, or the mediatized narcoleptics of North America – is another open question, and the only hope that goes unstated. The enigma of the fragmentary 'ancient Mayan prayer' lingers in 'The Pit,' introducing a note of doubt that is muted, but not forgotten, at the poem's end.

It is, finally, collective consciousness and memory as political events in themselves that longer poems such as 'Chacabuco' and *The Age of the Bird* foreground. By taking up 'topical' events in which North Americans might rather 'try to forget, to deny,' they were more or less directly implicated, Lowther attempted to intervene in the shaping of history, documenting what she saw as 'flickering' zones of cultural amnesia (*SD*, 25). And insisting, not just on the material effects of political economy, but on the material effects of a political *ecology* in which 'disease[d]' and 'broken' social orders held real consequences for individuals. As Lowther saw it, these consequences exceeded the metaphorical realm of the rotten body politic. The witness of 'Chacabuco' can for this reason assert that the documentary I/eye is permanently changed, at a 'cellular' level, by what it sees: 'that journey its / hardships its surprises / stay in our cells / our footprints in clay' (*SD*, 24).

It was a refinement and variation on a lesson she first learned at Rice Lake. Just as what came into the weir mattered, so are we also altered by any impurities we take in through the senses – organically altered, at an imperceptible 'cellular' level, below the threshold of conscious intellect or emotion. To witness violence and suffering on the scale of the Chilean crisis was, in this sense, to in-corporate events whose residual aftereffects or encrypted half-lives 'stay in our cells,' as though 'a virus' or 'violence among the cells' (*SD*, 71). The body of the witness becomes part of the documentary, storing its own 'topical data' – an active archive of 'something,' as she put it elsewhere, 'you know and can't remember knowing.'[22]

Lowther had no way of knowing that her husband was capable of taking the germ of a similar idea, perhaps plundered from her work, and

projecting it as one of his warped rationalizations for murdering her –
his 'sick' spouse. But she probably did appreciate the extent to which
her own personal circumstances supplied the censored subtext of her
political poem. It was not just that the torture 'pit' she envisioned and
descried was also that of her own broken-down marriage, an imprisonment 'counterpointed' only by the distant hope that someone from the
'outside,' like McNamara, represented. It was also that her poem's own
organic vision of 'the complicity between public acts and private lives'
(Quickenden 1977: 3) could not fail to remind her of that 'schizophrenic' tension at work within her own personal and professional lives.
This insoluble disjunction was exactly what Lowther was trying (and
unable) 'to forget, to deny,' and it implicated her uniquely in the problem targeted by 'Chacabuco's' social critique:

> but these places
> of death slowly inflicted
> we can't forgive, but writhe
> coiling in on ourselves
> to try to forget, to deny:
> *we have travelled so far*
> *and these are still with us?* (*SD* 25, italics in the original)

Privately, in her notebooks, on the other hand, she scribbled: 'actually,
it's my lifestyle / that's killing me/ this domestic chaos.'[23]

In the end, getting 'ready / to learn politics' meant acknowledging that
politics sometimes defied edification anyway. Consequently, not all of
Lowther's social protest poems are invested with such heavy ethical
imperatives or grim stakes as 'Chacabuco' or *The Age of the Bird*. Notably,
for instance, it was her own proclivity as a 'soapbox' preacher and public
intellectual with a 'message' that Lowther sent up as a parody in the very
first instalment of her 'City Slide' series. Speaker's Corner, in this case,
was a spot wedged between park statuary and 'a mens' – as in 'a men's'
public loo:

> Arranging my rectangular
> soapbox
> between a mens
> and a stone lion

> thereby eclipsing the sun
> for anything shorter than me,
> I declaim:
> My Fellow Conspirators,
>
> Citizens, file your teeth (*SD*, 67)

Like many of her other works, 'City Slide 1' reveals a poet entirely capable of tweaking the declamatory and prophetic modes that Lowther was elsewhere trying on in earnest, and finding a slightly uncomfortable misfit – as though a 'tourista' who had wandered to a wrong address. Certainly, its parody makes a serious point, touching again upon those questions of legitimacy that role models like Neruda raised, as Lowther reached ambitiously, but uncertainly, for a wider public voice and vocation as a poet. However, unlike the earlier 'Regard to Neruda,' this poem explicitly underlines the importance of the *position* from which one speaks as a determining factor of authority. The effect is a well-aimed poke at pretensions to stature, and the gamesmanship of politics, as an art of strategic self-positioning.

In this sense, politics, as Lowther discovered, was really 'a lesson' in 'perspective,' part of an on-going preoccupation that also played itself out in her oeuvre as conundrums related to size and spatial dimensions. As she tried out her voice in relation to various others – 'on/against' those of Small Small, Neruda, or Handel and Bach's choral 'towers of sound' – so she also tried on different experimental self-images, from the microscopic or 'small small' persona to the towering shadow, facetiously 'eclipsing the sun.' These oscillations in the self's scale and imaginary dimensions sometimes occur as the focus of individual poems. 'In the Continent behind My Eyes' features a speaker who treads an interior landscape that echoes with the giant footsteps and 'barbaric yawp' of Walt Whitman, but not with Whitman's confidence that she, too, is 'large enough to contain multitudes':

> White as silence I walk
> and can not determine my size
> If I am large
> enough to contain the universe
> in a pattern of cells
> still sometime I must scrape my knees
> on ice-heaved ground

and bark
with an unused throat (*MS*, 22)

At other moments that recall Small Small's contraction to 'the pupil of that eye' in 'Woman on/against Snow,' Lowther frequently figures herself as 'getting smaller,' and 'dwindling / to a dot' or an 'ellipsis.' In 'Greetings from the Incredible Shrinking Woman,' the speaker protests, 'it's not that / i'm getting smaller': 'Actually, it's that / i'm finally learning / perspective' (*SD*, 50).

The morphing poetic persona reflects the art of a life gaining new 'perspective' on powers of perception and self-projection. Projecting a physical presence was something that Lowther – the girl whose shoes at the door were all that once announced her return home – had to work at consciously. Topping out at a petit height of five feet, three inches, small-boned, thin, and rather shy, it was definitely not Lowther's physical stature that Livesay was describing when she referred to her as 'elongated.' Like her 'soapbox' speaker, Lowther would have needed a booster box in analogous situations – though the stairs of the old courthouse in downtown Vancouver also served, in a pinch, when she girded the troops for battle at anti-Vietnam rallies. Her diminutive frame was something she couldn't change, but nor did that mean she had to be seen – or see herself – as 'small small.'

Her poetry suggests an extension of her struggle to liberate herself from 'imposed self-images,' and image was something Lowther was actively cultivating in the final years of her life, especially after she assumed the position of Chair for the League of Canadian Poets. To the extent that she could afford to, she began to put care into her appearance for this more public role – treating herself, for example, to some brand new clothes more often. In doing so, she was beginning to shed alter egos that she had earlier projected. The 'welfare mother' was disappearing, as was at least one 'skinny, witchy-looking girl with clothes a little too big, a little too grown-up looking for her.'[24]

Lowther's eldest daughter, Kathy, remembers this period of incipient transformation well. She recalls one shopping jaunt, in particular, just before her mother's fortieth birthday:

I took her shopping. I gave her a wallet and I gave her a gift certificate for Sears. And then I came and picked her up and took her shopping for some new clothes. And she wanted to get a size nine pair of pants. I said, 'No, no, no, try a seven.' And she goes, 'No, no, no, I take a nine, I take a nine.' I said, 'Just put on the sevens!' And she came out [of the fitting room] and she said, 'Do you know I've been sticking out my stomach to hold my pants up all this time?'[25]

It wasn't that she was 'getting smaller.' 'Actually,' she was 'finally learning / perspective,' and realizing that oversized clothes only deflated her. That was not the appearance she wished to project as spokesperson for the League. For this role, she wanted a perfect fit, a chance to prove that the britches were definitely not too big for the woman.

Chapter 14

Welcome to the League

There was an ice jam in the North Saskatchewan River and snow flurries in the forecast when, in late November 1969, Lowther had stepped off the train for her very first taste of life east of the Rockies. She had arrived in Edmonton for Dorothy Livesay's 'Poet and Critic' conference, hoping to counteract the sense of loneliness that settled in on her after the departure of some of her closest friends from Vancouver in the late sixties: 'Uncle Miltie,' her Very Stone House friends, and, especially, Livesay, who had accepted a professorial appointment that would keep her at the University of Alberta until 1971. In the absence of Dee and her 'salon des autres' on West 8th, Lowther was left to complain: 'There is no "poetry circle" that I know of here. When poets meet, it's at formal readings, sandwiched between other things, and there's no discussion of work in process or just general shop talk.' So when Livesay mentioned her conference, Lowther didn't take too long to think about it. 'Sounds like just what I need,' she declared: 'if I'm going on any trip, that's where I should be going ... I really feel desperately in need of stimulation of this kind.' By the way, she added, at the end of her letter: 'How cold does it get in November?'[1]

At the conference, and at Livesay's nearby Garneau apartment 'for drinks and readings,' Lowther first met a group of 'poets and critics' who had all – like Livesay herself – been members of the League of Canadian Poets since its formal debut: people like Michael Ondaatje, Tom Marshall, and D.G. Jones.[2] Here, if Dee hadn't already filled her in, Lowther would have learned about the League, established only two years earlier 'as a national organization to further poetry in Canada.' From the start, it had been conceived of as a cross between a 'lobby' group and 'a trade union.' Membership was by invitation only. The original founders – including Earle Birney, Al Purdy, Raymond Souster, and J.R. Colombo – had sent out eighty invitations on 1 January 1967. 'We have decided to invite all the serious Canadian poets we could think of,' their first circular announced: 'regardless of age, reputation, or "school."'[3] After its inaugural 1968 meeting in Toronto, it was decided that membership in the new League would be open 'to all practicing poets who are either resident in Canada or Canadians living outside of Canada'; new members, however, had to be nominated from within, by at least three current League members.

By November 1969, Lowther may or may not have known that Earle Birney, along with Joe Rosenblatt, had already that spring indicated to Raymond Souster, the League's first Chair, their willingness to nominate both her and Daphne Marlatt for membership. Souster soon sent off an invitation to Marlatt. 'I'll check on Pat Lowther,' he added, 'and hope to get an invite to him shortly.' Birney promptly corrected his colleague – 'lowther, by the way, is a She, tho' named pat' – but while League records show that Marlatt's nomination and acceptance went through promptly, it wasn't until the spring of 1971 that Lowther's name was actually forwarded and approved.[4] It is difficult to avoid the conclusion that Souster, or someone else on the executive, blocked Lowther's first nomination, since technically she met the membership requirements just as well as Marlatt. Both had just published their first books, and theoretically it should have been no problem for Birney and Rosenblatt to find a third League member – Livesay, for instance – to support Lowther's nomination. In any case, it was her would-be Ingluvin publisher, Seymour Mayne, who eventually spearheaded Lowther's 1971 nomination to the League, on the strength of *This Difficult Flowring* and, interestingly, on her apparent inclusion 'in the forthcoming anthology by Al Purdy' – *Storm Warning*.[5]

If she was aware of any delay in being welcomed into the League's fold, however, Lowther didn't say so. On the contrary, she recorded having had a great time at the Edmonton conference; it had just the effect she'd hoped it would. 'I've really been writing frantically since I got back,' she informed Livesay by mail. 'Not from the impressions gained while I was away, strangely, but maybe the distance and new people gave me a fresh view of things that are always with me.'[6] And when her invitation to join the League did come, a few years later, her only problem with it was scrounging together the $7.50 for annual membership dues. At that point, Raymond Souster and his executive committee proposed to put 'Miss Pat Lowther' to work right away, as regional representative for the West Coast. Lowther responded:

Dear Ray Souster,

I'd be happy to stand as West Coast Rep. I'm not sure, though, just what is involved, other than writing reports for the newsletter. And there doesn't seem to be anybody accessible around here right now who does know.

If it involves being very closely in touch with large numbers of people, I might not be the right one, as I'm rather tied down with family, and don't get around much as most people.

Otherwise, fine. As you probably know, the League has invited me to do the Western tour with Atwood. It seems the least I can do in appreciation is take on this position. Actually, I feel honored to be asked. I just want to be sure I can do it properly.

Sincerely,

Pat Lowther[7]

Lowther's allusion to her 1972 readings with Atwood reveals her keen awareness of – and gratitude for – the social capital that membership in the League conferred upon her, officially placing her, as it did, *in league* with 'all the serious Canadian poets.' As with her first Canada Council grant, her inclusion in the League also bestowed material advantages. It opened actual new horizons and opportunities, as opposed to imaginary longitudes: in a very real sense, her League membership was Lowther's passport to the widest world she would encounter, subsidizing travels across Canada – to Edmonton, Regina, Saskatoon, Toronto, Thunder Bay, Fredericton, and Charlottetown, among other places – that she would not otherwise have been able to afford.

And, of course, within the space of a few short years, she would not only quell the apprehensive doubt that she 'might not be the right one' to serve as a regional representative, but, in fact, gamely replace Souster and his successors as the League's principal officer – a position that certainly would 'involv[e] being very closely in touch with large numbers of people.' As the first woman and the first writer with no other primary professional livelihood to take on this post, Lowther soon discovered it to be, as she put it, 'an immersion in more work than I ever bargained for.'[8] But this, too, was work that would prove an excellent education in politics.

⚮

The League that Lowther joined around the same time that Joy Kogawa, Marya Fiamengo, and Eugene McNamara also did, in the early seventies, was in the process of significant transitions, both demographic and geographic. Between 1966 and 1970, Raymond Souster and his founding colleagues had devoted copious amounts of time and energy to getting the infant association up and running, seeking (and obtaining) Canada Council funding; organizing the first two biennual meetings; drafting a constitution, by-laws, and membership procedures; and implementing a series of initiatives, ranging from funded reading tours for members to organized lobbying for government support of 'indigenous publishing' with bloc grants. By the spring of 1970, Souster was understandably tired, and looking to unload his duties.[9] He first approached two senior names as potential successors: F.R. Scott and Dorothy Livesay. Professor Scott, then heading into his seventies, was gracious but firm: '... it was good of your committee to think of me as next President of the League,' he wrote, 'but I am afraid this is a responsibility greater than I am ready to assume.' Noting that he had 'virtually no secretarial help' during summer months, Scott also felt that 'it should be a younger person who assumes the guidance of the League's activities for the future.'[10] Livesay was altogether more cagey, first indicating an openness to considering the job, but blowing smoke for several months before also declining: 'To be honest, I should admit that I have much work of my own to do, and the coming year will afford me some leisure (from teaching) to do it.'[11] Back to square one, Souster and his outgoing team decided to act upon Scott's advice to turn the leadership over to a younger set, one with the energy and ambition to prove itself through such service.

By nominating two youthful academics and poets, Douglas Barbour and Stephen Scobie, to assume the reins in 1972, the original League executive also had firmly in mind the motive that the new leadership 'should be based in a centre outside of Ontario.' Since its founding, the League's activities, they noted, 'tended to centre around Toronto,' a fact reflected in early membership lists. In 1968, forty-three of sixty-four paid members resided in Ontario; there were only two members from the Maritimes (Fred Cogswell and Alden Nowlan), a smattering from the Prairies and the West Coast, and none from Quebec. Though by 1970 regional representation had increased, Ontario members still weighed in to comprise 50 per cent of the League's membership.[12] 'Now,' however, 'with the possibility of a newly elected Executive based in Western Canada,' the old guard felt optimistic that a 'badly needed' change was taking place: '... we are at last taking on a truly national identity.'[13]

It was to Barbour and Scobie in Edmonton, then, that Lowther reported in her capacity as West Coast representative. In the fall of 1972, she wrote to Barbour, 'urgently' requesting membership lists and 'any other material you can give me, such as publication times for [the League newsletter], or even a definition of my duties, which I didn't get from Ray Souster.' Souster had written in his original letter of request that 'the work is pretty well what you decide you have time for.' That she didn't have a lot of time was, of course, a major part of Lowther's 'current constellation of anxieties,' but she approached her potentially open-ended duties pragmatically. She kept her 'tabs on poetic happenings in bc,' said her hellos to League readers, and sent in her newsletter reports when she could. 'Feel free to cut or whatever,' she appended in a note to one of these reports: 'I have no temperament connected to this kind of prose.'[14]

The third biennial meeting of the League in 1972 was one of the first membership perks Lowther enjoyed along with her new responsibilities. In early October of that year, she headed back to Edmonton – only this time, her $82.00 return-trip train fare was paid in full, and she was allotted $60.00 toward food and accommodation. Lowther applied to get the cash in advance. It was the first such League meeting held 'outside Upper Canada,' and the young co-convenors, Barbour and Scobie, were 'nervous' as bridegrooms as they 'awaited the first arrivals in the foyer' of the grand old CP Hotel MacDonald. 'Between fifty and sixty poets from all over Canada converged' for the meeting, 'shaking hands, and passing into the Rupert's Land Suite to gather and talk' over highballs (80¢) and 'bottled Western beer' (65¢).[15] Earle Birney was there, and F.R. Scott, and P.K. Page, as well as Miriam Waddington, Daphne Marlatt, Michael Ondaatje, and Victor Coleman of Coach House Press. Here, Lowther also happily reunited once again with old friends: bill bissett, Seymour Mayne, and Joy Kogawa, who had come from Ottawa. Livesay, who had relocated to Vancouver Island by then, also returned for the gathering. And then there was that copper-haired writer from Windsor, the editor of *Mainline*, Eugene McNamara. Their encounter in Edmonton coincided roughly with the appearance of some of Lowther's poems in the fall 1972 issue of *Mainline*. Clearly, McNamara admired her work; he would later publish more of her poetry, including the title poem of *A Stone Diary*, in the *University of Windsor Review*, a journal he founded and also edited. Vancouver must have seemed light years away from Lowther that weekend. Over a Friday night banquet featuring 'Hip of Beef' and 'Assorted Rainbow Jellos,' she was smitten.

But it wasn't all *soirée*. On Saturday morning, a bus shuttled the poets across the river valley to the university campus, where they settled in for a talk on 'The Poet in the Changing World'; a screening of Michael Ondaatje's film on bp Nichol, 'Sons of Captain Poetry'; and a symposium on the plight of small independent publishers. That night, there was a gala reading, and Lowther took to the stage, along with F.R. Scott, P.K. Page, Marya Fiamengo, Eugene McNamara, and others. Open to the public, the reading drew an audience of over three hundred. The Edmonton gathering was declared 'a complete success.' 'The divisiveness and bad feelings that sometimes seemed to be threatening the meeting at Ottawa in 1970,' one League member observed, 'didn't show up at Edmonton.'[16]

If Barbour and Scobie could breathe a sigh of relief at the outcome of the 1972 assembly, it wasn't just because they and their Western venue were testing new precedents for the League. As the allusion to latent tensions at previous meetings suggests, the League's early history revealed that differences of 'age, reputation, and "school"' (not to mention race, gender, nationality, and region) could not just be overridden 'regardless' but, instead, would sometimes result in internal 'divisiveness and bad feelings.' Indeed, if League members by and large did not see themselves as a coherent group or 'class,' this was not surprising: even from a strictly socio-economic point of view, their membership spanned a significant continuum that ranged from itinerant labourers and bohemian nomads like bissett, to pillars of ostensibly conventional middle-class respectability, some of whom supported their under- or non-salaried colleagues either informally, or through their institutional connections and influence. Aside from a host of academics, for example, the League's artistic ranks included a banker (Souster), an ex–law dean (Scott), and a diplomat's wife (Page). Nevertheless, like other national arts organizations born in the late sixties and early seventies, the League aimed *in effect* at the social definition and professionalization of this 'creative class,' an otherwise relatively heterogeneous and individualized group bound mainly by their common occupational interests and concerns as 'serious' poets.

To the extent that the League immediately set about addressing problems related to standards of working conditions and the protection of (intellectual) labour, its 'trade union' analogy held. Prior to the 1972 conference, for instance, delegates were given questionnaires which asked them about 'specific topics' they wanted to discuss. Livesay responded with one emphatic word – '*Copyright*' – which Lowther, in turn, would later pick up as an issue when she assumed the position of Chair. Similarly, one of the resolutions passed at the Edmonton meeting called for legal assistance to draw up a contractual prototype, stipulating 'minima for rights, payment, scales, etc.,' to be 'made available to members to use at their discretion.'[17]

On the other hand, the League's peer-adjudicated exclusiveness and emphasis on 'serious' literary standards were designed to distinguish it from 'the great morass of Sunday poets,' and to project a distinctly professional 'reputation and complexion' that was rather different from that of a tradesman's union. To this end, the League executive announced in 1971 that it had 'secured the services of Gerald Lampert as a professional organizer and publicity director.'[18] Careful to portray its hand-picked members as both skilled craftspersons *and* polished professionals, the League mobilized white-collar connotations of higher calling and careerism at the same time that it deployed the blue-collar model of working-class solidarity in its self-representations. As part and parcel of the institutionalization of literary culture during the seventies, artists' organizations such as the League and the contemporaneous Writers' Union of Canada also more broadly reflect the rise of the so-called 'no-collar' post-industrial 'creative class' (Florida 2002: 13).

To her Little Mountain NDP friend Shirley Miller, Lowther thus described her new literary confraternity as 'not quite a union' of poets, although, sounding very much like James Wilks's grand-daughter, she also went on to suggest 'that the League might become more of a union in the future' (Miller 1975: 18). While it was distinct from the traditional 'trade unionism' that had provided her grandfather's livelihood, Lowther appears almost immediately to have recognized the significance of the League as part of a burgeoning arts bureaucracy that was creating new forms of work and possibilities for employment (even as it also tightened the regulation of artistic production itself). Widening opportunities for actually making some form of modest living in an arts-related field seem to be the muted substance of a letter that she wrote to Livesay, for instance, during her first year as a full-fledged League member. She was awaiting news, she said, on a 'summer grant' for which she, Seymour Mayne, Allan Safarik, and Brian Brett had applied – they were pitching an anthology chronicling West Coast literary history. A hasty postscript to the letter later informs Livesay that the application was, in fact, rejected – 'O Hell.' But even though she 'just wish[ed] at the moment' that she 'could find some way to make money' – 'it always helps' – she expressed a significant hope: 'As the whole society becomes more pluralistic, I begin to see openings for myself too – alternatives that, if they don't exist at the moment, are developing, and will eventu-

ally be there if I need them.'[19] A few months later, she got her second
Canada Council grant.

The small windfall of $750 arrived just in time for the autumn of
1972, which continued as a blur of new faces and places after the Edmonton conference. There were the joint readings with Atwood, of
course, in Vancouver, Regina, and Saskatoon (where Lowther visited
with her friend Elizabeth Brewster). But in November, she also flew off
for a reading at the invitation of McNamara's department at the University of Windsor, where the creative writing program was in its heyday,
and where she met the American writer Charles Bukowski. When she
finally got back home and dropped the luggage she had borrowed from
her mother, she told Roy about the people she had most recently met,
mentioning Bukowski, in particular. Already unhappy about her
repeated absences from home, Roy, for all his labour-poet rhetoric, was
even unhappier about his wife consorting with the likes of the rough-
edged Bukowski: 'Bukowski's books have to be read to be believed. As
far as pornography and obscenity in poetry is [*sic*] concerned, he leads
all the rest' (RLJ, 1:52). Finally home again with her daughters, and
drawn back again into the rip tide of her resentful husband's moods,
she sat down and typed a quick note to McNamara:

> Very down and it's difficult to write. Fortunately, my clones are pursuing
> their destinies and dragging me with them ...
>
> On your scale of worries, what's major? Is the world coming to an end?
> Should I repent? Again?
>
> I'm bogging down. As the sun sinks slowly into the gray Pacific and
> somebody in the neighborhood plays a blue guitar, electronically ampli-
> fied. Very down and lonely. Hold my hand. Sorry.[20]

On Lowther's 'scale of worries' at the time, sheer financial survival
outstripped the compunction to 'repent' over her distant 'double' life.
The readings she was beginning to undertake were exciting, but the
income, on top of being irregular, was scarcely enough to supplement
her soon dwindling grant money and any contributions from Roy's occasional stints as a substitute teacher. Money problems meant concentrat-
ing on other forms of short-term employment for most of 1973. The
momentary self-indulgence expressed in her 'hold-my-hand' note to
McNamara passed, as usual, and she took matters into her own hands by
landing the secretarial job with the NDP constituency office. But while
she did manage to write poems like 'Chacabuco,' Lowther invariably

found her writing 'bogging down' when she attempted to juggle it with outside work, her volunteer political commitments, and motherhood: 'I'm not writing,' she informed McNamara. 'I've been blaming it on my job, which is to a large extent social work and uses a lot of psychic energy.'[21]

She might more accurately have said jobs, for in addition to her secretarial post, she was teaching a creative writing course out in New Westminster by the fall of 1973. It was a night school program, and she was slightly irritated and slightly bemused when she told Fred Cogswell that the leaflet advertising her course had arrived in the mail: 'I just got a night school brochure, discovering my course listed under "personal development" along with hair styling and palmistry.' But, she added, she was prepared to make the best of any experience as an instructor: 'I'm looking forward to it anyway – maybe getting other people writing will get me writing again too.' She concluded her letter to Fred by noting,

> Yesterday was the hottest day of the year here. Today it's pouring rain. Depressing.
>
> I think maybe I'll go bottle some wine, maybe get a little drunk from the syphon. I hope.[22]

The occasional snort of home-made wine aside, her brief flight to rendezvous with McNamara at Livesay's cabin on Cadboro Bay was one of Lowther's few escapes from home in 1973. 'You can't imagine how much this means to me,' she wrote to Livesay then. 'Or maybe you can, knowing something of the way I've been living.'[23]

With the turn of the new year, however, the pace and intensity of Lowther's career changed almost immediately and, in the end, dramatically. Ushering in 1974 was an invitation to appear as a visiting reader at the University of Ottawa in January. It was in the nation's capital that she made her initial contact with the eventual publisher of *Milk Stone*, Glenn Clever of Borealis Press. During her visit, she stayed with Joy Kogawa, who recalled a healthy turnout of 'about 60–70 people' for the reading, and who threw a party in Lowther's honour afterward. Many in the audience that day were students, whose 'warmth and receptiveness' Lowther commented upon gratefully afterward.[24] But another forthcoming Borealis poet, a little-known writer named Carol Shields, was also among them. Soon enough, both Shields's and Lowther's new books, *Intersect*

and *Milk Stone*, would be reviewed together in *Canadian Forum*. Thirty years later, the celebrated author of *The Stone Diaries* did not remember any conscious intention to echo *A Stone Diary* in her novel's title, nor could she recall thinking of Lowther in relation to *Swann*. What she did still vividly remember is one of the poems she heard Pat read that day in Ottawa, 'Mr. Happyman Is Coming' – a poem, she said, 'brimming with life.'[25]

But the vast majority of Lowther's new trails now came as a direct result of her increasing contacts with the League. By 1974 the League's only paid administrator, Gerald Lampert, was sufficiently overburdened to begin sharing his workload with his wife, Arlene. As a regional representative, Lowther had begun to correspond regularly with both Arlene and Gerald – the 'Dear Lamperts,' as she called them. Two thousand dollars of Canada Council grant funds had been set aside by the League for B.C. reading tours in the spring of 1974, which Pat and Arlene began to co-organize. Because of her contacts in the government, Lowther, on her own initiative, proposed to seek additional travel funds from the provincial minister of education 'so the whole $2000 can go to poets.' She did a quick cut, glue, and copy job with recycled stationery for her government application.'(ALWAYS) mention the Canada Council Grant,' Arlene advised.[26] In return for Lowther's efforts, which proved successful, the Lamperts soon proposed to organize an Ontario reading tour for her in the fall. Her first stop would be in Toronto. 'We'll use this as a starting point,' Arlene wrote, 'and build your tour around it.'[27]

Elated, Lowther purchased her new briefcase and a few new blouses that summer, and began to plan for her trip. She would be gone for eleven whole days, from October 3rd to the 13th. This was 'much longer than any previous trip,' Roy noted, adding stiffly: 'I was agreeing to look after the children' (RLJ, 1:50). The venue for her first Toronto reading was willing to pay Lowther's air fare in advance, but the financial logistics of the trip were complicated by the fact that she was also planning on heading from there to the League's next congress in Fredericton, October 11–13. Stephen Scobie advised League members that they would be reimbursed for expenses, 'but only after the meeting': 'The procedure is that you all submit bills to me ... once you get home. I add it all up and write to C[anada] C[ouncil] for the money. They send it to me, and then I send it to you. By this time, it will probably be arriving as a Christmas present.' Obviously, for Lowther, among other cash-strapped poets, this would not do. 'Dear Stephen Scobie,' she immediately wrote: 'I am, as usual, one of those people who *needs* an advance for convention expenses.' 'Hate to be always the first in the bread line, but I really have no choice.'[28]

With her cash advances secured, and her newly minted author copy of *Milk Stone* arriving just in the nick of time, Lowther bought her plane tickets and prepared for departure. On the 3rd, Roy drove her as far as the nearest Airporter bus stop. According to him, 'as she got out of the car, she looked at the girls,' Christie and Beth, in the back seat, 'and said "I'm going to miss *you*"' (RLJ, 1:50; emphasis in the original). Greeted by the 'dear Lamperts' on the other end, Lowther kicked off her tour the next day, a Friday, at A Space, a small art gallery on St Nicholas Street, where her audience sat in a circle on the floor around her. She had the weekend to enjoy the big city before she flew to Lakehead University in Thunder Bay, where – with her sharp affinity for rock formations and stones – she caught her first glimpse of the Canadian Shield around the northern expanse of Lake Superior. By Tuesday, the 8th, she was back in Toronto for more readings, first at Ryerson Polytechnic, and then at a place called, intriguingly, 'The School for Experiential Education.' No records or sound recordings from these readings appear to have survived. But her first visit to Toronto apparently absorbed her. So much so that 'by mistake,' she packed the Lamperts' city street map home with her.[29]

There would be more readings in Fredericton, where Lowther landed on the 10th, never anticipating that she would leave as the League's newly nominated Chair. The conference was held on the hilltop campus of the University of New Brunswick, with its quaint brick colonial buildings, overlooking the Saint John River. Here, amid the brilliant foliage of a maritime autumn, Lowther reunited once again with her favourite gang: Dee, Joy, Seymour, bill, Elizabeth Brewster, Joe Rosenblatt, and, of course, native son Fred Cogswell, who gave a talk to the assembled delegates on 'The Nature and Function of Poetry.' McNamara was there too. According to one contemplative male attendee, the men generally behaved themselves over the weekend; it was the women who let loose during the 'F'town' gathering: 'I can't believe how many have left husbands and families and are going it alone. Something is afoot in the world.'[30] As for the business part of the meeting, it was run as well as any passel of poets might be expected to conduct business. The conference scribe described it as marked by 'a period of confusion ... in which all kinds of subjects were brought up and discussed, in defiance of the declared agenda. But what the hell.' Fred Cogswell and Robert Gibbs, the conference organizers, were the candidates originally proposed to take over from Barbour and Scobie as the new executive. This 'proved unworkable for geographic reasons,' however, 'and a new slate was prepared and endorsed ... by acclamation': Lowther as Chair, Fred Candelaria as vice-Chair, and Leona Gom as the newsletter editor – 'the West Coast Troika,' as Pat would come to refer to her trio, after their election.[31]

It was an astonishing culmination to her longest solo journey yet.

All told, she was gone less than two weeks, barely enough time for the two postcards she had sent (one each, to Christie and Beth) to make it home before she returned. She got back late on the 13th, indulging in the rare luxury of taking a taxi from the airport (only because it was an expense she could claim). Though exhausted, she evidently could not contain her excitement, giving Roy, he said, 'a long, interesting, detailed report of the events of the convention.' He was floored by the news that 'she had been elected Chairperson of the whole kit-and-caboodle.' She explained, he said, that her election was less a result of 'her own popularity' than it was a reflection of the League's 'desir[e] to have the chairmanship located on the West Coast in this new, two-year period.' She also told him, he said, that 'she gave the best reading of her life' in Fredericton, and that the trip as a whole had been 'a smash success.' In Roy's account of her homecoming, pride and awe struggle with the conscious rancour of his exclusion from her 'league,' an exclusion he mistakenly attributes solely to Pat's own personal volition. While Pat provided an 'enthusiastic account of some event' or 'exciting experience,' he complained, she 'never ... did ... reveal any concern ... related to her husband and fellow poet from which experiences she was expressly banning him.' In fact, of course, regardless of Pat's own definite inclinations to keep their literary spheres apart, Roy was just as 'expressly bann[ed]' from such 'experiences' by the formal mechanisms of the League itself, as a professional organization whose 'intellectualist' membership criteria he did not meet. But that, to Roy, would probably be splitting hairs. If not in dollars, he would see to it that his wife would pay for such selfish 'exciting experience.' She was a negligent mother, he determined, for not having called or made contact to check on him and the children during her absence (RLJ, 1:51). The house, as usual, was a mess. Yes, she was home again.

'Am writing this during a long bus trip, which will, I hope, explain the eccentric handwriting,' Lowther scribbled to Glenn Clever, in a letter thanking him for the advance copies of *Milk Stone* and the 'little cheque' that followed:

> I really do feel ashamed at the long delay in communication. My copies of *Milk Stone* arrived on the eve of my departure for Ontario, where I did a reading tour, and Fredericton, where I was elected chairman of the League of Canadian Poets – an unforeseen development which has kept me unbelievably busy ever since.[32]

She wasn't kidding. Within a few days of her return from Fredericton, she received one of her first new business letters from Arlene, who took the time to say, 'it's great that you're the new Chairman of the League,' before launching into a detailed itemization of enclosures to be scrutinized, accounts to be opened, records to be kept, invoices to be expected, and information to be obtained from the out-going executive. Within a few days of that missive, Lowther began petitioning Barbour and Scobie about matters 'we really should get at quickly' – and confessing by return mail to Arlene that she seemed to have lost or misplaced a cheque she was supposed to have. 'Isn't that a scary thing to find out about our new chairman?' she joked. Sort of. But, she concluded, 'we'll start muddling through as soon as Edmonton gets off the dime.'[33]

But 'Edmonton,' it seems, was not that fast getting 'off the dime.' In mid-November, Fred Candelaria informed the Lamperts that he and Lowther were still awaiting 'information on the procedure for applying to the Canada Council' for the League's next round of grants: '... it's a bit of a chore getting things moved from Edmonton to Vancouver.' Like Barbour and Scobie, Candelaria also led a busy life as an English professor – in his case, at Simon Fraser University. As he explained to the Lamperts, therefore, what with 'keeping several other balls up in the air like full-time teaching, editing the *West Coast Review,* writing, composing, getting out two books, university committees,' and so forth, he was quite stretched for time. Most of the work related to the League's grant applications, he added, 'as we've divided our work, will fall to Pat.' Though frequently referred to as Lowther's 'co-Chair,' Candelaria was clear from the start that he could not afford to accept the League's principal role. 'Pat,' as he wrote, shortly after the 1974 conference, 'deserves whatever honor attaches to the position': 'I'll work as well as I can to help her.'[34]

With Candelaria eventually taking on the task of treasurer, Lowther assumed the bulk of responsibilities that came along with 'whatever honor' attended her new position. She immediately set about trying to prepare the League's next Canada Council application and to establish a budget for the forthcoming year. 'How do you like our new letter-head?' she asked the Lamperts in November. 'Fred had it done.' She had some compunction about the imposing title of 'Executive Commit-tee' on the stationery stamp, but she clearly liked it, because she stamped away with it faithfully from then on. More typically, though, she peppered the Lamperts with continual questions, bringing herself up to speed on the endless intricacies connected to the administration of aes-thetics. 'Who would be a bureaucrat?' she sighed to Arlene.[35] In one of her first 'progress reports' to members, she compared 'getting broken in to all this' to 'learning to ski while playing the tuba.'[36] By December, she was, as she phrased it, 'up to my eyebrows in correspondence,' and more than a little concerned about the workload she'd only just taken on. 'Sorry,' she wrote to Arlene over the holidays, 'I just had to knock off for a while over Christmas or my family wouldn't have had one.' 'This job wouldn't be so bad if I could keep my anxieties under con-trol.'[37]

Given her habitual disorganization and absent-mindedness about her own work, Lowther's 'anxieties' about her new role might seem well founded. But despite the one missing cheque and the disarray of the paperwork piling up at home, she was, if anything, strikingly adept at 'learning to ski while playing the tuba,' addressing League business promptly, effectively, and imaginatively. Still awaiting financial state-ments from Edmonton to tell her 'how much it costs on an average to run this outfit,' she was frustrated by delays that were exacerbated by distance, intermittent postal disruptions, and others' tardiness. Care-fully, she kept track of how much she and Candelaria were spending per month, on supplies like stamps and phone calls. League matters begin to cross increasingly into her letters to McNamara, from whom she now sometimes solicited advice. The occasional migraine makes its appear-ance. 'Don't be anxious,' Arlene urged. 'You're doing an amazing job.'[38]

In an inaugural state-of-the-union address which she drafted, Lowther outlined some of the real bases of her 'anxieties' about the job. They were problems intrinsic to the position she now occupied, more so than to the occupant herself:

The LCP has, in the past few years, confined its activities mainly to organiz-ing poetry reading tours throughout Canada ... [However,] at the 1974 general meeting of the League, the incoming executive was directed

toward a considerable expansion of activities in terms of both more services toward members and more involvement in cultural events throughout
the country. Among these would be providing guidelines, and, when necessary, special assistance to poets in their negotiations with publishers, participation in local and international arts festivals, etc.

Two factors are making it difficult, if not impossible, for the League to
engage in new activities in more than a token way: 1. Time. The present
small executive, working necessarily on a part-time basis, tends to get hopelessly bogged down in administrative detail. 2. Funds: The League's grants
from the CC have been firmly tied to poetry reading tours. They have covered reading fees and travel fares for poets, but no allowance for administrative costs ... As things stand at the present, the League has no 'seed
money' to initiate new programs, nor do we have a travel fund to allow for
... meetings of regional reps.[39]

If Lowther's new job tapped into 'anxieties' she struggled to control,
perhaps it was in part because the 'two factors' that she identified as
working against the League's desired 'expansion' mirrored exactly the
largest stresses in her personal life. Time and money, the two things she
always worried about, she could now worry about even more.

But the problem was not just the serious gap she discovered between
the expanded mandate placed upon the 'the incoming executive,' on
the one hand, and the actual resources available to her and the
Lamperts, on the other. The League's 1974 call for 'a considerable
expansion of activities' is in itself significant for its historical coincidence
with the appointment of its first woman president – or 'Chair Creature,'
as she told Shirley Miller one League member chose to address her
(Miller 1975: 17).[40] As an untested feminine novelty, it is very likely that
Lowther felt all the more intensely the heightened expectations that now
confronted her as the new Chair. Suddenly, she would have to accom-
plish more while still 'working necessarily on a part-time basis.' Not only
should she continue to keep the League afloat with funds, help the
Lamperts organize national and regional reading tours, and pull
together the next (and, notably, first *annual*) meeting; but, henceforth,
it would also be desirable if she could somehow implement a wider –and
if need be, personalized – array of professional services, as well as more
'local and international' programs for League members. She was, after
all, 'just a housewife' in her life beyond the League. Perhaps she could,
and would, be able to do even more for the organization than the previous full-time professionals who held the executive?

Back on the bus, when she was writing her post-Fredericton letter to
Glenn Clever, Lowther mentioned a few bookstores that might, she
thought, take orders for *Milk Stone*. A few weeks later, after she'd
'knocked off' for her brief respite over the Christmas holidays, she
wrote to her publisher again. 'Where in Vancouver is *Milk Stone* available?' she wanted to know. It wasn't at Duthie's, 'which is *the* main book
store here,' and she knew for a fact that people had been looking for
copies over Christmas. What about reviews – had Glenn seen any yet?
'I'm trying to promote myself some work,' she explained, '(paid work,
that is) and every little blurb helps.' 'Maybe it's the damp climate,'
Clever responded, but 'Vancouver book stores' seemed 'singularly
insensitive' to offerings by local writers: '... we have canvassed them all
by mail and by a personal sales representative, with no avail.' 'On the
other hand,' he continued, 'sales in the more enlightened areas of Canada prosper, so all is not lost.' And he expected the reviews to appear in
due course.[41] Which they did.

Though she once again needed some 'paid work' herself, one of
Lowther's earliest initiatives as League Chair was in fact to 'promote'
exactly that, *not* for herself, but for Arlene Lampert. Given the hours
Arlene steadily volunteered, Lowther felt strongly that Arlene should
receive an official position and title as the League's executive secretary.
Accordingly, the Canada Council application Pat prepared and submitted in the spring of 1975 included a request for 'a full-time paid secretarial position,' which would help relieve the League's officers from 'day
to day administrative duties.' Between the Canada Council and the
Ontario Arts Council, the League did manage to secure a small salary
for Arlene. Moreover, together with the Lamperts, Lowther now set
about energetically ferreting out other potential sources of funding.
She investigated the possibility of accepting donations from private
foundations. That got her 'depressed,' because she quickly discovered
how 'horribly complicated' it would be from the standpoint of Canadian taxation laws. But, of course, by spring of 1975 there was also her
new 'in' with the B.C. Arts Board to consider. That position, as Arlene
mused, 'sounds like a great way to get our foot in the door. If anyone
can do it, you can.' By the way, she suggested casually, in another one of
her letters to Pat, 'when you apply to the B.C. Arts Board, see if they'll
throw in an extra $500, at least, for yourself as co-ordinator.'[42]

There is no evidence to indicate that Lowther actually pursued this
tempting tidbit of advice. But it must have come as an interesting
thought. In tandem with the consultant's honorarium she began to

receive from the B.C. Arts Board in summer of 1975, and her successful efforts in winning some remuneration for Arlene, the possibility of cobbling together a livelihood through administrative work, or through a combination of administration and teaching, was likely beginning to take hold in Lowther's mind, if it hadn't already. At the very least, Arlene's suggestion would have reinforced Lowther's sense of potential 'openings' and 'alternatives that,' as she'd written to Livesay, 'if they don't exist at the moment, are developing.' If she could perform capably in the positions she was now assuming, who knows what new doors might open down the line – doors that she might get her own 'foot' into?

In the meantime, she redoubled her focus, meeting regularly with her 'West Coast Troika' at Leona Gom's apartment; sending out 'omnibus' letters to her regional representatives in the name of efficiency; smoothing ruffled feathers and placating egos with aplomb, when necessary. She confessed to Arlene at one point that she had 'trouble delegating responsibility, not because people aren't willing [to cooperate],' but 'just because I'm the only one with all the separate bits of information that have to be brought together.' Nevertheless, she also spent a good deal of time simply pleading with various people for the 'separate bits of information' that she needed to do the job, in the first place. Four months after her election, for instance, despite repeated requests to assorted members, she had still not managed to obtain a copy of the League's constitution, the document spelling out the rules and procedures of its governance. Exasperated, she tried one last source: 'If you have a copy to spare, *please* send us one. This is ridiculous!'[43]

Along with preparing the budget and grant application for 1975 reading tours, however, the single biggest task facing Lowther was organizing the League's next meeting. As part of the League's proposed 'considerable expansion of ... activities,' this newly annualized event would need extra funding – to the tune of some $16,000. Though it wasn't going to happen until the fall – a year from the time of her Ontario tour and the 'F'town' gathering – the planning for it had to begin almost immediately since applications for conference funds were due, along with those for operating grants, in March. The total request Lowther submitted to the Canada Council that spring was in excess of $30,000. Meanwhile, according to neighbour Shirley Miller, 'the Hydro Co.' swung by the Lowther house 'threatening cut off of service for a bill of something like $30' (1975: 18). Moreover, the Council deadline approached just as sporadic postal strikes that month rendered the mails a painfully 'slow peristalsis': in the end, Fred Candelaria hand delivered the League's application while he was on a trip to Ottawa.[44]

By soon settling on the landmark Empress Hotel in Victoria as a proposed venue, Lowther hoped to strike 'a compromise between the Big City and rustic bliss.' But the elegant ambience of the Empress wasn't going to come cheap. With the conference, Lowther's usual refrain to the Lamperts – *money is a real worry* – found a whole new impetus. 'Keeping fingers, eyes, legs, etc. crossed re our various and sundry grant applications. If Canada Council doesn't come through with the [funds for the] general meeting, we'll really suffer a set back.'[45] Indeed, the League's critical dependency on the lifeline of the Canada Council was an issue of increasing concern. Relations between the two organizations had become somewhat strained over the Council's decision, in 1974, to stop funding joint reading tours of the sort from which Lowther, and other lesser known poets, had benefited in the recent past. It was a decision that League members had protested with a vociferous letter-writing campaign, but to no avail. The question of the League's relationship to the Canada Council, which had already arisen at Fredericton, was important enough that Lowther and Candelaria decided to allocate a block of time at the 1975 meeting to address it specifically. Lowther also made sure to invite Council officials to attend the Victoria meeting and participate in the panel discussion. Privately, though, she fretted to Fred Cogswell about keeping certain members 'from roasting the Council representative alive.'[46]

It wasn't just relations with the Council that were prickly, either. League members had recently felt slighted at having been overlooked by a publishers' congress at which the Writers' Union of Canada had been duly represented. League members, Arlene notified Pat, wished her to redress this wrong with 'a strong letter': 'They'd like you to word it something to the effect that we're a bonafide organization of some of the top Canadian poets – in operation for so many years, etc., and we'd like to be informed and consulted, like The Writers' Union, whenever decisions are being made that directly affect Canadian writers.'[47] At the time, the 'Poets' league' was characterized by the press as a 'parallel' 'sister-group' to the Writers' Union, but when Lowther took over the Chair, the League was already finding itself struggling increasingly against cultural perceptions of the genre – and its practitioners – as 'esoteric' and, therefore, probably dispensable. Vis à vis its more conglomerate literary counterpart, the Writers' Union, the League was thus beginning to feel, not entirely without cause, less an equal sibling than a little sister. As she strategized publicity for the 1975 meeting, then, Lowther was careful to differentiate the issues highlighted in the League's press releases from those currently emanating from the Writers' Union. Using the topic of 'Canlit in schools' as a leader, she pointed out to the Lamperts, 'could look as though we're just tagging along after the WU, especially as that may be how it in fact turns out.'[48] Liaison work with the Writers' Union also got pencilled into the October meeting agenda.

Partially because the League was competing for public visibility and recognition with other professional arts groups like the Writers' Union, the Lamperts wanted to ensure a 'big promotional campaign' in advance of the Victoria conference: a nationwide blitz of press releases targeting newspapers, magazines, TV and radio stations, as well as 'key reviewers and critics' (including *Saturday Night*'s Robert Fulford). The idea was 'to get as much publicity mileage as we can.'[49] As part of this campaign, Lowther soon enough found herself, as chief spokesperson for the League, doing a few media interviews, during which she called attention to the issues facing her group. In June, she went on record with the arts newspaper *Performance* by criticizing the Canada Council's 'system of grant allocation' as 'quite unrealistic.' Not only were senior-level awards too few and far between, but she was sharp about the lack of any intermediate category for grants. 'The junior arts bursary will keep one person at or near the poverty line,' she is quoted as saying: 'For a person with dependants, it is totally unrealistic ... There needs to be an intermediate category, but the main problem is that the government is not committed to really support the arts.' 'Poetry has a place in so many areas today,' she argued, leading her interviewer to report that 'the league is sorely aware of the lack of promotion given to Canadian Literature, and poetry in particular.'[50]

Between promoting the League, attending to the endless details of conference organization, and assuming her Arts Board work, Lowther still managed to promote her own career too, resubmitting her *Stone Diary* manuscript around this time and taking another cross-country reading jaunt and business trip in July. She even squeezed in a brief holiday in the Gulf Islands. When she returned by mid-August, though, she reported to Arlene: 'I came home to eight inches of stacked mail, three days of Arts Board meetings, etc. And start officially at UBC tomorrow. (Small scream).' Now 'time is closing in,' Arlene admitted, and the pressure was on. The 'disaster warning' of another looming postal strike came just as Lowther was trying to finalize the Victoria agenda and get a sense of how many delegates were confirmed. 'In fact,' she quickly informed her regional representatives, 'we've got a very tightly squeezed agenda with a large blank space at the end for unfinished business.' Then she signed off, 'yours in haste.'[51]

Though she hoped, optimistically, that the 'large blank space at the end' of the agenda would allow the meeting space 'to set its own priorities,' the 'unfinished business' she anticipated was more likely related to one of the spontaneous debates that had derailed the business agenda in Fredericton, and gone unresolved in the interim. This was not the essential matter of the League's dependency on the Canada Council, nor its uneasy kinship with the Writers' Union. It was, however, an 'unfinished' argument interwoven with those pressing issues.

By the time Lowther was planning the Victoria meeting, the League had grown in size to approximately 160 members. Though by any measure still a highly select community of writers, rumblings over the fundamental nature of the League's constituency and its standards for membership eligibility began to emerge almost immediately with the rapid changes that took place after the departure of Souster's original executive, around the time that Lowther had first joined. The concern, in some quarters, was basically that expansion was coming at the cost of artistic integrity, and was sooner or later bound to undermine the influence of the League as 'a bonafide organization of some of the top Canadian poets' – to reprise Arlene's phrase to Pat. The 'impulses informally expressed' at the initial 'founding of the League of Canadian Poets' had, after all, specifically exhorted 'there be strictness in the selection of members,' and had envisioned the group as an 'authoritative body of poets ... to safeguard the welfare of the art and its practitioners': 'The prestige of this body must command official reference in the matter of national awards, juries, anthologies, and the like.'[52] By 1970 an amendment to Article 4 of the Constitution added the rider that, while the League was, in principle, open to nominations of 'all practicing and published poets in Canada,' '[m]embership in the LCP implies a serious commitment to the art of poetry ... and constitutes a recognition of achievement in the pursuit of [the] craft.'[53] Intended as a general directive for League members proposing new candidates, this caveat obviously allowed for a wide margin of interpretation and disagreement, a margin that only widened as the League's membership lists lengthened.

To address the problem, some members began to call for an overhaul of the League's organizational structure, advocating the replacement of a one-size-fits-all membership with graduated tiers of membership, each with corresponding levels of fees, rights, and privileges. One such proposal envisioned a complicated pyramid scheme, whereby members at each of three levels would vote on an annual basis to promote a select few from their own tier up to the next rung. At the very apex of this architecture was 'The Great Poets' Council' – lifetime appointees with full membership privileges. 'This three level structure,' the proposal reasoned, 'would have the advantage of including all Canadian poets in the basic organization, yet it would award privilege and power to those members who most deserve it, in the estimation of the whole community.'[54]

In early September, at another one of her publicity junkets, Lowther gave the local press a rundown of the forthcoming conference agenda. While she made it clear that the poets were meeting to discuss a range of problems, including copyright protection and distribution, she also singled out the issue of membership, which, she explained, had come to a head in Fredericton. 'There has been an enormous debate on whether we should be a kind of union of all poets or a select body of writers with a strong professional clout,' she is quoted as saying in the *Vancouver Sun*. The article points out that 'since members questioned criteria for membership at the last meeting,' the League had temporarily suspended the adjudication and acceptance of 'any new applicants.' Lowther did not attempt to disguise her frustration over this impasse:

> 'We have to think not only of the quality of the person's work, but also of the energy the poet is willing to put into the League's activities,' Lowther said. 'We have about 25 very qualified and valuable people waiting for this matter to be cleared up. But until the problem goes before the general membership, no new members can be accepted.'[55]

Her own position was pretty clear: as she stated to her friend Shirley Miller, it was 'that the League might become more of a union in the future.'

Pretty clear, but not easy or simple for that reason. Of all the things that drove Lowther 'hairy' about her League job, the contested issue of membership qualification was easily the most fraught. She confessed as much to Eugene McNamara barely two months after she began her tenure as Chair, when she wrote to him asking for advice about the delicate matter of 'setting up the League membership committee' for 1975: there had already been 'a long delay' in striking this committee because, as she observed, 'it does seem to be an emotional issue.'[56] In many ways, this 'emotional issue' recapitulated the tensions and contradictions she grappled with while drafting her 'Notes Toward a Socialist Cultural Policy for B.C.' during the summer of 1975. In this case, her democratic inclinations put her at odds with those who wished the League to become a more 'select body of writers,' and who wished more finely to articulate the hierarchies of 'privilege and power' within it. She told Arlene that she was deeply disconcerted by what she saw as the 'extremely elitist position' taken by some members, including one or two poised to sit on the new membership committee, which was all set to review fresh nominees, once the temporary embargo on admissions was lifted. 'I'm really worried about this committee,' she confided, 'but I don't know what the hell I can do at this distance.'[57]

On the other hand, as the League's Chair, she could appreciate, probably more than anyone, the importance of cultivating an 'authoritative body of poets' with a 'strong professional clout,' if for no other reason than that it was necessary to the organization's financial survival. Federal government agencies like the Canada Council wouldn't continue to fund anything else, as the case with the Canadian Authors Association illustrated. At any rate, her 'Socialist Cultural Policy' paper also eventually compelled Lowther to recognize that her own inclusiveness had definite functional limits, too. Hers was a vision of socialist democracy ultimately anchored upon the categorical integrity and coherence of the idea of the 'professional' artist. The 'kind of union of all poets' that she had in mind for the League was still not really a 'union of *all* poets,' at least not 'amateur' poets like Roy and his Vancouver Writers' Guild.

But what, then, did it mean to argue that literary ability alone should not stand as the sole criterion for membership in a 'professional' artistic clan? That the League, in the interests of its own self-perpetuation, also needed to recognize the pragmatic value of 'the energy the poet is willing to put into the League's activities'? That a willingness to pitch in with the day-to-day housework counted, too? 'Someone,' as she once informed a startled journalist, 'has to do the job, just as somebody has to dispose of the garbage.'[58] In this sense, what exactly defined a 'serious commitment to poetry,' anyway? Who was more 'serious' about 'the craft' than he or she willing to do the janitorial work on behalf of the entire 'outfit'? Come to think of it, given that vanity presses – the detritus of sub-literary 'amateur' culture – did not exactly exist in airtight opposition to the 'literary' press publications of the 'serious' or 'arty' cognoscenti, just how persuasively did her own primary division between amateur and professional hold up?

And yet, all the same, it was not for nothing that she had long since tired of tinkling her teacup at the Vancouver Poetry Society and seeing her poems in its members-only magazine, *Full Tide*. Gary Geddes observed of Lowther around this time that 'she ... understands ... something of the politics of literature' (1975: 327). One such 'something' she had come to understand was that processes of literary recognition and judgment were always 'political' and thus problematic. But another 'something' she also understood (all too well) was that simply abandoning problematic things usually didn't solve problems either, so much as 'exchange' them for 'a more interesting set,' as she'd said at the outset of her second marriage. If she only pushed at them a bit, some of the key distinctions she wanted and needed to rely upon in the weeks ahead did not promise to prove especially reliable. The unsavory fact was that the terms of the League's argument over membership involved some seriously complicated claims, of which, as a socialist thinker, she was acutely aware. But this awareness coexisted with a countervailing conviction: her firm belief in the inherent legitimacy of working artists' efforts to organize in their own professional self-interests and collective well-being.

In any case, the more practical problem facing Lowther by the time she did her *Vancouver Sun* interview in early September 1975 was that she would soon need to broker some sort of an agreement on these divisive and troubling questions at Victoria. Whichever way it went, the 'enormous debate' about 'criteria for membership,' that 'emotional issue' brewing since Fredericton, boded a crucial test of her new leadership. To Fred Cogswell, she wrote apprehensively: 'I won't breathe easily until after October's over.'[59] Looking to find some traction for her position, she also conferred with others in advance of the conference. Unsurprisingly, one person she tapped for council was her mentor and fellow advocate of 'people's culture,' Livesay. Four years earlier, Livesay had declined the League's Chairship – perhaps, in part, to avoid the quandaries of conscience that Pat now faced. Now, writing from her new home in Winnipeg, Livesay advised the League Chair to tell 'all the young poets who are whining about high fees and lack of readings ... that "poetry must be served, not the poets" – in the first instance.' She then went on to address the membership question directly, energetically reaffirming Lowther's own democratic leanings:

We must bring good poetry to the people and good criticism to the poets! ... I think that any young starting poet who is willing to give time to [the] organization of the League should be given membership. Let us be a confraternity (God forgive me, not consorority!) And work for the common cause! ... Salud! Dee [60]

Lowther may never have received this letter, which was dated 18 September 1975. Within the space of the next week, Arlene Lampert would start phoning Vancouver, repeatedly.

❧

With a characteristic mixture of hyperbole and accuracy, the press coverage of the 1975 meeting of the League in Victoria mobilized the metaphor of war. It was Don McLellan, the same reporter who would later pen the parodic crime melodrama 'Verses and Verdicts,' who interviewed Lowther about the conference agenda for the *Vancouver Sun* in early September. The piece appeared under the heading 'Into the Trenches Go Canada's Poets.' The subtitle elaborated: 'They've clearly got battles ahead, these people who court the muse, if their meeting agenda gives any indication.' Covering the conference itself in the following month, the *Toronto Star* chose a similarly combative sub-heading of 'War Imminent' to report on the League's issues with the Writers' Union of Canada: 'Literary civil war is imminent, but the League of Poets representatives hope to avoid it by negotiating a truce and a compromise peace with the Union.' 'Victoria poet' Pat Lowther, 'in her early 30s,' this article also reported, had not been heard from in weeks.[61]

Somewhere within the mock-heroic exaggeration of such returns on the Lamperts' earnestly planned publicity campaign is a disturbing element of truth. By the time she died, Lowther had received plenty of evidence of the genuinely aggressive animosity that the seemingly pacific 'craft' of poetry could provoke. In one of her newsletter reports as a new Chair, she had reproduced the partial text of a rambling, raving (possibly liquor-fuelled) letter addressed to her:

> To: Pat Lowther, Chairperson
> League of Canadian Poets
> (Elite of Some Canadian Poets)

She was reprinting this communication for all League members to see, she wrote, because 'I believe the view expressed in the letter is equally as important as other issues we are considering.' Ever tactful, she reprinted it anonymously.

Dear Pat,

Bitter. Resentful. Frustrated. Mixed-up. What is my status as League member? Zero? ...

During three years as a very junior member of the League, ... [it] did nothing for me in practical terms ... You see, I could never (and still cannot) fill out those forms for poetry reading tours. SUCH FORMS ARE DISCRIMINATORY AGAINST UNSURE EGOES [sic] AND UNESTABLISHED POETS LIKE ME, who don't have recent legitimate books and reviews published, etc. EXCLUSION BEGINS WITH FORMS.

... I belong to [the League's] majority. The majority that does not make decisions, the majority that cannot afford to attend conferences in Fredericton and Vancouver [sic] where decisions are made for them by the minority. Dues were increased threefold. Do I now pay ... still more [for] practical nothing [sic] in return? ... Sense of rage. Who survives in literary circles in this nation? Who are the successes? Those who are allergic to forms (Canada Council grant forms, etc.) die off, slowly, like the dodoes that they are.[62]

This was probably one of the instances Lowther had written to Livesay about, prompting the latter's reply from Winnipeg about how to counter 'all the young poets who are whining about high fees and lack of readings.'

Except for the fact that it was written by a 'Bitter. Resentful. Frustrated. Mixed-up' member *within* the League, the raw 'sense of rage' and direly aggrieved tone expressed in this missive could be Roy Lowther's. The wounded cry of an 'unsure' ego's conviction of exclusion and discrimination; the biting hostility directed to the formal trappings of 'legitimate' literary officialdom; the desperate sense of competitive 'survival' and fear of impending extinction – these are all keynotes which recall only too vividly Roy's hatred of the 'hungry and vociferous professionals' of his wife's dominant 'minority' 'establishment' group, and his lament for the old 'bread-and-butter' rhymes and 'writers of a now despised generation.' From the alienated 'amateur' outsider, Roy, to the alienated, marginal League insider, these reactions only reflect extreme variants of the usually more restrained, but nevertheless palpable, sore points of rivalry and contestation within and among groups such as the League and the Writers' Union. Only Roy was driven to murder. And loss of sexual control over his wife was an obvious factor in that crime. But the other central obsessions that fed his sense of impotence – literary jealousy, envy of the 'privilege and power' of a

318 Ready to Learn Politics

dominant group, and cringing fear of irrelevance or mediocrity – these were very much symptoms endemic to the increasingly administered, competitive, professionalized, and striated literary culture that Pat found herself uneasily patrolling by 1975, a border guard on the front lines of a 'literary civil war' that had 'battles' brewing on multiple fronts.

'EXCLUSION BEGINS WITH FORMS,' as the anonymous League member shrieked, but then, of course, so does inclusion: most 'forms,' whether bureaucratic paper rituals, social hierarchies, literary class divisions, or conceptual categories, are – in and of themselves – equally capable of enabling as well as imposing, of enriching as well as restricting, of helping as well as hindering. For Lowther personally, such 'forms' were working to advantage. Despite all the zoning disputes and boundary migraines that her work with the League entailed, her 'executive' position with that body offered a tangible means of social, literary, and (possibly and indirectly) financial advancement – and therein, at least the possibility of a viable future escape from her marriage. And yet it was to a large extent the doubleness of Lowther's position in relation to who was inside and who was outside of the League formation she now monitored that made her tenure as its chief 'officer' – on watch 'to safeguard the welfare of the art and its practitioners,' as the League's founders had put it – such a difficult tour of duty.

Given her own route 'the hard way' up, through North Vancouver night courses that quaintly 'behooved' her to write properly, and through the 'ageing heart' of the Vancouver Poetry Society, Lowther could scarcely have avoided a sharp sense of inner conflict as she set about performing her new role as keeper of the League. When in 1961, a Vancouver Poetry Society member named Alice Fry first founded the splinter group Vancouver Writers' Guild, which Roy Lowther would later take over, it was called 'The Scribbler's Club.' Alice had been a friend once, when Pat was still thinking little further than having some fun by 'fiddling around with words.' And Pat hung onto the gift book – *The Selected Poems of Malcolm Lowry* – that Miss Fry had once inscribed to her and Roy. Now, Alice Fry, Roy, and their sort – the scribblers, the dilettantes, the 'great morass of Sunday poets' – were the people Pat was invested with 'safeguarding' her own new club from – for the League's good, and for her own good too. 'One did not think of Pat as being part of the poetry wars,' Patrick Lane says, thinking back to 'the kind of fervour that was going on' around the postmodernist experiments inspired by *Tish* during the sixties. Nevertheless, he muses later, slowly, 'I always believed that's why he killed her, that she was killed over poetry.'[63]

In Lowther's absence, the poets at the Empress Hotel in Victoria faced their agenda, the one with the 'large blank space at the end for unfinished business.' The membership eligibility debate that was supposed to fill that 'large blank space' was one that implicitly raised into question, among other things, the history of the missing Chair's own, apparently forestalled, induction to the League she had risen to lead, briefly, for a year. One more year down the line, Arlene Lampert wrote to Dorothy Livesay: 'You can't believe the trouble we've had trying to keep things together without Pat': 'To this day, I don't think [League] members realize how many things she was just at the point of initiating and how it all dissipated.' 'I still have a thick file of her concerned and intelligent letters.'[64]

PART IV

Philosophy's First Molecule

The plainness of first things
trees
gravel
rocks
naive root atom
of philosophy's first molecule
                    – *A Stone Diary*

Chapter 15

Infinite Mirror Trips

'Here, the road ends,' Lowther wrote of her first beginnings – the 'Watershed' years at the Lynn Creek intake station. 'The dog barks / my father goes out / "end of the road" ': 'between mountains the air / shakes like a bell / with echoes.'[1] While a pre-school Pat was busily enchanted by *The Wizard of Oz* books that her mother steadily supplied, the 'end of the road' that echoed with such resonance for the adult poet was not paved with yellow bricks but, rather, owed its existence to a pipeline, the conduit for a more liquid commodity. Lynn Valley Road, originally named, plainly, 'Pipeline Road,' cuts with ruler-straight precision up and away from the City of North Vancouver in a north-easterly direction. Eventually, the road intersects with Lynn Creek – an understated localism for what is more usually a thundering, white-water river. Fed by the meltwaters that trickle and run through innumerable gullies and gorges down the slopes of Lynn Peak, the 'creek' has carved a deep, spray-misted canyon to the bedrock. In the thirties, near this juncture where the road met the river, one arrived at the streetcar's terminal stop and, apparently, the last, lonely street lamp. Residents who lived beyond this outpost needed their own 'bug lights' – usually, candles in tin cans – after dark.

Although a vehicle bridge crossed the river canyon at this point, continuing east along a road that stopped at Rice Lake, the Tinmouths probably walked or drove the more direct route along the west side of the river from the streetcar stop to their home at the intake station further up Lynn Creek – at the absolute 'end of the road.' The first of two intakes along the creek – there was another, yet more remote station further up the mountain – Arthur's intake was designed as a back-up water supply system, and so was connected by pipelines running south-east from the creek intake about a kilometre to the Rice Lake 'emergency' reservoir. The caretaker's house, which still stands today, is a modest wood-frame semi-bungalow box, tucked neatly into a forest clearing.

In a photograph taken in the yard several months after Pat's birth, Arthur crouches in the grass behind his happy baby, looking tanned and toned in his undershirt. The family hound, Ricky, lounges languidly in the background. The picture was probably taken by Virginia, for whom, of course, the relative isolation at the 'end of the road' weighed more heavily. 'We were way out there, by ourselves out there,' she emphasized in retrospect.[2] With only Pat to occupy her for most of their six years at the intake, Virginia's loneliness 'out there' could only have been exacerbated by the fact that for every camera-worthy day of sunshine there were many more that were low-ceilinged, fog-enshrouded, and dripping wet, especially over the winters. For the sociable and adventurous Virginia, the house at the intake was a far cry from 'The Romance of the Roxy,' rain or sun. 'Bug lights' could not have held a candle to the bright lights of Broadway.

But the moody, shape-shifting features and brooding solitude of the Lynn Valley catchment region also drew artistic types specifically for these reasons. A year before the Tinmouths took up residence at the intake, Group of Seven painter F.H. Varley moved into a house in the vicinity to sketch and paint his impressions of the landscape. It was an area he had previously frequented as a hiker; hence, the Varley Trail, which today still bears his name. As variations of filtered light in the valley drew the studied attention of the painter in such works as *Lynn Peak and Cedar* (1934) and *Weather — Lynn Valley* (1935), so the little poet-in-progress, Patsy Lou, would also eventually come to take note how 'the sun opening the clouds ... change[s] everything,' 'chang[es] everything, as every word written onto paper changes everything.'[3] Like Varley, too, she would come to respond deeply to the austere beauty of a valley that, although protected as a watershed by the thirties, also bore the blackened scars of previous mining and logging operations – not to mention, of course, the construction of waterlines and weirs. As Maria Tippet observes, Lynn Valley was perhaps not 'the most picturesque' spot around the stunning Burrard Inlet, but artists like Frederick Varley liked 'the bare-bones landscape' of 'fire-blackened stumps and swamp-soaked trees around Rice Lake' (1998: 205). So, too, did Lowther, who decades later accurately recorded in 'Watershed' 'the dead spars ris[ing] / from a lace of green / second growth.' The result of fires in the area in 1910, 1921, and 1939, that 'green / second growth' infused the humid air with a heightened fragrance of coniferous rainforest and its fecund ground cover: western hemlock and red cedar, red huckle-berry, bunchberry, ferns and fireweed. In this often mist-enveloped world, sounds, too, took on an amplified life: the sounds of water, fun-nelled along at various velocities, or the sounds of birds, as with the echoing 'hammer tap' rings of the woodpeckers in 'Watershed.' It was like 'the whole world swelling out at you,' Lowther wrote elsewhere, in her notebooks: 'forcing itself in at your eyes and ears and nose.'[4]

Today, stray remnants of the old pipes leading from the Tinmouths' intake by the creek down to Rice Lake are still discernible among the bushes. So named for the wild rice that grew around its sedgy margins, that lake is, of course, the spot where a young Pat discovered the joy of 'walk[ing] on water' under her father's watchful eye (*MS*, 24). Photo-graphs from the late twenties reveal little obvious evidence of man-made tampering around the lake; even today, surrounded by a popular park-land, the spot looks incredibly peaceful and serene. An ancient glacial impression, the lake is a sheltered, clay-bottomed bowl, fed by surface rainwater. The stillness of its waters appears in sharp contrast to the foaming run-off at nearby Lynn Creek and its sister 'creek,' Seymour. Where it was not papered over with the leaves that her father collected and cleared from the intake grates, Rice Lake was, quite possibly, the most perfect mirror Patsy Lou first looked into.

Fantastic and sensual, the solitary setting at the end of the Lynn Valley Road proved a fertile foundation for a poet's reflective life, providing Lowther with the (super)naturalistic themes of even her earliest fairy poems and adolescent writings, such as 'Song of the Forestland' and 'Legend of the Hills.' But reflection, as she would reiterate over and over again in her mature work, was a gift that, like most, came at a cost. An early, 1966 appearance in 'Dear Dr. Cogswell's' *The Fiddlehead* maga-zine included a poem whose title, 'A Water Clock,' carries the imprint of her early life at the watershed, where Arthur 'worked with water' as a unit of measurement, 'adjusting flow and level' (*MS*, 24), much as the water-driven precursors to mechanical clocks also required. 'A Water Clock' rewrites the myth of origins offered in Genesis, superimposing the legend of Narcissus on the story of Adam and Eve. At the moment he first stoops, 'snuffling on the brink' of 'cool water, rank and sweet,' Adam becomes aware of Eve's presence, 'woman in her heat / across the wind.' Their encounter is imminent, though unrealized by the poem. Instead, the intriguing paradox Lowther develops is that the

326   Philosophy's First Molecule

moment which marks Adam's awareness of Eve is also the moment
which marks his own sense of self-division, as a now strangely separate
self is mirrored back to him in the water. 'The water that, ticking,
drip[s]' from Adam's cupped hands thus measures his fall into self-
consciousness, sex, time and death:

> Atom from atom.
> He who had been whole
> As an amoeba or an apple's perfect sphere,
> Began his first disintegration, bit
> Into the round, unbroken fruit of here
> And now, and tense
> Began, declensions, seconds, alternatives,
> Peeling away, endlessly, never stopping,
> Like the tick of water dropping
> From his fingers to the trodden-under slime.
> Man born of crossed purpose, Adam
> Broke his bond with all the rest that lives –
> That veined integrity, whole skin of innocence –
> And looked into the water, mirror, time. (*TC*, 196–7)

Kin to the mythical figure of Lowther's 'Penelopes,' and other poems
which reveal experience and self-knowledge as, usually, ambiguous and
difficult blessings, the initially oblivious Adam in 'A Water Clock' is
replaced in other poems by the unselfconscious child. 'Child, Child,'
published in the anthology *West Coast Seen* (1969), re-stages the process
of Adam's division, 'atom from atom,' through the eyes of an adult
observing a scene of classroom instruction – a math lesson about the
'multiplication of fractions.' But as the speaker conveys in a direct
address to the child, formal tuition is not equivalent to knowledge,
which is – as she 'knows' – already 'in you':

> Child   you are a molecule of light
> in a glittering dark ocean
> you are the giant atom
> that begins the universe
> you are swimmer and sea
> in an orchestrated flow
> and the key to its orchestration
> is in you. (Brown and Phillips 1969: 106–7)

In the 'orchestrated flow' of the preconscious world there is no separation between 'swimmer and sea,' creature and creation, self and other. The child, that weightless 'molecule of light,' is as 'the round, unbroken fruit' of a molecule that has not yet split, 'atom from atom,' or as a whole number that has not yet begun its 'first disintegration' in the fractious world of 'here / And now and tense.' For all that the adult speaker can claim to 'know' throughout the poem, it is precisely this world without gravity, without divisional boundaries of space and time, that she can no longer fully fathom, for as she concludes: 'I can't turn my eyes upon my eyes / and know' (Brown and Phillips 1969: 107). Like Adam, once inducted into the world of 'water, mirror, time,' the speaker's sense of self is fractured: her 'eyes' can 'know' the embryonic indivisibility of 'swimmer and sea' only as an imperfect memory, a nostalgic longing.

That there is no recapturing this oceanic Proteus, these nebulous origins of the universe, is also the lesson underscored in the brief lyric 'On Reading a Poem Written in Adolescence,' where adulthood is attained at the price of relinquishing a direct, organic connection to the natural world. As with swimmer and sea, so, then, with speaker and 'tree':

> Couldn't write then maybe
> but how I could love –
> When I said 'Tree'
> my skin grew rough as bark.
> I almost remember how all the leaves
> rushed shouting shimmering
> out of my veins.
>
> Even now
> I can almost remember
> how many hands I had
> hooked in the sky (*DF,* 12)

The poet's adolescent ability to experience herself *becoming* the thing she names indicates her affiliation to the prelapsarian Adam and the child of 'Child, Child.' Each, in turn, prefigures what Lowther would soon call, in 'Coast Range,' the 'naive root atom / of philosophy's first molecule': they are precursors to those apparently more insentient 'first things' – 'trees / gravel / rocks' – that some of her most powerful landscape and nature poems would bring to life within a few years (*SD*, 37).

Such specimens from the mid-sixties period of Lowther's difficult flowering are significant, in other words, for what they reveal of her transition away from fairly predictable romantic preoccupations with nature, innocence and experience, and self-alienation to a more contemporary and distinctive poetic idiom and vision. The pointed reliance on what is '*almost* remembered' about prior, pristine states of being signals the poet's own retrospective reconstructions as incomplete facsimiles of past truths, for one thing. But even more striking is Lowther's nascent turn, by this time, to the vocabulary and models of the physical sciences – the world of 'molecules,' 'atoms,' and 'amoebas' – to rework traditional *meta*physical problems of human dualism or lost unity and 'origins,' themes more usually filtered through the frameworks of existentialism, religion, or (especially in the sixties) psychoanalysis. However tentatively, the painful journey of the subject's formation and individuation is linked instead by such poems as 'A Water Clock' to processes of molecular biology and particle physics. An early instance of that peculiar blend of romantic materialism that emerges as a distinguishing feature of Lowther's poetics over the next decade, works like 'A Water Clock' begin to suggest the range of her subsequent engagements with science, and with scientific theories of time, energy, ecology, evolution, entropy, gravity, and space, in particular. It was a creatively sidelong engagement, of course – a 'bumsliding' encounter, as she might have called it, 'splat into' the incredible facts of an incredibly elemental, physical world ('Coast Range,' in *SD*, 35).

Seymour Mayne gestured toward this dimension of Lowther's poetic life and 'legacy' shortly after her death. 'Future generations,' he said, 'may pick her up because she had a great interest in science fiction, in genetic engineering, in scientific imagery, in trying to incorporate that kind of material into her poetry, and into the language of her poetry.'[5] Lowther's surviving notebooks and correspondence, especially from the early seventies on, reinforce this 'interest,' bearing out an eclectic scope of reading in fields that encompassed biology, geology, archaeology, palaeontology, theoretical physics, cosmology, and astronomy. Her sources included everything from lay publications such as *Scientific American* to classical modernist works by philosophers of science, such as Henri Bergson's *Creative Evolution* (1907). Working with such material, Lowther began to consolidate her focus on the physical cosmos in the *Infinite Mirror Trip*, a multimedia show she conceived and began producing after the appearance of *This Difficult Flowring*. Roughly contemporaneous with the years of her quest to get *Milk Stone* published, Lowther's work in the *Infinite Mirror Trip* embarked upon an exploration of galactic evolution that overlapped with similar concerns at the sublunary realm in *Milk Stone, A Stone Diary,* and beyond.

This intellectual life and the work it generated – 'a nice welding / of science and art,' to borrow a phrase of her own ('Magellan,' in *TC,* 224) – are the most under-recognized facets of Lowther's 'legacy' today. They are also her most timely contribution for readers of today, given the ascendancy of science and technology as virtually unquestionable benchmarks of 'progressive' economic stimulus and cultural enlightenment. Indeed, the question of *time* – or, more precisely, the energy of matter in relation to time – was central to her preoccupation across the whole range of scientific disciplines that caught her attention. In essence, science reformulated problems of matter in time that she – as *mater* – lived out in experience most days, while attempting to navigate the continual demands of her home and work lives. In this sense, the cornerstone of modern science, Einstein's famous '$\in = mc^2$' equation, rearticulated the concerns she had already explored through mythological archetypes like Penelope and Arachne – those 'spinning female things' of finite energy and duration. In spinning out such feminine archetypes, Lowther had also already begun to tap the etymological roots of a word that would now return to her during the seventies with a new scientific valence. 'Evolution,' from the Latin *evolvere:* 'to unfold, to roll out,' to change over time.

Lowther turned increasingly to the physical world and to the primordial 'atom' of the sciences at a time in her life when, with her second family, order and control were slipping away, incrementally, into the day-to-day chaos of hungry youngsters, rebellious teens, unpaid bills, an unkempt house, and – worst of all – the unnameable 'it' of 'nasty surprises always lying in wait.' Perhaps the 'hard' sciences, with their neat taxonomies and tables, their insistence on stable laws, logical causality, and predictable outcomes, held a particular appeal to her for this reason. At the same time, however, her forays into the realms of science also unmistakably led her to the very limits of the observationally verifiable world: to subatomic and pre-biotic worlds where – stubborn exceptions like Albert Einstein aside – the scientists themselves were often the first to confess that physical theory broke down and shaded off into distinctly other forms of reality. To her delight, Lowther discovered zones of science governed by bizarre time warps and four-dimensional 'space-time' force fields, by uncertainty principles and random probabilities, by astonishing questions about the limits of logic and human knowledge itself. For the poet, the possibilities and postulates of *theoretical* science, in particular, were literally limitless – an *Infinite Mirror Trip*.

Whether astrophysical or geophysical in nature, the universe that Lowther reinterpreted would be marked, above all, by the murky fact of temporal relativity. It would prove a world in which the glacial metamorphosis of matter in geologic time coexisted with the weird, sub-nuclear flux of quantum time: a world in which rocks eroded to smoothness over eons, while bees buzzed erratically as 'ions' ('Ion,' in *TC*, 194). Rocks, bees, buried cities, life forms past and present, great and small: in Lowther's cosmos, most matter could be reduced to charged particles, elemental energy forces persisting, transforming, and eventually disappearing over variable rates and scales of time. The enigma of time as a dimension of reality, and the trace of matter's energy through measures of time, emerge as a signature trope in her later poetry. Along the way, Lowther invented some of the half-lives of her own, best making.

Having inadvertently double-submitted 'A Water Clock' to both *Northwest Review* in Oregon and *The Fiddlehead* in New Brunswick, Lowther wrote Fred Cogswell a sheepish letter when she discovered that both had accepted the poem for publication. She hoped 'to have it in both magazines, if possible,' she wrote to Fred.[6] Yet though she thought well enough of her 'atom from atom' poem to wish its publication in two magazines, 'A Water Clock' was ultimately set aside with a bulk of work Lowther produced during the mid- to late sixties that did not find its way into *This Difficult Flowring*. Much of this work indicates how the preoccupations more clearly discernible in her later books – time, history, geology, ecology, science – were already germinating during her earlier 'domestic' phase during the sixties.[7] But as Gary Geddes would remind her, it was an 'age of *theme* or *subject* books,' and the appearance of 'flow' or thematic 'unity' mattered to publishers.[8] It certainly appears to be the case that in selecting work for *This Difficult Flowring*, Lowther was consciously attempting to reinforce her essentially domestic '*theme*' of 'space/time tamed' by the 'interlocking conventions' of social order (*DF*, 7, 27). Poems which she apparently deemed not to fit this '*theme*' so well – lovely lyrics such as 'Split Rock,' 'Rocks in Copper-Bearing Water,' and 'Creek Delta,' among them – were thus, like 'A Water Clock' itself, gradually edited out of preliminary 'table of contents' lists for the manuscript.

Of the poems that did appear in *This Difficult Flowring*, 'Leaning from

City Window' offers perhaps the strongest hint of the poet's desire to escape the straitjacket of her domestic '*theme*' and take those laws of 'space/time tamed' for a playful 'carnival' 'ride':

> Leaning from city window
> absorbing heavy October sunset, clouds apricot and wool,
> leaning far out to grasp traffic lights, cars and substantial people
> (a Diesel truck bruises my heart in passing)
> leaning far out, far out, til the wind is an arm at my back,
> is a paratrooper sergeant.   I'm out!
> See how the pavement receives me, shatters me,
> see all my life spread in glittering shards on the cool cement,
> glittering fragments of traffic lights, of sunset reflect.
> Now the girls from the factory grind me beneath their sharp heels.
> I am a sparkle of powdered glass on the sidewalk,
> a smear of frost.   Now a boy scuffs his toe and whirls me to air.
> I am frost crystals, separate and dazzling.
> I disseminate, claim all the city for my various estate.
> Bidding myself farewell, I ride a stenographer's eyelash,
> enter the open collar of a labourer's coat
> and nest in the warm mat of hair at the base of his throat
> and carousing above the street
> ride like a carnival the wild loops of light in a neon sign. (*DF,* 24)

There are echoes of Whitman here, but this 'dissemina[tion]' of self into 'separate and dazzling crystals' that 'ride' 'wild loops of light' already points the way to the particularized and energized forms of matter Lowther would before long 'claim' as a favoured poetic 'estate.'

In January of 1968, when she was still finalizing her *Difficult Flowring* for Very Stone, the unthinkable happened and it actually snowed in Vancouver. In her little black notebook, Lowther recorded this striking event in 'Snow Sky, Vancouver,' an unfinished sketch whose images, in part, anticipate 'Early Winters' of *A Stone Diary.* 'In a temperate city,' the 'snow itself' seemed to her 'bizarre as a Time machine': it transformed the landscape to remind her of 'vast' primeval 'ice forests.' 'The next step now / will be the first falling / out of the world.'[9] And the 'next step' in the little black notebook continued this 'falling / out of the world' with the draft of a poem called 'Riding Past.'

Here, the poet who earlier leaned from a city window to become 'wild loops of light in a neon sign' is replaced by a poet who steps out of an open front door to witness the 'wild loops' of the earth's rotation and orbit in the galaxy:

> Long streets of houses
> with lighted roofs
> black against
>
> winter sky blue as Venetian glass
> with Venus hanging
> like a small yellow moon
>
> In the houses people
> are cooking food and scolding children
> the ones home from work
>
> are hanging their coats up
> telephones are ringing
> behind the yellow windows
>
> Come, open the doors
> yellow rectangles and steam
> of meat and potatoes
>
> Stand on the front steps
> stare at the sky and wave
> Look, we're riding past Venus (*TC*, 220)

Though early North Vancouver friends like Lorraine Plowman had always suspected Pat of having a head that was 'somewhere up in the clouds,' in the late sixties, when Lowther drafted poems like 'Riding Past,' there were also compelling reasons to go outside, 'stare at the sky and wave.' The American and Soviet 'race into space' had entered its climactic years, and at the time, Lowther, like millions of other earthlings, was paying pretty well rapt attention. When the Russian cosmonaut Yuri Gagarin died at the age of thirty-four in 1968, she attempted to write about this event. Having made history as the first human to survive space travel in 1961, Gagarin had returned to earth only to be killed in a crash during a routine jet test flight. It is a fact to which Lowther's poem gently alludes as the speaker gazes up at the night sky: 'I stand and watch a chip of light / travel across my cloud-ringed night / straight past the random spill of stars, / straight as men's purposes are not ...'[10] 'In Memory of Gagarin' never made it past the initial draft stage. Lowther seemed to be having trouble integrating two different generic impulses, one eulogistic and one – well, one something else. The poem was about the cosmonaut's death in the present, but alternate stanzas kept reverting back in time to prehistoric, cave-dwelling 'beginnings,' and, in this case, the two time-lines never did come together effectively.

Along with history, she moved on. More precisely, it took her only ten days, after Neil Armstrong and Buzz Aldrin made their famous 'giant step for mankind,' to commemorate the moon landing with a poem, 'Moonwalk Summer.' The Apollo 11 landed on 20 July 1969. On July 30th, a day after her thirty-fourth birthday, she wrote to Livesay: 'I've already written my moon poem, which surprised me. That sort of made-to-occasion thing doesn't usually come so readily. But I was tremendously moved by the fact, weren't you?'[11]

Though she was 'moved' in the immediacy of the moment, the remarkable age of Apollo 11 was also the repugnant age of missile crises, chemical warfare, and atomic bomb tests, and the ideologically pitched significance of the American space mission was definitely not lost on the Little Mountain socialist. Despite its dreamy title, 'Moonwalk Summer' insists on celebrating the scientific milestone of Apollo only as the 'whole flower / of human working,' a fruition that draws as much as anything on the unsung labour of women, who 'are accustomed / to hold in our sleep / the whole curve, / birth,   silence,   again birth.' In staking that feminist claim in 'mankind's' giant step, the poem also identifies an element of 'phallic' fantasy in the Apollo enterprise, one that 'comforts the men' with a specious sense of fulfilment in a thing made after their own image (MS, 67).

And when Lowther was 'moved' to revisit the moon landing a few years later, in her 'Anniversary Letter to Pablo,' the tone also carried a distinctly critical edge where it came to the imperialist stakes implied by those 'indelible' American 'footprints':

> That first time
> on the moongravel
> they jumped like clumsy fawns.
> They were drunk in love
> with their own history;
> Satori flash lighted
> their indelible footprints.

'You own also the moon / now where they touched,' Lowther delicately, but firmly, reasserts at the end of this poem, addressing the departed communist, Neruda (*SD*, 52). No doubt, she would have maintained the same for the Russian cosmonaut, Yuri Gagarin.

* confic*

'As for the "starry idea," it's still only an idea,' she wrote, again to Livesay, this time in May 1972. '*Must* do something about it soon.' With *The Age of the Bird* now in the works, and *Milk Stone* in the hands of a pre-'splosh' Ingluvin, Lowther did 'do something' about her 'starry idea' soon. The concept was for an experimental multimedia show, and within a month after first mentioning the 'idea,' she wrote to Livesay again: 'Practically on the spur of the moment, I applied for a short-term CC grant to do my planetarium thing. I hope you won't feel I presumed too much – I used your name as one of the referees.'[12] It was this 'planetarium thing,' an innovative performance project – not *Milk Stone* or *A Stone Diary* – for which Lowther soon enough, then, received her second Canada Council award.

Livesay was not likely to object being listed as a referee without prior consultation; she had already expressed an interest in the one multimedia production her younger friend had only just recently staged. That first show, entitled 'Canadian Mosaic,' had come off sometime during the spring of 1972, at an unspecified 'local coffee house' – perhaps some incarnation of the Advance Mattress. Lowther's own references to the production in a couple of letters are the only tangible source of information that seem to exist. They offer a piecemeal glimpse at the 'mosaic,' which she described to Margaret Atwood as 'a multi-media Canadian poetry thing': 'among other things, we used (without permission, of course) excerpts from *The Journals of Susanna Moodie*. Read with slides alternating between forest scenes and engravings of pioneer times. We thought it was very effective. But too small an audience.'[13] In a more relaxed copyright era, 'Canadian Mosaic' seems to have been conceived as a sort of postmodern collage: in addition to the citation of Atwood's work, for instance, Lowther featured excerpts of works by Leonard Cohen, Tom Wayman, Milton Acorn, and Emily Carr, along with various visuals (including images of the Arctic). She also borrowed a recording of Livesay reading from 'Night and Day,' and later reported to Dee:

Thanks so much for the use of the tape. It arrived exactly at the right time, just when we were getting everything together. We used your readings from

'Night and Day,' together with a slide presentation, mostly cityscapes, a foundry, boxcars, crane, & etc.

I'll enclose a list of the material we used. The whole thing went off really well, but only about a dozen people showed up, despite good advertising. I guess it's just not possible to do something like this away from downtown.[14]

Staged for 'about a dozen' intrepid coffee-house souls, the 'Canadian Mosaic' show only whetted Lowther's appetite for working in performance-based, experimental art. And the 'planetarium thing' she now had in mind was altogether more ambitious. For this show, which she eventually titled *Infinite Mirror Trip: A Multi-Media Experience of the Universe*, she wanted the high-end technical effects that only an actual planetarium could afford. This show would be 'downtown'; it would be based on a script of her own creation; and, in addition to images and a light show, it would also feature music and song. Livesay had suggested radio adaptation as a possibility for 'Canadian Mosaic,' a work that Lowther felt was 'too strongly tied to visuals' for that medium. But she was also keeping that in mind this time around.[15]

A few references in letters, some notebook draft fragments, an audio tape of a partial rehearsal session, a home-made advertising flyer, and a brief newspaper review are all the records that remain of *Infinite Mirror Trip*, which took two years' work to see through, in the end. Apparently, the directors of Vancouver's H.R. MacMillan Planetarium had never before sanctioned the use of its technical resources in the service of contemporary art, and balked at Lowther's 'starry idea,' 'chang[ing] their minds off and on for a year.' It was not until the summer of 1973 that she managed to persuade David Rodgers, the planetarium director, to support her show and 'apply for a grant to produce' it. On 8 August 1973 she reported triumphantly to Fred Cogswell: 'I finally got a contract with the planetarium after more than a year of [their] vacillating. The show won't be produced until next spring, at the earliest, but at least I know it will happen sooner rather than later.'[16] Or, as it turned out, later rather than sooner: the performances didn't happen until August 1974, another full year from the time she wrote to Fred. In the meantime, of course, her 'short-term' Canada Council grant, which she officially held from August through November of 1972, had long since dried up.

But the project was also complicated because of the amount of collaboration it involved. She had 'completed' the 'written portion of the script' by the time she filed her final report to the Canada Council in the spring of 1973. But the script was only step one. Once she finally got the official go-ahead from the planetarium, she began to cast about for assistance with the 'music & visuals to be performed' along with her 'suite of poems.'[17] To this end, she approached her friend Hilda Thomas for help finding 'a girl (preferably soprano) who might be interested in doing a little work with me at some indefinite future date and no pay.' (No word on whether such a selfless soprano ever appeared on the horizon, but Lowther did have luck enlisting the skills of her musical sibling, John, as a vocalist and guitarist.)[18] Eventually, she also took the unusual step of involving Roy to write some music for the show. Whether she actually 'turned to' him to write the score of 'the melody for her finishing verse,' as Roy claims in his journal – or whether he offered, cajoled, or pleaded to do so – is another question (RLJ, 2:126).

Notwithstanding his signal failure as a teacher of music, 'Roy did have musical talent,' according to Allan Safarik. Safarik attended one of the *Infinite Mirror Trip* performances and remembers the 'little tune' that Roy wrote as a refrain for the show as being 'beautiful.'[19] Though for years now Lowther had maintained a principle of creative independence from her husband, this one time, for whatever reason, she ignored her own ground rule. But she must have thought well of that 'little tune' too, or she wouldn't have used it.

While she worked up the music that was to accompany her poetry, both spoken and sung, by various voices, her script was also, as she put it, 'out of my hands, and in the hands of technicians.' It wasn't until about six months prior to the show, right around the time that a lascivious Milton Acorn reappeared in her town, that she became 'actively involved' on the project's visuals too, with the planetarium's technical producer, Michael Koziniak.[20] Her notebook entries provide some insight to the sorts of visual effects she wanted, and the 'starry ideas' they were intended to reinforce:

Wiggles – stars with planetary systems
Link observatory film (speeded) of quasar 3C345
Being inside the exploded universe is perceptually like being underwater.
Crab nebula with IR and UV filters
Dwarf → neutron star → shrinks → red disc → black hole, bottomless pit.
May constitute mini-universe, may appear in another, different universe, may reappear anywhere/time in our universe. Quasars may be reappearances.
Thumbprint, pollen grain in daisy.[21]

'The resulting show' was later described by a reporter as 'very much a creative mix between the poet and Michael Koziniak, the special effects technician.' Appearing just below a scathing review of a concert by the American funk pop band *The Fifth Dimension*, the *Vancouver Sun*'s review of *Infinite Mirror Trip* virtually glowed by comparison. Praising 'the gentle hand of Vancouver poet, Pat Lowther' for 'the first use ... of the planetarium as a total art form,' the reviewer, Susan Mertens, described the performance as 'a seamless composite of star show, music, and Lowther's poetry':

> In a complexity of juxtaposition, the images – visual, imaginative, and auditory – explored the ageless mystery of the relationship between inner and outer space ...
>
> Running counter to the current concern with mysticism and the supernatural, [Lowther's] aim was to show the excitement and complexity of the natural world ...
>
> The correspondences between man and universe are sometimes whimsical, sometimes witty, sometimes mysterious. 'We are the universe made flesh,' we are told, as Da Vinci's conception of the universal man wheels side by side with a whorl of galactic dust.
>
> 'Elegant as a music box,' the universe with its 'jewelled precision of moons' is the macrocosm and man is the microcosm. Whatever moves this cosmos – 'law or love' – moves us too. (1974: 29)

There was only one problem, and it was fairly serious. The show 'bombed.'

The 'very good contract' Lowther told Eugene McNamara that she had secured for *Infinite Mirror Trip* turned out to be less than so. Vancouver's 'starry' science world, it seems, was unprepared to actually advertise the show it was hosting. Moreover, it scheduled *Infinite Mirror Trip* for a Monday-night slot – the slowest night of the week, when even the nearby museum was closed. Allan Safarik tallied up the damage for Patrick Lane:

> Her planetarium thing bombed. They forgot to advertise, and shifted her to Monday nights – of course that's the night the museum is closed so its [*sic*] not there as a crowd catcher. The planetarium thing she worked on for a year with a technition [*sic*] is drawing nobody. 12 people to the first show, 6 to the second. Of course, Pat had some screwy arrangement where she gets a percentage of the gate.[22]

With attendance levels that anaemic, and at one dollar per admission, Safarik was right; it didn't matter how generous 'a percentage of the gate' Lowther had negotiated. Any hopes she may have had to make a bit of extra coin from the show evaporated rapidly.

Safarik suggests in his letter that Lowther tried to salvage *Infinite Mirror Trip* once she realized that it had not been adequately publicized. She phoned him on the morning after the first performance, asking him 'to come over and pick up some brochures that she hand printed and [to go] run around nailing them up.' With a colourful turn of phrase, Safarik then expressed his strong disinclination to help out; he felt that Pat called him 'as usual only when she wants a favor.'[23] Of her own tendency to reach out impulsively when she was under stress, Lowther had once confided, only half-jokingly: 'My best friends hate me because I don't write letters except in times of crisis.'[24]

Not even the last-minute flyers rescued her show in the end, but the *Vancouver Sun*'s Susan Mertens put a more positive spin on the disappointing outcome of this 'experimental program': 'The planetarium could have a good thing going for it if, in future, it takes more care in publicizing such experimental programs. A statistical failure, the *Infinite Mirror Trip* was an artistic success, and set a precedent for further planetarium efforts' (1974: 29). But even this was perhaps small consolation to Lowther. She was, after all, especially interested in forging connections between the 'masses and mainstream' of 'people's culture' and a world of contemporary art often perceived as rarefied or 'esoteric.' Yet despite her novel attempts to integrate the 'high arts' of modern poetry and classical music with the newest bells and whistles of modern techno-culture, 'the people' were not coming. Apparently, they went to uninspired concerts by *The Fifth Dimension* instead.

The dismal audience turnout, worse even than for the more off-the-cuff, coffee-house 'Canadian Mosiac,' meant that the hugely unprofitable *Infinite Mirror Trip* did not even fulfil its modestly scheduled run. As Safarik noted, it had opened to its fullest house of a whole dozen on its inaugural Saturday night premier. Thereafter, it had been scheduled to run twice every Monday night, at eight and nine o'clock, for three consecutive weeks, during August 12–26. But Mertens's review, from Tuesday, August 27th, specifically emphasized that after only 'five shows with disappointing attendance, the *Infinite Mirror Trip* concluded' (1974: 29). At least twice over the course of that three-week run, then, the cast and crew of *Infinite Mirror Trip* got to go home early, because they themselves were the only human beings under the planetarium's dome of whorled galactic dust.

Though she listed it in subsequent contributor's notes for publications, Lowther never again mentioned her 'planetarium thing' in any of her subsequent surviving correspondence. Not even to her closest confidants. Not to Livesay, not to Gene McNamara, not to 'Dear Fred' at the helm of *The Fiddlehead*.

⟡

Only two years prior to the 'starry' inception of *Infinite Mirror Trip*, in 1970, the British physicist Roger Penrose and his student Stephen Hawking published an article contending that 'the universe must have had a beginning in time' – a 'big bang' theorem that aroused 'a lot of opposition' within the scientific community then. The term 'black hole' first entered the lexicon around this time too (Hawking 1998: 53, 83). According to Hawking, after the interregnum of the Second World War, 'the problem of gravitational collapse,' first taken up by physicists like Robert Oppenheimer during the thirties, 'was largely forgotten as most scientists became caught up in what happens on the scale of the atom and its nucleus. In the 1960s, however, interest in the large-scale problems of astronomy and cosmology was revived' (87). Disseminating this new ferment in the arcane world of physics and 'large-scale' astrophysics were not only Lowther's local press, but also periodical publications such as *Nature* and *Scientific American*, magazines geared toward wide audiences that included the curious, non-technical reader. During the early seventies, such magazines began running articles – by Penrose and Hawking, among others – on such topics as 'Black Holes,' 'The Evolution of Quasars,' 'Black Hole Explosions?' and 'The Origin of Galaxies.'[25]

In one of her notebooks, Lowther referred to an article she'd read in *Scientific American*, a piece on the neurological underpinnings of autism – reading related to an early draft of her poem 'The Electric Boy' (*MS*, 87).[26] It may well have been some such 'popular' science journal that was among the sources she consulted while making her notebook jottings on wiggles, quasars, and black holes for *Infinite Mirror Trip*. Years earlier, astrophysics had also been a field of particular interest for her old North Vancouver lover, the inventor Ward Carson. He may have initially introduced her to some scientific literature on astronomy and physics back in the fifties.[27]

Gauging from her notebook entries and the rehearsal session audio tape of the planetarium show, what is more generally certain is that it was evolutionary cosmology, the field 'revived' by contemporary science over the sixties, which provided the basic impetus for Lowther's 'starry idea.' In a way, *Infinite Mirror Trip* signalled her return to questions of origin and change posed by earlier works such as 'Child, Child' and 'A Water Clock.' Here she was again, back in a world that queried the fate of the first 'atom' and 'molecule of light.' Only this time, the nebulous origins she explored concentrated her attention literally on nebular matter, and on a 'cosmological hypothesis that the world began with the explosion of a primordial atom containing all the matter in the universe' (Rees and Silk 1977: 53). By turning to processes of cosmic formation, Lowther was now giving full rein to the fact that she found herself, as she told the *Vancouver Sun* reporter, '"very much moved by science, by the images of science"' (Mertens 1974: 29)

Though Susan Mertens aptly described it as a star show that plumbed 'the ageless mystery of the relationship between inner and outer space,' the records that exist suggest that Lowther's 'planetarium thing' was also quite precisely concerned to accentuate the age of the apparently 'ageless,' and the finitude of the seemingly 'infinite.' In contrast to her show's title, for instance, the text from her 'suite of poems' actually reinforced the space- and time-bound nature of a universe that only *appeared* virtually 'timeless' and 'infinite' by human measures. Drawing a correlation between the buoyancy of being in outer space and under water, she thus invited her audience to 'imagine' 'limits':

> Imagine yourself a deep sea fish
> a water-breather.
> At the limits of your sight
> light breaks on broken water.
> Those planes and breaking webs
> of light mark off a universe's end.[28]

Similarly, of the various 'correspondences' that the show charted between 'man and universe,' 'microcosm' and 'macrocosm' (Mertens 1974: 29), the subjection of each to finite natural life cycles figured prominently. As with the image of da Vinci's 'universal man,' Lowther's plans to include in her show images of a human 'thumbprint' or 'pollen grain in daisy' were intended as markers of the ephemeral lifespans on earth, imprints of matter and energy both replicated (or 'mirrored') *and* contradicted, on a much vaster spatio-temporal scale, by the image patterns of 'a whorl of galactic dust.'

That even the most spectacular brush of distant 'galactic dust' also presented a *memento mori* of inherently mortal 'dust' was an idea that Lowther's performance piece intended to reinforce with accelerated clips of 'observatory film (speeded)' and a pointed thematic focus on the evolution of stars, galaxies, and quasars. No doubt precisely because of the poetic appeal of stars as emblems of timeless transcendence *par excellence*, Lowther was intrigued by the science that was now busy calculating the actual lifespan of stars – including her beloved, but skin-wise troublesome sun – in measures of hundreds of millions or billions of years. As she 'speeded up' the visual images depicting this immensely long evolution, so, in the text of her poem suite, she also compressed the cosmic time frame by linking it metaphorically to the organic lifespan of ripening plants and trees: 'stars and the seed of stars' 'fall out / like petals shaken / or like fruit / in their generation.'

If stars and whole galaxies of them, too, were 'seeds' of finite energy, bound to burn up their nuclear fuel, expand, cool, contract, and die on some distant day, then even more fascinating was the overarching question being posed by physicists like Roger Penrose in 1972: 'What can be their ultimate fate?' (38). Penrose and his colleagues were in the midst of proving the inevitable expiration of stars into not one, but many, possible final stages, and Lowther's workbook reveals her interest in this rather remarkable fact. Some, as she duly noted, reddened and then shrank into different forms of so-called 'cold' stars that went by names like 'dwarf' and 'neutron.' Others, like the 'Crab Nebula' that she wanted to show through 'IR and UV filters,' exploded as supernovas, their un-ejected cores thereafter surrounded by luminous clouds. Yet other stars, those with great mass, could suffer the complicated 'catastrophic gravitational collapse' that went by the new nomenclature of the 'black hole': they imploded to an 'infinite' point of gravitational density and zero volume, creating in their wake a singular, funnel-like 'region of space-time' from which it was impossible for anything, including light, to escape (Hawking 1998: 87–8; Penrose 1972: 39). In Lowther's show, a segment of her poem, chanted on the rehearsal tape by multiple voices, seems to envision the process of a dying 'cinder star' forming a black hole: a singularity 'smaller than worlds / heavier than cluster / heavier / heavier / drawing in all your weight / to darkness / drawing space itself.'

For Lowther, who found herself contemplating 'bottomless pits' more and more frequently over the course of her second marriage, the intelligibility of cosmic black holes was likely intuitive and immediate. In attempting to explain the idea in non-mathematical language, scientists themselves often resorted to metaphors of prison and hell. 'Labor camps' was the grim synonym Russian physicists initially used for black holes, 'since nothing can come out of them' (Davies 1995: 119). As a precipice in space 'with a definite edge over which anything can fall and nothing can escape' (Thorne 1977: 63), one could say of the black hole's boundary 'what the poet Dante said of the entrance to Hell: "All hope abandon, ye who enter here"' (Hawking 1998: 92). As the physicists conscripted the language of poetry and metaphor as an aid to explication, so Lowther, in turn, focused her poetic sensibilities on their seemingly abstruse science, a strange astrophysical field which probably 'moved' her, in part, because its 'images' spoke so directly to her own darkest moments of despair.

Among other things, she would have commiserated with the scientists' greatest dilemma. It was one thing to make 'fantastic'-sounding black holes comprehensible to an incredulous public – most science writers at the time agreed that this was an issue. But black holes also presented one of those instances where theoretical science anticipated reality as a mathematical imperative before the existence of such things could actually be verified. To empirically detect a black hole, which was both light years away and, by definition, an energy vacuum that sucked back even light – this was the biggest problem of all. It was 'a bit like looking for a black cat in a coal cellar,' Stephen Hawking allows (1998: 96–7). Perhaps the creator of *Infinite Mirror Trip* found some comfort in the fact that even the best scientific minds on the planet could not easily locate the 'holes' that they knew would be 'catastrophic' if one were to fall into them. Or perhaps she was more struck by the fact that the existence of invisible black holes could best be 'deduced' from their gravitational 'influence' on a 'companion star' or stellar 'cluster' – by the fact that it was the behaviour of astral bodies nearest to the suspected void that might provide all the crucial clues (Thorne 1997: 67).

The new science of black holes reverberated with reminders of her own personal situation, but the subject also touched off other, more purely exciting frequencies for Lowther, as well. Since the funnels created by the implosion of huge stars enclosed vapour-locked voids inaccessible to any form of direct observation, what happened 'on the other side,' as it were, formed the finest point of conjecture for physicists studying the phenomenon. Their theory held that, as with the fate of the star which first made the 'hole,' altering the very structures of space and time in the process, any matter that fell into the 'hole' would inevitably be compacted out of existence – in a sense, crushed back into something like that 'primordial atom' of 'zero volume and infinite density' which once started the universe. So 'what we have is a model of the creation of the universe in reverse and on a much' smaller scale' (Penrose·1972: 42–3). According to such an 'idealized mathematical model,' the 'anti-world,' 'parallel' world, or 'other universe' beyond the black hole constituted 'a mirror image of our own, stretching away to infinity' in a 'time-reversed' way (Davies 1995: 224; Penrose1972: 43). The black hole scientists were, then, basically describing a kind of 'Infinite Mirror.' And Lowther's notebook entry to the effect that black holes '[m]ay constitute [a] mini-universe, may appear in another, different universe' also begins to make sense in this context.

Indeed, it is exactly where her notebook records start to sound as though she may have taken a little space 'trip' herself – perhaps nipped into the Curacao or home-made wine again – that astrophysics also got really interesting. As her show's 'juxtaposition' of microcosmic and macrocosmic realms suggests, Lowther was struck by the fact that the same science which took up the extraordinarily 'large-scale' problems of the physical universe often did so by attempting to trace cosmic matter and structure back down to the most extraordinarily minuscule realm – to the very sub-physical roots of matter known as quantum particles. In the early seventies, quantum cosmologists like Penrose and Hawking were taking the old idea of studying 'the universe in a grain of sand' (or daisy pollen) to incredible new subatomic levels involving the scrutiny of molecules, neutrons, protons, photons, electrons, and other super-tiny particles. Along with 'images' of quasars, galaxies, and black holes, it was to such molecular components that Lowther also began to turn, increasingly, by way of building up the 'elemental' poetic vocabularies of *Milk Stone, Infinite Mirror Trip,* and *A Stone Diary.*

As on the cosmic scale of black holes, most of the normal laws of science, of space, time, and causality, terminate at the quantum level: '... suddenly, all the rules of behavior with which we are familiar no longer hold' (Aczel 2002: x). The renowned physicist Werner Heisenberg invoked Aristotle's notion of *potentia* to explain this anomaly. It was because 'atoms or elementary particles are not as real' as 'things that are facts': '... they form a world of potentialities and possibilities rather than of things or facts' (quoted in Polkingthorne 2002: 85). Applying this basic principle of quantum 'logic' to the phenomenon of black holes, cosmologists could proceed to formulate a 'many worlds' hypothesis: '... at every act of measurement, physical reality divides into a multiplicity of separate universes ... Reality is a multiverse, rather than a simple universe' (Polkingthorne 2002: 52–3). Perhaps this, in essence, also best summed up Lowther's 'multi-media experience of the universe': a 'many worlds' 'experience' of multiple, coexisting realities and temporalities.

While she also experimented with the very big and the 'small small' in terms of the personae and voice projected in her poetry, Lowther was attracted to the physical study of these extremes because they represented for her, as she told Susan Mertens, the real 'excitement and complexity' of a '*natural* world' running '*counter to* current concerns with mysticism and the supernatural' (Mertens 1974: 29; emphasis added). Bracketing the outer limits of empirical science, the study of both cosmic and atomic phenomena marked the fascinating peripheries where science met epistemology – or, in her terms, 'philosophy' joined the 'molecule.' Both realms presented semi-detectable 'behaviour' that seemed to stretch the very concepts of 'science' and of 'reality.' Just as 'black holes' appeared 'much more at home in science fiction or in ancient myth' (Thorne 1977: 62), so the study of elemental substrata uncovered 'an experience as baffling and bizarre as Alice's adventures in Wonderland' (Azcel 2002: x).

Physicists describe the 'logic' of their quantum order as 'unreal,' 'random,' 'counterintuitive,' 'schizophrenic,' 'cloudy,' and 'fitful,' almost as though it presents a sort of subatomic unconscious. Enacting a world of 'potentialities' rather than of 'things or facts,' the behavior of atomic elements confounds such basic categorical distinctions as solid or fluid, 'here' and 'there,' or 'then' and 'now.' As in the non-sense of a dream, energy quanta like photons, tiny filaments of light, register in the spectroscopic world as fluid waves *and* discrete particles at one and the same time. They also seem to exist simultaneously here *and* there, then *and* now. The implication is 'a schizophrenic world in which both alternatives coexist in a sort of hybrid reality' (Davies 1995: 170).

As the famous 'uncertainty principle' named by Werner Heisenberg underscores, answers for the scientist who would make sense of this 'cloudy' elemental disorder are always elusive. In effect, Heisenberg's principle predicts that any attempt to actualize a quantum 'potentiality' in order to know it as a concrete 'thing or fact' in space *and* time will always result in only half an answer (*either* the location *or* the momentum of the particle measured). 'Observables,' as one physicist puts it, 'come in pairs that epistemologically exclude each other': 'in the quantum world,' 'half-truth' or 'half-knowledge is the best that we can manage' (Polkingthorne 2002: 33, 44). This quandary seems to represent 'a fundamental limitation on knowledge inherent in the laws of nature, not merely some sort of human failing' (Davies 1995: 167).

Lowther may or may not have come across Heisenberg's Uncertainty Principle over the course of her science reading. But she had read some Aristotle along with her Plato, and she certainly understood the intricacies of transmuting 'actualities' from 'potentialities.' Growing up as she did in the age of the atom (and the advent of the 'nuclear' family), she knew enough about the regime of the very tiny – or what she called 'the neat mechanics of molecules' (*TC*, 243) – to draw upon it as an image bank for what could seem stranger than reality, but was nevertheless firmly based in the material world. If not the means, she also understood the principal end of principles like Heisenberg's. It didn't require any technical grasp of physics to understand the frustration of arriving at conundrums of 'half-knowledge' and mutually exclusive answers – dilemmas very much like the one she described to Patrick Lane, in the spring of 1973, as resulting in 'the kind of situation psychologists devise to drive white rats crazy.' Perhaps, in part, because she too, like an atomic element, had come to inhabit a sort of 'fitful' 'hybrid reality,' a 'here *and* there' existence that she called a 'schizophrenic life,' Lowther was by the early seventies irresistibly drawn to the strange 'wave/particle duality' of the elemental realm. The 'cloudy' idea of *Milk Stone*, which she'd sent off to Ingluvin Press some months before embarking on her 'starry idea,' already suggested this much.

Incidentally, 'milk,' she had insisted to Eugene McNamara, was intended as a transitive 'verb' in that title (McNamara 1977: 23). Elsewhere, in her letters to Windsor, she amused herself wistfully with the potential possibilities of being 'here' and 'there' instantaneously: 'Will teleportation be developed in our time?'[29] Free radicals like 'ions' could 'buzz off' faster than one could say 'the bee has been / here' (*TC*, 194–5). Would that she could, too.

୬

Just where modern science tapered off into logical constraints of 'half-truth,' then, it also beckoned as an invitation to invention, 'sometimes whimsical, sometimes witty, sometimes mysterious' (Mertens 1974: 29). 'They have postulated microbes / building cities on a mucous membrane,' Lowther observed in 'The Origin of the Universe,' first published in 1971 as a short poem, but begun as part of a longer poem cycle in her notebooks. Unlike the microbiologists, though, Lowther preferred a few other theories: that the 'universe' began in the condensation of 'laughter / visible / as in absolute cold,' or alternatively, with a braggart boy's 'all-time champion / distance spit' (*MS*, 29). In a less flippant mood, about a year into her 'planetarium thing,' she wrote to Fred Cogswell on 3 May 1973 with an interesting announcement. She was 'researching Hatshepsut, first female Pharaoh of Egypt,' for a 'group of science fiction poems,' she said. In the same sentence, she also mentioned a debate she was organizing, on 'alternative futures between Old and New Left in my NDP constituency.'[30]

There seems to be no trace of this 'research' in Lowther's notebooks, and no surviving poems about Hatshepsut or ancient Egypt. But her interest in the 'first female pharaoh' in connection to a 'group of science fiction poems,' and political debates about 'alternative futures,' is nevertheless telling. Hatshepsut, who ascended to power after her father, Tuthmose I, ruled in the fifteenth century BC. A rare species of 'liberated' ancient womanhood, she was a cross-dressing queen, remembered for both her love of art and her political acumen (which included having herself represented as male in all statuary). So the material Lowther was thinking of using for her new poems not only pointedly encompassed art and politics as well as science, but also promised to feature the historical past as much as any possible future. While there is nothing new about time travel or politics as staples of modern science fiction, Lowther's interest in exploring the possibilities of 'science fiction' for *feminist poetry* signals an unusual aspiration for its time.

In one sense, the Egyptian queen Hatshepsut was none other than a grown-up version of that fearless warrior-heroine 'Sea Bird, the King's daughter and princess of the mer-people,' which a very young Pat, daughter of one Arthur Tinmouth II, had sketched out in big, loopy pencil scrawl decades earlier. But such plans for future work were also exactly consistent with the 'science fictions' of the 'planetarium' project Lowther was deeply into by 1973, as well as the 'core sequence' of *Milk Stone* – those poems that were still wending their long way into print while *Infinite Mirror Trip* was in process. As its title indicated, the long, three-part poem at the 'core' of *Milk Stone*, 'In the Continent behind My Eyes,' also explored reflections between 'inner and outer space.' In terms that clearly anticipate the concept of 'time reversed' travel central to both *Infinite Mirror Trip* and Lowther's plans for her Hatshepsut poems, this long poem was first summed up by Eugene McNamara as 'an interior cinemascope of the whole evolutionary process beginning with the present urban scene and spiraling back into prehistory':

[The poem] merges the archetypal and the personal in a blend of reality [and] hallucination ... which approximates the form of a speeded up film

... There is a constant process of interrelating the self living in a here and now with past selves ... so we are right back there at the moment of the evolutionary scale just after the death of the reptiles, and the cave bears whose claw marks on the walls may have taught our ancestors the rudiments of painting. (McNamara 1977: 23–4)

Fascinated by the optical illusion of how 'clocks in mirrors' seemed to 'tell time backwards,' Lowther was essentially mobilizing that illusion as a formal principle in her re-winding, or un-winding, of the history of natural evolution in this 'core sequence' of *Milk Stone*.[31] Between the performances of *Infinite Mirror Trip* in August 1974, then, and the first publication of 'In the Continent behind My Eyes' in November of that same year, Lowther offered not one but two 'models' of 'creation ... in reverse' (Penrose 1972: 42): mirror-reversals of the evolutionary process on both the cosmological and biological levels.

Though self-explanatory in relation to her unhappy marriage, this growing preoccupation with un-doing or reversing the trajectory of 'time's arrow' was also part of a more complex 'blend of reality [and] hallucination' in Lowther's newest work, as McNamara suggested. He was being precise when he characterized 'In the Continent behind My Eyes' as a poem '*spiraling* back into prehistory.' Like a milky galactic swirl or a 'thumbprint,' the movement implied is circuitous and recursive, rather than linear or unidirectional. The poem's composition and structure reinforce this 'spiral' relation between continuous time curves or loops of past and present. Lowther originally wrote her long poem around a few shorter poem drafts, which she eventually embedded as italicized segments of the final text. The original poems, 'Killing the Bear' and an 'Ice Age' cycle, were all concerned with those atavistic 'past selves' – or 'the primitive self within, dormant but alive' – that McNamara's essay specifically isolated and linked, with some due cause, to the example of James Dickey (24).[32]

But the text that Lowther scripted around these 'prehistorical' origins complicates the poem's temporal 'flow,' which does not devolve straightforwardly from present into past. The 'present' moment which lays out 'the city like an open brain' of 'lights' at the outset, for example, comes around again as the evolutionary 'present' (but personal *past*) in the speaker's account of her Rice Lake origins in the poem's third section (*MS*, 18, 24). Indeed, that speaker, a 'star-shaped I,' 'stumble[s] nauseated / through millennia,' both backwards and forwards in time (*MS*, 24, 26). Backwards, she witnesses the extinction of the dinosaurs –

'your world, old Rex' – as well as the stick-and-stone beginnings of art
that the cave dwellers learned from 'Greatbrother bear' (*MS*, 20, 21).
Forwards, on the other foot, she also 'stumbles' into the anticipation of
a possible future, a distinctly cybernetic 'world web in time' that will
have 'invited us out of our bodies':

> A petal's weight brought down
> your world, old Rex,
> and grew this furled and ruffled
> flower in my head
>
> A photon's weight
> a deflection of light
> across a jelly
> was it?   invited us
> out of our bodies
> to make a world web in time,
> to build on the rock Death (*MS*, 20)

Lowther could as readily envision the Darwinian fall of 'old Rex' as
she could intuit the rise of a new order, something born at the intersec-
tions of biology and technology, something akin to the virtual realities
of our present. Rather than heralding her power as part of a 'mystical
vanguard,' however, Lowther's intuitive grasp of this present resulted
from her firm belief that the 'business' of the poet was 'mainly to stay
alert.'[33] And where it came to the 'business' of contemporary science, as
elsewhere, she was pretty 'alert.' During the early- to mid-seventies, the
'world web in time' that would eventually become the Internet was
already evolving. Inaugural intimations of networked computers and a
new matrix for human-machine relations began to emerge from the
fields of bionics and computer science, fields widely popularized by
(among other things) mid-seventies 'sci-fi' television shows like *The Six
Million Dollar Man*. These cutting-edge technologies were also implicit in
the new 'media' that critics like Marshall McLuhan had started to sound
warnings about, as 'hypnotizing' mass audiences with fantasies of 'the
amputation and extension of [their] own being in a new technological
form' (1971: 144).

It is not surprising, then, that the 'continent' of *in*–sight 'behind'
Lowther's eyes absorbed immediately the first portents of a future that
had already begun to arrive. Nor is it especially peculiar that the vision-

ary materialist of *Milk Stone* should see that future coming at a cost – the 'weight' of one insubstantial 'photon,' enough, perhaps, to bring down our world, just as a fluttering 'petal' might have been what toppled big 'old Rex.' The post-human epoch in which experimental technology – like a laser beam's 'deflection of light' – might 'invite us out of our bodies' and possibly efface, or even replace, corporeal feeling, is precisely the refrain of *Milk Stone*'s withdrawn and rock-numb 'Electric Boy,' tethered to his plethora of imaginary electrical prostheses: 'This wire breathes me / This wire moves my heart'; 'This wire lets me see / and this connection / is my feeling' (*MS*, 87–8). It is also 'The Face' of the dehumanized present glimpsed in Lowther's experimental prose piece of that title, the final section of which imagines 'The Machinery' of a 'centrifuge' which 'holds us motionless': 'our muscles flatten, our veins and arteries spread out like maps.'[34]

Milk Stone's circuitous reach back into 'prehistory' thus spirals *from* a proto-future in which being human was itself being reconfigured as a matter of 'hardwired' brains and bodies, networked neural systems designed like so many electrical grids or 'circuit breakers.' Twigging, no doubt, to some version of the argument that emergent technologies affected 'human affairs' by introducing a 'change of scale or pace or pattern' in social relations (McLuhan, 1971: 141), Lowther constructed the long poem at the 'core' of *Milk Stone* as a 'funnel of twilight' 'forms' (*MS*, 19). The eye of this storm deliberately commingled 'hybrid realities' of the coming post-human with the distant prehistoric. When the open-brained 'city' of the present and future conditional is reinvoked again, at the end of the poem, it thus 'throw[s]' the 'voice' of both the primeval collective past and the recent personal past of Rice Lake, 'melting a mountain range / into a mirror' (*MS*, 28). In the very last stanza, the super evolved /devolved 'star-shaped I' traces the 'gouge' marks of 'Greatbrother bear' 'on the wall.' Then she concludes: 'I will take a sharp stick / and begin' (*MS*, 19, 28).

Lowther had presumably put the 'statistical failure' of *Infinite Mirror Trip* behind her by the time she packed up her new copies of *Milk Stone* and went touring Ontario in the fall of 1974. But the attraction to her 'starry idea' and the cosmos beyond persisted. Even as she was preparing her *Stone Diary* manuscript for re-submission by the spring of 1975, she was still writing poems that strained against gravity, just as she had earlier leaned out – leaned 'far out, far out' of city windows – looking for release

(*DF,* 24). Down at the 'intersection of Fraser & Marine,' by the Blue Boy Motor Hotel, the Gulf and Esso gas stations, and the Shop Easy, where she sometimes caught the bus, she also discovered that she could walk into a 'phone booth / and step out between the planets' (*SD,* 79). Even a windy, nondescript Vancouver intersection could prove the 'axis' of a special threshold, one that sent the thread of her 'thumb end' spiralling out, even further than Spiderman's, to galaxies still unfolding: 'the thumb end / where you press / and the whole universe twirls out / a long seamless skin / a rill of piano music' (*SD,* 76). 'Intersection' goes some way toward explaining why Lowther's daughter Beth can recall her mother one day lost in thought at a crosswalk, staring blankly until the 'walk' sign went *off,* and then almost stepping out into traffic. Either she had pressed out 'between the planets' again, or perhaps the automated signal prompting her to 'WALK' arrested her attention for another reason. It was such a simple instruction. And yet, in terms of the unfurling parallel universe of her marriage, that microcosm of 'lives / unwinding like a roll / of bloody bandage' (*TC,* 243) – one so very difficult to follow.

There is strong evidence for Lowther's abiding interest in cosmological matters right up to her last publications in small magazines. As a result of her visit to Thunder Bay, for instance, she contributed 'Planetarium Poems' to *A Lake Superior Journal* for the spring, 1975 issue. Not a part of her *Infinite Mirror Trip,* this sequence of three short 'planetarium' poems was, like the projected Hatshepsut work, 'science fiction' poetry. It may have been related to the file she eventually flagged as her 'Time Capsule' project, a file which no longer appears to exist. In part, the 'Planetarium Poems' provide a succinct summation of that 'planetarium thing' that hardly anyone turned out to see. *Here's the show you missed,* she seemed to say, *and we were waiting for you!*

> While we've been in this
> darkened theatre
> years have passed
>
> we have to play them back,
> spin the sun backward
> ...
> set the white and golden
> planets swooping
> retracing their courses

Look! Three planets
in opposition. when?
March of some future year?

Not satisfied with just 'rewind[ing] the cosmos' of her *Infinite Mirror Trip*, she replayed her concerns with terrestrial evolution on the 'continents,' too:

In an afternoon
we could unmake continents;
species could rise
people the earth and die

while we rewind the cosmos,
slower now, steady the
planets, station the sun
at *now. (TC,* 217)

As always, it was a matter of time. Time, '*now*' more than ever, the preoccupation of the overextended new 'chair creature' of Canadian poets. If she didn't find some time soon, when would she ever get back to Henri Bergson – 'matter / is what falls back / from the luminous high- / arching parabola / of energy'? That was a hasty 'paraphrase' (*SD*, 87). Wasn't it Bergson who took issue with mechanistic conceptions of time – talked instead about the reality of subjective, 'durational' time, 'this time which is the very fluidity of our internal life'? What was Roy bellowing about in the background *now*? What was it that she might have been thinking about time – as it related to film? Interesting how a film, played backwards, rewound, could seem to undo the in-built direction of time ... running motion backwards like that. But right *now,* she was on the red pleatherette, typing another letter, and probably smoking a cigarette. 'Dear Arlene': 'Racking my brains about replacements for our [19]75–76 [readers'] list.' Not much time for reading or watching films while she waded through 'very conscientious and rather depressing' correspondence from League members. Letters that occasionally reminded her, helpfully, to just 'stop worrying and write poetry.'[35]
    Whenever she got back to the second segment of her 'Planetarium Poems,' she was thinking about sleep. Or the *now* of attempting it, at least:

now I attempt sleep
my ceiling's grained with stars
windows let in light leaks
compulsively I arrange
spaces. Even with eyes
closed, my head's a dome
with projectors stuck
and will not dim out. (*TC*, 218)

Especially for the migraine sufferer, the 'dome' of the planetarium, with its special effects and dazzling light displays, captured something more than just a recurring metaphor. As the architecture for 'a total art form,' in Susan Mertens's phrase, it was fitting that Lowther gravitated to the playhouse of the planetarium, an amphitheatre uniquely capable of staging the illuminations of her own 'compulsive' hyper-consciousness, if not the auras of her blinding 'sick headaches,' as well. The domed planetarium externalized perfectly what her 'star-shaped I' also called 'this huge bowl my head,' filled with 'shavings of light' and 'sphere[s] of ringing sound' (*MS*, 25). Using the planetarium as both a physical and figurative extension of her head, Lowther discovered in it a space to reimagine her 'being in a new technological form' (McLuhan 1971: 144) – a prospect as tantalizing as it was also potentially terrifying.

Brilliantly, Lowther began the third and last section of her 'Planetarium Poems' in the 'assurance' of a lucid dream – the only rest attained, restlessly aware of itself as such: 'Sleeping at last / dreaming, moving in / the assurance of dream / I know that what we / order is reality' (*TC*, 218). Busy even asleep, anxiously ordering 'reality,' 'engaged in pattern recognition' and 'choice of data,' the self-conscious sleeper tries to end the poem. But it is exactly at its attempted closure that the poem also falters, dissipating, in the last stanza, into vague anticipations of 'wait[ing] for' 'some thing / some new order we could / never have imagined' (*TC*, 219). It was as though, all of a sudden, Lowther literally could not envision the sense of an end – neither for her poem, nor for 'compulsive' consciousness in general – and so simply admitted as much.

The under-finished conclusion of 'Planetarium Poems' signalled an element of haste that was also deliberately highlighted by the title of the companion poem which appeared in the same issue of *A Lake Superior Journal*. 'Losing My Head' reconfigures the 'huge bowl' of the 'head' as a 'sorcerer's globe,' a 'precious object' 'lost' as the speaker recounts her fall into 'the emptiness of [her] body.' But it is precisely to the 'empty'

space of the body's cavity that Lowther's cosmos relocates itself imagisti-
cally. 'Invited' *into* her body, the speaker is once again transported into
outer space:

> now there is no
> where dark where the light
> does not trouble
> the galaxies shine like whales
> the light moves
> in slow waves[36]

Once before, she had overseen the transformation of a 'now' into a
'no,' the wave of one small 'w' swimming away, like a detached particle
of light. But in its quest for a quiet place of rest, a place where 'the
light / does not trouble,' 'Losing My Head' also *finds* the satisfying conclusion that is missing at the end of the 'Planetarium Poems':

> does the light trouble?
> the galaxies swim away
> at the speed of light
> we can never know them

   Of course, by the time these poems appeared in the spring of 1975,
she was occasionally writing to Fred Cogswell twice a day, not remembering what she'd said from one letter to the next. 'Waiting for my trank to
work,' she explained.[37] Those were the very bad days, the days when she
may have thought back longingly to the tranquil mirror of Rice Lake.
Or, to a lake's mirror opposite: a dot of land, surrounded by sea. A quiet
little island, not too far away.

Chapter 16

The Land Is What's Left

Tucked between Galiano and Saturna Islands like a loose-fitting jigsaw puzzle piece, Mayne Island is one of the smaller links in the spectacular chain of Gulf Islands sprinkled along the Strait of Georgia between Vancouver Island and the mainland. Part of the southern Gulf Island group, it can be traced on a map as the tip of a triangle drawn from the roughly equidistant and opposite points of Nanaimo, to its north-west, and Vancouver City, to its north-east. In this respect, the island where two of Virginia Tinmouth's brothers had purchased large tracts of land during the forties completes, in geographical outline, the home range of Lowther's family history, from its pioneer beginnings near the coal mines around Nanaimo, to Lowther's big city present on the mainland, to those intervals of 'rustic bliss' at her favourite Gulf Island refuge, her 'main' island. For Lowther, who perceived the 'geo-metry' of geography better than she sometimes cared to let on (*MS*, 39), some such design was perhaps apparent. As with those definite constellations of astronomical bodies in space, the continents and contents of the earth kept offering up suggestive shapes. For the poet, as always, it was a matter of constant 'pattern recognition' amid the 'random spill' of raw 'data.'

Strategically positioned along the steamship routes and salmon runs through Active Pass, and blessed with an abundance of arable land, as well as lush forest growth, Mayne Island first attracted White settlers and farmers around the mid-nineteenth century, soon after it was surveyed by the British Royal Navy, in which served the Lieutenant Mayne who left behind his name. Archaeological evidence, however, suggests that human habitation of the island reaches back at least five thousand years to ancestors of the Cowichan and Nanaimo tribes (Elliott 1984: 2–4). But it is, ultimately, around its outermost edges that Mayne Island best shows its actual age, some forty million years of it. Here, among pungent kelp beds and small inlets crammed with driftwood, the effects of water on rock told Lowther about time. Quite 'in love with Mayne' since her first childhood visits, she used to 'wander on the beach' frequently, according to her cousin Barry Wilks.[1] Along these margins, she could observe a natural sort of 'water clock' in action, waves that marked off rhythms of time both sensually immediate and enduring, as the sea perpetually covered and un-gloved the smooth fingers of stone that the island extended out into it. As did the adjacent Gulf Islands that she also visited, Mayne Island featured rocks of what she might have called many 'characters.' Some of these 'characters' were fissured by clefts and encrusted with white barnacles, which she likened to 'minute pimples of salt.' Others conveyed the plastic 'character' of her 'milk stone,' lavishly webbed and sculpted over time into formations resembling honeycombs, bone tissue, shallow bowls, melted wax, or strange cathedrals by Antoni Gaudí.

It is important that these ancient, stony 'characters' and Pat Tinmouth had more than a few good decades to get well acquainted. Before Virginia's people moved to Mayne Island around 1945, the Tinmouths had made only the odd sprint to Bowen Island, near Vancouver, for family holiday excursions. But over the post-war years, once the relatives resettled on Mayne, the family – or, at least, Virginia and her children – could afford to venture to the Gulf Islands for regular vacations, instead. Barry Wilks, whose father, William, was one of the brothers who had relocated to Mayne, remembers Pat as a girl coming to visit. One day, 'she had a great big idea to put on a show,' he recollects. Apparently, the young dramatist who produced 'Song of the Forestland' wanted her cousin's help to clean out a barn and convert it into 'a theatre.' Already the proto-performance artist of *Infinite Mirror Trip*, 'she had fantastic ideas,' Barry says.[2] But this was, after all, the Wilks clan. It was due to his ideas that a young James Wilks had managed the fantastic feat of extricating himself from the coal mines that blew up his father. James's daughters, Virginia and Isabelle Wilks, had once quite literally acted on ideas that led them to perform in the fantastic theatres of New York and Chicago. And James's son, William, namesake of the William Wilks from Northumberland, had some 'great big ideas' of his own. This William, who could evidently divine lucrative Gulf Island real estate when he saw it, also practised as a diviner, even self-publishing a book on the subject, entitled *Science of a Witch's Brew*. There was no shortage of 'fantastic ideas' – and ambition – in the Wilks family.

Lowther herself referred to Mayne as, simply, 'The Island,' as though there were no others around as far as she was concerned. And indeed, there weren't any others quite so much like a second home to her. In fact, shortly after Virginia's brothers resettled there, some of the Wilks siblings, including Virginia, had sought to 'get a family enterprise going' by running a general store on the island – much as their grandfather, the would-be hotelier, William Wilks, had once attempted a 'family establishment' near the mines on Vancouver Island, a few generations earlier.[3] Around 1947, Virginia took the children to Mayne, leaving Arthur behind at his shipyard job in North Vancouver. Pat was twelve at the time, her sister Brenda two years younger – neither of them much older than Beth and Christine Lowther when Roy packed them off to Mayne during a futile run from the law, a generation later. Arden, Virginia's youngest child at the time, was just a baby, and not well. There were no readily accessible phones, much less medical facilities, on Mayne Island in 1947. For these reasons, and because the 'family enterprise' didn't prosper as hoped, it was bound to be a brief adventure for Virginia and her children. Nevertheless, at the time, Lowther actually lived on Mayne Island for about a year, she and Brenda traipsing off together to attend its one-room school for the duration of their stay.

In an unpublished narrative poem called 'The Island,' written during her St George Street period during 1963–5, Lowther remembered her youth on Mayne in lines that echoed Dylan Thomas's 'Fern Hill':

> I was young and the island was orchards,
> dark starry swell of sea
> fishes' shimmering ballet
> ...
> Starfish clutching like hands
> under the wharf,
> gulls crying,
> arbutus lifting their bodies like poems.
> I was young and the island
> was anticipated dream,
> fruition,
> honey under the tongue,
> salt flowers opening.

The 'salt flowers opening' under the 'honey' are the poem's first indication that the speaker's perception of 'The Island' changes over time, from the 'sugary siren' call and 'romantic music' of youth, to something else, more complicated, more 'real and detailed':

> I came back to the island, grown
> soft girl flesh seared away,
> grown lean and acid with the acid years
> and saw,
> beneath the soft flesh of my dream,
> the real and detailed island:
> the sea's bones
> shouldering through thin soil,
> the pale burnt slopes
> of empty pastures,
> the signs:
> No Smoking in these Woods,
> leaves snapping like thin glass underfoot;
> here and there houses
> given over
> to wild rose, nettle and bird dung ...[4]

However harsh, the more 'real and detailed' vision that comes with the adult's 'lean' and 'acid years' proves productive, dispelling 'the soft flesh of [a] dream' to make way for an awareness of both the vulnerability *and* the tenacity of the physical world. Degraded by 'signs' of human habitation, 'The Island' is a 'scab' of exposed shoulder bones and 'leaves' fragile as 'thin glass.' But it is also a complex organism that fights to reclaim its space, as the overgrown houses splattered with 'bird dung' suggest. The adult's 'real and detailed' knowledge of the place is poignantly ironic – or sweetly acidic. It is typical of Lowther that her poem directs attention to the 'pale burnt slopes' of the farmers' cleared 'pastures' just before its focus diverts to 'the signs: / No Smoking in these Woods.'

Long after all the 'soft girl flesh' was 'seared away,' Lowther's visits to Mayne remained a constant source of pleasure and inspiration, as a great many poems that she wrote around the time of her marriage to Roy attest. One such draft records the effects of a 'Full Moon' that leaves 'the islands defined' at night, throwing into vivid relief 'the vertical chain of red / from the power transmitter / on Saturna.' Another records the tribulations of a speaker 'hunched down among the skulls of rock, / out of sight of the windowed hotel / or boys on the smooth

sand beach.' The anticlimax is swift and ludicrous: 'I crouch to pee /
Secure in my privacy.' And this revelation is again playfully undercut:
'But, crammed in a rock, a crimson crab / with grouchy, suspicious old-
bachelor's eyes / is watching me.'[5] Other unpublished lyrics from this
time, such as 'After a Day Canoeing' or 'Creek Delta,' reproduced
below, were probably written with the North Shore in mind, but capture
also the vital energy she derived from contact with Mayne Island 'characters' made of stone, and the surrounding 'breath of the sea':

> Now, the rocks change character,
> furred with flat green tongue-fuzz
> and minute pimples of salt
> and I smell the breath of the sea
> that has breathed
> mouth to mouth with me
> ...
> I am restored
> walking among sea mud
> and weed-expropriated rocks
> to the stretching-away sea.[6]

At the time, with Kathy and Alan in tow, Pat and Roy used to visit
Mayne 'more than twice a year,' according to cousin Barry: 'they really
liked the good weather,' and, as always, staying with relatives made for
an inexpensive holiday. In later years, Barry recalls the family arriving
with Beth and Christie, Roy's broken-down old cars 'stuffed with their
junk.'[7] By 1973, probably as a result of Lowther's intensifying work
schedule, the family seems to have limited its Gulf Island migrations to
an annual summer vacation – a high summer trip that was, however,
almost as consistent as clockwork throughout the final three years of
Lowther's life.

Along with the 'high energy environment' of the North Shore Mountains, with their cataracts, 'steep granitic slopes, gulleys, glacial valleys
and cirques' (Kahrer 1989: 5), Mayne Island and the surrounding Gulf
Islands provided the central touchstones for virtually all of Lowther's
landscape poetry, including those nature poems which she wrote in the
early seventies and compiled in her final, and most consistently accomplished book, *A Stone Diary*. Ubiquitous, immediate, and detailed in a

way that her partly 'mythic' Arctic and Atacama Desert settings could not be, Lowther's mountainous North Vancouver backyard and 'The Island' of her youth together comprise the grounds for her most brilliant poems about the physical world, as even the Anansi editors who declined her *Stone Diary* manuscript in 1974 acknowledged.

The galaxies, 'wiggles,' and stars that preoccupied Lowther during her work on the planetarium show also exert their presence in contemporaneous poems about the sublunary physical world. Being in deep space was, after all, as she'd carefully noted, 'perceptually like being underwater.' As befitting poems forged on earth's 'dark / anvil,' however, Lowther's nature-based work accentuates her complementary interests in the earth sciences, not only geology, but also biology and archaeology (*TC*, 244). In doing so, she turned her attention from cosmic to organic forms of energy, including everything from 'ugh ugh,' slugs, to winter deer with 'jewels in their antlers,' to the 'fat red lanterns' of huckleberries at Furry Creek, and, of course, to 'stones': 'do you know / stones are alive [?]' (*SD*, 45, 11, 29, 27). 'I'm having a tremendous love affair with invertebrates,' she confessed gleefully at this point.[8] And falling 'madly in love' with 'invertebrates' like 'stone' would become the substance of her very first entry in 'A Stone Diary' (*SD*, 9).

Coming from the author of *Milk Stone*, the mad 'love affair' 'with stone' announced in the title poem of *A Stone Diary* was, obviously, another of Lowther's open secrets. When Oxford University Press eventually accepted the revised manuscript in the fall of 1975, the only thing that the editor, William Toye, objected to was the repetition of 'stone' in what he termed its 'flat and unappealing' title: 'As "stone" was in the title of your last (?) book, perhaps it doesn't bear repeating, for this reason alone. (It is called *Milk Stone* is it not?)'[9] Had she lived to respond, one senses Lowther would have held her ground – or hugged her 'stone' – on this point, just as she once did with the title of *This Difficult Flowring*. And perhaps the word did 'bear repeating,' not only because she loved it, but because, chronologically speaking, stone poems like 'Coast Range' formed the bedrock of *A Stone Diary* from its first inception.

Written around the time Arthur died in 1970, 'Coast Range' is one of the 'older' poems in her last book. Exuberantly, it celebrates the mountain range 'just north of town': those giants who wear their 'high stubbled meadows' as a 'back-of-the-head-buzz' cut, stone scalps showing through. Rather like the typically amiable Arthur, 'they're not snobs, these mountains, / they don't speak Rosicrucian.' 'First things' made of 'gravel' and 'rocks,' the mountains are 'humble' to a fault, 'talk[ing]' in their 'casual tongues,' and letting humans 'blast highways through them.' Ancient 'things,' they are simpler than the fussy meanings that poets, shamans, philosophers, statesmen, or scientists might project upon them. Just 'intractably there,' they are 'a bare fact' of pure materiality and presence. 'The land is what's left / after the failure / of every kind of metaphor':

> The mountains reject nothing
> but can crack
> open your mind
> just by being intractably there
>
> Atom: that which cannot
> be reduced
>
> You can gut them
> blast them
> to slag
> the shapes they've made in the sky
> cannot be reduced (*SD*, 36–7)

In its continuation of work begun in simpler poems like 'The Island,' 'Coast Range' refracts a set of interlocking concerns and tensions that are representative of the geophysical thrust of *A Stone Diary* in general, and also indicative of Lowther's political and intellectual involvements with the environmental movement that was under way by the early seventies. Her poem's familiar emphasis on the literally elemental or 'atomic' afterlife of the gutted and blasted mountain reveals itself as subtly double-edged in this context. On its surface, 'Coast Range' rings with an affirmation of the natural world as irreducible in its ultimate ability to withstand alterations wrought upon it in the name of modernity. But those 'highways' dynamited through massive 'iron and granite' mountain shoulders also leave in their wake disquieting reminders of damage done: 'sunset-coloured bones / broken for miles' (*SD*, 35).

'Do you know / stones are alive'? Lowther's conviction of the animation of 'first things' was partly indebted to First Nations mythologies, which she absorbed through books, films, and Native leaders like Leonard George. But it was also a belief informed by her keen interests in politics, science, and technology. From these perspectives, the 'sunset-coloured bones' of 'Coast Range' and its concluding image of 'atomic' after-shadows of 'shapes ... made in the sky' also cast darker implications. The poem's opening 'splat' into its subject matter, so joyous and uninhibited in its 'casual' tongue, makes it easy to go 'bumsliding' right over the 'bare fact' that its first publication in 1971 happened to coincide with a particularly pitched episode in nuclear weapons testing – testing that, beginning in 1965, had been hitting awfully close on the Northwest Pacific rim. In the fall of 1971, the U.S. military and Atomic Energy Commission conducted the *third* in a series of extremely contentious nuclear tests in Alaska's Aleutian Islands. The nuclear bombs were all the more environmentally catastrophic because the men in charge of exploding them chose a National Wildlife Refuge area as ground zero for their test site. 'Life, ecology, evolutionary processes: all essential features of the worldwide heritage of mankind to which a ... Refuge ... is devoted, were violated,' the anguished Refuge caretaker protested after the first bomb. And that was just the start of the 'corrosive evil' which he and the Aleut people would be forced to live with from then on.[10]

And, to a lesser extent, Vancouverites and Canadians too. Around the time of the first Amchitka bomb in 1965, health officials across the country had already begun to solicit mothers to volunteer the baby teeth of their children to determine 'amounts of radioactive strontium-90 ingested by Canadians as a result of fallout from nuclear weapons tests.' At the time, Lowther clipped this news article from the *Vancouver Sun* and duly sent in one of Kathy's baby teeth. In return, nine-year-old Kathy stood to receive an 'I gave my tooth to science' button.[11]

In at least one other of her notebook poem drafts, Lowther imaginatively fused the Amchitka bomb tests in Alaska with dynamite rock blasting 'up north.'[12] Perhaps she had heard of the rock falls and turf slides caused by the underground bombs in the Aleutians, land collapses that effectively smothered intertidal marine life in some areas (Kohlhoff 2002: 110). Notably, in 'Coast Range,' it is exactly the obsolete definition of the 'atom' as 'that which cannot / be reduced,' which is cleanly split by the scalpel of the poet's line break for a new age of nuclear fission. At the same time that she was reasserting the endurance of a 'Coast Range' gutted 'to slag,' Lowther was using the faint after-image of the mountains' atomic dispersal as a reminder of the coexisting reality of an arms race that threatened all life forms on the planet. When it came to the nuclear test 'blasts' of the Cold War, she was extremely conscious of the 'bare fact' that 'shapes' once 'made in the sky / cannot be reduced.' Nature, even when decimated by ordnance crafted from an atom halved, would continue, at that same imperceptibly atomic level, on 'intractably' self-regulating terms of its own. Consequences like radio-chemical fallout could be 'irreducible' too. Those 'first things' which appeared 'so humble' and 'broken,' then, might not prove so endlessly forgiving, after all. As though to reinforce the point, the poem which follows 'Coast Range' in *A Stone Diary* is entitled 'Dark': 'The darkness comes down like meteors / petals of hot black' (*SD*, 38).

As events spurring the formation of many environmental alliances, including the West Coast Greenpeace group, in 1969, the Amchitka bomb tests marked a pivotal stake in the ground for a new politics of ecology. 'Suddenly, environmental concerns were at the forefront of public attention,' and the movement which 'quickly took shape' after the first international Earth Day in 1970 soon 'achieved general recognition ... in the realm of public debate' (Torgerson 1999: xiii). Aside from her poetry, Lowther participated in this 'public debate' through her work with the NDP, which, like most leftist groups, officially endorsed the overlapping environmental and social concerns spearheaded by leaders of the 'green' movement. So, when the first dozen Greenpeacers set out (in the recycled tub of a halibut packer) to disrupt the 1971 Amchitka test, it was Lowther, once again acting as her party's faithful recording secretary, who set down its 'message of good wishes to the Greenpeace, *en route* to the Aleutians to protest the Amchitka bomb.'[13]

In this context, her line 'The land is what's left,' in 'Coast Range' is perfectly accurate as a synopsis for a cultural moment in which the cause of 'the land' was becoming ever more crucially identifiable with what was Left. Moreover, as a socialist, Lowther would have been very clear on exactly why it was that 'the promise of green politics' (Torgerson 1999) depended on some shade of red. Like ecologist James O'Connor, she would have understood the problem along the lines of Marx's analysis of 'the contradictions of capitalism':

> On the one hand, capitalism is a self-expanding system of economic growth. Its aim is limitless growth, or money in search of more of itself ... On the other hand, nature is not self-expanding: forests reach climax stages; fresh water is limited by geography and climate; fossil fuels and minerals are physically fixed. Nature is far from stingy and enables, as well as constrains human production, but its rhythms and cycles are governed by a different logic than the rhythms and cycles of capital. (1999: 10)

By virtue of her early roots in such environments as the Gulf Islands and the Lynn Creek watershed, of course, Lowther was already well versed in the self-limiting and finite 'rhythms and cycles' of the natural world by the time the seventies arrived. If nothing else, her father's live-lihood at the intake station conditioned her ecocentric sensibilities, serving as her first introduction to the importance of conservation and protection. The lesson conveyed by Arthur's job was elementary and essential: whatever leeched into soil and water mattered to anything that depended on them for life. Mayne Island advanced this lesson further, as another example of a particularly delicate biosphere, one in which any imbalance or contamination could pose especially dire conse-quences. So it was not merely the case that she was fully prepared to lend some support to the eco-movements of her time while she wrote *A Stone Diary*. Instead, one of the unforgettable 'first things' she literally drank in as she grew was that her own survival depended on that of 'the land.'

It was with the *sang froid* of a lifelong non-driver that Lowther regarded 'the automobile.' 'Besides being a major source' of air pollution and 'resource depletion,' cars annoyed her as the pre-eminent 'symbol' of a 'materialistic, gadget-ridden society.'[14] It is tempting to think that she therefore spurned the driver's seat herself as a matter of principle. But, in fact, she did attempt to get a driver's licence, once, early on. She failed the test. Her daughter Kathy attributes this to the fact that her mother was 'too high strung'– 'extremely high strung.' Her sister Brenda draws the opposite conclusion: 'She had too slow of a reaction,' she recalls, of the ill-fated driver's test. 'They gave her several tries ... She couldn't brake in time.'[15] Perhaps too languid, perhaps too jittery, or perhaps both, at different times – whatever the case, she never darkened the door of a motor vehicle branch again.

'The automobile' was only one target of a range of environmental reforms being proposed by the newly elected NDP under David Barrett during the early seventies. At their 1973 provincial convention, which Lowther attended as an elected delegate for her Little Mountain riding, the NDP passed a series of environmental motions that called for improvements in recycling, sewage, and sanitation, as well as reduction of industrial waste. The meeting also passed the following motion, directed at the critical issue of water pollution:

> WHEREAS the Fraser River is turning into an open sewer,
> WHEREAS Georgia Strait is also in danger of pollution,
> WHEREAS the NDP is committed to maintain a clean environment,
> BE IT RESOLVED that

1. A law be enacted to make it unlawful to dump raw sewage into   B.C. waters (fresh water and salt water).
2. Crown Corporations (such as the B.C. Ferry Authority) set an example by being the first ones to honour this law.[16]

Effluents in the water from sources like the ferries which plied the Burrard Inlet and the Georgia Strait were thus one of the dangers now preoccupying the intake caretaker's daughter. Cars may have been particularly galling as 'symbols' of consumption – if not also of a test once 'failed.' But public transportation like the *Mayne Queen* or the *Queen of the Islands*, which Lowther routinely relied upon to get to 'her' Island, was not exactly problem-free either.

And paradise was being lost in other disturbing ways, as well. After her 1973 annual summer holiday in the Gulf, Lowther alluded to another new ecological concern in a letter to Eugene McNamara:

We spent a week at my uncle's cabin on Mayne Island, in the Gulf of Georgia [*sic*] between here and Victoria. The Islands are incredibly beautiful, though I suppose they'll inevitably be spoiled by the sub-dividing that's going on now. Still, some things can't be changed, like the view from the cabin, which looks out on a bay and chains of beautifully shaped small islands. I think I've been badly needing a few days away from the city.[17]

The 'lean' and 'acid years' of Lowther's adult visits to Mayne were years of witness to an island slowly transformed by a real estate boom during the sixties and seventies, as it and the other Gulf Islands became the focus of increasing demand for recreational and leisure property, and the 'urban shadows' of Victoria and Vancouver loomed ever larger (Elliott 1984: 95ff, 117). The consequence was not only a 'sub-dividing' alteration of the face of islands like Mayne, but also the outright purchase of many of those 'beautifully shaped small islands' that Lowther took pleasure in viewing from her relatives' residences on Horton and Bennett Bays, and, sometimes, visiting by canoe.

Such was the fate of Curlew Island, 'beautifully shaped' like a pelvic bone and jutting just off Horton Bay, the spot where, as a girl, Lowther had entertained grand, theatrical plans for her Uncle William's barn. Curlew's passage into 'Private Ownership' is sardonically commemorated in a poem by that title in *A Stone Diary*.[18] 'Curlew Island' is, we are informed, now 'owned by a Texas Millionaire' and 'guarded by Fierce Dogs.' 'Don't beach a boat there,' the poet warns: 'you'll be savaged by mastiffs.' Though '[n]obody's ever seen' the Texas Millionaire, 'we hear his voice: / Shuddup, you gawdam dogs! / Shuddup!' (*SD*, 13). All around the islands, audibly as well as visibly, there were now proliferating signs of what Marx once called 'our friend, Moneybags' (1995: 107).

Not surprisingly, Lowther approached the question of 'Private Ownership' from the perspective of a tenant and temporary resident. It was a philosophy of tenure on Earth that she articulated as early as her pre-'flowring' Vancouver Poetry Society days, in poems like 'After Rain,' where the speaker, like a 'pear tree,' 'puts forth green hands – / Not to hold you, never to hold you fast – / Only to touch you gently as you pass.'[19] As she would write of the business of 'Inheritance' in *A Stone Diary*, she usually felt quite 'useless at owning things' (14). Even her hymn to Mayne Island in *A Stone Diary*'s 'Song' consistently counters its own, almost exaggerated claims to proprietorial 'ownership' of the land. Here, the speaker envisions herself in control of comings and goings on what she calls 'my island.' But all of her exhortations to the potential visitor aim to minimize any signs of their human presence:

> If I take you to my island
> you'll have to remember
> to speak quietly
> you'll have to remember
> sound carries over water
> You must come by night
> we'll walk through the dark
> orchards to the sea
> and gather crystal jellyfish
> from the black water
> we'll lie on the sand
> and feel the galaxy
> on our cheeks and foreheads
> you'll have to remember
> to wear warm clothing
> follow where I go
> and speak very softly
> if I take you (*SD*, 40)

Part of her family 'Inheritance' through the lineage of James Wilks and Annie McCain, Mayne Island also presented some facts that Lowther herself would 'have to remember.' Her own relatives were now landholders of sufficient estate to warrant not only a road named after them but also a lane that branched from it, named for the pioneering Isabella Wilks. Their own rapidly appreciating and 'sub-dividing' lands were, like that of the 'Texas Millionaire's' on Curlew, exclusive 'private' properties – the antithesis of the 'public beach' next to 'the windowed hotel' at Bennett Bay. And yet, it was only by virtue of the Wilks family's 'Private Ownership,' and their on-going hospitality, that Lowther could afford to be in the Gulf in the first place, sensually absorbing the islands' impressionable 'characters,' slowly changing, over time. Such, too, were the 'contradictions of capitalism.'

After Anansi's rejection of both *Milk Stone* and *A Stone Diary* in early 1974, the almost immediate rescue of 'the albatross' manuscript by Borealis Press meant that Lowther could let go of the idea she flirted with at Atwood's suggestion, of fusing the two collections into one. But that still left the task of finding a home for *A Stone Diary*. As she told Fred Cogswell in February 1974, she apparently shipped that revised manuscript out again when she sent Borealis *Milk Stone*. There are no records indicating where she sent her *Stone Diary* at that time, but it was still in her hands later that year. With no apparent prompting, now, from friends like Lane or Livesay, Lowther got strategic. Sometime after her Ontario tour and acclamation as League Chair, she contacted one of her newer League colleagues, Gary Geddes. Geddes, a critic, editor, and fellow West Coast writer, also happened to have some good publishing connections. The letter that Lowther composed contained a request, at once careful and direct in its wording and tone:

> I've been trying to get up the nerve to ask you a favor. I'm really anxious to get a reliable publisher for my next book (ie one who'll distribute the eff-ing thing). I could a tale of woe unfold you've probably heard dozens of times and maybe even experienced yourself. I'm wondering if you could see your way to giving me a recommendation to your editor at Oxford. I've become convinced that just sending a *ms* out blind is like playing roulette.
>
> Naturally, you can see the *ms* first if you want to. And naturally, if this is embarrassing and you'd rather not do it, just say so. I won't aggress you.[20]

'Naturally,' Geddes wanted to 'see the *ms*' he was being asked to recommend. And though he 'didn't know Pat Lowther terribly well' at the time, it was also 'naturally' enough that she came to set her sights on him. Having 'met her at League of Poets meetings, and watched her become Chairman,' Geddes still 'hadn't really seen much of [Lowther's] work up until that point,' aside from 'the odd poem in journals here and there.' Among the 'odd' poems he *had* seen so far, however, was 'Coast Range,' first published in *Blackfish* magazine. As an editor, Geddes was about to accord pride of place to this poem as the opening piece in his anthology of West Coast poetry, *Skookum Wawa*, published in 1975 by his scholarly colleague and friend, William Toye, for none other than Oxford University Press. 'I think,' Geddes surmises of Lowther's initiative, 'having that connection and being in an Oxford anthology, [she felt] that she could write to me.' He was 'very, very impressed' with the *Stone Diary* manuscript Lowther packed off to him shortly after her query letter. On 2 April 1975, he responded with a quick assessment of the manuscript's strengths and weaknesses, along with what Lowther had hoped for most of all: an indication of his willingness to vouch for her manuscript's merits with William Toye.[21]

Giving herself just enough time to assimilate some of the suggestions Geddes made, Lowther submitted the manuscript to Oxford on 22 May 1975. By July 19, William Toye was writing to say that he liked 'very much' her work 'in Gary's *Skookum Wawa*,' and that, though he could not yet promise anything definite in regards to her manuscript, 'it would be nice to publish a collection by you (in the fall of 1976).' Could she continue to be patient a little longer, while he checked into the possibility of a Canada Council grant for the book?[22] Lowther didn't get this letter for awhile – it arrived while she was away on her cherished Mayne Island, for her last summer vacation. But as far as the new book was concerned, the rest, as they say, is history. 'Rank has its privileges,' Lowther once half-joked to Arlene Lampert: 'or, I've got to have some reward for doing all this work.' She was referring then to having tweaked a minor string in the League's readings roster to indulge a personal gratification. But it was the connection to people occupying even more instrumental positions than her own that were the real 'rewards' and 'privileges' of her new 'rank' – and 'all the work' that 'rank' entailed.[23]

In his preliminary evaluation of the *Stone Diary* manuscript, Geddes suggested expunging several poems that struck him as 'trite, and rather thin.' Lowther left virtually all of the poems he identified as such, including 'Slugs,' for example, intact in the revised collection. But she must have found his remarks on structure and organization somewhat more to her own thinking, because she did act on his advice to divide the volume into tripartite segments – a triptych form to which she frequently gravitated in individual poems, anyway. Even on this point, however, she reserved her own counsel. Geddes envisioned one section for 'the BCish stuff, like "Coast Range," "Early Winters,"' and what he called 'the beast poems' – those 'brief, evocative cameos, like "Octopus" [and] "Craneflies [in Their Season]."' 'Then, put the Neruda poems together ... [and] then a third and final section of tough poems about current events, women's lib (God help us for this term), and the city scapes, including "Intersection." That would be really strong.'[24]

While composed along these general lines, Lowther scored her arrangements for three somewhat more unpredictable sets. In the midst of 'the BCish stuff' that comprises the bulk of *A Stone Diary*'s first part – poems like 'A Stone Diary,' 'Coast Range,' 'Early Winters,' and 'Notes from Furry Creek,' for instance – yawns the Chilean hell hole of 'Chacabuco, the Pit.' Conversely, 'the beast poems' about 'BCish' creatures like octopuses and craneflies, she tucked instead alongside the Neruda poems in the second part. And in the book's 'third and final section of tough poems,' she not only collected most of what Geddes called those 'gutsy media pieces' – the poems about 'current events, women's lib ... and the city scapes' – but also one very unusual long poem, 'The Dig,' based as much or more in the remote archaeological past as in the modern present.

'There's such a diversity here,' Geddes had written to her: 'you'll need to make your book flow, or at least appear unified.'[25] But containing 'diversity' was never one of Lowther's strong suits, as her pro-environmental politics and the state of her household equally testified. The deliberately porous divisions of her book's new, three-part numerical structure reflected this fact as well. If she was going to have to sort out her poems according to some kind of coherent logic, then she would use both an atomic logic that accurately mirrored the 'cloudy' and 'hybrid' realities of that 'here *and* there' elemental realm, as well as the eco-logic of a natural world based on the primary fact of systemic interdependence. 'It's the vision of interconnectedness or [a] holistic vision' of 'all living things,' as Suniti Namjoshi explained, in an early review of *A Stone Diary*: 'the vegetable and the human, the animate and the inanimate, the "civilized" and the "natural,"' the 'regional' and the global (1977: 51).

As the structural principle of her book, the idea of 'diversity' and differentiation within an integrative whole offered Lowther's readers virtually a textbook definition of the physical cosmos, and of the key to 'life, ecology, [and] evolutionary processes,' as enumerated by the Amchitka wildlife parks warden. At the same time, it pointed as well to the grounds of long-standing scientific debates about those 'evolutionary processes' in which Lowther took a strong interest – one carried over to *A Stone Diary* from works like *Infinite Mirror Trip* and *Milk Stone*. Charles Darwin, that 'child of Victorians' whom she occasionally thought about, if she hadn't also read, argued in *On the Origin of Species* that evolutionary change progressed not only from simple to increasingly complex and heterogeneous life forms, but that this divergent evolutionary process also signalled an intrinsically benevolent 'progress towards perfection' (1964: 489). The progressive philosophy implied by Darwin's positivist science was, in turn, taken up by a later generation of thinkers, including the Continental modernist philosopher Henri Bergson, whom Lowther certainly did read. In *Creative Evolution*, Bergson argued similarly that 'the directing causes' of evolutionary processes expressed a 'vital' or 'original impetus' that aimed *naturally* toward the betterment and advancement of life: 'I mean an internal push that has carried life, by more and more complex forms, to higher and higher destinies' (1949: 74).

On the other hand, as a generalist reader also attracted to the field of evolutionary *cosmology* and its underpinnings in physics, Lowther would have known at least a little something about a competing theory of divergence and change over time, a counter view wherein biology and physics often seemed to remain at loggerheads. Indeed, contemporary with Darwin's theory of evolution, the second law of thermodynamics posited instead a 'universal principle of degeneration,' by which 'every closed system tends towards a state of total disorder or chaos.' The same mechanisms that some biologists and philosophers would construe as signs of an 'impetus' onwards and upwards to better things – diversification, differentiation, subdivision, and proliferation – were also, then, processes that physicists spoke about, instead, in terms of the physical laws of entropy, whereby 'almost all natural changes' occurring in matter and energy within the cosmos signalled a 'remorseless' 'downhill process' of self-expenditure and disintegration (Davies 1995: 34–5).

When it came to competing ideas about entropic devolution versus 'progressive' evolution, Lowther *wanted* to side with Darwin and Bergson. However, as she intimated in her prefatory comments in Elaine Gill's *Mountain Moving Day*, this desire bespoke only 'a tentative kind of hope' at the best of times: 'I went through a time when I believed we humans were coming to the end of our evolutionary cycle – devolving like dandelions. Now I see the half-breeds of the future passing like migrating birds, and I begin to have a tentative kind of hope.'[26] The 'tentativeness' of this 'hope' also marks the arrangement and tenor of *A Stone Diary*, which records, among other things, Lowther's struggle, during the last half decade of her life, to believe in the possibilities of 'creative evolution' in the midst of an unprecedentedly destructive world. The ominous 'Dark' that descends after 'Coast Range,' closing out the first instalment of her *Diary*, was only one manifestation of this struggle.

In more ways than one, it made sense that she chose to surround 'Chacabuco, the Pit' with many of her 'BCish' landscape poems in *A Stone Diary*'s opening section. As the example of 'Coast Range' suggests, even while such landscape works revel in the natural splendours of her region, they also tend to evoke the destructive abuses of 'a broken world' (*SD*, 28). In this way, like her longer 'documentary' poem about Chacabuco, Lowther's nature-based lyrics also work to witness a form of atrocity: 'the horrors of / what we allow to be done' to the living *and* the living world that sustains us, the 'specific magic / of land alive' (*SD*, 26, 27). Not all such works are as understated as 'Coast Range' in conveying this message. Inspired by an anti-Vietnam war rally, 'The Earth Sings Mi-Fa-Mi,' for instance, takes its unusual title from a quotation by Johannes Kepler that leaves little doubt as to the poem's imperative from the very outset: '... so we can gather even from this that MIsery and FAmine reign on our habitat' (*SD*, 32; ellipsis and emphasis in the original). The peace protesters gathered '[o]utside the U.S. consulate' sing, 'hoping [their] soft noise / will spread outward / from the centre.' But this harmonious music of the spheres is ultimately drowned out by the shrill, discordant 'noise' and chaos of a planet reeling in pain: 'the wind screams' 'like whipped wires,' 'and the earth spinning,' 'the earth sings Mi-Fa-Mi' (*SD*, 33).

The wretched earth that 'sings' of 'misery' and 'famine' seems a planet from another galaxy, arranged, as it is, right next to one of *A Stone Diary*'s best-known and most soothing landscape poems, 'Notes from Furry Creek.' Everything in this setting seems 'perfect,' from the 'ruler-straight' orderliness of a fallen log across the creek, to the bountiful munificence of the 'fat red' huckleberries:

> The water reflecting cedars
> all the way up
> deep sonorous green –

> nothing prepares you
> for the ruler-straight
> log fallen across
> and the perfect
> water fall it makes
> and the pool behind it
> novocaine-cold
> and the huckleberries
> hanging
> like fat red lanterns (*SD*, 29)

But the tranquility of the creek's 'pool' of water is disturbed even as it is also reinforced by the comparison of its effect to a 'novocaine-cold' tranquillizing drug, a sedative not unlike those soothing 'tranks' Lowther was relying upon by the time she wrote this final version of her poem. The 'cold' spot of anaesthetized numbness amid the 'deep sonorous green' of Furry Creek creates a ripple, a dissonance, that Lowther was also slyly preparing to amplify even as she invoked those jovial 'fat red lanterns' of the huckleberries at the very end of her poem's first section. Suggestively, those 'fat red lanterns' are left 'hanging' over the second sequence, which begins as follows:

> The dam, built
> by coolies, has outlived
> its time; its wall
> stained sallow
> as ancient skin
> dries in the sun (*SD*, 30)

In first announcing the arrival of the Chinese into the landscape's historical past, the red huckleberries of the poem's opening stanza gradually transmute into ethnic emblems of those famous 'fat red' Chinese 'lanterns,' as well. Structurally speaking, the image accomplishes nothing less than the paradox of anticipating a *coming past.*

'Red,' usually a flag for politics in Lowther's books, here reminds readers once again that the 'dam' 'is a pit' too. If not a formal prison, then still, like Chacabuco, it is also a structure that carries a trace of 'the wretched of the earth,' in Franz Fanon's phrase – in this case, the underpaid 'coolie' labourers whose sweat and energy built the 'dam' whose 'wall' has 'outlived' them all. As for the natural inhabitants of this dammed 'pit' site, 'the royal animals,' they may be 'quiet,' but, the poet warns, they are 'dangerous' too:

> The dam foot
> is a pit
> for the royal animals
> quiet and dangerous
> in the stare
> of sun and water (*SD*, 30)

Henri Rousseau's *The Sleeping Gypsy* (1897) was one of Lowther's favourite paintings, as she told her Regina audience in 1972, one she had already written about in a poem by the same title in her first book. In Rousseau's painting, the 'royal animal' of a lion hovers directly over the shoulder of a sleeping human, its nostrils just inches away from the sleeper's exposed neck. The animal is simply staring at the prostrate figure, evoking an encounter that is 'quiet' but 'dangerous,' too. Like a cloud of unsettled silt in water, a similarly suspended mood begins to infiltrate 'Notes from Furry Creek' – where the only 'shapes' made by Lowther's beloved 'characters' of 'rock,' incidentally, are of that 'royal animal,' the 'lion' (*SD*, 30).

   And in the poem's riddling and reflective third and final section, it is rock that the speaker eventually becomes. 'Swallowed' by 'stones,' she bows out as an 'Incredible Shrinking Woman' once again, simultaneously 'seduced' and reduced 'to smaller and smaller / ellipses,' ground down to a living particle in /of the landscape she began by taking 'notes' on for her 'diary.' Such reduction, moreover, will happen to 'you,' the 'opposite' of her 'eyes' / 'I,' too – when 'you' understand 'the secret' imparted by becoming 'stone' (*SD*, 31).

   The place that inspired 'Notes from Furry Creek' – Roy's old childhood stomping grounds – eventually generated a more obscure companion piece, as well, which Lowther did not include in her *Stone Diary* manuscript. Also about the 'dam' near Furry Creek, and also in a triptych form that mirrored its predecessor perfectly, 'Elegy for the South Valley' recounts how that 'perfect' weekend retreat just north of town, like her own subdividing Mayne Island, was visibly altering over time. In this case, it was literally a 'down hill' devolution that Lowther 'noted': more and more puke outs of 'slid scree' 'over broken banks.' 'The dam that served / a mine that serviced empire' is still there, though 'crumbling slowly.' 'For this country,' 'where a few generations / do for antiquity,' the South Valley dam might as well be one of the 'pyramids' of ancient Egypt, but 'the work of men / will all be undone' eventually (*TC*, 205–6).

'The work of men / will all be undone' by 'the work of men,' because the South Valley dam is slowly being undermined by the enterprise of a new 'empire' that is 'eating' the valley:

> The gravel pit is eating
> South Valley, the way you'd
> eat a stalk of asparagus,
> end to end, saving the tender
> tip for last. It starts
> at the highway end
> gouging alder and huckleberry
> off the creek banks;
> dust loosed in the air
> precipitates slowly on water
> and smooth wet stones. (*TC*, 206–7)

The 'asparagus' analogy tempts readers with a false 'tip': the 'gravel pit' 'gouging' the valley and dusting up the dam below with silt is no connoisseur of delicacies. If it saves the 'tender / tip for last,' that's only because it *has* to eat its way up the mountainside. The 'gravel pit' does not savour with appreciation that which it consumes: 'each year,' its 'tooth marks' just 'go deeper' and 'higher into the green' mountain slopes (*TC*, 206–7). The 'gravel pit' is a predator with a bottomless appetite and incisors that mean business. The effects it leaves behind are no more 'civilized' than those of 'Chacabuco, the Pit,' or the 'gouge' marks of 'Greatbrother Bear,' or, say, the 'tooth marks' of a hungry 'lion.'

At the end of her 'Elegy,' Lowther left the South Valley dam tilting precariously 'between time's jaw's': 'waiting for either / the weight of its past / or the hard bite of the future / to bring it down' (*TC*, 207). Evidence of environmental degradation was piling up against the 'ancient skin' of the straining old dam, but she once again preferred to close on a note of suspended animation, a 'waiting' period that reiterated once more her fascination with 'potentialities,' and with the relativity of 'time's arrow,' which might point 'either' to causal antecedents 'or' in the direction of a 'hard bite' yet ahead.

Lowther published 'Elegy for the South Valley' in Geddes' 1975 *Skookum Wawa*, but excluded this poem from her *Stone Diary* manuscript.

Perhaps it and 'Notes from Furry Creek' were not closely related in her mind, despite their rather obvious connections. 'Notes from Furry Creek' had a long prehistory, spanning back over multiple drafts to the early period of her marriage to Roy. Having 'done a lot of [his] growing up there,' Roy was particularly attached to the Furry Creek area, professing himself 'extremely fond' of it for sentimental reasons (RLJ, 1:16). Among the cardboard boxes that house Pat's papers are photographs of her at Furry Creek, dating from the time Roy first took her out there. In one, she sports the short hair she wore at the time of her second marriage, and smiles broadly while propped up on her elbows, risking a bit of sunbathing. On the back of the photo is written, 'Glamour Puss, Furry Creek.'

The earliest draft of 'Notes from Furry Creek,' entitled simply 'From Furry Creek,' dates from this honeymoon period as well. In both it and a lightly revised subsequent draft, a pair of lovers 'come to Furry Creek / and to the South Valley,' 'these trees and mountains / in our weekend reach.' The place is a respite and refuge for the couple, 'searching out a private joy': 'here we can be naked in the water / in the secretive forest.' Already in these drafts, the couple's 'private joy' is juxtaposed against the 'private' 'dreams' and 'nightmares' of the 'coolies' who built the South Valley dam and 'fathered' the 'tiny lake' behind it, its 'deep jade' waters a gemstone 'always beyond their purse.'[27] Overly discursive, the early drafts bear little resemblance to the fine focus and clean technique of the 'Notes' that appear in *A Stone Diary*. Nor is it surprising that the original couple, unlike the Chinese labourers, are gradually written out of the landscape by the time of the final 'Notes from Furry Creek.' On the other hand, the personal past erased from the drafts may help account for those 'novocaine-cold' spots that linger in the final text, like the faint under-image of a painting.

'Elegy for the South Valley,' by contrast, originated much later, in 1974. 'Elegy' may have been one of those newer poems that Lowther told William Toye she had written for 'another (distant future, at this rate) collection,' but which she also felt 'might fit in with "Stone Diary" if you feel that would be desirable.'[28] According to Roy, Pat wrote the poem based upon his reports of changes in the area when he returned from a solitary trip there (RLJ, 1:16). Whether or not this was the case, it was true that, despite her own attraction to Furry Creek, Lowther was by this time no longer accompanying her husband to his favourite old spot, unless it was to take the girls for family picnics. Not only had the 'secretive' Eden of that original pair of lovers long since disintegrated, but by now, the 'Glamour Puss' of 1963 had also evolved, creatively, into a very different species – a 'Chair Creature.'

That painter, Henri Rousseau, whom Lowther spoke about in Regina as 'a very strange and charming sort of person,' was, among other things, a 'primitive' modernist known for creating 'very strange and charming' sorts of landscape paintings in which he deliberately assembled flora and animal species that actually belonged to entirely disparate habitats. Sometimes, he also 'intermingled real and imaginary' species, as his 'fancy' dictated (Shattuck et al. 1985: 226, 231). From this point of view, the middle part of *A Stone Diary* reflects a similarly 'charming' eccentricity: with its 'strange' concatenation of 'beast poems' (as Geddes called them) and Neruda poems, it was as though Lowther was also experimenting with an imaginative zoology of specimens from distinct environments.

At the same time, her 'BCish' habitat did not just overlap with Neruda's Chilean one, climatically and geographically. Lowther also felt that her 'beast' poems *belonged* with Neruda – though not the epic Neruda of the *Canto General*. Instead, her short 'cameo' works resonated with a series of books Neruda published over the fifties, the *Elemental Odes*, in which he began to document the everyday world of humble objects and activities, including onions, apples, socks, feet, ironing. So too, Lowther's 'beast poems,' which turned from earlier 'beast poems' like the domesticated but dramatic 'Killer Whale' (*DF*, 30) to examine, now, the other, so-called 'lesser' life forms of her coastal marine region: the 'invertebrates' like 'Anemones,' 'Octopus,' 'Craneflies in Their Season,' 'Hermit Crabs,' 'Slugs.' Her choice of (presumably) less evolved or lowly subject matter carries implications similar to those of Neruda's *Odes*, which are often characterized as a direct extension of his Marxist ideology. Likewise there is a clear relationship between Lowther's own commitments to democratic socialism and the materialist poetics of her landscape works, in general, as well as her 'invertebrate' poems, in particular. In this specific respect, Neruda was not entirely problematic as a literary mentor, especially in combination with other salient influences, like the painter Rousseau.

Naturally enough, the 'invertebrate' poems, all written between 1972 and 1974, follow Lowther's 'Song' to 'her' Island in *A Stone Diary*. Certainly not 'odes' in the form of those of Horace or Pindar, or even in the looser sense of Keats's 'irregular' odes, the 'beast poems' are nevertheless ode-like in the Nerudian sense of their praise and elevation of the 'simple' life forms they examine, almost microscopically. There are 'the sea anemones' 'under our feet' on 'the wharf at Saturna,' whose 'velvet bodies' are inspected and promoted to mammalian and even avian heights as 'gorgeous animals' 'feeding / in the sky' (*SD*, 41). There are the tiny 'Hermit Crabs,' their 'brindle legs' 'fine' as a ladies' 'fine-tooth' 'comb,' and yet groomed for fierce self-defence with 'pincers / thin as bronze wire' (*SD*, 44). There is the fabulous 'Octopus':

> The octopus is beautifully
> functional as an umbrella;
> at rest a bag of rucked skin
> sags like an empty scrotum
> his jelled eyes sad and bored
>
> but taking flight: look
> how lovely purposeful
> in every part:
> the jet vent smooth
> as modern plumbing
> the webbed pinwheel of tentacles
> moving in perfect accord
> like a machine dreamed
> by Leonardo (*SD*, 42)

With models culled from as far afield as the Chilean South and the Inuit North, 'Patsy Lou' was returning home to find a 'beautifully / functional' aesthetic stamped all over her own habitat. Everywhere – in the water, under docks, on the beaches – were forms 'lovely purposeful / in every part.' Even those gross, disgusting 'Slugs,' 'heaving themselves' so 'gracelessly' over the earth, could be seen to transform in the act of reproduction, 'twined / together / in a perfect spiral / flowing,' a double helix of life's chemistry itself (*SD*, 44–5).

And yet. Though nature offered examples of as 'nice' a 'welding / of science and art' as any 'machine dreamed / by Leonardo,' 'Leonardo' also dreamt up some fairly weird 'machines.' In this, the Renaissance artist-scientist was copying nature too. This was a fact Lowther was also prepared to record in her 'diary.' Contradicting 'in every part' the 'beautifully / functional' design of the octopus, for instance, are the ungainly 'Craneflies in Their Season,' on *A Stone Diary*'s facing page:

> Struggling in the grass
> or splayed against walls and fences,
> they seem always somehow askew.
> Even their flights in air
> appear precarious
> and all their moves seem
> to be accidents.
>
> Dead, they form windrows
> of bent wires,
> broken delicate parts
> of some unexplained machine.
> And the wind sweeps them
> like evidence of an accident
> out of sight. (*SD* 43)

Long, slender-legged insects like mosquitoes, craneflies do not bite, and they do not live long. Swept away after their ephemeral lives, like the 'bent wires' and 'broken delicate parts' of one of 'Leonardo's' more inexplicable inventions, these small insects, like those tinier quantum particles of the molecular realm, too, begged for Lowther bigger questions about the aims and ends of evolutionary processes. Far from revealing any 'lovely purposeful' logic, her craneflies seemed to offer 'evidence' of the existence of an entire species 'somehow askew': 'evidence' of a collective energy fated to self-expenditure in repeated struggle, 'accidents,' and breakdown. The mass death marking the insects' quick end seemed entirely forgettable – just so much predictably failed debris, dusted away again at the end of another 'season.'

'[R]eflecting on accidents / of *all kinds*' – evolutionary as well as domestic, phylogenetic as well as ontogenetic (*SD*, 72, emphasis added) – the rhythms and mood of *A Stone Diary* enact what Lowther called elsewhere 'the delicate polar dance / of atoms,' 'the lovely and necessary / balance of opposites.'[29] For every anemone, octopus, or hermit crab supplying 'evidence' of a 'progressive' evolution toward 'higher destinies' there were 'windrows' of dead craneflies to belie that scenario. 'A Sometime Waffler' by more than just her political affinities, Lowther absorbed the apparent discrepancies of her natural habitat, along with its 'lovely' accord. And as she kept making her 'notes,' so she kept doing her 'delicate polar dance' between 'opposites.'

∽

During the mid-sixties, around the time she was working in that '#@! insurance office' and firing off mostly so-so poems to magazines like *Ganglia*, Lowther found herself thinking about a 'news item' she had recently read. 'It was weeks ago now, but it's lodged in my mind, and keeps repeating itself': 'o Sybaris o Sybaris.' The 'news item' about 'the ancient city of Sybaris' so intrigued her that she took the time to scribble it down for herself 'weeks' later:

> Archeologists in Southern Italy have discovered the site of the ancient city of Sybaris, where life was reputed to be so sweet that the adjective 'sybaritic' originated in its name ... But it's the way that it was found that has hooks and barbs. Someone has invented an instrument which measures disturbances in the earth's magnetic field. And the thousands-of-years-dead city had made a change in the earth's magnetic pattern. Not the buildings, nor even the excavations, the cutting and shaping men do to create their livable geometries, but the people themselves, the press of living, moving, interacting people gathered in Sybaris have left their magnetism printed into the structure of the world, detectable even now.[30]

The stone diarist who would eventually come to record her own metamorphosis into rock began then by thinking about 'ancient' places where people actually had once been 'swallowed' by 'stones,' but left a trace of their presence 'printed into the structure of the world, detectable even now.' In this vein, one of the first archaeologically based poems she attempted was 'Skin over Pompeii,' which begins: 'That city houses in / my hollow self / ... my skin tents over catacombs / populous as all sub-cellars.' The 'hooks and barbs' of Sybaris, however, extended also to such works as 'Imagine Their Generations,' unpublished during Lowther's lifetime.[31] As with 'the stone bone and breath / of those dry mouths' of Pompeii, 'Imagine Their Generations' reimagines once again her notebook entry's excited 'press of living, moving, interacting people,' long dead, but yet somehow still alive, 'their magnetism' imprinted in earth and stone. Buried 'in a vertical frieze,' these 'generations' also compose a *tableau vivant* of 'ambiguous' postures and gestures. Their arrested 'shapes' form the 'calyx' of a past present which is frozen and contained. But 'theirs' is a time frame also specifically linked, at the poem's end, to coal, an energy source in and for the future: 'Imagine now time itself grown dense / as coal, impacted' (*TC*, 188).

Carbon-14, the coal derivative, has one of the longest half-lives known to science – longer even than the strontium-90 Lowther worried about as a result of nuclear tests. And in her case, the compaction of 'time' into 'coal' was certainly apt, not in the least because of the prominence of that mineral in her own family history. Once recorded in her note-books, the idea of the past's *physical* persistence into the present – whether by way of electromagnetic waves, chemical energy traces, or more purely solid artifacts – was also one that would just not let go, its 'hooks and barbs' persisting right through to the work of her last book. There, in *A Stone Diary*'s final section, surrounded by what Geddes termed those 'tough poems about current events, women's lib ... and ... the city scapes,' the ancient, 'thousands-of-years-dead city' reappears most vividly in the form of 'The Dig.'

A three-part poem originally published in the *Antigonish Review* in 1974, 'The Dig' consists of a prologue and two titled, subsequent sec-tions, 'The Diggers' and 'The Bones.' In *A Stone Diary*, the untitled pro-logue is typographically suppressed to the very bottom of the page, obliging the reader's eye to 'dig' down in order even to hit print. It is a *modern* city to which the reader's gaze is initially drawn – but one whose busy byways and 'conduits' quickly open up to the Pompeii- or Sybaris-like 'populous sub-cellars' of 'the ancient world' below:

> Even where traffic passes
> the ancient world has exposed
> a root, large and impervious,
> humped like a dragon
> among the city's conduits.
> *Look, they say,*
> *who would have thought*
> *the thing so tough,*
> *so secretive?* (*SD*, 89, emphasis in the original)

Recalling the 'naive root atom / of philosophy's first molecule,' the 'large and impervious' 'root' of the material past now becomes 'the thing' philosophized by the scientists, 'the diggers' of the present: '*who would have thought ...?*' But the italicized voice that obtrudes in the poem's opening sequence also immediately raises further questions.

Who is the speaker who thus relays the words of the awestruck archaeologists at 'The Dig' site? And where is that voice speaking from, in time and space?

The prologue hints at the structural ambiguity of 'The Dig' in general. The two-part sequence which follows the prologue *seems* to set up a straightforward series of oppositions between 'the diggers' and the dug-up: between, respectively, present and past, male and female, subject and object, living and dead, unfinished and unpredictable versus 'finished' and 'completed' (*SD*, 90–1). But these neat demarcations between 'now' and 'then' and their correlative attributes are almost completely destabilized by the poem's strangely disembodied speaker and its slippery pronominal shifts between 'them' and 'we.' In 'The Diggers,' as in the preceding prologue, 'they' refers clearly enough to the male 'diggers,' as set against the 'we' of the italics, the voice of the feminine 'bones': '*Will our bones tell / what we died of?* (*SD*, 90). At least initially, the poem appears to inscribe the speaker as the choric mouthpiece of the excavated, 'ancient' feminine past. At the same time, the future conditional form of the question she poses also opens the possibility of a speaker who interjects from the contemporary present of 'the diggers' themselves.

The poem's final section, 'The Bones,' further complicates matters. It begins with an indeterminately anchored 'we' and segues into an italicized interjection that is no longer the voice of '*our* bones' from the past – or the present:

> The men we see always swift
> moving, edged with a running light
> like fire; their hands infinitely
> potent ...
>
> The women we see finished
> completed like fat jars,
> like oil floating on water:
> breasts   bellies   faces
> all round and calm.
>
> *Their bones should thrash*
> *in the diggers' baskets,*
> *should scream against the light.* (*SD*, 91)

'We' now appears to refer, inclusively, to a contemporary feminist consciousness, thinking about perceptions of men and women; about the violation of 'the bones" extraction; and about the conditions of life for our 'ancient' sisters in a phallocentric culture that 'worshipp[ed] the cock.' 'Bent' and broken 'over and over' by the 'miraculous' fertility of 'their' own desires and domestic labours – childbirth and grinding grain alike – 'they fell away at last / they became bone' (*SD*, 91–2). Subsequently, though, the poem's last italicized passage, its final stanza, reverts once more to the voice that speaks of '*our* bones':

> *Will our bones tell*
> *sisters, what we died of?*
> *how love broke us*
> *in that helplessly desired*
> *breaking, and men*
> *and children ransacked our flesh,*
> *cracked our innermost bones*
> *to eat the morrow* (*SD*, 92)

Like that 'star-shaped I' who 'stumbled nauseated' backwards and forwards through time in *Milk Stone*'s 'In the Continent behind My Eyes,' the undifferentiated voice(s) of 'The Dig' are multidimensional in space and multidirectional in time, situated both within and beyond the archaeological past, both inside and outside of the modern present. Lowther underscored the doubleness of her poem's temporality even in its last line, whose pun on bone 'marrow' is perhaps less to the point than its infinite aim at the future – '*to eat the morrow*' – by means of an archaism or 'ancient' relic dug up, as it were, from the linguistic past. But then, she was, after all, writing 'The Dig' by 1973, right around the time she was also working on the space-time curves of her *Infinite Mirror Trip*, and telling Fred Cogswell about her plans for 'science fiction poems' featuring Hatshepsut. The possibilities of travel in time and space – and language – were clearly on her mind anyway.

The intriguing effect of 'The Dig' is rather like that of a deliberately squinting modifier, moving meaning in two directions at once and, no doubt, accounting for the fact that the poem has been read by reviewers as *either* a past-oriented address about 'the role of women in history' (Levenson 1978: 353) *or* a 'speculat[ion]' 'on what future archeologists will make of the bones of twentieth-century women when they dig them up' (Fulford 1977: 71). In addition to the shell game she was playing with the subject in the plural addresses of 'The Dig,' Lowther's highly conscious use of verb tenses and mood was essential to achieving this effect. (These were among the morphological issues she had considered while comparing Inuktituk words and phrases to English structures.) And the implications of her technique in this regard are once again far-reaching. Earlier, she dangled 'fat red lanterns' to illuminate the paradox of a historical past that was yet to arrive at 'Furry Creek.' Now, in choosing a future conditional and interrogative mode for a choric voice that seems to speak, at least in part, *for* and *from* the past, Lowther was suggesting more than merely that past's persistence in – or return to – the present as a physical fact. In this case, the past, far from being 'finished' or 'complete,' also specifically announces itself as an incomplete and undecided 'thing' – '*Will our bones tell / sisters, what we died of ?*' When heard as the voice of 'bones' long buried, the italicized portions of the poem articulate a historical past that is never really past, over, done with, fixed, or determined at all. It is a past that, in its incompletion, is instead much like the present; and, in its as-yet-undecided open-endedness, much like the future, too.

Lowther's 'Dig' thus reiterated the 'cloudy' idea of time operative in that 'counterintuitive' elemental realm that she found so engrossing. As the scientists at 'Sybaris' had suggested to her, archaeological time had plenty to do with kinetic energy at molecular levels – with electrically charged particles, for example, and with the distribution of mass and energy in electromagnetic and gravitational 'force fields.' 'But it's the way that it was found that has hooks and barbs,' she'd emphasized then, marvelling over the technology that now allowed researchers to measure 'disturbances in the earth's magnetic field.' Notably, *the way that it was found* is the one question that never does surface in 'The Dig,' a poem which simply proceeds from the mouth of the excavation pit without ever indicating how – or exactly where – 'it was found.' Those were questions that Lowther quietly, cleverly displaced onto the formal structure of her poem instead, rerouting as queries to be asked about how and from where the poem is told. In doing so, she ultimately directs readers' attention to a speaker who herself functions, in effect, as a kind of 'magnetic force field,' altering or 'disturbing' readers' experience and perception of space-time, as force fields tend to do. And all the while conveying also the incredible 'magnetism' of old 'bones,' 'printed into the structure of the world, detectable even now.'

Wherever in the world it may have been that Lowther imagined 'The Dig' of her *Stone Diary,* what is recovered of women's lives there is not very 'sybaritic.' The archaeological site, too, 'is a *pit*' (*SD*, 30, emphasis added). 'Before their falling away,' the women are hardened by 'an anger' against those they also 'helplessly desired,' 'the men / and children' who 'ransacked our flesh / cracked our innermost bones':

> But before their falling away
> was an anger,
> a stone in the mouth.
> They would say there is
> a great fall like water,
> a mask taking shape on air,
> a sound coming nearer
> like a heavy animal
> breaking twigs. (*SD*, 92)

Here, near the end of her *Stone Diary,* Lowther was once again sounding the notes of what Eugene McNamara had stressed as her work's preoccupation with 'the primitive self within, dormant but alive' (1977: 24). By way of a closing movement for her collection, she allowed the influx of an atavistic vision which was followed up, after 'The Dig,' with the thunder of a 'Cataract' ('a great fall like water') and, in the last poem, with the ominous stirring of 'a heavy animal' 'coming nearer' (*SD*, 93, 94). Whereas the opening, title poem of *A Stone Diary* had offered another happy fusion with the 'first things / trees / gravel / rocks' (*SD*, 37), the closing poem presented an altogether different kind of 'beast.' Using a musical time signature as her operative metaphor, Lowther now listened to 'the silence between' intervals of sound, artfully composed and arranged: 'In the silence between the / notes of music / something is moving: / an animal / with the eyes of a man' (*SD*, 94). 'It is as if,' the poem continues, 'huge' 'migrations take place / between the steps of music' (*SD*, 94). But it is *not* 'as if' these 'migrations' take to wing as 'migrating birds,' those 'half-breeds of the future' which once gave Lowther a 'tentative kind of hope' that 'we humans' had avoided the terminal end 'of our evolutionary cycle' (*MMD*, 80).

Perhaps, the last poem allows, we 'advance' the 'progressions' of our civilizations intermittently, with 'civilized' pursuits like music and science. But the 'journey' that here begins, once again, in particles of light, with 'photons / from the outer / galaxies,' ultimately issues in a consciousness that balances precariously 'between' its mutual recognition of the human in the animal, and the animal in the 'civilized' or 'evolved' human. So while 'we begin also / advancing / between / progressions of music,' 'we' are finally left 'suspended' 'between earths / our heads full of leaves / our eyes like / the eyes of humans' (*SD*, 94, 95). With this one final simile that not even 'Dee' Livesay would have wanted to edit, the latent animality of the human is literally the last 'print' made in *A Stone Diary*, a book that began with the poet making 'blood prints' with her hands on the stones that she saw *lived* all around her, 'breathing as naturally / as animals' (*SD*, 8).

Like the lion of Henri Rousseau's *Sleeping Gypsy*, it is an ambiguously complex and unpredictable 'animal' that moves in the 'silences' between the lines of *A Stone Diary*. To some degree, the *Diary* is, 'naturally,' an autobiographical 'beast': a record of Lowther's own growth into feminist consciousness, and the 'animal' of that 'anger'; a record of her own 'stone in the mouth' 'anger' at the circumstances to which her personal life had devolved; and a record of her awareness, too, of the 'heavy animal' of male 'anger' that she knew she was living with, that she could hear 'breaking twigs' and tramping around 'in the silences between' the noise and the music, the arguments and the happier distractions, that filled her everyday family life.

But the haunting spectre of 'an animal / with the eyes of a man' is also of a piece with the emphasis of Lowther's ecological vision in general, a vision distinctively refined in her late poetry, and taken up through her environmental involvements as well. The 'beasts' bestirred in *A Stone Diary* are always also, first and foremost, the 'royal animals' disturbed by human intrusions; the atomic after-shadows of blasted rocks; the slowly accumulating, retributive 'weight' of gravel and trees devoured without restraint or thanks. All of these, like the detritus of 'thousands-of-years-dead' cities, or 'the dung and debris' of more recent 'generations' (*SD*, 56), insist as material energies 'printed into the structure of the world, detectable even now.' Together, they make for what she called elsewhere a 'twitching frothing planet' that 'stings' the 'nerves / like clouds of insects' (*TC*, 225). Most creatures, as Lowther knew, would bite back, especially when provoked.

She had already poked the hermit crabs to test this out.

'The work of men / will all be undone' by 'the work of men' (*TC*, 205). Evidence of environmental tampering and what Lowther recognized as the 'cellular memory' of its biological and social effects is still piling up, and still pressing on toward impending crises – to the end point, perhaps, of an 'evolutionary cycle' or the survival of any species, never mind whatever 'land is left.' Thirty years later, we are still shoring up our South Valley dams, and still 'waiting' for either 'the weight' of our 'past' or 'the hard bite' of our 'future' to bring us down, like 'old Rex.'

'Our minds will create counter-arguments to ecological awareness,' the American poet William Heyen points out. 'Our minds will find a hundred intricate ways to distract attention from what, it seems to me, must be the central thing we must be thinking about.' It is not as though we are unaware of the inevitably self-sabotaging and immoral consequences of a whole host of collective behaviours that throw the future into question, he stresses: 'Do we have to be struck over the head with a hammer? ... Will we get used to the warnings until we're bored, or will we, with all the intensity we can call up in ourselves, keep this precariousness of our existence on earth in mind?' He questions the very possibility of sustaining the latter sort of 'intensity.' 'It may be that the one thing we are physiologically unable, *unable* to think about is this coming death': '... we can't concentrate on this possibility, can't imagine our beloved earth within a silence devoid of human presence' – devoid of us (1998: 90–1, 94, 96; emphasis in the original). Not really, or not for long. Because industry and avoidance usually go on hand in hand, constructing, as Lowther herself quite rightly noted, 'green living rooms built / on the edge of denial' (*TC*, 214).

Chapter 17

'History, and Context, and Continuity'

While she was plotting her moves for the manuscript of *A Stone Diary* in the spring of 1975, Lowther received an exciting invitation from afar. Réshard Gool, a political scientist, novelist, and editor with Square Deal Publications, based in Charlottetown, was organizing a series of summer readings for a 'Poetry & Music' festival in his home province. The program, 'very generously funded by the Canada Council,' would feature performances by such writers as Alden Nowlan, Miriam Waddington, Joe Rosenblatt, Milton Acorn, Austin Clarke, Eli Mandel, and Dave Godfrey, reading at various parks and heritage sites on Prince Edward Island. As coordinator of the event, Gool wrote to offer Lowther a spot also – for, as it turned out, the inaugural date of the summer series, in mid-July. Of course, she jumped at the prospect: aside from the chance to promote her work, the idea of visiting an island on the nation's Atlantic seaboard was too enticing to resist. And, since she had some League business to take care of anyway, the trip would be an opportune time to stop by Toronto again. Perhaps, if she had not already done so, this would be her chance to return that inadvertently purloined Toronto city map to Arlene. 'Your plan sounds really great,' she wrote to Gool, confirming the date shortly after his invitation arrived in March. 'It all sounds like great fun.'[1]

As usual, however, there was that troublesome matter of the 'bread' that would have to be brought to the table before the 'great fun' could begin. 'P.S.' she scrawled across the bottom of her typewritten reply to Gool: 'Is there any chance Canada Council might advance fares for those of us who have to come across country?' At the time, Lowther's personal finances were on the upswing. The Interim Arts Board honorarium was about to kick in, and, as she informed Arlene Lampert,

Gool's invitation arrived the same month that she also discovered she would be 'taking George McWhirter's place at UBC, at least part time, while he's on sabbatical. Damn good thing the League's getting a secretary!'[2] But that was 'bread' in the future, not present, tense and didn't solve the problem of purchasing a $400 plane ticket by July. That was simply an astronomical sum, almost three times the $160 that the Lowthers barely scraped together for monthly rent.

In reminiscences he recorded around 1977, Réshard Gool recollects Lowther also phoning him about the air-fare issue, and sounding 'apologetic' for asking him to approach the Canada Council for an advance on her behalf. He suggested finding a Vancouver travel agency willing to advance credit. But for a family still relying sporadically on social assistance, with a husband unemployed and a wife under-gainfully employed, this was not likely to happen. In fact, Gool expressed amazement at Lowther's evident amazement that such credit was an option – for some people. He said he realized then 'how lacking in confidence she was.'[3] By June, not having heard back from Gool, Lowther was getting nervous, because what she really 'lacked' was cash. She wrote to 'Dear Réshard' again:

> It occurs to me I should find out exactly where in P.E.I. I'll be reading July 12. I guess it will make some difference in travel arrangements. I assume Canada Council turned thumbs down on advance fares, so I'll do my best to find a wealthy patron ...
>
> Also, is there a cheap accommodation? I would assume my best plan would be to arrive in Charlottetown on the night of the 11th. The other flight, that arrives there in the afternoon, is really impossible. One would arrive exhausted. And I intend to enjoy my stay there![4]

In the end, Gool played the role of 'wealthy patron' by advancing the money for Lowther's trip, and between them, they also practised 'a little deception' (as Lowther called it) on the Canada Council, apparently to pay for the extra cost of her stopping in Toronto.[5]

And while Lowther did indeed make good on her intentions to enjoy her trip, when the time came, her journey barely qualified as a 'stay' anywhere. She left Vancouver on Saturday, July 12, and was back by Thursday, the 17th, because Roy insisted that anything longer was too long for her to be gone. During that time, she also made a point of phoning home, no doubt to deflect the kind of criticism that had greeted her upon her return from the ten-day Ontario tour the fall before. This time, however, Roy brushed off the gesture of her phone call as 'hardly need-ful for a 5-day jaunt, and besides the girls were asleep' when she called. And besides that, he knew she'd packed in her luggage a rather sexy new blouse of which he did not approve (RLJ, 1:67).

Though she left a day before her reading, she 'arrive[d] exhausted' anyway. Among other hassles, the long flight to Montreal had been delayed, and her luggage was not on the connecting flight to Charlot-tetown with her, as she discovered upon arrival. In the luggage she had once again borrowed from her mother, Lowther had packed most of the new clothes she had recently purchased; there had been hopes that the CBC might televise this reading series, and she wanted to look her best. Still worse, most of the poems she planned to read were also stowed in that wayward suitcase, which Air Canada promptly reunited her with – the day *after* her reading.

In the meantime, her maritime hosts, Réshard Gool and his partner, Hilda Woolnough, did what they could to help re-compose the 'flus-tered' new arrival. Hilda, a visual artist, lent her guest an elaborately embroidered caftan dress of heavy cotton to wear for her appearance at the Howatt Fruit Farm reading the next day. The two women hit it off immediately, according to Hilda, and talked away 'most of the night' before the reading. In a letter Hilda wrote many years later to Christine Lowther, she recalled her conversations with Pat, that night, about 'her life, family, the poets' league, B.C., etc.':

I asked her what she most wanted to do in her life + she said, 'One day – to be organized.' She felt very inadequate domestically, and was trying des-perately to be what she thought was expected of her at home. She said she thought she could manage to keep a houseboat in order, and hoped one day ... to live on one.

In the same letter, Hilda also recounted in fine detail the day of the reading, a spectacular summer's day on the Island:

The reading was way out in the country at Howatt's Fruit Farm in Tyron, a beautiful heritage spot by the sea with a magnificent, prize-winning gar-den. We drove to the farm in an old white Ford ½ ton truck with Pat try-ing to remember her poems. Writing down bits of what she could remember with a borrowed red pen on scrap paper. The paper balanced on a library book on her knees. (R. got the University library to open up on a Sunday!)

With her artist's eye, Hilda recalled how, as Lowther read that afternoon, the sunlight picked up 'golden flecks of light' in her long hair and in the threads of the borrowed dress. The audience lounged 'on the dappled grass' around her, 'people eating huge red strawberries from wicker baskets,' fruit provided by Everett and Betty Howatt. Standing beneath a 'hundred-year-old willow tree,' Lowther looked, Réshard said, like 'a slip of a woman, frizzy wisps of hair' blowing gently across her pale face.[6]

Unnerved by her unexpected separation from the texts she wanted to read, Lowther was struggling with her memory on that bucolic afternoon, trying – with her 'borrowed red pen'– to remember exactly phrases and fragments from the works she had packed into the suitcase. Memory, as she knew, was a 'complex kind of witness.' Especially under pressure, it was a 'witness' that could often be 'buried' more easily than 'dug up' on demand. On the audiotape recording of this reading, she candidly addressed her strawberry-munching audience:

One of the few poems that survived the journey with me, ... got to Prince Edward Island with me, is from a thing that is still in progress, called 'Time Capsule.' Which is sort of envisioned as a complex kind of witness that maybe has been buried, or – and is dug up at some time in the future ... It starts out with a physical description of human beings that goes something like this [reads poem 'Bipeds']. And then it goes on through some things I've forgotten, like skin,'clown's coat,' 'spectrum of odor,' 'arena of all our wars and meeting place,' and, uh, things about the hands, 'agile pentacles,' and so on. And eventually it gets into things like history, and context, and continuity.

The 'thing' that was 'still in progress, called "Time Capsule,"' may have been that 'collection (distant future, at this rate)' to which Lowther alluded, that same summer, in her letter to her *Stone Diary* publisher, William Toye. But her comments on July 13 also imply that the 'Time Capsule' in question, beginning with the short poem 'Bipeds,' may have been conceived as a poem sequence in the vein of short-poem series she had attempted before, such as the largely abandoned 'The Origin of the Universe.' In either case, whether it was a book-length collection or merely a title cycle she had in mind, she was outlining work-in-progress that, rather like 'The Dig' of her *Stone Diary*, pointed in two directions simultaneously: to future work that promised 'eventually' to return to questions of the past, and to that past's flexible 'continuities' with the present.

In the midst of her remarks under the old willow tree that day, Lowther read 'Bipeds' as an example of the 'physical description of human beings' at the outset of her 'Time Capsule' project. The poem, which she later reworked and retitled as 'The Animals Per Se' (*TC*, 185), went 'something like this':

> Bipeds, but that is not important
> what's important is
> the structure is inside
> like an idea, the act shaping the will
>
> The student should bear in mind
> the corollary of internal structure:
> the creatures were unbelievably fragile.

Mid-way through 1975, Lowther was still searching for that ideal of immanent form she had first carved out for herself in such works as 'Woman on/against Snow,' still on the lookout for that elusive 'corollary of internal structure' that would present the nicest 'welding' of a 'thing' and its 'idea,' of the material and the metaphysical.

Contrary to its cheeky first line, moreover, the bipedalism of 'the creatures' in 'Bipeds' *was* 'important' – as 'important' as the 'sinewy pentacles' of 'Their Hands,' another 'Time Capsule' poem, which zeroed in on the evolutionary milestone of 'the creatures'' opposable thumbs 'in their / oiled sockets': 'infinite shape makers / stubborn and daring movers' of ingenuity, craft, and 'daring' folly all at once (*TC*, 186). The 'Time Capsule' poems may have been leaving the 'invertebrate' order behind, but again, these examples suggest unmistakable 'continuities' with the evolutionary, anthropological, and archaeological substance of work Lowther produced from *Milk Stone* onwards.

Like a galactic spiral with its constant and contiguous loops of 'beginning again,' hers was indeed 'the structure of a peculiarly historical consciousness' (White 1978: 41). It was not just that was she was still 'digging' around in some of the same sciences and social sciences that had drawn her attention even before the decade's advent. The constant retrieval and rearticulation of evolutionary (and devolutionary) concerns in each of her successive 'new' works – *Milk Stone, Infinite Mirror Trip, A Stone Diary*, and 'Time Capsule' – also add up to a body of work that in itself enacts an idea of 'creative evolution,' as she would have been familiar with that concept through Henri Bergson. Bergson stressed that his theory of 'durational time' was, above all, based upon plural, open-ended, and overlapping orders of temporal reality:

> [D]uration is not merely one instant replacing another; if it were, there would never be anything but the present – no prolonging of the past into the actual, no evolution, no concrete duration. Duration is the continuous progress of the past which gnaws into the future and which swells as it advances. And as the past grows without ceasing, so also there is no limit to its preservation. (1949: 60)

The perfusion of the past within the flux of the present and forming future was also the 'first molecule' animating the 'philosophy' of Lowther's poetics and politics. From her unwritten Hatshepsut poems to her unfinished 'Time Capsule,' and in most of what she accomplished in between, the sum of her life's work speaks directly to the 'continuous progress of the past,' a cumulative, recombinant work-in-process, on-going into the present.

Not accidentally, it was the subject of history that the author of *This Difficult Flowring* once remembered having almost failed – having been granted merely 'a conditional pass' as a 'final mark' in her 'Mid-Term Exam' (*DF,* 20). Not really recognizing the past as past might have made for problems with history teachers. Unlike her driver's test, however, this was one score Lowther was compelled to re-address.

Aside from her broad focus on the natural history of the cosmos and 'the origin of species' in general, Lowther quietly but continuously re-evaluated her cultural 'heritage,' her family 'inheritance,' and her personal relationship to a family past that also changed over time. These were facets of her own 'history, and context, and continuity' that she did not generally share with her literary friends, or with her NDP acquaintances on 'pub nites' at Hillcrest Hall, either. In fact, for a writer every bit as preoccupied with 'origins' and 'beginnings' as she was with death and ends, it is striking how rarely she seems to have discussed her family history with friends, virtually none of whom can recall her speaking about her mother, her father, or her early North Vancouver origins. Nevertheless, her marriages to William Domphousse and to Roy Lowther were not the only intimate bonds affected by her 'creative evolution,' especially with the increasing success and demands of her career during the seventies.

Though philosophers like Bergson spoke, theoretically, of 'no limit' to the 'preservation' of the accumulating and 'advancing' past, Lowther also recognized that the living past was nevertheless, to recoup a phrase from 'Bipeds,' 'unbelievably fragile.' It would linger as an energy to be 'mined' in the present only so long as its physical traces were also actively preserved. Conservation of the past was a keynote she had stressed all along. 'Visit to Olympus,' from 1968, offers a case in point. A comment on 'generations' of resource industries as shaping factors in the cultural history of her province, 'Visit to Olympus' was written after a trip to one of British Columbia's 'ghost towns' from the fifties, as she explained:

> The terrible thing that happens to a lot of the towns on the Coast is that you'll have a little mining town or a logging settlement that's built and owned entirely by one company, and when it's no longer profitable to them, they simply ... shut down, and the people have to move away. And not only do they shut down, but eventually – and particularly, if anyone shows any interest in the site – they'll go and burn it to the ground so there's nothing left ... I think possibly the rationale might be, 'Oh, some-body'll go into one of those buildings and have a beam fall on them and sue us' or something, but I find it very annoying. There's a certain ambi-ence about these places that really should be a part of our heritage. It makes me angry when some capitalist – usually foreign capitalist – comes and burns it all down.[7]

As an extension of her 'documentary' political poetry, historically based works such as 'Visit to Olympus' reiterate Lowther's sense of the archival nature of the writer's job, her obligation to ensure that certain pasts not be eliminated from the visible and official record – and certainly not for the purposes of assuaging the litigious paranoia of 'some capitalist – usually foreign.'

Along the same lines, among the drafts in one of her *last* notebooks, the 'Music Dictation' scribbler, is a poem entitled by a date alone, '1913.' About two mining brothers – Eastern European immigrants, gauging from their names, 'Antol' and 'Stan' – '1913' is a late poem that 'gets into things like history, and context, and continuity.' Along with 'The Animals Per Se,' 'Their Hands,' and 'Imagine Their Genera-tions,' '1913" may have been among the handful of works which Lowther envisioned as part of her next 'Time Capsule' project. At least, since 'Imagine Their Generations,' with its mineral-based metaphor of time, seemed to figure as part of the 'Time Capsule' project, it would make sense that Lowther may also have planned to include a vein of poems like '1913,' works that continued to excavate the 'generations' of mining history so central to her home territory and her own personal past.

A brief narrative poem, '1913' chronicles 'Stan's' death in the 'lice / and stench of the bunkhouse.' When 'Antol goes to the boss' to collect 'his brother's pay,' he is informed that he, in fact, 'owes the boss / for his brother's keep': 'sick time, board on rainy days / overalls towels a pick handle' all amount to more than Stanislaw's pitifully small, accumulated wage. Whereupon Antol 'curses the boss / and jumps work,' disappearing into a 'big' country with 'a pocketful of matches / and a few sentences of English' (*TC*, 215). Lowther essentially highlights the obscurity of the immigrant labourers, both the brother who dies in the bunkhouse, and the one who takes off after that tragedy. 'Maybe he makes town' – maybe not: 'the country's too big / for anyone to ask' (*TC*, 216).

The apparently fictitious historical vignette of '1913' resonates with the story of Lowther's own family history. For one thing, the date itself coincides with a 1913 Nanaimo miners' strike to which Lowther appears to allude, elsewhere, in another of her 'History Lessons' (*TC*, 191). Discernible also are faint shades of the fate of her immigrant great-grandfather, William Wilks, and the son who also 'jumped work' in the mines after his father's death, with a head full of ideas as incendiary as any 'pocketful of matches.' Once again an exercise in 'Imagin[ing] Their Generations,' '1913' directs attention to all but anonymous individual lives of toil. At the same time, it also points up the entanglement of public 'heritage' and personal history in Lowther's imagination. The threats posed by corporate monopolies of 'foreign capital' were one matter, and fairly easy game for socialist critique. But where it came to the record of her own family past, Lowther often found herself more conflicted. Particularly down on through the Wilks-McCain branch of the family tree there were more than one or two sprouting 'capitalists' whom she could count among her own people. Even the firebrand James Wilks had, after all, aged into a much more conservative, liquor-vending version of his youthful trade unionist self.

'History Lessons,' from 1967, provides an early indication of this ambivalence, which is perhaps why Lowther did not include the poem, along with her 'Mid-Term Exam,' in *This Difficult Flowring*.[8] The 'family legends' recounted in the first two sequences of 'History Lessons' alternately spoof the entrepreneurial aspirations running through her family history, and celebrate that family's defiant spunk. The first 'legend' is of a 'great-uncle' who returns from the Klondike panhandle as a 'diamond-fingered / pearl-pinned' wealthy man, not because he ever 'put hand to shovel / or panned a stream,' but because 'he opened barber shops.' The second 'legend' evokes the memory of Eliza McCain, the English-born mother of Lowther's grandmother, Annie. 'Slip' of a woman though she was reputed to have been, Eliza is called up by her great-granddaughter as a heroic figure of resistance during a coal miners' strike in which the militia are summoned – possibly, the famous fracas of 1913, in which the regiment of 'Bowser's Seventy Twa' was called · in:[9]

> Eliza McCain,
> height five foot one,
> when the government ordered striking coal miners
> (and everyone else)
> off the streets of Nanaimo,
> threatened to thrash a six-foot militiaman
> with her umbrella (*TC*, 191)

In the poem, the militiaman wisely gives way to Eliza's umbrella, and both these family stories, apocryphal 'legends,' pave the way for the third and last 'History Lesson.' This last 'lesson' illustrates the retroactive power of the present as a filter of the past to much less amusing effect: after the fall of the Nazis, a soldier stationed in Japan contemplates the impossibility of ever recovering the original integrity of the 'old so old' symbol of the swastika (*TC*, 192).

Steadily, slowly, and in no particular chronological order, Lowther worked her way through subsequent 'generations' of her family over the course of her writing career. Eventually, she moved on from 'Eliza McCain' to Eliza's daughter, Annie. Annie McCain-Wilks died in 1949, when her granddaughter was only fourteen. Even as an adolescent, however, Pat had apparently begun to argue with her grandmother over politics. Her cousin Barry remembers one such stand-off between the two, over the issue of Annie's disdain for the Chinese.[10] Consequently, long after Annie's passing, it was a complicated 'Inheritance' that Lowther was left to sort out. 'Annie McCain bequeathed to me / her lace,' *A Stone Diary*'s 'Inheritance' begins. 'Yards and yards' of 'doilies and tablecloth edging':

> She must have imagined me
> in the citrus smell
> of furniture polish
> gleaming walnut and oak
> pouring tea from a silver pot
>
> She should have known even then
> I'd be something else
> useless at owning things
> up to my head in books (*SD*, 14)

Annie's 'tatting' is pretty, but pretty much 'useless' to the granddaughter: it 'runs through my all-thumbs / like something I can't / even regret.' The grandmother is guilty of having *mis*-imagined the future generation in her own image: 'She should have known even then / I'd be useless at owning things.'[11]

But Lowther's resentment over the assumption that she should covet the same middle-class 'things' – gleaming furniture and silver tea pots – that her grandmother evidently valued is also tempered by an adult poet's affectionate longing. 'I'd rather have had / her old corsets,' she eventually confesses, 'or her brass bed,' or 'her rocking chair' – all the heirloom 'things' that might bear the imprint of Annie's now absent body. And finally, the granddaughter also comes to recognize a powerful parallel between Annie's 'long life of making' and her own creativity: lace doilies and 'hard-edged' poems were but different expressions of a 'spinning female thing' they shared. In the end, the lace was like one of those suspension bridges Lowther was familiar with from the rugged environs around North Vancouver: it was a tie that bound the different sides of a divide, as much as it measured the gulf between them.

In one of her notebook entries, Lowther once made a cryptic remark to the effect that all of her 'ghosts' were women. Strictly speaking, this wasn't entirely true – the presence of James Wilks lingered, as did her father, after his death, in poems such as 'Posthumous Christmas Eve,' among others (*TC*, 200). But part of Lowther's feminist flowering did involve a kind of deliberate thinking back through her foremothers, as Virginia Woolf once styled it. In the notebook entry, her remark about the femininity of her 'ghosts' was specifically linked to a 'long ago' memory of 'Annie, weeping with shame and anger at a friend's betrayal.'[12] But Lowther's familiar female ghosts were clearly multi-generational, including not only Eliza McCain, as well as Annie, but Annie's daughters, too. So when she conjured her 'grandmother's house' in the poem 'Haunting,' it was a 'house' peopled by the 'ghosts' of 'grandma and all the Aunts,' still walking about, though now 'without / their crinkled, flower-talcumed flesh' (*MS*, 70). Most palpable among those 'Aunts' was the 'ghost' of Virginia's older sister, Isabelle.

The life that had awaited Isabelle upon her return to North Vancouver in 1929 had fallen far short of the 'brilliant future' which the press had been forecasting for the lovely and talented star of 'The Speeders' touring musical revue during the 'roaring twenties.' Her handsome American lover, the pianist-composer Harry Stover, seems inexplicably to have faded from the scene. She never did marry, or pursue her stage career. Age, and an eventual diagnosis of multiple sclerosis put an end to that, and left her to live, toward the end of her life, on a meagre disability pension. After Isabelle died, in 1965, Lowther noted that among the possessions her aunt left behind was a box filled with 'posed and costumed photos, / programmes, / sheet music / beiged clippings attesting [to her] triumphs, / applause of crowds, / fragrance like dusty flowers.' Along with the press clippings and assorted mementos of Isabelle's American stage career are dozens and dozens of letters and cards from the long gone Harry Stover.

Lowther's lines about her aunt's 'posed and costumed photos' come from a poem she drafted upon Isabelle's death, entitled 'The Comet: An Elegy.' Attaining nothing near the subdued undercurrents of the 'Inheritance' connected to Annie McCain, 'The Comet' remained unpublished during Lowther's lifetime.[13] It is of interest mainly as a record of her fraught relation with the 'Belle' of her mother's family. Sharply, even violently ambivalent in more than its tone alone, it is the tremendous struggle of 'The Comet' with its own 'elegiac' mandate that is most remarkable. The poem recounts in retrospect the brutal and protracted process of Isabelle's final illness and death. It is a deathbed attended by the niece, as she admits, only out of 'duty,' with 'clumsy pity' and 'false smalltalk' (*TC*, 176, 178). 'Belle' is characterized bluntly as 'a woman full of pretenses, / enacting a rich and peopled life / among borrowed children / and lovers only dreamed' (*TC*, 175). Though Lowther is not unmoved by the 'animal ignominy of death,' it is only at the end of nine pages that are almost as painfully drawn out as Isabelle's last decline that the elegist can finally recall having summoned from herself an *intention* to offer a meaningfully compassionate gesture. And by then, it's too late: 'For as I remembered / and planned what I would say to you / you died / with my one gift   unreturned' (*TC*, 179).

The 'one gift,' ungiven as much as 'unreturned,' was the *intention* to prompt the dying Isabelle to remember one of her most vivid memories, the fabulous spectacle of a comet which she witnessed one sultry night of her youth, and still spoke of 'thirty and forty and fifty years / later' (*TC*, 177, 172). Even in this 'one' last, would-be 'gift' there is a barbed edge, a hook to which Lowther's 'elegy' appears genuinely blind. There were probably reasons why the spectacle of a downward diving 'comet' lodged in the memory of an older Isabelle, the former vaudeville star, and they could not have been all happy. Just as well, perhaps, that this was one 'gift' too late for the giving.

Seven years before she took another 'starry idea' toward entirely new and more encompassing astrophysical ends, 'The Comet' is about the strongest evidence Lowther left behind regarding her conflicted perceptions of the more recent 'generations' of her female forebears on her mother's dominant side of the family. As measured against the historical memory of the scrappy 'Eliza' – a 'family legend' idealized – women like Annie and Isabelle could only fall short. Actual, tangible relatives, they lived and died with their own complicated private stories of 'betrayal,' loss, and heartache – and with all their imperfections open to Lowther's precocious and sharp-eyed scrutiny. Not even their own distinctly creative aspirations, so like her own, could entirely curb Lowther's impatience with what she saw as her grandmother's staid conventionalism and her aunt's superficial vanity.

But if her reaction to Isabelle was especially pitched, then perhaps that was because, as with her grandmother, Lowther also recognized certain points of commonality with 'Belle' too. And these were emergent 'continuities' more difficult to confront. 'The Comet' is a reluctant 'elegy' to an actress characterized as living her life in a vain attempt to keep up promising appearances with 'rouge, lotion, perfume, / the right soap, / the right tooth powder' until – '"Miracle, miracle"' – her own mortality finally strips her down to make her 'become real' (*TC*, 174, 176). By the time she wrote these lines, Lowther obviously knew quite a lot about the desire to maintain appearances: to tinker with the spelling of one's surname, if it looked too uncouth, for example, or to get married quickly if a child was on the way. But more than that, around 1965, she was also just beginning to respond to much stronger internal compulsions to create unreal new appearances of her own, to divide her existence like an atom, unobserved, into separate parts. This fragmentation also implied a kind of duplicity, as she began to acknowledge elsewhere in her writing. 'How strange to see / two faces in one mirror,' she mused in one such instance.[14] By 1974 she would publish her prose piece 'The Face,'[15] with its 'cut out ... woman shape' of a narrator, routinely performing her 'woman' role like an empty charade. 'All faces change minute by minute,' she wrote then. In 'The Face,' this fact testifies not only to the instability of the present moment, but also to the inspiration behind the 'ancient' human invention of 'masks.'

And one year after 'The Face,' precisely a decade after Belle's death, Lowther also drafted a poem called 'Continuity: A Masque for Two Interchangeable Players.'[16] Here, she called up the elaborately theatrical form of the aristocratic 'masque' to question a love affair associated throughout with a dramatic performance or a 'game' in which the lovers /players need to ask themselves: 'what faces are we wearing?' There is, however, nothing theatrical about the paradoxical self-disclosure with which this poem opens: 'unconscious as a weed / as a bird scratching / I prepare my lies / – always astonished / at catching / myself in my own line.' Another attempt to address the stress fractures of her own by now 'schizophrenic' life, 'Continuity' emphasizes, above all, the idea of sameness through substitution, the idea of 'Two Interchangeable Players.' This was an idea even more painful than the poem's spectacle of a pair of lovers wearing face masks in a gilded 'masque,' a tacit acknowledgment of the duplicity of her long-distance affair with McNamara. For this was one performance also necessarily 'haunted' by the 'ghost' of Aunt Isabelle. By 1975 there was no longer any way Lowther could overlook the fact that, at least in one sense, she and Isabelle were 'Interchangeable Players' too. Though she herself didn't 'rouge,' or need to 'borrow' any 'children,' 'the face' that looked back at her in the mirror some days could have been Isabelle's: 'a woman full of pretenses, / enacting a rich and peopled life / among ... lovers only dreamed' (*TC*, 175). Astonished at 'catching' herself living a lie, an older Lowther came to appreciate just how hair-fine and flickering the 'line' was between attempting a life of art, and crossing over into one of artifice.

Along with erect carriage and opposable thumbs, the capacity for lying, as many have pointed out, is unique to the 'evolved' human animal, the linguistic mammal. The 'physical description of human beings' at the projected outset of Lowther's 'Time Capsule' summed up the species best, in the past tense: 'The creatures were unbelievably fragile.'

Thankfully, Virginia, that most central of foremothers in Lowther's personal 'history' and 'context,' was not a ghost. After her Prince Edward

Island visit and her last reading at Toronto's Harbourfront Centre, Lowther, in fact, probably thought about her mother during the flight home on July 17 – wondered how Virginia had fared with the girls, and with her husband, during the five days of her absence. Still, she left very few records, private or public, about the nature of her adult relationship with her mother, the woman she could rely upon for childcare support when necessary, and also for the occasional loan of small sums of money.

Where the 'mother' figure does appear in Lowther's notebooks, she tends to be equated, like Annie McCain, with forces of social decorum and discipline that are resisted or parodied. 'I laughed at the whole world of mothers and studies and boundaries,' as one of her early fictional protagonists proclaims, deliberately sabotaging the piano lesson enforced upon him by his mother. Similarly, in the early poem draft 'Mother':

> Mother stands
> with proverbs in her hand
> like a ring of keys,
> smooth worn keys
> trying at the keyhole
> one after one.
> Waste not, want not.
> Spare the rod, spoil the child.
> Early to bed and early to rise ...
> Fumbling and jumbling them,
> jingling like money
> but they will not fit.[17]

Lowther's perception of a 'mother's' ineffectual reliance on the 'worn' currency of proverbial wisdom accords with Virginia's own apprehensive sense of her inadequacy as a mother who 'wasn't much help' to her book-inclined daughter.[18] Self-consciously aware of the close kinship that her daughter had forged over the past decade with a female mentor who *was* 'much help' to Pat in this regard, Virginia wrote to Dorothy Livesay in the spring of 1976. Her letter drew a rather anxious and direct comparison between their respective relationships with Pat: 'Pat was very fond of you, mentioned you a lot and I know she admired you very much. Pat and I were not as close as I would have liked, but I loved her very deeply.' Pat and Virginia were not particularly 'close' in the same sense as many mothers and daughters of their respective generations: the first had exchanged her early personal aspirations for marriage and motherhood, whereas the second took on her challenges in reverse, struggling to claim and integrate personal aspirations only after marriage and motherhood. As widely acknowledged, it was 'pioneering' feminist foremothers like Livesay, defying the social norms of the earlier generation, who also provided women of Lowther's cohort with some stamina for their own struggle.

All the same, in her apologetic self-assessments as a mother, Virginia seemed to forget that it was she who had been instrumental in first instilling a love of words in her daughter; that it was she who had marched about the nursery singing 'The Red Flag'; and that it was she, the adventurous Broadway dancer, who decades later had those suitcases ready, when her daughter's opportunities for wider horizons arose. Her own life may have settled, gradually, into something her daughter would disavow as stifling in its bourgeois predictability. But the decades never entirely domesticated Virginia, either. In her letter to Livesay, Virginia was not only impelled to declare that she loved her own daughter deeply. She also recorded frankly her equally deep satisfaction that Pat had found moments of happiness with a lover, furtive and infrequent though those moments had been. 'We all feel very grateful to Gene [McNamara] and admire him, and thank God that Pat loved him.'[19]

If anything, Lowther's cordial but distant connection to her immediate relations by 1975 was both a natural outgrowth of the private child she had always been, and an index of the strange 'creature' she had evolved into. No one in the family had as yet tried to make a living by 'fiddling around with words' in quite the same way. They weren't sure what to make of the poems she wrote, nor this 'League of Poets' with which she seemed to be involved. They knew her as 'Patsy Lou,' the quiet, unobtrusive one, the one who loved rocks and 'things' like that.

⌘

It was to that special outcropping of rock, 'her' Mayne Island, that Lowther made a beeline, almost immediately upon her return from Prince Edward Island. By July 22, she was readying her family for their annual summer expedition. Along with her kids' toys, she packed her typewriter, or one of them that was in working order, anyway. Once the ferry crossing was accomplished, and they were settled into Uncle Bill's guest cabin, she started typing. First, a letter to Réshard Gool and Hilda

Woolnough. 'I'm writing from Mayne Island,' she told them, 'where we have no red earth, but we do have red trees. I enclose a piece of arbutus bark to remind you of the west coast.'[20] Though she was no longer so young, and it was no longer 'The Island' of her youth, the arbutus were still 'lifting their bodies like poems' for her, and when she walked through the forest, she could hear that arbutus bark crack, and see it peel away in copper-red curls, and trace with her fingers the smooth, pistachio-coloured flesh that opened up beneath.

A few days after she sent Réshard and Hilda this small souvenir of bark from the Gulf, Beth and Christie presented their mother with a necklace, purchased on Mayne Island, in honour of her fortieth birthday. If at forty, she was no longer quite so young, then neither were her children, either – her two youngest now well into self-propelled girlhood, and her two elder, Kathy and Alan, already leading their own independent lives. With her forties now stretching before her, she was beginning, again, as she'd once told Livesay, 'to see openings for myself too.' 'Alternatives,' which, if they didn't exist 'at the moment,' were indeed 'developing,' and bringing with them possibilities for the kinds of 'alternate futures' she liked to imagine, and to debate with her political allies on the left.

On this summer holiday, Lowther could take some time to think about her work with the League. That work now connected her across the entire nation, even to big cities like Toronto, where, conceivably, a woman with a few good friends and a handy street map might, someday, successfully disappear. But she was also thinking about work closer in space and time: her forthcoming job at the university. That job would start shortly after her Gulf Island rest, when Professor Lowther would begin bussing to the Point Grey campus, weeks in advance of the official fall term, to begin reviewing student portfolios and preparing her course – the first one she could be fairly sure she would not see listed in any brochure next to hairdressing and palmistry. 'It looks as though I'm going to have a lot more students than I ought to for what they're paying me,' she quipped (sort of) to Fred Cogswell.[21] The $4,500 sessional stipend would be a good start, very good. But in return for big class sizes and further teaching experience, she could envision 'a wanting' beyond this, too.

At Bennett Bay, the road named after the Wilks family runs behind the spot where the guest cabin that was called 'Sleepy Hollow' once stood. Through a forest lanced with light and scented by pine and sumac, fat blackberries and salal, moist ferns and moss, Wilkes Road eventually curves east where Isabella Lane branches from it in a westerly direction. It is a short walk down Isabella Lane to the tip of Campbell Point, a peninsular finger pointing out over the Gulf in the direction of Washington State. Campbell Point was only the closest of many such spots – like Edith Point, or the lighthouse at Georgina Point – to which Lowther could have strolled or bicycled for a little visit to see how her favourite 'characters' were doing. Inevitably drawn to the beaches and shores, she probably smoked a lazy Matinée or two, listening to the seagulls, the water, and the subtler sounds of those stony 'invertebrates' 'breathing as naturally / as animals' all around her (*SD*, 8). Then, as in 'Now,' she could 'stand caliper-legd / on land and water'– one foot in either element, taking a physical measure of the intricate wave / particle 'continuities' between 'the water / and its continents' (*MS*, 39).

On clear days, from Campbell Point, she could see the white snow cap of Mount Baker in the distance, rising out over the salt haze across the Gulf, and creating the illusion of a mountain peak levitating in mid-air. On overcast days that threatened of rain and migraine, days when she felt 'a sound coming nearer / like a heavy animal / breaking twigs,' she could watch and wait for a break in the sky (*SD*, 92). In the Gulf archipelago, as in Lynn Valley, and East Vancouver, all it took was one single 'opening' in the clouds – even the smallest 'molecule of light' – to 'change everything.' She *knew* this, as she needed also to believe that 'every word written onto paper' could, already had, was now, and would again, 'change everything.' No matter how 'small small' the inscriptions on paper, the histories scratched into stone, the figures notched out of bone, or even into snow. There was, in fact, no matter too 'small small.' It was the tiniest thing, the scientists said, that created the universe.

Acknowledgments

Pat Lowther, for starters. There are others who have 'gone to spirit,' in bill bissett's gentle phrase, whom I also need to acknowledge here, so I may as well begin with the obvious. My immersion in Pat Lowther's life and art provided an education in 'context, and continuity, and history' that I never remotely anticipated at the outset. Difficult though it sometimes was, I am grateful for the journey she took me on.

This work would not have been possible without the generous cooperation and assistance of members of the Lowther family, on both Pat's and Roy's sides. I am especially grateful to Beth Lowther, Christine Lowther, Kathy Domphousse Lyons, John Tinmouth, Arden Tinmouth, Brenda Marshall, and Ruth Lowther Lalonde, all of whom were crucial to the progress of this book. Beth Lowther and her son, Rowan, made space for me to work in their home for repeated stretches, sometimes days on end, and sometimes on short notice. Never once did they turn down my request to view material, and never once did they make me feel an imposition. Likewise, Christine Lowther shared with me not only memories and photographs but also her Tofino homes, and at least one unforgettable meal of wild chanterelles. Kathy Lyons responded faithfully to queries that got increasingly recondite over the years. A truly gracious Brenda Marshall also answered every last request for help and went out of her way (literally) to ensure my access to some of Pat's childhood writing. Ruth Lowther Lalonde spoke candidly and courageously to me about her family past and gave me permission to consult Roy Lowther's casebook journals. For various forms of prompt assistance and many kindnesses, Barry Wilks, Chris Jang, Warren Rudd, and David Lowther also deserve my hearty thanks. I am indebted to the Estate of

Pat Lowther for granting permission to print previously published and unpublished materials that appear here.

Many friends, acquaintances, and individuals connected to Pat and Roy Lowther granted me time for interviews; allowed me access to archived papers; responded to my queries by mail and phone; and otherwise supplied helpful information and permissions: the Estate of Milton Acorn, Margaret Atwood, Michelle Benjamin, Pauline (Bennett) Farrell, the Estate of Earle Birney, bill bissett, Brian Brett, Brian Campbell, Fred Candelaria, Ward Carson, Glenn Clever, John R. Colombo, Frank Davey, Robert Fulford, Gary Geddes, Leona Gom, the Estate of Réshard Gool, Ken Hale, John Hall, Robert Harlow, Alex Henderson, Anne Henderson, Lionel Kearns, Joy Kogawa, Rita Lalik, Arlene Lampert, Patrick Lane, the Estate of Dorothy Livesay, Jean Mallinson, Seymour Mayne, Gail McKay, David Morgan, Lorraine (Plowman) Orbeck, P.K. Page, Joe Rosenblatt, Allan Safarik, Andreas Schroeder, Bethoe Shirkoff, Dona Sturmanis, Hilda Thomas, William Toye, Lorraine Vernon, Andy Wainwright, Tom Wayman, and Hilda Woolnough. Fred Cogswell proved an exceptionally cooperative source of valuable information, and I regret that he did not live to see this work completed. Thanks to Madam Justice Kirkpatrick of the Family Court Division at the B.C. Law Courts; to the retired judge who oversaw the trial of Roy Lowther; and to 'Tammy' in the office at the Law Courts, for allowing me a comfortable room to work, and liberal access to the photocopy machine. I also owe special thanks to Toby Brooks, a generous predecessor. Among her many acts of assistance, I am especially grateful for Toby Brooks's offer to share with me some of her previously taped interviews, including one with Virginia Tinmouth, who died suddenly in 1998, just as I was trying to arrange my own interview with her.

For assistance and permission to reprint records in their respective holdings, I would like to acknowledge library staff at the following institutions: New York Public Library for the Performing Arts, Billy Rose Theatre Collection (Mary Ellen Rogan, Senior Archivist); University of Prince Edward Island, Harriet Richardson Library, Special Collections (Simon Lloyd and Leo Cheverie); University of New Brunswick archives (Linda Baier and Mary Flagg); Queen's University archives (George Henderson); Thomas Fisher Rare Books Library, University of Toronto; York University Special Collections and Archives (Kent Haworth and Sean Smith); University of Windsor Archives (Michael Owens and Karen Marerro); Ryerson Polytechnic University Archive; Lakehead University Archives; National Archives, Ottawa (Anne Goddard, Michael

MacDonald, and Martin Lanthier); National Library, Ottawa (Karen Raymond); University of Manitoba Archives and Special Collections; University of Regina Special Collections and Archives (Selina Coward); Cameron Library Map Division, and Bruce Peel Special Collections Library, University of Alberta (Jeannine Green and John Charles); UBC Archives and Special Collections (George Branak, Erwin Wodarczak, Anne Wilkins, and Sarah Wilkinson); UBC Map and Atlas Library; Simon Fraser University Library and Special Collections; City of Nanaimo Community Archives (Christine Meutzner); Vancouver Public Library; City of Vancouver Archives. Special thanks to archivists Francis Mansbridge and June Thompson at the North Vancouver Museum and Archives, who took an expert interest in this work from the start, and helped me obtain original records and photographs. Thanks also to Leslie Broscomb of the Lower Seymour Conservation Reserve, and to the staff at the District of North Vancouver Public Library, who put me in touch with Helen Dickinson, who searched through the apple boxes in her attic for unpublished research to supplement her excellent published work on library history. At the City of North Vancouver Public Library, Information Services and Collection Librarian John Black likewise shared valuable unpublished research with me. My knowledge of North Vancouver's geography and physical history is specifically indebted to local watershed authority Eric Crossin (thanks for the directions) and to Russell Thornton, who enhanced a guided tramp around Rice Lake with excellent conversation and valuable correspondence.

The following also supplied assistance, records, and/or permission to reprint materials in their holdings: Oxford University Press (Canada); B.C. Provincial Archives (Victoria); Province of British Columbia, Vital Statistics; Provincial Law Courts, B.C.; Washington State Office of Corrections; U.S. Federal Bureau of Corrections; University of California (Berkeley), Office of Student Records; UBC Student Records Office; The Peak (SFU); the League of Canadian Poets; Status of Women, Canada; St James Society (Vancouver); the New Democratic Party (Little Mountain); and the Center for Continuing Education, University of Regina. Excerpts from Gzowski on FM appear courtesy of CBC Radio Network Archives © (thanks to Gail Donald, Norbert Boiley, Barbara Brown, and Scott Heaney).

Most of this work was supported by a grant from the Social Sciences and Humanities Research Council of Canada. The Faculty of Arts, University of Alberta, provided seed funding and partial teaching relief to make on-going progress with the research possible. The inspiring writers in my 2001 West Coast Women's Poetry seminar, and in my 2001 and 2003 Non-fiction Writing courses, also spurred this work along. At various times, research assistants Renée Ward, Hagit Hayada, and (especially) Kim Larsen were sent off with incomplete information and/or tight time-lines, and not only came through, but for the most part still speak to me today. Josefina Estrada and Barbara Bucknell provided translation services. Trustworthy technical support came from Linda Pasmore and from Karin Fodor at the Imaging Center, Creative Services, University of Alberta.

For a lively life-writing friendship that began, by chance, in Beijing, I remember Gabi Helms. *Ruhe in Frieden, freundin.* Numerous other colleagues and friends provided assistance and advice at various stages of this project, and also shared with me their own work: Lynn Adam, David Arnason, Douglas Barbour, Ted Bishop, Tim Bowling, Mary Chapman, Daniel Coleman, Dennis Cooley, Chris Gittings, Isobel Grundy, Orval Henderson, Daniel Horowitz, Linda Hutcheon, Peggy Kelly, Myrna Kostash, Ian Maclaren, Suzanne Matheson, Alex McKay, Daphne Read, Michael Trussler, Janice Williamson, and Dr Yasmin Jiwari of the FREDA Centre for Research on Violence against Women and Children. Lisa Rosenberg valiantly explained the 'half-lives' of her realm and let me play (supervised) in her chemistry lab one day. Juliet McMaster and Theresa Shea read parts or all of this manuscript with a critical clarity that reminded me once again why I so value their judgments, and their friendship. Rebecca Helfer, Jan Wesselius, and our friend, Buffy, got me through the final revisions stage.

Ken Lewis and Frances Mundy supplied superb editorial assistance. Siobhan McMenemy showed enthusiasm about this project from the start. Her advice and patience throughout its coming into being have made essential contributions.

One way or another, I owe most of the important things in my present life to my late parents, Renate Müller and Dieter Wiesenthal. These include the family members and close friends who offered me the encouragement that meant the most, and who humoured me with a wide berth while I was absorbed by this work: Di, Perry, and Cole; 'the two G's,' Geoff and Gail; Troni Grande, Loren McMaster, Rowland McMaster, and Toni Samek. Pamela Banting swapped notes on biography and cheered me on innumerable occasions, including the day she finally married Fred Stenson. Special Vancouverites Lisa Johnson and Glenn Wiesenthal ran me to and from the airport dozens of times; took on some odd requests without raising an eyebrow; and, most of all, gave me their terrific company every time I was in town.

Finally, this book would have been less possible and more painful without Brad Bucknell, who influenced it into being from the very start, and who in due course brought home purple knee-pads to expedite the floor work. The knee-pads were only among the more colourful and tangible of countless contributions that he made from day to day, and draft to draft. My gratitude to him goes beyond words.

CSW
MILL CREEK, EDMONTON

Notes

Introduction

1 Robert Fulford, 'Poet on Edge of Fame Beaten to Death,' *Ottawa Citizen*, 25 Oct. 1975, p. 82.

2 University of Manitoba Special Collections, Dorothy Livesay Papers, undated typescript, MSS 37, box 20, folder 4; diary entry, 31 Oct. 1975, MSS 37, box 3, folder 5.

3 Roy MacSkimming, 'Poets' League Discusses Interests with Writers,' *Toronto Star*, 14 Oct. 1975, p. F8.

4 Dorothy Livesay, 'Pat Lowther Tribute,' CBC Radio, *Gzowski on FM*, 2 Nov. 1975.

5 The editors of the bilingual quarterly *Ellipse: Writers in Translation* paired a selection of Lowther's poems with those of the talented young Québécois poet Marie Uguay, who succumbed to cancer at the age of twenty-six. Lowther's poems, translated into French, are introduced by Judith Cowan in 'La poésie de Pat Lowther.' Sagaris included Lowther as one of twelve Canadian poets in her Spanish anthology (1986).

6 Nicholson 2003. This essay appeared as the present work was being prepared at press. A new unpublished dissertation by Richard Almonte (2003), which deals in part with Lowther's posthumous representations, also appeared as this work was being prepared at press; I have not yet been able to obtain a copy of the latter.

7 Interview with Gary Geddes. Edmonton, 8 March 2001.

8 '*Gzowski on FM,*' CBC Radio, 2 Nov. 1975.

9 See McNamara 1977. McNamara, whose relationship with Lowther had come under painful public scrutiny during Roy Lowther's trial, arranged with George Woodcock to obscure the authorship of the essay (Queen's Uni-

versity Archives, George Woodcock Papers, A. Arch 2095, box 2, George Woodcock–Eugene McNamara correspondence). In the interests of a full and accurate understanding of the public record, it is important to be able to affix meaningful credentials to the non-existent 'Sean Ryan.' McNamara declined a request to participate in the research for this book. However, while his papers were deposited at the University of Windsor, they had no access restrictions placed on them.

10 'Rumpelstiltskin, Dr. Freud, Adam and Eve, and Others,' undated typescript and undated looseleaf typescript, in the possession of Beth Lowther. Lowther's comment regarding the 'mystical vanguard' appears in a draft version of her author statement for Elaine Gill's *Mountain Moving Day* anthology (1973).

11 'Split Rock,' undated entry, Fred C. Myers notebook, in the possession of Beth Lowther.

Chapter 1

1 On Neruda's death and the doubts raised over the final pages of Neruda's *Memoirs*, which discuss Allende's death, see Bizzarro 1979: 149–64. On the situation in Chile in the immediate aftermath of the 1973 coup, see Sobel 1974, esp. 144. On Chile's 'slow and still unfinished transition' back to democracy after the end of Pinochet's reign, see Riesco 1999.

2 'It's Chile in North,' *Vancouver Province*, 6 Sept. 1973, p. 21. This article cites American perceptions of British Columbia's new socialist government: 'In April, *Barron's*, a Wall Street weekly, blew the whistle loud enough for the entire Wall Street financial district to hear when they called B.C. "The Chile of the North"' (21).

3 Letter to the author, 4 Nov. 2000.

4 Letter to Eugene McNamara, 22 Sept. 1973, in the possession of Beth Lowther. Beth Lowther possesses her mother's letters to McNamara because they were subpoenaed as evidence for Roy Lowther's trial; after his conviction, some (not all) of the exhibits were returned to Pat Lowther's family.

5 Letter to Doug Barbour, 28 Sept. 1973, National Archives, Ottawa, League of Canadian Poets fonds, MG 28, I301, Vol 1, file 15.

6 Letter to Fred Cogswell, 6 Sept. 1973, University of New Brunswick (UNB) Archives and Special Collections, Fred Cogswell fonds, MS 2.1963. In the next breath, Lowther added, about her growing children: 'But I don't know how old they have to be before I can stop worrying about them.'

7 Letter to Fred Cogswell, 8 Aug. 1973, UNB Archives and Special Collections, Fred Cogswell fonds, MS 2.1920.

8 Letter to Eugene McNamara, 31 Dec. 1973, in the possession of Beth Lowther.

9 RLJ, 1:57, 35, 60. See also CATT, 3:425, 437; 4:564.

10 Letter to Dorothy Livesay, 15 Jan. 1970, Queen's University Archives, Dorothy Livesay Papers, box 4A, file 84. The reference to '*eros über alles*' is here in relation to a review of Livesay's *Plainsongs,* but the comment applies as well to Lowther's conflicted attitudes toward some of her own sexual affairs.

11 RLJ, 1:53–4, 58. Among other things, Roy's claim is substantiated by a letter from Lowther to Eugene McNamara in which she specifically directed him: 'Please write to me at home' (12 April 1974, in the possession of Beth Lowther).

12 RLJ, 1:70. The *West Coast Review* issue in question was January 1975.

13 Letter to Eugene McNamara, 11 Dec. 1974, in the possession of Beth Lowther.

14 bill bissett, personal communication with the author, 4 March 2002.

15 Letter to Fred Cogswell, 3 May 1975, UNB Archives and Special Collections, Fred Cogswell fonds, MS 2.2423.

16 Letter to Eugene McNamara, 22 Sept. 1973, in the possession of Beth Lowther.

17 Letter to Rita Lalik, undated, in the possession of Beth Lowther. Similarly, in the same letter, Roy refers to 'Pat Lowther on the program' and to his wife's unwillingness to advocate for him: 'Pat Lowther just keeps hands off.' During Roy's trial, the Lalik letter was entered as evidence, and prosecutor John Hall called attention to this same anomaly: 'I suggest it manifests a degree of estrangement between you [and your wife]' (CATT, 3:399–400).

18 RLJ, 1:6. Roy Lowther's court testimony offers basically a parallel account, including the description of the 'wave' of 'pity' which overcame him as he sat on the trunk in the bedroom (CATT, 3:350–1; 4:542).

19 RLJ, 1: unpaginated, handwritten insert opposite page 67; and 1:61E. In this latter sense, 'what she had become, what she was becoming' conveyed Roy's delusion that 'Pat the poet's whoring around was bringing her, as it often does, to a contempt of the male sex' (1:68A).

20 The text, from *Pegasus* (6.3 [Winter 1974]: 30), is reproduced below. Roy indicated the parenthetical line as borrowed from his father, who also wrote verse.

> Summer died last night
> In a yowling iceberg death,
> The leaves turned rattles,
> Silent things alive in the soil
>   slipped under stones

And the cats balled themselves tight
  in the back porch
And the one great season died

This afternoon the corpse lies serene
In the new sun
    ('agewise–aloof–austere')*
The cedars, green mourners,
    philosophically sigh,
And white water plays a mighty dirge
On the vast black organ of the rocks.
We pay our respects,
    turn from our quiet internal weeping
To this night's long rest.

My God, someone
Give me a death like that.
(I say I have summer's soul
Even yet.)

21 Interview with Alex Henderson, Supreme Court of British Columbia, Vancouver, 16 Jan. 2000.
22 Ibid.
23 'Pat Lowther Tribute,' *Vancouver Review,* August 1985, p. 9.
24 University of Manitoba Special Collections, Dorothy Livesay Papers, MSS 37, box 20, folder 4; emphasis added.
25 Undated pencil entry, 'Music Dictation' notebook, in the possession of Beth Lowther. The notebook is Lowther's, but this entry, a musical score with lyrics, is in Roy's hand, not Pat's.
26 Elsewhere, too, Roy appropriated celestial imagery from Lowther's *Infinite Mirror Trip* for his own purposes, using it to focus on issues of competitive measurement and rivalry, as I am suggesting is also implicit in his conjoining of Pat with Pablo in death. That symbolic union is but another version of his similarly condescending pronouncements about his wife's impressive but still relatively diminutive status in relation to a 'major' male Canadian poet: 'Pat Lowther stands as second to Milton Acorn as a poet in Canada' (CATT, 3:385).
27 Interview, with Alex Henderson, Supreme Court of British Columbia, Vancouver, 16 Jan. 2000.
28 Phone interview with Alex Henderson, 13 March 2002.
29 Interview with Gail McKay, 19 July 2001.

Chapter 2

1 Rita Lalik, the NDP administrator whom Roy had lobbied for a spot on the Ironworkers' program, had also called that week – on September 23 – to inform Roy that she was unable to add him to the roster of poets. Lalik testified that Roy responded to this news by saying, 'It's too late now anyway' (PHTT, 7:504–5).

2 Roy's phrase, as recalled in testimony of Detective R.E. Chapman (PHTT, 7:537).

3 In 'Clue Followed on Missing Poet,' the *Vancouver Province* reported on 11 October 1975 that an unnamed woman claimed to have seen Lowther on Sept. 27th, at an NDP fund-raising dinner attended also by Premier Dave Barrett, in Coquitlam.

4 RLJ, 1:19; this was a detail also divulged in court: 'I removed nothing from the purse. There was a dollar in it and I left it' (CATT, 4:562).

5 RLJ, 1:20. Of the briefcase, Roy also testified in court: '... that was the one thing, the only thing I did not want to see again' (CATT, 3:477–8, 545).

6 Virginia Tinmouth, interview with Toby Brooks, 23 Feb. 1989.

7 Interview with Kathy [Domphousse] Lyons, Vancouver, 12 Jan. 2000.

8 Virginia Tinmouth, interview with Toby Brooks, 23 Feb. 1989.

9 Ken Hale, testimony, PHTT, 9:707; Interview with Ken Hale, Vancouver, 13 Dec. 2000.

10 'She has dropped completely out of sight' and 'People don't disappear that completely,' Hale or Chapman is cited as saying in an early report, which goes on to note that Lowther had no money with her, nor were there any new charges on her credit cards ('City Poet Missing, Case Handed to Homicide,' *Vancouver Province*, 9 Oct. 1975).

11 Interview with Ken Hale, Vancouver, 13 Dec. 2000; Detective Roy Chapman, testimony, PHTT, 8:650.

12 Interview with Brenda Marshall, North Vancouver, 17 Feb. 2000. Roy may have shipped some of the couple's books up to a friend's place on Saturna Island. Very few survive in the archive now in possession of Beth Lowther.

13 Interview with Ken Hale, Vancouver, 13 Dec. 2000; Roy Chapman, testimony, PHTT, 8:654.

14 Interview with Ken Hale, Vancouver, 13 Dec. 2000. At the time, Roy's anomalous social role as a sort of house husband to a successful career woman was another basis for the 'sympathy' accorded him by some people — especially, though not exclusively, men. For example, Hale at one point suggested to Roy that Don Cummins, the downstairs boarder, 'must have sided with you [in matters of domestic dispute] because of you having to look after the kids

and do all the work' (CATT, 4:540). A few women neighbours were sympathetic to Roy for similar reasons.

15 'City Poet Missing, Case Handed to Homicide,' *Vancouver Province*, 9 Oct. 1975; 'Body Identity Confirmed,' *Vancouver Sun*, 17 Oct. 1975.

16 Letter to Arlene Lampert, 23 June 1975, National Archives, Ottawa, League of Canadian Poets fonds, MG 28, I301, Vol. 1, file 1–19.

17 Interview, with Ken Hale, Vancouver, Dec. 13, 2000.

18 Christine Lowther's memory of the image of her father receding to 'a dot' on the dock at Miner's Bay is recounted by her in Anne Henderson's film, *Water Marks* (2002).

19 'Poet's Husband Granted Bail,' *Vancouver Sun*, 11 Dec. 1975, p. 49.

20 Interview with Ken Hale, Vancouver, 12 Dec. 2000. The parking lot mishap is recounted in 'Helpful Policemen End Up with Damaged Cruiser,' *Vancouver Sun*, 2 Jan. 1976.

21 Interview with Ken Hale, Vancouver, 12 Dec. 2000.

22 Interview with Alex Henderson, Vancouver, 16 Jan. 2000.

23 RLJ, 2: 'Biographical,' n.pag.

24 Interview with Alex Henderson, Vancouver, 16 Jan. 2000.

25 'In 1949, the Immigration Department of the United States ... refused to renew my student visa. They held a kangaroo court and ... I was deported after being held in Immigration Jail in San Francisco for five weeks. A year later, I returned to the U.S. illegally. I was in love with a girl in California' (CATT, 4:548).

26 Bethoe Shirkoff, typescript of personal diary, 7 Feb. 1996; emphasis in the original (in the possession of Christine Lowther).

27 U.S. Federal Bureau of Prisons, letter to the author, 5 June 2001. The case file has since been destroyed.

28 Interview with Hilda Thomas, Vancouver, 17 Aug. 1998. Thomas is another observer inclined to think that Roy Lowther 'actually believed' the 'not ... very well put together story' he told in the 'aftermath of the murder.

29 Interview with Hilda Thomas, Vancouver, 17 Aug. 1998.

30 Interview with Alex Henderson, Vancouver, 16 Jan. 2000.

31 'Wife-Killer's Appeal Frivolous, Says Court,' *Vancouver Province*, 29 June 1978. What is remarkable about Roy's appeal is not so much the familiar attempt to cast the balance of responsibility onto the victim by pleading justifiable 'provocation,' as the fact that it was even tried. Lawyer James Hogan tried to argue that the assize judge 'erred in law in failing to leave [the lesser charge of] manslaughter [open] to the jury,' and secondarily, in failing to charge the jury 'upon the defense of provocation' (*Crim. Rep.*, 238–49). In other words, 'the French notion of a *crime passionnel*' was raised to suggest that

'Patricia Lowther's possible stated intention to leave her husband ... could have provided sufficient lawful provocation to excuse the husband of an act of murder' (Larry Still, '"*Crime Passionnel*" Angle Raised in Murder Appeal,' *Vancouver Sun*, 20 June 1978). The appeal court judge rejected both arguments, pointing out that 'the very nature' of the initial defence 'precluded the consideration' of either: 'The accused's evidence, if accepted by the jury, freed him from all criminal responsibility. If not accepted, the remaining evidence pointed overwhelmingly to murder and murder alone ... The sole defence was that the appellant was not present at the killing' (*Crim. Rep.*, 246–7).

32 The influence of New Critical philosophy is particularly evident in the 'principles for procedure' outlined in the judge's Charge to the Jury at the end of the trial (CATT, 4:490–8).

33 Chapters 5, 10, and 14 elaborate upon aspects of the amateur and professional literary cultures of Pat Lowther's time; the conflicts she experienced as a result of straddling these spheres; and Roy's position in those conflicts.

34 Interview with Alex Henderson, Vancouver, 16 Jan. 2000.

35 Jim Fairley, 'Lowther Murder Case Goes to Jury Today,' *Vancouver Province*, 22 April 1977. Sources for headlines, in order of appearance: Larry Still, *Vancouver Sun*, 13 April 1977, p. 16; Michael Findlay, *Vancouver Sun*, 18 Oct. 1975, p. 16; Jim Fairley, *Vancouver Province*, 16 April 1977; Jim Fairley, *Vancouver Province*, 14 April 1977; Larry Still, *Vancouver Sun*, 15 April 1977, p. 25; [no by-line], *Vancouver Province*, 21 April 1977. Most of the local press clippings related to the Lowther trial have been collected in a folder at the Vancouver Public Library. The trial was less heavily publicized in other regions, though articles did appear in Ontario newspapers (including the *Ottawa Citizen* and the *Windsor Star*). Dorothy Livesay also collected press clippings related to Lowther's disappearance and Roy's trial, many from Victoria newspapers (University of Manitoba Special Collections, MSS 37, box 20, folder 4).

36 Bethoe Shirkoff, trial diary typescript of 18–22 April 1977, pp. 10, 4, 2, 14 (in the possession of Christine Lowther). Years later, Shirkoff typed up the diary notes she had taken while attending the hearings, for Beth and Christine Lowther.

37 Don McLellan, 'Verses and Verdicts,' *Vancouver Sun*, 29 April 1977, p. 3A.

38 Don McLellan, 'Into the Trenches Go Canada's Poets,' *Vancouver Sun*, 5 Sept. 1975, p. 29.

39 Newspaper reports over the course of the trial are, for instance, inconsistent in assigning the role of the 'poet,' which the headlines almost as often attribute to Roy as to Pat Lowther: 'Poet Tells Court of Panic in Finding Wife's Body'; 'Protesting Poet Found Guilty'; 'Poet's Murder Appeal Fails'

(*Vancouver Sun*, 20 April 1977, p. 7; 23 April 1977, pp. 1–2; 22 Aug. 1978, p. D6). There is an obvious irony in this conflation, given the importance that Pat Lowther's distinction as the legitimate 'professional' poet of the two would prove to play in her husband's motive for murder. Similarly, in 'Verses and Verdicts,' the roles of 'lover, madman and poet' go unattached to any one individual: the 'lover' could refer to McNamara but could also apply to the 'missing woman,' Pat Lowther; the 'poet' could refer to any one of the three principals; the 'madman' could be the 'maniac' Roy postulated – the article certainly does not allege outright that Roy Lowther is insane. It does note, however, that 'Meg' thinks he looks like 'the type to spend the last twenty years of his life writing poems in an attic,' which implies as much – again, by way of a very 'Victorian' trope. But, of course, to the extent that all poets are stereotypically mad anyway, this character function is also fluid.

40 *Vancouver Sun*, 21 April 1977, Sect. 2, p. 22.

41 Interview with Ken Hale, Vancouver, 13 Dec. 2000.

42 Roy's action during his final remarks is reported in a newspaper account, 'Lowther Guilty in Wife's Murder,' *Vancouver Province*, 23 April 1977.

43 Interview with John Hall, Vancouver, 15 Feb. 2000.

44 Interview with Alex Henderson, Vancouver, 16 Jan. 2000. Though 'the famous trial–lawyers' story' 'may be exaggerated by now,' this account of Hall's dramatic flair also accords with the impressions of others, including Bethoe Shirkoff, Detective Ken Hale, and Don McLellan, whose 'Verses and Verdicts' describes Hall's habit of 'waltz[ing] around the accused with one hand up against the side of his face, as if to massage a migraine,' thus conjuring the presence of the migraine-afflicted Pat Lowther.

45 Interview with John Hall, 15 Feb. 2000. According to Hall, there's 'more scope' to be 'dramatic' in 'defending' than prosecuting.

46 Interview with Alex Henderson, Vancouver, 16 Jan. 2000.

47 Both Dorothy Livesay and Allan Safarik resorted to the 'star-crossed' metaphor in the wake of Lowther's death, the former in the *Gzowski on FM* radio tribute, 2 Nov. 1975, the latter in Michael Findlay's article, 'Slain Vancouver Poet Wrote of Bloody Death,' *Vancouver Sun*, 18 Oct. 1975. Lorraine Vernon is quoted by Brooks as comparing her friend's life to 'a Greek tragedy' (2000: 171).

48 Letter to Eugene McNamara, 1 June 1973 (in the possession of Beth Lowther); David Morgan, interview, Vancouver, 11 Dec. 2000, and personal correspondence with the author, October 2000.

49. Interview with Justice J.G. — , Vancouver, 12 Dec. 2000. The retired judge requested not to be cited by name. It does appear in public records related to the case, and in Toby Brooks's biography.

50 Interview with Justice J.G. — , Vancouver, 12 Dec. 2000.

Chapter 3

1 Atwood acknowledges her personal acquaintance with both poets under review: 'I will try not to let that fact or my sorrow at these premature deaths influence what I have to say about the poetry. In this I will of course be unsuccessful, but the reader is warned' (1982: 308).
2 Dorothy Livesay and Hilda Thomas, CBC Radio 'Pat Lowther Tribute,' *Gzowski on FM*, 2 Nov. 1975. Arlene Lampert's comment that 'the tragic news of Pat has knocked so much out of my head' occurs in a letter to Livesay (20 Oct. 1975, University of Manitoba Special Collections, Dorothy Livesay Papers, MSS 37, box 60, folder 11). Caruth traces Freud's literary source for the 'trauma' of the speaking wound in *Beyond the Pleasure Principle* to Torquato Tasso, but Shakespeare utilizes the same figure in *Julius Caesar* when Marc Antony compares 'sweet Caesar's wounds' to 'poor, poor dumb / mouths,' and 'bid[s] them speak for me' (3.2.226–8). The inability to assimilate crisis experience – the paradoxical 'belatedness' of trauma's intelligibility, or the even more radically persistent atemporality of its experience for the survivor, despite compulsive mental returns to it – is also underscored by recent theorists (Langer 1997; Felman and Laub, 1992; Caruth 1996).
3 See Michelle Benjamin's preface to *Time Capsule*, which in its closing remark echoes the final sentence of Gzowski's introduction to the 1975 radio tribute: 'What follows in this special report is an attempt to capture something of the person Pat Lowther was, and the person she might have been: woman, mother, artist.'
4 Peter Gzowski, *Gzowski on FM*, 2 Nov. 1975; emphasis added to indicate voice inflection on the tape. When Gzowski refers to this 'true nightmare,' he is citing Lowther herself, who, as she told her Prince Edward Island audience, apparently based the poem on 'the true transcript' of an actual dream.
5 It is like night and day to set Acorn's assessment of Lowther's career next to that of Roy, who had this to say about the 'poet-establishment' he deemed Pat to represent: 'So here was the poet who at 35 had one book, and occasionally sent poems to magazines; and who at 40 was not only national head of the chief poets' union but was developing government policy for her poetic employers. Talk about influence!' (RLJ, 1:81).
6 Allan Safarik, 'A Final Tribute,' *Canadian Review* 4.5 (June 1977): 31. See also Safarik's comments in Michael Findlay, 'Slain Vancouver Poet Wrote of Bloody Death,' *Vancouver Sun*, 18 Oct. 1975.
7 On the same radio tribute, Lane did acknowledge, however, Lowther's

national reputation by the time of her death: 'The country as a unit was finally saying, "goddamn it, this woman has got something to say; she's speaking for us."' Similarly, Dorothy Livesay readily acknowledged Lowther's professional reputation and credentials, but also stressed the modest amounts of the Canada Council grants Lowther had received during her career: 'In the two times I supported her requests to the Canada Council I stressed the fact that she was penniless, that she had no way unless she got help. But the help was small, compared to what other poets have had.'

8 Undated draft letter, Hilroy '500' notebook, in the possession of Beth Lowther.

9 See Seymour Mayne's 'For Pat Lowther (1935–75)' (1981: 118).

10 Andy Wainwright, letter to the author, 6 Nov. 2000.

11 *Gzowski on FM*, 4 and 5 Nov. 1975.

12 'A Kind of Wrestling,' undated 'Standard Life' notebook entry and loose typescript, in the possession of Beth Lowther. Both drafts are undated, but the address at the top of the typescript dates this essay during 1963–5; my quotation is from the typescript.

13 See also, for example, Sturmanis 1985a, where the measure of who was 'closest' to Lowther gets cast as a matter of who had the best 'ringside seats on her life before she died,' as though at a boxing match or circus sideshow (6). If Cathy Caruth (1996) and others are right about trauma as involving 'unclaimed experience,' then it is one of the paradoxes of traumatic experience that it should so often manifest itself socially as precisely the opposite.

14 Because Lowther had not yet signed a contract at the time of her death, Oxford University Press was obliged to settle contractual details for the publication of *A Stone Diary* through her estate's lawyers and the Office of Public Trustee for the Province of British Columbia. In this case, the estate could not be settled until an official guardian, one vested with the legal authority to sign the contract on behalf of the estate, was declared. As Lowther's two daughters by her marriage with Roy were made wards of the province, this authority eventually settled with the Office of the Public Trustee. Oxford University Press records also include original correspondence between Lowther and William Toye, the editorial director at Oxford, regarding the manuscript's submission, review, and eventual acceptance; letters between Toye and writers such as Gary Geddes, Allan Safarik, and Margaret Atwood, who helped to prepare, review, and promote *A Stone Diary* upon its publication; and correspondence related to grants in aid of publication and photo credit permissions. David Morgan, who took the author photo which appears on the back cover of *A Stone Diary*, turned over his fee to the Coalition for Solidarity with Chile. Two thousand copies of *A Stone Diary* were originally

printed at a list price of $3.95. Finally, the file also includes correspondence related to Oxford's submission of *A Stone Diary* for the 1977 Commonwealth Poetry Prize. The award that year went to Indian poet Arun Kolatkar; *A Stone Diary* made it to the short list, however, and 'several of the judges,' who that year included Fleur Adcock, 'thought highly of Ms. Lowther's book' (letter from Michael Foster, CPP juror, to Richard Teleky, 1 Sept. 1977). Thanks to Toby Brooks for assistance in accessing this material.

15 University of Manitoba Special Collections, Dorothy Livesay Papers, MSS 37, box 20, folder 4. In this draft editorial typescript, Livesay also expresses resentment against 'Robert Fulford, the Toronto critic who never knew Pat.'

16 'The Premonition' was first published in Livesay's *CV/II* tribute (2.1 [Jan. 1976]: 16) before being reprinted in Dempster's 1978 anthology. A variation on the theme of survivor guilt occurs in Lorraine Vernon's 'On the Business of Being: A Practical Friend' (*CV/II* 2.1 [Jan. 1976]: 17).

17 'Two Lives' was first published in Livesay's *Feeling the Worlds* (1984: 23). It has been reprinted in *The Self-Completing Tree: Selected Poems* (1999: 220); my references are to this edition.

18 'The Continuum' was first published in *The Fiddlehead* 119 (Fall 1978): 11. Dean Irvine, who reprints the poem in *Archive for Our Times*, indicates a typescript date of 1975 (Livesay 1998: 213, 278). My references are to his edition.

19 In 1977 Atwood forwarded a copy of *A Stone Diary* to Nina Finkelstein, editor of *Ms* magazine, with the comment: 'I think some of these poems are very good and deserve a wider audience ... I also feel that Pat's life was in some way representative' (Margaret Atwood, letter to Nina Finkelstein, 4 April 1977, Oxford University Press archives; ellipsis in original).

20 Moses' 'Our Lady of the Glacier' (1988: 46–7) is an exception in this body of poetic tribute literature, in that there is no internal or extra-textual evidence (such as a dedication) to indicate that it is necessarily 'about' or 'for' or 'to' Pat Lowther at all. The poem's content alludes to memories of a 'murdered' creative-writing instructor, which would certainly appear to suggest this much, however, since Moses was, very briefly, one of Lowther's students at UBC in the fall of 1975. In a letter of 6 December 1996 to Christine Lowther, Moses suggested that his poem was based only vaguely on emotions surrounding Pat's death. He later re-titled it 'Grandmother of the Glacier.'

21 Frank Davey, letter to the author, 23 Nov. 2000. McKay herself prefers to think of Lowther in sororal terms as an older '*sister,* artist,' as she is also presented in the book. Of her book, McKay now says, 'I did think of it at the time as a tribute to her, as a way of continuing my relationship with her, pulling the relationship into the future somehow and quoting her, making our voices speak back and forth for other people to share' (interview, 19 July 2001).

22 Gom recalls that 'Patricia's Garden' began as an unrelated poem until
    Lowther's death conditioned its completion: '... as I went back to it, my mind
    was still so full of Pat (and Roy) that the poem became about her' (letter to
    the author, 9 Jan. 2001).

23 Catherine Firestone, 'Tone, Tune of True Poet.' A clipping of this newspaper
    review (without source identification) is in the Dorothy Livesay's Papers,
    University of Manitoba Special Collections, MSS 37, box 20, folder 4. I have
    been unable to trace the original.

24 Letter to William Toye, 23 Nov. 1976, Oxford University Press archives. Ged-
    des was referring to having come across the *Stone Diary* manuscript that
    Lowther had sent him for an informal assessment, while cleaning up his study.

25 The morbid rumour that Lowther 'gave a friend a copy of one of her poetry
    books, *Milk Stone*, with the inscription "Pat Lowther R.I.P., 1935–1975,"' is
    repeated by Dona Sturmanis (1985a) and Paul Grescoe in 'Eulogy for a
    Poet,' among others. See Brooks (2000: 231–2), who accurately 'separate[s]
    fact from fiction' on this point.

26 Similarly, in a second article published by Sturmanis in 1985, entitled
    'Lowther's Legacy,' Lowther's mis-routed luggage during her Prince Edward
    Island reading trip is more sensationally (and erroneously) rendered as a
    case of 'stolen' 'manuscripts' (1985b: 4).

27 The second article, published a few months later in *Books in Canada*, begins
    with the observation that 'the late Vancouver poet Pat Lowther is very much
    alive these days ... Random reminders of her legacy have popped up in the
    most surprising contexts in the decade since she was murdered' (1985b: 4–
    5). The article then basically recapitulates the vague history of *Final Instruc-
    tions* offered in 'A Poet's Haunting Legacy,' also curiously neglecting to men-
    tion Sturmanis's own role in the transmission of texts that became *Final
    Instructions*.

28 Pat's account of how Bill Domphousse threatened to use evidence of her
    relationship with Carson as 'grounds ... to take the children away from me,'
    and her denial of any impropriety in her relation with Carson, came only in a
    confidential written statement to the judge who finalized her divorce, a letter
    that had remained sealed since 1963 (FCR, D & M, 1001/62).

29 Ward Carson, interview with Toby Brooks, Vancouver, 28 and 31 May 1997,
    emphasis added. Brooks does not pursue the implication of Carson's ambig-
    uous wording in the interview. In conversation with Brooks, as in my own
    interview with Carson, he also makes a claim very similar to Roy Lowther's
    'case' against his wife's poetry; namely, that some of Lowther's early poems
    were 'directly written to me, about me.' Thanks to Toby Brooks for lending
    me a copy of her taped interview.

30 Interview with Ward Carson, Vancouver, 21 June 2002.
31 Phone interview with Dona Sturmanis, 24 June 2002. Sturmanis could not recall considering the provenance of the written poems as a potential factor in compiling the collection.
32 Interview with Fred Candelaria, Vancouver, 11 Dec. 2000.
33. Interview with Brenda Marshal, Surrey, 15 June 2002.
34 League records kept by Dorothy Livesay indicate that, even at the time of its conception, the Pat Lowther Memorial Award was a contentious issue among members of the League's feminist caucus for reasons articulated by Rona Murray: 'The award distresses me. Should we have it? Should we support yet another competition that sets all of us against each other? ... Is this the kind of award of which Pat Lowther would have approved? ... [C]an something be done to change the award from a competition to a celebration?' (University of Manitoba Special Collections, Dorothy Livesay Papers, MSS 37, box 13, folder 1).
35 Michelle Benjamin, letter to Kathy Lyons, Christine Lowther, and Beth Lowther, 27 March 1997 (in the possession of Beth Lowther). 'By *integrity*,' Benjamin recalls, 'I meant that we were searching for the "best" poems from Pat's entire collection – best, as in best quality, most literary, most complete, most accessible ... The "almost" probably refers to some poems that are included because they were important to the family, or they are representative of a kind of Pat's writing that might not be reflected elsewhere – perhaps we made some decisions based on these reasons rather than quality' (letter to the author, 14 June 2002).
36 *Time Capsule*, for example, welds two different poems from *This Difficult Flowring* (16, 17) into one extended text (*TC*, 29–30).
37 'Did Pat have a tap root into a special level of awareness? ... She may have had an enlightened premonition about the manuscript that she called *Time Capsule* [*sic*], her project at the time of her death' (Brooks 2000: 232–3). Among other problems, *Pat Lowther's Continent* does not distinguish meaningfully between Polestar's posthumous *Time Capsule* and Lowther's unfinished project by that name.
38 Thesis 'IX' of the 'Theses on the Philosophy of History' (1940):

> This is how one pictures the angel of history. His face is turned toward the past. Where we perceive a chain of events, he sees one single catastrophe which keeps piling wreckage upon wreckage and hurls it in front of his feet. The angel would like to stay, awaken the dead, and make whole what has been smashed. But a storm is blowing from Paradise ... This storm irresistibly propels him into the future to which his back is turned, while the pile of debris before him grows skyward. This storm is what we call progress. (Benjamin 1978: 257–8)

39 It is, of course, the slippage between actual and apparent biographical evidence – not the validity or value of 'new ways of thinking about' literature which are not biographically 'authorized' – which is at issue here.

40 Interview with Gary Geddes, Edmonton, 8 March 2001.

41 'Pat Lowther is the most arresting writer of this selection,' Diane Bessai also wrote, in a review of Borealis books that included both Lowther's *Milk Stone* and Carol Shields's *Intersect* (Bessai 1975: 36). In his review article, George Woodcock explicitly compared Lowther (favourably) to Miriam Mandel, whose prize-winning *Lions at Her Face* he went on to (harshly) critique (1975, 94). Woodcock's article may have been a factor in *Eli* Mandel's negative response to Gary Geddes' decision to include Lowther in *Fifteen Canadian Poets Plus Five*. My letter (through Brick Books) to Michael Ondaatje received no reply.

42 Interview with Seymour Mayne, Ottawa, 17 May 2001.

43 J.R. Colombo, letter to the author, 12 Feb. 2002.

44 Hutcheon adds an essential caveat, pertinent also to the present study: 'To say that the past is only *known* to us through textual traces, is not, however, the same as saying that the past is only textual, as the semiotic idealism of some forms of poststructuralism seems to assert' (1989: 81; emphasis in the original).

45 Interview with Hilda Thomas, Vancouver, 17 Aug. 1998. In 1975 the standard UBC sessional stipend for an academic year was around $4,500, usually disbursed in two equal payments of $2,250. UBC financial statements for the period from 1 April 1975 to 31 March 1976 list Lowther's remuneration for this period as only $500, which may have been an advance on her September 1975 term's salary.

46 The most problematic aspect of Harrison's 'non-fictional novel' is that while some of his characters critically question the role of Lowther's murder in her posthumous 'mystique' (118), the novel's fictionalized focus on that sensational murder case also contributes to it. Ultimately, Harrison's stated aim 'to imagine a fictive shape for Pat Lowther's *actual life*' (213, emphasis added) only succeeds in imagining 'a fictive shape' around her *death*, which it does not (and insofar as it *is* 'fictive') cannot move beyond.

Chapter 4

1 Virginia Tinmouth, interview with Toby Brooks, North Vancouver, 23 Feb. 1989. The family surname appears under variant spellings as 'Tinmouth' (the official name) and 'Tinmuth' — the version that Virginia used. Similarly, Virginia's maiden surname, 'Wilks,' also appears in some earlier records as

'Wilkes.' For sake of consistency and clarity, I use the legal name 'Tinmouth,' unless otherwise specifically noted in relation to Virginia's preference; and the modern spelling of 'Wilks' unless citing instances where the variant is used.

2 District of North Vancouver Municipal Public Library, Annual Report, 1964, Lynn Valley Branch, North Vancouver District Library, n.pag.

3 'Brilliant Future Awaiting Actress,' *Portland Telegram*, 1 June 1923; 'Native Daughter Stars in Musical Comedy at Pantages Next Week,' *Vancouver Daily World*, 12 May 1923, p. 19.

4 Virginia Tinmouth, interview with Toby Brooks, North Vancouver, 23 Feb. 1989.

5 Jack Alicoate, 'The Romance of the Roxy: A Fascinating Stroll through the Fairyland of the World's Largest and Greatest Theatre,' in *The Roxy: A History* (New York: The Film Daily, 1927), 9–13; 'The Evolution of a Roxy Stage Setting,' scrapbook clipping (Radio City Music Hall collection of the papers of James Stewart Morcom and John William Keck, Billy Rose Theatre Collection, New York Public Library).

6 Virginia Tinmouth, interview with Toby Brooks, North Vancouver, 23 Feb. 1989; *Christian Science Monitor*, 26 May 1971, p. 13 ('Russell Markert' clipping file, Billy Rose Theatre Collection, New York Public Library).

7 Unidentified press clipping, 19 May 1929; *New York Sun*, 23 March 1933 ('The Roxyettes' and 'Russell Markert' clipping files, Billy Rose Theater Collection, New York Public Library). For a history of the 'dance routine' which Virginia took up, a form of precision dance actually based in part on military drills of the late-nineteenth century, see Stratyner 1996. It is often inaccurately suggested that Virginia was a Radio City 'Rockette.' But her connection to the 'Russell Markert Dancers' at the Roxy Theatre predates the formation of that more famous dance troupe, a group that began with the opening of Radio City Music Hall – the Roxy Theatre's successor – on 27 Dec. 1932.

8 Virginia Tinmouth, interview with Toby Brooks, North Vancouver, 23 Feb. 1989.

9 Ibid.

10 'During the Depression when we were first married, my husband worked for a hundred and fifty dollars a month for a long time [\$37.50 per week]' (ibid.).

11 Interview with Brenda Marshall, and John and Arden Tinmouth, North Vancouver, 17 Feb. 2000.

12 'During the early months of 1940 the number of men employed in the North Vancouver shipyards was estimated at 800. By the end of 1942 that number had risen to 12,000, with a corresponding increase in office staffs'

(Woodward-Reynolds 1943: 159). See also Barman (1996), who cites a
'severe housing shortage' and a provincial figure of 'over 30,000 men and
women' employed in shipbuilding during the peak years in Vancouver and
Victoria (262). Stott records extra ferries imported from the States 'to help
handle the crowds of workers at the ship yards' (1950: 17).

13 Interview with Brenda Marshall, and John and Arden Tinmouth, North Vancouver, 17 Feb. 2000.

14 Virginia Tinmouth and Brenda Marshall, interview with Toby Brooks, North
Vancouver, 23 Feb. 1989.

15 See, for example, Brooks 2000: 27, 30. Brooks asserts that 'at three and a
half, Pat wrote what may have been her first poem: "I love to sit on the cool
green grass, / Sit there on my little ass"' (25), but her source is Paul Grescoe,
who quotes the lines in an unattributed parenthetical clause in his 'Eulogy
for a Poet' (1976: 16). The information may originally have come from Virginia, though in her interview with Brooks, Virginia does not recall this
poem (or any others) when asked about Pat's early childhood writing (interview with Toby Brooks, North Vancouver, 23 Feb. 1989). I have not come
across this little rhyme in any of the juvenilia in the possession of Beth
Lowther and Brenda Marshall.

16 Looseleaf newspaper clipping, 1939, in the possession of Christine Lowther.

17 Black, unlined folder notebook, in the possession of Brenda Marshall.

18 'Smooth Ivory' notebook, in the possession of Beth Lowther. Although an
inscription on the cover in Virginia's hand indicates the play as a collaborative effort by 'Pat Tinmuth' and a girlfriend, 'Lorraine Plowman,' Plowman
'definitely doesn't remember' having written it, or anything else, with her
former childhood friend (interview, 12 July 2002). Plowman may have forgotten, or, as Brenda speculates, Virginia may have made an error in attribut-
ing it to her.

19 Roy Lowther's account, which cites as a source Elsie Wilks, Pat's aunt, is
headed 'Re: Pat as child' and reads in part as follows: 'It is the story of a child
prodigy reading to family and other audiences from books at age four, suddenly eclipsed, as she saw it, by the baby sister (see the nipple poem ...
["Watershed"]), then neglected again ... as she saw it ... when her brother.
Arden is born (RLJ, 2:100). While there is probably some truth in this 'story,'
Roy's account reflects his own preoccupations with 'competition' for attention as much as anything else.

20 'Watershed' was first published in *Event* 4.3 (1975): 69; it has not been
reprinted since.

21 Undated draft entry, coverless notepad, blue binding (in the possession of
Beth Lowther).

22 Interview with Brenda Marshall, and John and Arden Tinmouth, North Vancouver, 17 Feb. 2000.
23 Virginia Tinmouth, interview with Toby Brooks, North Vancouver, 23 Feb. 1989.
24 Brenda Marshall and Virginia Tinmouth, interview with Toby Brooks, North Vancouver, 23 Feb. 1989. Virginia recounts a very similar memory of her daughter's characteristically distracted absorption in books on the Gzowski radio tribute.
25 Virginia Tinmouth, interview with Toby Brooks, North Vancouver, 23 Feb. 1989.
26 Loose typescript, in the possession of Beth Lowther.
27 'University Entrance Examination Certificate,' June 1951, in the possession of Beth Lowther; *Columbae* [North Vancouver High School Yearbook], 1950–1, n.pag., City of North Vancouver Museum and Archives.
28 Virginia Tinmouth, interview with Toby Brooks, North Vancouver, 23 Feb. 1989; interview with Brenda Marshall, North Vancouver, 17 Feb. 2000.
29 Virginia Tinmouth, interview with Toby Brooks, North Vancouver, 23 Feb. 1989.
30 Undated pencil draft, coverless notepad, blue binding (in the possession of Beth Lowther).
31 Loose mss., in the possession of Beth Lowther.
32 Virginia Tinmouth, interview with Toby Brooks, North Vancouver, 23 Feb. 1989.
33 Interview with Kathy (Domphousse) Lyons, Vancouver, 12 Jan. 2000.
34 Phone interview with Lorraine Plowman, 12 July 2002.
35 Virginia Tinmouth, interview with Toby Brooks, North Vancouver, 23 Feb. 1989.
36 Mimeographed pamphlet, in the possession of Beth Lowther.
37 Spanning the decades 1930–90, the *Alberta Poetry Yearbook* was the longest-running of several such series published at various times by affiliate branches of the Canadian Authors Association – in Montreal, Toronto, Ottawa, and Manitoba, as well as Alberta. The contests did represent a form of vanity publication since would-be authors paid to enter and were also obliged to pay for the anthology if their work was chosen. As Peggy Kelly notes, though, 'most poetry publications, especially chapbooks, have constituted vanity publishing throughout literary history ... Frank Scott paid $200 to Macmillan Canada in 1935, to publish *New Provinces: Poems of Several Authors* (1936),' a form of 'financial self-support' that 'has not kept Scott or his colleagues in the *New Provinces* outside the Canadian literary canon' (2000: 4).
38 Roy Lowther, 'In Praise of Petitions,' *Alberta Poetry Yearbook*, 1959.

39 Interview with Kathy (Domphousse) Lyons, Vancouver, 12 Jan. 2000.
40 FCR, D & M, 1001/62.
41 Virginia Tinmouth, interview with Toby Brooks, North Vancouver, 23 Feb. 1989.

Chapter 5

1 Virginia Tinmouth, interview with Toby Brooks, North Vancouver, 23 Feb. 1989.
2 Brooks claims that the couple met at the Vanguard Book Store, citing Roy's journals as a source for her information (2000: 57, 261). But I have not been able to find the information where she indicates, or elsewhere, in Roy's journal. Family sources such as Kathy, Brenda, Arden, and John remember that it was through a writing workshop that the two first met, and this would seem to point in the direction of the Vancouver Poetry Society.
3 RLJ, 2: 'Biographical,' n.pag. Directories for 1955 and 1959 list his occupations as 'paymaster' for a roofing company and 'cost clerk' for another firm.
4 Virginia Tinmouth, interview with Toby Brooks, North Vancouver, 23 Feb. 1989; interview with John Tinmouth, North Vancouver, 17 Feb. 2000.
5 Interview with Hilda Thomas, Vancouver, 17 Aug. 1998.
6 Bethoe Shirkoff, 'Pat Lowther,' unpublished typescript, Oct. 1975, in the possession of Christine Lowther.
7 Lionel Kearns, letter to the author, 24 Sept. 2001.
8 According to his eldest daughter, Roy spoke of being rather mercilessly bullied in Britannia Beach as a young man, memories he rued to his dying day (interview with Ruth Lowther Lalonde, Surrey, 13 Dec. 2000).
9 Not only was California, for example, the jurisdiction of the zealous *über*-patriot Senator Jack B. Tenney and his 'Fact-Finding Committee on Un-American Activities,' but the university at Berkeley, where Roy arrived in 1946, had just been transformed during the Second World War: formerly regarded as little more than an intellectual outpost on the West Coast, the institution which housed J. Robert Oppenheimer and his fellow scientists, as they developed the first atomic bomb, had proven a key beneficiary of lucrative and top-secret National Defense Program research contracts – 57 million dollars worth during 1940–5 alone (Stadtman 1970: 311, 307–10). As a consequence of its newly acquired strategic significance for the American government, Berkeley came under heightened scrutiny for any signs of 'subversive taint' in the immediate post-war years. 'The dead embers of the student radical movements of the Depression years were raked over,' and the faculty, likewise 'raked over,' were forced to sign loyalty oaths disclaiming any

communist affiliations – or be fired (as psychologist Erik Erikson, among others, was) – in an unprecedented clampdown on civil liberties and academic freedom (Stadtman 1970: 320ff). In other words, at that particular place, during those years, it would not have taken much to be deemed suspiciously 'un-American,' and worthy of an FBI file, deportation, or other such harassment. Patricia Domphousse, however, would have had no way to know that Roy's status as an opinionated non-American, who was failing to make any progress toward his graduate degree, could have served as sufficient grounds for the Americans to turf him, rather than renew his student visa.

10 Interview with Hilda Thomas, Vancouver, 17 Aug. 1998.

11 Phone interview with Bill Bissett, 4 March 2002; Tom Wayman, letter to the author, 4 Nov. 2000.

12 Roy's nephew David Lowther recalls that as 'an outdoorsman' Roy was 'really good with canoes': '... technically, he was excellent. And I can observe that [because] I took the Outward Bound course after [canoeing with Roy], and none of the instructors was as good as Roy' (interview, Victoria, 17 April 2001).

13 Plaintiff's Statement of Claim, 5, FCR, D & M, 1001/62.

14 William Domphousse, Affidavit, 7 Aug. 1963, FCR, D & M, 1001/62. In a statement that she filed during her March divorce hearing, Pat already signalled to the judge her 'intent to marry' Roy and so solemnize the union. But that this step was prematurely hastened into being by Bill's threat to revoke access to their son seems an unavoidable conclusion: in a letter sent by Pat's lawyer six days after her marriage to Roy, Bill Domphousse was officially notified of his ex-wife's remarriage and instructed to make 'the necessary arrangements' for Pat to have Alan for summer holidays that August.

15 Roy Lowther, letter to Gerry Anderson, 24 Aug. 1963, City of Vancouver Archives, VPS fonds, #Add. MSS. 294.

16 Dr W.G. Wallis, letter, 12 March 1962, Exhibit 'B' of Affidavit filed by William Domphousse, 7 Aug. 1963, FCR, D & M, 1001/62.

17 Handwritten draft poem, undated, coverless notebook, in the possession of Beth Lowther.

18 Handwritten draft letter, undated, coverless notebook, in the possession of Beth Lowther.

19 'It could be posited that Modernist poetry did not assemble an anthology in Vancouver because from 1915 to 1945 Vancouver was a hick town in which any poets were trying to be Kipling' (Bowering 1994: 139). Unlike 'official' centres of modernism like Montreal, Vancouver could have been the sort of place Robert Kroetsch was thinking about when he said, 'I don't see much Modernism in our literature ... There is a gap between older Canadian writ-

ing and most contemporary work,' in part because 'Modernism was a product of a high urban civilization and we just didn't have any' (1982: 111). See, however, Shirley Neuman's critique of the 'trend to a master narrative for post-modernist poetry' (1990: 60). Neuman argues persuasively that the term 'postmodernism' has not so much 'describ[ed] Canadian poetry of the last twenty-five years' as it has 'inscrib[ed] a new set of inclusions and exclusions in a shifting canon' (55) – one that has tended to neglect the post-sixties' work of writers like Dorothy Livesay, P.K. Page, and Earle Birney, all of whom 'adapted the language practices of the 1960s poetic revisionism without entirely adopting its sense of language's relations to the world' (60). Much of her argument can be seen to apply as well to the work of a younger writer like Pat Lowther, another 'undecidable' figure in a more ambiguous 'post(modern)/modern' narrative (59).

20 Mabel T. McIntyre, 'The Vancouver Poetry Society,' [1957], 3, 1, Vancouver City Archives, VPS fonds, # Add. MSS 294.

21 A generation before Roy Lowther occupied the position, Duncan Mcnair also acted as secretary of the VPS, during 1937–8. Livesay herself gave an address at the Society's 'twenty-first season' (University of Manitoba Special Collections, Dorothy Livesay Papers, MSS 37, box 15, folder 6). The title of her talk, 'New Directions in Poetry,' suggests an attempt to nudge the VPS in 'new directions,' even back in the thirties, by a poet whose exposure to modernism (through such publications as *Poetry Chicago*) extended back to her childhood upbringing in Winnipeg. For Lowther, by contrast, though she had also read some of the low moderns (such as C. Day Lewis and Stephen Spender) by the early 1960s, the VPS years were still part of a much steeper learning curve.

22 Mabel T. McIntyre, 'The Vancouver Poetry Society' [1957], 2. Vancouver City Archives, VPS fonds, # Add. MSS 294. Similarly, Peggy Kelly records the 'lofty goals' of the CAA-affiliated editors of the *Alberta Yearbook* series: 'to encourage Canadians to write poetry and to develop a national literature' (2000: 4).

23 I am drawing on Paul Litt's analysis in *The Muses, the Masses, and the Massey Commission*: 'The recommendations made by the [Massey] commissioners flowed naturally from the premises of liberal humanist nationalism. Their general goal was to promote high culture as national culture and make it more accessible to the average Canadian' (214).

24 Quoted in Keith Cronshaw, 'An Ode to Rhyme and Reason,' undated newspaper clipping [1968?], Vancouver City Archives, VPS fonds, #Add. MSS 294.

25 The historical bases for conflicts between amateur and professional literary groups is only beginning to attract the attention it deserves. Harrington's history of the CAA in *Syllables of Recorded Time* is a valuable start in this direc-

tion, but I am also indebted to recent work by Peggy Kelly. In her discussion of the CAA-sponsored *Alberta Poetry Yearbook* contests, Kelly makes an important observation that is pertinent to understanding (not excusing) Roy Lowther's resentful and defensive posture vis à vis 'professional' 'modern' poets like his wife: 'The serious-popular continuum gets mapped onto the Victorian-modernist struggle in Canadian literary history. Although it's logical to argue that each genre, Victorian and modernist, produces examples ranging along the serious-popular continuum, the modernist hegemony in our present educational and critical arena situates all Victorian writing at the popular, feminized, devalued end of this continuum, because it's considered formulaic and out-dated' (2000: 4).

26 'On It Being Resolved that a Poetry Group Should Write on Ookpik,' undated draft poem entry, coverless notebook, in the possession of Beth Lowther. The poem continues: 'whatever little gems be wrought / they won't demand the pain of thought / nor ask that hard-won honesty/ that is the mark of poetry.'

27 Roy's correspondence with Cogswell begins in spring of 1954 and tapers off in 1966, around the time Pat was beginning to enjoy success with her own submissions. Cogswell did accept one poem by Roy during the fifties, but after that, the tone of his rejection letters becomes a little more blunt (UNB Archives and Special Collections, Fred Cogswell fonds, MS 1.410, 428, 671, 867, 1008, 2898, 2935, 3248, 3671, 5029, 5202, 5937, 8564, MS 3.233).

28 Letters to Fred Cogswell, 18 Jan. 1965 and 30 May 1965, UNB Archives and Special Collections, Fred Cogswell fonds, MS 1.7647, 1.7929.

29 Letter to Fred Cogswell, 20 March 1964, UNB Archives and Special Collections, Fred Cogswell fonds, MS 1.7.7170.

30 Interview with Patrick Lane, Victoria, 17 April 2001.

31 Roy Lowther, letter to Fred Cogswell, 3 April 1966, UNB Archives and Special Collections, Fred Cogswell fonds, MS 1.8564. In this letter, Roy mentions Acorn's presence as a current house guest.

32 Interview with Gary Geddes, Edmonton, 8 March 2001.

33 Draft letter to Jacob Zilber, undated, coverless notebook, in the possession of Beth Lowther.

34 Coverless notebook entry, undated [ca. 1964], in the possession of Beth Lowther.

35 Interview with Patrick Lane, Victoria, 17 April 2001.

36 Draft letter entry, undated [ca. 1964], 'Standard Life' notebook, in the possession of Beth Lowther. Lowther's draft quotes the following statement by the VPS member testifying against Roy at his custody hearings: 'I am a member of VPS. I know Roy Lowther through VPS and other groups. I have

observed his behavior in this area to be abnormal. He is extremely arrogant, and doesn't want to let anyone else's poetry be heard but his own. I have seem him get violently angry over a point of discussion in a poem. He will then yell and become purple in the face ...' Lowther's draft concludes: 'It was truly a performance which it will be very difficult to erase from our memories.'

37 Kathy (Domphousse) Lyons, letter to the author, 22 Feb. 2002.

38 'Thrift,' undated draft entry [ca. 1963–4], Standard Life notebook, in the possession of Beth Lowther.

39 Lane's 'first really strong memory' of Lowther stems from one of these poetry evenings: 'bill bissett and I went over to Roy and Pat's place ... Roy invited a bunch of poets over for an evening where we would talk about poetry. Both bill and I went and both bill and I hated it ... It was pretentious ... And what made it so pretentious was the pomposity of Roy ... he was the poet and Pat was just this little added thing that he called a wife, who happened to dabble' (interview, Victoria, 17 April, 2001).

40 Letter to Barry Nichol, 19 Oct. 1965, Simon Fraser University, Special Collections, Ganglia papers, CLC MSC 12b.3.6.1–6.

41 The phrase 'Black Mountain offspring' is Seymour Mayne's, in a letter to Robert Bly, 16 July 1966; Livesay's letter to Mayne testifying to her sense of alienation on the Coast is from 9 July 1966 (National Archives, Ottawa, Seymour Mayne Papers, MG 31, D253, Vol. 1, file 16, and Vol. 1, file 14). On Livesay's first summer back in Canada and her unique adaptations of 'Black Mountain techniques,' see also McInnis 1994: 55–8. Mayne's reference to Livesay's '*salon des autres*' is from an interview, Ottawa, 17 May 2001.

42 Letter to Dorothy Livesay, 26 Nov. 1966, Queen's University Archives, Dorothy Livesay Papers, box 4A, folder 84; postcard to Lorraine Vernon, loose mss. in the possession of Beth Lowther.

43 Letter to Dorothy Livesay, 26 Nov. 1966, Queen's University Archives, Dorothy Livesay Papers, box 4A, folder 84.

44 Undated typescript, loose mss., in the possession of Beth Lowther. Livesay may have recommended such books as Friedan's; her papers contain annotated feminist bibliographies listing *The Feminine Mystique*, among other key feminist texts from the fifties, sixties, and seventies (University of Manitoba Special Collections, Dorothy Livesay Papers, MSS 37, box 15, file 5).

45 See Horowitz 1998, which carefully documents Friedan's distancing of herself from an early past that included links to communism, progressive feminism of the 1940s, Popular Front social reform causes, and a career as a radical labour journalist. Horowitz attributes Friedan's liberal re-emergence

in the sixties to the 'devastating' effects of McCarthyism (145). Friedan's career thus complicates conventional historical accounts of 1960s feminism as 'middle-class,' suggesting instead 'additional origins – anti-fascism, radicalism, and labor union activism of the 1940s' (7). He traces the 'central thesis' of *The Feminine Mystique* to Friedan's notebook transcription of the following passage from Friedrich Engel's 1884 essay 'The Origin of the Family, Private Property, and the State': 'We see already that the emancipation of women and their equality with men are impossible and will remain so as long as women are excluded from socially productive work and restricted to housework, which is private. The emancipation of women becomes possible only when women are enabled to take part in production on a large, social scale, and when domestic duties require their attention only to a minor degree' (quoted in Horowitz 1998: 201).

Chapter 6

1 Earle Birney, letter to Seymour Mayne, 4 July 1966, National Archives, Ottawa, Seymour Mayne Papers, MG 31, D253, Vol. 1, file 12.
2 Wynne Francis, letter to Seymour Mayne, 6 Feb. 1967, and Seymour Mayne, letter to Tom Marshall, 9 July 1969, National Archives, Ottawa, Seymour Mayne Papers, MG 31, D253, Vol. 1, file 15, Vol. 1, file 20, Vol. 2, file 10.
3 Seymour Mayne, letter to Louis Dudek, 19 June 1966, National Archives, Ottawa, Seymour Mayne Papers, MG 31, D253, Vol. 1, file 17. In the same letter, Mayne mentions displeasure with the promotion of 'only Tishites' by certain presses such as Contact Press.
4 Interview with Patrick Lane, Victoria, 17 April 2001.
5 Ibid.
6 Interview with Seymour Mayne, Ottawa, 17 May 2001.
7 Patrick Lane, letter to Seymour Mayne, 15 May 1967, National Archives, Ottawa, Seymour Mayne Papers, MG 31, D253, Vol. 1, file 24.
8 Pauline Bennett, undated letter to the author; and interview, 13 Feb. 2000.
9 Interview with Patrick Lane, Victoria, 17 April 2001.
10 Interview with Seymour Mayne, Ottawa, 17 May 2001.
11 Letter to Ralph Gustafson, 20 Nov. 1974, Queen's University Archives, Ralph Gustafson Papers, box 2, 'Lowther' file.
12 Patrick Lane, letter to Seymour Mayne, 8 Nov. 1968; Seymour Mayne, letter to Patrick Lane, 11 Nov. 1968: National Archives, Ottawa, Seymour Mayne Papers, MG 31, D253, Vol. 2, file 3.
13 Letter to Dorothy Livesay, 15 Dec. 1968, Queen's University Archives, Dorothy Livesay Papers, box 4A, folder 84.

Chapter 7

1 Acorn's recent biographer, Richard Lemm, states that Acorn moved into the Lowther basement 'in early 1968' and stayed for 'two months' (1999: 145), but Acorn had stayed there intermittently prior to this time as well: not only in 1966, when Roy mentioned his presence to Fred Cogswell, but also in the fall of 1967, when Acorn was preparing flyer notices for meetings of the activist group 'Artists against Viet Nam,' giving Lowther's address (National Archives, Ottawa, Seymour Mayne Papers, MG 31, D253, Vol. 1, file 26). He does not appear to have stayed at the Lowthers' during his return visit in 1974, as Lemm reports (146).
2 Interview with Kathy (Domphousse) Lyons, Vancouver, 12 Jan. 2000.
3 Letter to Dorothy Livesay, 23 April 1969, Queen's University Archives, Dorothy Livesay Papers, box 4A, folder 84.
4 Ibid., 30 July 1969.
5 Ibid.
6 Letter to Fred Cogswell, 5 Dec. 1973, UNB Archives and Special Collections, Fred Cogswell fonds, MS 2.2177.
7 Interview with Patrick Lane, Victoria, 17 April 2001.
8 Letter to Fred Cogswell, 5 Dec. 1973. UNB Archives and Special Collections, Fred Cogswell fonds, MS 2.2177; letter to Eugene McNamara, 13 Dec. 1973, in the possession of Beth Lowther.
9 Letter to Dorothy Livesay, 17 June 1972, University of Manitoba Special Collections, Dorothy Livesay Papers, MSS 37, box 61, folder 42; letter to Fred Cogswell, 28 Dec. 1973, UNB Archives and Special Collections, Fred Cogswell fonds, MS 2.2140.
10 Letter to Arlene Lampert, 27 Jan. 1974 [1975], emphasis in the original, National Archives, Ottawa, League of Canadian Poets fonds, 1975 correspondence, MG 28, I301, Vol. 1, file 1–19.
11 Letters to Dorothy Livesay, 28 Dec. 28, 1973 and 9 Jan. 1974, University of Manitoba Special Collections, Dorothy Livesay Papers, MSS 37, box 61, folder 42.
12 Interview with Patrick Lane, Victoria, 17 April 2001.
13 Undated typescript, in the possession of Beth Lowther.
14 The poem provides mixed cues on this point. On the one hand, it suggests Penelope's faithfulness, as in the original story: 'She *could have* spun her hanging of her hair / or made her bed a market thoroughfare – / he didn't care' (*MS*, 57, emphasis added). On the other hand, Penelope's attitude toward the 'old boy' who 'interrupt[s] forever' her suitors' 'sweet songs' also conveys her jaded dissatisfaction with Odysseus (*MS*, 56).

15 Letter to Dorothy Livesay, 26 June 1972, University of Manitoba Special Collections, Dorothy Livesay Papers, MSS 37, box 61, folder 42.
16 Interview with Brenda Marshall, and John and Arden Tinmouth, North Vancouver, 17 Feb. 2000.
17 Letter to Dorothy Livesay, 29 Oct. 1973, University of Manitoba Special Collections, Dorothy Livesay Papers, MSS 37, Box 61, folder 42.
18 Letter to Eugene McNamara, 11 Dec. 1974, in the possession of Beth Lowther.
19 Letter to Fred Cogswell, 3 May 1973, UNB Archives and Special Collections, Fred Cogswell fonds, MS 2. 1856.
20 Letter to Eugene McNamara, 17 April 1973, in the possession of Beth Lowther.
21 Letter to Joy Kogawa, 20 April 1973, UBC Archives and Special Collections, Joy Kogawa papers, MSS Col. 50-4.
22 Lorraine Vernon, witness statement, PHTT, court dossier, Vancouver, B.C. Law Courts.
23 'After,' in *Beware the Months of Fire*, 51.

Chapter 8

1 Letter to Patrick Lane, 6 April 1973, UBC Archives and Special Collections, Patrick Lane Papers, MSS Coll, box 3, folder 7.
2 Letter to Seymour Mayne, 5 Jan. 1973, in the possession of Beth Lowther.
3 Phone interview with Gail McKay, 20 Aug. 2002.
4 PL, testimony, Proceedings at Trial transcript, 13 (FCR, D & M, 1001/62).
5 Lorraine Vernon, pre-trial statement, PHTT court dossier, Vancouver, B.C. Law Courts. See also Brooks 2000: 142.
6 Interview with Joy Kogawa, Toronto, 25 Jan. 2001. Kogawa, who had herself been through an anguished divorce, also recalls Lowther worrying about the effects on her children of a second divorce.
7 Leona Gom, letter to the author, 9 Jan. 2001.
8 Interview with Patrick Lane, Victoria, 17 April 2001.
9 Interview with Fred Cogswell, Fredericton, 21 Feb. 2001.
10 Lorraine Vernon, pre-trial statement, PHTT court dossier, Vancouver, B.C. Law Courts.
11 Interview with David Morgan, Vancouver, 11 Dec. 2000.
12 Letter to Eugene McNamara, 2 Dec. 1974, in the possession of Beth Lowther.
13 Lorraine Vernon, pre-trial statement, PHTT court dossier, Vancouver, B.C. Law Courts.

14 Interview with Brenda Marshall, and John and Arden Tinmouth, North Van-couver, 17 Feb. 2000.

15 Interview with Patrick Lane, Victoria, 17 April 2001.

16 Letter to Arlene Lampert, 23 June 1975. National Archives, Ottawa, League of Canadian Poets fonds, MG 28, I301, vol. 1, file 1–19.

17 Interview with Brenda Marshall, and John and Arden Tinmouth, North Van-couver, 17 Feb. 2000.

18 Virginia Tinmouth, interview with Toby Brooks, North Vancouver, 23 Feb. 1989.

19 Interview with Beth and Christine Lowther, Vancouver, 14 Aug. 1998.

20 Lorraine Vernon, pre-trial statement, PHTT court dossier, Vancouver, B.C. Law Courts.

21 Interview with Patrick Lane, Victoria, 17 April 2001.

22 Lorraine Vernon, pre-trial statement, PHTT court dossier, Vancouver, B.C. Law Courts.

23 Undated looseleaf typescript, in the possession of Beth Lowther.

24 The site of the speaker's impossible non-'choice' in 'City Slide / 6' conveys a similar aporia, for as a nexus of potential fatalities, or 'accidents / of all kinds,' the cross-road marks 'love's' 'intersection' with or by its opposite, death. The intersection also figures the speaker's own double-consciousness: the 'sick headache' of her own hyper-'reflective' lucidity, her own sometimes double-crossing mind.

25 Undated looseleaf draft, in the possession of Beth Lowther.

26 PL, Howatt Fruit Farm, Prince Edward Island tape recording (in the posses-sion of Beth Lowther).

27 Letter to Fred Cogswell, 25 Feb. 1974, UNB Archives and Special Collections, Fred Cogswell fonds, MS 2.2191.

28 Arlene Lampert, letter to Pat Lowther, 25 March 1975, National Archives, Ottawa, League of Canadian Poets fonds, 1975 correspondence, MG 28, I301, Vol. 1, file 1–19; Lorraine Vernon, pre-trial statement, PHTT court dos-sier, Vancouver, B.C. Law Courts.

29 Interview with Patrick Lane, Victoria, 17 April 2001.

30 *The Peak*, 1 Nov. 1972; Margaret Atwood, letter to the author, 8 Dec. 2000.

31 There is no record of Lowther having read Ibsen's 1881 play, but her poem's ironic prescription to 'take the sun' and the line's subsequent repetition by the speaker do seem to echo the conclusion of *Ghosts*, which ends with the slowly dying Oswald repeating: 'give me the sun ... The sun. The sun ... The sun ... The sun' (Ibsen 1981: 163–4). If she did read it there are reasons Lowther may have remembered Ibsen's 'Domestic Drama in Three Acts,' a play about hereditary illness and the false partitions between public and private lives.

32 Letter to Fred Cogswell, 3 May 1973, UNB Archives and Special Collections, Fred Cogswell fonds, MS 2.1856.

33 *Columbae* [North Vancouver High School Yearbook], (1950–1), n.pag., City of North Vancouver Museum and Archives.

34 Fred Cogswell, letter to the author, 24 Nov. 2000.

Chapter 9

1 Virginia Tinmouth, interview with Toby Brooks, 23 Feb. 1989. For a detailed history of British immigrant mining communities on Vancouver Island, see Belshaw 2002.

2 Virginia Tinmouth, interview with Toby Brooks, 23 Feb. 1989.

3 See Bowen 1999: 49–50; Belshaw 2002: 153–4, 208–10; and Phillips 1967: 'The casualty list was staggering: April 17, 1879 – eleven killed in Wellington explosion; Jan. 24th, 1881 – sixty-five killed in Wellington explosion; July 1st, 1884 – twenty-three killed in South Wellington explosion; May 3rd, 1887 – 148 killed in Nanaimo explosion; Jan. 24th, 1889 [*sic*, 1888] – seventy-five killed in Wellington gas explosion; Feb. 15th, 1901 – fifty-five buried in Cumberland; September 30th, 1901 – seventeen killed in Extension fire; Oct. 25th, 1909 – thirty-two killed in Extension explosion; and this toll out of a labour force that probably never exceeded four thousand miners' (8–9). The Wellington and Extension mines were not far from Nanaimo; Cumberland was further up the Island.

4 *Daily Colonist* [Victoria]: 'The Nanaimo Disaster,' 26 Jan. 1888, p. 1; 'Mining Disaster,' 27 Jan. 1888, p. 1.

5 *Daily Colonist* [Victoria]: 'Mining Disaster,' 25 Jan. 1888, p. 1; 'Mining Disaster,' 27 Jan. 1888, p. 1; 'The Last Sad Rites,' 28 Jan. 1888, p. 1; 'The Nanaimo Disaster,' 26 Jan. 1888, p. 2.

6 See Phillips 1967; Reksten 1991; Bowen 1999; and Belshaw 2002, esp. 25–6, 209.

7 'James Wilks Laid to Rest,' undated newspaper clipping, in the possession of Barry Wilks; 'James Wilks, B.C. Pioneer, Is Dead' *Vancouver Province*, 2 March 1937, p. 19; 'James Wilks, North Shore Pioneer, Dead,' *Vancouver Sun*, 2 March 1937, p. 10.

8 'My father ... would go ahead to a little town where Gerry McGeer was going to campaign. He would go ahead and arrange for the hall, and arrange for local people to support, and all this sort of thing, sort of a front man or whip' (Virginia Tinmouth, interview with Toby Brooks, 23 Feb. 1989). The newspaper article published at James Wilks's death also notes him as a 'well known former Liberal organizer.'

9 Interview with Barry Wilks, Mayne Island, 1 Aug. 2001. According to Christine Lowther, Virginia 'often emphasized how different [James] was from his
wife Annie' in this regard (letter to the author, 6 July 2004).

10 Virginia Tinmouth, interview with Toby Brooks, 23 Feb. 1989.

11 'James Wilks Laid to Rest,' undated newspaper clipping, in the possession of
Barry Wilks.

12 Virginia Tinmouth, interview with Toby Brooks, 23 Feb. 1989.

13 'Smothered in Bunker Fuel: Shipyard Worker Found in Oil Tank on Liner
Niagara,' *Daily Province* [Vancouver], 29 May 1923, p. 24.

14 Ibid.; 'Falls Down Tank; Killed,' *Vancouver Sun*, 29 May 1923 p. 12; 'Card of
Thanks' and 'Vancouver Port's Splendid Record,' *North Shore Press*, 1 June
1923, pp. 1, 5.

15 'Police Ban on Pickets in Force Today after Twenty-Eight Injured in Rioting,'
Vancouver Province, 19 June 1934, p. 1.

16 'Tear Gas Bombs Halt Strikers at Ballantyne Pier; Longshore Leader Jailed,'
Vancouver Province, 18 June 1934, p. 1; 'Will Not Tolerate Communist Agitators,' *Vancouver Province*, 19 June 1934, p. 2.

17 During the expansive 'boom' years of the war, for example, communist leadership became a contentious issue for unions such as the Boilermakers and
Shipyard Workers of Vancouver. See Mansbridge, 2002: 97ff and Phillips
1967: 133 for a more detailed account of the workplace politics which would
have affected Arthur Tinmouth as a new employee and union man at the
Burrard Dry Docks.

18 'Everybody was talking about being communist,' Virginia put it, '[as if] that's
what we needed to bring the country out of the Depression' (interview with
Toby Brooks, 23 Feb. 1989).

19 'Problems Outlined: Heavy Reduction Bonded Debts of City and District,'
North Shore Press, 21 June 1935, pp. 1, 4.

20 Virginia Tinmouth, interview with Toby Brooks, 23 Feb. 1989.

21 Undated black, unlined folder, circa 1943, in the possession of Brenda Marshall.

Chapter 10

1 Robert Patchell, CBC *Regional Tales* producer, letter to Pat Domphousse,
8 April 1959, in the possession of Beth Lowther.

2 'Red,' undated typescript, in the possession of Beth Lowther.

3 Employee records show that Bill Domphousse, who began at the Burrard
Dry Docks in 1942, was laid off fourteen times between 1948 and 1950 alone.

4 Interview with Brian Campbell, Vancouver, 14 Feb. 2000.

5 Ibid.

6 Ibid.

7 National Archives, Ottawa, Seymour Mayne Papers, MG 31, D253, box 1, file 26.

8 Interview with Patrick Lane, Victoria, 17 April 2001.

9 Interview with Hartley Dent, *Mountaineer* 4.3 (April 1970): 3; 'Why You Should Boycott Kraft,' *Mountaineer* (June 1973); 'Beating the Backlash,' *Mountaineer* (Nov. 1974); 'Film Night,' *Mountaineer* 4.8 (Nov. 1971): 1. The second and third cited issues of *Mountaineer* do not have volume, issue, or page numbers. All the issues cited are located in UBC Special Collections, NDP Little Mountain fonds, box 3, files 1–6. Undated draft film reviews appear in 'Woodward's' exercise book, in the possession of Beth Lowther. The biographical sketch of Tom Anderson appears in draft notebook form and in a circular from Fred Miller, 7 March 1973, UBC Special Collections, NDP Little Mountain fonds, box 1, file 2. Submissions by Roy Lowther also appear in *Mountaineer*; usually, he is grumbling about lack of credit for his work, or his exclusion from one committee or another.

10 *Mountaineer* 4.5 (July–Aug. 1971): 7, UBC Special Collections, NDP Little Mountain fonds, box 3, files 1–6.

11 Undated entries, 'Little Children' notebook, in the possession of Beth Lowther. Clearly, even if they had been implemented, the forms of state assistance advocated by feminists on the left of the left at this time would not have solved all the obstacles facing women in Lowther's particular position. But – as with Waffle proposals related to day care and better working conditions for part-time employees – they would have eased some.

12 Undated entry, 'Canada' looseleaf exercise book, in the possession of Beth Lowther.

13 Bethoe Shirkoff, 'Pat Lowther, 1935–1974 [*sic*],' unpublished memoir, in the possession of Christine Lowther.

14 Letter to Eugene McNamara, 27 June 1973, in the possession of Beth Lowther.

15 Phone interview with Rita Lalik, 21 Aug. 2001. Lalik is emphatic that Lowther was not terminated or forced from the position because of her 'radicalism,' as has sometimes been suggested. 'I can say very strongly we did not ask her to leave'; Phyllis Young and her staff were 'very happy with Pat' and her 'very satisfactory' work.

16 *Mountaineer* 4.3 (April 1970), UBC Special Collections, NDP Little Mountain fonds, box 3, files 1–6.

17 'This Movie Is Not Over (For Claire Culhane),' undated draft, looseleaf poem typescript, in the possession of Beth Lowther.

18 Bethoe Shirkoff, 'Pat Lowther, 1935–1974 [*sic*],' unpublished memoir, in the possession of Christine Lowther.
19 Miller 1975: 18. Miller's brief introduction to 'Penelopes' in this issue of the NDP's *Priorities* underscores Lowther's own appreciation of disparate audiences, not all of whom might be literarily inclined: 'Sometimes reading poetry can be intimidating, involving dictionaries and concentration.'
20 Undated draft letter, 'Hilroy 500' notebook, in the possession of Beth Lowther.
21. Seymour Mayne, letter to Patrick Lane, 5 June 1975, UBC Special Collections, Patrick Lane Papers, box 3, file 14.
22 Undated draft entry, 'Music Dictation' notebook, in the possession of Beth Lowther.
23 'Notes toward a Socialist Cultural Policy for British Columbia,' undated typewritten/handwritten draft, looseleaf material, in the possession of Beth Lowther.
24 *Pegasus* 6.2 (Summer 1974): 2; emphasis in the original. 'It should also mean,' the editorial continues, 'audiences – much larger than the present minuscule ones; now indifferent or 'turned off' the arts – who may respond to us' (2).

Chapter 11

1 Letter to Patrick Lane, 23 April 1973, UBC Special Collections, Patrick Lane Papers, box 3, file 7.
2 Undated newspaper clipping, UBC Special Collections, Patrick Lane Papers, MSS Col, box 3, file 7.
3 In his preface to *Storm Warning*, Purdy admits to a compunction over this 'arbitrary' editorial principle and mentions a few poets whose 'comparative senility ... precluded [their] inclusion' (1971: n.pag.). A glance at the back-cover blurb suggests that aside from the age requirement, Lowther fitted the criteria of *Storm Warning*, which was intended to showcase emergent 'writers who are not yet widely known' and who had not yet 'published a large, "commercial" book of poetry to date.'
4 Allan Safarik to Patrick Lane, undated letter, UBC Special Collections, Patrick Lane Papers, box 3, file 14.
5 The lack of representation given to women writers in the earliest *Storm Warning* anthologies was a subject Purdy was made to address when the time came for him to compile a subsequent edition. 'I'm involved with female poets right to my hackles and withers and wattles,' as he put it to George Woodcock in a letter of 25 July 1975: 'Jack McC. put out a press release to the

effect that we didn't have enough females in Storm Warning 2, and now
Roblin Lake is awash with soggy poems ... I am shrieking loudly at Jack McC.
TO SEND AN EDITOR DOWN HERE QUICKLY to save me from iambics' (in Galt 1983:
143).

6 Phone interview with Brian Brett, 9 Feb. 2002.
7 'At the last Judgement we shall all be trees,' 'The Origin of the Universe,'
several parts of 'Five Diptyches,' and 'Vision' also appeared in *Blackfish* 2
(Fall 1971). 'Vision' was previously published by Dorothy Livesay in *The
Merry Devil of Edmonton* (1969–70).
8 Phone interview with Allan Safarik, 3 Feb. 2002.
9 Phone interview with Brian Brett, 9 Feb. 2002.
10 Undated draft entry, 'Woodwards School Exercise' notebook, in the possession of Beth Lowther.
11 There is a flurry of correspondence regarding 'confusion with Pat Lowther'
in relation to her reading tour with Atwood in the LCP's national tours correspondence from 1972. Some of the 'mix-up' stemmed from scheduling
errors with the Saskatchewan venues, but there also seems to have been a
misunderstanding between Lowther and Gerald Lampert regarding the Vancouver reading at Simon Fraser University. Lampert apparently wanted to
'give someone else a turn in Vancouver,' but, as he eventually reported in a
letter of 10 October 1972 to Allan Safarik, 'plans are changed and Pat will be
reading with Peggy' (National Archives, Ottawa, League of Canadian Poets
fonds, MG 28, I301, Vol. 8, folder 8–14; see also files 8–17, 8–20, 8–24, 8–25).
12 Letter to Margaret Atwood, 11 Oct. 1972, Thomas Fisher Rare Book Library,
University of Toronto, Margaret Atwood Papers, MS Coll. 200, box 160 –
Lowther.
13 Letter to Dorothy Livesay, 26 Nov. 1966, Queen's University Archives, University of Manitoba Special Collections, Dorothy Livesay Papers, box 4A, file 84.
14 Andrew Robertson, letter to PL, 15 Sept. [1972], in the possession of Beth
Lowther.
15 University of Regina Archives and Special Collections, Collection 81–13:
Department of Extension, Canada Lecture Series, Audio Cassette #11: Pat
Lowther and Margaret Atwood, 24 Oct. 1972.
16 'Chilko Kid,' 'Iris and the Silver,' *Peak* [SFU], 1 Nov. 1972, p. 4.
17 'A Reading of Fine Poetry,' *Vancouver Province*, 31 Oct. 1972, p. 27.
18 Letter to Gerald Lampert, 5 Nov. 1972, National Archives, Ottawa, League of
Canadian Poets national tours correspondence, MG 28, I301, Vol. 8, file 8–24.
19 David Stouck, letter to PL, 18 Nov. 1972, in the possession of Beth Lowther.
20 Letter to Eugene McNamara, 11 Nov. 1972, in the possession of Beth
Lowther.

21 Letter to Margaret Atwood, 27 Dec. 1972, Thomas Fisher Rare Book Library, University of Toronto, Margaret Atwood Papers, MS Coll. 200, box 160 – Lowther.
22 Interview with Seymour Mayne, Ottawa, 17 May 2001.
23 Seymour Mayne, letter to PL, 31 Dec. 1972, in the possession of Beth Lowther.
24 Draft letter to Seymour Mayne, 5 Jan. 1973; emphasis in the original (in the possession of Beth Lowther).
25 Margaret Atwood, letter to PL, 16 Jan. 1973, Thomas Fisher Rare Book Library, University of Toronto, Margaret Atwood Papers, MS Coll. 200, box 160 – Lowther.
26 Letter to Fred Cogswell, 3 May 1973, UNB Archives and Special Collections, Fred Cogswell fonds, MS 2.1856.
27 Interview with Seymour Mayne, Ottawa, 17 May 2001.
28 Letter to Eugene McNamara, 1 June 1973, in the possession of Beth Lowther.
29 Letter to Eugene McNamara, 1 March 1973, in the possession of Beth Lowther.
30 Letter to Dorothy Livesay, 30 Sept. 1973, University of Manitoba Special Collections, Dorothy Livesay Papers, MSS 37, box 61, folder 42.
31 Margaret Atwood, letter to PL, 17 Dec. 1973, National Library of Canada, Ottawa, House of Anansi fonds, LMS-0150 1988–13/1989–16.
32 Letter to Margaret Atwood, 30 Dec. 1973, Thomas Fisher Rare Book Library University of Toronto, Margaret Atwood Papers, MS Coll. 200, box 160 – Lowther.
33 Letter to Shirley Gibson, 4 Jan. 1974, National Library of Canada, Ottawa, House of Anansi fonds, LMS-0150 1988-13/1989-16.
34 James Polk, letter to PL, 29 Jan. 1974, National Library of Canada, Ottawa, House of Anansi fonds, LMS-0150 1988-13/1989-16. Permission to quote directly from this letter was denied.
35 Allan Safarik, letter to Patrick Lane, 10 Aug. 1974. UBC Special Collections, Patrick Lane Papers, box 4, file 4.
36 Lorraine Vernon, letter to the author, 29 Aug. 1998.
37 'To Milton Acorn,' undated looseleaf typescript, in the possession of Beth Lowther.
38 Letter to Fred Cogswell, 25 Feb. 1974, UNB Archives and Special Collections, Fred Cogswell fonds, MS 2.2191.
39 Interview with Fred Cogswell, Fredericton, 21 Feb. 2001.
40 'Pat Lowther Tribute,' Gzowski on FM, 2 Nov. 1975.

Chapter 12

1 'B.C. is becoming a mecca for women artists,' Lowther wrote in her spring 1973 regional report for the League, which mentions the publication of Mar-

latt's *Vancouver Poems* (undated notebook entry, 'Imperial' notebook, in the possession of Beth Lowther).

2 The original passage in *Milk Stone* is marred by a printer's error: 'A hillside suburb / lights up like a bloc / of dogman [*sic*] memorized' (*MS*, 18).

3 The original title for *Milk Stone* is mentioned in Lowther's contributor's note for *The Fiddlehead* 93 (Spring 1972): 118.

4 Dorothy Livesay, 'Pat Lowther Tribute,' *Gzowski on FM*, 2 Nov. 1975, emphasis added.

5 Letter to Dorothy Livesay, 29 Oct. 1973, University of Manitoba Special Collections, Dorothy Livesay Papers, MSS 37, box 61, folder 42.

6 *Mountaineer* 4.8 (Nov. 1971): 1, UBC Special Collections, NDP Little Mountain fonds, box 3, files 1–6.

7 Undated entry [ca. 18 Nov. 1971], 'Woodwards School Exercise' notebook, in the possession of Beth Lowther.

8 Dorothy Livesay, letter to PL, 8 Aug. 1971, in the possession of Beth Lowther.

9 University of Regina, Archives, Collection 81-13: Department of Extension, Canada Lecture Series, Audio Cassette #11, Pat Lowther / Margaret Atwood, 24 Oct. 1972; emphasis in the original.

10 Mallinson's initial connection to Lowther came while she was teaching a course in Canadian poetry for UBC's Continuing Education faculty. In 1968, shortly after the appearance of *This Difficult Flowring*, Mallinson invited several local poets, Lowther, Joy Kogawa, and John Hulcoop, among others, to record audio tapes of their poetry. Mallinson's recording of Lowther from this time hasn't survived (personal communication with the author, 4 Aug. 2001).

11 Carpenter basically lifts Hearne's story as a rhetorical embellishment, using it as a fetching opening narrative in the first two paragraphs of his essay, because it illustrates his thesis that 'when life there [in the Arctic] is reduced to its barest essentials, art and poetry turn out to be among those essentials.' In relocating Hearne's encounter with the Dogrib woman somewhere vaguely 'in the desolate Canadian tundra,' he deliberately suppresses details of place supplied by the explorer to suit the world of 'the ice-bound arctic,' the proper purview of his discussion (206). Conversely, Hearne's original report of his encounter with the lone Dogrib woman might have touched an additional chord for Lowther in that it leads directly to an account of how his Native guide, Matonabbee, enraged by criticism from one of his wives, 'fell on her with both hands and feet, and bruised her to such a degree, that after lingering some time she died' (Hearne 1958: 170–1).

12 See also, for example, Hamilton 1994; essays by Coates and Morrison, and Ray, in the special issue of *Essays on Canadian Writing*, 'Representing North' (1996); and Grace 2001.

13 Undated looseleaf typescript, in the possession of Beth Lowther.

14 This was a principle of Inuit art which Lowther read about in Carpenter's article, which was accurate enough on this aspect of 'Image Making in Arctic Art': 'As the carver holds the unworked ivory lightly in his hand, turning it this way and that, he whispers, "Who are you? Who hides there?" ... He rarely sets out to carve, say, a seal, but picks up the ivory, examines it to find its hidden form and, if that is not immediately apparent, carves aimlessly until he sees it' (206). Of course, the idea of immanent form was already evident in some of Lowther's earliest work, including the black-canvas painting in the story 'Thrift.'

15 'Scatter Poem' is the title of a work which Lowther published in bp Nichol's *Ganglia* 6 (July 1966), n.pag. The notebook text of 'Woman on/against Snow' in the 'Canadian Exercise' scribbler appears to post-date the 1971 *White Pelican* version since the notebook includes the lines Lowther added to Small Small's first monologue by the time of her Regina reading. This suggests that she took the earlier draft apart, deliberately scrambling the stanzas in her notebook, before reconstructing the final version that appears in *Milk Stone* and *Time Capsule.*

16 As Mallinson notes, Lowther's main source of information about Nuliajuk was probably Paul Riesman's essay in Kepes 1966. Riesman recounts versions of this myth, the basic events of which remain constant: Nuliajuk is originally rejected, thrown into the water from a boat. In some versions, she is a young girl, thrown overboard by her father; in others, she is a mother thrown by her own children; in yet others, she is 'an orphan whom nobody wants' (Riesman 1966: 231).When Nuliajuk tries to get back into the boat, her fingers are cut off. 'The joints fall off and become the animals of the sea on which men feed, and Nuliajuk falls back into the water and becomes ... "the most feared of all spirits, the most powerful, and the one who more than any other controls the destinies of men"' (231). Riesman's source, whom he is quoting in the last sentence, is the Danish anthropologist Knud Rasmussen, from the *Report of the Fifth Thule Expedition, 1921–24.* The quotations in Riesman's essay are attributed, so Lowther may also have consulted Rasmussen's account of 'The Sea Spirit Nuliajuk, the Mother of the Sea Beasts' (1931; rpt. 1976: 225–9).

17 See Carpenter 1966: 206, 212, 224, and Mallinson 1986: 12, 15–16, on the correspondences between the linguistic features of Inuktitut and Lowther's poem. Lowther's notebook indicates that she also used other unspecified sources in her research of the Inuit's language.

18 It is interesting to compare the poem's final stanza with its earlier versions in *White Pelican* and in Lowther's notebook, where the poem concludes: 'and

her hands stiffen working / the human statement / and her breath will go out / on a song.' The revisions show how Lowther tightened the ending, making the fate of Small Small's 'breath' more ambiguous, while still nevertheless ending on the affirmative note of 'still working.'

19 'Welfare Rate Ups City Bill by $500,000,' *Vancouver Province*, 6 April 1973, p. 31.
20 'Notes Toward a Socialist Cultural Policy for British Columbia,' in the possession of Beth Lowther.
21 See also, for example, 'Lydia's Children,' *Prism* (Summer 1965): 52.
22 Letter to Glenn Clever, 13 Feb. 1974, in the possession of Beth Lowther and Glenn Clever, Borealis archive (Ottawa).
23 Interview with Seymour Mayne, Ottawa, 17 May 2001.
24 Letter to Glenn Clever, 20 March 1974, in the possession of Beth Lowther and Glenn Clever, Borealis archive (Ottawa).
25 Sending on a copy of *Milk Stone* to Ralph Gustafson, Lowther wrote on 20 November 1974: 'I send you my new book in the hope that you'll forgive the embarrassing back cover [blurb] and the multitude of misprints, some of which I'm sure I can remember correcting. This poor book has had many misadventures, long before getting into print, and is now actually about four years old' (Ralph Gustafson Papers, Queen's University, box 2, 'Lowther' file).

Chapter 13

1 Dorothy Livesay letter to PL, 17 Dec. 1973, in the possession of Beth Lowther; Dorothy Livesay letter to PL, 2 Jan. 1974. University of Manitoba Special Collections, Dorothy Livesay Papers, MSS 37, box 61, folder 42.
2 Letter to Dorothy Livesay, 9 Jan. 1974. University of Manitoba Special Collections, Dorothy Livesay Papers, MSS 37, box 61, folder 42.
3 As well as through translations of Neruda and Vallejo, Bly directed attention to contemporary South American poetry in his influential little magazine, *The Sixties* (later renamed *The Seventies*), which attracted a wide readership that included Allen Ginsberg, Galway Kinnell, Denise Levertov, Robert Creeley, Gary Snyder, James Wright, and many others; see Marras 1984: 34.
4 That is, if stray notes by Roy Lowther, mixed up in his wife's papers, are any indication (undated, looseleaf entry, in the possession of Beth Lowther). Before Bly's 1972 work, translations available to Lowther would have included those by Angel Flores (1946), Ben Belitt (1961), Carlos Lozano (1961), and Nathaniel Tarn (1967).
5 Letter to Doug Barbour, 28 Sept. 1973, National Archives, Ottawa, League of Canadian Poets fonds, MG 28, I301, box 1, file 1–15.

6 Walter Lowenfels, the American editor of this anthology, wrote to Stephen Scobie early in 1974, soliciting Canadian contributions: 'I have only one or two Anglo poems from Canada,' he lamented. 'Could you possibly notify all Canadian poets asking them to submit poems to me about Neruda or Chile [?]' Scobie sent on the call for submissions – to Lowther, at least, who, in turn, sent it on to others (PL, letter to Pat Lane, 28 Feb. 1974, UBC Special Collections, Patrick Lane Papers, MS Col, box 3, file 7). In *For Neruda, for Chile*, Lowenfels took the unusual step of interspersing his poets' voices with short, prose eye-witness accounts and documents of the events in Chile: the text of Allende's final radio address on Sept. 11; an autobiographical report of Neruda's death (by his widow); a journalist's account of the overflowing morgues of Santiago; and a publishing house editor's testimony of folk singer Victor Jara's unspeakably awful execution in the National Stadium, where memories of soccer World Cups gave way to torture after the overthrow.

    The poem that Lowther contributed to Lowenfels's book was 'Anniversary Letter to Pablo,' which appears in *A Stone Diary* as the first in her sequel 'letters' to Neruda. The composition date of this particular 'letter' is uncertain. Its appearance in the context of a posthumous tribute to Neruda suggests that, like 'Last Letter to Pablo,' this poem was written after Neruda's death to commemorate that 'anniversary.' However, before it was published in Lowenfels's 1975 anthology, 'Anniversary Letter to Pablo' had already appeared in an American magazine called *Inscape*, which I have not been able to trace. It is possible that she wrote the poem soon after Neruda's death and first published it in *Inscape* during 1974, anticipating the first 'anniversary' of his death. But her comments about the Neruda cycle to Livesay from February 1974 (cited above) make mention of only 'Last Letter' as a posthumous addition to the series, and imply that the others are all earlier works. Moreover, both the poem's placement at the head of the series in *A Stone Diary* and its internal imagery link it to earlier work. In this case, the 'anniversary' of the poem's title could refer to the 'anniversary' of having written her own first 'Regard for Neruda.'

7 As Wayman notes, unlike many English translations, sources like *Masses and Mainstream* would have allowed Lowther a glimpse of some of Neruda's more 'extremely Communist, even Stalinist, works' (letter to the author, 4 Nov. 2000; see also Wayman 1993: 90).

8 Letter to Eugene McNamara, 13 Dec. 1973, in the possession of Beth Lowther.

9 Virginia, in fact, was inclined to compare her bookish daughter to her father, James – a parallel that the family likely drew to Pat's attention over the years

(Virginia Tinmouth, interview with Toby Brooks, 23 Feb. 1989). As equally ambitious women in their respective generations, it is perhaps not surprising that both Virginia and Pat identified strongly along paternal lines.

10 See Wayman 1993: 105. Neruda's *Memoirs* recount various sexual conquests and adventures, the most disturbing of which involves a Tamil servant woman who persistently ignored Neruda's advances during his service as Chilean consul in Colombo, Ceylon (Sri Lanka). He then recounts his effectual rape of the unnamed servant, whom he compared to 'a statue' as he gratified himself sexually: 'She kept her eyes wide open all the while, completely unresponsive. She was right to despise me. The experience was never repeated' (1977: 100).

11 Lowther probably met Gill, an American from up-state New York, through her Very Stone House connections and through Livesay, at one of 'Dee's' parties during the late sixties (undated letter from Elaine Gill to PL, in the possession of Beth Lowther). Along with the likes of Marge Piercy and Erica Jong, Lowther is one of five Canadian women poets represented in Gill's anthology (the others are Atwood, Brewster, MacEwen, and Webb).

12 Undated draft entry, photocopied notebook, in the possession of Beth Lowther.

13 One of most compelling sources of current information on Chacabuco is Gastón Ancelovici's documentary film, *Chacabuco: Memories of Silence* (2001). The film interviews surviving prisoners and ex–prison guards to narrate the experiences and memories of both. Chacabuco operated for only a year, holding about 1,200 prisoners from all classes of Chilean society. Ancelovici's film reveals that, unlike notorious Santiago torture houses such as Villa Grimaldi or London 38, there were no executions at Chacabuco; the people held there suffered primarily from demoralization and depression due to 'head stew' (or boredom and loneliness). As a counterpoint to Lowther's 'Chacabuco,' see also Neruda's poems 'Ananconda Copper Mining Co.,' 'United Fruit Co.,' and 'The Nitrate Men,' in Canto V, Sections II and III of *Canto General.*

14 This is, for example, Neruda's recurrent posture in Canto V of the *Canto General,* 'The Sand Betrayed,' which includes a warning to the interfering 'hordes' of 'North America' that 'we'll rise from the stones and the air / to bite you': 'we'll rise from the furrow so that the seed / will pound like a Columbian fist, / we'll rise to deny you bread and water, / we'll rise to burn you in hell' (1991: V, iv, 266).

15 Dorothy Livesay, letter to Seymour Mayne, 22 Nov. 1968, National Archives, Ottawa, Seymour Mayne Papers, MG 31, D253, Vol. 2, file 1.

16 PL, letter to Dorothy Livesay, 23 April 1969, Queen's University Archives, Dorothy Livesay Papers, box 4A, folder 84.

17 Shirley Neuman observes that, for many *Tish* poets, 'the most significant aspect' of their postmodern poetics was 'a phenomenological relation between language and the "real" that, like [Charles] Olson, they termed proprioceptive' (1990: 62). The 'phenomenological stance' of this postmodern school is especially evident in Olson's theory of 'projective verse,' which privileges direct subjective experience in its conceptualization of the poem as an 'energy' construct. As Beverley Mitchell pointed out in 1976: 'What Olson is concerned with ... is a poem in which the poetic experience is transferred to the reader with as much immediacy as the poet can summon – that is, *with the experience itself rather than thought about the experience*' (Mitchell 1976: 82; emphasis added). In her poetry, by contrast, Lowther was more and more interested in doing precisely the opposite: in 'thinking about' experience and calling attention to its replication and manipulation as simulacra.

18 Undated, looseleaf entry, 'High Flyer' airmail notepad, emphasis added; and undated draft entry, pale green, unlined, stapled notebook (in the possession of Beth Lowther). The latter notebook with the draft of 'newsreel' also contains the draft version of '[Chacabuco,] the Pit.'

19 See Kroker's critique of McLuhan's 'curious and somewhat constricted' 'technological humanism,' which 'omitted any analysis of the precise historical conditions surrounding the development of the technological experience in North America' (1984: 52, 79–80).

20 UBC Special Collections, NDP Little Mountain Constituency fonds, box 4, files 4–5. The article, 'A State of Siege,' dates from a few years after Lowther's death. However, as the constituency secretary for Phyllis Young, Lowther would have seen similar literature.

21 Letter to Eugene McNamara, 31 Dec. 1973, in the possession of Beth Lowther.

22 'Darwin,' undated draft entry, photocopied notebook in the possession of Beth Lowther.

23 'Gretel,' undated draft entry, 'Canadian Music Dictation' notebook, in the possession of Beth Lowther.

24 Undated fiction entry, blue-bound coverless notepad, in the possession of Beth Lowther.

25 Interview with Kathy (Domphousse) Lyons, Vancouver, 12 Jan. 2000.

Chapter 14

1 Letter to Dorothy Livesay, 19 Oct. 1969. University of Manitoba Special Collections, Dorothy Livesay Papers, MSS 37, box 61, folder 42.

2 Dorothy Livesay, letter to Seymour Mayne, 28 Nov. 1969, National Archives, Ottawa, Seymour Mayne Papers, MG 31, D253 Vol. 2, file 2.

3 Circular memo, 1 Jan. 1967, signed by J.R. Colombo, provisional coordinator, National Archives, Ottawa, League of Canadian Poets (LCP) fonds, Executive Committee files, MG 28, I301, Vol. 1, file 1–2.

4 Earle Birney, letter to Raymond Souster, 19 March 1969; Raymond Souster,
letter to Earle Birney, 23 March 1969; Earle Birney, letter to Raymond
Souster, 9[?] April 1969: Thomas Fisher Rare Book Library, University of
Toronto, Earle Birney Papers, MS Coll. 49, box 18, folder 55A.

5 Daphne Buckle Marlatt, letter to Raymond Souster, 2 April 1969; Douglas
Lochhead, letter to Michael Yates and Douglas Barbour, 15 March 1971; Seymour Mayne, letter to Douglas Lochhead, 8 Feb. 1971: National Archives,
Ottawa, LCP fonds, MG 28, I301, Vol. 1, files 1–4, 1–5, 1–9. Joe Rosenblatt
has no recollection of the circumstances around Lowther's apparently
delayed League nomination, other than to observe that 'the League then
was very elitist, and had a rigid system for selecting members' (personal communication with the author, 2 Feb. 2003).

6 Letter to Dorothy Livesay, 6 Dec. 1969, Queen's University Archives, Dorothy
Livesay Papers, box 4A, folder 84.

7 Letter to Raymond Souster, 26 June 1972, National Archives, Ottawa, LCP
fonds, MG 28, I301, Vol. 1, file 1–12.

8 Draft letter to Ernest Hall, December [1974], 'Hilroy' coil notebook, in the
possession of Beth Lowther.

9 National Archives, Ottawa, LCP fonds, Executive Committee files, MG 28,
I301, Vol. 1, file 1–6.

10 F.R. Scott, letter to Raymond Souster, 10 April 1970, National Archives,
Ottawa, LCP fonds, MG 28, I301, Vol. 1, file 1–6.

11 Dorothy Livesay, letter to Raymond Souster, 12 July 1970, National Archives,
Ottawa, LCP fonds, MG 28, I301, Vol. 1, file 1–6. Their correspondence discussing the issue of taking on the League Chairship began in April, shortly
after Scott's declension.

12 Raymond Souster, letter to Francis Sparshott, 11 Oct. 1971; 1970 biennial
conference literature; General Membership Lists: National Archives, Ottawa,
LCP fonds, MG 28, I301, Vol. 1, files 1–8, 1–6; Vol. 5, file 1–16.

13 1970 biennial conference literature; Raymond Souster, letter to Dorothy
Livesay, 6 May 1970: National Archives, Ottawa, LCP fonds, MG 28, I301,
Vol. 1, file 1–6.

14 PL, letter to Doug Barbour, 26 Oct. 1972; Doug Barbour, letter to PL, 29 Oct.
1972; Raymond Souster, letter to PL, 17 June 1972; PL, letter to Doug Barbour, 5 Dec. 1972: National Archives, Ottawa, LCP fonds, MG 28, I301, Vol.
1, files 1–10, 1–11, 1–12.

15 Executive report of the 1972 meeting, National Archives, Ottawa, LCP fonds,
MG 28, I301, Vol. 4, file 4–12.

16 Itinerary of Edmonton conference and report on 1972 general meeting, by
   Francis Sparshott, National Archives, Ottawa, LCP fonds, MG 28, I301, Vol. 4,
   file 4–12. The fracas alluded to at the 1970 League meeting related to the
   nationalist concerns of some League members that Canadian citizens be
   given priority for government grants and League benefits. This debate was
   covered in Lowther's local press by Andreas Schroeder, 'Nationalism Splits
   Canadian League of Poets,' *Vancouver Province*, 17 Oct. 1970, p. 53.
17 Lowther's response to the same questionnaire declared that she wished to
   address 'the social role of poetry.' 'All this is hypothetical with me,' she
   added, 'as at present, I can't even scrape up the money for dues'. (National
   Archives, Ottawa, LCP fonds, MG 28, I301, Vol. 4, file 4–10; report and minutes of the 1972 LCP meeting, Vol. 4, file 4–12).
18 Dennis Lee, letter to Douglas Lochhead, 20 Aug. 1971; report to the League
   executive, 1 Feb. 1971: National Archives, Ottawa, LCP fonds, MG 28, I301,
   Vol. 1, files 1–9, 1–8.
19 Letter to Dorothy Livesay, [?] April 1972, University of Manitoba Special Collections, Dorothy Livesay Papers, MSS 37, box 61, folder 42.
20 Letter to Eugene McNamara, 11 Nov. 1972, in the possession of Beth
   Lowther.
21 Letter to Eugene McNamara, 22 Sept. 1973, in the possession of Beth
   Lowther.
22 Letter to Fred Cogswell, 6 Sept. 1973, UNB Archives and Special Collections,
   Fred Cogswell fonds, MS 2.1963. In addition to her teaching and secretarial
   jobs, Lowther also attended a large 'Arts Access' conference sponsored by
   the provincial government in October 1973, which she reported on to Gerald and Arlene Lampert: 'The conference elected an interim committee
   with representatives from all arts disciplines to continue negotiations with
   the [B.C.] govt. I'm a member of that committee and will certainly push for
   help for poets. So, great manna will fall from the sky in B.C. Maybe. Sometime. But I can't see this as a substitute for the League of Canadian Poets'
   (letter to Gerald Lampert, 23 Oct. 1973, National Archives, Ottawa, LCP
   fonds, National Tours, 1973–4, MG 28, I301, Vol. 9, file 7).
23 Letter to Dorothy Livesay, 29 Oct. 1973, University of Manitoba Special Collections, Dorothy Livesay Papers, MSS 37, Box 61, folder 42.
24 Joy Kogawa, letter to Fred Cogswell, 10 Feb. 1974, UNB Archives and Special
   Collections, *Fiddlehead* Papers, MS 5; PL, letter to Glenn Clever, 13 Feb. 1974,
   in the possession of Beth Lowther and Glenn Clever, Borealis archives,
   Ottawa.
25 Thanks to Juliet McMaster for relaying these responses from Carol Shields
   during their phone conversation, 30 May 2001.

26 Arlene Lampert, letter to PL, 15 July 1974; PL, undated letter to Arlene Lampert; Arlene Lampert, letter to PL, 16 Sept. 1974: National Archives, Ottawa, LCP fonds, 1974 correspondence, MG 28, I301, Vol. 1, file 1–18.

27 Arlene Lampert, letter to PL, 16 Sept. 1974, National Archives, Ottawa, LCP fonds, 1974 correspondence, MG 28, I301, Vol. 1, file 1–18.

28 Stephen Scobie, undated League correspondence; PL, letter to Stephen Scobie, 20 Sept. 1974, emphasis in the original: National Archives, Ottawa, LCP fonds, MG 28, I301, Vol. 4, file 4–14.

29 PL, letter to Arlene Lampert, 22 Oct. 1974, National Archives, Ottawa, LCP fonds, 1974 correspondence, MG 28, I301, Vol. 1, file 1–18. League records indicate that Lowther was also slated to read at Queen's University in Kingston on Oct. 9, though it is unclear whether this reading actually came off in the end (National Archives, Ottawa, LCP fonds, National Tours, 1974–5, MG 28, I301, Vol. 9, file 23).

30 Mike Friendly, letter to Stephen Scobie, 23 Oct. 1974, National Archives, Ottawa, LCP fonds, MG 28, I301, Vol. 4, file 4–17.

31 Francis Sparshott, report on 1974 elections, National Archives, Ottawa, LCP fonds, MG 28, I301, Vol. 4, file 4–16.

32 Letter to Glenn Clever, 12 Nov. 1974, in the possession of Beth Lowther and Glenn Clever, Borealis archives, Ottawa.

33 Arlene Lampert, letter to PL, 16 Oct. 1974; PL, letter to Stephen Scobie, 18 Oct. 1974; PL, letter to Arlene Lampert, 22 Oct. 1974: National Archives, Ottawa, LCP fonds, 1974 correspondence, MG 28, I301, Vol. 1, files 1–17, 1–18.

34 Fred Candelaria, letter to Gerald and Arlene Lampert, 21 Nov. 1974; Fred Candelaria, undated letter to Stephen Scobie: National Archives, Ottawa, LCP fonds, 1974 correspondence, MG 28, I301, Vol. 1, file 1–18; Vol. 4, file 4–17.

35 PL, letters to Arlene Lampert, 8 Nov. 1974 and 18 Nov. 1974, National Archives, Ottawa, LCP fonds, 1974 correspondence, MG 28, I301, Vol. 1, file 1–18.

36 'Chair Creature's Progress Report,' LCP Newsletter 14 (Winter 1975), in University of Manitoba Special Collections, Dorothy Livesay Papers, MSS 37, box 13, folder 2.

37 Letter to Gerald and Arlene Lampert, 5 Dec. 1974; PL, letter to Arlene Lampert, 27 Dec. 1974: National Archives, Ottawa, LCP fonds, 1974 correspondence, MG 28, I301, Vol. 1, file 1–18.

38 PL, letter to Arlene Lampert, 27 Dec. 1974; Arlene Lampert, letter to PL, 31 Dec. 1974: National Archives, Ottawa, LCP fonds, 1974 correspondence, MG 28, I301, Vol. 1, file 1–18.

39 Undated draft looseleaf, in the possession of Beth Lowther.

40. Even as the previous League executive sounded out Fred Cogswell about his willingness to take over the Chairship in 1974, it also felt that 'it would be nice, perhaps, to have a woman' in that position for a change (Doug Barbour, letter to Fred Cogswell, 24 Aug. 1973, National Archives, Ottawa, LCP fonds, Executive Committee files, MG 28, I301, Vol. 1, file 1–14).

41 PL, letter to Glenn Clever, 25 Jan. 1975, in the possession of Beth Lowther; Glenn Clever, letter to PL, 30 Jan. 1975, in the possession of Beth Lowther and Glenn Clever, Borealis archive, Ottawa.

42 Executive Committee files; PL, letter to Arlene Lampert, 10 Feb. 1975; Arlene Lampert, letter to PL, 25 March 1975; Arlene Lampert, letter to PL, 6 Feb. 1975: National Archives, Ottawa, LCP fonds, 1975 correspondence, MG 28, I301, Vol. 1, file 1–26; Vol. 1, file 1–19.

43 PL, letter to Arlene Lampert, 13 Aug. 1975; PL, letter to Francis Sparshott, 16 Feb. 1975, emphasis in the original: National Archives, Ottawa, LCP fonds, 1975 correspondence, MG 28, I301, Vol. 1, file 1–19.

44 Francis Sparshott, letter to PL, 9 March 1975; PL, letter to Arlene Lampert, 14 March 1975: National Archives, Ottawa, LCP fonds, 1975 correspondence, MG 28, I301, Vol. 1, file 1–19.

45 PL, letter to Arlene Lampert, 23 June 1975; PL, letter to Arlene Lampert, 10 Feb. 1975, emphasis in the original; PL, letter to Arlene Lampert, 20 May 1975: National Archives, Ottawa, LCP fonds, 1975 correspondence, MG 28, I301, Vol. 1, file 1–19.

46 Letter to Fred Cogswell, 7 Sept. 1975, UNB Archives and Special Collections, Fred Cogswell fonds, MS 2.2430.

47 Arlene Lampert, letter to PL, 6 Feb. 1975, National Archives, Ottawa, LCP fonds, 1975 correspondence, MG 28, I301, Vol. 1, file 1–19.

48 PL, letter to Arlene and Gerald Lampert, 6 Sept. 1975, National Archives, Ottawa, LCP fonds, 1975 correspondence, MG 28, I301, Vol. 1, file 1–19.

49 Arlene Lampert, letters to PL, 25 Aug. 1975 and 28 July 1975, National Archives, Ottawa, LCP fonds, 1975 correspondence, MG 28, I301, Vol. 1, file 1–19.

50 Chris Potter, 'Pat Lowther: "A Culture Is Judged by Its Literature,"' *Performance* (June 1975), clipping in National Archives, Ottawa, LCP fonds, 1975 correspondence, MG 28, I301, Vol. 1, file 1–19.

51 PL, letter to Arlene Lampert, 13 Aug. 1975; Arlene Lampert, letter to PL, 25 Aug. 1975; PL, omnibus letter, 'To all regional representatives,' 17 Aug. 1975: National Archives, Ottawa, LCP fonds, 1975 correspondence, MG 28, I301, Vol. 1, file 1–19.

52 'The Founding of the League of Canadian Poets,' loose typescript, University

of Manitoba Special Collections, Dorothy Livesay Papers, MSS 37, box 13, folder 3.

53 Constitution of the League of Canadian Poets as adopted Oct. 19, 1968 and amended ... in 1970 ... 1975 ... and 1977, Article 4.1, National Archives, Ottawa, LCP fonds, Constitution and By-laws, 1968–91, MG 28, I301, Vol. 22, file 22–1.

54 'A Sketch of a New Structure for the League of Canadian Poets,' National Archives, Ottawa, LCP fonds, 1975 correspondence, MG 28, I301, Vol. 1, file 1–20.

55. Don McLellan, 'Into the Trenches Go Canada's Poets,' *Vancouver Sun*, 5 Sept. 1975, p. 29.

56 Letter to Eugene McNamara, 29 Dec. 1974, in the possession of Beth Lowther. The letter reveals that the frustration Lowther expressed over the League's suspension of new admissions arose from a decision she had made earlier with Fred Candelaria, over which she had misgivings from the start: 'To wit: after a long delay we're setting up the League Membership committee. We kept hoping for some Big Name to volunteer, since there seems to be a feeling that the committee should have a Big Name. I can see the point, since it does seem to be an emotional issue. If somebody bitches about the recommendations, we can say, with Him on [the committee], it must be Above Reproach ... Fred ... was quite adamant that we do nothing about processing applications until this committee is in operation. And since I'm easily talked into doing nothing, I went along. I'm beginning to wonder now whether this was the right decision.'

57 Letter to Arlene Lampert, 10 Feb. 1975, National Archives, Ottawa, LCP fonds, 1975 correspondence, MG 28, I301, Vol. 1, file 1–19.

58 Quoted in Chris Potter, 'Pat Lowther: "A Culture Is Judged by Its Literature,"' *Performance* (June 1975), clipping in National Archives, Ottawa, LCP fonds, 1975 correspondence, MG 28, I301, Vol. 1, file 1–19.

59 Letter to Fred Cogswell, 7 Sept. 1975, UNB Archives and Special Collections, Fred Cogswell fonds, MS 2.2430.

60 Dorothy Livesay, letter to PL, 18 Sept. 1975, National Archives, Ottawa, LCP fonds, 1975 correspondence, MG 28, I301, Vol. 1, file 1–20.

61 *Vancouver Sun*, 5 Sept. 1975, p. 29; Roy MacSkimming, 'Poets' League Discusses Interests with Writers,' *Toronto Star*, 14 Oct. 1975, p. F8.

62 *LCP Newsletter* 16 (Summer 1975): 14.

63 Interview with Patrick Lane, Victoria, 17 April 2001.

64 Arlene Lampert, letters to Dorothy Livesay, 6 Jan. 1976 and 22 Dec. 1976, University of Manitoba Special Collections, Dorothy Livesay Papers, MS 37, box 60, folder 11.

Chapter 15

1 'Watershed' was first published in *Event* 4.3 (1975): 69. It has not been reprinted since.
2 Virginia Tinmouth, interview with Toby Brooks, 23 Feb. 1989.
3 Undated notebook entry, coverless notepad, blue binding, in the possession of Beth Lowther.
4 Ibid.
5 'Pat Lowther Tribute,' *Gzowski on FM*, 2 Nov. 1975.
6 Letter to Fred Cogswell, 7 April 1965. UNB Archives and Special Collections, Fred Cogswell fonds, MS 1.7840.
7 Like 'A Water Clock,' some works produced during the sixties, such as 'History Lessons' and 'Skin over Pompeii,' appeared in small magazines at the time, but were never included in any of her collections. In other cases, she deferred publication to later books: a number of poems from *Milk Stone*, for example, appear in a small black notebook that she used around 1967–8, which also contains many poems from *This Difficult Flowring*. These include 'Stone Deaf,' early versions of 'The Falconer,' and, ironically, a poem entitled 'Now,' which was also made to wait for the 'albatross' book to appear. Other works such as 'Clock Watching,' 'Ion,' and 'Snow Sky, Vancouver' exist only as unpublished notebook drafts or typescripts that date roughly from Lowther's residence on St George Street. Some of the poems from this period would appear for the first time in collected form only in the 'Time Capsule' section of the posthumous *Time Capsule*, and these include 'A Water Clock,' 'Ion,' 'Salt Wafers,' 'History Lessons,' and 'Riding Past.'
8 Gary Geddes, letter to PL, 2 April 1975, emphasis in the original (in the possession of Beth Lowther).
9 Undated draft, lined black notebook, in the possession of Beth Lowther.
10 Ibid.
11 Letter to Dorothy Livesay, 30 July 1969, Queen's University Archives, Dorothy Livesay Papers, box 4A, folder 84. 'Moonwalk Summer' is another poem apparently composed by way of Lowther's 'scrabble' method of composition, with various stanzas rearranged and re-sequenced in one draft version (undated draft entry, three-hole coverless notebook, in the possession of Beth Lowther).
12 Letters to Dorothy Livesay, 16 May 1972 and 17 June 1972, University of Manitoba Special Collections, Dorothy Livesay Papers, MSS 37, box 61, folder 42.
13 Letter to Margaret Atwood, 27 Dec. 1972, Thomas Fisher Rare Book Library,

University of Toronto, Margaret Atwood Papers, MS Coll. 200, box 160 – Lowther.

14 Letter to Dorothy Livesay, April [?] 1972, University of Manitoba Special Collections, Dorothy Livesay Papers, MSS 37, box 61, folder 42. Neither the letter to Livesay nor Atwood mentions whom Lowther may have been working with on this apparently collaborative project. The 'enclosed' list of 'material' that she mentions in her letter to Livesay is no longer with the letter in Livesay's papers; however, one of Lowther's notebook entries, which appears next to entries related to *Infinite Mirror Trip*, seems to provide such a list:

> Arctic with slides
> Atwood with pics from archives
> Notes from a Native Land
> Klee Wyck and Carr film?
> Roots
> I Shout Love
> from Beautiful Losers
> Rob – three poems
> Wayman – two poems
> singing
> end
> Pat: time readings (Undated journal entry, photocopied journal, in the possession of Beth Lowther)

15 PL, letter to Dorothy Livesay, 16 May 1972, University of Manitoba Special Collections, Dorothy Livesay Papers, MSS 37, box 61, folder 42.

16 Letters to Eugene McNamara, 22 Sept. 1973, and to Hilda Thomas, 18 July 1973, in the possession of Beth Lowther; letter to Fred Cogswell, 8 Aug. 1973, UNB Archives and Special Collections, Fred Cogswell fonds, MS 2.1920.

17 Undated notebook draft (ca. March 1973), 'Imperial White' notebook, in the possession of Beth Lowther.

18 Letter to Hilda Thomas, 18 July 1973, in the possession of Beth Lowther. John Tinmouth's musical contributions to *Infinite Mirror Trip* were prerecorded at the planetarium, but he did not actually attend any of the shows (interview, North Vancouver, 17 Feb. 2001).

19 Phone interview with Allan Safarik, 3 Feb. 2002.

20 PL, letter to Fred Cogswell, 25 Feb. 1974, UNB Archives and Special Collections, Fred Cogswell fonds, MS 2.2191.

21 Undated journal entry, photocopied journal, in the possession of Beth Lowther.

22 Allan Safarik, letter to Patrick Lane, 10 Aug. 1974, UBC Special Collections, Patrick Lane Papers, MSS Coll., box 4, file 4.

23 Ibid.

24 Letter to Doug Barbour, 26 Oct. 1972, National Archives, Ottawa, League of Canadian Poets fonds, MG 28, I301, Vol. 1, file 1–11.

25 Roger Penrose, 'Black Holes' *Scientific American* (*SA*) 226.5 (May 1972); Stephen Hawking, 'Black Hole Explosions?' *Nature* 248 (1974): 30; Maarten Schmidt and Francis Bello, 'The Evolution of Quasars,' *SA* 224.5 (May 1971); Martin J. Rees and Joseph Silk, 'The Origin of Galaxies,' *SA* (June 1970), rpt. in Gingerich 1977: 53–62. Lowther's local press also ran news items on black holes at the time she was working on her show (e.g., 'Grain of Dust Weighed Million Billion Tons,' *Vancouver Province*, 24 Sept. 1973, p. 9), sources she probably also consulted.

26 'Circuit Breakers,' undated draft, 'Fred C. Myers' notebook, in the possession of Beth Lowther.

27 Carson studied astronomy and physics in his spare time, and spent years working on a mathematical theory for calculating the masses and distances of the planets (interview, Vancouver, 21 June 2002). In her magazine profile of Carson, Dona Sturmanis notes that this theory emphasized 'proportions and ratios observable in atoms as well as galaxies' (1980: 3, 4).

28 Undated notebook entry, photocopied journal, in the possession of Beth Lowther.

29 Letter to Eugene McNamara, 30 Nov. 1973, in the possession of Beth Lowther.

30 Letter to Fred Cogswell, 3 May 1973. UNB Archives and Special Collections, Fred Cogswell fonds, MS 2.1856.

31 'Clock-Watching,' undated poem draft, black, lined notebook, in the possession of Beth Lowther.

32 McNamara recommended James Dickey to Lowther, and she did read Dickey's *Eyebeaters* (PL, letter to Eugene McNamara, 27 June 1973, in the possession of Beth Lowther). 'In the Continent behind My Eyes,' however, also suggests the influence Lowther herself was beginning to exert on other writers, including Dorothy Livesay, who at one point accepted 'Killing the Bear' for publication in *White Pelican* in 1971. By the time she published her own *Ice Age* in 1975, Livesay seemed to have picked up on some of the same themes Lowther had been reworking.

Lowther's original two 'Ice Age' segments and 'Killing the Bear' appear in the final text of 'In the Continent behind My Eyes' as the italicized portion of the sixth section of Part I (*MS*, 21) and the italicized portions of the second section of Part III (*MS*, 26–7), respectively.

33 Undated looseleaf draft of author statement for *Mountain Moving Day*, in the possession of Beth Lowther.
34 'The Face' was first published in *Prism* 13.3 (1974): 39–41. It has not been reprinted since.
35 PL, letter to Arlene Lampert, 14 March 1975, National Archives, Ottawa, League of Canadian Poets fonds, 1975 correspondence, MG 28, I301, Vol. 1, file 1–19.
36 'Losing My Head' was first published in *A Lake Superior Journal* 1.1 (Winter/Spring 1975): 20–3. It has not been reprinted since.
37 Letter to Fred Cogswell, 3 May 1975, UNB Archives and Special Collections, Fred Cogswell fonds, MS 2.2423.

Chapter 16

1 Interview with Barry Wilks, Mayne Island, 10 Aug. 2001.
2 Ibid.
3 Ibid.
4 Undated looseleaf typescript [ca. 1963–5], in the possession of Beth Lowther.
5 Undated drafts [ca. 1963–5], coverless lined notepad, in the possession of Beth Lowther.
6 Undated draft, [ca. 1965], 'Fred C. Meyers' notebook, in the possession of Beth Lowther.
7 Interview with Barry Wilks, Mayne Island, 10 Aug. 2001.
8 Howatt Fruit Farm, Prince Edward Island reading, audiotape, in the possession of Beth Lowther.
9 William Toye, letter to PL, 9 Sept. 1975, Oxford University Press archives.
10 Robert D. Jones, quoted in Kohlhoff 2002: 55. Kohlhoff's work offers an excellent historical account of the bombs' devastating impact on the Aleutian Islands' people and environment, and the widespread protest movements which the tests galvanized across North America, including Canada, where the Liberal government announced its support of 'a total nuclear test ban' as a result (108).
11 Looseleaf clipping, 'Now Scientists Take Baby Teeth,' *Vancouver Sun*, 20 Feb. 1965, and looseleaf information sheet, in the possession of Beth Lowther.
12 Undated, untitled poem draft, looseleaf typescript, in the possession of Beth Lowther. The poem is a parody in which Lowther envisions her brother, 'Amchitka Ardie,' in the role of 'Mad Bomber,' 'going/ up north to set the dynamite charges.'

13 Undated entry, notes on NDP provincial convention, photocopied journal, in the possession of Beth Lowther.

14 Undated handwritten entry, 'Woodward Narrow Rule' notebook, in the possession of Beth Lowther.

15 Interview with Kathy Domphousse, Vancouver, 12 Jan. 2000; interview with Brenda Marshall, North Vancouver, 17 Feb. 2000.

16 UBC Special Collections, NDP Little Mountain fonds, box 2, file 1. *The Waffle Manifesto* also provides a useful source of information for the environmental platforms of that wing of the federal NDP.

17 Letter to Eugene McNamara, 27 June 1973, in the possession of Beth Lowther.

18 See Derksen 1994 for a brief discussion contrasting Lowther's 'social and economic' perspective on landscape in 'Private Ownership' with Atwood's more existential vision in 'The Islands' of *The Circle Game* (146).

19 *Full Tide* 27.1 (Dec. 1962).

20 Undated draft letter entry, 'Hilroy 500' notebook, in the possession of Beth Lowther.

21 Interview with Gary Geddes, Edmonton, 8 March 2001; Gary Geddes, letter to PL, 2 April 1975, in the possession of Beth Lowther.

22 William Toye, letter to PL, 18 July 1975, Oxford University Press archives.

23 PL, letter to Arlene Lampert, 27 Jan. [1975], National Archives, Ottawa, League of Canadian Poets fonds, 1975 correspondence, MG 28, I301, Vol. 1, file 1–19.

24 Gary Geddes, letter to PL, 2 April 1975, in the possession of Beth Lowther.

25 Ibid.

26 Undated looseleaf draft, in the possession of Beth Lowther. I am quoting from Lowther's draft, but an edited version of this statement appears in Gill's *Mountain Moving Day* (80).

27 Undated looseleaf typescripts, 'From Furry Creek' and 'Notes from Furry Creek,' in the possession of Beth Lowther.

28 Letter to William Toye, 11 Aug. 1975, Oxford University Press archives.

29 'The Room and the Wind,' undated looseleaf typescript, in the possession of Beth Lowther.

30 'O Sybaris,' undated notebook draft entry [ca. 1965], 'Fred C. Myers' notebook, ellipsis in the original (in the possession of Beth Lowther).

31 'Skin over Pompeii' appears in the same notebook as the 'O Sybaris' entry; the published version is in *West Coast Review* 4.2 (Fall 1969): 40. Though not published until *Time Capsule*, 'Imagine Their Generations' may date from the late sixties as well.

Chapter 17

1 'Pat Lowther,' typescript of proposed radio program, by Réshard Gool, National Archives, Ottawa, Réshard Gool Papers, MG 31, D220, Vol. 35 interim; PL, letter to Réshard Gool, 10 March 1975, in the possession of Beth Lowther.

2 Letter to Arlene Lampert, 18 March 1975, National Archives, Ottawa, League of Canadian Poets fonds, 1975 correspondence, MG 28, I301, Vol. 1, file 1–19.

3 Réshard Gool, 'Pat Lowther,' 1977 recording, in the possession of Beth Lowther.

4 Letter to Réshard Gool, 10 June 1975, in the possession of Beth Lowther.

5 Letter to Réshard Gool, 27 July 1975, in the possession of Beth Lowther. Lowther's initial plan, as she informed Arlene Lampert, had been to use League funds to pay for 'the relatively small cost of having me stop over at Toronto on the way back' (letter to Arlene Lampert, 29 April 1975, National Archives, Ottawa, League of Canadian Poets fonds, 1975 correspondence, MG 28, I301, Vol. 1, file 1–19).

6 Hilda Woolnough, letter to Christine Lowther, 18 May 1996, in the possession of Christine Lowther, Réshard Gool, 'Pat Lowther,' typescript of proposed radio program, National Archives, Ottawa, Réshard Gool Papers, MG 31, D220, Vol. 35 interim.

7 University of Regina Archives, Collection 81-13: Department of Extension, Canada Lecture Series, Audio Cassette #11: Pat Lowther and Margaret Atwood, 24 Oct. 1972. 'Visit to Olympus' was first published in *West Coast Seen* (1969) and later reprinted in *Milk Stone*.

8 'History Lessons' was first published in *Fiddlehead* 72 (Summer 1967): 4–5.

9 The 1913 strike was not the only confrontation between miners on Vancouver Island and militiamen called in by 'the government' (that is, the Dunsmuirs), but it was one of the largest and most violent; see Phillips 1967: 58–61.

10 Interview with Barry Wilks, Mayne Island, 10 Aug. 2001; phone interview, July 2002.

11 Lowther changed the wording of this last line from a previous draft's 'useless at *woman* things' ('Inheritance,' undated draft entry, 'Imperial White' notebook, in the possession of Beth Lowther).

12 Undated entry, blue-bound coverless notepad, in the possession of Beth Lowther. This remark comes in the long prose entry Lowther made early during her marriage, when she began to gauge the suicidal depths of Roy's

misery. The entry does not elaborate on the circumstances around Annie's 'betrayal.'

13 'The Comet' was first published in *Final Instructions* and is reprinted in *Time Capsule*. It exists as a draft in the notebooks kept by Beth Lowther.

14 Undated poem draft, '#10,' photocopied journal, in the possession of Beth Lowther. '#10' is one of the original poems in Lowther's 'The Origin of the Universe' sequence, which she wrote around the time of her planetarium work for *Infinite Mirror Trip*. '#10' constructs a speaker with a kind of binocular, halved vision, with two fields of sight, one specific to each 'eye.'

15 See note 34, p. 455.

16 Undated looseleaf typescript, in the possession of Beth Lowther. 'Continuity' was one of the poems entered into the evidence in Roy Lowther's trial. Although its title suggests otherwise, Roy stated that it was not part of the 'Time Capsule' file, which no longer exists. In any event, 'Continuity: A Masque for Two Interchangeable Players' was part of Lowther's general thinking around the problems of 'history, and context, and continuity' shortly before her death.

17 Undated prose fiction fragment, blue-bound coverless notepad, and 'Mother,' undated entry, small black lined notebook, in the possession of Beth Lowther.

18 Virginia Tinmouth, interview with Toby Brooks, 23 Feb. 1989.

19 Virginia Tinmouth, letter to Dorothy Livesay, 29 April 1976, University of Manitoba Special Collections, Dorothy Livesay Papers, MSS 37, box 72, folder 40. In mentioning her gratitude to McNamara, Virginia was alluding to the trial testimony he provided, which, she said, 'did Pat honor.'

20 Letter to Réshard Gool, 29 July 1975, in the possession of Beth Lowther.

21 Letter to Fred Cogswell, 7 Sept. 1975, UNB Archives and Special Collections, Fred Cogswell fonds, MS 2.2480.

Bibliography

Abley, Mark. 1975. 'Between the Banal and the Beautiful.' Rev. of *Milk Stone*. *CVII* 1.2: 35–6.

Aczel, Amir D. 2002. *Entanglement: The Greatest Mystery in Physics*. Vancouver: Raincoast.

Adams, Ian. 1970. *The Poverty Wall*. Toronto: McClelland and Stewart.

Adorno, Theodor. 1997. *Aesthetic Theory*. Trans. and ed. Robert Hullot-Kentor. Minneapolis: U of Minnesota P.

Agosin, Marjorie. 1986. *Pablo Neruda*. Trans. Lorraine Roses. Boston: Twayne.

Almonte, Richard. 2003. 'Posthumous Praise: Biographical Influence in Canadian Women Writers.' PhD diss., McMaster University.

Althusser, Louis. 1971. 'Ideology and State Ideological Apparatuses.' In *Lenin and Philosophy*. New York: Monthly Review P.

Angus, H.F., F.W. Howay, and W.N. Sage. 1970. 'The American Mining Advance into Southern British Columbia, 1864–1910.' In *British Columbia and the United States*, ed. H.F. Angus, pp. 264–99. New York: Russell and Russell [1942].

Arnason, David. 1986. 'Dorothy Livesay and the Rise of Modernism in Canada.' In *A Public and Private Voice: Essays on the Life and Work of Dorothy Livesay*, ed. Lindsay Dorney, Gerald Noonan, and Paul Thiessen, pp. 5–18. Waterloo: U of Waterloo P.

Atwood, Margaret. 1961. *Double Persephone*. Toronto: Hawkshead P.

– 1970. *The Journals of Susanna Moodie*. Toronto: Oxford UP.

– 1971. *Power Politics*. Toronto: Anansi.

– 1972. *Survival: A Thematic Guide to Canadian Literature*. Toronto: Anansi.

– 1982a. 'Last Testaments: Pat Lowther and John Thompson' [1978]. In *Second Words: Selected Critical Prose*, pp. 307–12. Toronto: Anansi. Originally published in *Parnassus: Poetry in Review* 6.2 (Spring/Summer 1978): 193–8.

– ed. 1982b. *The New Oxford Book of Canadian Verse*. Toronto: Oxford UP.

Aubert, Rosemary. 1981. Rev. of *Final Instructions. Quill & Quire*, March: 61.

Banting, Pamela, and Kristjana Gunnars, eds. 1986. *The Papers of Dorothy Livesay: A Research Tool.* Foreword by David Arnason. Compiled with assistance of the Department of Archives and Special Collections. Winnipeg: U of Manitoba.

Barbour, Douglas, 1975–6. 'The Poets and Presses Revisited: Circa 1974.' *Dalhousie Review* 55: 338–60.

Barman, Jean. 1996. *The West beyond the West: A History of British Columbia.* Rev. ed. Toronto: U of Toronto P.

Barton, John. 1997. 'The Message inside *Time Capsule*: Pat Lowther's Legacy.' *ARC* 39: 64–70.

Belshaw, John D. 2002. *Colonization and Community: The Vancouver Island Coalfield and the Making of the British Columbian Working Class.* Kingston and Montreal: McGill-Queen's UP.

Benjamin, Walter. 1978. 'Theses on the Philosophy of History.' In *Illuminations*, ed. and introd. Hannah Arendt, trans. Harry Zohn, 5th ed., pp. 253–64. New York: Schocken.

Bergson, Henri. 1949. *Selections from Bergson.* Ed. and introd. Harold A. Larrabee. New York: Appleton-Century-Crofts Inc.

Bessai, Diane. 1975. 'Poetry from Ottawa.' *Canadian Forum*, July: 36–8.

Bizzaro, Salvatore. 1979. *Pablo Neruda: All Poets the Poet.* Metuchen, NJ: Scarecrow Press.

Black, John. 1992. 'History of North Vancouver City Library.' Unpublished lecture, North Vancouver.

Blum, John Morton. 1991. *Years of Discord: American Politics and Society, 1961–74.* New York: W.W. Norton.

Boland, Eavan. 1995. *Object Lessons: The Life of the Woman and the Poet in Our Time.* New York: W.W. Norton.

Bourdieu, Pierre. 1984. *Distinction: A Social Critique of the Judgement of Taste.* Trans. Richard Nice. Cambridge: Cambridge UP.

– 1993. *The Field of Cultural Production: Essays on Art and Literature.* Ed. and introd. Randal Johnson. Oxford: Polity P.

Bowen, Lynne. 1999. *Robert Dunsmuir: Laird of the Mines.* Lantzville, BC: XYZ Publishing.

Bowering, George. 1994. 'Vancouver as Postmodern Poetry.' In *Vancouver: Representing the Postmodern City*, ed. Paul Delany, pp. 121–43. Vancouver: Arsenal Pulp P.

Bowling, Tim, ed. 2002. *Where the Words Come From: Canadian Poets in Conversation.* Roberts Creek: Nightwood.

Brett, Brian. 1977. 'Where Was Praise When She Needed It?' *Vancouver Province*, Aug. 15, p. 22.

Brewster, Elizabeth. 1976. 'For Pat Lowther.' *CVII* 2.1: 16.

Bridgeman, J.M. 2000. 'Living on Rorschach.' Rev. of *Furry Creek*, by Keith Harrison. Http://www. januarymagazine.com/fiction/furrycreek.html

Brooks, Toby. 2000. *Pat Lowther's Continent: Her Life and Work*. Charlottetown: Gynergy.

Brown, Jim, and David Phillips, eds. 1969. *West Coast Seen*. Vancouver: Talon Books.

Bruffee, Kenneth. 1983. *Elegiac Romance*. Ithaca: Cornell UP.

Cain, Louis P. 1976. 'Water and Sanitation Services in Vancouver: An Historical Perspective.' *B.C. Studies* 30: 27–43.

Carpenter, Edmund. 1966. 'Image Making in Arctic Art.' In *Sign, Image, Symbol*, ed. Gyorgy Kepes, pp. 206–25. New York: George Braziller.

Caruth, Cathy. 1996. *Unclaimed Experience: Trauma, Narrative and History*. Baltimore: Johns Hopkins UP.

Chaisson, Eric J. 2001. *Cosmic Evolution: The Rise of Complexity in Nature*. Cambridge, MA: Harvard UP.

Cogswell, Fred. 1978. 'Little Magazines and Small Presses in Canada.' In *Figures in a Ground: Canadian Essays on Modern Literature Collected in Honor of Sheila Watson*, ed. Diane Bessai and David Jackel, pp. 162–73. Saskatoon: Western Producer Prairie Books.

Colombo, John Robert, ed. 1978. *The Poets of Canada*. Edmonton: Hurtig Publishers.

Cooney, Seamus, ed. 1983. *The Bukowski/Purdy Letters: A Decade of Dialogue, 1964–74*. Sutton West, ON; Santa Barbara, CA: Paget.

Cowan, Judith. 1983. 'La poésie de Pat Lowther.' *Ellipse: Writers in Translation* 31: 86–93.

Cunningham, M. Wayne. 2000. Rev. of *Furry Creek*, by Keith Harrison. *Canadian Book Review Annual*, p. 3036.

Darwin, Charles. 1964. *On the Origin of Species*. Introd. Ernst Mayr. Cambridge, MA: Harvard UP.

Davey, Frank. 1976. 'Introduction.' In *The Writing Life: Historical and Critical Views of the Tish Movement*, C.H. Gervais, pp. 15–24. Coatsworth, ON: Black Moss P.

Davies, Paul. 1995. *About Time: Einstein's Unfinished Revolution*. New York: Simon & Schuster.

Davis, Chuck, ed. 1976. *The Vancouver Book*. North Vancouver: J.J. Douglas.

– 1990. *Reflections: One Hundred Years; a Celebration of the District of North Vancouver's Centennial*. Vancouver: Opus Productions for the District of North Vancouver.

Day Lewis, C. 1992. *The Complete Poems of C. Day Lewis*. Stanford: Stanford UP.

Dempster, Barry, ed. 1978. *Tributaries: An Anthology, Writer to Writer*. Oakville: Mosaic P.

Denham, Paul. 1986. 'Lyric and Documentary in the Poetry of Dorothy Livesay.' In *A Public and Private Voice: Essays on the Life and Work of Dorothy Livesay*, ed. Lindsay Dorney, Gerald Noonan, and Paul Thiessen, pp. 87–106. Waterloo: U of Waterloo P.

Derksen, Jeff. 1994. 'Sites Taken as Signs: Place, the Open Text, and Enigma in New Vancouver Writing.' In *Vancouver: Representing the Postmodern City*, ed. Paul Delany, pp. 144–61. Vancouver: Arsenal Pulp P.

Derrida, Jacques. 1994. *Specters of Marx: The State of the Debt, the Work of Mourning, and the New International*. Trans. Peggy Kamuf. Introd. Bernd Magnus and Stephen Cullenberg. New York: Routledge.

Dickinson, Helen. 1964. 'The Capilano Public Library Association.' *British Columbia Library Quarterly* 28.1–2: 25–32.

Doyle, John. 1997. '"For My Own Damn Satisfaction": The Communist Poetry of Milton Acorn.' *Canadian Poetry* 40: 74–87.

Duffy, Ann, and Julianne Momirov. 1997. *Family Violence: A Canadian Introduction*. Toronto: James Lorimer.

Eliot, T.S. 1994. 'Tradition and the Individual Talent.' [1919]. In *Contemporary Literary Criticism: Literary and Cultural Studies*, ed. Robert Con Davies and Ronald Schleifer, 3rd ed., pp. 27–33. New York: Longmans.

Elliott, Marie. 1984. *Mayne Island and the Outer Gulf Islands: A History*. Mayne Island, BC: Gulf Islands P.

Energy, Mines and Resources Canada. 1976. *Mining Communities*. Mineral Policy Series Bulletin, MR 154.

Essays in Canadian Writing. 1996. Special Issue: 'Representing North.' 59 (Fall).

Felman, Shoshana. 1985. *Writing and Madness (Literature/Philosophy/Psychoanalysis)*. Trans. Martha Noel Evans, Brian Massumi, and the author. Ithaca, NY: Cornell UP.

Felman, Shoshana, and Dori Laub. 1992. *Testimony: Crises of Witnessing in Literature, Psychoanalysis and History*. New York: Routledge.

Felstiner, John. 1980. *Translating Neruda: The Way to Macchu Picchu*. Stanford: Stanford UP.

Fiamengo, Marya. 1978. 'Requiem.' *West Coast Review* 12.3: 15.

Finn, Geraldine. 1981. 'Why Althusser Killed His Wife.' *Canadian Forum*, Sept./Oct.: 28–9.

Florida, Richard. 2002. *The Rise of the Creative Class: And How It's Transforming Work, Leisure, Community, and Everyday Life*. New York: Basic Books.

Frederick, John T. 1972. *William Henry Hudson*. New York: Twayne Inc.

Freiwald, Bina. 2001. 'Revisiting That Difficult Continent.' *ARC* 47: 67–9.

Freud, Sigmund. 1959a. 'Thoughts on War and Death' [1915]. In *Sigmund Freud: Collected Papers*, Vol. 4, ed. Ernst Jones, trans. Joan Riviere, pp. 288–317. New York: Basic Books.

– 1959b. 'The Uncanny' [1919]. In *Sigmund Freud: Collected Papers*, Vol. 4, ed. Ernst Jones. trans. Joan Riviere, pp. 368–407. New York: Basic Books.

Fulford, Robert. 1975a. 'Murdered Vancouver Poet Was on Brink of Recognition.' *Toronto Star*, Oct. 25.

– 1975b. 'Poet on Edge of Fame Beaten to Death.' *Ottawa Citizen*, Oct. 25, p. 82.

– 1977. 'The Death-Haunted Poetry of Pat Lowther.' *Saturday Night* 92.4: 71.

Galt, George, ed. 1988. *The Purdy-Woodcock Letters: Selected Correspondence 1964–1984*. Toronto: ECW P.

Gasparini, Len. 1969. Rev. of *This Difficult Flowring*. *Canadian Forum* 48: 232–3.

Geddes, Gary, ed. 1975. *Skookum Wawa: Writings of the Canadian Northwest*. Toronto: Oxford UP.

– 1977. Rev. of *A Stone Diary*, *Globe and Mail*, April 9, p. E27.

Geddes, Gary, and Phyllis Bruce, eds. 1978. *Fifteen Canadian Poets Plus Five*. Toronto: Oxford UP.

Gervais, C.H., ed. 1976. *The Writing Life: Historical and Critical Views of the Tish Movement*. Introd. Frank Davey. Oakville, ON: Black Moss P.

Gibbs, Robert. 1998. 'A Voice from the Past for the Present.' *Fiddlehead* 196: 157–61.

Gill, Elaine, ed. and introd. 1973. *Mountain Moving Day: Poems By Women*. Trumansburg, NY: The Crossing P.

Gingerich, Owen, ed. 1977. *Cosmology + 1: Readings from Scientific American*. San Francisco: W.H. Freeman and Co.

Golland, Della. 1994. 'Metaphor as a Second Language: Vision and Revision in the Poetry of Pat Lowther.' MA thesis, Department of History and Philosophy of Education, University of Toronto.

Gom, Leona. 1991. *The Collected Poems*. Victoria: Sono Nis.

González Echevarría, Roberto. 1991. 'Introduction: Neruda's *Canto General*, the Poetics of Betrayal.' In *Canto General*, by Pablo Neruda, trans. Jack Schmidt, pp. 1–12. Berkeley: U of California P.

Gotlieb, Phillis. 1977. Rev. of *A Stone Diary*. *Quarry* 26.3: 86–8.

Grace, Sherrill. 2001. *Canada and the Idea of the North*. Kingston and Montreal: McGill-Queen's UP.

Greco, Heidi. 1997. 'Time Capsule of Cruelty and Talent.' *Columbia Journal*, July: 10.

Grescoe, Paul. 1976. 'Eulogy for a Poet.' *Canadian Magazine*, June 5, pp. 13, 16–19.

Grimal, Peter. 1990. *The Penguin Dictionary of Classical Myth*. Harmondsworth: Penguin.

Guillory, John. 1993. *Cultural Capital: The Problem of Literary Canon-Formation*. Chicago: U of Chicago P.

– 1995. 'Canon.' In *Critical Terms for Literary Study*, ed. Frank Lentricchia and Thomas McLaughlin, 2nd ed, pp. 233–49. Chicago: U of Chicago P.

Gustafson, Ralph, ed. 1975. *The Penguin Book of Canadian Verse*. 2nd rev. ed. Harmondsworth: Penguin.

Gutstein, Donald. 1975. *Vancouver, Ltd.* Toronto: James Lorimer & Co.

Hamilton, David. 1994. *Arctic Revolution: Social Change in the North West Territories, 1935–1994*. Toronto: Dundurn.

Harrington, Lyn. 1981. *Syllables of Recorded Time: The Story of the Canadian Authors Association, 1921–1981*. Foreword by Harry J. Boyle. Toronto: Simon & Pierre.

Harrison, Keith. 1997. 'Notes on "Notes from Furry Creek."' *Canadian Literature* 155: 39–48.

– 1999. *Furry Creek*. Lantzville, BC: Oolichan Books.

Hawking, Stephen. 1998. *A Brief History of Time*. 2nd rev. ed. New York: Bantam Books.

Hearne, Samuel. 1958. *A Journey from Prince of Wales's Fort in Hudson's Bay to the Northern Ocean, 1769–72*. Ed. and introd. Richard Glover. Toronto: Macmillan.

Herman, Ellen. 1995. *The Romance of American Psychology: Political Culture in the Age of Experts*. Berkeley: U of California P.

Heyen, William. 1998. 'Open Letter to the SUNY Brockport College Community' and 'The Host: An Address to the Faculty at SUNY Brockport.' In *Pig Notes and Dumb Music: Prose on Poetry*, pp. 90–102. Rochester, NY: BOA Editions.

Hiebert, Daniel. 1999. 'Immigration and the Changing Social Geography of Greater Vancouver.' *BC Studies* 121: 35–82.

Higgins, Iain. 1997. Rev. of *Time Capsule*. *Canadian Literature* 155: 191–3.

Horowitz, Daniel. 1998. *Betty Friedan and the Making of the Feminine Mystique: The American Left, the Cold War, and Modern Feminism*. Amherst: U of Massachusetts P.

Hosek, Chaviva, 1978. Rev. of *A Stone Diary*. *The Fiddlehead* 118: 162–5.

Howard, Cori. 1999. 'Success, So Very Late in the Day.' *National Post*, Dec. 10, p. B4.

Hudson, William H. 1944. *Green Mansions: A Romance of the Tropical Forest*. Introd. John Galsworthy. New York: Modern Library.

Hunan, Renée. 1996. 'Literary Field Notes: The Influence of Ethnography on Representations of the North.' *Essays on Canadian Writing* 59: 147–63.

Hutcheon, Linda. 1988. *A Poetics of Postmodernism: History, Theory, Fiction*. London: Routledge.

– 1989. *The Politics of Postmodernism*. London: Routledge.

Huyssen, Andreas. 2002. 'High/Low in an Expanded Field.' *Modernism/Modernity* 9.3: 363–74.

Ibsen, Henrik. 1981. *Ghosts: A Domestic Drama in Three Acts* [1881]. In *Henrik Ibsen: Four Major Plays*, trans. James McFarlane and Jens Arup, introd. James Macfarlane, pp. 89–164. Oxford: Oxford UP.

Jarman, Mark Anthony. 2000. 'Lowther "Novel" a Labour of Love.' *Globe and Mail*, Jan. 29, p. D10.

Kahrer, Gabrielle. 1989. *The Seymour River Valley, 1870–1980*. Vancouver: Greater Vancouver Regional District.

Kelly, Peggy. 2000. 'Is *Poetry Contest* an Oxymoronic Term? An Enquiry into the Alberta Poetry Year Book Series, 1, 1955.' Paper presented to the History of the Book in Canada Conference, Toronto, 2000. Published on-line: http://www.library.utoronto.ca/hbic/new/kelly.htm

– 2001. 'Politics, Gender, and *New Provinces* (1936): Dorothy Livesay and Frank Scott.' Unpublished manuscript.

Kepes, Gyorgy, ed. 1966. *Sign, Image, Symbol*. New York: George Braziller.

Kleinman, Arthur, Veena Das, and Margaret Lock, eds. 1997. *Social Suffering*. Berkeley: U of California P.

Kohlhoff, Dean W. 2002. *Amchitka and the Bomb: Nuclear Testing in Alaska*. Seattle: U of Washington P.

Kroetsch, Robert. 1982. *Labyrinths of Voice: Conversations with Robert Kroetsch*. Ed. Shirley Neuman and Robert Wilson. Edmonton: Newest P.

Kroker, Arthur. 1984. *Technology and the Canadian Mind: Innis, McLuhan, Grant*. New York: St Martin's P.

Lacey, A.R. 1989. *Bergson*. London: Routledge.

Lane, Patrick. 1974. *Beware the Months of Fire*. Toronto: Anansi.

– 1995. 'Pat Lowther, c. 1973.' *Geist* 17 (Spring): 30.

Lane, Patrick, and Russell Thornton. 2002. 'A Brooding upon the Heart of Things.' Interview in Bowling 2002: 62–74.

Langer, Lawrence L. 1997. 'The Alarmed Vision: Social Suffering and Holocaust Atrocity.' In Kleinman, Das, and Lock 1997: 47–68.

Lawrence, Scott. 1977. 'Sharing Dream Passions.' *Vancouver Sun*, April 22, p. 3.

Lemm, Richard. 1999. *Milton Acorn: In Love and Anger*. Ottawa: Carleton UP.

Lennox, John, ed. and introd. 1993. *Margaret Laurence – Al Purdy: A Friendship in Letters*. Toronto: McClelland & Stewart.

Levenson, Christopher. 1978. Rev. of *A Stone Diary*. *Queen's Quarterly* 85: 352–4.

Litt, Paul. 1992. *The Muses, the Masses, and the Massey Commission*. Toronto: U of Toronto P.

Livesay, Dorothy. 1967. *The Unquiet Bed*. Toronto: Ryerson Press.

– 1968. *The Documentaries*. Toronto: Ryerson P.

– 1971. 'The Documentary Poem: A Canadian Genre' [1969]. In *Contexts of Canadian Criticism*, ed. and introd. Eli Mandel, pp. 267–81. Chicago: U of Chicago P.

– 1972. *The Collected Poems: The Two Seasons*. Toronto: McGraw Hill.

– ed. 1974. *Woman's Eye: Twelve B.C. Poets*. Vancouver: AIR.

– 1984. *Feeling the Worlds: New Poems*. Fredericton: Goose Lane Editions.

– 1998. *Archive for Our Times: Previously Uncollected and Unpublished Poems of Dorothy Livesay*. ed. Dean Irvine. Foreword by Miriam Waddington. Vancouver: Arsenal Pulp.

– 1999. *The Self-Completing Tree: Selected Poems*. 2nd ed. Vancouver: Beach Holme.

Livesay, Dorothy, and Seymour Mayne, eds. 1971. *Forty Women Poets of Canada*. Montreal: Ingluvin.

MacEwen, Gwendolyn. 1977. Rev. of *A Stone Diary*. *Quill & Quire* 43.6: 44.

MacLaren, Ian. 1996. 'Tracing One Discontinuous Line through the Poetry of the Northwest Passage.' *Canadian Poetry* 39: 7–48.

Mallinson, Jean. 1981. 'Versions and Subversions: Formal Strategies in the Poetry of Contemporary Canadian Women.' PhD diss., Simon Fraser University.

– 1986. '"Woman On/Against Snow": A Poem and Its Sources.' *Essays on Canadian Writing* 32: 7–26.

Mansbridge, Francis. 2002. *Launching History: The Saga of Burrard Dry Dock*. Vancouver: Harbour.

Marras, Emma. 1984. 'Robert Bly's Reading of South American Poets: A Challenge to North American Poetic Practice.' *Translation Review* 14: 33–9.

Marx, Karl. 1995. *Capital*. Ed. and introd. David McLellan. Oxford: Oxford UP.

Marx, Karl, and Friedrich Engels. 1998. *The Communist Manifesto*. Trans. Terrell Carver. ed. Mark Cowling. New York: New York UP.

Matthews, Glenna. 1987. *'Just a Housewife': The Rise and Fall of Domesticity in America*. Oxford: Oxford UP.

Mayne, Seymour. 1981. *The Impossible Promised Land: Poems New and Selected*. Oakville, ON: Mosaic P.

McInnis, Nadine. 1994. *Dorothy Livesay's Poetics of Desire*, Winnipeg: Turnstone Press.

McKay, Gail. 1978. *The Pat Lowther Poem*. Toronto: Coach House.

McLellan, Don. 1975. 'Into the Trenches Go Canada's Poets.' *Vancouver Sun*, Sept. 5, p. 29.

– 1977. 'Verses and Verdicts.' *Vancouver Sun*, April 29, p. 3A.

McLuhan, Marshall. 1971. 'The Medium Is the Message' [1964]. In *Contexts of Canadian Criticism*, ed. and introd. Eli Mandel, pp. 140–53. Chicago: U of Chicago P.

McNamara, Eugene [pseud. Sean Ryan]. 1975. 'Florence McNeil and Pat Lowther.' *Canadian Literature* 74: 21–9.

Mertens, Susan. 1974. 'Multimedia without the Pain.' *Vancouver Sun*, Aug. 27, p. 29.

Miller, D.A. 1988. *The Novel and the Police.* Berkeley: U of California P.

Miller, Shirley. 1975. 'Poetry.' *Priorities: A Publication of the NDP Women's Committee* 3.5: 17–20.

Mitchell, Beverley. 1976. 'The Genealogy of *Tish.*' In *The Writing Life: Historical and Critical Views of the Tish Movement,* ed. C.H. Gervais, introd. Frank Davey, pp. 70–93. Coatsworth, ON: Black Moss P.

Mitchell, W.J.T. 1994. *Picture Theory.* Chicago: U of Chicago P.

Morehouse, Val. 1977. Rev. of *A Stone Diary. Library Journal Book Review,* p. 384.

Morton, Desmond. 1977. *NDP: Social Democracy in Canada.* 2nd ed. Toronto: Samuel Stevens Hakkert & Co.

Moses, Daniel David. 1988. *First Person Plural.* ed. Judith Fitzgerald. Windsor: Black Moss P.

Musgrave, Susan. 1997. 'Slain Poet's Work Eerily Prescient.' *Vancouver Weekend Sun Review of Books,* May 31, pp. G1, G8.

Namjoshi, Suniti. 1977. 'Inscribed on Stone.' *Canadian Forum,* June–July: 51.

Nelson, Cary. 1989. *Repression and Recovery: Modern American Poetry and the Politics of Cultural Memory, 1910–1945.* Madison: U of Wisconsin P.

Neruda, Pablo. 1970. *Isla Negra: A Notebook.* Trans. Alastair Reid. Afterword by Enrico Mario Santí. New York: Farrar, Straus and Giroux.

– 1974. 'Towards an Impure Poetry.' In *Pablo Neruda: Five Decades, a Selection,* trans. Ben Belitt. New York: Grove P.

– 1977. *Memoirs.* Trans. Hardie St Martin. London: Penguin Books.

– 1991. *Canto General.* Trans. Jack Schmidt. Introd. Roberto Gonzáles Echevarria. Berkeley: U of California P.

Neuman, Shirley. 1990. 'After Modernism: English-Canadian Poetry since 1960.' In *Studies on Canadian Literature: Introductory and Critical Essays,* ed. Arnold E. Davidson, pp. 54–73. New York: MLA.

Nicholson, Mervyn. 2003. 'Lowther, Neruda and the Secret Wisdom of Food.' *Essays on Canadian Writing* 78: 220–42.

Norris, Ken. 1982. 'The Beginnings of Modernism.' *Canadian Poetry* 11: 56–66.

– 1984. *The Little Magazine in Canada, 1925–80: Its Role in the Development of Modernism and Post-Modernism in Canadian Poetry.* Toronto: ECW P.

O'Connor, James. 1999. *Natural Causes: Essays in Ecological Marxism.* New York: Guilford P.

Oliver, Michael. 1991. *Alden Nowlan and His Works.* Toronto: ECW P.

Ormsby, Eric. 1998. 'In the Dark Peninsula of Self.' *Books in Canada,* April: 33–4.

Page, P.K. 1997. *The Hidden Room: Collected Poems.* 2 vols. Erin, ON: Porcupine's Quill.

Page, P.K., and Christine Wiesenthal. 2002. 'Looking at the World Through Topaz.' Interview in Bowling 2002: 11–30.

Pauls, Naomi, and Charles Campbell, eds. 1997. *The Georgia Straight: What the Hell Happened?* Vancouver: Douglas and McIntyre.

Penrose, Roger. 1972. 'Black Holes.' *Scientific American* 226.5: 38–46.

Perry, Adele. 2001. *On the Edge of Empire: Gender, Race and the Making of British Columbia, 1849–71.* Toronto: U of Toronto P.

Phillips, Paul. 1967. *No Power Greater: A Century of Labour in British Columbia.* Vancouver: B.C. Federation of Labour and the Boag Foundation.

Polkinghorne, John. 2002. *Quantum Theory: A Very Short Introduction.* Oxford: Oxford UP.

Precosky, Don. 1983. '"Back to the Woods Ye Muse of Canada": Conservative Response to the Beginnings of Modernism. *Canadian Poetry* 12: 40–5.

Purdy, Al, ed. 1971. *Storm Warning: The New Canadian Poets.* Toronto: McClelland & Stewart.

– 1993. *Reaching for the Beaufort Sea: An Autobiography.* Maderia Park, BC: Harbour Publishing.

Quickenden, Robert. 1977. 'Language in the Hiss of Blood.' Rev. of *A Stone Diary. CVII* 3.2: 3–5.

Rasmussen, Knud. 1976. *The Netsilik Eskimos: Social Life and Spiritual Culture.* Vol. 8, nos. 1–2. *Report of the Fifth Thule Expedition, 1921–24* [1931]. Rpt. New York: AMS Press.

Ravel, Aviva. 1975. Rev. of *In Search of Eros,* by Elizabeth Brewster, and *Milk Stone,* by Pat Lowther. *The Fiddlehead* 105: 116–20.

Rees, Martin J., and Joseph Silk. 1977. 'The Origin of Galaxies' [1970]. In Gingerich 1977: 53–62.

Reksten, Terry. 1991. *The Dunsmuir Saga.* Vancouver: Douglas and McIntyre.

Riesco, Manuel. 1999. 'Chile, A Quarter Century On,' *New Left Review* 238: 97–125.

Riesman, Paul. 1966. 'The Eskimo Discovery of Man's Place in the Universe.' In Kepes 1966: 226–35.

Safarik, Allan. 1977. 'A Final Tribute.' *Canadian Review* 4.5: 31.

Sagaris, Lake, ed. and trans. 1986. *Un Pajaro Es Un Poema.* Ottawa and Dunvegan, ON: Casa Canada and Cormorant Books.

Scobie, Stephen. 1991. 'Leonard Cohen, Phyllis Webb, and the End(s) of Modernism.' In *Canadian Canons: Essays in Literary Value,* ed. Robert Lecker, pp. 57–70. Toronto: U of Toronto P.

Scott, F.R. 1945. *Overture: Poems by F.R. Scott.* Toronto: Ryerson P.

Shaidle, Kathy. 2000. 'Women, Poetry and the Cult of the Victim.' *Toronto Star,* Feb. 6, p. B2.

Shakespeare, William. 1982. *Hamlet.* ed. Harold Jenkins. Arden Edition. London: Methuen.

– 1986. *Julius Caesar.* Ed. T.S. Dorsch. Arden Edition. London: Methuen.

Shattuck, Roger, et. al. 1985. *Henri Rousseau.* New York: Museum of Modern Art.

Smith, William. 1967. *Dictionary of Greek and Roman Mythology.* Vol. 3. New York: AMS Press.

Smythe, Karen. 1992. *Figuring Grief: Gallant, Munro and the Poetics of Elegy.* Kingston and Montreal: McGill-Queens UP.

Sobel, Lester A., ed. 1974. *Chile and Allende.* Introd. Jordan M. Yong. New York: Facts on File Inc.

Souster, Raymond, ed. and introd. 1966. *New Wave Canada: The New Explosion in Canadian Poetry.* Toronto: Contact P.

Stadtman, Verne A. 1970. *The University of California: 1868–1968.* New York: McGraw-Hill.

Stott, William. 1950. 'The Early Story of North Vancouver.' *Museum and Art Notes,* 2nd ser., 1.2: 11–19.

Stratyner, Barbara. 1996. *Ned Wayburn and the Dance Routine: From Vaudeville to the Ziegfeld Follies.* Studies in Dance History, no. 13. Madison, WI: Society of Dance History Scholars.

Sturmanis, Dona. 1980. 'Investigation of an Inventor.' *Vancouver Province* [*Sunday Magazine Supplement*], March 30, pp. 3–5.

– 1985a. 'A Poet's Haunting Legacy.' *Vancouver Province* [*Sunday Magazine Supplement*], Aug. 4, p. 6.

– 1985b. 'Lowther's Legacy.' *Books in Canada* 14.8: 4–5.

Sullivan, Rosemary. 1983. 'Pat Lowther.' In *The Oxford Companion to Canadian Literature,* ed. William Toye, pp. 473–4. Toronto: Oxford UP.

– ed. 1989. *Poetry by Canadian Women.* Toronto: Oxford UP.

– 1995. *The Shadow Maker: A Life of Gwendolyn McEwan.* Toronto: Harper Collins.

– 1997. 'Pat Lowther.' In *The Oxford Companion to Canadian Literature,* 2nd ed., ed. William Toye and Eugene Benson, pp. 682–3. Toronto: Oxford UP.

– 1998. *Red Shoes: Margaret Atwood Starting Out.* Toronto: Harper Flamingo.

Tallman, Warren. 1976. 'Wonder Merchants: Modernist Poetry in Vancouver during the 1960s.' In Gervais 1976: 27–69.

Tennant, Paul. 1976. 'Vancouver Politics.' In *The Vancouver Book,* ed. Chuck Davis, pp. 178–80. Vancouver: J.J. Douglas.

Thesen, Sharon. 1997. 'Earth's Dark Anvil.' *Vancouver Review* 24: 19.

Thom, Ian M. 2000. 'Home Environment, 1968, 1985 and 1986.' In *Gathie Falk*, ed. Robin Laurence et al., pp. 34–50. Vancouver: Douglas & McIntyre.

Thomas, Hilda. 1986. 'Pat Lowther.' In *The Dictionary of Literary Biography*, Vol. 53, *Canadian Writers since 1960: First Series*, ed. W.H. New, p. 278. Detroit: Gale Research.

Thorne, Kip S. 1977. 'The Search for Black Holes' [1974]. In Gingerich 1977: 63–74.

Tippet, Maria. 1998. *Stormy Weather: F.H. Varley, a Biography*. Toronto: McClelland & Stewart.

Toner, Patrick. 2000. *If I Could Turn and Meet Myself: The Life of Alden Nowlan*. Fredericton: Goose Lane Editions.

Torgerson, Douglas. 1999. *The Promise of Green Politics: Environmentalism and the Public Sphere*. Durham, NC: Duke UP.

Trehearne, Michael. 1989. *Aestheticism and the Canadian Modernists*. Kingston and Montreal: McGill-Queen's UP.

UNESCO. 1977. *Statistics of Educational Attainment and Illiteracy: 1945–1974*. Paris: UNESCO.

Waffle. 1969. *The Waffle Manifesto for an Independent Socialist Canada*. Vancouver: Canadian League of Rights.

Wayman, Tom. 1993. *A Country Not Considered: Canada, Culture, Work*. Toronto: Anansi.

Webb, Phyllis. 1982. *The Vision Tree: Selected Poems*. ed. Sharon Thesen. Burnaby: Talonbooks.

White, Hayden. 1978. 'The Historical Text as Literary Artifact.' In *The Writing of History: Literary Form and Understanding*, ed. Robert H. Canary and Henry Kozicki, pp. 41–62. Madison: U of Wisconsin P.

Woodcock, George. 1975. 'Purdy's Prelude and Other Poems.' *Canadian Literature* 64: 92–8.

Woodward-Reynolds, Kathleen. 1943. 'A History of the City and District of North Vancouver.' MA thesis, Department of History, University of British Columbia.

York, Lorraine. 1993. 'The Ivory Thought: The North as Poetic Icon in Al Purdy and Patrick Lane.' *Essays on Canadian Writing* 49: 45–56.

– 1993–4. 'Home Thoughts or Abroad? A Rhetoric of Place in Modern and Postmodern Canadian Poetry.' *Essays on Canadian Writing* 51–2: 321–39.

Illustration Credits

Estate of Pat Lowther: James Wilks and four of his children; Isabelle 'Belle' Wilks; Arthur Tinmouth Jr; Patsy Lou and grandmother; big sister with charges (photograph by Virginia Tinmouth); Mrs Domphousse and two babies; the newlyweds; Christine and Beth Lowther; notebook draft page.

North Vancouver Museum and Archives: photograph #26-28-3, Rice Lake reservoir.

Vancouver Sun: the League 'Chair Creature' (photograph by Ian Lindsay).

Christine Wiesenthal: 'Milk stone' on Mayne Island.

Index

Thomas, Dylan, 356
Thomas, Hilda, 5, 7, 52, 75, 115, 139,
141, 226, 229, 335
Thompson, John, 7, 71, 118, 336,
453n18
Thorne, Kip, 342, 344
Time Capsule (Polestar), 6, 9, 75, 98,
109, 111, 114, 116, 172, 195, 201,
452n7; publication history and
appearance of, 104–8. *See also*
Lowther, Pat, unpublished manuscripts and notebook entries
Tinmouth, Arden (PL's brother), 44,
127, 130, 143, 154, 356, 426n2,
455n12
Tinmouth, Arthur, Sr (PL's grandfather), 126, 218, 219
Tinmouth, Arthur, Jr (PL's father),
92, 121, 126–7, 133, 134, 139, 143,
218, 219, 275, 323, 324, 325, 346,
356, 359, 363, 395, 436n17; death
of, 172–3; family history of, 126,
218–19; marriage to Virginia Wilks,
126–7, 131, 219–20
Tinmouth, Brenda. *See* Marshall,
Brenda
Tinmouth, Harriet (PL's grandmother), 126, 218, 219
Tinmouth, John (PL's brother), 44,
45, 46, 127, 130, 139, 336, 426n2,
453n18
Tinmouth, Virginia Wilks (PL's
mother), 36, 44, 45, 54, 75, 105, 138,
139, 140, 186, 425n24, 436n18;
early career as dancer, 124–6, 128,
423n7; family history of, 124, 211–
17, 255, 354, 355, 395–7, 435n8;
marriage to Arthur Tinmouth, Jr,
126–7, 131, 219–20, 324, 356,
423n10; motherhood, 121–2, 130,

132, 133, 135, 143, 188, 193–4, 217–
18, 220, 398–400, 444–5n9, 458n19
Tippet, Maria, 324
Tish, 5, 17, 79, 146, 150, 155, 239,
255–6, 284, 318, 446n17
'To a Woman Who Died of 34 Stab
Wounds,' 196, 198–9
'To Capture Proteus,' 90
Torgerson, Douglas, 362
Toronto Star, 5, 78, 316
'Touch Home,' 160
'Toward a Pragmatic Psychology,'
167–8
Toye, William, 359, 367, 389
Trotskyism, 150, 170, 224
Trower, Peter, 30, 237–8
Tuthmose I (pharaoh), 346
'Two Babies in Two Years,' 161

Uguay, Marie, 6, 7, 118
UNESCO, 133, 155
University of British Columbia, 4, 28,
29, 39, 41, 51, 60, 94, 99, 102, 115,
141, 146, 158, 192, 256, 311, 387,
401, 422n45
University of California (Berkeley),
51, 141, 426n9
University of Windsor Review, 297

Vallejo, César, 272
Vancouver, City of, 25, 121, 123, 154,
190, 214, 244, 250, 255, 256, 261,
305, 331, 350, 354, 355; political
history of, 216, 219, 225, 226–7,
361; socio-economic geography of,
144, 226, 252. *See also* literary culture and politics
Vancouver Area Council. *See* New
Democratic Party of British Columbia